Sport Psychology: Stress Management in Sport

Sport Psychology: Stress Management in Sport

Edited by Erica Glover

SYRAWOOD
PUBLISHING HOUSE
New York

Published by Syrawood Publishing House,
750 Third Avenue, 9th Floor,
New York, NY 10017, USA
www.syrawoodpublishinghouse.com

Sport Psychology: Stress Management in Sport
Edited by Erica Glover

International Standard Book Number: 978-1-64740-360-7 (Hardback)

Cataloging-in-publication Data

Sport psychology : stress management in sport / edited by Erica Glover.
p. cm.
Includes bibliographical references and index.
ISBN 978-1-64740-360-7
1. Sports--Psychological aspects. 2. Stress (Psychology). 3. Stress management.
4. Competition (Psychology). I. Glover, Erica.
GV706.4 .S66 20233
796.01--dc23

TABLE OF CONTENTS

PREFACE

This book aims to highlight the current researches and provides a platform to further the scope of innovations in this area. This book is a product of the combined efforts of many researchers and scientists, after going through thorough studies and analysis from different parts of the world. The objective of this book is to provide the readers with the latest information of the field.

Sport psychology refers to the study of the impact of psychological factors on athletic performance, physical activity, sports and exercise. It is helpful for athletes in handling the pressures of competition, improving athletic performance and achieving their goals. The various techniques used in sport psychology have different functions such as improving self-confidence, and reducing stress and anxiety. Stress management in sport is necessary for athletes to control their anxiety and stress. The management of anxiety and stress is important for athletes performing in high-pressure situations. Some of the techniques used in sport psychology for managing stress include biofeedback, progressive relaxation, cognitive behavioral therapy and hypnosis. This book aims to shed light on the role of sport psychology for managing stress in sports. It consists of contributions made by international experts. The book will serve as a valuable source of reference for graduate and postgraduate students.

I would like to express my sincere thanks to the authors for their dedicated efforts in the completion of this book. I acknowledge the efforts of the publisher for providing constant support. Lastly, I would like to thank my family for their support in all academic endeavors.

Editor

1

Challenge and Threat: A Critical Review of the Literature and an Alternative Conceptualization

Mark A. Uphill[1], Claire J. L. Rossato[2], Jon Swain[1] and Jamie O'Driscoll[1]*

[1]*Section of Sport and Exercise Sciences, Canterbury Christ Church University, Canterbury, United Kingdom,* [2]*Department of Psychology, Social Work and Counselling, Old Royal Naval College, University of Greenwich, London, United Kingdom*

Correspondence:
Mark A. Uphill
mark.uphill@canterbury.ac.uk

In this article, the authors describe a new theory, the Evaluative Space Approach to Challenge and Threat (ESACT). Prompted by the Biopsychosocial model of challenge and threat (BPS: Blascovich and Tomaka, 1996) and the development of the Theory of Challenge and Threat States in Athletes (Jones et al., 2009), recent years have witnessed a considerable increase in research examining challenge and threat in sport. This manuscript provides a critical review of the literature examining challenge and threat in sport, tracing its historical development and some of the current empirical ambiguities. To reconcile some of these ambiguities, and utilizing neurobiological evidence associated with approach and avoidance motivation (c.f. Elliot and Covington, 2001), this paper draws upon the Evaluative Space Model (ESM; Cacioppo et al., 1997) and considers the implications for understanding challenge and threat in sport. For example, rather than see challenge and threat as opposite ends of a single bipolar continuum, the ESM implies that individuals could be (1) challenged, (2) threatened, (3) challenged and threatened, or (4) neither challenged or threatened by a particular stimulus. From this perspective, it could be argued that the appraisal of some sport situations as both challenging *and* threatening could be advantageous, whereas the current literature seems to imply that the appraisal of stress as a threat is maladaptive for performance. The ESACT provides several testable hypotheses for advancing understanding of challenge and threat (in sport) and we describe a number of measures that can be used to examine these hypotheses. In sum, this paper provides a significant theoretical, empirical, and practical contribution to our understanding of challenge and threat (in sport).

Keywords: stress, coactivation, parasympathetic, emotions, ambivalence

Understanding individuals' response to stressors is important across a range of domains such as medicine, business, sport, military, and for a range of consequences including performance, health, and economy (e.g., through absenteeism). We begin this paper by providing a brief and critical summary of the two prevailing models that have guided research on challenge and threat (in sport), namely the biopsychosocial model (e.g., Tomaka et al., 1993; Blascovich and Tomaka, 1996; Blascovich et al., 2004), and the Theory of Challenge and Threat States in Athletes (TCTSA; Jones et al., 2009). Coupled with the limitations in the literature on challenge and threat, we then consider several lines of converging evidence in related areas of research, which act as the impetus for proposing what we consider to be a unique, significant, and valuable contribution to the literature on challenge and threat: namely the Evaluative Space Approach to Challenge and Threat (ESACT). We conclude the paper by considering some applied implications and directions for future research.

Predicated on Kramer's (2013) six criteria to evaluate a theory, in comparison to both the BPS model and the Theory of Challenge and Threat States in Athletes, we elucidate how the ESACT approach demonstrates greater (1) comprehensiveness (the scope of the theory in describing, explaining, controlling, and predicting constructs and behavior), (2) precision (the extent to which constructs are clearly defined and open to valid and reliable testing through falsifiable assumptions), (3) parsimony (all things being equal, the simpler the explanation, the more likely it is to be the correct one), (4) empirical validity (the manner in which a theory correctly predicts and controls phenomena, and the extent to which it handles disconfirming evidence), (5) heuristic value (its ability to generate unique thoughts and perspectives in other fields), and (6) applied value (the extent to which the theory offers solutions to life's challenges).

Specifically, we propose that the ESACT extends our understanding of challenge and threat beyond existing conceptualizations in several important ways:

1. Rather than see challenge and threat as endpoints of a bipolar continuum, challenge and threat are reconceptualized as at least partially independent and bivalent states;
2. Individuals, then, may be challenged, threatened, or both challenged and threatened in motivationally relevant situations;
3. A constellation of appraisals allow flexibility for evaluating stimuli as either a challenge (perceiving there to be an opportunity for gain or growth), threat (perceiving anticipated harm or loss), or as both challenge and threat;
4. Describing contexts in which athletes may experience emotions of mixed valence (e.g., anxiety and excitement);
5. Recognizing that approach and avoidance goals can be coactivated;
6. The autonomic response associated with challenge and threat is extended beyond the sympathetic nervous system to include indices of the parasympathetic nervous system;
7. Threat is not necessarily unhelpful to performance;
8. The development of applied interventions that recognize the utility of threat among athletes.

CHALLENGE AND THREAT: A CONCISE AND CRITICAL REVIEW

Influenced by the biopsychosocial (BPS) model of challenge and threat (e.g., Tomaka et al., 1993; Blascovich et al., 2003; Seery, 2013), and prompted by the development of the TCTSA (Jones et al., 2009), research on challenge and threat in sport has grown in recent years. To illustrate, a literature search confined to the PsycInfo database using the terms "challenge" and "threat" and "sport," limited in scope to English language periodicals and the period 2000 to present, revealed 46 articles. In this section, we first briefly describe the BPS and TCTSA approaches, and second, outline what we perceive to be several limitations associated with these perspectives.

Briefly stated, the biopsychosocial (BPS) model of challenge and threat provides a framework which suggests that motivated performance situations can be appraised as either a challenge or threat and that these psychological states differ in the constellation of physiological (particularly cardiovascular) markers (e.g., Blascovich et al., 2003). The physiological indices associated with challenge and threat have their roots in Dienstbier's (1989) notion of "physiological toughness," and the appraisals of challenge and threat have parallels with Lazarus and Folkman (1984), Folkman and Lazarus (1985, 1986), and Lazarus's (1999) approach to stress. According to this theory, a challenge state occurs when the situation is appraised as self-relevant and the individual perceives sufficient (or nearly sufficient) personal resources to meet or exceed the demands of the task. In a threat state, the situation is also appraised as self-relevant, but the individual perceives insufficient personal resources to meet the demands of the task (c.f., Blascovich and Tomaka, 1996; Tomaka et al., 1997; Seery, 2011). The theory further suggests that these cognitive evaluations precede the physiological responses to a stressful situation (Tomaka et al., 1993; Blascovich et al., 2003) and that a challenge state is typically associated with a more efficient cardiovascular pattern and improved performance (see also Hase et al., 2018).

The TCTSA (Jones et al., 2009) extended the BPS model by suggesting that three antecedents (self-efficacy, perceived control, type of motivational goals) influence whether individuals feel they have the resources to cope with a stressful situation. Specifically, it is contended that higher levels of perceived control and self-efficacy coupled with the adoption of approach goals elicit a challenge state, whereas lower perceived control and self-efficacy coupled with the adoption of avoidance goals evoke a threat state. Similar to Blascovich and colleagues, Jones et al. suggest that the physiological markers that differentiate challenge from threat states are Cardiac Output (CO) and Total Peripheral Resistance (TPR). Cardiac output is computed as heart rate x stroke volume (amount of blood expelled from left ventricle on a heart beat) and total peripheral resistance as the resistance to flow in the vascular network (Wright and Kirby, 2003). Challenge is characterized by relatively greater cardiac reactivity (increased CO) and a decrease in TPR. In contrast threat is characterized by no change or an increase in TPR and no change or a small increase in CO (Blascovich and Tomaka, 1996; Blascovich and Mendes, 2000). Alongside the cardiovascular (CV) changes, challenge and threat states in the TCTSA model also shape the valence and interpretation of emotions (i.e., positively valenced emotions are more typical of challenge and perceived to be helpful; negatively valenced emotions more typical of threat and perceived to be unhelpful). Although these patterns may be typical, it is also plausible according to TCTSA that negatively toned emotions such as anger can be experienced in a challenge state.

On the one hand, there is considerable evidence supporting many of the tenets of the BPS model (e.g., Tomaka et al., 1993; Blascovich and Tomaka, 1996) and a growing body of literature supporting a number of the hypotheses associated with the TCTSA (e.g., Turner et al., 2012, 2013). Indeed, evidence to date suggests that both the BPS model and TCTSA have made valuable and important contributions to our understanding of challenge and threat broadly, and in sport specifically. Why then is an alternative conceptualization needed? As outlined below, we contend that (1) there are two significant measurement limitations currently inherent in both the BPS model and TCTSA that constrain the questions we ask, the research we conduct, and the applications we espouse and (2) research in related areas suggests that current models of challenge and threat are insufficient to capture the complexity and array of responses that humans have evolved to manage stressful situations.

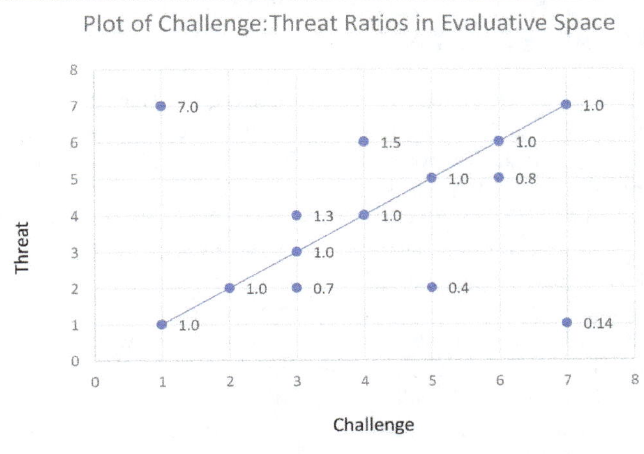

FIGURE 1 | Illustration of challenge: threat ratio plotted in evaluative space.

MEASUREMENT LIMITATIONS ASSOCIATED WITH BIOPSYCHOSOCIAL MODEL AND THEORY OF CHALLENGE AND THREAT STATES IN ATHLETES

The first major limitation of the BPS model is that challenge and threat states represent opposite ends of a unidimensional continuum rather than two dichotomous states, allowing researchers to examine relative (rather than absolute) differences in challenge and threat (i.e., greater vs. lesser challenge or threat; Blascovich, 2008; Seery, 2011). Similarly, the TCTSA draws upon the BPS model (at least in its physiological measures) such that challenge and threat physiological indices have been operationalized in a similar way.

In terms of operationalizing demand and resource appraisals, typically, in this literature, two items (e.g., on a Likert-type scale of range 1–7) – one measuring demands or threat, the other measuring resources or perceived challenge – are used to construct either a ratio measure (e.g., demands/resources; Quigley et al., 2002) or difference score (e.g., resources minus demands; Chalabaev et al., 2009). Others have used a single item to assess the degree of challenge or threat (c.f. Turner et al., 2012). The ratio measure is limited as depicted in **Figure 1**. For example, the same ratio score could denote very different locations in evaluative space and ratio measures also possess a largely nonlinear distribution (Hase et al., 2018). As we highlight in the section outlining the ESACT, this bipolar conceptualization (and the reciprocal activation assumed) is subsumed as just one mode of activation in our Evaluative Space Approach to Challenge and Threat (ESACT).

Second, in both the BPS model and TCTSA, the constellation of cardiovascular indices reflects alterations in the activity of the sympathetic-adrenomedullary (SAM) and hypothalamic–pituitary–adrenal (HPA) axes (Seery, 2011). Wright and Kirby (2003) have arguably provided the most elaborate critique of the cardiovascular correlates of the biopsychosocial approach to challenge and threat. In brief, there are both conceptual and empirical grounds for questioning the CV responses associated with the BPS model of challenge and threat. On conceptual grounds, Wright and Kirby argue that Blascovich and colleagues' derivation of CV indices from the work of Dienstbier (1989) is misguided. Specifically, whereas Dienstbier (1989), (and the ESACT model outlined herein), assumes that challenge occurs when there is opportunity for growth, and threat occurs when there is potential for harm or loss, the BPS model proposes that challenge and threat occur as a function of the relation between demands and resources. Wright and Kirby argue that this difference is not trivial and therefore assumptions regarding the activity of SAM and PAC associated with challenge and threat are not well founded. Similarly, SAM activation is associated with the release of both epinethrine and norepinethrine – and circulating norepinethrine is exclusively constrictive. Thus the vasodilatory effect associated with challenge (and predictions associated with the index of TPR more generally) may be viewed somewhat cautiously.

Importantly, innervation of the cardiac muscle is by efferent branches of *both* sympathetic and parasympathetic arms of the autonomic nervous system (e.g., Berntson et al., 1994; Cacioppo et al., 2011), and drawing on the doctrine of autonomic space (Berntson et al., 1991, 1993), we contend that by embracing the activity of the parasympathetic branch of the autonomic nervous system to investigate cardiovascular indices associated with challenge and threat, we advance understanding of the characterization of challenge and threat and concomitantly potential strategies for applied practice. For example, Respiratory Sinus Arrhythmia (RSA) or low-frequency Heart Rate Variability (Billman, 2011) is widely purported to be an index of parasympathetic activation, has been associated with the behavioral activation system (Blair et al., 2004) and the ability to optimally cope and engage with environmental perturbations (Beauchaine, 2001; Porges, 2007), characteristics that are theoretically symptomatic of a challenge state. Moreover, breathing interventions have been demonstrated to facilitate RSA and to lower blood pressure responses to a stressor (Steffen et al., 2017).

RESEARCH EVIDENCE POINTING TO AN ALTERNATIVE CONCEPTUALIZATION

Whether it is improved measurement or clarification of moderating and mediating variables that may explain departures from hypotheses proposed by the BPS model or TCTSA, these improvements alone will not suffice to reconcile the more fundamental difficulties associated with the BPS model and TCTSA. Specifically, the essence of the bipolar configuration of challenge and threat upon which these models are based are arguably not in accord with evidence emerging from related literature, and collectively begin to explain why, when not placed in artificial experimental procedures, individuals report experiencing both challenge and threat (e.g., Campbell and Jones, 2002; Cerin, 2003; Sirsch, 2003; Meijen, et al., 2013). We summarize these briefly below.

Bivalent Activation of Appraisals

Whereas Lazarus and Folkman's (1984) original conceptualizations of challenge and threat appraisals were distinct and independent, the BPS model ostensibly reconfigured this as a bipolar measure, in effect considerably reducing the explanatory power of challenge and threat evaluations in understanding experience and behavior. Here, we briefly outline evidence supporting the bivalent activation of appraisals.

There is a growing body of research that supports the proposition that the same mental representation is linked in memory to both positive and negative evaluations (Zayas and Shoda, 2015). Such a stance is consistent with approaches that consider the human mind as being highly attuned to both rewarding and punishing aspects of the environment (e.g., Cacioppo and Berntson, 1994). More specifically, there is growing support for the contention that evaluations of positivity and negativity reflect two distinct and separable neural systems: one that is sensitive to appetitive cues and the other to aversive cues. These initial evaluations occur in parallel and independently (e.g., Zayas and Shoda, 2015). Indeed, in a review of neuroscience literature, Man et al. (2017) argue that the architecture of the brain permits the simultaneous processing of positive and negative information. This suggests that conceiving a situation as an opportunity *both* for gain *and* loss is consistent with the idea that challenge and threat can be activated independently (i.e., individually), and together coactivated (see also Sirsch, 2003). Dual models of attention further corroborate the notion that more than one feature of a stimulus can be attended to simultaneously (e.g., de Gelder and Vroomen, 2000).

Coactivation of Approach and Avoidance Goals

Across a number of areas that focus on approach and avoidance motivations, there is philosophical, conceptual, and empirical support for the distinction between, and coactivation of, approach and avoidance goals (e.g., neuroevolutionary, Gray's, 1970; Elliot and Covington, 2001; Corr, 2004; Berntson and Cacioppo, 2008; Law et al., 2012). Indeed, and associated with appraisal judgments more broadly, Zajonc (1998) asserts that "approach/avoidance discriminations are the primary and most elemental reaction of organisms to environmental stimuli, the initial response on which all subsequent responses are based" (p. 592).

Reviewing the literature on approach and avoidance motivations and goals is beyond the scope of this literature. For the purposes of this argument, we present a synopsis of what we perceive to be several important observations regarding approach and avoidance goals for the advancement of understanding of challenge and threat. First, there have been considerable psychometric studies (exploratory and confirmatory factor analyses) that support the separation of performance-approach, and performance-avoidance goals. Second, in a meta-analysis, Hulleman et al. (2010) observed a mean correlation of $r = 0.4$ between performance-approach and performance-avoidance goals. From a practical perspective, a moderate correlation suggests that in naturalistic domains such as sport, the active pursuit of performance-approach goals may easily be coactivated with performance-avoidance goals (c.f. Law et al., 2012). Third, Law et al. (2012) provide some empirical support for the coactivation of performance-approach and performance-avoidance goals (as specified in the TCTSA). As described by Law et al. (2012), obtaining a future positive outcome and avoiding a future negative outcome can sometimes be construed quite similarly (e.g., as "opposite sides of the same coin") and can become commingled in goal pursuit. If approach and avoidance goals can be activated not only independently, but in combination, this represents a subtle but important conceptual distinction that, allied to the bivalent activation of appraisals (described above) and mixed emotional experiences (described below), suggests that the bipolar approach to challenge and threat represents at best a partial and incomplete picture of the evaluative space. Indeed, similar to performance-approach and performance-avoidance goals, there is theoretical and practical utility in identifying the unique precursors associated with the independent and coactivated challenge and threat states.

Mixed Emotional Experiences

Recent literature has adopted a similar approach when examining constructs such as emotion. For example, Larsen et al. (2001) suggested that happiness and sadness can be experienced simultaneously rather than being viewed as bipolar (Russell and Carroll, 1999). Larsen et al. (2001) suggested that happiness and sadness should be viewed as bivariate, for example, graduating college students may have experienced happiness and sadness simultaneously.

Moreover, Larsen et al. (2001) further explain their rationale for using a bivariate approach to happiness and sadness by exploring how university students felt during a move-out day compared to a typical day. Individual's emotions were recorded *via* a self-report tool to capture emotion. University students were given the measure on a typical day and then on a move-out day (leaving university). Participants were more likely to report experiencing both happiness and sadness when they completed the self-report measure on a move-out day compared to a typical day. This was similar to findings on graduation day, among graduates and nongraduates, with graduates experiencing both happiness and sadness simultaneously. In the sport domain, athletes reported experiencing a mix of emotions, indicative of experiencing both challenge and threat in anticipation of a competition (Cerin, 2003). Beyond emotions experienced subjectively, at a psychophysiological level, these mixed emotional reactions (i.e., positively valenced + negatively valenced) are not simply characterized by the net physiological response; mixed emotional reactions seem to comprise an emergent physiology such that the physiological response associated with mixed emotions is unique (c.f. Kreibig et al., 2015). In a similar way, and as outlined below, the bipolar configuration of challenge and threat states does not allow for the possibility being *both* challenged *and* threatened and is characterized by an emergent and unique constellation of physiological indices distinct from being either challenged or threatened.

Summary

In sum, this section illustrates several lines of converging evidence that supports an alternative conceptualization of challenge and threat. Specifically, the extant bipolar configuration, although it has some utility in circumstances where challenge and threat are reciprocally activated, does not adequately capture the full range of challenging and threatening experiences that individuals can experience. Indeed, this contrasts with the earlier views of Lazarus and Folkman (1984), and other researchers (e.g., Skinner and Brewer, 2004), who considered challenge and threat as independent cognitive appraisals that can occur simultaneously.

AN EVALUATIVE SPACE APPROACH TO CHALLENGE AND THREAT

In what is a complex and dynamic world, the ability to respond quickly and flexibly to a stimulus that is hostile, hospitable, or has features of both is critical to our social interactions, and from an evolutionary perspective, our survival (c.f. Norris et al., 2010). Indeed, it is proposed that the differentiation of hostile from hospitable stimuli is so fundamental to mammalian survival that this behavioral organization is found at multiple levels of the neuraxis, ranging from the spinal cord to the neocortex (Ito and Cacioppo, 1999; Berntson and Cacioppo, 2008). According to Cacioppo and colleagues, although the primary function of the affect system is to discriminate harmful from helpful, good from bad, appetitive from aversive, the structure of the underlying system is not constrained to a bipolar configuration; rather, our affective system is organized in a bivalenced manner defined (at least partially) by separable systems for processing positive and negative stimuli. For example, would a golfer who anticipated a $120,000 win but received only $50,000 feel pleased about the win or displeased because it fell well short of expectations (c.f., Kahneman, 1992)? The structure of the question implies that evaluative judgments about such disappointing wins (Larsen et al., 2004) fall along a bipolar scale ranging from good to bad and precludes examination of whether the golfer could feel both good *and* bad (Larsen et al., 2009).

The literature on challenge and threat broadly, and in sport specifically, is severely limited by the bipolar conceptualization and may benefit from an alternative conceptualization: namely one in which challenge and threat can be coactivated (Cacioppo and Berntson, 1994). From this perspective, the bipolar argument is not completely rejected; instead the bipolar conceptualization (and assumption of reciprocal activation) is subsumed within a model that affords multiple modes of activation. Moreover, as Crum et al. (2017) contend, there may be times when it is difficult to reduce the (perceived) demands of a situation, or enhance (perceived) resources (from a BPS perspective), and perhaps equally importantly, trying to minimize the experience of threat precludes the possibility that there might be (performance) gains to be realized from experiencing and managing threat (see also Bell et al., 2013).

Whereas the BPS model and TCTSA have adopted a bipolar approach to challenge and threat, these only allow for a reciprocal mode of activation, that is, as one (e.g., threat) increases, the other (e.g., challenge) decreases. This notion of reciprocal activation is not rejected by the ESACT, but rather subsumed within it. Namely, challenge and threat can be characterised by (1) reciprocal activation (i.e., when a stimulus has opposing effects on challenge and threat), (2) uncoupled activation (i.e., when a stimulus evokes only challenging or only threatening evaluations), and (3) nonreciprocal or coactivation (i.e., when a stimulus increases – or decreases – both evaluations of challenge and threat). For example, a rally which an individual wins would likely enhance challenge (opportunity for gain) and reduce threat (potential for loss). An example of a scenario in which only challenge would be evoked is when runners set a spontaneous self-referenced goal to enhance their split times during a training session. A singular threat may be evoked when there is no perceived opportunity for gain. Consider a darts player afflicted by dartitis approaching a competition with the expectation of a recurrence of the symptoms. Thus, in our estimation, "pure" challenge and threat are relatively rare occurrences in the performance domain, and are perhaps more marked by a combination of both challenge and threat. On the one hand, this is not conceptually dissimilar to existing notions of being relatively more challenged or more threatened (see Seery, 2011). Yet, on the other, positioning challenge and threat as independent, separable modes of activation affords opportunity to explore circumstances where conflict might arise (between opportunity for gain and anticipation of loss), and to explore the unique precursors of challenged, threatened, and challenged and threatened states.

The ESACT approach also differs from the BPS and TCTSA approaches in how threat is conceptualized. In our view, a threat by definition is aversive and warrants extinguishing, withdrawal, or avoidance. While the former (i.e., extinguishing a threat) could involve approach-related behavior, *the underlying motivation and affective response is one of avoidance and unpleasantness respectively*. This differs from the BPS conceptualization insofar as threat is characterized by an approach motivation (Blascovich, 2008).

Physiological Indices of Challenge and Threat

Inferences about psychological states from psychophysiological indices have a long history (c.f. Cacioppo and Tassinary, 1990; Blascovich and Mendes, 2000). The "identity thesis" (Cacioppo and Tassinary, 1990) suggests that all mental (and *vis-à-vis* psychological) states and processes are incorporated bodily. Nevertheless, as Blascovich and Mendes (2000) caution, one of the challenges facing researchers is how to choose among the plethora of psychophysiological indices available. On the one hand, Blascovich and Mendes (2010) suggest that researchers could search for validated neurophysiological indices of that construct. Yet, as we have argued above, there are some difficulties in assuming that the extant "validated" psychophyisiological measures of challenge and threat (specifically CO and TPR) are "fit-for-purpose" in lieu of the ESACT's broader scope. From this perspective, at the least, there should be complementary measures (i.e., in addition to CO and TPR) that represent coactivated challenge and threat states. Against this backdrop, in the absence of such a measure, one can "take on the task of melding appropriate neurophysiological theory with psychological processes underlying the target construct" (Blascovich and Mendes, 2000, p. 243). It is to this end that we now turn.

As we have argued above, one significant limitation associated with the extant literature on challenge and threat is the almost exclusive reliance on sympathetic markers of cardiovascular activity. Expanding consideration of cardiovascular markers of challenge and threat that are illustrative of parasympathetic influence is predicated on several grounds pertinent to the current thesis. First, there is evidence the parasympathetic nervous system is associated with psychological states broadly and appraisal processes specifically (see Ito and Cacioppo, 1999; Kreibig et al., 2012). Second, and consistent with the ESACT's emphasis on adaptive flexibility, changes in CO could be brought about by either enhanced sympathetic activation, a withdrawal of parasympathetic activation, or a combination of the two (see Stratton and Pfeifer, 1987). From this angle, given that CO is considered to change simply by *degree* in both challenge and threat states (i.e., a relatively larger change in challenge compared to threat), the assessment of the branches of the autonomic system that influence CO would perhaps represent a more nuanced marker of challenge and threat states.

Accordingly, we posit that challenge states and threat states (and challenge *and* threat states) may be differentiated by both quantitative differences (e.g., in magnitude or rate of change), and qualitative differences (i.e., differences in type) in cardiovascular markers (see **Table 1**) and elaborate further below.

In order to differentiate individuals characterized by challenged, threatened, and both challenged and threatened states, noninvasive hemodynamic and cardiac autonomic assessment as well as invasive biomarker analysis may have considerable utility. To recap, from BPS and TCTSA perspectives, challenged states are associated with sympathetic activation and threat states are associated with sympathetic and hypothalamic pituitary adrenocortical (HPA) activation (Blascovich and Mendes, 2000; Seery, 2011). As such, hemodynamic responses differ with an augmented cardiac output and attenuated total peripheral resistance in challenge states, compared to a combined increase in cardiac output and total peripheral resistance in threat states. However, as detailed above, we postulate that these indices are severely limited as measures of challenge and threat specifically, but also do not afford an appropriate assessment of individuals evaluating a scenario as both a challenge and threat.

TABLE 1 | Appraisal and psychophysiological indices of (1) challenge, (2) threat, and (3) challenge and threat states.

	Challenge	Threat	Challenge and threat
Appraisal elements			
Opportunity for growth	Y	N	Y
Opportunity for loss	N	Y	Y
Psychophysiological index	Challenge	Threat	Challenge and threat
PEP	↑	↑↑	↑
Total HRVms2	↓	↓↓↓	↓↓
HFms2	↓	↓↓↓	↓↓
LFms2	↓	↑↑	↑
LF/HF ratio	↓	↑↑	↑
HFnu	↑	↓↓	↓
LFnu	↓	↑↑	↑
Cortisol	↔	↑	↔
CAB	↔	↓	↔/↑
CAR	↑↑	↓	↔/↑
HPA axis Gcs	↔	↑	↔
TPR	↓	↑↑	↑
CO	↑↑	↑	↑

↑↓, direction and ↑↑ magnitude of change; ↔, no change; Δt+, fast rate of change; Δt–, slow rate of change.

Heart rate continuously fluctuates around its mean and is under the control of complex neural and endocrine mechanisms aimed at maintaining cardiovascular stability. Heart rate variability reflects the activity of cardiovascular control mechanisms and has evolved to become a widely applied tool as a noninvasive index of the cardiac autonomic nervous system. A healthy heart is symbolized by significant oscillating fluctuations around its mean, or rather significant beat-to-beat variability. Conversely, medical conditions that are associated with and accelerate cardiovascular disease morbidity and mortality, including prevalent psychiatric disorders (Chalmers et al., 2014), are characterized by a significant attenuation of this beat-to-beat variability (O'Driscoll and Sharma, 2015). As such, individuals who appraise a given task as challenging are likely to have higher overall HRV, with a stepwise decrease in those with mixed appraisal (challenge and threat), being lowest in individuals who appraise a given task as threatening. This hypothesis is partially supported from the work of Casad and Petzel (2018). The oscillating changes in heart rate (R-R intervals) are caused by continuous alterations in sympathetically and parasympathetically mediated neural impulses. The sympathetic and parasympathetic nervous activity can be assessed by the oscillating fluctuations in the frequency and amplitude of each R-R interval. The R-R intervals from an electrocardiogram recording oscillate around two main frequencies: high frequency (HF; 0.15–0.40 Hz), which corresponds to parasympathetic outflow to the heart and low frequency (LF; 0.04–0.10 Hz), which has been shown to reflect sympathetic and parasympathetic neural outflow. Due to the ambiguities surrounding LF-HRV, the pre-ejection period (PEP) is commonly used as a measure of sympathetic cardiovascular control (Berntson et al., 2008). The PEP is a measure of cardiac performance, representing cardiac sympathetic activity that can be measured noninvasively. The ventricles of the heart are richly innervated by cardiac sympathetic neurons and an increase in sympathetic activity (beta-adrenergic stimulation) elicits a positive inotropic response, which increases myocardial contractility.

It is conceivable that individuals with challenged appraisals will present with a greater proportion of their HRV in the HF domain (higher HFnu and LF/HF ratio), indicative of greater parasympathetic activity, which declines as individuals move along the continuum to threat appraisals. Additionally, as individuals move along the continuum from challenge to threat, there is greater sympathetic activity, which is reflected by changes in PEP, which is required in order to overcome the increased afterload (increased total peripheral vascular resistance), which is documented in threat appraisals.

The increase in total peripheral vascular resistance results from activation of the HPA axis. Although HPA activation under ideal control mechanisms is of critical importance, with beneficial actions on the immune system, metabolism, and cardiovascular function, inappropriate or prolonged HPA axis activation is linked with numerous physiological and psychological disease states (Herman et al., 2016). Activation of the HPA axis, as seen during stress, promotes higher levels of glucocorticoids (primarily cortisol in humans). Although there are numerous cellular pathways, which are beyond the scope of this work, glucocorticoids are the end product of HPA axis activation and their release can be beneficial or detrimental. Chronic stimulation of the HPA axis and greater glucocorticoid release suppresses the production of vasodilators, such as nitric oxide and enhances vasoconstrictors, such as Endothelin-1, which promotes an increase in total peripheral resistance. These cellular changes, although in the short term has anti-inflammatory effects, when chronically stimulated, may promote inflammation.

Although, we have outlined some stepwise changes that may occur in individuals who evaluate a situation as both challenging and threatening, we also posit some unique markers that we feel may differentiate this from individuals who evaluate a situation as only challenging or threatening. Evaluations of mixed valence are thought to be precipitated by parallel automatic processing or a rapid oscillation between appraisals (Cacioppo et al., 2011). With regard to the former, it has been suggested by Kreibig and Gross (2017) that behavioral reflexes may be associated with bivariate mixed emotions. Specifically, the postauricular reflex remains relatively unchanged during neutral and negatively valenced emotional states, yet is potentiated during positive emotions. In contrast, the eyeblink startle reflex is potentiated in response to negative emotions, but remains relatively unchanged in neutral and positively valenced emotional conditions. While Kreibig and Gross (2017) contend that these measures have different neural circuitries and can be concurrently evoked and measured, to date, there remain no studies that have used these measures in examining mixed emotions. With regard to the latter, it is conceivable that rapid oscillation between evaluative judgments may exhibit nonlinear patterns of HRV (c.f. Paton et al., 2005).

Summary

The narrative and accompanying table illustrate quantitative and qualitative differences associated with challenge, threat, and challenge and threat states. With regard to the qualitative differences, multiple markers may offer strength in inferring the presence of varying psychological constructs. To illustrate with just two markers, a two-step process would hypothetically differentiate, challenge, threat, and challenge and threat. TPR lowers in challenge, compared to threat groups and challenge and threat groups. In contrast, cortisol is hypothesized to increase in threatened but not for challenged or challenged and threatened individuals. In short, the combination of these indices offers potential for differentiating individuals who are challenged, threatened, or both challenged and threatened (**Table 2**).

In order to support these conceptual responses, future research should investigate the cardiac autonomic (HRV analysis), myocardial (electrocardiogram/imaging), and biomarker (inflammatory and vascular adhesion molecules) responses in individuals who present with challenge, threat, and mixed appraisals.

Self-Report Measures of Challenge and Threat

Alongside limitations of cognitive appraisal ratio measures reviewed above, it may be erroneous to assume that the measures such as the Primary and Secondary Appraisal Scale (PASA: Gaab et al., 2005), Cognitive Appraisal Scale (CAS: Skinner and Brewer, 2002), and Challenge and Threat Construal (McGregor and Elliot, 2002) developed in one population transfer to other contexts and situations (c.f. Hagger and Chatzisarantis, 2009). Notwithstanding the debate regarding the accessibility of individuals' appraisal processes, our stance is that self-report measures offer the potential for valuable insight into individuals' experience of challenge and threat, rather than privilege one "level" of measure as opposed to

TABLE 2 | Illustrative qualitative differences in psychophysiological indices associated with different states.

	Challenge	Threat	Challenge and threat
TPR	↓	↑	↑
Cortisol	↔	↑	↔

another. For example, where physiological indices of anxiety (HR) differed from individuals' self-report, it was noted that individuals' tendency toward defensiveness may explain the incongruence between the two (Weinberger et al., 1979).

Among athletes, Rossato et al. (2016) undertook a series of studies to develop a measure of Challenge and Threat in Sport (CAT-Sport) scale. More recently, Tomaka et al. (2018) developed an instrument to assess individuals' disposition to appraise events as challenging or threatening. The aim here is not to provide a thorough review of these instruments; rather the aim is to provide visibility to the range of instruments that are available to the discerning researcher, and to consider some of the issues in the use of measures across situations and contexts. Importantly, each of the latter two instruments afford the opportunity to assess challenge and threat independently of one another which enables interaction effects of challenge and threat on a range of outcome variables to be examined.

Self-Report Measures of Emotional Experience

There are a plethora of measures that examine individuals' emotions (see Jones et al., 2005 for a review). In terms of the ESACT approach, the Evaluative Space Grid (ESG: Larsen et al., 2009) provides a brief, effective instrument to assess positivity and negativity associated with particular contexts and stimuli. The ESG is a 5 × 5 grid in which respondents indicate how positive and negative they feel along the x-axis and y-axis respectively from 0 (not at all) to 4 (extremely). In a series of studies, Larsen and colleagues concluded that the ESG was more efficient than simple bipolar measures of positivity and negativity, and also afforded the assessment of ambivalence.

Given the importance of ambivalence and mixed emotions to our current model, it is perhaps helpful to explicate a little more fully how ambivalence in affect or challenged and threatened states might be assessed from self-report data. Ambivalence is typically defined as simultaneously holding positive and negative orientations toward an object (Ashforth et al., 2014). For example, consider a football player's reaction to a newly appointed manager. It is plausible that this individual could hold a positive appraisal of this coach's technical ability and simultaneously hold a negative appraisal of his/her interpersonal qualities. We draw upon the Griffin formula which has been demonstrated as an effective tool in assessing bivalent attitudes (Thompson et al., 1995). Specifically, it is proposed that there are two necessary and sufficient conditions of ambivalence. First, the two (bivalent) components (i.e., challenge and threat) must be similar in magnitude. Second, with similarity held constant, ambivalence increases directly with intensity. In short, ambivalence is equal to similarity plus intensity. For example, if we measured challenge and threat on 2, 4-point scales, similarity of components is assessed by subtracting the absolute difference of the challenge (C) and threat (T) components from 4 (so that similarity scores range from 4, when the C and T components are equivalent in magnitude, to 1, when the C and T components are maximally different). Intensity of components is assessed by averaging the challenge and threat components to give a formula of $4 - (C - T) + (C + T)/2$ (see **Table 3** for illustration). Similar to evaluations of Challenge and Threat, mixed emotions could also be assessed in a similar fashion using the ESG.

TABLE 3 | Illustration of ambivalence calculation.

	Evaluation of loss			
Evaluation of gain	**1**	**2**	**3**	**4**
1	1.0	0.5	0	−0.5
2	0.5	2.0	1.5	1.0
3	0	1.5	3.0	2.5
4	−0.5	1.0	2.5	4.0

RESEARCH IMPLICATIONS OF EVALUATIVE SPACE APPROACH TO CHALLENGE AND THREAT

Much of the research on challenge and threat, in sport at least, has been directed toward performance consequences. Because theoretical models guide and constrain our thinking, this is unsurprising. Although the ESACT may provide a framework for examination of the precursors and consequences of challenge and threat including performance, we take this opportunity to outline some novel paths regarding challenge and threat that hitherto have remained untrodden.

First, ambivalence associated with holding mixed evaluations about situations (and the concomitant emotions) is typically considered discomfiting (Ashforth et al., 2014), and that individuals will seek to resolve this dissonance. Both the ESM and literature on coactivation of goals (Gernigon et al., 2015) lend themselves to a dynamical systems approach and the processes by which individuals achieve stability in their appraisals, and the situations that perturb this stability arguably warrant exploration.

Second, the experience of being "pulled in more than one direction" that accompanies ambivalence has been demonstrated to be embodied in movement (Schneider et al., 2013). Schneider et al. for instance found that side-to-side movements on a Wii Balance Board were heightened in participants experiencing ambivalence compared to those participants who were not. The same research team (Schneider et al., 2015) asked participants to control a computer mouse while observing univalent and ambivalent attitude objects. Schneider et al. (2015) observed that computer mouse response times were lengthened and that more "pull" was exhibited when evaluating ambivalent rather than univalent attitude objects. It was speculated that opposite evaluations are often represented on a horizontal plane in mental space and that such mental representations may activate accompanying motor programs. Whether such findings extrapolate to performance in gymnastics for example in a task that is familiar to participants remains uncertain, yet the embodiment of challenge and threat states and the implications for performance and behavior represent an interesting line of enquiry.

Third, and indicative of the potential for both losses and gains, concerns the relationships between challenge, threat, and interpersonal relationships. According to Gable and Gosnell (2013), the nature of social bonds (such as coach-athlete relationships) is that they simultaneously offer both incentives and threats. Importantly, such relationships are integral to both performance (Jowett and Cockerill, 2003) and well-being (e.g., Hold-Lunstad et al., 2010). Hope for affiliation perhaps coupled with the fear of rejection may offer utility in explaining behaviors such as sacrifice (Prapavessis and Carron, 1997), and compromise and avoidance (Ashforth et al., 2014), variables that are important in understanding interpersonal functioning and performance.

Finally, examining the immunological and health consequences of adopting challenge and/or threatened states is likely beneficial. With regard to the latter for instance, in a 10-year longitudinal study, Hershfield et al. (2013) found that the co-occurrence of positive and negative emotions was not only associated with good physical health, but increases of mixed emotions over many years attenuated age-related health declines.

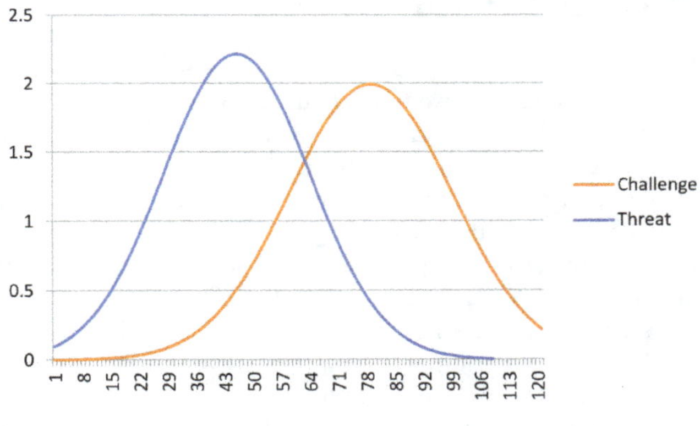

FIGURE 2 | Distribution of scores on Cardiac Output (derived from reported Mean and SD).

APPLIED IMPLICATIONS OF EVALUATIVE SPACE APPROACH TO CHALLENGE AND THREAT

Given the preceding arguments, we feel that although the ESACT may have utility in explaining aspects of sport performance, this is likely to heavily be influenced by a myriad of both individual and environmental factors such that the explanatory power of challenge, threat, and challenge and threat states *per se* may not explain much variance (i.e., beyond those indices that in TCTSA terms influence challenge and threat states, namely SE, perceptions of control, and performance goals). Against the backdrop of a body of research to suggest that a challenge state is associated with better performance compared to that of a threat state, in a range of both cognitive and sport-related activities (c.f. Hase et al., 2018), are a growing number of studies that refute the posited performance advantage associated with being in a challenge compared to a threat state. For example, Turner et al. (2012) found inconsistent relations between self-report and cardiovascular indices. Specifically, for some individuals exhibiting cardiovascular reactivity associated with threat, those reporting higher self-efficacy performed well in comparison to others exhibiting threat reactivity, but reporting low levels of self-efficacy. Indeed, consideration of the means and standard deviations reported in Turner et al.'s (2012) first study (see **Figure 2**) illustrates that there is considerable overlap in the distribution of scores on cardiac output.

Although establishing psychophysiological indices associated with challenged, threatened, and challenged and threatened states have a number of advantages, the extent to which the markers have a bearing on performance in and of themselves is somewhat questionable, and it is feasible to ask why relatively small changes in cardiovascular parameters associated with challenge and threat would have an impactful effect on sport performance. Phrased a little differently, physiological variables may be associated with challenged and threatened states, but the extent to which these parameters are mechanisms (e.g., energy efficiency) by which changes in performance are brought about are debatable, and for which there is mixed evidence (e.g., Moore et al., 2013; Wood et al., 2018).

In comparison, to performance outcomes, there is perhaps particular utility in the ESACT framework for guiding interventions to support individuals in developing adaptive and flexible motivational approaches to competition and life events more broadly. Specifically, whereas threat is typically viewed as unhelpful for performance, the ESACT model proposes that there is adaptive value in some situations to construe a performance situation as either threatening or as challenging *and* threatening. From this perspective, just as anxiety may not necessarily be unhelpful to performance, there can be some advantages associated with acknowledging and recognizing that sometimes there are losses as well as gains to be held. Anticipated threat associated with freefalling from an aeroplane for example may elicit some valuable preparative strategies in terms of checking the parachute! Moreover, when personal relevance is high, individuals may engage in more systematic processing to resolve the conflict, or when conflicting evaluations are difficult to change, individuals create order (see Schneider and Schwarz, 2017). This "meaning making" arising from ambivalence and specifically holding *both* positively *and* negatively valenced appraisals simultaneously may be valuable in the long term (compared to holding either positively or negatively valenced appraisals alone) and can help turn adversity to advantage (see Larsen et al., 2003). Furthermore, ambivalent attitudes are perhaps more pliable and more open to persuasive messaging interventions (Armitage and Conner, 2000).

Drawing on Gray's Reinforcement Sensitivity Theory (Gray, 1970; Corr, 2004), the threat of potential punishment has been advocated as one strategy to facilitate the development of resilience among athletes and the military (e.g., Bell et al., 2013). Anecdote, empirical data, and psychological models of change suggest that rather than reappraise a threat as a stressor (although this might at times be beneficial), there may be times when it is difficult to reduce the (perceived) demands of a situation, or enhance (perceived) resources (Crum et al., 2017).

CONCLUSION

Whereas the BPS model and TCTSA have been directed toward performance domains, we feel that the ESACT offers a number of advantages both in terms of research and practice moving forward. Although we have outlined a number of avenues that warrant scrutiny, the ESACT provides a broad framework for researchers and practitioners to forge their own paths. Extending the evaluative space to times (e.g., athlete transitions such as retirement), people (e.g., exercisers), and places (e.g., performance academies) away from the temporally restricted and somewhat myopic focus on performance offers opportunities to ask new questions and deliver practically important and impactful answers. The place of loss, threat, and suffering is evident in a range of psychotherapeutic approaches, and rather than dismiss threat as an undesirable state that we wish to avoid, reconceptualizing threat as having some advantages in some circumstances may confer flexibility to individuals experiencing threat and to those practitioners working alongside individuals to help enhance well-being and functioning. In particular, examining ambivalence through a motivational interviewing lens considers ambivalence a normal reaction to behavioral change and addressing ambivalence represents a key process in the behavioral change process (Miller and Rose, 2015). In critiquing the BPS model and TCTSA, and outlining an alternative Evaluative Space Approach to Challenge and Threat, we have provided a unique and significant contribution to the literature that sharpens our understanding, research, and practice.

AUTHOR CONTRIBUTIONS

Emerging from CR's doctoral studies (MU and JS were supervisors), MU led this review and alternative conceptualization, with MU, CR, and JOD contributing distinct sections to the first draft of the manuscript. JS provided a critical oversight, suggesting areas to strengthen, areas of omission, and matters of emphasis and priority. Several team meetings were held thereafter interspersed with revised drafts to refine the manuscript, complete revisions, and additions. All authors reviewed the final draft and played a significant part in the conceptualization and dissemination of this review.

REFERENCES

Armitage, C. J., and Conner, M. (2000). Attitudinal ambivalence: a test of three key hypotheses. *Pers. Soc. Psychol. Bull.* 26, 1421–1432. doi: 10.1177/0146167200263009

Ashforth, B. E., Rogers, K. M., Pratt, M. G., and Pradies, C. (2014). Ambivalence in organisations: a multilevel approach. *Organ. Sci.* 25, 1453–1478. doi: 10.1287/orsc.2014.0909

Beauchaine, T. (2001). Vagal tone, development, and Gray's motivational theory: toward an integrated model of autonomic nervous system functioning in psychopathology. *Dev. Psychopathol.* 13, 183–214. doi: 10.1017/S0954579401002012

Bell, J. J., Hardy, L., and Beattie, S. (2013). Enhancing mental toughness and performance under pressure in elite young cricketers: a 2-year longitudinal intervention. *Sport Exerc. Perform. Psychol.* 2, 281–297. doi: 10.1037/a0033129

Berntson, G. G., and Cacioppo, J. T. (2008). "The functional neuroarchitecture of evaluative processes" in *Handbook of approach and avoidance motivation.* ed. A. J. Elliot (New York, NY, US: Psychology Press), 307–321.

Berntson, G. G., Cacioppo, J. T., Binkley, P. F., Uchino, B. N., Quigley, K. S., and Fieldstone, A. (1994). Autonomic cardiac control. III. Psychological stress and cardiac response in autonomic space as revealed by pharmacological blockades. *Psychophysiology* 31, 599–608. doi: 10.1111/j.1469-8986.1994.tb02352.x

Berntson, G. G., Cacioppo, J. T., and Quigley, K. S. (1991). Autonomic determinism: the modes of autonomic control, the doctrine of autonomic space, and the laws of autonomic constraint. *Psychol. Rev.* 98, 459–459. doi: 10.1037/0033-295X.98.4.459

Berntson, G. G., Cacioppo, J. T., and Quigley, K. S. (1993). Cardiac psychophysiology and autonomic space in humans: empirical perspectives and conceptual implications. *Psychol. Bull.* 114, 296–322. doi: 10.1037/0033-2909.114.2.296

Berntson, G. G., Normon, G. J., Hawkley, L. C., and Cacioppo, J. T. (2008). Cardiac autonomic balance versus cardiac regulatory capacity. *Psychophysiology* 45, 643–652. doi: 10.1111/j.1469-8986.2008.00652.x

Billman, G. E. (2011). Heart rate variability – a historical perspective. *Front. Physiol.* 2:86. doi: 10.3389/fphys.2011.00086

Blair, C., Peters, R., and Granger, D. (2004). Physiological and neuropsychological correlates of approach/withdrawal tendencies in preschool: further examination of the behavioural inhibition system/behavioural activation system scales for young children. *Dev. Psychobiol.* 45, 113–124. doi: 10.1002/dev.20022

Blascovich, J. (2008). "Challenge and threat" in *Handbook of approach and avoidance motivation.* ed. A. J. Elliot (New York, NY, US: Psychology Press), 431–445.

Blascovich, J., and Mendes, W. B. (2000). "Challenge and threat appraisals: the role of affective cues" in *Feeling and thinking: The role of affect in social cognition.* ed. J. P. Forgas (Paris: Cambridge University Press), 59–82.

Blascovich, J., and Mendes, W. B. (2010). "Social psychophysiology and embodiment" in *Handbook of social psychology.* 5th edn. eds. S. T. Fiske, D. T. Gilbert, and G. Lindzey, vol. 1 (New York, NY: Wiley), 194–227.

Blascovich, J., Mendes, W. B., Tomaka, J., Salomon, K., and Seery, M. (2003). The robust nature of the biopsychosocial model challenge and threat: a reply to Wright and Kirby. *Pers. Soc. Psychol. Rev.* 7, 234–243. doi: 10.1207/S15327957PSPR0703_03

Blascovich, J., Seery, M. D., Mugridge, C. A., Norris, R. K., and Weisbuch, M. (2004). Predicting athletic performance from cardiovascular indices of challenge and threat. *J. Exp. Soc. Psychol.* 40, 683–688. doi: 10.1016/j.jesp.2003.10.007

Blascovich, J., and Tomaka, J. (1996). The biopsychosocial model of arousal regulation. *Adv. Exp. Soc. Psychol.* 28, 1–51.

Cacioppo, J. T., and Berntson, G. G. (1994). Relationship between attitudes and evaluative space: a critical review, with emphasis on the separability of positive and negative substrates. *Psychol. Bull.* 115, 401–423. doi: 10.1037/0033-2909.115.3.401

Cacioppo, J. T., Berntson, G. G., Norris, C. J., and Gollan, J. K. (2011). "The evaluative space model" in *Handbook of theories of social psychology.* eds. P. A. M. Van Lange, A. W. Kruglanski, and E. T. Higgins, vol. 1 (London: Sage), 50–72.

Cacioppo, J. T., Gardner, W. L., and Berntson, G. G. (1997). Beyond bipolar conceptualisations and measures: the case of attitudes and evaluative space. *Pers. Soc. Psychol. Rev.* 1, 3–25.

Cacioppo, J. T., and Tassinary, L. G. (1990). Inferring psychological significance from physiological signals. *Am. Psychol.* 45, 16–28. doi: 10.1037/0003-066X.45.1.16

Campbell, E., and Jones, G. (2002). Cognitive appraisal of sources of stress experienced by elite male wheelchair basketball players. *Adapt. Phys. Activ. Q.* 19, 100–108. doi: 10.1123/apaq.19.1.100

Casad, B. J., and Petzel, Z. W. (2018). Heart rate variability moderates challenge and threat reactivity to sexism among women in STEM. *Soc. Psychol.* 49, 191–204. doi: 10.1027/1864-9335/a000341

Cerin, E. (2003). Anxiety versus fundamental emotions as predictors of perceived functionality of pre-competitive emotional states, threat, and challenge in individual sports. *J. Appl. Sport Psychol.* 15, 223–238. doi: 10.1080/10413200305389

Chalabaev, A., Major, B., Cury, F., and Sarrazin, P. (2009). Physiological markers of challenge and threat mediate the effects of performance-based goals on performance. *J. Exp. Soc. Psychol.* 45, 991–994. doi: 10.1016/j.jesp.2009.04.009

Chalmers, J. A., Quintana, D. S., Abbott, M. J., and Kemp, A. H. (2014). Anxiety disorders are associated with reduced heart rate variability: a meta-analysis. *Front. Psychiatry* 5:80. doi: 10.3389/fpsyt.2014.00080

Corr, P. J. (2004). Reinforcement sensitivity theory and personality. *Neurosci. Biobehav. Rev.* 28, 317–332. doi: 10.1016/j.neubiorev.2004.01.005

Crum, A. J., Akinola, M., Martin, A., and Fath, S. (2017). The role of stress mindset in shaping cognitive, emotional, and physiological responses to challenging and threatening stress. *Anxiety Stress Coping* 30, 379–395. doi: 10.1080/10615806.2016.1275585

de Gelder, B., and Vroomen, J. (2000). The perception of emotions by ear and by eye. *Cognit. Emot.* 14, 289–311. doi: 10.1080/026999300378824

Dienstbier, R. A. (1989). Arousal and physiological toughness: implications for mental and physical health. *Psychol. Rev.* 96, 84–100. doi: 10.1037/0033-295X.96.1.84

Elliot, A. J., and Covington, M. V. (2001). Approach and avoidance motivation. *Educ. Psychol. Rev.* 13, 73–92. doi: 10.1023/A:1009009018235

Folkman, S., and Lazarus, R. S. (1985). If it changes it must be a process: study of emotion and coping during three stages of a college examination. *J. Pers. Soc. Psychol.* 48, 150–170. doi: 10.1037/0022-3514.48.1.150

Folkman, S., and Lazarus, R. S. (1986). Dynamics of a stressful encounter: cognitive appraisal, coping, and encounter outcomes. *J. Pers. Soc. Psychol.* 50, 992–1003. doi: 10.1037/0022-3514.50.5.992

Gaab, J., Rohleder, N., Nater, U. M., and Ehlert, U. (2005). Psychological determinants of the cortisol stress response: the role of anticipatory cognitive appraisal. *Psychoneuroendocrinology* 30, 599–610. doi: 10.1016/j.psyneuen.2005.02.001

Gable, S. L., and Gosnell, C. L. (2013). Approach and avoidance behaviour in interpersonal relationships. *Emot. Rev.* 5, 269–274. doi: 10.1177/1754073913477513

Gernigon, C., Vallacher, R. R., Nowak, A., and Conroy, D. E. (2015). Rethinking approach and avoidance in achievement contexts: the perspective of dynamical systems. *Rev. Gen. Psychol.* 19, 443–457. doi: 10.1037/gpr0000055

Gray, J. A. (1970). The psychophysiological basis of introversion-extraversion. *Behav. Res. Ther.* 8, 249–266. doi: 10.1016/0005-7967(70)90069-0

Hagger, M. S., and Chatzisarantis, N. (2009). Assumptions in research in sport and exercise psychology. *Psychol. Sport Exerc.* 10, 511–519. doi: 10.1016/j.psychsport.2009.01.004

Hase, A., O'Brien, J., Moore, L. J., and Freeman, P. (2018). The relationship between challenge and threat states and performance: a systematic review. *Sport Exerc. Perform. Psychol.* 8, 123–144. doi: 10.1037/spy0000132

Herman, J. P., McKlveen, J. M., Ghosal, S., Kopp, B., Wulsin, A., Makinson, R., et al. (2016). Regulation of the hypothalamic-pituitary-adrenocortical stress response. *Compr. Physiol.* 6, 603–621. doi: 10.1002/cphy.c150015

Hershfield, H. E., Scheibe, S., Sims, T. L., and Carstensen, L. L. (2013). When feeling bad can be good: mixed emotions benefit physical health across adulthood. *Soc. Psychol. Personal. Sci.* 4, 54–61. doi: 10.1177/1948550612444616

Hold-Lunstad, J., Smith, T. B., and Layton, J. B. (2010). Social relationships and mortality risk: a meta-analytic review. *PLoS Med.* 7:e1000316. doi: 10.1371/journal.pmed.1000316

Hulleman, C. S., Schrager, S. M., Boadmann, S. M., and Harackiewicz, J. M. (2010). A meta-analytic review of achievement goal measures: different labels for the same constructs or different constructs with similar labels? *Psychol. Bull.* 136, 422–449. doi: 10.1037/a0018947

Ito, T. A., and Cacioppo, J. T. (1999). "The psychophysiology of utility appraisals" in *Well-being: The foundations of hedonic psychology*. eds. D. Kahneman, E. Diener, and N. Schwarz (New York, NY, US: Russell Sage Foundation), 470–488.

Jones, M., Meijen, C., McCarthy, P. J., and Sheffield, D. (2009). A theory of challenge and threat states in athletes. *Int. Rev. Sport Exerc. Psychol.* 2, 161–180. doi: 10.1080/17509840902829331

Jones, M. V., Lane, A. M., Bray, S. R., Uphill, M., and Catlin, J. (2005). Development and validation of the sport emotion questionnaire. *J. Sport Exerc. Psychol.* 27, 407–431. doi: 10.1123/jsep.27.4.407

Jowett, S., and Cockerill, I. M. (2003). Olympic medallists' perspective of the athlete–coach relationship. *Psychol. Sport Exerc.* 4, 313–331. doi: 10.1016/S1469-0292(02)00011-0

Kahneman, D. (1992). Reference points, anchors, norms, and mixed feelings. *Organ. Behav. Hum. Decis. Process.* 51, 296–312. doi: 10.1016/0749-5978(92)90015-Y

Kramer, K. M. (2013). Six criteria of a viable theory: putting reversal theory to the test. *J. Motivation Emot. Personal.* 1, 9–16. doi: 10.12689/jmep.2013.102

Kreibig, S. D., Gendolla, G. H., and Scherer, K. R. (2012). Goal relevance and goal conduciveness appraisals lead to differential autonomic reactivity in emotional responding to performance feedback. *Biol. Psychol.* 91, 365–375. doi: 10.1016/j.biopsycho.2012.08.007

Kreibig, S. D., and Gross, J. J. (2017). Understanding mixed emotions: paradigms and measures. *Curr. Opin. Behav. Sci.* 15, 62–71. doi: 10.1016/j.cobeha.2017.05.016

Kreibig, S. D., Samson, A. C., and Gross, J. J. (2015). The psychophysiology of mixed emotional states: internal and external replicability analysis of a direct replication study. *Psychophysiology* 52, 873–886. doi: 10.1111/psyp.12425

Larsen, J. T., Hemenover, S. H., Norris, C. J., and Cacioppo, J. T. (2003). "Turning adversity into advantage: on the virtues of the coactivation of positive and negative emotions" in *A psychology of human strengths: Fundamental questions and future directions for a positive psychology*. eds. L. G. Aspinwall and U. M. Straudinger (Washington, DC: American Psychological Association), 211–255.

Larsen, J. T., McGraw, A. P., and Cacioppo, J. T. (2001). Can people feel happy and sad at the same time? *J. Pers. Soc. Psychol.* 81, 684–696. doi: 10.1037/0022-3514.81.4.684

Larsen, J. T., McGraw, A. P., Mellers, B. A., and Cacioppo, J. T. (2004). The agony of victory and thrill of defeat: mixed emotional reactions to disappointing wins and relieving losses. *Psychol. Sci.* 15, 325–330. doi: 10.1111/j.0956-7976.2004.00677.x

Larsen, J. T., Norris, C. J., McGraw, A. P., Hawkley, L. C., and Cacioppo, J. T. (2009). The evaluative space grid: a single-item measure of positivity and negativity. *Cognit. Emot.* 23, 453–480. doi: 10.1080/02699930801994054

Law, W., Elliot, A. J., and Murayama, K. (2012). Perceived competence moderates the relation between performance-approach and performance-avoidance goals. *J. Educ. Psychol.* 104, 806–819. doi: 10.1037/a0027179

Lazarus, R. S. (1999). *Stress and emotion: A new synthesis*. (New York: Springer Publishing Co).

Lazarus, R. S., and Folkman, S. (1984). *Stress, appraisal, and coping*. (New York: Springer Publishing Co).

Man, V., Nohlen, H., Melo, H. U., and Cunningham, W. A. (2017). Hierarchical brain systems support multiple representations of valence and mixed affect. *Emot. Rev.* 9, 124–132. doi: 10.1177/1754073916667237

McGregor, H. A., and Elliot, A. J. (2002). Achievement goals as predictors of achievement-relevant processes prior to task engagement. *J. Educ. Psychol.* 94, 381–395. doi: 10.1037/0022-0663.94.2.381

Meijen, C., Jones, M. V., McCarthy, P. J., Sheffield, D., and Allen, M. S. (2013). Cognitive and affective components of challenge and threat states. *J. Sports Sci.* 31, 847–855. doi: 10.1080/02640414.2012.753157

Miller, W. R., and Rose, G. S. (2015). Motivational interviewing and decisional balance: contrasting responses to client ambivalence. *Behav. Cogn. Psychother.* 43, 129–141. doi: 10.1017/S1352465813000878

Moore, L. J., Wilson, M. R., Vine, S. J., Coussens, A. H., and Freeman, P. (2013). Champ or chump?: challenge and threat states during pressurized competition. *J. Sport Exerc. Psychol.* 35, 551–562. doi: 10.1123/jsep.35.6.551

Norris, C. J., Gollan, J., Berntson, G. G., and Cacioppo, J. T. (2010). The current status of research on the structure of evaluative space. *Biol. Psychol.* 84, 422–436. doi: 10.1016/j.biopsycho.2010.03.011

O'Driscoll, J., and Sharma, R. (2015). Non-invasive assessment of the autonomic nervous system. *Int. J. Clin. Ther.Diagn.* 3, 85–91. doi: 10.19070/2332-2926-1500017

Paton, J. F. R., Boscan, P., Pickering, A. E., and Nalivaiko, E. (2005). The yin and yang of cardiac autonomic control: vago-sympathetic interactions revisited. *Brain Res. Rev.* 49, 555–565. doi: 10.1016/j.brainresrev.2005.02.005

Porges, S. W. (2007). The polyvagal perspective. *Biol. Psychol.* 74, 116–143. doi: 10.1016/j.biopsycho.2006.06.009

Prapavessis, H., and Carron, A. V. (1997). Sacrifice, cohesion, and conformity to norms in sport teams. *Group Dyn. Theory Res. Pract.* 1, 231–240. doi: 10.1037/1089-2699.1.3.231

Quigley, K. S., Barrett, L. F., and Weinstein, S. (2002). Cardiovascular patterns associated with threat and challenge appraisals: a within-subjects analysis. *Psychophysiology* 39, 292–302. doi: 10.1017/S0048577201393046

Rossato, C. J. L., Uphill, M. A., Swain, J., and Coleman, D. A. (2016). The development and preliminary validation of the challenge and threat in sport (CAT-sport) scale. *Int. J. Sport Exercise Psychol.* 16, 1–14. doi: 10.1080/1612197X.2016.1182571

Russell, J. A., and Carroll, J. M. (1999). On the bipolarity of positive and negative affect. *Psychol. Bull.* 125, 3–30. doi: 10.1037/0033-2909.125.1.3

Schneider, I. K., Eerland, A., van Harreveld, F., Rotteveel, M., van der Pligt, J., van der Stoep, N., et al. (2013). One way and the other: the bidirectional relationship between ambivalence and body movement. *Psychol. Sci.* 24, 319–325. doi: 10.1177/0956797612457393

Schneider, I. K., and Schwarz, N. (2017). Mixed feelings: the case of ambivalence. *Curr. Opin. Behav. Sci.* 15, 39–45. doi: 10.1016/j.cobeha.2017.05.012

Schneider, I. K., van Harreveld, F., Rotteveel, M., Topolinski, S., van der Pligt, J., Schwarz, N., et al. (2015). The path of ambivalence: tracing the pull of opposing evaluations using mouse trajectories. *Front. Psychol.* 6:996. doi: 10.3389/fpsyg.2015.00996

Seery, M. D. (2011). Challenge or threat? Cardiovascular indexes of resilience and vulnerability to potential stress in humans. *Neurosci. Biobehav. Rev.* 35, 1603–1610. doi: 10.1016/j.neubiorev.2011.03.003

Seery, M. D. (2013). The biopsychosocial model of challenge and threat: using the heart to measure the mind. *Soc. Personal. Psychol. Compass* 7, 637–653. doi: 10.1111/spc3.12052

Sirsch, U. (2003). The impending transition from primary to secondary school: challenge or threat? *Int. J. Behav. Dev.* 27, 385–395. doi: 10.1080/01650250344000082

Skinner, N., and Brewer, N. (2002). The dynamics of threat and challenge appraisals prior to stressful achievement events. *J. Pers. Soc. Psychol.* 83, 678–692. doi: 10.1037/0022-3514.83.3.678

Skinner, N., and Brewer, N. (2004). Adaptive approaches to competition: challenge appraisals and positive emotion. *J. Sport Exerc. Psychol.* 26, 283–305. doi: 10.1123/jsep.26.2.283

Steffen, P. R., Austin, T., DeBarros, A., and Brown, T. (2017). The impact of resonance frequency breathing on measures of heart rate variability, blood pressure and mood. *Front. Public Health* 5:222. doi: 10.3389/fpubh.2017.00222

Stratton, J. R., Pfeifer, M. A., and Halter, J. B. (1987). The hemodynamic effects of sympathetic stimulation combined with parasympathetic blockade in man. *Circulation* 75, 922–929. doi: 10.1161/01.cir.75.5.922

Thompson, M. M., Zanna, M. P., and Griffin, D. W. (1995). "Let's not be indifferent about (attitudinal) ambivalence" in *Attitude strength: Antecedents and consequences*. eds. R. E. Petty and J. A. Krosnick (Mahwah, NJ: Lawrence Erlbaum), 361–386.

Tomaka, J., Blascovich, J., Kelsey, R. M., and Leitten, C. L. (1993). Subjective, physiological, and behavioural effects of threat and challenge appraisal. *J. Pers. Soc. Psychol.* 65, 248–260. doi: 10.1037/0022-3514.65.2.248

Tomaka, J., Blascovich, J., Kibler, J., and Ernst, J. M. (1997). Cognitive and physiological antecedents of threat and challenge appraisal. *J. Pers. Soc. Psychol.* 73, 63–72. doi: 10.1037/0022-3514.73.1.63

Tomaka, J., Palacios, R. L., Champion, C., and Monks, S. (2018). Development and validation of an instrument that assesses individual differences in threat and challenge appraisal. *J Depression Anxiety* 7:313. doi: 10.4172/2167-1044.10003

Turner, M., Jones, M., Sheffield, D., Slater, M., Barker, J., and Bell, J. (2013). Who thrives under pressure? Predicting the performance of elite academy cricketers using the cardiovascular indicators of challenge and threat states. *J. Sport Exerc. Psychol.* 35, 387–397. doi: 10.1123/jsep.35.4.387

Turner, M. J., Jones, M. V., Sheffield, D., and Cross, S. L. (2012). Cardiovascular indices of challenge and threat states predict competitive performance. *Int. J. Psychophysiol.* 86, 48–57. doi: 10.1016/j.ijpsycho.2012.08.004

Weinberger, D. A., Schwartz, G. E., and Davidson, R. J. (1979). Low-anxious, high-anxious, and repressive coping styles: psychometric patterns and behavioural and physiological responses to stress. *J. Abnorm. Psychol.* 88, 369–380. doi: 10.1037/0021-843X.88.4.369

Wood, N., Parker, J., Freeman, P., Black, M., and Moore, L. (2018). The relationship between challenge and threat states and anaerobic power, core affect, perceived exertion, and self-focussed attention during a competitive sprint cycling task. *Prog. Brain Res.* 240, 1–17. doi: 10.1016/bs.pbr.2018.08.006

Wright, R. A., and Kirby, L. D. (2003). Cardiovascular correlates of challenge and threat appraisals: a critical examination of the biopsychosocial analysis. *Pers. Soc. Psychol. Rev.* 7, 216–233. doi: 10.1207/S15327957PSPR0703_02

Zajonc, R. B. (1998). "Emotion" in *The handbook of social psychology*. 4th Edn. eds. D. T. Gilbert, S. T. Fiske, and G. Lindzey (New York: McGraw-Hill), 591–632.

Zayas, V., and Shoda, Y. (2015). Love you? Hate you? Maybe it's both: evidence that significant others trigger bivalent-priming. *Soc. Psychol. Personal. Sci.* 6, 56–64. doi: 10.1177/1948550614541297

2

The Power of Faith: The Influence of Athletes' Coping Self-Efficacy on the Cognitive Processing of Psychological Stress

Tengfei Guo[1†], Yakun Ni[1†], Qiaoling Li[1] and Hao Hong[2]*

[1] School of Educational Science, Henan University, Kaifeng, China, [2] School of Physical Education, Henan University, Kaifeng, China

Correspondence:
Qiaoling Li
lqlinger@163.com

†These authors have contributed equally to this work

Coping self-efficacy (CSE) has a positive mental health effect on athletes' ability to cope with stress. To understand the mechanism underlying the potential impact of CSE, event-related potentials (ERPs) were used to explore the neural activity of the cerebral cortex under acute psychological stress in athletes with different CSE levels. Among 106 high-level athletes, 21 high-CSE athletes and 20 low-CSE athletes were selected to participate in the experiment. A mental arithmetic task was used to induce acute psychological stress. The results showed that high-CSE athletes responded more quickly than low-CSE athletes. In the stress response stage, the N1 peak latency of low-CSE athletes was longer than that of high-CSE athletes, and the N1 amplitude was significantly larger than that of high-CSE athletes. In the feedback stage, the FRN amplitude with error feedback of high-CSE athletes was larger than that of low-CSE athletes, and the P300 amplitude with correct feedback was larger than that with error feedback. The results indicate that high-CSE athletes can better cope with stressful events, adjust their behaviors in a timely manner according to the results of their coping, and focus more on processing positive information.

Keywords: coping self-efficacy, psychological stress, N1, FRN, P300, athletes

INTRODUCTION

As a high-stress group expected to perform in an intensely competitive environment, athletes face various stressful events. Factors such as the time pressures of the game, noise from the audience, and the uncertainty of competition, all place athletes in a state of high tension, cause acute psychological stress. Unlike the physiological stress caused by situations such as pain and hunger, psychosocial stress is mainly induced by socially threatening situations such as social evaluation, social exclusion, and achievement/cognitive stress and occurs when an individual's psychological homeostatic process is threatened (Pruessner et al., 2010; Kogler et al., 2015). Studies show that stress is the main cause of athletes' mental health problems (Gulliver et al., 2015; Rice et al., 2016; Sabato et al., 2016; Gerber et al., 2018). Many athletes cannot withstand psychological pressure before and during competition, thus affecting their physical and technical performance and eventually preventing them from achieving the desired results (Moritz et al.,

2000; Nicholls et al., 2010). Therefore, it is particularly important for athletes to be able to cope with the pressures of competition.

Ideal athletic performance occurs when an athlete successfully copes with various adverse situations during competition. The pressure cognitive interaction theory argues that coping is an important regulatory variable of the psychosocial stress that affects individuals' physical and mental health (Lazarus and Folkman, 1984; Edwards and Cooper, 1988). As a pressure buffer and resource replenishment device, coping helps athletes self-regulate and eliminate the interference caused by stress and helps them quickly adapt to stressful situations that arise in competition (Nicholls and Perry, 2016). When facing a stressful situation, the more that an athlete can mobilize resources such as cognitive level, self-confidence, experience, and willpower, the higher the motivation level is, and the more active the involvement is. Bandura (1997) proposes that individuals' motivation level, emotional state, and behavior are based more on what they believe than on what is objective and true. Coping self-efficacy (CSE) is an extension of self-efficacy theory in the field of coping and refers to an individual's confidence about his/her ability to cope successfully with stress (Benight et al., 1997). CSE is considered an important influencing factor in athletes' ability to effectively cope with the stress of competition (Gyurcsik et al., 2010).

As an intrinsic and relatively stable individual belief, CSE directly affects an athlete's ability to cope effectively with stress. Therefore, exploring the mechanism of CSE as a potential belief helps illuminate why some athletes feel more confident than others about their ability to cope effectively with stress. This study uses the event-related potential (ERP) technique to reveal the cortical neurological activity induced by acute psychological stress in athletes with different CSE levels. The brain is believed to be the organ that plays a core role in stress reactivity, coping, and recovery processes (McEwen, 2009; McEwen and Gianaros, 2010). In response to stress, the brain activates several neuropeptide-secreting systems. The brain first processes various stimuli deemed threats and then induces endocrine responses *via* the hypothalamus-pituitary-adrenal axis (HPA axis) and the sympathetic adrenal medulla axis (De Kloet et al., 2005; Foley and Kirschbaum, 2011), which in turn generate physiological and behavioral responses to the stimuli. Therefore, attention-related brain cognitive processes are particularly important in competitive sports. Individuals' information processing ability is limited. Therefore, in fast ball sports such as basketball, athletes must select prominent key information for processing from a large corpus of information (Isoglualkac et al., 2018). Using the ERP technique in a high temporal resolution enables understanding the intracerebral temporal dynamic changes during the attention-processing process of athletes under stress.

Uncontrollability and social-evaluated threats are the two key stressors responsible for acute psychological stress (Dickerson and Kemeny, 2004). Based on previous studies (Yang et al., 2012; Qi et al., 2018), this study used the multiplication estimation task and designed an experimental situation to induce the psychological stress response of participants by limiting the time available for decision-making (to induce uncontrollability) and informing the participant that his/her correct answer rate would be compared with that of another participant, and a reward would be given accordingly (to induce social-evaluated threat). The study by Qi et al. (2016) showed that the individual's salivary cortisol content significantly increased after a mental arithmetic task, confirming the task's successful induction of acute psychological stress response. When stressed, high-CSE individuals are more confident about their ability to face the challenges of stress and adopt effective coping strategies to maintain their physical and mental health. In contrast, low-CSE individuals have insufficient self-confidence and cannot effectively or timely relieve various psychological and physical symptoms caused by stress, resulting in threats to their health (Watson and Watson, 2016). To understand the potential influencing factors of athletes' CSE and improve the ability of high-level athletes to cope with stress, this study used the ERP technique to explore differences in the neurological activities of athletes with different CSE levels under psychological stress and stress assessment feedback, thereby further illuminating the mechanism underlying the effect of CSE on individuals under stress.

Acute psychological stress causes the body to be in a state of high vigilance and high arousal, making early sensory coding sensitive (Löw et al., 2015). If the stimulus requires an individual to respond quickly, attention should be directed to the perception process that primarily manifests in the N1 component, and the increased vigilance should trigger a more negative N1 component (Shackman et al., 2011). Low-CSE individuals often show insufficient confidence when they are under stress, unable to effectively control stress situations, and are in a state of high tension and anxiety (Nicholls et al., 2010). Therefore, we predicted that, compared with high-CSE athletes, low-CSE athletes would show a larger amplitude of N1 under stress. Stress also has a regulatory effect on the allocation of attention resources (Shackman et al., 2011; Sänger et al., 2014; Löw et al., 2015). Some studies have shown that, stress is helpful in narrowing the focus of attention and has a negative impact on the allocation of attention resources (Dambacher and Hübner, 2015; Qi et al., 2016). As a "control switch" for allocating decision resources, the P2 component is linked to attention selection and control processing. The larger the P2 amplitude, the higher the individual's attention level (Yuan et al., 2016). Since the high-CSE individual is more confident in accepting the tasks of stress and challenge, and the attention resources are weakened by the reduction of stress, in this sense, we predicted that the P2 amplitude of high-CSE athletes is larger than that of athletes with low CSE under stress.

"Assessment" is the core concept in the theory of stress-cognitive interaction (Lazarus and Folkman, 1984). To adapt to a changing environment, individuals must monitor the appropriateness of their current behavior and adjust their behavior accordingly. For example, after erring or receiving an error feedback, individuals must adjust their behavior to reduce the possibility of committing a similar error. In a stressful environment, the assessment of coping outcomes affects an individual's subsequent coping efforts (Crocker et al., 2015). Previous studies showed that the result assessment process consisted of two main stages: the early stage of elementary automatic rapid assessment processing, as characterized by feedback-related negativity (FRN), and the late stage of top-down sophisticated control processing, which affected the allocation of attention resources and was characterized by P300 (Wu and Zhou, 2009; Leng and Zhou, 2010). The existing literature still lacks ERP evidence related to the assessment of stress results. This study uses FRN and P300 as indicators to investigate the temporal dynamic characteristics of the process of feedback assessment under stress. When facing the wrong response or getting the wrong feedback, they have to adjust their behavior in a timely manner to reduce the possibility of making errors. FRN reflects cognitive processing of expected error monitoring (Holroyd and Coles, 2002), an individual with high CSE can make self-evaluation of the effectiveness of responding more promptly to dangerous situations (Benight et al., 1999). In this sense, we hypothesize that in the wrong feedback phrase, the FRN amplitude of athletes with high CSE is larger than that of athletes with low CSE. In addition, previous study of the impact of stress on executive control resources (Shields et al., 2016) suggests that stress will reallocate the executive control resources from working memory and cognitive flexibility to selective attention, in order to focus on processing current stress-related information. P300, which reflects the allocation of cognitive resources in the late stage of information processing, is a neurological index of selective attention; the more the cognitive resources are occupied, the larger the P300 component is induced (Kopp and Lange, 2013). When interacting with the environment, the athletes with high CSE are inclined to positively control the environment and events that may cause stress, while the athletes with low CSE are inclined to think about personal deficiencies and take the potential difficulties more seriously than they really are (Nicholls et al., 2010). Therefore, on the basis of "mood congruent effect," we assume that, the athletes with high CSE will have larger P300 amplitudes in positive feedback processing, while the athletes with low CSE will have a larger P300 amplitude in negative feedback processing.

MATERIALS AND METHODS

Participants

We recruited high-level basketball players from several universities located in central part of China. The participants consisted of 106 high-level basketball players who were mostly players of Chinese University Basketball Association (CUBA). They had to pass rigorous physical and cognitive tests to become CUBA registered athletes. Before the participants registered for the experiment, the researcher explained the purpose of the project and asked them for their consent to participate. Firstly, we employed coping self-efficacy scale (Chesney et al., 2006) to test the degree of coping self-efficacy (CSE) of 106 high-level basketball players. Secondly, according to their CSE scores' ranking, the participants whose CSE scores were ranking in top 27 percent of all participants were assigned to the high-CSE group (including 29 participants) and the participants whose CSE scores were ranking in the bottom 27 percent of all participants were assigned to the low-CSE group (including 29 participants). The CSE scores of high-CSE group ranged from 66 to 75 points (M = 69.21, SD = 2.93), and the CSE scores of low-CSE group ranged from 43 to 58 points (M = 53.97, SD = 3.86). For 1 week before the start of the experiment, all participants were allowed to refrain from taking any coffee and getting plenty of rest. Finally, 41 athletes also volunteered later to participate in the experiment, of which the high-CSE group consisted of 21 high-level basketball players (including 17 males and 4 females), and the low-CSE group consisted of 20 high-level basketball players (including 15 males and 5 females). Participants in the high-CSE group had an average age of 20.9 ± 1.34 years and included four national first-class athletes and 17 national second-class athletes, who played the forward (9), center (5), and defender (7) positions in the field. Participants in the low-CSE group had an average age of 20.7 ± 1.03 years and included two national first-class athletes and 18 national second-class athletes, who played the forward (10), center (4), and defender (6) positions in the field. The CSE score of the high-CSE group (69.52 ± 2.94) was significantly higher than that of the low-CSE group (52.80 ± 4.06), with $t(39) = 15.16$, $p < 0.001$, and Cohen's $d = 4.74$. All participants in the experiment were right-handed, with normal naked eyesight or corrected visual acuity, and were participating in such experimental research for the first time. Before participating in the experiment, the participants were asked to refrain from taking any coffee and having a good sleep. In accordance with experimental ethical principles, all basketball players participating in the experiment signed an informed consent form prior to the experiment and received an honorarium of 40 CNY cash after completing the experiment.

Design and Materials

The multiplication estimation task imposed a time limit for answering and included a social-evaluated threat. This task was used to induce a psychological stress response in participants (Qi et al., 2018). Two hundred and forty multiplication arithmetic problems were presented. The problems consisted of two numbers less than 10 and with two decimals (for example, 2.36 × 4.59). The numbers were selected from a series of Gaussian distributed numbers in the range of 1–10, with an average of 5 and a standard deviation of 2.5. The participants were required to determine whether the result of each arithmetic problem was less than 10 and press the "1" key if so and the "2" key otherwise. After an answer was submitted, the result was displayed as "correct," "wrong," or "time out."

A single-factor inter-participant design was used. The independent variable was the type of basketball player participating in the experiment, namely, high-CSE or low-CSE basketball player. The dependent variable was the response time, the accuracy rate of the participant under stress, and the electroencephalographic (EEG) data of the participants in the stress stage and the feedback stage.

Procedure

The experiment was conducted in a quiet and soundproof EEG laboratory. The participant wore an electrode cap, which positioned both eyes approximately 80 cm from the computer screen. Stimulating materials were presented using E-Prime 2.0 (Psychology Software Tools, Inc., Sharpsburg, USA) and appeared in black on a white background at the center of a

19-inch computer screen at a viewing angle of 6.66° × 4.87°. After the experiment started, the participants familiarized themselves with the experimental tasks and keyboard operations through the instructions and then performed the corresponding practice experiments. After they fully understood and could independently and skillfully complete the experimental procedures, the experiment formally began.

At the beginning of the experiment, a "+"-shaped gaze point appeared in the center of the screen for 500 ms to remind the participants to focus on the experiment, after which an arithmetic problem was displayed. The participants were asked to quickly and accurately complete the mental arithmetic problem and submit their answer by pressing one of two keys. If the answer to the arithmetic problem was less than 10, the number "1" key was pressed, and the number "2" key was pressed otherwise. The time limit for answering a problem was 2,000 ms, and a red countdown was displayed at the bottom of the screen, decreasing as "3-2-1" over time. After the "1" or "2" key was pressed or after time expired, a blank screen appeared for 500 ms, followed by feedback, i.e., correct, wrong, and timeout, for 1,000 ms. Then, the next trial began. The experiment consisted of 240 trials, and after every 60 trials, there was a rest time controlled by the participants. The detailed experimental procedure is shown in **Figure 1**.

Electrophysiological Recordings

The EEG information was recorded using a BrainAmp system with 64-channel electrodes (Brain Products, Germany) extended with the 10-20 International EEG Recording System. The vertical electrooculogram (VEOG) signal above the left eye and the horizontal electrooculogram (HEOG) signal outside the right eye were recorded with the reference electrodes at the bilateral mastoids behind the left and right ears. The ground electrode was placed at the midpoint AFz of the line connecting FPz and Fz. Before the start of the experiment, the resistance of the connecting point between each electrode and the scalp was reduced to less than 5 kΩ, the sampling frequency was set to 500 Hz, and the filter bandpass was set to 0.05–100 Hz.

Data Analysis

To analyze the behavioral data, the participants' reaction time and accuracy were recorded using E-prime 2.0, and the data for both variables were combined and extracted. A *t*-test was then performed using the SPSS 20.0 statistical software program.

The EEG data were processed offline using BrainVision Analyzer version 2.04 (Brain Product GmbH; Gilching, Germany). The ICA method was used to correct the ocular power. The EEGs were segmented into 1000 ms epochs surrounding the onset of the probe stimulus. The filter passband frequency was 0.01–30 Hz, and artifact signals with an amplitude greater than ±80 μV were removed. Based on the experimental design, the EEG in the stress stage was superimposed by participant type, and the EEG component in the feedback stage was superimposed and analyzed by participant type and feedback type (correct/wrong). Data with excessive artifacts and insufficient times of superimposition were eliminated. Two participants in the low-CSE group were deleted due to excessive artifacts, which resulted in EEG data that could not be superimposed or averaged. The average numbers of superimposition for the retained cases were as follows. In the high-CSE group, the number for the stress stimulus was 179.2 ± 44.9, with a range of 91–236; the number for correct feedback was 83.1 ± 32.3, with a range of 33–133; and the number for error feedback was 74.7 ± 20.2, with a range of 33–128. In the low-CSE

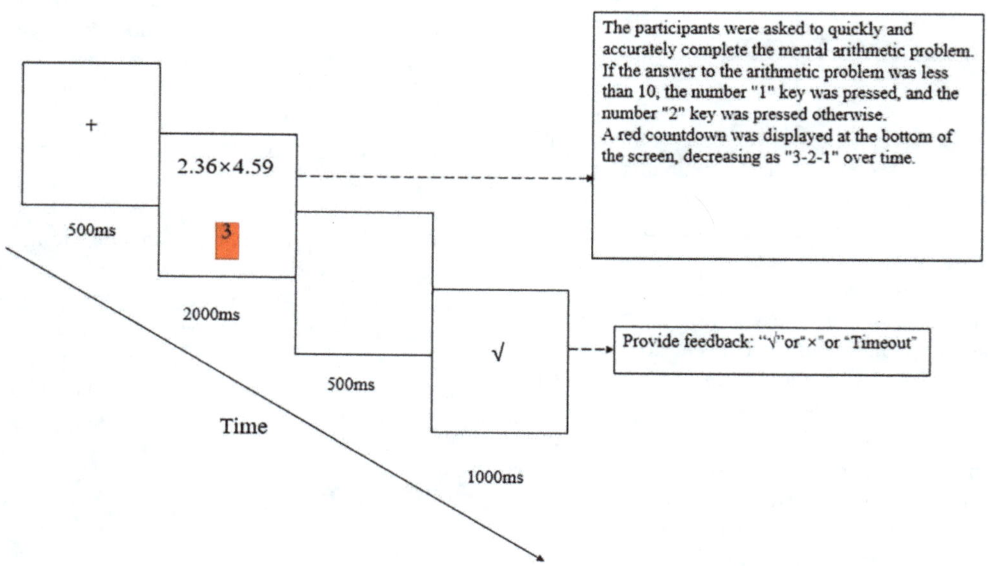

FIGURE 1 | Experimental procedure and sample materials. Each trial began with a fixation cross of 500 ms, after which an arithmetic problem was displayed. The time limit for answering a problem was 2,000 ms. After the "1" or "2" key was pressed or after time expired, a blank screen appeared for 500 ms, followed by feedback for 1,000 ms and the next trial started.

group, the number for the stress stimulus was 175.7 ± 41.3, with a range of 78–231; the number for correct feedback was 80.9 ± 34.1, with a range of 32–146; and the number for error feedback was 70.9 ± 29.1, with a range of 30–110.

In the stress stage, based on the total average waveform and previous studies (Yang et al., 2012; Qi et al., 2018), the N1 and P2 components were mainly analyzed. For the N1 component, the peak latency and average amplitude of the left (PO7, O1) and right (PO8, O2) sides of the cerebral palpebral area within the time window of 150–220 ms after the presentation of the stimulus were selected for analysis. For the P2 component, the average amplitudes of the frontal (F3, Fz, F4), the front-central (FC3, FCz, FC4), and the central (C3, Cz, C4) zones of the brain within the time window of 180–260 ms after the presentation of the stimulus were analyzed. N1 was subjected to a 2 (group: high/low) × 2 (hemisphere: left/right) mixed variance analysis. P2 was subjected to a 2 (group: high/low) × 3 (brain area: anterior/middle/posterior) mixed variance analysis. The grand-averaged ERPs at the Fz, FCz, Cz, PO7, and PO8 electrode sites for high- and low-CSE athletes under psychological stress stage is shown in **Figure 2**.

In the feedback stage, the ERP waveforms of the participants were analyzed for both correct and error feedback. Following previous studies on outcome evaluation (Chen et al., 2013; Ma et al., 2015), two ERP components, FRN and P300, which were related to outcome evaluation, were selected for analysis. Previous studies (Hajcak et al., 2005, 2007) showed that the maximum amplitude of FRN occurred in the anterior middle of the scalp. Therefore, the average amplitude of three electrode points at Fz, FCz, and Cz in the anterior middle of the brain at 250–350 ms after the presentation of feedback was selected for FRN analysis. The maximum amplitude of P300 appeared in the posterior of the scalp (Yeung and Sanfey, 2004). Therefore, the average amplitude of two electrode points at CPz and Pz in the posterior of the brain at 300–500 ms after the presentation of feedback was selected for P300 analysis. Because the analysis time courses for the FRN component and the P300 component partially overlapped, the FRN was defined as the most negative peak within 250–350 ms (Rigoni et al., 2010), and the FRN difference wave for error and correct feedback (dFRN, the amplitude of the brain wave caused by error feedback minus the amplitude caused by correct feedback) was analyzed (Holroyd and Krigolson, 2007). The dFRN indicator for analysis is the average amplitude of the difference wave within the time window of 250–350 ms. The FRN was subjected to a 2 (group: high/low) × 2 (feedback type: correct/error) × 3 (electrode point: Fz, FCz, Cz) mixed variance analysis, and the P300 was subjected to a 2 (group: high/low) × 2 (feedback type: correct/error) × 2 (electrode point: CPz, Pz) mixed variance analysis. The difference wave dFRN was subjected to a 2 (group: high/low) × 3 (electrode point: Fz, FCz, Cz) mixed variance analysis. When the statistical results did not pass the spherical test, the Greenhouse-Geisser method was used to correct degree of freedom. Main effects were followed by Bonferroni-corrected pairwise comparisons. The grand-averaged ERPs at the Fz, FCz, Cz, CPz, and Pz electrode sites for high- and low-CSE athletes under the feedback stage are shown in **Figure 3**.

RESULTS

Behavioral Data

Statistical analysis was conducted on the average response time of the participants under stress. The average response time of the athletes in the high-CSE group under stress

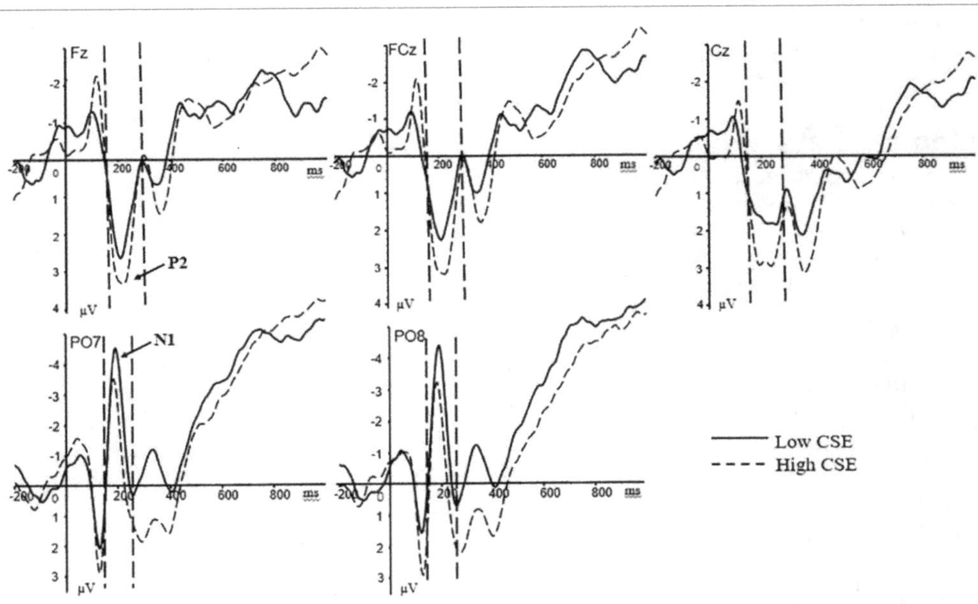

FIGURE 2 | Grand-averaged ERPs at the Fz, FCz, Cz, PO7, and PO8 electrode sites for high- and low-CSE athletes under psychological stress. The P2 component (180–260 ms) at Fz, FCz, and Cz. The N1 component (150–220 ms) in PO7 and PO8.

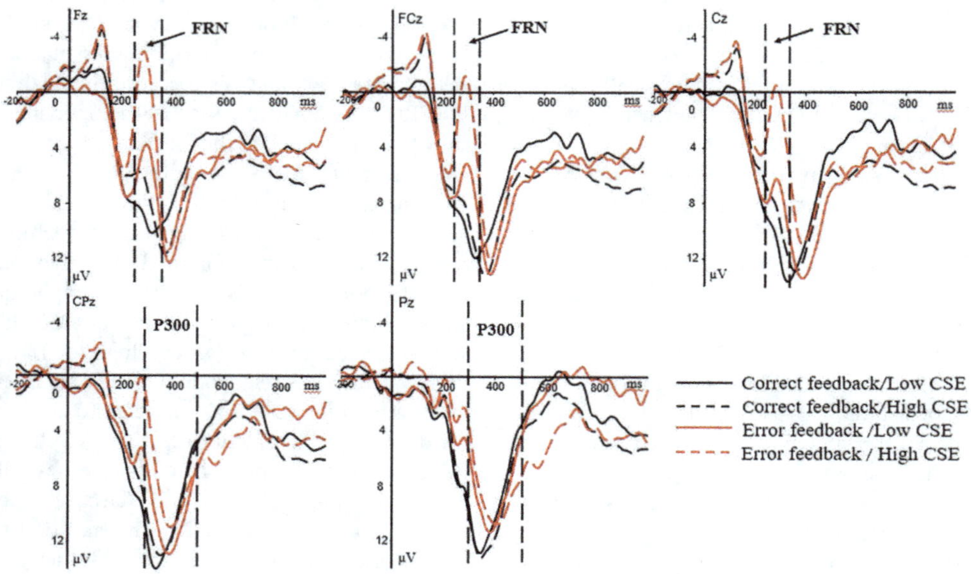

FIGURE 3 | Grand-averaged ERPs at the Fz, FCz, Cz, CPz, and Pz electrode sites for high- and low-CSE athletes under the feedback. The FRN component (250–350 ms) at Fz, FCz, and Cz. The P300 component (300–500 ms) at CPz and Pz.

(M = 1,472.23 ms, SD = 190.62) was significantly faster than that of the low-CSE group (M = 1,613.16 ms, SD = 229.65), with $t(39) = -2.14$, $p = 0.038$, $d = -0.669$. Thus, athletes in the high-CSE group responded more quickly under stress.

Statistical analysis was also conducted on participants' accuracy rate. The accuracy rates of athletes in the high-CSE group (M = 53.85%, SD = 2.87) and the low-CSE group (M = 53.02%, SD = 4.32) were not significantly different, with $t(39) = 0.73$, $p = 0.473$. The participants' accuracy rate also suggested that the difficulty of the arithmetic problems in the experimental materials was appropriate and that the experimental materials were scientifically prepared.

Electrophysiological Data

For stress response phase, regarding the N1 peak latency, the main effect of the right/left hemisphere was significant [$F(1, 37) = 6.88$, $p = 0.013$, $\eta_p^2 = 0.157$]. The N1 peak latency in the left hemisphere (M = 183.29 ms, SD = 2.35) was significantly longer than the right hemisphere (M = 178.69 ms, SD = 2.87). The main effect of the subject groups was significant [$F(1, 37) = 4.76$, $p = 0.036$, $\eta_p^2 = 0.114$]. The N1 peak latency of the low-CSE group (M = 186.39 ms, SD = 3.63) was significantly longer than the high-CSE group (M = 175.59 ms, SD = 3.36). For N1 peak latency, there were no other interaction effects. For N1 amplitude, the main effect of the groups was significant [$F(1, 37) = 6.06$, $p = 0.019$, $\eta_p^2 = 0.141$]. The N1 amplitude of the low-CSE group (M = −3.95 μV, SD = 0.68) was significantly larger than the high-CSE group (M = −1.68 μV, SD = 0.63). There were no other interaction effects for N1 amplitude.

For P2 amplitude, the main effect of the brain region was significant [$F(1.4, 74) = 6.79$, $p = 0.007$, $\eta_p^2 = 0.155$]. The P2 amplitude of the frontal region of the brain (M = 2.57 μV, SD = 0.55) was significantly greater than the frontal-central zone (M = 2.33 μV, SD = 0.50) and the central zone (M = 1.86 μV, SD = 0.49). The main effect of the groups was not significant [$F(1, 37) = 0.60$, $p = 0.442$]. There were no other interaction effects for P2 amplitude.

For reaction feedback phase, regarding the FRN amplitude, the main effect of the feedback type was significant [$F(1, 37) = 42.97$, $p < 0.001$, $\eta_p^2 = 0.558$]. The FRN amplitude under error feedback (M = 3.37 μV, SD = 1.11) was significantly larger than the correct feedback (M = 9.05 μV, SD = 1.07). There is a significant interaction between groups and feedback type [$F(1, 37) = 17.25$, $p < 0.001$, $\eta_p^2 = 0.337$]. Simple effects analysis revealed that high-CSE group has significant difference in FRN amplitude on feedback type [$F(1, 37) = 64.50$, $p < 0.001$, $\eta_p^2 = 0.655$]. The FRN amplitude under error feedback (M = −0.32 μV, SD = 1.48) is greater than under the correct feedback (M = 8.97 μV, SD = 1.42). Low-CSE group has no significant difference in feedback types. For FRN amplitude, there was a significant difference between the groups in the error feedback [$F(1, 37) = 11.09$, $p = 0.002$, $\eta_p^2 = 0.246$], and the FRN amplitude of error feedback in high CSE group (M = −0.32 μV, SD = 1.48) was significantly larger than the low CSE group (M = 7.05 μV, SD = 1.65). For dFRN amplitude, the main effect of the groups was significant [$F(1, 37) = 10.14$, $p = 0.003$, $\eta_p^2 = 0.215$]. The dFRN amplitude of high CSE group (M = −8.71 μV, SD = 1.23) was significantly larger than the low CSE group (M = −2.94 μV, SD = 1.33).

For P300 amplitude, the groups × feedback type interaction was significant [$F(1, 37) = 6.19$, $p = 0.018$, $\eta_p^2 = 0.154$]. Simple effects analysis revealed that high-CSE group has significant difference in P300 amplitude on feedback type [$F(1, 37) = 5.48$, $p = 0.025$, $\eta_p^2 = 0.138$]. The P300 amplitude of correct feedback

(M = 10.86 μV, SD = 1.54) is larger than error feedback (M = 7.39 μV, SD = 1.62). For P300 amplitude, neither the main effects nor interaction effects was significant.

DISCUSSION

This study used arithmetic problems with the characteristics of uncontrollability and social-evaluated threat to examine differences between athletes with high and low CSE levels under acute psychological stress. The behavioral results of the reaction time and accuracy rate indicated that among athletes with comparable accuracy rates, the reaction time of athletes in the high-CSE group was significantly faster than that of the athletes in the low-CSE group, and thus, athletes in the high-CSE group had a competitive advantage in terms of response speed, agility, and action speed under acute psychological stress. To further explore the reasons for this advantage, differences in cortical neurological activity under acute psychological stress between high- and low-CSE athletes were analyzed in both the stress reaction and response feedback stages.

Competitive sports are mostly performed under intense time pressure, requiring athletes to perform rapid sensory perception and movement initiation (Hülsdünker et al., 2018). When stressed, the brain must quickly and effectively detect information and re-integrate physiological and psychological resources to effectively cope with the stressful stimuli. Therefore, when athletes are stressed, effective cognitive processing is crucial for optimal performance (Sanchez-Lopez et al., 2016). The N1 component primarily reflects the functional role of stress in regulating early sensory coding (Löw et al., 2015; Qi et al., 2018). The results of this study show that in the state of stress, the N1 amplitude of athletes in the low-CSE group was significantly larger than that of athletes in the high-CSE group, and the peak latency of N1 was significantly longer than that of athletes in the high-CSE group. Amplitude is generally believed to reflect the excitability of the brain, whereas the latency period reflects the speed and evaluation time of neurological activity and processing (Wang et al., 2012; van Dinteren et al., 2014). Previous studies have shown that when the perception load caused by high vigilance is increased, the individual's recognition and processing of stimuli become difficult, prompting an increase in the amplitude of N1 (Yang et al., 2012; Qi et al., 2018). The study by Wang et al. (2012) showed that older people experience larger N1 amplitudes due to slower perception processing and increased difficulty in identifying the target stimuli. In this study, low-CSE athletes had a poorer self-evaluation of their coping ability. Under acute psychological stress, they were more likely to experience a "blank brain," resulting in increased vigilance and enhanced sensory input. Consequently, both the difficulty of stimulation recognition and processing and the time required for individual perceptual analysis increased, thus reducing response speed. By contrast, high-CSE athletes displayed the confidence of "keep calm even in face of danger" under stress. Therefore, when facing the same stimulating materials, they exhibited low levels of attention and perception load; hence, they could locate and process the related information more quickly, resulting in improved efficiency in processing information and quicker reaction times compared with low-CSE athletes.

Qi et al. (2017) compared electrophysiological responses under stress and no stress and found that the attention processes and cognitive control were regulated by acute psychological stress, which negatively impacted early perception processes, as evidenced mainly by the reduction of the P2 component. The P2 component was a distinct positive waveform in the prefrontal region that occurs after the N1 component and has a latency period of approximately 200 ms. The P2 component was more specifically a cognitive processing component that influences the early process of decision-making and indicated the choice of attention resources and the early outcome of decision-making (Rigoni et al., 2010). Paynter et al. (2009) showed that the larger the P2 amplitude, the more an individual was inclined to adopt a smooth intuitive heuristic strategy. In the present study, the difference in P2 amplitude between the two groups of athletes was not significant, possibly due to factors such as the number of participants and experimental materials. The psychological stress state in this study was stimulated by time-stressed arithmetic problems, which were not the type of sports problems at which athletes are proficient. Therefore, there was no difference in attention resource selection and decision-making processing strategy. In the future research, motor imagery (MI) task can be considered to study (Cebolla et al., 2015), and the distinguishing sports problems that athletes are good at solving can be used as the experimental materials for analysis.

Athletes' evaluation of the outcome of stress events directly affects their arousal level and emotional state and determines whether they can recover quickly and adapt to the stressful environment during competition (Anshel and Anderson, 2002). Therefore, this study analyzed the changes in the brain activity of athletes with different CSE levels following feedback from transient stress events. FRN and P300 are the two most common EEG components in outcome evaluation; they characterize, respectively, the early warning and early signaling stages that must be changed and the late stage involving the integration of information from the updated behavioral characterization provided by the neural mechanism of outcome evaluation and behavioral regulation (Wu and Zhou, 2009; Leng and Zhou, 2010). In the early stage of primary automated processing, error feedback triggered a larger FRN amplitude, suggesting that negative feedback can also induce an individual's stress response (Atchley et al., 2017). FRN originates from the anterior cingulated cortex (ACC), which is a negative waveform that appears in the central part of the forehead approximately 250 ms after the presentation of the feedback stimulus (Miltner et al., 1997; Holroyd and Coles, 2002). Mars et al. (2004) stated that FRN mainly transmitted an early warning signal concerning whether the result was "good" or "bad." Therefore, FRN is sensitive to correct feedback and error feedback stimuli reflects the rapid and difficult process of evaluating the importance of the stimuli, thus providing information for behavioral adjustment. The results of the current study showed that both the FRN and dFRN amplitudes of athletes in the high-CSE group were significantly larger than those of the low-CSE group. Accordingly, in the early stage of feedback processing, athletes with high-CSE were more alert to the error signal of the response. This type of vigilance is highly adaptive because it conveys early warning signals for adjustment, which is conducive to behavioral adjustment in a stressful environment full of uncertainties and can thereby help athletes avoid repeating mistakes.

The anterior cingulated cortex (ACC) conveys the warning that behavior must be adjusted. This information only indicates the occurrence of an error and the necessity of change. The specific behavior adjustment required should be determined by the integration of all information to ensure that behavioral characterization is appropriately updated. This processing is a slower, more detailed, and more sophisticated form of information processing, which may be reflected in the P300 component in the late stage (Mars et al., 2004; Polich, 2007). As a late control evaluation process based on motivation/emotional meaning or attention resource allocation, P300 reflects the transfer of attentional resources or the update of working memory and is positively correlated with the amount of invested psychological resources (Yu and Sun, 2013). The study by Kopp and Lange (2013) showed that in the cued task-switching paradigm, unexpected signal switching triggered a larger P300 amplitude. Similarly, the study by Chase et al. (2011) showed that the behavioral reversal based on explicit rules induced a greater P300 amplitude than that caused by information without behavioral reversal. These studies suggested that the P300 wave may be an EEG indicator that guided behavioral regulation, possibly because P300 reflected the renewal and adjustment of behavioral characterization. In this study, in the late sophisticated processing stage, the P300 amplitude of high-CSE athletes was significantly larger with correct feedback than with error feedback. By contrast, the P300 amplitude in low-CSE athletes was greater with error feedback than with correct feedback, while the difference was not statistically significant. Consequently, after the approximate and automatic early detection of feedback had provided early warning information indicating the necessity of change, the athletes paid greater attention to the stimulus information and engaged in controlled processing. Athletes in the high-CSE group invested more attention resources to correct feedback during stimulation processing to update behavioral characterization and guide behavioral regulation. This positive sophisticated processing is conducive to maintaining the individual's coping confidence under stress and encouraging the individual to develop positive coping strategies (Snyder, 1999).

The perception of athletes depends on the interaction of the physical characteristics of the object and the athletes' ability in the environment (Gray, 2014). Coping self-efficacy as an individual resource can affect coping behavior by regulating cognition, emotion, and inclination (Bandura, 1997). The study on the cerebral cortical nerve activity of athletes with high and low CSE levels under acute psychological stress showed that low-CSE athletes lacked confidence and hence were more likely to not know what to do when facing stress. When the stress feedback results were presented, high-CSE athletes were more alert to the error feedback compared with low-CSE athletes and transmitted an early warning signal indicating the necessity of behavioral adjustment. High-CSE athletes could also recover quickly from frustration and disappointment and focus on positive information. By contrast, low-CSE athletes paid greater attention to negative information and the consequences of failure, not only causing them to lose confidence in their abilities but also affecting their subsequent coping behavior. Therefore, coping effectiveness training (CET) and an attention modification program should be incorporated in the training of athletes (Amir et al., 2009; Reeves et al., 2011). Through measures such as improving athletes' confidence, suppressing attention to negative stimuli to complete the search for positive stimuli, and changing the attention mode, the individual's self-efficacy can be improved. Athletes can thus better cope with and eliminate interference caused by competitive pressures and eventually achieve their best performance.

Despite these contributions, some limitations in our work should be noted that may shed light on future research directions. The first concern is the use of mental arithmetic exercise for inducing athletes' psychological stress response. Although mental arithmetic exercise as an effective approach to induce individual psychological stress response, (Dedovic et al., 2005; Qi et al., 2016), whether there is consistency across different kinds of laboratory-induced stress and whether different types of stress sources can trigger the same pattern of electrophysiological response still need to be further studied and tested. Therefore, motor imagery (MI) can be used for psychological simulation of sports stress in future research, for MI can be applied to event-related potential technologies without any interference of real movement (Machado et al., 2013; Cebolla et al., 2015). At the same time, the time-frequency measurement of ERP has been reliably applied to MI (Machado et al., 2013; Tabrizi et al., 2013), and the time-frequency analysis with time-frequency characteristics of EEG oscillations can better reveal brain function activities of athletes under stressful scenarios. Second, another limitation of our study is that we did not measure the objective physiological indicators of psychological stress. In future studies, research findings can be more convincing by increasing the measurement frequency of heart rate, saliva cortisol and other objective stress indicators, raising the sample size, and establishing a correlation test between ERP components and physiological data, which makes the results more convincing.

CONCLUSION

The results of the current study show that, under the acute psychological stress, the athletes with low CSE have higher level of vigilance and sensory input which affects the speed of recognition and processing of stimulation and increases the time required for individual perceptual analysis. It eventually will show a decrease in the rate of response. However, in the process of stress response evaluation, athletes with high CSE are more alert to the wrong signal of the result and have adaptive significance in the early feedback result processing stage of providing early warning information. And in the late sophisticated processing stage of affect behavior adjustment, athletes with high and low CSE showed obvious mood congruent effect.

ETHICS STATEMENT

All procedures performed in studies involving human participants were in accordance with the ethical standards of the institutional and/or national research committee and with the 1964 Helsinki Declaration and its later amendments or comparable ethical standards with written informed consent from all subjects. This research was approved by the Human Research Ethics Committee (HREC) at Henan University.

AUTHOR CONTRIBUTIONS

YN contributed to developing the theoretical framework, data analysis, organization, and overall writing of the paper. QL contributed to the editing and organization of the paper as well as the overall design. TG contributed to the design, data analysis, and editing of the paper. HH was concerned with drafting the work and revising it critically.

REFERENCES

Amir, N., Beard, C., Burns, M., and Bomyea, J. (2009). Attention modification program in individuals with generalized anxiety disorder. *J. Abnorm. Psychol.* 118, 28–33. doi: 10.1037/a0012589

Anshel, M., and Anderson, D. (2002). Coping with acute stress in sport: linking athletes' coping style, coping strategies, affect, and motor performance. *Anxiety Stress Coping* 15, 193–209. doi: 10.1080/10615800290028486

Atchley, R., Ellingson, R., Klee, D., Memmott, T., and Oken, B. (2017). A cognitive stressor for event-related potential studies: the Portland arithmetic stress task. *Stress* 20, 277–284. doi: 10.1080/10253890.2017.1335300

Bandura, A. (1997). *Self-efficacy: the exercice of control.* New York: W. H. Freeman & Co, 610.

Benight, C. C., Antoni, M. H., Kilbourn, K., Ironson, G., Kumar, M. A., Fletcher, M. A., et al. (1997). Coping self-efficacy buffers psychological and physiological disturbances in hiv-infected men following a natural disaster. *Health Psychol.* 16, 248–255. doi: 10.1037/0278-6133.16.3.248

Benight, C. C., Ironson, G., and Durham, R. L. (1999). Psychometric properties of a hurricane coping self-efficacy measure. *J. Trauma. Stress.* 12, 379–386. doi: 10.1023/A:1024792913301

Cebolla, A. M., Petieau, M., Cevallos, C., Leroy, A., Dan, B., and Cheron, G. (2015). Long-lasting cortical reorganization as the result of motor imagery of throwing a ball in a virtual tennis court. *Front. Psychol.* 6:1869. doi: 10.3389/fpsyg.2015.01869

Chase, H. W., Swainson, R., Durham, L., Benham, L., and Cools, R. (2011). Feedback-related negativity codes prediction error but not behavioral adjustment during probabilistic reversal learning. *J. Cogn. Neurosci.* 23, 936–946. doi: 10.1162/jocn.2010.21456

Chen, Q., Wang, Y., and Huang, Y. (2013). Social exclusion modulates fairness consideration in the ultimatum game: an ERP study. *Front. Hum. Neurosci.* 7:505. doi: 10.3389/fnhum.2013.00505

Chesney, M. A., Neilands, T. B., Chambers, D. B., Taylor, J. M., and Folkman, S. (2006). A validity and reliability study of the coping self-efficacy scale. *Br. J. Health Psychol.* 11, 421–437. doi: 10.1348/135910705X53155

Crocker, P. R., Tamminen, K. A., and Gaudreau, P. (2015). "Coping in sport" in *Mellalieu, contemporary advances in sport psychology: A review.* ed. D. Stephen (New York: Routledge), 28–67.

Dambacher, M., and Hübner, R. (2015). Time pressure affects the efficiency of perceptual processing in decisions under conflict. *Psychol. Res.* 79, 83–94. doi: 10.1007/s00426-014-0542-z

Dedovic, K., Renwick, R., Mahani, N. K., Engert, V., Lupien, S. J., and Pruessner, J. C. (2005). The Montreal Imaging Stress Task: using functional imaging to investigate the effects of perceiving and processing psychosocial stress in the human brain. *J. Psychiatr. Neurosci.* 30, 319–325.

De Kloet, E. R., Joëls, M., and Holsboer, F. (2005). Stress and the brain: from adaptation to disease. *Nat. Rev. Neurosci.* 6, 463–475. doi: 10.1038/nrn1683

Dickerson, S. S., and Kemeny, M. E. (2004). Acute stressors and cortisol responses: a theoretical integration and synthesis of laboratory research. *Psychol. Bull.* 130, 355–391. doi: 10.1037/0033-2909.130.3.355

Edwards, J. R., and Cooper, C. L. (1988). Research in stress, coping, and health: theoretical and methodological issues. *Psychol. Med.* 18, 15–20. doi: 10.1017/S0033291700001847

Foley, P., and Kirschbaum, C. (2011). Human hypothalamus-pituitary-adrenal axis responses to acute psychosocial stress in laboratory settings. *Neurosci. Biobehav. Rev.* 35, 91–96. doi: 10.1016/j.neubiorev.2010.01.010

Gerber, M., Best, S., Meerstetter, F., Walter, M., Ludyga, S., Brand, S., et al. (2018). Effects of stress and mental toughness on burnout and depressive symptoms: a prospective study with young elite athletes. *J. Sci. Med. Sport* 21, 1200–1205. doi: 10.1016/j.jsams.2018.05.018

Gray, R. (2014). Embodied perception in sport. *Int. Rev. Sport Exerc. Psychol.* 7, 72–86. doi: 10.1080/1750984X.2013.871572

Gulliver, A., Griffiths, K. M., Mackinnon, A., Batterham, P. J., and Stanimirovic, R. (2015). The mental health of Australian elite athletes. *J. Sci. Med. Sport* 18, 255–261. doi: 10.1016/j.jsams.2014.04.006

Gyurcsik, N. C., Brawley, L. R., and Langhout, N. (2010). Acute thoughts, exercise consistency, and coping self-efficacy. *J. Appl. Soc. Psychol.* 32, 2134–2153. doi: 10.1111/j.1559-1816.2002.tb02067.x

Hajcak, G., Holroyd, C. B., Moser, J. S., and Simons, R. F. (2005). Brain potentials associated with expected and unexpected good and bad outcomes. *Psychophysiology* 42, 161–170. doi: 10.1111/j.1469-8986.2005.00278.x

Hajcak, G., Moser, J. S., Holroyd, C. B., and Simons, R. F. (2007). It's worse than you thought: the feedback negativity and violations of reward prediction in gambling tasks. *Psychophysiology* 44, 905–912. doi: 10.1111/j.1469-8986.2007.00567.x

Holroyd, C. B., and Coles, M. G. (2002). The neural basis of human error processing: reinforcement learning, dopamine, and the error-related negativity. *Psychol. Rev.* 109, 679–709. doi: 10.1037/0033-295X.109.4.679

Holroyd, C. B., and Krigolson, O. E. (2007). Reward prediction error signals associated with a modified time estimation task. *Psychophysiology* 44, 913–917. doi: 10.1111/j.1469-8986.2007.00561.x

Hülsdünker, T., Strüder, H. K., and Mierau, A. (2018). Visual but not motor processes predict simple visuomotor reaction time of badminton players. *Eur. J. Sport Sci.* 18, 190–200. doi: 10.1080/17461391.2017.1395912

Isoglualkac, U., Ermutlu, M. N., Eskikurt, G., Yücesir, İ., Demirel, S. T., and Temel, T. (2018). Dancers and fastball sports athletes have different spatial visual attention styles. *Cogn. Neurodyn.* 12, 201–209. doi: 10.1007/s11571-017-9469-6

Kogler, L., Müller, V. I., Chang, A., Eickhoff, S. B., Fox, P. T., Gur, R. C., et al. (2015). Psychosocial versus physiological stress—meta-analyses on deactivations and activations of the neural correlates of stress reactions. *NeuroImage* 119, 235–251. doi: 10.1016/j.neuroimage.2015.06.059

Kopp, B., and Lange, F. (2013). Electrophysiological indicators of surprise and entropy in dynamic task-switching environments. *Front. Hum. Neurosci.* 7:300. doi: 10.3389/fnhum.2013.00300

Lazarus, R. S., and Folkman, S. (1984). *Stress appraisal and coping*. New York: Springer. (Chapter 3).

Leng, Y., and Zhou, X. (2010). Modulation of the brain activity in outcome evaluation by interpersonal relationship: an ERP study. *Neuropsychologia* 48, 448–455. doi: 10.1016/j.neuropsychologia.2009.10.002

Löw, A., Weymar, M., and Hamm, A. O. (2015). When threat is near, get out of here: dynamics of defensive behavior during freezing and active avoidance. *Psychol. Sci.* 26, 1706–1716. doi: 10.1177/0956797615597332

Ma, Q., Hu, Y., Jiang, S., and Meng, L. (2015). The undermining effect of facial attractiveness on brain responses to fairness in the ultimatum game: an ERP study. *Front. Neurosci.* 9:77. doi: 10.3389/fnins.2015.00077

Machado, S., Arias-Carrión, O., Paes, F., Ribeiro, P., Cagy, M., Piedade, R., et al. (2013). Changes in cortical activity during real and imagined movements: an ERP study. *Clin. Pract. Epidemiol. Ment. Health* 9, 196–201. doi: 10.2174/1745017901309010196

Mars, R. B., De Bruijn, E. R. A., Hulstijn, W., Miltner, W. H. R., and Coles, M. G. H. (2004). "What if I told you: 'You were wrong'? brain potentials and behavioral adjustments elicited by performance feedback in a time-estimation task" in *Errors, conflicts, and the brain. Current opinions on performance monitoring*. eds. M. Ullsperger and M. Falkenstein (Leipzig: MPI of Cognitive Neuroscience), 129–134.

McEwen, B. S. (2009). The brain is the central organ of stress and adaptation. *NeuroImage* 47, 911–913. doi: 10.1016/j.neuroimage.2009.05.071

McEwen, B. S., and Gianaros, P. J. (2010). Central role of the brain in stress and adaptation: links to socioeconomic status, health, and disease. *Ann. N. Y. Acad. Sci.* 1186, 190–222. doi: 10.1111/j.1749-6632.2009.05331.x

Miltner, W. H., Braun, C. H., and Coles, M. G. (1997). Event-related brain potentials following incorrect feedback in a time-estimation task: evidence for a "generic" neural system for error detection. *J. Cogn. Neurosci.* 9, 788–798. doi: 10.1162/jocn.1997.9.6.788

Moritz, S. E., Feltz, D. L., Fahrbach, K. R., and Mack, D. E. (2000). The relation of self-efficacy measures to sport performance: a meta-analytic review. *Res. Q. Exerc. Sport* 71, 280–294. doi: 10.1080/02701367.2000.10608908

Nicholls, A. R., and Perry, J. L. (2016). Perceptions of coach–athlete relationship are more important to coaches than athletes in predicting dyadic coping and stress appraisals: an actor–partner independence mediation model. *Front. Psychol.* 7:447. doi: 10.3389/fpsyg.2016.00447

Nicholls, A. R., Polman, R., and Levy, A. R. (2010). Coping self-efficacy, pre-competitive anxiety, and subjective performance among athletes. *Eur. J. Sport Sci.* 10, 97–102. doi: 10.1080/17461390903271592

Paynter, C. A., Reder, L. M., and Kieffaber, P. D. (2009). Knowing we know before we know: ERP correlates of initial feeling-of-knowing. *Neuropsychologia* 47, 796–803. doi: 10.1016/j.neuropsychologia.2008.12.009

Polich, J. (2007). Updating P300: an integrative theory of P3a and P3b. *Clin. Neurophysiol.* 118, 2128–2148. doi: 10.1016/j.clinph.2007.04.019

Pruessner, J. C., Dedovic, K., Pruessner, M., Lord, C., Buss, C., Collins, L., et al. (2010). Stress regulation in the central nervous system: evidence from structural and functional neuroimaging studies in human populations-2008 Curt Richter Award Winner. *Psychoneuroendocrinology* 35, 179–191. doi: 10.1016/j.psyneuen.2009.02.016

Qi, M., Gao, H., Guan, L., Liu, G., and Yang, J. (2016). Subjective stress, salivary cortisol, and electrophysiological responses to psychological stress. *Front. Psychol.* 7:229. doi: 10.3389/fpsyg.2016.00229

Qi, M., Gao, H., and Liu, G. (2017). Effect of acute psychological stress on response inhibition: an event-related potential study. *Exp. Brain Res.* 323, 32–37. doi: 10.1016/j.bbr.2017.01.036

Qi, M., Gao, H., and Liu, G. (2018). The effect of mild acute psychological stress on attention processing: an ERP study. *Exp. Brain Res.* 236, 2061–2071. doi: 10.1007/s00221-018-5283-6

Reeves, C. W., Nicholls, A. R., and McKenna, J. (2011). The effects of a coping intervention on coping self-efficacy, coping effectiveness, and subjective performance among adolescent soccer players. *J. Sport Exerc. Psychol.* 9, 126–142. doi: 10.1080/1612197X.2011.567104

Rice, S. M., Purcell, R., De Silva, S., Mawren, D., McGorry, P. D., and Parker, A. G. (2016). The mental health of elite athletes: a narrative systematic review. *Sports Med.* 46, 1333–1353. doi: 10.1007/s40279-016-0492-2

Rigoni, D., Polezzi, D., Rumiati, R., Guarino, R., and Sartori, G. (2010). When people matter more than money: an erps study. *Brain Res. Bull.* 81, 445–452. doi: 10.1016/j.brainresbull.2009.12.003

Sabato, T. M., Walch, T. J., and Caine, D. J. (2016). The elite young athlete: strategies to ensure physical and emotional health. *Open Access J. Sports Med.* 7, 99–113. doi: 10.2147/OAJSM.S96821

Sanchez-Lopez, J., Silva-Pereyra, J., and Fernandez, T. (2016). Sustained attention in skilled and novice martial arts athletes: a study of event-related potentials and current sources. *PeerJ* 4:e1614. doi: 10.7717/peerj.1614

Sänger, J., Bechtold, L., Schoofs, D., Blaszkewicz, M., and Wascher, E. (2014). The influence of acute stress on attention mechanisms and its electrophysiological correlates. *Front. Behav. Neurosci.* 8:353. doi: 10.3389/fnbeh.2014.00353

Shackman, A. J., Maxwell, J. S., McMenamin, B. W., Greischar, L. L., and Davidson, R. J. (2011). Stress potentiates early and attenuates late stages of visual processing. *J. Neurosci.* 31, 1156–1161. doi: 10.1523/JNEUROSCI.3384-10.2011

Shields, G. S., Sazma, M. A., and Yonelinas, A. P. (2016). The effects of acute stress on core executive functions: a meta-analysis and comparison with cortisol. *Neurosci. Biobehav. Rev.* 68, 651–668. doi: 10.1016/j.neubiorev.2016.06.038

Snyder, B. C. R. (1999). *Coping: The psychology of what works*. Oxford: Oxford University Press. (Chapter 6).

Tabrizi, Y. M., Mazhari, S., Nazari, M. A., Zangiabadi, N., Sheibani, V., and Azarang, S. (2013). Compromised motor imagery ability in individuals with multiple sclerosis and mild physical disability: an ERP study. *Clin. Neurol. Neurosurg.* 115, 1738–1744. doi: 10.1016/j.clineuro.2013.04.002

van Dinteren, R., Arns, M., Jongsma, M. L., and Kessels, R. P. (2014). P300 development across the lifespan: a systematic review and meta-analysis. *PLoS One* 9:e87347. doi: 10.1371/journal.pone.0087347

Wang, Y., Fu, S., Greenwood, P., Luo, Y., and Parasuraman, R. (2012). Perceptual load, voluntary attention, and aging: an event-related potential study. *Int. J. Psychophysiol.* 84, 17–25. doi: 10.1016/j.ijpsycho.2012.01.002

Watson, J. C., and Watson, A. A. (2016). Coping self-efficacy and academic stress among hispanic first-year college students: the moderating role of emotional intelligence. *J. Coll. Couns.* 19, 218–230. doi: 10.1002/jocc.12045

Wu, Y., and Zhou, X. (2009). The P300 and reward valence, magnitude, and expectancy in outcome evaluation. *Brain Res.* 1286, 114–122. doi: 10.1016/j.brainres.2009.06.032

Yang, J., Qi, M., Guan, L., Hou, Y., and Yang, Y. (2012). The time course of psychological stress as revealed by event-related potentials. *Neurosci. Lett.* 530, 1–6. doi: 10.1016/j.neulet.2012.09.042

Yeung, N., and Sanfey, A. G. (2004). Independent coding of reward magnitude and valence in the human brain. *J. Neurosci.* 24, 6258–6264. doi: 10.1016/j.neulet.2012.09.042

Yu, R., and Sun, S. (2013). To conform or not to conform: spontaneous conformity diminishes the sensitivity to monetary outcomes. *PLoS One* 8:e64530. doi: 10.1371/journal.pone.0064530

Yuan, Y., Leung, A. W. S., Duan, H., Liang, Z., Kan, Z., Wu, J., et al. (2016). The effects of long-term stress on neural dynamics of working memory processing: an investigation using ERP. *Sci. Rep.* 6:23217. doi: 10.1038/srep23217

3

Advancing our Understanding of Psychological Stress and Coping among Parents in Organized Youth Sport

Chris G. Harwood[1], Sam N. Thrower[1,2], Matthew J. Slater[3], Faye F. Didymus[4] and Lucy Frearson[1]*

School of Sport, Exercise and Health Sciences, Loughborough University, Loughborough, United Kingdom, [2] Department of Life Sciences, University of Roehampton, London, United Kingdom, [3] School of Life Sciences and Education, Staffordshire University, Stoke-on-Trent, United Kingdom, [4] Institute for Sport, Physical Activity and Leisure, Leeds Beckett University, Leeds, United Kingdom

***Correspondence:**
Chris G. Harwood
c.g.harwood@lboro.ac.uk

The current study investigated psychological stress among parents of competitive British tennis players. Adopting a multipart concurrent mixed method design, 135 British tennis parents completed a cross sectional online questionnaire to examine their primary appraisals, emotions, and coping strategies associated with self-disclosed stressors. Hierarchical content analysis was conducted on open ended questionnaire responses to identify key stressors and coping strategies, and descriptive and inferential statistics were utilized to explore the differences between various components of the process. The findings revealed a range of organizational, competitive, and developmental stressors. These stressors were predominantly appraised as harm or challenge, and anxiety and anger were the most prominent emotions that the parents experienced. Statistically, parents experienced greater anger in relation to competition (compared to organizational and developmental) stressors, whilst harm appraisal increased negative emotions, and challenge appraisal increased positive emotions. Findings also highlighted how parents used a number of mastery, internal regulation, and goal withdrawal coping strategies, which varied statistically in degrees of reported effectiveness. The contribution of these findings to the stress literature and their applied implications are discussed.

Keywords: sport parents, stressors, appraisal, emotion, coping, coping effectiveness, mixed method

INTRODUCTION

Psychological stress among athletes and coaches has been well documented in the sport psychology literature (e.g., Didymus and Fletcher, 2012; Didymus, 2017). Transactional and relational theories of stress are some of the most widely used and tested in sport [see e.g., transactional stress theory; Lazarus and Folkman, 1984; cognitive-motivational-relational theory (CMRT) of stress and emotion; Lazarus, 1999, 2000]. These theories posit that stress is a transaction between an individual and his or her environment, and that individuals appraise stressors in relation to their goals, values, and beliefs. According to the CMRT (Lazarus, 1999, 2000), appraising is an evaluative process during which individuals construct relational meanings about the stressors they encounter. Relational meanings may relate to challenge, threat, harm, or benefit, and each has different implications for emotions, coping, and other outcomes (e.g., well-being and performance). If a stressor is appraised as relevant to an individual, coping will ensue. The degree to which coping optimizes stress transactions is known as coping effectiveness. Drawing on transactional theories, researchers have used qualitative and quantitative methods to unearth stressors (i.e., competitive, organizational, and personal) that athletes experience (e.g., Nicholls et al., 2005), the ways in which they are appraised (e.g., Didymus and Fletcher, 2012; Doron and Martinent, 2017), the emotions experienced (Nicholls et al., 2011; Moore et al., 2012), and the strategies used to cope (see, for a review, Nicholls and Polman, 2007). Researchers have also, more recently, started to explore the relationships and interactions between different components of stress transactions (e.g., stressors, appraisal, emotion, and coping; Nicholls et al., 2012; Doron and Martinent, 2017; Gomes et al., 2017).

Although the stress literature has predominantly focused on the experiences of athletes and coaches, researchers have offered initial understanding of the stressors associated with parenting in youth sport (Harwood and Knight, 2009a,b; Harwood et al., 2010). Initiating this line of inquiry, Harwood and Knight (Harwood and Knight, 2009a,b) explored the stressors that British tennis parents experienced at different stages of their children's development. Data were collected during these studies via 123 open-ended surveys and 22 semi-structured interviews with tennis parents. Parental stressors centered on the organizational aspects of children's tennis (e.g., injuries, finances, and time), competition demands (e.g., watching matches, players/opponents cheating, and limited effort), and developmental concerns (e.g., players' future in tennis and transitional decisions regarding schooling). Taken together, these findings illustrate how parents' experiences are influenced by the nature of the sport, the sport organizational system, and their children's developmental stage. This supports the notion that stress is a context-dependent and temporal process (Lazarus, 1999).

Alongside this body of work, a small number of studies have explored the emotions that parents experience in youth sport settings (e.g., Goldstein and Iso-Ahola, 2008; Omli and LaVoi, 2012). For example, Omli and LaVoi (2012) identified the sources of anger for parents at youth sport competitions based on the assumption that anger fuels negative parental behavior at sporting events. Surveys with 773 parents of young athletes (aged 5–19 years) revealed that 98% of participants had experienced anger during sport competitions and that the parents experienced stressors such as the unjust, uncaring, and incompetent behaviors of coaches, other parents, officials, and athletes. Whilst anger appears to be a particularly salient emotion experienced by parents in youth sport, research has also illustrated how parents often feel disappointment (Wiersma and Fifer, 2008; Dorsch et al., 2009) and embarrassment if their child is underperforming or behaving poorly (Dorsch et al., 2009; Harwood and Knight, 2009a,b). Although these studies have offered initial insight into emotions among sport parents, it is not clear how parents' appraisals shaped their emotional responses or the types of appraisals that parents experience. Furthermore, very little is known about the other theoretically proposed emotions that parents may experience when watching their children compete (e.g., anxiety, dejection, happiness, and excitement; Jones et al., 2005). Developing a more robust body of evidence in this area is important if we are to understand the psychological processes that determine parents' experiences of stress and, in turn, the behaviors that they exhibit and the support (or lack thereof) that they are able to offer to their children (cf. Webster-Stratton, 1990; Lazarus, 1999).

Many approaches to the classification of coping have been proposed (see e.g., Lazarus and Folkman, 1984; Connor-Smith et al., 2000; Skinner et al., 2003; Gaudreau and Blondin, 2004) yet a consensus on how best to classify coping is yet to be reached. To address this challenge, Nicholls et al. (2016) reviewed the strengths and limitations of various approaches and, during a meta-analysis, found support for a three-factor classification system (i.e., mastery, internal regulation, and goal withdrawal). Despite other approaches to coping classification holding promise, this three-factor approach appears useful for enhancing conceptual clarity and informing future research. There is limited empirical research that has specifically set out to explore the coping strategies that parents use. One notable exception is a recent study by Burgess et al. (2016) who used interpretive phenomenological analysis (IPA) to examine how parents (n = 7) of elite youth gymnasts cope with stressors. Their findings suggest that the parents encountered a variety of competitive, organizational, and developmental stressors and employed a range of coping strategies, including detaching, normalizing experiences, having a willingness to learn, and managing emotional reactions (Burgess et al., 2016). This study provided initial insight to the coping strategies employed by youth sport parents and suggests that parents utilize multiple strategies in combination when attempting to cope with stressors. Nevertheless, it is not clear which strategies are effective for parents. As Nicholls (2016) suggested, understanding more about coping effectiveness and the factors that influence coping (i.e., stressors, appraisals, and emotions) would help applied researchers and practitioners to develop more effective and tailored interventions (see Thrower et al., 2017).

Considered collectively, the aforementioned studies have offered preliminary understanding of different components of psychological stress transactions among sport parents. Nevertheless, by focusing on the discrete components of transactions, these studies have overlooked the crucial associations between stressors, appraisals, emotions, and coping that have implications for parents' behavior, health, and well-being (Lazarus and Folkman, 1984; Lazarus, 1999). In addition, extant literature almost entirely overlooks the concept of appraising among parents, which is problematic given the central role that it has in determining the outcomes of stress transactions. There is clearly a need to go beyond fragmented studies and give more holistic consideration to stress transactions. As Harwood and Knight (2009b) suggested, "future research should pay closer attention to understanding the full stress and coping process in sport-parents to furnish practitioners, parents, and organizations with more precise intervention ideas, education, and skills" (p. 34). Such studies represent a significant methodological challenge for researchers due to the contextual nature of stressors and the absence of measures that capture the complexity and idiographic nature of stressors and coping. With this in mind, Nicholls (2016) suggested that exploring the nuanced ways in which individuals cope with stressors might require more sophisticated and novel research designs. The aim of this study was, therefore, to build on the aforementioned sport parent research and explore more fully psychological stress among parents of competitive British tennis players. To achieve this aim, the current study used a multipart mixed method design to answer a series of interconnected questions: (a) What are the prominent stressors that tennis parents experience? (b) How are these stressors appraised? (c) What emotions are associated with such stressors? (d) What coping strategies do parents use? (e) How effective are these coping strategies? and (f) Does perceived effectiveness vary as a function of stressor type, appraisal, and coping strategy used?

METHODOLOGY AND METHODS

Research Design

This study was conducted from a post-positivistic philosophical position which acknowledges that some aspects of the social world cannot be directly measured but seeks to retain an objective approach that is free from bias (Weed, 2009). As such, post-positivists loosen the strict positivistic belief in value-free inquiry, yet still test theories, often quantify their data, and adopt traditional evaluation criteria (Krane and Baird, 2005; Denzin and Lincoln, 2011). Consistent with this philosophical position, a novel multipart concurrent mixed method design (Morse, 2003; Morgan, 2013) was adopted in which multiple qualitative and quantitative data were collected simultaneously within one study to answer the research questions. Both types of data were collected at the same time and were given equal emphasis and priority (i.e., QUAL + QUANT; Morse, 2003). Specifically, a cross-sectional online questionnaire was used where qualitative components were included to identify prominent stressors and coping strategies (Harwood and Knight, 2009a; Burgess et al., 2016) and quantitative elements captured primary appraisals, emotions, and coping effectiveness (Jones et al., 2005; Hanton et al., 2012). Qualitative data was subsequently transformed (i.e., quantified) to allow for combined analyses to be conducted which in turn enabled the data to be merged and interpreted within both the results and discussion sections.

Participants and Sampling

Following institutional ethical approval, homogeneous purposeful sampling was used to recruit parents of British junior tennis players (aged 5–18 years). An email invitation was sent from the national governing body (i.e., the Lawn Tennis Association) to parents of an estimated 1,500 British tennis players who met the selection criteria (i.e., parents of children who regularly participate in tennis between the ages of 5–18 years). One hundred and thirty five parents (41 men, 93 women, one parent chose not to report gender) responded to this invitation and agreed to participate in the study (9.0% response rate). Most participants identified as being their child's biological parent (97.77%), were in a relationship (94.77%), and had between 2 and 17 years (M = 6.88; SD = 3.07) experience as a tennis parent. Participants' children were between the ages of 6 and 18 years of age (M = 12.29; SD = 2.52) and were predominantly male (65.18%). Thirty-six participants' children played 'mini tennis' (5–10 years) and had ratings between Red 4 (starting/lowest possible rating) and Green 1* (the best/highest possible rating) specific to 'mini-tennis'. Ninety-nine participants' children played junior tennis and had ratings between 10.2 (starting/lowest possible rating) and 2.2 (M = 6.13; SD = 1.98). The highest (i.e., best) possible rating in British Tennis across junior and adult players is 1.1.

Procedure

Those parents who responded favorably to the invitation were emailed a link to the online questionnaire where participant information for informed consent was provided. Parents who consented to participate at this point were then provided with an introductory guide containing instructions on how to complete the questionnaire. This guide was designed to enhance parents' understanding of psychological stress, define key terms (e.g., stressors, primary appraisals, emotion, coping, and coping effectiveness), and provide worked examples. Once parents had read the introductory guide, they were asked to record up to five of the most prominent stressors that they had faced as a tennis parent. Participants were then asked to record the ways that they appraised each stressor (i.e., harm/loss, threat, challenge, and benefit; Lazarus, 1999) and the emotions associated with it (i.e., anger, dejection, anxiety, happiness, and excitement; Jones et al., 2005). Finally, parents were asked to record up to three strategies that they used to cope with each stressor in an open-ended format and how effective they considered each strategy to be.

Qualitative Data Collection

In line with previous research (i.e., Harwood and Knight, 2009b; Levy et al., 2009; Burgess et al., 2016) a qualitative approach was used to identify the individual and subjective stressors that parents experienced and the ways in which they attempted to cope in their own words (Lazarus, 2000). Specifically, questionnaires with open-ended answer boxes were used to collect qualitative data about parents' most pertinent stressors and associated coping strategies (Harwood and Knight, 2009b). Parents were given specific instructions about what to include in each open-ended box. For example, parents were asked to: "Record the coping strategies that you used in response to the stressor using the boxes below. Each coping strategy should go in a separate box. You can enter one or more (up to three) coping strategies depending on what you did to cope with that stressor." Each open-ended question box offered unlimited space and parents were encouraged to provide as much depth and detail as possible.

Quantitative Data Collection

Primary Appraisals

Drawing on the procedures outlined by Hanton et al. (2012), parents in the current study were asked to self-report whether they appraised each stressor as harm/loss (i.e., damage to goals, values, or beliefs that has already occurred), threat (i.e., future damage), challenge (i.e., anticipated gain), or benefit (i.e., gain that has already occurred; Lazarus, 1999). Parents were asked to select the most relevant primary appraisal for each stressor. The current study focused solely on primary appraisals because this part of appraising is thought to have salient implications for coping, emotion, performance, and well-being (see e.g., Lazarus, 1999; Didymus, 2017). Secondary appraising, which refers to evaluations of available coping resources, is also relevant as a determinant of emotional responses in Lazarus' model. Nevertheless, given the complexity of the current design and anticipated analyses, an examination of this part of stress transactions was deemed beyond the scope of the current work.

Emotion

Based on the Sport Emotion Questionnaire (SEQ; Jones et al., 2005), which has demonstrated validity and internal consistency in a number of sport settings, participants were asked to record how anxious (i.e., uneasy, tense, nervous, apprehensive, or anxious), dejected (i.e., upset, sad, unhappy, disappointed, or dejected), excited (i.e., exhilarated, excited, enthusiastic, or energetic), happy (i.e., pleased, joyful, happy, or cheerful), and angry (i.e., irritated, furious, annoyed, or angry) they felt in response to each documented stressor. Specifically, participants were asked to record the extent to which they experienced each emotion on a 5-point rating scale of zero (not at all), one (a little), two (moderately), three (quite a bit), and four (extremely).

Coping Effectiveness

A coping effectiveness score was used to understand whether the strategies employed were perceived to be successful in alleviating the negative outcomes of stressors. In accordance with previous studies (Nicholls et al., 2007; Levy et al., 2009; Didymus and Fletcher, 2012), participants were asked to rate on an 11-point scale (0–10) how effective they perceived each individual coping strategy to be. For the purpose of this study, a perceived coping effectiveness score of zero was considered to be completely ineffective, a score of five was moderately effective, and a score of 10 was considered completely effective.

Data Analyses

Qualitative Data

Qualitative data from the online open-ended questionnaire were analyzed using an abductive (i.e., inductive and deductive) approach to hierarchical content analysis. This approach has been applied elsewhere in the literature (e.g., Didymus, 2017) to encourage the creation of new ideas (i.e., inductive logic) whilst also applying theoretical frameworks or lenses to participants' experiences (i.e., deductive logic). Although inductive reasoning was used to guide the initial stages of analysis, existing stressor (Harwood and Knight, 2009a,b) and coping classifications (Nicholls et al., 2016) were subsequently and deductively used to promote consistency in the terminologies that are applied within published literature. In line with the procedures outlined by Sparkes and Smith (2014), qualitative data were read and re-read to promote content familiarity and each open-ended response was labeled as a lower order theme. Following initial labeling, ideas that represented stressors or coping strategies reported by parents were grouped together to create meaningful higher order themes and general dimensions. Next, themes were crosschecked and thoroughly re-examined by the second named author and then confirmed by the first named author (Sparkes and Smith, 2014). Finally, tables were produced to reflect the hierarchical nature of the chosen method of analysis, including the frequencies of each cited stressor or coping strategy.

Quantitative Data

Quantitative data analysis started by calculating the overall frequency with which each type of appraisal was reported (i.e., harm/loss, threat, challenge, and benefit). Providing sufficient power (Clark-Carter, 2010), the total dataset for emotions was $n = 342$, and for coping effectiveness $n = 646$. Descriptive statistics (i.e., means and standard deviations) for the emotions experienced (i.e., anxiety, dejection, happiness, excitement, and anger) and coping effectiveness were then calculated. Data were screened for parametric assumptions and detected the presence of outliers in happiness and excitement variables. Accordingly, when analyzing the data, sensitivity analyses were conducted without these extreme cases (i.e., the removal of $n = 4$ each for happiness and excitement). These exclusions did not materially change the pattern of results. The main and interaction effects were the same, whilst two additional pairwise comparisons emerged as significant (these points are highlighted in the "Results" section). To complement the descriptive data, differences in emotions experienced as a function of stressor category and appraisal were explored using a 3 (stressor: competition vs. organizational vs. developmental) × 3 (appraisal: harm vs. threat vs. challenge) multivariate analysis (MANOVA). Differences in coping effectiveness as a function of stressor category, appraisal, and coping strategy were then assessed using a 3 (stressor: competition vs. organizational vs. developmental) × 3 (appraisal: harm vs. threat vs. challenge) × 3 (coping strategy: mastery vs. internal regulation vs. goal withdrawal) analysis of variance (ANOVA). Any significant main or interaction effects were followed up with Bonferroni adjusted pairwise comparisons.

RESULTS

In accordance with guidance from Lazarus (1999), the results section is organized by the components of psychological stress that were examined to provide a full and comprehensive view of the data. Data relating to stressors are presented first, followed by primary appraisals, emotions, coping strategies, and coping effectiveness. The final sub-sections of the results explore the statistical differences in emotions experienced and coping strategy effectiveness.

Stressors

Data analysis generated three general dimensions of parental stressors: (a) organizational; (b) competitive; and (c) developmental. These three dimensions contained a total of 20 higher order themes, 51 lower order themes (see **Table 1**), and

TABLE 1 | The general dimensions, higher order themes, and lower order themes of stressors reported by parents (n = 135), including the frequency of which each was reported.

General dimensions	Higher order themes	Lower order themes	Frequency	
			N	%
Competition	Child's opponent		33	24.44
		Bad line calls and cheating	24	17.78
		Aggressive or inappropriate behavior	9	6.67
	Child's behavior		32	23.70
		Bad physical and verbal behavior	19	14.07
		Distress and limited emotional control	6	4.44
		Reluctance to challenge line calls/decisions	5	3.70
		Negative body language	2	1.48
	Other parents		21	15.56
		Bad behavior and attitude	9	6.67
		Interfering with play	7	5.19
		Intimidating and aggressive behavior	5	3.70
	Child's performance		20	14.81
		Not playing to full potential	18	13.33
		Limited effort	2	1.48
	Watching a match		20	14.81
		Feeling nervous/worried about child's performance	17	12.59
		Feeling helpless during a match	3	2.22
	Outcome of matches		16	11.85
		Consoling child/helping them to cope	7	5.19
		Child's reaction to match outcome	4	2.96
		Child losing a match	3	2.22
		Spouse's reaction to match outcome	2	1.48
	Child's psychological readiness to perform		9	6.67
		Pressure/expectation that child places on themselves	7	5.19
		Child's negative approach going into a match	2	1.48
	Poor refereeing		4	2.96
Organizational	Finances		34	25.19
		Cost of coaching, tournaments, and travel	29	21.48
		Financial impact on family and siblings	3	2.22
		Lack of player funding	2	1.48
	Time		30	22.22
		Limited family and partner time	13	9.63
		Time commitment	6	4.44
		Work/tennis role conflict	4	2.96
		Effect of unequal time spent on siblings	4	2.96
		Impact on social life/personal time	3	2.22
		Organization of tennis schedule	2	1.48
	Coaching and training		22	16.30
		Commitment, communication, and relations with coach	9	6.67
		Training program	6	4.44
		Specific disagreement with coach	4	2.96
		Access to training facilities	3	2.22
	Organizing bodies		20	14.81
		Lack of recognition and support	8	5.93
		Pressure of the rating system	6	4.44
		Problems with talent identification system	3	2.22
		Disorganization and management issues	3	2.22

(Continued)

TABLE 1 | Continued

General dimensions	Higher order themes	Lower order themes	Frequency	
			N	%
	Tournaments		17	12.59
		Issues with entry, draws, and seedings	6	4.44
		Traveling to tournaments	5	3.70
		Poor organization/communication at tournament	3	2.22
		Lack of umpire present	2	1.48
		Tournament schedules	2	1.48
	Injury		9	6.67
		Overuse injury	5	3.70
		Fear of injury	2	1.48
		Limited knowledge regarding injuries	2	1.48
Developmental	Child's progress in tennis		22	16.30
		Selection pressure	9	6.67
		Progression relative to peers	6	4.44
		Tennis rating	4	2.96
		Limited effort in training	3	2.22
	Tennis decisions		10	7.41
		Coaching decisions	4	2.96
		Tournament decisions	4	2.96
		Training decisions	2	1.48
	Child's education and social development		5	3.70
	Child's future in tennis		3	2.22
	Impact of tennis on other sports/hobbies		2	1.48
	Child's wellbeing and happiness		2	1.48
Other			8	5.93

342 individual raw data themes or stressors (eight stressors were not grouped into lower and higher order themes or dimensions due to limited relevance or coherence within the responses).

Competition Stressors

Eight higher order themes, 19 lower order themes (see **Table 1**), and 155 raw data themes were associated with junior tennis competitions. Specifically, 'child's opponent' (24.44%) was the most prominent cause of stress for parents during competitions and, in particular, 'bad line calls and cheating' (17.78%) and 'aggressive or inappropriate behavior' (6.67%). As one parent explained: "I find it difficult watching the behavior of my daughter's opponent (i.e., tantrums, persistent poor calls) and the effect this had on my daughter" (Parent 5). Parents also cited their own 'child's behavior' (23.70%) and, to a lesser extent, their 'child's performances' (14.81%) as prevalent stressors. The following quote from one mother illustrates how her daughter 'not playing to full potential' (13.33%) was a significant stressor:

> My daughter is a technically very able player, quite athletic, and plays really well in her 1-1 lessons and squads. Then she gets onto court in a tournament, playing against someone who is clearly a casual, 2 h-a-week player (not 10 h like my daughter!), and my daughter plays "down," doesn't use her technique, and loses. I wonder if it is even worth her putting all the hours training, if that is what happens in tournaments! (Parent 112).

The presence of 'other parents' (15.56%) during competitions was another stressor and included lower order themes such as 'bad behavior and attitude' (6.67%), 'interfering with play' (5.19%), and 'intimidating and aggressive behavior' (3.70%). Parents reported specific examples such as: "Parents of other players providing guidance beyond acceptable encouragement" (Parent 111) and "abusive parents who shout at your child during the match" (Parent 65) as pertinent stressors associated with other parents. In addition, parents self-reported stressors that related to 'watching a match' (14.81%), particularly if they thought their child should win or would lose badly: "I find watching my son play a stressful experience, especially if I know the score..." (Parent 65). Parents also reported the 'outcome of matches' (11.85%) as a stressor, especially their 'child losing a match' (2.22%), 'child's reaction to match outcome' (2.96%), and 'consoling child/helping them to cope' (5.19%). For instance, one parent stated: "If my child doesn't win/play well he gets very upset and is sometimes physically sick. He thinks he's letting everyone down... himself/me/coach" (Parent 53). Less frequently cited competition stressors included their 'children's psychological readiness to perform' (6.67%) and 'poor refereeing' (2.96%).

Organizational Stressors

Six higher order themes, 25 low order themes (see **Table 1**), and 135 raw data themes referred to organizational stressors associated with children's tennis involvement. A substantial number of participants mentioned 'finances' (25.19%) and particularly the 'cost of coaching, tournaments, and travel' (21.48%) as a source of stress. As one parent stated: "Finance. The cost of lessons, squads, competitions, and traveling to competitions" (Parent 11). Similarly, another parent added: "Financial – we have not had a family holiday for 2 years since my daughter started competing at a higher level!" (Parent 122). 'Time' (22.22%) was also a stressor for a large number of parents and, in particular, 'limited family and partner time' (9.63%) as demonstrated in the following quotes: "Lack of time. Tennis competitions (event time, traveling, and recently finding them) taking up too much family time" (Parent 11) and "competitions that are over two or more days present a constant problem for a family with more than one child, particularly where the other child does not play competitive tennis – it splits the family and creates rifts" (Parent 84). In terms of time related stressors, a small number of parents also appeared to be concerned about 'work/tennis role conflict' (2.96%), the 'effect of unequal time spent on siblings' (2.96%), and resented the time spent on tennis due to its negative 'impact on social life/personal time' (2.22%). One parent admitted: "I resent the way that the time (and money) involved in traveling to tennis squads and tournaments means my son is also put first leaving little time for anything I would like to be doing, and little money for anything else" (Parent 36).

Beyond the financial and time commitments of junior tennis participation, parents identified 'coaching and training' (16.30%) and 'organizing bodies' (14.81%) as stressors. Lower order themes included the 'lack of recognition and support' (5.93%), 'pressure of the rating system' (4.44%), 'problems with talent identification system' (2.22%), and general 'disorganization and management issues' (2.22%) as organizational stressors. The following quote captures parents' frustration with the current rating system:

> Too much emphasis for years on ratings, often non-reflective of ability, and until recently LTA refusal to acknowledge this. The LTA can't see how the system is 'abused' by some players, and when you get your rating behind (e.g., through injury and player withdrawals) virtually no opportunity to catch up (Parent 14).

Other organizational stressors related to 'tournaments' (12.59%), and specifically 'issues with entry, draws, and seedings' (4.44%), 'traveling to tournaments' (3.70%), 'poor organization/communication at tournaments' (2.22%), 'lack of umpire present' (1.48%), and 'tournament schedules' (1.48%). As one parent wrote: "Referees being poorly organized, not getting players on, leaving long times in between matches, making mistakes in informing both players about starting times, not being friendly and helpful" (Parent 68). A small number of parents made reference to 'injury' related stressors (6.67%) and, in particular, 'overuse injuries' (3.70%). As one parent wrote: "My child has been constantly injured as a result of the amount of tennis training he has being taking part in" (Parent 41). Other parents cited 'fear of injury' (1.48%) and their 'limited knowledge regarding injuries' as stressors (1.48%).

Developmental Stressors

Six higher order themes, seven lower order themes (see **Table 1**), and 44 raw data themes referred to stressors associated with children's development both within and outside of tennis. The most frequently cited developmental stressor within this dimension was their 'child's progress in tennis' (16.30%). Specifically, parents referenced 'selection pressures' (6.67%), 'progression relative to peers' (4.44%), 'tennis rating' (2.96%), and 'limited effort in training' (2.22%) as lower order stressors. The following quote captures the concerns of parents in relation to these developmental factors: "I feel stressed about trying to keep my son's ratings/rankings up with his peers/coaches' expectations" (Parent 115). Furthermore, parents felt that 'tennis decisions' (7.41%) in relation to 'coaching decisions' (2.96%), 'tournament decisions' (2.96%), and 'training decisions' (1.48%) were key stressors. As one parent wrote:

> I find it difficult to have to make choices and decisions about which tournaments my son should play and balancing out costs and aims from competition (i.e., good tough matches vs. easy points, not risking ratings losses, keeping up with other players who can travel further or fit in more tournaments vs. working on own goals) (Parent 36).

A small number of parents were concerned about the impact that tennis has on their 'child's education and social development' (3.70%). As one parent wrote: "[Child's name] spends 14 h a week doing sport outside school (tennis and football). I worry that this has an impact on both his school and his social development" (Parent 88). Beyond children's development, some parents also reported stressors regarding their 'child's future in tennis' (2.22%), the 'impact of tennis on other sports/hobbies' (1.48%), and their 'child's wellbeing and happiness' (1.48%).

Primary Appraisals

Of the total 342 separate self-reported stressors, 115 (33.65%) were appraised as a harm/loss, 113 (33.04%) were appraised as a challenge, 105 (30.70%) were evaluated as a threat, and 9 (2.63%) were evaluated as a benefit. **Table 2** illustrates differences in the way competition, developmental, and organizational stressors were appraised. The results suggest that organizational stressors were most commonly appraised as harmful (40.00%) whilst threat appraisals were most commonly made in response to both developmental (43.18%) and competition (35.55%) stressors. Challenge appraisals were the second most frequently used appraisal across all general stressor dimensions whilst benefit appraisals were rarely made irrespective of the nature of the stressor.

Emotions

Parents reported moderate levels of anxiety and anger, low levels of dejection, and very low levels of excitement and happiness in relation to the stressors recalled (see **Table 2**). Due to low numbers, stressors categorized as other ($n = 8$) and appraisals categorized as benefit ($n = 9$) were not included in analyses, resulting in a sample of 327 (two of the other stressors were appraised as benefit). Therefore, the means reported in text vary compared to **Table 2**, which includes the full stressor, appraisal, and emotion profile. A 3 (stressor) × 3 (appraisal) MANOVA indicated a significant main effect for stressor, Wilks' $\Lambda = 0.91$, $F(10,628) = 3.09$, $p = 0.001$, $\eta_p^2 = 0.05$, and appraisal, Wilks' $\Lambda = 0.88$, $F(10,628) = 4.03$, $p < 0.001$, $\eta_p^2 = 0.06$, on experienced emotion. There was a non-significant

TABLE 2 | The appraisals and emotional profile for all stressors (n = 342) and general stressor dimensions (n = 334).

General stressor dimensions	Appraisals	Frequency		Anxiety		Dejection		Excitement		Anger		Happiness	
		N	%	*M*	*SD*	*M*	*SD*	*M*	*SD*	*M*	*SD*	*M*	*SD*
All		342	100	2.81	1.03	1.80	1.37	0.66	1.03	2.06	1.41	0.52	0.94
	Harm/loss	115	33.63	2.94	1.01	2.17	1.40	0.32	0.79	2.49	1.42	0.27	0.64
	Challenge	113	33.04	2.72	1.04	1.61	1.28	0.82[c]	1.04	1.76	1.35	0.70	1.03
	Threat	105	30.70	2.87	0.94	1.71	1.36	0.67	0.95	2.06	1.34	0.39	0.74
	Benefit	9	2.63	1.78	1.48	0.67	1.12	2.89	1.45	0.33	0.50	2.89	1.45
Competition		155	100	2.88	1.07	1.79	1.41	0.56	0.92	2.39	1.43	0.40	0.85
	Threat	52	35.55	2.85	1.06	1.50	1.35	0.77	0.94	2.31	1.38	0.42	0.75
	Challenge	51	32.90	2.90	0.99	1.76	1.26	0.63	0.96	2.14	1.50	0.51	0.95
	Harm/loss	49	31.61	2.96	1.15	2.16	1.59	0.16	0.47	2.86	1.31	0.12	0.39
	Benefit	3	1.94	2.00	1.73	1.00	1.00	2.33	2.08	0.67	0.58	2.67	2.31
Organizational		135	100	2.79	0.97	1.86	1.31	0.64	1.03	1.93	1.32	0.54	0.90
	Harm/loss	54	40.00	2.94	0.92	2.06	1.23	0.50	1.004	2.22	1.46	0.43	0.79
	Challenge	45	33.33	2.53	1.10	1.58	1.36	0.80	1.06	1.58	1.12	0.76	1.11
	Threat	34	25.19	2.91	0.79	1.94	1.30	0.53	0.90	2.00	1.23	0.35	0.60
	Benefit	2	1.48	2.00	1.41	1.50	2.12	2.50	2.12	0.50	0.71	2.00	1.41
Developmental		44	100	2.70	0.95	1.80	1.37	0.98	1.21	1.27	1.23	0.75	1.16
	Threat	19	43.18	2.84	0.90	1.89	1.45	0.63	1.07	1.47	1.26	0.37	0.97
	Challenge	14	31.82	2.50	1.02	1.36	1.08	1.57	1.02	0.86	0.95	1.21	1.05
	Harm/loss	9	20.45	2.78	0.83	2.67	1.22	0.22	0.67	1.78	1.39	0.22	0.67
	Benefit	2	4.55	2.50	2.12	0	0	3.50	0.71	0	0	3.50	0.71

M, mean score; SD, standard deviation.

interaction between stressor and appraisal, Wilks' Λ = 0.94, $F(20,1042)$ = 1.02, p = 0.436, η_p^2 = 0.02. Regarding the stressor categories, follow up comparisons indicated greater anger in competition stressors (M = 2.43 ± 1.42) compared to both developmental (M = 1.33 ± 1.22, p < 0.001, CIs: 0.47, 1.65) and organizational stressors (M = 1.95 ± 1.32, p = 0.006, CIs: 0.12, 0.89). In addition, in the analyses with the extreme cases removed, greater anger was reported in organizational compared to developmental stressors (p = 0.037, CIs: 0.03, 1.22). Other comparisons were non-significant. Regarding the appraisal categories, follow up comparisons indicated greater dejection (M = 2.15 ± 1.40, p = 0.005, CIs: 0.18, 1.28) and anger (M = 2.46 ± 1.43, p = 0.003, CIs: 0.21, 1.31) in harm appraisal compared to challenge ($M_{dejection}$ = 1.64 ± 1.28, M_{anger} = 1.75 ± 1.35) appraisal. In addition, in the analyses with the extreme cases removed, greater dejection was reported in harm appraisal compared to threat (M = 1.67 ± 1.33) appraisal (p = 0.033, CIs: 0.04, 1.12). There was also greater excitement (M = 0.82 ± 1.04, CIs: −1.08, −0.33) and happiness (M = 0.70 ± 1.05, CIs: −0.91, −0.23, both p < 0.001) in challenge appraisal compared to harm ($M_{excitement}$ = 0.33 ± 0.80, $M_{happiness}$ = 0.28 ± 0.65) and threat appraisal ($M_{excitement}$ = 0.67 ± 0.95, p = 0.038, CIs: −0.70, −0.02; $M_{happiness}$ = 0.39 ± 0.74, p = 0.002, CIs: −0.75, −0.14). Other comparisons were non-significant. In sum, competitive stressors elicited greater anger compared to organizational and developmental stressors. Further, stressors appraised as harm elicited greater negative emotions (i.e., dejection and anger, but not anxiety) compared to challenge appraisals, while stressors appraised as a challenge elicited greater positive emotions (i.e., excitement and happiness) compared to both harm and threat appraisals.

Coping Strategies

A total of 653 individual coping strategies were reported by parents, which were categorized into 79 lower order themes, 20 higher order themes, and three general coping dimensions (see **Table 3**). Seven entries were not classified because no strategies were reported as being used. General coping dimensions included: (a) mastery coping; (b) internal regulation; and (c) goal withdrawal coping.

Mastery Coping

Eleven higher order themes, 49 lower order themes (see **Table 3**), and 374 coping strategies were categorized as mastery coping (i.e., parents attempting to take control of a stressful situation and eliminate the stressor; Nicholls et al., 2016). The most frequently cited mastery coping strategy by parents was 'communicating with child' (48.89%), which primarily included 'discussing the situation' (18.52%). As one parent explained: "Constant talking to him after matches to help deal with these emotions and try to make him see that if he carried on trying then matches can be turned round" (Parent 128). Other lower order themes included 'providing advice and guidance' (9.63%) before matches and 'providing comfort and reassurance' (9.63%) after defeats. For instance, in relation to the stressor of their child's opponent making bad line calls and cheating, one parent explained:

> Prior to the match I try and get him to realize that there will always be dodgy [line] calls that he needs to focus on his own game and

TABLE 3 | The general dimensions, higher order themes, and lower order themes of coping strategies including the frequency of parents (*n* = 135) reporting each strategy and coping effectiveness.

General dimension	Higher order theme	Lower order theme	Frequency		Coping effectiveness	
			N	%	*M*	*SD*
Mastery	Communicating with child		66	48.89	5.93	2.30
		Discussing the situation	25	18.52	6.29	1.83
		Providing comfort and reassurance	13	9.63	5.81	1.94
		Providing advice and guidance	13	9.63	5.20	3.00
		Providing positive feedback	9	6.67	7.30	1.25
		Providing encouragement	7	5.19	4.27	1.74
		Confronting and discussing behavior	7	5.19	3.50	2.83
		Involving child in decision making	6	4.44	6.57	1.90
		Emphasizing performance over outcomes	4	2.96	6.00	2.31
		Displaying positive body language	3	2.22	8.67	1.15
		Providing feedback at an appropriate time	3	2.22	7.75	2.63
		Setting process goals	3	2.22	6.67	1.53
		Emphasizing enjoyment	2	1.48	7.00	1.41
	Information seeking		36	26.67	6.44	2.18
		Seeking information from child's coach	25	18.52	6.50	2.39
		Researching information	6	4.44	6.75	1.58
		Seeking information from organizer	5	3.70	4.80	2.49
		Seeking information from physiotherapist	3	2.22	6.67	1.53
		Seeking information from strength and conditioning coach	2	1.48	7.50	0.71
		Seeking information from other parents	2	1.48	6.67	1.53
	Time management		33	24.44	6.59	2.03
		Planning, logistics, and being organized	20	14.81	6.39	1.99
		Selective tournament entry	9	6.67	6.90	2.38
		Scheduling time with siblings	6	4.44	6.33	2.34
		Sharing commitment with partner	6	4.44	8.22	1.20
		Scheduling family time	5	3.70	6.40	1.14
		Incorporating family trips and tennis	3	2.22	4.67	1.53
		Incorporating personal activities and tennis	1	0.74	4.00	0.00
		Training locally	1	0.74	8.00	0.00
	Financial management		25	18.52	6.11	2.09
		Budgeting	18	13.33	6.26	2.00
		Selective/limited tournament entry	5	3.70	5.00	2.10
		Setting up additional income	3	2.22	4.33	1.15
		Applying for funding	2	1.48	6.00	1.41
		Working full time	1	0.74	9.00	0.00
	Managing child's tennis progress and development		22	16.30	7.41	1.84
		Scheduling/enforcing break from tennis	9	6.67	7.00	2.26
		Changing coach/training center	6	4.44	7.83	1.60
		Employing a sport psychologist	5	3.70	6.83	1.17
		Ensuring child completes rehab exercises	2	1.48	7.00	2.83
		Moving child abroad	2	1.48	8.50	2.12
		Scheduling regular meetings with child's coach	1	0.74	8.00	1.41
		Changing physiotherapist	1	0.74	10.00	0.00

(Continued)

TABLE 3 | Continued

General dimension	Higher order theme	Lower order theme	Frequency		Coping effectiveness	
			N	%	*M*	*SD*
	Changing parenting behavior		20	14.81	5.72	2.73
		Concealing emotions	8	5.93	5.63	2.72
		Punishing child's behavior	5	3.70	4.25	2.66
		Allowing child to make own choices	4	2.96	7.80	1.92
		Giving child space to calm down	4	2.96	6.25	2.75
	Reducing negative impact of others		11	8.15	6.93	1.71
		Influencing opponent's parents	5	3.70	7.33	1.21
		Reducing negative impact of partner	5	3.70	7.00	2.00
		Maintaining presence courtside	2	1.48	5.5	2.12
	Involving the referee		11	8.15	4.64	2.73
	Preparation		9	6.67	4.50	2.59
		Preparing child mentally and physically for competition	7	5.19	5.00	2.67
		Planning communication with child	2	1.48	2.50	0.71
	Problem solving		8	5.93	6.22	2.22
	Overseeing child's overall development		6	4.44	6.75	2.25
		Ensuring balance with school and other hobbies	6	4.44	7.29	1.80
		Monitoring child's academic progress	1	0.74	3.00	0.00
Internal regulation	Cognitive reappraisal		46	34.07	6.41	2.08
		Placing stressor in perspective	15	11.11	5.78	2.10
		Focusing on the positives	14	10.37	6.60	1.73
		Rationalizing the situation	14	10.37	6.73	2.78
		Focusing on long term development	13	9.63	5.93	1.98
		Focusing on benefits of tennis participation	7	5.19	7.25	1.16
		Focusing on processes not outcomes	4	2.96	7.33	1.21
		Managing own expectations	4	2.96	5.25	0.50
	Seeking emotional support		26	19.26	6.15	1.68
		Talking about situation with other parents	11	8.15	5.94	1.24
		Talking about situation with partner/friend	10	7.41	6.83	1.80
		Talking about situation with multiple people	9	6.67	5.73	2.00
	Behavioral avoidance		26	19.26	6.62	2.15
		Watching match with a limited view/further away	9	6.67	7.33	1.66
		Avoiding contact with other parents	8	5.93	7.58	1.68
		Temporarily walking away	4	2.96	6.00	2.16
		Avoiding the LTA's system/tournaments	4	2.96	6.00	2.94
		Avoiding contact with child	2	1.48	4.00	0.00
		Avoiding watching the match closely	2	1.48	3.50	2.12
		Avoiding contact with coach	1	0.74	5	0.00
	Emotional regulation		19	14.07	6.08	1.85
		Trying to keep calm	13	9.63	6.33	1.91
		Deep breathing	7	5.19	5.30	1.16
		Smoking a cigarette	1	0.74	10.00	0.00
	Distraction		13	9.63	6.47	2.20
		Distraction with another task during a match	8	5.93	7.11	1.96
		Distraction by talking to other parents	3	2.22	5.75	2.50
		General distraction	2	1.48	5.00	2.83

(Continued)

TABLE 3 | Continued

General dimension	Higher order theme	Lower order theme	Frequency		Coping effectiveness	
			N	%	*M*	*SD*
	Cognitive avoidance		12	8.89	4.54	2.44
	Acceptance		9	6.67	6.12	2.74
Goal withdrawal	Behavioral disengagement		28	20.74	5.31	3.05
		Not watching the match/training	13	9.63	4.77	3.09
		Walking away from the match/training	12	8.89	6.15	3.18
		Stopped child playing tennis	2	1.48	5.00	0.00
		Stopped entering certain events	1	0.74	2.00	0.00
	Venting emotions		12	8.89	4.00	2.85
		Complaining	9	6.67	3.92	3.06
		Arguing	2	1.48	3.00	0.00
		Crying	1	0.74	7.00	0.00
No coping			6	4.44	2.86	3.48

M, mean score; SD, standard deviation.

> realize that he is handing the game to the other child if he lets it get to him. He needs to challenge the calls and call the referee over if it is too bad (Parent 53).

In addition to communicating with their child, parents regularly used 'time management' (24.44%) as a higher order coping strategy that consisted of 'planning, logistics, and being organized' (14.81%), 'selective tournament entry' (6.67%), 'scheduling time with siblings' (4.44%), and 'sharing commitments with partner' (4.44%). Similarly, parents also used 'financial management' (18.52%) as a coping strategy and, particularly, 'budgeting' (13.33%) as one mother self-reported:

> Looking to set up a small business alongside part time work so we have more money coming in and still be flexible for coaching and tournaments. But I will miss out on seeing my daughter play and the tournaments will be down to her dad (Parent 122).

'Information seeking' (26.67%) was another frequently cited coping strategy, with a number of parents 'seeking information from child's coach' (18.52%) as well as other key stakeholders (i.e., organizer, physiotherapist, strength and conditioning coach, and other parents). Some parents also used coping strategies such as 'managing child's tennis progress and development' (16.30%), including 'scheduling/enforcing a break from tennis' (6.67%), 'changing coach/training center' (4.44%), and 'employing a sport psychologist' (3.70%) as explained in the following quote:

> Engaged external professional help [sport psychologist] for our child and ourselves, utilize preparation routines and put our child at the center of the solution and recognize it is not a quick fix, give them the mechanisms and create an environment that will support them to help themselves supported by a team including ourselves as parents (Parent 110).

Less frequently cited higher order coping strategies included, 'changing parenting behavior' (14.81%), 'reducing negative impact of others' (8.15%), 'involving the referee' (8.15%), 'preparation' (6.67%), 'problem solving' (5.93%), and 'overseeing child's overall development' (4.44%).

Internal Regulation

Two hundred and twenty-nine coping strategies, 23 lower order themes, and seven higher order categories (see **Table 3**) were characterized as referring to internal regulation (i.e., attempting to manage the internal responses to stress; Nicholls et al., 2016). Over a third of parents used 'cognitive reappraisal' strategies (34.07%), which referred to: 'Placing stressor in perspective' (11.11%), 'focusing on the positives' (10.37%), 'rationalizing the situation' (10.37%), 'focusing on long-term development' (9.63%), or 'focusing on benefits of tennis participation' (5.19%). The following quote illustrates this finding and how parents cope by focusing on the benefits of tennis participation:

> I think about how much I love my children and how I want them to have as many different opportunities as possible. I think about the positive impact sport has had (and continues to have) on their self-esteem, confidence, motivation, determination, and discipline. They are aware of their bodies and how to stay healthy. I think about how sport has encouraged them to take risks, to try things, to learn how to cope with getting things wrong. They have benefitted from interacting with a wider circle of people through sport. I consider that the time I will get with them (of them wanting me around) is relatively short and I rationalize that I have plenty of time to treat myself later! Also, when I stop and add everything up and really think about it, I always come to the conclusion that even if I had more money I would spend it on them anyway! (Parent 11).

Parents also regulated their internal responses to stressors by 'seeking emotional support' (19.26%), which consisted mainly of 'talking about situation with other parents' (8.15%) or 'talking about situation with partner/friend' (7.41%). Other higher order themes included 'behavioral avoidance' strategies (19.26%), which included 'watching match with a limited view/further away' (6.67%), 'avoiding contact with other parents' (5.93%), and 'temporarily walking away' (2.96%). One parent explained why she watches with a limited view: "I sit so there is an obstruction in the way of the court to limit my view – again this stops me living every point" (Parent 50). Parents also used 'emotional regulation' (14.07%) coping strategies such as 'trying to keep calm' (9.63%) and 'deep breathing' (5.19%), as one parent disclosed: "If I go [to tournaments/matches] I try to take deep breaths and can't wait for it to be over and go home" (Parent 87). Less frequently cited higher order coping strategies included 'distraction' (9.63%), 'cognitive avoidance' (8.89%), and 'acceptance' (6.67%). For instance, one parent explained how he charts matches (i.e., recording match statistics) as a distraction technique: "I have started charting matches for something to focus on and then share stats with him sometime after match as part of conversation about how he felt and what the stats say" (Parent 130).

Goal Withdrawal

Two higher order themes, seven lower order themes (see **Table 3**), and 43 individual coping strategies referred to goal withdrawal coping strategies (i.e., parents ceasing efforts to achieve a goal; Nicholls et al., 2016). Specifically, 'behavioral disengagement' (20.74%) consisted of lower order themes such as 'not watching the match/training' (9.63%). As one parent admitted: "I try to avoid taking him to matches and hope my husband will take my son. It actually makes me feel sick" (Parent 87). Other lower order coping strategies included 'walking away from the match/training' (8.89%) as one parent explained:

> I removed myself from the match and walked away to get a coffee. [I was] angry and also feeling very concerned for my daughter who had done everything she is asked to when this happens but who was basically being bullied and cheated on court – disgraceful! Such inconsistency from official to official from tournament to tournament (Parent 3).

In a small number of cases, parents 'stopped child playing tennis' (1.48%). For instance, one parent wrote: "I supported my son but asked him to stop playing. The pressure was painful to watch and no one cares" (Parent 129). A small number of parents also attempted to cope by 'venting emotions' (8.89%). This higher order category was made up of lower order themes such as 'complaining' (6.67%), 'arguing' (1.48%), and 'crying' (0.74%).

Coping Effectiveness

Mastery Coping Effectiveness

As seen in **Table 3**, within the mastery coping dimension (n = 374), the most effective higher order coping strategy was 'managing child's tennis development and progress' (M = 7.41 ± 1.84), which included moderately effective lower order strategies such as 'changing coach/training center' (M = 7.83 ± 1.60), 'scheduling/enforcing break from tennis' (M = 7.00 ± 2.26), and 'employing a sport psychologist' (M = 6.83 ± 1.17). In addition, 'reducing negative impact of others' (M = 6.93 ± 1.71), 'time management' (M = 6.59 ± 2.03), and 'overseeing child's overall development' (M = 6.75 ± 2.25) were perceived as moderately effective higher order strategies. Other higher order strategies such as 'communicating with child' (M = 5.93 ± 2.30) included a combination of moderately effective [e.g., 'providing positive feedback' (M = 7.30 ± 1.25)] and ineffective lower order strategies [e.g., 'confronting and discussing behavior' (M = 3.50 ± 2.83)]. Similarly, within the 'changing parenting behavior' (M = 5.72 ± 2.73) higher order theme, 'allowing child to make own choices' (M = 7.80 ± 1.92) was moderately effective, whilst 'punishing child's behavior' (M = 4.25 ± 2.66) was considered to be a moderately ineffective strategy. 'Involving the referee' (M = 4.64 ± 2.73) and 'preparation' (M = 4.50 ± 2.59) were considered to be the most ineffective mastery higher order coping strategies.

Internal Regulation Coping Effectiveness

Turning attention toward internal regulation coping strategies (n = 229), 'behavioral avoidance' (M = 6.62 ± 2.15) was considered to be the most effective higher order strategy, with lower order strategies such as 'avoiding contact with other parents' (M = 7.58 ± 1.68) and 'watching match with a limited view/further away' (M = 7.33 ± 1.66) considered as moderately effective. Another higher order theme 'cognitive reappraisal' (M = 6.41 ± 2.08) was perceived as moderately effective, and included particularly effective lower order themes such as 'focusing on benefits of tennis participation' (M = 7.25 ± 1.16) and 'focusing on processes not outcomes' (M = 7.33 ± 1.21). Similarly, 'seeking emotional support' (M = 6.15 ± 1.68), 'emotional regulation' (M = 6.08 ± 1.85), 'acceptance' (M = 6.12 ± 2.74) and 'distraction' (M = 6.47 ± 2.20) were moderately effective higher order strategies and 'distraction with another task during a match' (i.e., charting, reading, and answering emails) was considered as a particularly effective lower order theme (M = 7.11 ± 1.96). In contrast, cognitive avoidance (M = 4.54 ± 2.44) was perceived to be moderately ineffective.

Goal Withdrawal Coping Effectiveness

Higher order goal withdrawal strategies (n = 43) such as 'behavioral disengagement' (M = 5.31 ± 3.05) was considered moderately effective. In contrast, 'venting emotions' (M = 4.00 ± 2.85) was perceived as a relatively ineffective coping strategy. Parents also considered 'not watching the match/training' (M = 4.77 ± 3.09) to be a moderately ineffective strategy and 'complaining' (M = 3.92 ± 3.06) was perceived as the least effective coping strategy within this coping dimension.

Overall Coping Effectiveness

Overall, the 646 coping strategies were considered by parents to be moderately effective (M = 6.10 ± 2.32). Due to low numbers, benefit appraisals (n = 15) were not included in statistical analyses, resulting in a sample of 631 strategies. Therefore, the means reported in text vary compared to **Tables 3, 4**. A 3 (stressor) × 3 (strategy) × 3 (appraisal) ANOVA indicated a non-significant main effect for stressor, $F(2,606) = 0.85$, $p = 0.430$, $\eta_p^2 = 0.003$ and appraisal, $F(2,606) = 1.69$, $p = 0.186$, $\eta_p^2 = 0.01$, on effectiveness. A significant main effect for strategy, $F(2,606) = 6.01$, $p = 0.003$, $\eta_p^2 = 0.02$, indicated greater effectiveness for mastery (M = 6.20 ± 2.27) and internal regulation (M = 6.15 ± 2.03) strategies compared to goal withdrawal (M = 4.77 ± 2.98). In terms of the two-way interactions, there was: (a) a significant interaction between stressor category and appraisal, $F(4,606) = 3.69$, $p = 0.006$, $\eta_p^2 = 0.02$; (b) stressor category and coping

TABLE 4 | The relationships between stressors, appraisals, coping strategies, and coping effectiveness (*n* = 646).

Stressor	Appraisal	Mastery coping strategy		Mastery coping effectiveness		Internal regulation coping strategy		Internal regulation coping effectiveness		Goal withdrawal coping strategy		Goal withdrawal coping effectiveness	
		F	%	*M*	*SD*	*F*	%	*M*	*SD*	*F*	%	*M*	*SD*
All	All	374	57.89	6.23	2.26	229	35.45	6.20	2.05	43	6.66	4.77	2.98
	Harm/loss	110	29.41	5.70	2.30	82	35.81	5.72	2.18	19	43.18	4.32	2.89
	Threat	125	33.42	5.90	2.32	71	31.00	6.01	1.83	17	39.53	4.65	3.08
	Challenge	132	35.29	6.89	2.03	68	29.69	6.82	1.89	7	16.28	6.29	2.93
	Benefit	7	1.87	7.86	1.07	8	3.49	7.38	2.33	0	n/a	0.00	0.00
Competition	All	164	43.85	5.81	2.42	113	49.34	6.27	2.07	28	65.12	4.96	3.01
	Harm/loss	45	27.44	5.11	2.43	41	36.28	5.73	2.24	10	35.71	3.60	2.63
	Threat	56	34.15	4.98	2.22	36	31.86	5.75	1.61	12	42.86	5.08	3.15
	Challenge	62	37.80	7.03	2.08	30	26.55	7.40	1.69	6	21.43	7.00	2.45
	Benefit	1	0.61	8.00	0.00	6	5.31	7.33	2.73	0	0.00	0.00	0.00
Developmental	All	52	13.90	6.31	2.14	33	14.41	5.88	1.65	2	4.65	4.50	4.95
	Harm/loss	9	17.31	5.44	1.74	5	15.15	4.80	2.28	0	0.00	0.00	0.00
	Threat	23	44.23	6.48	2.00	17	51.52	6.00	1.77	2	100	4.50	4.95
	Challenge	17	32.69	6.12	2.45	10	30.30	6.10	0.99	0	0.00	0.00	0.00
	Benefit	3	5.77	8.67	0.58	1	3.03	7.00	0.00	0	0.00	0.00	0.00
Organizational	All	158	42.24	6.63	2.05	83	36.24	6.23	2.18	13	30.23	4.38	2.90
	Harm/loss	56	35.44	6.21	2.17	36	43.37	5.83	2.14	9	69.23	5.11	3.10
	Threat	46	29.11	6.74	2.21	18	21.69	6.56	2.25	3	33.33	3.00	2.00
	Challenge	53	33.54	6.96	1.78	28	33.73	6.46	2.19	1	7.69	2.00	0.00
	Benefit	3	1.90	7.00	0.00	1	1.20	8.00	0.00	0	0.00	0.00	0.00

F, frequency; M, mean score; SD, standard deviation.

strategy, $F(4,606) = 3.69$, $p = 0.006$, $\eta_p^2 = 0.02$; and (c) a non-significant interaction between appraisal and coping strategy, $F(4,606) = 0.27$, $p = 0.898$, $\eta_p^2 = 0.002$. The three-way interaction between stressor category, appraisal, and coping strategy was non-significant, $F(6,606) = 1.57$, $p = 0.154$, $\eta_p^2 = 0.02$.

The two interaction effects were followed up with adjusted pairwise comparisons. First, regarding stressor category and appraisal: (a) challenge, but not harm or threat, appraisals were managed more effectively for competition stressors ($M = 7.20 \pm 1.97$, $n = 96$) compared to organizational ($M = 6.72 \pm 2.02$, $n = 85$), stressors only ($p = 0.035$, CIs: 0.11, 3.98); and (b) competition, but not organizational or developmental, stressors were managed more effectively following challenge appraisals ($M = 7.20 \pm 1.97$, $n = 96$) compared to both harm ($M = 5.24 \pm 2.43$, $p = 0.001$, CIs: 1.31, 3.38, $n = 95$) and threat ($M = 5.26 \pm 2.17$, $p < 0.001$, CIs: 0.89, 2.91, $n = 104$) appraisals.

Second, regarding stressor category and coping strategy: (a) mastery, but not internal regulation or goal withdrawal, coping was more effective for organizational ($M = 6.60 \pm 2.09$, $n = 160$) compared to competition ($M = 5.83 \pm 2.43$, $n = 160$), stressors only ($p = 0.001$, CIs: 0.28, 1.44); and (b) organizational, but not competitive or developmental, stressors were managed more effectively by mastery ($M = 6.60 \pm 2.09$, $p = 0.001$, CIs: 1.14, 5.34, $n = 160$) and internal regulation ($M = 6.21 \pm 2.18$, $p = 0.004$, CIs: 0.77, 5.06, $n = 82$) strategies compared to goal withdrawal ($M = 4.38 \pm 2.90$, $n = 13$).

To summarize, irrespective of stressor category or appraisal, mastery and internal regulation coping strategies were more effective than goal withdrawal. Furthermore, with challenge appraisal, competition stressors were managed more effectively than organizational but not developmental stressors. Within competition, but not organizational or developmental stressors, challenge appraisal was linked to more effective stressor management than both harm and threat appraisal. Mastery coping, but not internal regulation or goal withdrawal, was more effective for organizational stressors compared to competition stressors, but not developmental stressors. Organizational, but not competition or developmental, stressors were managed more effectively through mastery and internal regulation strategies compared to goal withdrawal.

Descriptive Relationships Between Stressors, Emotions, Coping, and Coping Effectiveness

The current study also provides initial insights into the descriptive relationship between parents' stressors, emotions, coping strategies, and coping effectiveness ($n = 646$). Focusing first on the relationship between emotions, coping, and coping effectiveness, mastery coping strategies ($n = 374$) were considered to be the most effective coping strategy and were used when

TABLE 5 | The relationship between competition, developmental, and organizational stressors, emotions, coping strategies, and coping effectiveness (*n* = 646).

Stressor	Emotion	Mastery					Internal regulation					Goal withdrawal				
			Coping strategy		Coping effectiveness			Coping strategy		Coping effectiveness			Coping strategy		Coping effectiveness	
		F	*M*	*SD*	*M*	*SD*	*F*	*M*	*SD*	*M*	*SD*	*F*	*M*	*SD*	*M*	*SD*
All	Anxiety	374	2.84	1.04	6.23	2.26	229	2.78	1.00	6.20	2.05	43	3.05	0.99	4.77	2.98
	Dejection	374	1.80	1.39	6.23	2.26	229	1.88	1.32	6.20	2.05	43	2.25	1.40	4.77	2.98
	Excitement	374	0.61	0.99	6.23	2.26	229	0.08	1.10	6.20	2.05	43	0.59	1.00	4.77	2.98
	Anger	374	1.99	1.39	6.23	2.26	229	1.98	1.40	6.20	2.05	43	2.75	1.48	4.77	2.98
	Happiness	374	0.44	0.87	6.23	2.26	229	0.65	1.03	6.20	2.05	43	0.43	0.93	4.77	2.98
Competition	Anxiety	164	2.90	1.10	5.81	2.42	113	2.95	1.01	6.27	2.07	28	2.97	1.15	4.96	3.01
	Dejection	164	1.91	1.46	5.81	2.42	113	1.87	1.38	6.27	2.07	28	2.00	1.46	4.96	3.01
	Excitement	164	0.46	0.79	5.81	2.42	113	0.71	1.06	6.27	2.07	28	0.79	1.15	4.96	3.01
	Anger	164	2.46	1.39	5.81	2.42	113	2.14	1.51	6.27	2.07	28	2.62	1.54	4.96	3.01
	Happiness	164	0.25	0.59	5.81	2.42	113	0.58	1.08	6.27	2.07	28	0.66	1.08	4.96	3.01
Developmental	Anxiety	52	2.94	0.92	6.31	2.14	33	2.24	0.79	5.88	1.65	2	3.00	0.00	4.50	4.95
	Dejection	52	1.60	1.42	6.31	2.14	33	1.79	1.24	5.88	1.65	2	3.00	1.41	4.50	4.95
	Excitement	52	1.15	1.24	6.31	2.14	33	0.79	1.05	5.88	1.65	2	0.00	0.00	4.50	4.95
	Anger	52	1.00	1.14	6.31	2.14	33	1.42	1.17	5.88	1.65	2	2.50	2.12	4.50	4.95
	Happiness	52	0.87	1.22	6.31	2.14	33	0.61	1.06	5.88	1.65	2	0.00	0.00	4.50	4.95
Organizational	Anxiety	158	2.74	1.01	6.63	2.05	83	2.76	1.01	6.23	2.18	13	3.23	0.60	4.38	2.90
	Dejection	158	1.76	1.31	6.63	2.05	83	1.95	1.29	6.23	2.18	13	2.69	1.18	4.38	2.90
	Excitement	158	0.59	1.04	6.63	2.05	83	0.93	1.18	6.23	2.18	13	0.23	0.44	4.38	2.90
	Anger	158	1.84	1.27	6.63	2.05	83	2.01	1.28	6.23	2.18	13	3.08	1.33	4.38	2.90
	Happiness	158	0.49	0.92	6.63	2.05	83	0.75	0.97	6.23	2.18	13	0.00	0.00	4.38	2.90

F, frequency; M, mean score; SD, standard deviation.

parents reported moderate levels of anxiety, low levels of dejection and anger, and very low levels of excitement and happiness (see **Table 5**). Parents who used internal regulation strategies (*n* = 229) also experienced moderate levels of anxiety, low levels of anger and dejection, and very low levels of excitement and happiness. In contrast, parents who used goal withdrawal strategies (*n* = 43) reported high levels of anxiety, moderate levels of anger and dejection, and very low levels of excitement and happiness (see **Table 5**).

Table 5 also illustrates the descriptive relationships between competition, developmental, and organizational stressors, emotions, coping strategies, and coping effectiveness. For example, mastery (*n* = 164), internal regulation (*n* = 113) and goal withdrawal (*n* = 28) coping strategies were used when parents experienced moderate levels of anxiety and anger, moderate to low levels of dejection, and very low levels of excitement and happiness in response to competition stressors. Of these strategies, internal regulation was considered to be most effective. Mastery (*n* = 52) and internal regulation (*n* = 33) coping strategies were used when parents experienced moderate levels of anxiety; low levels of dejection and anger; low to very low levels of excitement, and very low levels of happiness when facing developmental stressors. Goal withdrawal strategies (*n* = 2) were used when parents experienced high level of anxiety and dejection and moderate levels of anger. Mastery coping strategies (*n* = 158) were used when parents reported moderate levels of anxiety, low levels of dejection and anger, and very low levels of excitement and happiness when facing organizational stressors. Internal regulation strategies (*n* = 83) were used when parents reported moderate levels of anxiety and anger, low levels of dejection, and very low levels of excitement and happiness. Finally, goal withdrawal strategies (*n* = 13) were used when parents experienced high anxiety and anger, moderate levels of dejection, and very low levels of excitement in relation to organizational stressors. Mastery coping strategies were the most effective way of coping with both organizational and developmental stressors.

DISCUSSION

The aim of this study was to build on the existing sport parent research through a thorough investigation of psychological stress among parents of competitive British tennis players. As such, the current study extends existing research on the stressors that parents experience (Harwood and Knight, 2009a,b; Burgess et al., 2016), the ways that stressors are appraised, the range of emotions experienced (Omli and LaVoi, 2012), and the coping strategies employed (Burgess et al., 2016). The discussion that follows outlines the contributions that the findings make to scientific understanding within each of these areas and integrates the qualitative and quantitative elements of this study to provide novel insights into psychological stress among sport parents. We also offer a number of recommendations for applied practitioners, coaches, and national governing bodies.

Focusing initially on the stressors that tennis parents experience, this study provides the largest investigation ($n = 135$) to date of the situations that British tennis parents appraise as taxing or exceeding their resources. In line with previous studies (i.e., Harwood and Knight, 2009a,b; Harwood et al., 2010; Burgess et al., 2016), parents in the current study reported experiencing a range of competition, organizational, and developmental stressors. The consistency of these findings across various youth sport contexts (i.e., tennis, gymnastics, and soccer) is concerning because research within developmental psychology has shown that parents who experience a greater numbers of stressors consistently display more negative parenting styles and behaviors (e.g., higher levels of disciplinary punishment and harsher interactions with their children; see Knight et al., 2009). These studies also suggest that limited progress has been made within the past decade to reduce the number of stressors that British tennis parents experience in youth sport (see Harwood and Knight, 2009a,b). Although recent headway has been made by the Lawn Tennis Association to address competition-related stressors (see LTA Tennis, 2017), there still remains a need for policy level changes to reduce some of the organizational and developmental stressors (i.e., finances, time, tournament structure, ratings system, and education-related concerns) that are difficult to address through educational approaches alone (Thrower et al., 2016).

Beyond identifying the stressors that parents experience in British tennis, the current study was the first to explore parents' primary appraisals of self-disclosed stressors. The high frequency of negative appraisals (i.e., harm/loss or threat) in the current study is concerning given the implications that these types of appraisal have for parents' experiences within youth sport contexts. Research with athletes has found positive associations between threat appraisals and mastery avoidance, performance approach, and performance avoidance goals as well as challenge appraisals and mastery goals (e.g., Adie et al., 2010; Nicholls et al., 2014). In addition, Ntoumanis et al. (2009) reported that individuals are more likely to appraise demands as a challenge as opposed to a threat or harm/loss when they feel autonomous and competent during a stressful encounter. Taking these points into consideration, it is possible that working with parents to alter their beliefs about what constitutes success in youth sport, develop more task oriented achievement goals for their child, and strengthen perceptions of parenting competence may increase the chance of parents making more adaptive primary appraisals (i.e., challenge or benefit; see Thrower et al., 2017). From a theoretical perspective, such approaches are likely to be particularly effective when combined with efforts to optimize parents' secondary appraisals (Lazarus and Folkman, 1984; Lazarus, 1999) by, for example, helping parents to remain aware of the variety of coping options that they can use during stressful situations.

The present study was also the first to examine the range of emotions (i.e., pleasant and unpleasant) that arise during sport parents' stress transactions. Findings add to existing sport parent research (i.e., Omli and LaVoi, 2012) by highlighting that parents experienced greater anger in relation to competition but not organizational or developmental stressors. Consistent with Lazarus (1999) suggestions, the findings presented here also illustrate that harm appraisal generated greater negative emotions (i.e., dejection and anger, but not anxiety) compared to challenge appraisal, whilst challenge appraisal generated greater positive emotions (i.e., excitement and happiness) compared to both harm and threat appraisal. These findings are consistent with the results of similar studies conducted with athletes (see Nicholls et al., 2011, 2012) and illustrate how primary appraisals play a crucial role in shaping the subsequent emotional responses and experiences of sport parents. Furthermore, developmental stressors (in comparison to organizational and competitive stressors) in the current study were most frequently appraised as a threat (i.e., future damage to goal commitment, values, or beliefs) and associated with the high levels of anxiety. Such findings suggest that the temporal nature of stressors (i.e., past vs. future) may influence not only the appraisal (i.e., damage already occurred vs. future damage) but also the specific type of emotion (e.g., anxiety, anger, dejection, excitement, and happiness) sport parents experience.

Building on the aforementioned points, our findings suggest that the emotions parents experience influence the coping strategies they select. For instance, parents in the current study tended to use internal regulation or mastery coping strategies when they experienced moderate to low levels of unpleasant emotions (i.e., anxiety, anger, and dejection) and goal withdrawal strategies when they experienced moderate to high levels of unpleasant emotions (i.e., anxiety, anger, and dejection). From a practical perspective, these findings suggest that reducing levels of unpleasant emotions (e.g., by encouraging gain, rather than loss, appraisals) may enable parents to select more adaptive coping strategies (i.e., mastery or internal regulation). Although the mechanisms influencing this proposed relationship are not fully understood, it may be that experiencing less unpleasant emotions (particularly anxiety) reduces cognitive interference and enables parents to select a more effective coping strategy (McCarthy et al., 2013).

Turning attention toward coping strategies, novel insights have been reached in this study regarding the most effective coping strategies parents used in response to competition, organizational, and developmental stressors. For example, our findings suggest that organizational stressors (but not competition or developmental stressors) were managed more effectively by mastery and internal regulation strategies when compared to goal withdrawal strategies. Further, when appraised as a challenge, competition stressors were managed more effectively compared to organizational, but not developmental, stressors. These findings are consistent with Lazarus and Folkman's (1984) goodness-of-fit hypothesis of coping effectiveness, which proposes that coping strategies are most effective when matched to the level of controllability in any given situation. In line with transactional conceptualizations of stress (Lazarus and Folkman, 1984; Lazarus, 1999), coping strategies are not likely to be inherently effective or ineffective. Instead, it seems that coping effectiveness depends on the deployment of the most appropriate strategies at the right time (Knight and Holt, 2014). Some coping strategies (e.g., avoiding other parents) used by parents in the current study may, however, be viewed as maladaptive within the culture of British junior tennis, or may result in behaviors that are considered undesirable by young athletes (e.g., temporarily walking away; Knight et al., 2010). These suggestions are important for practitioners and should be taken into account when designing coping interventions for sport parents.

The current study and its applied implications should be considered in light of several limitations and insights that may enrich further research. First, only those stressors that were pertinent for parents at the time of data collection were explored. While this was a methodologically reasonable decision given the scope of this study, it does overlook the dynamic and recursive nature of stressors and stress more broadly. Future longitudinal research is needed to monitor stressors over time and build a more accurate and detailed picture of parents' experiences. Use of diaries, think aloud protocols, or video assisted interviewing may assist in this respect. It would also be interesting to consider how parents' level of experience or previous coping attempts influence their appraisals, emotions, and coping strategies. Second, the current study focused on primary appraising but secondary appraising is also an important part of stress transactions and one that can influence emotions and other outcomes (e.g., well-being, Lazarus, 1999, 2000). It was the complexity of analyses that were required to examine the components of stress transactions that meant secondary appraising was not investigated in the current work. Researchers are urged to consider methodologies that make possible more comprehensive explorations of appraising in sport. Third, although the parents in the current study identified multiple coping strategies, we did not explore the effectiveness of different combinations of coping strategies but, instead, focused on the effectiveness of each individual strategy. Future studies that examine the way in which multiple strategies are used together would progress this body of research and enable researchers to develop more effective coping interventions. Fourth, whilst sufficiently powered statistically, the investigation achieved a 9% response rate from the targeted parent population (n = 135). Challenges to engage parents with busy lifestyles were expected but researchers should carefully consider how to attract even more representative samples of a sport's parent community in future work. Finally, although nomothetic methods have afforded greater understanding of tennis parents' stress as a collective, more specific and idiosyncratic insights remain constrained. For example, exploring stress transactions among parents at different ages/stages of their child's sporting journey (see Harwood and Knight, 2009a) would build on the contribution of the current study.

To conclude, this study used a mixed method design to provide unique insights to various components of psychological stress among parents of British tennis players. Furthermore, exploring the relationships and interactions between each stage of stress transactions provided a number of novel insights into the most effective ways of mediating the relationships between appraisal and emotions and of managing the emotions arising from a stressor (Lazarus, 1999). Such insights not only add to the sport parent literature but also provide crucial recommendations for practitioners, coaches, and national governing bodies who work with sport parents.

ETHICS STATEMENT

This study was carried out in accordance with the recommendations of the Loughborough University ethics committee with informed consent from all subjects. All subjects gave informed consent in accordance with the Declaration of Helsinki. The protocol was approved by the Loughborough University Ethics committee.

AUTHOR CONTRIBUTIONS

CH was responsible for the conceptualization and management of research program. FD contributed to the study design and planning. LF was responsible for data collection. ST and MS analyzed the data. CH, ST, FD, and MS were responsible for manuscript preparation.

REFERENCES

Adie, J. W., Duda, J. L., and Ntoumanis, N. (2010). Achievement goals, competition appraisals, and the well-and ill-being of elite youth soccer players over two competitive seasons. *J. Sport Exercise Psychol.* 32, 555–579. doi: 10.1123/jsep.32.4.555

Burgess, N. S., Knight, C. J., and Mellalieu, S. D. (2016). Parental stress and coping in elite youth gymnastics: an interpretative phenomenological analysis. *Qual. Res. Sport Exerc. Health* 8, 237–256. doi: 10.1080/2159676X.2015.1134633

Clark-Carter, D. (2010). *Quantitative Psychological Research: The Complete Student's Companion*, 3rd Edn. London: Psychology Press.

Connor-Smith, J. K., Compas, B. E., Wadsworth, M. E., Thomsen, A. H., and Saltzman, H. (2000). Responses to stress in adolescence: measurement of coping and involuntary stress responses. *J. Consult. Clin. Psychol.* 68, 976–992. doi: 10.1037/0022-006X.68.6.976

Denzin, N. K., and Lincoln, Y. S. (2011). *The SAGE Handbook of Qualitative Research.* Thousand Oaks, CA: Sage.

Didymus, F. F. (2017). Olympic and international level sports coaches' experiences of stressors, appraisals, and coping. *Qual. Res. Sport Exerc. Health* 9, 214–232. doi: 10.1080/2159676X.2016.1261364

Didymus, F. F., and Fletcher, D. (2012). Getting to the heart of the matter: a diary study of swimmers' appraisals of organisational stressors. *J. Sports Sci.* 30, 1375–1385. doi: 10.1080/02640414.2012.709263

Doron, J., and Martinent, G. (2017). Appraisal, coping, emotion, and performance during elite fencing matches: a random coefficient regression model approach. *Scand. J. Med. Sci. Sports* 27, 1015–1025. doi: 10.1111/sms.12711

Dorsch, T. E., Smith, A. L., and McDonough, M. H. (2009). Parents' perceptions of child-to-parent socialization in organized youth sport. *J. Sport Exerc. Psychol.* 31, 444–468. doi: 10.1123/jsep.31.4.444

Gaudreau, P., and Blondin, J. P. (2004). Different athletes cope differently during a sport competition: a cluster analysis of coping. *Pers. Individ. Dif.* 36, 1865–1877. doi: 10.1016/j.paid.2003.08.017

Goldstein, J. D., and Iso-Ahola, S. E. (2008). Determinants of parents' sideline-rage emotions and behaviors at youth soccer games. *J. Appl. Soc. Psychol.* 38, 1442–1462. doi: 10.1111/j.1559-1816.2008.00355.x

Gomes, A. R., Faria, S., and Vilela, C. (2017). Anxiety and burnout in young athletes: the mediating role of cognitive appraisal. *Scand. J. Med. Sci. Sports* 27, 2116–2126. doi: 10.1111/sms.12841

Hanton, S., Wagstaff, C. R., and Fletcher, D. (2012). Cognitive appraisals of stressors encountered in sport organizations. *Int. J. Sport Exerc. Psychol.* 10, 276–289. doi: 10.1080/1612197X.2012.682376

Harwood, C. G., and Knight, C. J. (2009b). Understanding parental stressors: an investigation of British tennis-parents. *J. Sports Sci.* 27, 339–351. doi: 10.1080/02640410802603871

Harwood, C. G., Drew, A., and Knight, C. J. (2010). Parental stressors in professional youth football academies: a qualitative investigation of specializing stage parents. *Qual. Res. Sport Exerc.* 2, 39–55. doi: 10.1080/19398440903510152

Harwood, C. G., and Knight, C. J. (2009a). Stress in youth sport: a developmental investigation of tennis parents. *Psychol. Sport Exerc.* 10, 447–456. doi: 10.1016/j.psychsport.2009.01.005

Jones, M. V., Lane, A. M., Bray, S. R., Uphill, M., and Catlin, J. (2005). Development and validation of the sport emotion questionnaire. *J. Sport Exerc. Psychol.* 27, 407–431. doi: 10.1123/jsep.27.4.407/

Knight, C. J., Boden, C. M., and Holt, N. L. (2010). Junior tennis players' preferences for parental behaviors at tournaments. *J. Appl. Sport Psychol.* 22, 377–391. doi: 10.1080/10413200.2010.495324

Knight, C. J., and Holt, N. L. (2014). Parenting in youth tennis: understanding and enhancing children's experiences. *Psychol. Sport Exerc.* 15, 155–164. doi: 10.1016/j.psychsport.2013.10.010

Knight, C. J., Holt, N. L., and Tamminen, K. A. (2009). "Stress and coping among youth sport parents," in *Handbook of sports psychology*, ed. C. H. Chang (Hauppauge, NY: Nova Science), 347–359.

Krane, V., and Baird, S. M. (2005). Using ethnography in applied sport psychology. *J. Appl. Sport Psychol.* 17, 87–107. doi: 10.1080/10413200590932371

Lazarus, R. S. (1999). *Stress and Emotion: A New Synthesis.* New York, NY: Springer.

Lazarus, R. S. (2000). How emotions influence performance in competitive sports. *Sport Psychol.* 14, 229–252. doi: 10.1123/tsp.14.3.229

Lazarus, R. S., and Folkman, S. (1984). *Stress, Appraisal, and Coping.* New York, NY: Springer.

Levy, A., Nicholls, A., Marchant, D., and Polman, R. (2009). Organisational stressors, coping, and coping effectiveness: a longitudinal study with an elite coach. *Int. J. Sports Sci. Coach.* 4, 31–45. doi: 10.1260/1747-9541.4.1.31

LTA Tennis (2017). *Parents in Tennis: How to Support Your Child.* Available at: https://www.lta.org.uk/play-compete/getting-started/information-for-parents/ (accessed February 27, 2019).

McCarthy, P. J., Allen, M. S., and Jones, M. V. (2013). Emotions, cognitive interference, and concentration disruption in youth sport. *J. Sports Sci.* 31, 505–515. doi: 10.1080/02640414.2012.738303

Moore, L. J., Vine, S. J., Wilson, M. R., and Freeman, P. (2012). The effect of challenge and threat states on performance: an examination of potential mechanisms. *Psychophysiology* 49, 1417–1425. doi: 10.1111/j.1469-8986.2012.01449.x

Morgan, D. L. (2013). *Integrating Qualitative And Quantitative Methods: A Pragmatic Approach.* Thousand Oaks.CA: Sage.

Morse, J. M. (2003). "Principles of mixed methods and multimethod research design," in *Handbook of Mixed Methods In Social And Behavioural Research*, eds A. Tashakkori and C. Teddlie (Thousand Oaks, CA: Sage), 189–208.

Nicholls, A. R. (2016). "Adaptation, stress, and coping in sport," in *Routledge International Handbook of Sport Psychology*, eds R. J. Schinke, K. R. McGannon, and B. Smith (Abingdon: Routledge), 119–127.

Nicholls, A. R., Holt, N. L., Polman, R. C., and James, D. W. G. (2005). Stress and coping among international adolescent golfers. *J. Appl. Sport Psychol.* 17, 333–340. doi: 10.1080/10413200500313644

Nicholls, A. R., Levy, A. R., Jones, L., Rengamani, M., and Polman, R. C. J. (2011). An exploration of the two factor schematization of relation meaning and emotions among professional rugby union players. *Int. J. Sport Exerc. Psychol.* 1, 78–91. doi: 10.1080/1612197X.2011.563128

Nicholls, A. R., Perry, J. L., and Calmeiro, L. (2014). Precompetitive achievement goals, stress appraisals, emotions, and coping among athletes. *J. Sport Exerc. Psychol.* 36, 433–445. doi: 10.1123/jsep.2013-2266

Nicholls, A. R., Polman, R., Levy, A. R., Taylor, J., and Cobley, S. (2007). Stressors, coping, and coping effectiveness: gender, type of sport, and skill differences. *J. Sports Sci.* 25, 1521–1530. doi: 10.1080/02640410701230479

Nicholls, A. R., and Polman, R. C. (2007). Coping in sport: a systematic review. *J. Sports Sci.* 25, 11–31. doi: 10.1080/02640410600630654

Nicholls, A. R., Polman, R. C., and Levy, A. R. (2012). A path analysis of stress appraisals, emotions, coping, and performance satisfaction among athletes. *Psychol. Sport Exerc.* 13, 263–270. doi: 10.1016/j.psychsport.2011.12.003

Nicholls, A. R., Taylor, N. J., Carroll, S., and Perry, J. L. (2016). The development of a new sport-specific classification of coping and a meta-analysis of the relationship between different coping strategies and moderators on sporting outcomes. *Front. Psychol.* 7:1674. doi: 10.3389/fpsyg.2016.01674

Ntoumanis, N., Edmunds, J., and Duda, J. L. (2009). Understanding the coping process from a self-determination theory perspective. *Br. J. Health Psychol.* 14, 249–260. doi: 10.1348/135910708X349352

Omli, J., and LaVoi, N. M. (2012). Emotional experiences of youth sport parents I: anger. *J. Appl. Sport Psychol.* 24, 10–25. doi: 10.1080/10413200.2011.578102

Skinner, E. A., Edge, K., Altman, J., and Sherwood, H. (2003). Searching for the structure of coping: a review and critique of category systems for classifying ways of coping. *Psychol. Bull.* 129, 216–269. doi: 10.1037/0033-2909.129.2.216

Sparkes, A. C., and Smith, B. (2014). *Qualitative Research Methods In Sport, Exercise And Health: From Process To Product.* London: Routledge.

Thrower, S. N., Harwood, C. G., and Spray, C. M. (2016). Educating and supporting tennis parents: a grounded theory of parents' needs during childhood and early adolescence. *Sport Exerc. Perform. Psychol.* 5, 107–124. doi: 10.1037/spy0000054

Thrower, S. N., Harwood, C. G., and Spray, C. M. (2017). Educating and supporting tennis parents: an action research study. *Qual. Res. Sport Exerc. Health* 9, 600–618. doi: 10.1080/2159676X.2017.1341947

Webster-Stratton, C. (1990). Stress: a potential disruptor of parent perceptions and family interactions. *J. Clin. Child Psychology* 19, 302–312. doi: 10.1207/s15374424jccp1904_2

Weed, M. (2009). Research quality considerations for grounded theory research in sport & exercise psychology. *Psychol. Sport Exerc.* 10, 502–510. doi: 10.1016/j.psychsport.2009.02.007

Wiersma, L. D., and Fifer, A. M. (2008). "The schedule has been tough but we think it's worth it": the joys, challenges, and recommendations of youth sport parents. *J. Leis. Res.* 40, 505–553. doi: 10.1080/00222216.2008.11950150

4

Investigating the Protective Role of Mastery Imagery Ability in Buffering Debilitative Stress Responses

Mary Louise Quinton**, Jet Veldhuijzen van Zanten, Gavin P. Trotman, Jennifer Cumming and Sarah Elizabeth Williams

University of Birmingham, Birmingham, United Kingdom

****Correspondence:***
Mary Louise Quinton
m.quinton@bham.ac.uk

Mastery imagery has been shown to be associated with more positive cognitive and emotional responses to stress, but research is yet to investigate the influence of mastery imagery ability on imagery's effectiveness in regulating responses to acute stress, such as competition. Furthermore, little research has examined imagery's effectiveness in response to actual competition. This study examined (a) whether mastery imagery ability was associated with stress response changes to a competitive stress task, a car racing computer game, following an imagery intervention, and (b) the effects of different guided imagery content on pre-task cognitive and emotional responses. In Session 1, 78 participants (*M* age = 20.03 years, *SD* = 1.28) completed ratings of pre-task anxiety intensity and direction, confidence, and perceived control. Imagery ability was also assessed before completing the task. In Session 2, participants were randomly allocated to an imagery condition (positive mastery, negative mastery, relaxation) or control group (no imagery) before completing the task and outcome measures again. For the negative mastery group, greater positive mastery imagery ability was associated with greater perceived control and perceiving anxiety as more facilitative. Furthermore, mastery imagery ability moderated the relationship between anxiety intensity and direction. Altogether, results suggest that positive mastery imagery ability may act as a potential buffer against the effects of negative images.

Keywords: anxiety, confidence, sport imagery ability, coping, control

INTRODUCTION

Acute psychological stress is a common occurrence in everyday life, eliciting a range of psychological (e.g., increases in anxiety) and cardiovascular (e.g., increases in heart rate) responses (Turner, 1994; Skinner and Brewer, 2004; Moore et al., 2012). Excessive stress can be detrimental toward physical and psychological health (Schneiderman et al., 2005); therefore, individuals self-regulate stress responses by modifying the symptoms of stress (e.g., relaxing) or changing the perception of these symptoms (e.g., reappraisal; Jamieson et al., 2013). Stress can be appraised as facilitative or debilitative (Crum et al., 2013). Facilitative stress responses are characterized by better task performance, greater confidence, helpful anxiety perceptions, and/or a more favorable cardiovascular profile, whereas debilitative responses can consist of poorer performance, lower confidence, hurtful anxiety perceptions, and/or a less favorable cardiovascular profile

(Williams et al., 2010; Turner et al., 2014; Trotman et al., 2018b). Consequently, it is important to establish strategies to elicit more facilitative responses to stress.

Competition is a type of stress that individuals do not always try to avoid as readily as other types of stress. Thus, when developing strategies to elicit more facilitative responses to stress, considering situational factors such as the competition context may help researchers understand the stress responses experienced (Jones, 1995). For example, 30% of the population in England engage in some type of sport at least once a week (Sport England, 2016), a proportion of which would be classified as competition. Thus, in the sport setting, competition is typically not feared by individuals and is often enjoyed and actively engaged in. Unlike the clinical literature, responses to stress in the form of a competition can be more beneficial than experiencing no response (Skinner and Brewer, 2004). Indeed, although anxiety is one of the most common and debilitating responses to stress (NHS Digital, 2018), athletes often report higher anxiety levels and feeling "psyched up" to be helpful for performance in an upcoming competition (Hanton et al., 2008) and therefore do not want to reduce these levels.

In support of not simply reducing anxiety levels, Jones (1995) proposed that strategies to elicit more facilitative competitive anxiety responses should target both the intensity experienced (i.e., severity of anxiety symptoms) and the direction (i.e., facilitative or debilitative toward performance). Importantly, anxiety direction perceptions can be a stronger predictor of performance success than anxiety intensity (Chamberlain and Hale, 2007). This research suggests that interventions that regulate anxiety responses to stress in the form of competitions should focus more on the interpretation of the anxiety rather than reducing its intensity.

More positive perceptions of anxiety symptoms are thought to be influenced by perceptions of control (i.e., greater control leads to more facilitative anxiety; Jones, 1995). Furthermore, Jones et al. (2009) posit that in a motivated performance situation like competition, higher confidence and greater perceived control are associated with positively appraising stress as a challenge, which is a state characterized by more facilitative anxiety perceptions and better performance (Williams et al., 2010; Moore et al., 2012). By contrast, a threat appraisal, resulting from lower perceived control and less confidence, is associated with more debilitative anxiety perceptions and worse performance (Williams et al., 2010; Moore et al., 2012; Turner et al., 2014). Therefore, strategies for effectively regulating anxiety perceptions to competition could be focused on raising confidence and perceived control.

Imagery is a technique that can alter the intensity and perceptions of psychophysiological stress with athletes (Cumming et al., 2007; Williams et al., 2010, 2017). Given that imagery is more effective when people can image sufficiently (Williams et al., 2013), imagery ability has been identified as a key factor for effectively regulating stress (Williams et al., 2017). Imagery ability is "an individual's capability to form vivid, controllable images and retain them for sufficient time to effect the desired imagery rehearsal" (Morris, 1997, p. 37). Mastery imagery ability—the ease with which individuals can image mastering challenging or difficult situations—has been linked to more adaptive stress appraisals and more facilitative anxiety perceptions via greater self-confidence levels (Williams and Cumming, 2012b, 2015). Thus, those with higher mastery imagery ability, who are better at regulating their anxiety through self-confidence, may be less affected by negative imagery. Additionally, recent research has found that negative mastery imagery ability—the ability to image low feelings of confidence and a lack of control—predicted anxiety intensity and negative appraisals of stress, and both positive and negative mastery imagery ability were mediators between confidence and individuals' dispositional stress responses (Quinton et al., 2018). Altogether, this research highlights the important role played by mastery imagery ability in regulating stress. What is still unclear, however, is whether positive mastery imagery ability is associated with stress response changes to competition. Clarifying this question would advance theoretical thinking, provide clear guidelines to those with clients participating regularly in competition (e.g., sport), and encourage developing mastery imagery ability through techniques such as layered stimulus response training (LSRT; Cumming et al., 2016) for optimal performance.

Although the impact of mastery imagery ability on responses to competition stress is not yet known, hypotheses can be developed based on research demonstrating the effect of different imagery content on responses to various types of stress. Williams et al. (2010, 2017) and Williams and Cumming (2012a) studies found that imaging low feelings of confidence and control (termed threat imagery) led to the situation being perceived as more stressful, lower confidence, and more debilitative anxiety interpretations compared to imagery of feeling confident and in control of the stress (i.e., mastery type imagery) and neutral imagery. However, other findings from these studies were mixed, as one study found that a neutral script was most helpful toward regulating stress (Williams et al., 2017), whereas others found that the mastery type script was most effective (Williams et al., 2010; Williams and Cumming, 2012a). This difference is likely due to using different tasks (i.e., public speaking, dart throwing, and a competitive experience), and using an actual stress task (i.e., public speaking, dart throwing; Williams and Cumming, 2012a; Williams et al., 2017) compared to hypothetical stress (i.e., script based on previous competitive experience; Williams et al., 2010). However, research is yet to investigate imagery's effectiveness in altering responses to actual competition, which would be important to address to recommend particular imagery types for athletes regularly participating in competition. Therefore, it would be interesting to compare a mastery script, designed to enhance confidence and control, to a relaxation script (Cumming et al., 2007) to clarify which is most effective in regulating anxiety responses to actual competition. Clarifying this question could inform evidence-based imagery interventions and help practitioners to recommend particular types of imagery for athletes who find it difficult to cope with competition stress. As the revised applied model of deliberate imagery use (RAMDIU; Cumming and Williams, 2013) proposes that imagery content for a particular function can be influenced by the situation, it is likely that the findings of this study may be in line with Williams et al. (2010) due to a similar situation (competition), and therefore it could also be feasible that the mastery script would be more effective than a relaxation script.

Aims and Hypotheses

The primary aim was to determine whether mastery imagery ability is associated with, and moderates, stress response changes following an imagery intervention (positive mastery, negative mastery, or relaxation script). Affect imagery ability was included as a comparison imagery ability due to emotional content that is commonly associated with a stress response, such as nervousness and excitement (Williams and Cumming, 2011). Assuming the competition elicited a stress response, it was hypothesized that higher levels of positive mastery imagery ability would (a) be associated with more favorable stress responses for the positive mastery and relaxation intervention groups, and (b) be less detrimental for the negative mastery intervention group compared to those with lower positive mastery imagery ability in the same group. It was also hypothesized that (c) mastery imagery ability would positively moderate the relationship between anxiety intensity and direction at both sessions (i.e., greater mastery imagery ability would help participants perceive increased anxiety as more facilitative).

The secondary aim was to investigate how different types of imagery can alter cognitive and emotional responses to an actual competition task (state anxiety intensity and direction, state confidence, and perceived control), rather than hypothetical or different tasks used previously (Williams et al., 2010, 2017). It was hypothesized that (d) the positive script would elicit the most facilitative stress responses for the competition task and the negative script would elicit the most debilitative responses; (e) anxiety intensity would increase from Session 1 to Session 2 for the positive and negative groups, but decrease for the relaxation group; (f) compared to Session 1, anxiety would be perceived as more facilitative for the positive group and more debilitative for the negative group; and (g) confidence would increase from Session 1 for the positive and relaxation groups but decrease for the negative group.

MATERIALS AND METHODS

Participants

Seventy-eight male undergraduate athletes (*M* age = 20.03 years, *SD* = 1.28) participated in the study with the option of gaining course credit. Only males were recruited due to sex differences in stress responses (Bale and Epperson, 2015). The sample mainly consisted of team (*n* = 48) and individual (*n* = 25) sport athletes, with the majority coming from rugby (*n* = 16), golf (*n* = 16), and football (*n* = 14). Athletes ranged in competitive levels from elite (*n* = 10), regional (*n* = 14), club (*n* = 41), to recreational (*n* = 10). Participants were healthy with no history of epileptic seizures and cardiovascular, immune, metabolic, or kidney disease, and had no current illness or prescribed medication in the last 4 weeks at the time of the study. Participants were instructed to abstain from heavy exercise and alcohol consumption 24 h before testing and from eating and drinking caffeine 2 h before testing. Following ethical approval, participants provided informed written consent after being recruited by experimenters over an 8-week period through social media, emails, and class announcements at the university where the authors are based.

Psychological Measures

Mastery and Affect Imagery Ability

Participants completed the mastery and affect subscales of the Sport Imagery Ability Questionnaire (SIAQ; Williams and Cumming, 2011). Participants imaged three items reflecting positive mastery content (staying positive after a setback, giving 100% effort when things are not going well, and remaining confident in a difficult situation) and three items reflecting affect content (positive emotions felt while doing sport, anticipation and excitement associated with sport, excitement associated with performing) before rating ease of imaging on a seven-point Likert-type scale from 1 (*very hard to image*) to 7 (*very easy to image*). The ratings were averaged to give one mastery and one affect imagery ability score. The internal reliability in this study was just below adequate (Cronbach α mastery and affect = 0.66 and 0.69, respectively). However, validity and reliability evidence has previously been found in support of SIAQ test scores (Williams and Cumming, 2011; Quinton et al., 2018).

Imagery Script Evaluation

Six items evaluated the generated imagery on 7-point or 10-point Likert-type scales (Cumming et al., 2007). Two items asked how easily and vividly participants could image the scripts (1 = *very hard/no image at all*, 7 = *very easy/perfectly clear*). One item asked the extent to which participants were engaged when listening to the script (1 = *none of the time*, 10 = *all of the time*). Two items assessed how imagery was perceived to impact confidence and anxiety intensities (1 = *decreased confidence/anxiety symptoms a lot*, 7 = *increased confidence/anxiety symptoms a lot*). The final item assessed how imagery was perceived to influence anxiety symptom interpretation (1 = *anxiety viewed as being much more hurtful*, 7 = *anxiety viewed as being much more helpful*).

State Anxiety and Self-Confidence

The Immediate Anxiety Measurement Scale (IAMS; Thomas et al., 2002) assessed cognitive and somatic anxiety intensity and direction and self-confidence in relation to the task. Participants were provided with definitions of these constructs to ensure understanding. Participants rated the extent to which they felt cognitively anxious, somatically anxious, and self-confident on a seven-point Likert-type scale from 1 (*not at all*) to 7 (*extremely*) before indicating how they perceived these symptoms from -3 (*very debilitative/negative*) to +3 (*very facilitative/positive*). Validity and reliability evidence has been found in support of IAMS test scores (Thomas et al., 2002).

Perceived Control

A single item assessed perceived control prior to completing the task, asking "how much control do you think you will have over the outcome of the task?" Participants responded on a seven-point Likert-type scale from 1 (*none*) to 7 (*total*).

Task Evaluation

Three items assessed the level of task stressfulness, difficulty, and effort experienced (e.g., Williams et al., 2017). Ratings were made on a seven-point Likert-type scale from 1 (*not at all stressful/not at all difficult/did not try at all*) to 7 (*extremely stressful/extremely difficult/tried throughout the whole task*).

Cardiovascular Measures

Heart rate (beats per minute; bpm) was measured as a manipulation check to ensure the competition task elicited a stress response. Heart rate was recorded continuously using the Vrije Universiteit Ambulatory Monitoring System (VU-AMS5fs, TD-FPP, Amsterdam, Netherlands; De Geus et al., 1995; Willemsen et al., 1996). The VuAMS5fs used seven Ag/AgCl spot electrodes (Invisatrace, ConMed Corporation), three of which recorded electrocardiography (ECG). The ECG was recorded using three electrodes: below the right collar bone 4 cm to the right of the sternum, between the lower two ribs on the lateral right-hand side, and at the apex of the heart on the left lateral margin of the chest. Following automated R-peak detection, the interbeat interval signal was visually inspected and corrected if necessary.

Competition Task

The competition task was the car racing computer game Need for Speed: Underground (Electronic Arts Games). The primary objective was to win a car race in the quickest time possible against three computer-controlled opponents, while avoiding traffic and other obstacles. Game manipulations allowed the computer opponents to match the ability of the participant to ensure there was never a clear win or loss. To enhance task competitiveness, a leaderboard was displayed in the lab and participants were informed that the fastest time (for each session) at the end of the study would be awarded a £10 voucher. Pre-recorded instructions informed participants about the keypad controls, that their race position would be displayed throughout the race, and that they would have one practice lap (Session 1 only) before completing the three-lap race. The experimenters provided participants with verbal encouragement throughout (e.g., Veldhuijzen van Zanten et al., 2002). The conditions for both races were pilot tested and similar in difficulty but included a different car and track than Session 1 to ensure the novelty of the task was maintained. This task has been used as a competition task in previous research and was valid for eliciting a stress response (Trotman et al., 2018b).[1]

Imagery Scripts

The three imagery scripts (positive mastery, negative mastery, and relaxation) described the moments prior to the task, including cognitive and physiological responses. Scripts were based on those previously employed (Cumming et al., 2007; Williams et al., 2010) and included characteristics of positive and negative mastery imagery (Quinton et al., 2018). Scripts included stimulus (e.g., "you look around and notice the experimenters watching you"), response (e.g., "your heart is beating faster than usual"), and meaning (e.g., "...but you feel ready") propositions (Lang, 1979). Scripts were pilot tested but no further changes were made. All three scripts were matched in terms of the amount of content and script length and lasted approximately 3 min. The scripts were audio recorded and played on an mp3 player.

The positive and negative mastery scripts were matched for stimulus and response propositions and described how participants would cope with the task based on theories from the stress literature (Blascovich and Mendes, 2000; Jones et al., 2009). For example, altered meaning propositions were attempted through manipulating perceptions of self-efficacy and control, which influence how stressful situations are appraised (Jones et al., 2009). The relaxation script was developed with the aim of making participants feel comfortable and calm prior to completing the task. The script included details about cognitions, body position, and physiological responses. This script predominantly included response propositions to focus on inducing a state of relaxation.[2]

Procedure

Session 1

On arrival at the lab, eligibility criteria were confirmed and all procedures were explained to the participants. Participants were randomly allocated to an intervention group (1, 2, 3, or 4) from a randomly generated list devised by the experimenters: positive mastery (n = 18), negative mastery (n = 20), relaxation (n = 19), or control (n = 19). Session 1 was the same for all participants regardless of intervention condition.

Participants were connected to the cardiovascular recording equipment and comfortably seated where they remained throughout the session. A 15-min baseline period then ensued where participants watched a nature documentary to establish resting heart rate values. ECG recordings analyzed, in the 9th, 11th, 13th, and 15th min. Following baseline, participants were introduced to the task and completed the IAMS. Participants then completed the task, while heart rate was measured at 30 s and 2 min into the task. Participants completed the task evaluation form immediately after the task, had cardiovascular equipment removed, and were reminded about their second session.

Session 2

Session 2 for the control group was identical to Session 1. The protocol was also similar for the imagery groups except that on arrival at the lab, participants were provided with White and Hardy (1998) definition of imagery. Following baseline, but before participants listened to their allocated imagery script, they received LSRT (Cumming et al., 2016) from an experimenter trained in the technique to ensure they could image as clearly and vividly as possible. Next, participants received instructions for the task before listening to their allocated imagery script. Participants were instructed to image as clearly and vividly as possible in their preferred visual perspective. After listening to the script, participants completed the pre-task questionnaires and the

[1]Please note that this study marginally overlaps with the current study in terms of data (Session 1 only). However, the manuscripts are sufficiently distinct to not warrant concern.

[2]Scripts can be found in **Supplementary File 1**.

task. Finally, participants completed measures of imagery ability, imagery perceptions, and task evaluation before the removal of equipment and being thanked for participation. Each visit lasted between 90 and 120 min.

Data Reduction and Analyses

Data were analyzed using SPSS, including the process macro for moderation (version 24; Hayes, 2017). Data were first screened and cleaned in accordance with recommendations by Tabachnick and Fidell (2013), resulting in one participant (negative mastery group) excluded from the analysis as a result of univariate and multivariate outlier checks. Baseline measurements were averaged to give an overall baseline score for heart rate. Task scores were the average of the 30-s and 2-min values. Where dependent variables were correlated, to reduce the likelihood of a Type 1 error, multivariate analysis of variances (MANOVAs) were chosen over ANOVAs (Williams et al., 2010). Pillai's Trace values were reported for all MANOVAs as this multivariate test is most robust (Olson, 1976). For MANOVAs including repeated measures, Greenhouse Geisser values were reported if Mauchly's test of sphericity was violated. The probability value threshold for all analyses was set at 0.05 and 95% confidence intervals were reported. All significant effects were followed up with Bonferroni *post hoc* pairwise comparisons.

The Benjamini–Hochberg method was used to control for multiple comparisons in the analyses (Benjamini and Hochberg, 1995; McDonald, 2014). This method reduces the likelihood of Type 1 error while avoiding the loss of power associated with other alpha adjustments considered too conservative (e.g., Bonferroni; Shi et al., 2012). For each set of multiple analyses (e.g., correlations, MANOVAs), the p-values were ranked from smallest to largest and compared with Benjamini–Hochberg critical values at a false discovery rate of 0.05 (Benjamini and Hochberg, 1995; McDonald, 2014). This method has been used previously in laboratory-based stress-evoking research (Trotman et al., 2018a).

To verify that a stress response was elicited, two paired-samples t-tests examined differences in heart rate from baseline to the competition task at both sessions. To examine the extent to which mastery and affect imagery ability impacted the effects of the scripts, partial correlations (controlling for Session 1 scores) were conducted for each imagery group to investigate the relationships between mastery and affect imagery ability with Session 2 IAMS and perceived control scores. To investigate mastery imagery ability as a moderator between anxiety intensity and direction, analyses were separately conducted for cognitive and somatic anxiety using the process macro for SPSS (Hayes, 2017). To evaluate how well participants were able to image the scripts and the perceived effect on certain outcomes, a one-way ANOVA analyzed imagery script engagement, and two one-way MANOVAs analyzed ease and vividness of imaging the script, and the effect of the script on confidence, anxiety intensity, and anxiety perception.

To investigate if the different scripts influenced the task stress responses, two separate 2 Time (Session 1, Session 2) × 4 Group (positive mastery, negative mastery, relaxation, control) MANOVAs with repeated measures on the first factor were conducted to analyze differences in IAMS constructs (cognitive and somatic anxiety intensity and direction and confidence) and task stressfulness, difficulty, and effort. A 2 Time (Session 1, Session 2) × 4 Group (positive mastery, negative mastery, relaxation, control) repeated-measures ANOVA was also conducted to investigate if the scripts influenced perceived control prior to the task.

RESULTS

Stress Response

Two paired-samples t-tests revealed the competition task elicited significant heart rate responses from baseline at Session 1, $t(68) = -11.30$, $p < 0.001$, and Session 2, $t(66) = -8.05$, $p < 0.001$. Significant results remained following the Benjamini–Hochberg correction. Heart rate was significantly higher during the competition task at Session 1 ($M = 86.05$, $SD = 14.82$) and Session 2 ($M = 83.13$, $SD = 17.61$) in comparison to the respective baselines (Session 1: $M = 70.12$, $SD = 9.48$; Session 2: $M = 70.16$, $SD = 9.34$). These data were further supported by self-report task stressfulness ratings reported below.

Imagery

Positive Mastery Imagery Ability

Correlations

All correlations are shown in **Table 1**. There was a significant relationship between positive mastery imagery ability and confidence for the positive mastery group ($p = 0.043$). However, following the Benjamini–Hochberg correction, this correlation was no longer significant. For the negative mastery group, positive mastery imagery

TABLE 1 | Mastery and affect imagery ability correlations by imagery group for Session 2 variables, controlling for Session 1 scores.

	Positive mastery	Negative mastery	Relaxation
Variable		**Mastery IA**	
Cognitive intensity	−0.488	0.177	−0.189
Cognitive direction	0.269	0.723**	−0.400
Somatic intensity	−0.410	0.078	−0.029
Somatic direction	0.455	0.653*	−0.533
Confidence intensity	0.592†	0.398	−0.151
Perceived control	0.010	0.730**	−0.351
		Affect IA	
Cognitive intensity	−0.001	0.085	−0.307
Cognitive direction	−0.246	−0.079	0.134
Somatic intensity	−0.102	0.175	−0.326
Somatic direction	−0.334	0.176	−0.117
Confidence intensity	−0.106	0.386	0.262
Perceived control	0.217	0.160	0.096

*IA represents imagery ability. *p < 0.05. **p < 0.01. †No longer significant after Benjamini–Hochberg correction.*

ability was positively correlated with cognitive (p = 0.005) and somatic (p = 0.016) anxiety direction and perceived control (p = 0.005). These results remained significant following the Benjamini–Hochberg correction. Better imagery ability was associated with more facilitative anxiety symptom perceptions in Session 2 for the negative mastery group. There were no significant correlations for the relaxation group.

Moderation

At Session 2, mastery imagery ability moderated the relationship between cognitive [B = 0.24, $t(72)$ = 2.31, p = 0.024, 95% CI (0.03, 0.45)] and somatic [B = 0.26, $t(72)$ = 2.63, p = 0.01, 95% CI (0.06, 0.45)] anxiety intensity and direction. Significant results remained following the Benjamini–Hochberg correction. Graphs were then plotted to illustrate the simple slopes for low (M - 1 SD), average (M), and high (M + 1 SD) mastery imagery ability (**Figure 1**). For the low mastery imagery ability condition, there was a significant and negative relationship between cognitive [B = −0.30, $t(72)$ = −2.22, p = 0.029 (−0.57, −0.03)] and somatic [B = −0.29, $t(72)$ = −2.17, p = 0.033 (−0.56, −0.02)] anxiety intensity and direction. For those with lower mastery imagery ability, increased cognitive and somatic anxiety intensity was regarded as more debilitative. Although no significant relationships were found between anxiety intensity and direction for average and high mastery imagery ability (**Table 2**), there was a pattern for those with greater mastery imagery ability to regard increased anxiety as more facilitative (**Figure 1**).

Despite the non-significant Session 1 moderation results for cognitive [B = 0.12, $t(72)$ = 0.84, p = 0.406, 95% CI (−0.17, 0.42)] and somatic [B = 0.15, $t(72)$ = 1.18, p = 0.243, 95% CI (−0.10, 0.40)] anxiety, the data followed the same pattern whereby greater mastery imagery ability was associated with regarding increased anxiety as more facilitative (**Figure 2**).

Affect imagery ability

All correlations are shown in **Table 1**. There were no significant relationships between affect imagery ability and Session 2 variables.

Imagery script evaluation

Means and standard deviations are reported in **Table 3**. For script ease and vividness, there was a significant main effect for group at the multivariate level, Pillai's Trace = 0.21, $F(2, 53)$ = 3.09, p = 0.019. At the univariate level, significant group differences were for vividness, $F(2, 53)$ = 5.17, p = 0.009, η_p^2 = 0.16, but not ease (p = 0.079). *Post hoc* analyses showed that the positive mastery group imaged their scripts significantly more vividly than the negative mastery group (p = 0.007). For script engagement, there was a significant difference between groups, $F(2, 53)$ = 10.29, p < 0.001,

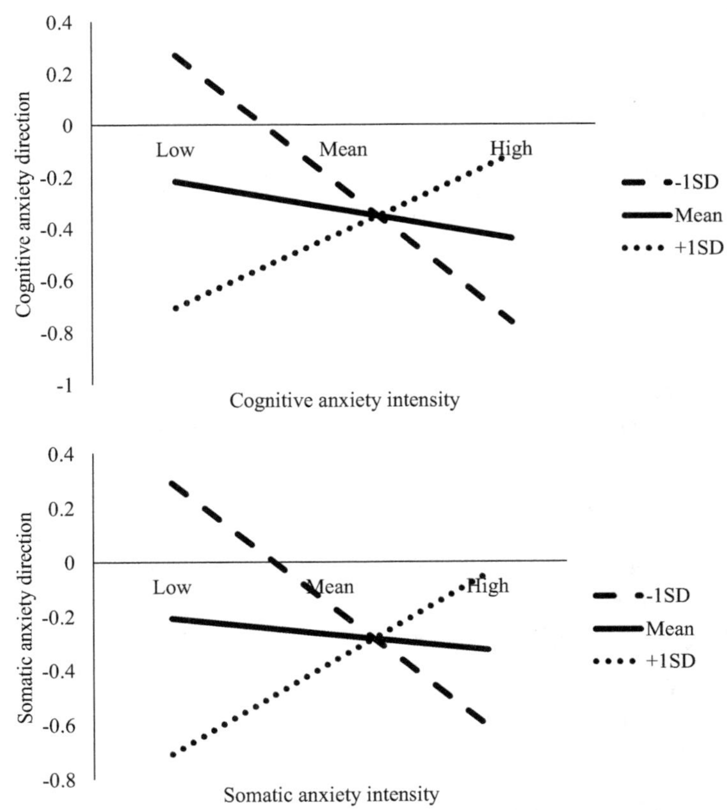

FIGURE 1 | Plots for the interaction effects of cognitive and somatic anxiety intensity and mastery imagery ability on anxiety direction at Session 2.

TABLE 2 | Simple slopes for differing levels of mastery imagery ability moderating between anxiety intensity and direction at Session 2.

	Levels of mastery imagery ability		
	−1 SD	**Mean**	**+1 SD**
Cognitive intensity → Cognitive direction	$B = -0.30$, $t(72) = -2.22$, $p = 0.029$ (−0.57, −0.03)	$B = -0.06$, $t(72) = -0.66$, $p = 0.513$ (−0.26, 0.13)	$B = 0.17$, $t(72) = 1.15$, $p = 0.250$ (−0.12, 0.47)
Somatic intensity → Somatic direction	$B = -0.29$, $t(72) = -2.17$, $p = 0.033$ (−0.56, −0.02)	$B = -0.04$, $t(72) = -0.39$, $p = 0.695$ (−0.23, 0.15)	$B = 0.21$, $t(72) = 1.54$, $p = 0.128$ (−0.06, 0.49)

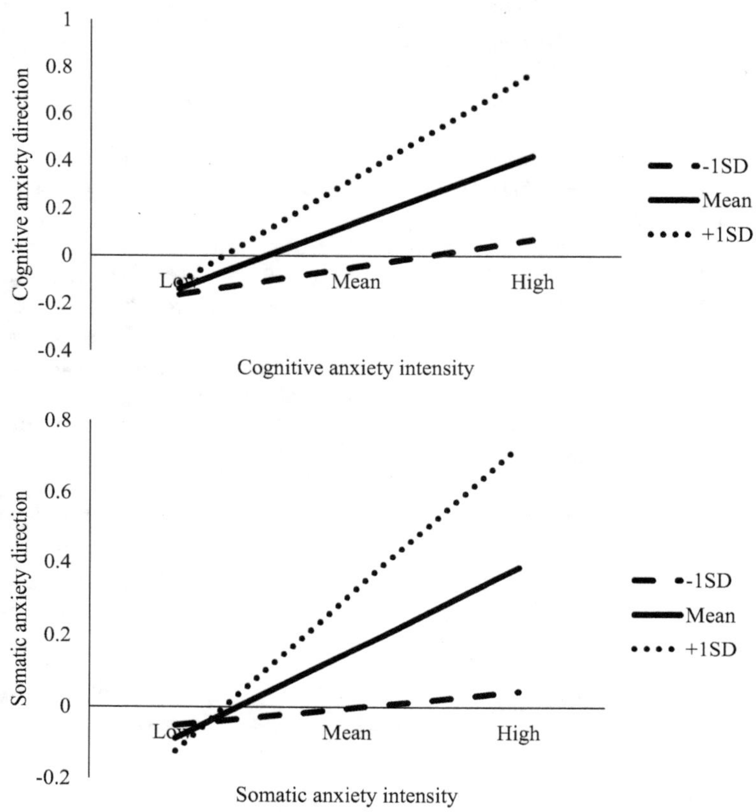

FIGURE 2 | Plots for the interaction effects of cognitive and somatic anxiety intensity and mastery imagery ability on anxiety direction at Session 1.

$\eta_p^2 = 0.28$. The positive mastery and relaxation groups were significantly more engaged than the negative mastery group ($p = 0.011$, $p < 0.001$, respectively). For the scripts' effect on confidence, overall anxiety, and anxiety direction for both tasks, results of the one-way MANOVA revealed that there was a significant main effect for group, Pillai's Trace = 0.52, $F(2, 53) = 6.15$, $p < 0.001$. At the univariate level, there were significant group differences for confidence, $F(2, 53) = 8.62$, $p = 0.001$, $\eta_p^2 = 0.25$, anxiety intensity, $F(2, 53) = 13.27$, $p < 0.001$, $\eta_p^2 = 0.33$, and anxiety direction, $F(2, 53) = 4.77$, $p = 0.012$, $\eta_p^2 = 0.15$. The positive mastery and relaxation scripts elicited a greater effect on confidence than the negative mastery script ($p = 0.009$; $p = 0.001$, respectively). The positive and negative mastery scripts were more anxiogenic than the relaxation script ($p = 0.008$, $p < 0.001$), and the positive mastery script was perceived as more helpful for anxiety symptoms than the negative mastery script ($p = 0.010$). Significant results remained following the Benjamini–Hochberg correction.

State Anxiety and Self-Confidence

All means and standard deviations are reported in **Table 4**. Note that higher direction scores mean that anxiety was perceived as more facilitative. A 2 Time (Session 1, Session 2) × 4 Group (positive mastery, negative mastery, relaxation, control) MANOVA revealed a significant multivariate main effect for time, Pillai's Trace = 0.24, $F(5, 68) = 4.17$, $p = 0.002$, and a significant time by group interaction, Pillai's Trace = 0.42, $F(3, 72) = 2.24$, $p = 0.006$. Significant results remained following the Benjamini–Hochberg correction. Univariate analyses revealed that the main effect was for cognitive intensity, $F(1, 72) = 12.87$, $p = 0.001$, $\eta_p^2 = 0.15$, 95% CI (0.30, 1.05), cognitive direction,

TABLE 3 | Means (standard deviation) for imagery evaluation items according to intervention group.

Imagery item	Imagery script		
	Positive mastery	Negative mastery	Relaxation
Imagery script engagement (1 = none of the time, 10 = all of the time)	7.29(1.31)[a*]	5.95(1.47)	7.85(1.23)[a***]
Ease of imaging script (1 = very hard, 7 = very easy)	5.29(1.11)	4.45(1.32)	5.25(0.85)
Vividness of imaging script (1 = no image at all, 7 = perfectly clear)	5.18(0.95)[a**]	4.16(1.11)	4.60(0.75)
Effect on confidence (1 = decreased confidence a lot, 7 = increased confidence a lot)	5.00(0.61)[a**]	4.05(1.13)	5.20(0.89)[a**]
Effect on anxiety intensity (1 = decreased anxiety symptoms a lot, 7 = increased anxiety symptoms a lot)	3.76(1.15)[b**]	4.37(0.90)[b***]	2.70(1.03)
Effect on anxiety direction (1 = anxiety viewed as being much more hurtful, 7 = anxiety viewed as being much more helpful)	4.88(1.22)[a*]	3.53(1.26)	4.20(1.44)

*[a]Significantly greater than the negative mastery script. [b]Significantly greater than the relaxation script. *p < 0.05. **p < 0.01. ***p < 0.001.*

$F(1, 72) = 9.54, p = 0.003, \eta_p^2 = 0.12$, 95% CI (−0.85, −0.18), and somatic direction, $F(1,72) = 10.38$, $p = 0.002$, $\eta_p^2 = 13$, 95% CI (−0.63, −0.02). Participants had higher cognitive anxiety levels and perceived both cognitive and somatic symptoms as more debilitative at Session 2 compared to Session 1.

For the time by group interaction, univariate analyses revealed that this effect was for somatic intensity, $F(3, 72) = 3.45$, $p = 0.021$, $\eta_p^2 = 0.13$, and approached significance for somatic direction, $F(3, 72) = 2.55$, $p = 0.063$, $\eta_p^2 = 0.10$. Participants in the positive mastery, $p = 0.035$, 95% CI (0.06, 1.50), and negative mastery, $p = 0.006$, 95% CI (0.30, 1.70), groups had higher somatic intensity levels at Session 2 than at Session 1. For somatic direction, there was a trend for the positive mastery and control groups to perceive their symptoms as more debilitative at Session 2 compared to Session 1. At the multivariate level, there was no main effect for group and no time by group interaction for confidence intensity, cognitive intensity, or cognitive direction.

Perceived Control

All means and standard deviations are reported in **Table 4**. A 2 Time (Session 1, Session 2) × 4 Group (positive mastery, negative mastery, relaxation, control) ANOVA revealed no main effects for time, $F(1, 71) = 0.05$, $p = 0.823$, or group, $F(3, 71) = 1.41$, $p = 0.246$, and no time by group interaction, $F(3, 71) = 1.67, p = 0.182$.

Task Evaluation

All means and standard deviations are reported in **Table 4**. A 2 Time (Session 1, Session 2) × 4 Group (positive mastery, negative mastery, relaxation, control) MANOVA revealed a significant multivariate main effect for time, Pillai's Trace = 0.18, $F(3, 69) = 4.63$, $p = 0.004$. Significant results remained following the Benjamini–Hochberg correction. Univariate analyses revealed that this effect was for task stressfulness, $F(1, 71) = 7.57$, $p = 0.008$, $\eta_p^2 = 0.10$, 95% CI (0.12, 0.78), and task effort, $F(1, 71) = 4.80$, $p = 0.032$, $\eta_p^2 = 0.06$, 95% CI (−0.65, −0.03), but not for difficulty. Participants found Session 2 significantly more stressful, but put in significantly less effort compared to Session 1. There was no significant multivariate main effect for group, or time by group interaction.

DISCUSSION

The present study examined whether positive mastery imagery ability was associated with stress response changes to a competition task following an imagery intervention, while also investigating how positive mastery, negative mastery, and relaxation imagery influenced the cognitive and emotional (anxiety, confidence, and perceived control) pre-task responses. The task elicited a stress response in accordance with previous literature (Veldhuijzen van Zanten et al., 2002). Also, when considering manipulation checks, the mean values support that participants appeared motivated and engaged in the task.

A key strength of the present study, in comparison to previous research (e.g., Williams et al., 2010, 2017), is the theoretical underpinning of the RAMDIU (Cumming and Williams, 2013). The use of this framework allowed for the discovery of a new buffering role for mastery imagery ability against the debilitative effects of imagery and therefore a novel theoretical contribution to existing literature. Another strength of this study was the use of actual competition as a stress task. Competition is a unique type of stress that people approach rather than avoid compared to most types of stress studied, which means these results can contribute to the broader implications of what can be learned from a type of stress that people choose to engage in, and the strategies used to regulate such stress (e.g., mastery imagery ability).

Key Findings and Implications: Primary Aim

In support of our hypotheses, results suggest that the imagery's effectiveness was determined by imagery ability. In particular, for the negative mastery group, greater positive mastery imagery

TABLE 4 | Means (standard deviation) by session and intervention group.

Imagery group	Session 1	Session 2
	Cognitive anxiety intensity	
Positive mastery	2.94 (1.16)	3.72 (1.74)
Negative mastery	2.47 (1.22)	3.89 (1.82)
Relaxation	3.15 (1.57)	3.60 (1.93)
Control	3.37 (1.30)	3.42 (1.47)
Total	2.99 (1.34)	3.66 (1.73)[a**]
	Cognitive anxiety direction	
Positive mastery	0.06 (1.59)	0.11 (1.64)
Negative mastery	−0.21 (1.58)	−0.74 (1.41)
Relaxation	0.20 (1.51)	−0.45 (1.64)
Control	0.42 (1.58)	−0.53 (1.07)
Total	0.12 (1.55)	−0.41 (1.46)[a**]
	Somatic anxiety intensity	
Positive mastery	2.67 (1.28)	3.44 (1.76)[a*]
Negative mastery	2.42 (1.12)	3.42 (1.54)[a*]
Relaxation	3.15 (1.46)	2.95 (1.54)
Control	3.37 (1.17)	3.11 (1.45)
Total	2.91 (1.30)	3.22 (1.55)
	Somatic anxiety direction	
Positive mastery	0.67 (1.41)	0.06 (1.55)
Negative mastery	−0.21 (1.51)	−0.68 (1.16)
Relaxation	−0.45 (1.57)	−0.30 (1.46)
Control	0.58 (1.35)	−0.37 (1.07)
Total	0.13 (1.52)	−0.33 (1.32)[a**]
	Self-confidence	
Positive mastery	4.17 (1.65)	4.44 (1.20)
Negative mastery	4.11 (1.20)	3.79 (1.08)
Relaxation	4.55 (.95)	4.35 (1.31)
Control	4.68 (1.38)	3.89 (.99)
Total	4.38 (1.31)	4.12 (1.17)
	Perceived control	
Positive mastery	5.61 (1.29)	5.50 (1.15)
Negative mastery	5.26 (1.15)	4.79 (1.40)
Relaxation	5.45 (1.00)	5.80 (1.11)
Control	5.39 (1.04)	5.50 (1.04)
Total	5.43 (1.11)	5.40 (1.22)
	Task stressfulness	
Positive mastery	3.44 (1.46)	3.44 (1.58)
Negative mastery	3.53 (1.02)	4.32 (1.11)
Relaxation	3.70 (1.26)	4.10 (1.25)
Control	3.17 (1.51)	3.78 (1.31)
Total	3.47 (1.31)	3.92 (1.33)[a**]
	Task difficulty	
Positive mastery	3.72 (1.36)	3.78 (1.59)
Negative mastery	4.32 (1.16)	4.32 (1.06)
Relaxation	4.05 (1.00)	4.25 (1.48)
Control	3.56 (1.42)	3.89 (1.13)
Total	3.92 (1.25)	4.07 (1.33)
	Task effort	
Positive mastery	5.61 (1.50)	5.67 (1.28)
Negative mastery	5.89 (1.10)	5.68 (1.25)
Relaxation	6.40 (1.05)	5.80 (1.80)
Control	6.28 (.96)	5.67 (1.28)
Total	6.05 (1.18)	5.71 (1.40)[a*]

[a] *Significantly different than Session 1. *$p < 0.05$. **$p < 0.01$. ***$p < 0.001$.*

ability was associated with greater perceived control and a lower reduction in anxiety direction (i.e., less likely to perceive anxiety symptoms as debilitative). In other words, those in the negative imagery group with poorer positive imagery ability were more greatly impacted by their assigned imagery condition, suggesting that positive mastery imagery ability acts as a buffer against imagery eliciting debilitative stress responses (e.g., debilitative anxiety). This finding supports the RAMDIU as imagery ability influenced outcomes experienced from a stress task (Cumming and Williams, 2013). However, the novelty of our finding provides an additional theoretical contribution to this model by suggesting that imagery ability can also buffer against the debilitative effects of negative imagery, therefore extending beyond what the revised model hypothesized.

Support that mastery imagery ability acts as a buffer against negative imagery was demonstrated using moderation analyses: those with lower mastery imagery ability perceived increased levels of anxiety as more debilitative. Although the moderation relationships were not significant at Session 1, this could be explained by increased task stressfulness ratings at Session 2. At the first visit, participants were likely still acclimatizing to the laboratory conditions and learning how to perform the task. Although there were some differences introduced in Session 2 to maintain a degree of task novelty (e.g., different race track), the learning from Session 1 would enable participants to focus more on performing and the results, hence the increased ratings of stressfulness but reduced effort. That this moderation effect was significant for all participants, regardless of their condition, indicates that the stress-inducing factors of competition were strong enough to elicit an anxiety response for all groups. Moreover, this anxiety response was of a sufficient level for participants' mastery imagery ability to exert a moderating effect. Recent research has found positive mastery imagery ability to be associated with either anxiety intensity or anxiety direction (Quinton et al., 2018; Williams et al., under review). However, the current study extends these findings by suggesting that the role of mastery imagery ability as a correlate of anxiety may be more complex than previously thought, playing a moderating role in perceiving anxiety as more facilitative. This novel finding should be explored in future research to determine its replicability and generalizability to other settings (e.g., other competitive and stress-evoking situations). If replicated, developing mastery imagery ability could be a significant strategy for promoting more facilitative anxiety interpretations during stress.

During stressful scenarios, spontaneous negative images can be experienced (Van de Braam and Moran, 2011). The present results allude to the importance of mastery imagery ability in protecting against the debilitative effects of negative images. The importance was further emphasized by the lack of any significant results with affect imagery ability. Although research shows that the ability to image intervention content can influence imagery's effectiveness (McKenzie and Howe, 1997), this study highlights the importance of more general imagery ability, positive mastery, by demonstrating that the ability to image this content may play a role in the effectiveness of a particular imagery intervention. More broadly, findings demonstrate the importance of imagery ability impacting upon the effectiveness of imagery use and, in line with Jones (1995) framework, suggest that individual factors such as imagery ability should be considered when investigating responses to stress and how they are perceived.

Another type of imagery ability in this study, although employed as a manipulation check, could be imagery script engagement. Supported by the computational theory of imagery (Kosslyn et al., 2006), the ability to remain engaged in a script could reflect the maintenance stage of image generation. The negative mastery group was less engaged in their script, which, although could be noted as a limitation, could also imply that lower script engagement acts as a protective factor against debilitative imagery. It is possible that higher engagement with facilitative imagery could elicit more positive responses. Although engagement is crucial for imagery effectiveness in clinical settings (Steenbergen et al., 2009), scarce research has explored engagement within other settings, such as sport and competition. As debilitative imagery can be more powerful in eliciting stress responses than facilitative imagery (Nordin and Cumming, 2005), it is important to understand this relationship and what strategies (e.g., imagery rescripting) may be most effective to prevent debilitative stress responses and poor performance.

Key Findings and Implications: Secondary Aim

In accordance with our hypotheses and previous research (Williams et al., 2010, 2017), the scripts containing positive and negative mastery content reported higher cognitive and somatic anxiety levels. However, in contrast to our hypothesis, there was a trend for anxiety to be perceived as more debilitative for the positive mastery and control groups but not the negative mastery group. These results were unexpected and also in contrast to research where participants who imaged neutral or coping-based content perceived anxiety symptoms as facilitative (Cumming et al., 2007; Williams et al., 2010, 2017) and those who imaged negative content perceived anxiety as debilitative (Cumming et al., 2007; Williams et al., 2010). Although some of these studies included hypothetical competitions or low stress-evoking situations, the scripts provided stimulus propositions based on personal experiences, which likely contributed to an increased meaning, and therefore effectiveness, of the imagery (Lang, 1979). In this study, the unexpected results could be due to the imagery of the task being less familiar compared to previous studies, and subsequently less meaningful and effective for participants. This notion is supported by the RAMDIU (Cumming and Williams, 2013), which posits that the meaning of an image influences what function (e.g., anxiety producing) the image content (e.g., positive mastery) serves. Importantly, when using positive mastery imagery, results suggest that practitioners should ensure imagery is meaningful and that it has the intended facilitative effect for actual performance scenarios.

Interestingly, additional results were also in contrast to our hypotheses and previous research. In contrast to Williams et al. (2010, 2017), Williams and Cumming (2012a) studies, there were no significant group differences for confidence or perceived control in relation to the competition task. Furthermore, although Williams et al. (2017) found that the neutral script was occasionally more facilitative than the challenge script, this was not the case for the relaxation script used in this study. These results could be due to the variation between these imagery groups in the vividness and engagement of the scripts. Although there were no group differences in ease of imaging (i.e., one indicator of imagery ability), the positive mastery group imaged their scripts significantly more vividly than the negative mastery group, and the positive and relaxation groups were significantly more engaged in their scripts than the negative group. These findings suggest that participants found it easier to image the positive script content compared to negative, which could have influenced the effect of the imagery on task responses (i.e., confidence and perceived control). Therefore, researchers and practitioners conducting imagery interventions should ensure adherence to scripts and verify during the intervention (i.e., rather than after) whether participants can sufficiently image all aspects of the scripts, providing extra training where necessary (e.g., LSRT; Cumming et al., 2016).

Findings expand on Williams et al. (2010, 2017), Williams and Cumming (2012a) research by investigating imagery's effect on responses to actual competition, and highlights the importance of considering the situation associated with the imagery (i.e., public speaking or competition, hypothetical or real). This study supports that responses to an actual competition task are different to a real task in the form of dart throwing (Williams and Cumming, 2012a), a speech preparation task (Williams et al., 2017), and hypothetical competition (Williams et al., 2010). The collective results from these studies may demonstrate that imagery scripts (challenge or positive mastery, threat or negative mastery, or relaxation) might not be as effective for a stressful task where stimuli are constantly presented (i.e., car racing competition) and performance was evaluated, in comparison to a hypothetical task or a task which involves greater internal concentration (i.e., public speaking preparation task or dart throwing). Thus, in accordance with the RAMDIU (Cumming and Williams, 2013), the content (e.g., imagery script), situation (e.g., stress task, hypothetical or real), and individual components (e.g., positive mastery imagery ability) appear crucial to consider when implementing imagery interventions for stressful situations.

Limitations and Future Research

Although the current study provides some important contributions to the literature, it is not without limitations. Numerous tests were run in a small sample; however, multiple comparisons were controlled for using a conservative method that allowed statistical power to be maintained (Benjamini and Hochberg, 1995). Task novelty may have been influenced by previous task experiences; thus, research should test this consideration as a confounding variable (e.g., Williams and Cumming, 2012a). Also, the competition task differed in stressfulness across sessions. Although these tasks could have been counterbalanced (e.g., race track) to rule out the order being a confounding variable, the nature of the imagery intervention meant that participants had to be exposed to the task twice and therefore it was likely that the novelty, and stress response, would be reduced. Stress research makes the issue of novelty difficult to control, as the unique aspect of stress is that it is often associated with fear of the unknown. Therefore, undertaking a task twice is likely to yield differences in the stress response. However, this difference could also be viewed as a strength as completing a task twice often results in a loss of stressfulness of the task, but in this case, the task was more stressful the second time. Future research should expand on combining imagery interventions in repeated exposures to stress tasks and the subsequent influence on the stress response experienced. Future research should also ensure daytime is controlled for between laboratory visits.

CONCLUSION

Findings demonstrated that positive mastery imagery ability can determine the effectiveness of imagery's use. Results found a new buffering role for mastery imagery ability against the debilitative effects of negative imagery (e.g., debilitative anxiety), providing a novel theoretical contribution to the RAMDIU (Cumming and Williams, 2013) and a new understanding of how this type of imagery interacts with anxiety intensity and direction. Results also suggested, in contrast to Williams et al. (2010, 2017), that the imagery type used may not be more/less beneficial for a novel computer car racing task, which may be due to the different nature of hypothetical vs. real competition experiences or competition vs. other stress tasks (e.g., public speaking). Altogether, in accordance with and extending the RAMDIU (Cumming and Williams, 2013), positive mastery imagery ability varied across individuals and acted as a buffer, which together with the situation (e.g., competition task) likely influenced what function (e.g., anxiogenic) the image content (e.g., positive mastery) served, and therefore the outcomes experienced (e.g., more debilitative anxiety interpretations). Positive mastery imagery ability should be developed to reduce the impact of debilitative imagery and maladaptive responses to stress.

ETHICS STATEMENT

This study was carried out in accordance with the recommendations of the University of Birmingham's ethical review board, with written informed consent from all subjects. All subjects gave written informed consent in accordance with the Declaration of Helsinki. The protocol was approved by the University of Birmingham's ethical review board.

AUTHOR CONTRIBUTIONS

MQ made substantial contributions to the study design, data collection, entry, and analysis, and drafting of the manuscript. GT made substantial contributions to the study design, data collection and entry, and provided feedback on the manuscript. JC provided critical analysis of, and feedback on the manuscript. SW and JVvZ made substantial contributions to the study design, analysis, and provided feedback on drafts of the manuscript.

REFERENCES

Bale, T. L., and Epperson, C. N. (2015). Sex differences and stress across the lifespan. *Nat. Neurosci.* 18, 1413–1420. doi: 10.1038/nn.4112

Benjamini, Y., and Hochberg, Y. (1995). Controlling the false discovery rate: a practical and powerful approach to multiple testing. *J. R. Stat. Soc.* 57, 289–300. doi: 10.1111/j.2517-6161.1995.tb02031.x

Blascovich, J., and Mendes, W. B. (2000). "Challenge and threat appraisals: the role of affective cues," in *Feeling and Thinking: the Role of Affect in Social Cognition*, ed. J. Forgas (New York, NY: Cambridge University Press), 59–82.

Chamberlain, S. T., and Hale, B. D. (2007). Competitive state anxiety and self-confidence: intensity and direction as relative predictors of performance on a golf putting task. *Anxiety Stress Coping* 20, 197–207. doi: 10.1080/10615800701288572

Crum, A. J., Salovey, P., and Achor, S. (2013). Rethinking stress: the role of mindsets in determining the stress response. *J. Pers. Soc. Psychol.* 104, 716–733. doi: 10.1037/a0031201

Cumming, J., Cooley, S. J., Anuar, N., Kosteli, M., Quinton, M. L., Weibull, F., et al. (2016). Developing imagery ability effectively: a guide to layered stimulus response training. *J. Sport Psychol. Action* 7, 1–11. doi: 10.1080/21520704.2016.1205698

Cumming, J., Olphin, T., and Law, M. (2007). Self-reported psychological states and physiological responses to different types of motivational general imagery. *J. Sport Exerc. Psychol.* 29, 629–644. doi: 10.1123/jsep.29.5.629

Cumming, J., and Williams, S. E. (2013). Introducing the revised applied model of deliberate imagery use for sport, dance, exercise, and rehabilitation. *Mov. Sport Sci.* 82, 69–81. doi: 10.1051/sm/2013098

De Geus, E. J. C., Willemsen, G. H. M., Klaver, C. H., and Van Doornen, L. J. (1995). Ambulatory measurement of respiratory sinus arrhythmia and respiration rate. *Biol. Psychol.* 41, 205–227. doi: 10.1016/0301-0511(95)05137-6

Hanton, S., Neil, R., and Mellalieu, S. D. (2008). Recent developments in competitive anxiety direction and competition stress research. *Int. Rev. Sport Exerc. Psychol.* 1, 45–57. doi: 10.1080/17509840701827445

Hayes, A. F. (2017). *Introduction to Mediation, Moderation, and Conditional Process Analysis: A Regression-Based Approach*, 2nd Edn. New York, NY: Guilford Publications.

Jamieson, J. P., Mendes, W. B., and Nock, M. K. (2013). Improving acute stress responses: the power of reappraisal. *Curr. Dir. Psychol. Sci.* 22, 51–56. doi: 10.1177/0963721412461500

Jones, G. (1995). More than just a game: research developments and issues in competitive anxiety in sport. *Br. J. Psychol.* 86, 449–478. doi: 10.1111/j.2044-8295.1995.tb02565.x

Jones, M., Meijen, C., McCarthy, P. J., and Sheffield, D. (2009). A theory of challenge and threat states in athletes. *Int. Rev. Sport Exerc. Psychol.* 2, 161–180. doi: 10.1080/17509840902829331

Kosslyn, S. M., Thompson, W. L., and Ganis, G. (2006). *The Case for Mental Imagery.* Oxford: Oxford University Press.

Lang, P. J. (1979). A bio-informational theory of emotional imagery. *Psychophysiology* 16, 495–512. doi: 10.1111/1469-8986.197901511

McDonald, J. H. (2014). *Handbook of Biological Statistics*, 3rd Edn. Maryland, MD: Sparky House Publishing.

McKenzie, A. D., and Howe, B. L. (1997). The effect of imagery of self-efficacy for a motor skill. *Int. J. Sport Psychol.* 28, 196–210. doi: 10.1016/j.apmr.2013.06.031

Moore, L. J., Vine, S. J., Wilson, M. R., and Freeman, P. (2012). The effect of challenge and threat states on performance: an examination of potential mechanisms. *Psychophysiology* 49, 1417–1425. doi: 10.1111/j.1469-8986.2012.01449.x

Morris, T. (1997). *Psychological Skills Training in Sport: an Overview*, 2nd Edn. Leeds: National Coaching Foundation.

NHS Digital (2018). *Mental Health of Children, and Young People in England* Available at: https://digital.nhs.uk/data-and-information/publications/statistical/mental-health-of-children-and-young-people-in-england/2017/2017 (accessed March 20, 2019).

Nordin, S., and Cumming, J. (2005). More than meets the eye: investigating imagery type, direction, and outcome. *Sport Psychol.* 19, 1–17. doi: 10.1123/tsp.19.1.1

Olson, C. L. (1976). On choosing a test statistic in multivariate analysis of variance. *Psychol. Bull.* 83, 579–586. doi: 10.1037/0033-2909.83.4.579

Quinton, M. L., Cumming, J., and Williams, S. E. (2018). Investigating the mediating role of positive and negative imagery ability. *Psychol. Sport Exerc.* 35, 1–9. doi: 10.1016/j.psychsport.2017.10.011

Schneiderman, N., Ironson, G., and Siegel, S. D. (2005). Stress and health: psychological, behavioral, and biological determinants. *Annu. Rev. Clin. Psychol.* 1, 607–628. doi: 10.1146/annurev.clinpsy.1.102803.144141

Shi, Q., Pavey, E. S., and Carter, R. E. (2012). Bonferroni-based correction factor for multiple, correlated endpoints. *Pharm. Stat.* 11, 300–309. doi: 10.1002/pst.1514

Skinner, N., and Brewer, N. (2004). Adaptive approaches to competition: challenge appraisals and positive emotion. *J. Sport Exerc. Psychol.* 26, 283–305. doi: 10.1123/jsep.26.2.283

Sport England (2016). *Sport England Annual Report and Accounts*. London: Sport England.

Steenbergen, B., Craje, C., Nilsen, D. M., and Gordon, A. M. (2009). Motor imagery training in hemiplegic cerebral palsy: a potentially useful therapeutic tool for rehabilitation. *Dev. Med. Child Neurol.* 51, 690–696. doi: 10.1111/j.1469-8749.2009.03371.x

Tabachnick, B. G., and Fidell, L. S. (2013). *Using Multivariate Statistics*. Essex: Pearson Education Limited.

Thomas, O., Hanton, S., and Jones, G. (2002). An alternative approach to short-form self-report assessment of competitive anxiety. *Int. J. Sport Psychol.* 33, 325–336.

Trotman, G. P., Gianaros, P. J., Veldhuijzen van Zanten, J. J. C. S., Williams, S. E., and Ginty, A. T. (2018a). Increased stressor-evoked cardiovascular reactivity is associated with reduced amygdala and hippocampus volume. *Psychophysiology* 56, 1–13. doi: 10.1111/psyp.13277

Trotman, G. P., Williams, S. E., Quinton, M. L., and Veldhuijzen van Zanten, J. J. C. S. (2018b). Challenge and threat states: examining cardiovascular, cognitive and affective responses to two distinct laboratory stress tasks. *Int. J. Psychophysiol.* 126, 42–51. doi: 10.1016/j.ijpsycho.2018.02.004

Turner, J. R. (1994). *Cardiovascular Reactivity and Stress*. New York, NY: Plenum Press.

Turner, M. J., Jones, M. V., Sheffield, D., Barker, J. B., and Coffee, P. (2014). Manipulating cardiovascular indices of challenge and threat using resource appraisals. *Int. J. Psychophysiol.* 94, 9–18. doi: 10.1016/j.ijpsycho.2014.07.004

Van de Braam, M., and Moran, A. (2011). The prevalence and effects of negative mental imagery in tennis. *J. Med. Sci. Tennis* 16, 34–37.

Veldhuijzen van Zanten, J. J. C. S., de Boer, D., Harrison, L. K., Ring, C., Carroll, D., Willemsen, G., et al. (2002). Competitiveness and hemodynamic reactions to competition. *Psychophysiology* 39, 759–766. doi: 10.1111/1469-8986.3960759

White, A., and Hardy, L. (1998). An in-depth analysis of the uses of imagery by high-level slalom canoeists and artistic gymnasts. *Sport Psychol.* 12, 387–403. doi: 10.1123/tsp.12.4.387

Willemsen, G. H. M., De Geus, E. J. C., Klaver, C. H., Van Doornen, L. J., and Carroll, D. (1996). Ambulatory monitoring of the impedance cardiogram. *Psychophysiology* 33, 184–193. doi: 10.1111/j.1469-8986.1996.tb02122.x

Williams, S. E., Cooley, S. J., and Cumming, J. (2013). Layered stimulus response training improves motor imagery ability and movement execution. *J. Sport Exerc. Psychol.* 35, 60–71. doi: 10.1123/jsep.35.1.60

Williams, S. E., and Cumming, J. (2011). Measuring athlete imagery ability: the sport imagery ability questionnaire. *J. Sport Exerc. Psychol.* 33, 416–440. doi: 10.1123/jsep.33.3.416

Williams, S. E., and Cumming, J. (2012a). Challenge vs. threat: investigating the effect of using imagery to manipulate stress appraisal of a dart throwing task. *Sport Exerc. Psychol. Rev.* 8, 4–21.

Williams, S. E., and Cumming, J. (2012b). Sport imagery ability predicts trait confidence, and challenge and threat appraisal tendencies. *Eur. J. Sport Sci.* 12, 499–508. doi: 10.1080/17461391.2011.630102

Williams, S. E., and Cumming, J. (2015). Athlete imagery ability: a predictor of confidence and anxiety intensity and direction. *Int. J. Sport Exerc. Psychol.* 14, 268–280. doi: 10.1080/1612197X.2015.1025809

Williams, S. E., Cumming, J., and Balanos, G. M. (2010). The use of imagery to manipulate challenge and threat appraisal states in athletes. *J. Sport Exerc. Psychol.* 32, 339–358. doi: 10.1123/jsep.32.3.339

Williams, S. E., Veldhuijzen van Zanten, J. J. C. S., Trotman, G. P., Quinton, M. L., and Ginty, A. T. (2017). Challenge and threat imagery manipulates heart rate and anxiety responses to stress. *Int. J. Psychophysiol.* 117, 111–118. doi: 10.1016/j.ijpsycho.2017.04.011

5

Action Monitoring Through External or Internal Focus of Attention does not Impair Endurance Performance

Francesca Vitali[1], Cantor Tarperi[1], Jacopo Cristini[1], Andrea Rinaldi[1], Arnaldo Zelli[2], Fabio Lucidi[3], Federico Schena[1], Laura Bortoli[4] and Claudio Robazza[4]*

[1] Department of Neurosciences, Biomedicine and Movement Sciences, University of Verona, Verona, Italy, [2] Department of Movement, Human and Health Sciences, Foro Italico University of Rome, Rome, Italy, [3] Department of Developmental and Social Psychology, La Sapienza University of Rome, Rome, Italy, [4] BIND–Behavioral Imaging and Neural Dynamics Center, Department of Medicine and Aging Sciences, Università degli Studi G. d'Annunzio Chieti e Pescara, Chieti, Italy

***Correspondence:**
Francesca Vitali
francesca.vitali@univr.it

Attentional focus in endurance sports has been found to largely affect performance. To deal with discomfort, fatigue, and pain associated with endurance performance under pressure, athletes tend to direct attention to both internal (e.g., bodily) sensations and external (e.g., environmental) stimuli. The purpose of this study, framed within the multi-action plan (MAP) model, was to examine whether different levels of action monitoring through external or internal focus of attention could influence endurance performance. Action monitoring has been conceptualized as awareness of the current experience without necessarily influencing the course of action or disrupting automated motor processes. Thirty-two male participants (M_{age} = 29.12 years, *SD* = 6.12 years) were engaged in a treadmill, time-to-exhaustion running task across seven visits to the laboratory (i.e., task familiarization, baseline, four experimental conditions, and follow up). Assessment involved performance (i.e., time to exhaustion), oxygen uptake ($\dot{V}O_2$), blood lactate levels, ratings of perceived exertion (RPE), and perceived arousal and hedonic tone. Across four visits, participants were prompted to use the four attentional strategies (one per session) deriving from the interaction of low/high conscious monitoring level by external/internal attention focus in a counterbalanced experimental design. Repeated measures analysis of variance did not yield significant results in any variable of the study, performance included. Consistent with predictions of the MAP model, study findings showed that participants were able to attain same performance levels irrespective of whether they used a high or low level of action monitoring through an external or internal focus of attention. Findings suggest practical indications to help athletes deal with stress in endurance sports.

Keywords: action monitoring, attentional focus, fatigue, hedonic tone, multi-action plan model, endurance

INTRODUCTION

Attentional focus in endurance sports, such as running, cycling, orienteering, swimming, triathlon, rowing, and cross-country skiing, has been acknowledged to largely impact performance (e.g., Brick et al., 2016a; McCormick et al., 2018; Robazza et al., 2018). To deal with task demands and perform optimally, athletes need to pay attention to and monitor both internal (e.g., bodily) sensations and external (e.g., environmental) stimuli, especially under competitive pressure (Carson and Collins, 2016; Gropel, 2016; Buchanan et al., 2018). Over the last decades, cognitive functioning and motivational issues in endurance sports have received increased research interest, and study findings have been interpreted in light of different theoretical approaches in the attempt to understand decision making and metacognitive processes (e.g., Smits et al., 2014; Brick et al., 2016b), attentional focus and cognitive control (e.g., Brick et al., 2014, 2016a), and mental fatigue (e.g., Marcora et al., 2009; Marcora and Staiano, 2010; Boccia et al., 2018). Beyond psychological approaches, the role of central fatigue in endurance tasks has been explained in light of metabolic, neurochemical, physiological, and psychophysiological processes (e.g., Martin et al., 2018; McMorris et al., 2018; Pedrinolla et al., 2018). Notwithstanding the substantial progresses in the field, and general agreement of the importance of self-monitoring processes to deal with physical and mental exertion, a number of questions remain to be investigated. In this regard, a specific research question that we addressed in the current study is whether different levels of action monitoring through external or internal focus of attention could influence endurance performance.

In one of the most influential works on marathon runners, Morgan and Pollock (1977) differentiated between an associative (task related) and a dissociative (task unrelated) attentional strategy. This classification was based on the observation that elite runners tended to monitor (i.e., to associate) sensory information and adjust their pace accordingly, whereas less expert runners tended to focus more on distracting stimuli (i.e., to dissociate) to divert attention away from physical strain, exhaustion, pain, and mental exertion. Later, Stevinson and Biddle (1998, 1999) proposed a two-dimensional classification system by adding an internal-external (body related/unrelated) dimension to the associative-dissociative (task related/unrelated) dimension. In a muscular endurance task (i.e., a wall-sit isometric posture), Lohse and Sherwood (2011) combined the internal-external with the associative-dissociative dimensions. In particular, the wall-sit task was completed under three attention focus conditions: internal-associative (thighs position), external-associative (drawing imaginary lines between knee and hip), and external-dissociative (drawing imaginary lines between pylons in front of the participant). While the two types of external focus were equally effective, they were superior to the internal focus in increasing the time taken to failure and in reducing perceived exertion. More recently, Brick et al. (2014) proposed a working model to better categorize cognitive processes. They suggested an extension to the internal associative category of Stevinson and Biddle's (1998) classification to include internal sensory monitoring (e.g., breathing, muscles soreness, and fatigue) and active self-regulation (e.g., cadence, pacing, technique, strategy, maintaining a relaxed state). They also differentiated between active, voluntary distraction and involuntary distraction (passive thoughts).

Despite the large body of research in endurance sports, (Schücker et al., 2016a,b) noted that research findings regarding attentional focus effects on endurance performance are controversial. An external focus of attention on the intended movement effects has been found to benefit movement efficiency in endurance activities (e.g., optimized muscular activity and oxygen consumption), as well as motor learning, movement effectiveness (e.g., precision in hitting a target, exerting a specific amount of force, keeping balance) independent of skill level, task, and age (Wulf, 2007, 2013). This effect has been explained with the constrained action hypothesis (Wulf et al., 2001). According to this hypothesis, an external attentional focus determines a more automatic mode of control through unconscious and fast processes of movement control. In contrast, an internal focus on movement execution is contended to induce a conscious type of control that interferes with automatic control processes regulating movement coordination (Wulf, 2007).

Although performance advantages of an external focus of attention have been found across many studies conducted on discrete and short-time motor tasks (for reviews, see Wulf, 2013; Wulf and Lewthwaite, 2016), controversial research findings have been reported in endurance sports and long-lasting cyclic motor tasks requiring sustained attention over time (see Brick et al., 2014). One explanation of the inconsistent results can lie on the equivocal or vague definition of the notion of attention focus operationalized in different manners. For example, an internal focus of attention can involve physical sensations or technique, while an external focus can include visual or auditory information. It is therefore unsurprising that studies manipulating attention in endurance sports led to different practical recommendations on whether it is more beneficial to focus attention internally or externally. Schücker et al. (2014) tried to resolve this issue by classifying an internal focus of attention into two subclasses: A focus on physical sensations exerting beneficial effects on performance, and a focus on automated processes exerting detrimental effects. Schücker et al. (2014) used this framework in a study on runners involved in a 24 min treadmill task. In particular, they examined the effects on running economy of an internal focus on physical sensations and an internal focus on automated processes. In the internal focus on physical sensations, participants were asked to direct attention on feelings of the body, perceived effort, and body responses during the exercise. In the internal focus on automated processes runners were asked either to pay attention to their breathing dynamic or to monitor their running movement (i.e., feet and legs action). According to the study hypotheses, both the internal foci of attention directed on automated processes (i.e., breathing or running movement) were detrimental to movement economy measured through oxygen consumption ($\dot{V}O_2$), whereas a focus on internal physical sensations did not impair movement efficiency.

The finding that an internal focus is not harmful as long as it does not disrupt automated processes is not in contrast with the constrained action hypothesis (Wulf et al., 2001) or other theoretical approaches, such as reinvestment theory (Masters, 1992; Masters and Maxwell, 2008) and explicit monitoring theory (Beilock and Carr, 2001; Beilock, 2011). All approaches, indeed, agree that focusing attention on movement execution impairs automaticity. As van Ginneken et al. (2017) pointed out, the beneficial or detrimental effects of an internal focus may depend on its relative emphasis on conscious monitoring or control, respectively. Monitoring involves movements "observation" and awareness of what is currently happening without necessarily influencing the course of action. This is much like a "mindful" moment-to-moment awareness and task relevant attention on current behavior. A mindful attitude is contended to promote a modified relationship with internal experiences (i.e., cognitions, emotions, and physiological sensations) rather than trying to change them (Gardner and Moore, 2007). Conversely, control entails both observation and influence—a conscious manipulation of the mechanics of the action during motor output (Masters and Maxwell, 2008).

van Ginneken et al. (2017) compared the effects of conscious monitoring and conscious control on performance in a darts task using specific instructions to manipulate both internal and external foci of attention. Conscious monitoring instructions emphasized awareness of arm movements (internal focus) or awareness of dart flight (external focus), whereas conscious control requests were to produce an ideal arm movement (internal focus) or an ideal dart flight (external focus). Based on the results of this study and previous research (e.g., Malhotra et al., 2015), the authors concluded that conscious monitoring can leave motor performance unaffected or even influence it positively (Zhang et al., 2016), whereas conscious control disrupts motor performance. Predictions concur with the reinvestment theory (Masters and Maxwell, 2008), explicit monitoring theory (Beilock and Carr, 2001), and the constrained action hypothesis (Wulf et al., 2001). Although using different perspectives, the three approaches place emphasis on the detrimental effects deriving from trying to consciously control the course of the action. However, the effect of consciously monitoring the action has not been examined or explicitly recognized in the different theoretical views.

The contention that an internal focus of attention is not always associated with detrimental effects and that can even benefit performance is also endorsed by action and motor-centered frameworks (Hanin and Hanina, 2009; Carson and Collins, 2016; Hanin et al., 2016; for a review, see Robazza and Ruiz, 2018). The multi-action plan (MAP) model, in particular, has been proposed to account for the multiple performance states of athletes, and to help them reach and maintain high execution standards in training and competition (Bortoli et al., 2012; Robazza et al., 2016). In the MAP model, high and low levels of performance are categorized in function of high and low levels of action control. In essence, four performance states are identified through this interaction: (1) Type 1, optimal-automated performance state, in which high performance is attained with a low focus of attention aimed at "supervising" the correct flow of movement execution; (2) Type 2, optimal-controlled performance, wherein high performance is reached through attention focused on the core component(s) of the action to prevent step-by-step movement control and to ensure the action be properly run; (3) Type 3, non-optimal-controlled performance, with undue and effortful attentional focus toward action control; and (4) Type 4, non-optimal-automated performance, with unfocused or wandering attention. In a laboratory cycling task (Bertollo et al., 2015; di Fronso et al., 2018), participants were asked to focus attention on a metronome reproducing an individual preferred pedaling rate (i.e., Type 1 state, external attention) or to pay attention to the preferred pedaling rate (i.e., Type 2 state, internal attention). Both conditions led participants to attain a better time-to-exhaustion performance than attending to feelings of muscle pain, tension, and fatigue (i.e., Type 3 state, internal attention). No differences were found in terms of performance outcomes between Type 1 and Type 2 states.

The Schücker et al. (2014) classification of attention focus either on physical sensations or on automated processes, as well as the van Ginneken et al. (2017) proposal to differentiate between monitoring and controlling the action, could be framed within the MAP conceptualization (Bortoli et al., 2012; Robazza et al., 2016). Specifically, directing attention to physical sensations in the running task (Schücker et al., 2014) can be viewed as a mental strategy to attain a Type 2 state functional for performance, whereas attempts to control automated processes would determine a Type 3 dysfunctional state. In the same vein, action monitoring and action control in darts throwing (van Ginneken et al., 2017) can be considered as characterizing a Type 1 functional state and a Type 3 dysfunctional state, respectively. A common assumption across the outlined perspectives is that a monitoring ("mindful," "supervising," and attending to action core components) attitude is beneficial, whereas controlling automated motor processes is detrimental. Although scant, research evidence is in favor of action monitoring rather than action control. What remains to be established is whether different levels of external or internal monitoring influence performance differently. Thus, the purpose of the current study was to determine whether low or high levels of external or internal conscious monitoring influence performance differently in a treadmill endurance task.

To manipulate the level of conscious monitoring, we alternated task requirements during execution according to the contextual interference paradigm applied to the learning of motor skills (for review, see Farrow and Buszard, 2017). Low contextual interference (low cognitive load) is created when different tasks are executed randomly or in serial order, one after another, usually allowing enough time to the performer to familiarize with one task before switching to the other. High contextual interference (high cognitive load) occurs when tasks change more frequently in random order or serial order, thus leaving less time to the performer to become acquainted. A high contextual interference schedule is deemed to produce a high cognitive effort reflecting the amount of cognitive processing needed to perform a skill (Patterson and Lee, 2008). To manipulate cognitive load and, as a consequence, action monitoring levels, we constrained participants to adjust less frequently (low interference) or more frequently (high interference) their attention focus (see **Table 1**). Shifting the focus of attention (external or internal) from task to task every minute is expected to determine a higher conscious monitoring associated with the higher cognitive effort than shifting the focus every 3 min. Drawing on previous research findings showing the benefits of conscious monitoring (e.g., Bortoli et al., 2012; Schücker et al., 2014; van Ginneken et al., 2017), we hypothesized to find same levels of performance across the four conditions stemming from the relationship between monitoring levels and the external/internal focus. Moreover, we

TABLE 1 | Four Experimental Schedules derived from the interplay between Low/High conscious monitoring and External/Internal attention focus.

Attention focus	Conscious monitoring	
	High – Type 2 performance	Low – Type 1 performance
External	On a metronome for 1 min On a bellows for 1 min On a ball for 1 min	On a metronome for 3 min On a bellows for 3 min On a ball for 3 min
Internal	On feet rhythm for 1 min On breathing rhythm for 1 min On arms and shoulders rhythm for 1 min	On feet rhythm for 3 min On breathing rhythm for 3 min On arms and shoulders rhythm for 3 min

The sequence in each schedule is repeated until exhaustion.

expected the four conditions to result in better performance and running economy compared to a baseline and a follow up without attentional constraints. Together with performance and running economy, measured as time-to-exhaustion and rate of oxygen consumption, we assessed perceived exertion and core affect (i.e., arousal and hedonic tone). Higher levels of exertion during the endurance task were expected to be accompanied by higher levels of perceived exertion, and lower levels of perceived arousal (less energy) and hedonic tone (more displeasure). These predictions are consistent with previous research results. For instance, in a study with orienteering athletes Robazza et al. (2018) showed a similar pattern of results between perceived exertion and emotion-related (psychobiosocial) states dysfunctional for performance.

MATERIALS AND METHODS

Participants

Sample size was determined using G*Power 3.1 (Faul et al., 2007). Consistent with previous studies using similar designs (Schücker et al., 2016a,b), we set the following input parameters for *a priori* power analysis: $f = 0.25$, $\alpha = 0.05$, $1\text{-}\beta = 0.95$, 1 group, 6 measurements, $r_{\text{repeated measures}} = 0.50$, $\varepsilon = 1$. The required sample size was 28 participants. To account for possible dropouts, we involved in the study 34 participants. Two of them discontinued participation from the study due to personal reasons. Therefore, 32 male participants, aged between 20 and 44 years ($M_{age} = 29.12$ years, $SD = 6.12$ years) were engaged in this investigation on a voluntary basis. All of them were healthy and free from injuries, engaged regularly in different physical activities of low to moderate intensity, and were accustomed to treadmill running. On the initial visit, baseline assessment, obtained by an incremental cardiopulmonary exercise test (CPET; American College of Sports Medicine, 2018), showed that the fitness level of participants was $\dot{V}O_2$max $M = 54.02$ ml Kg^{-1} m^{-1}, $SD = 9.05$, HRmax $M = 184.41$, $SD = 10.88$. Participants were informed about the procedure, the measurements, and the general purpose of the study, and provided written informed consent before participation. The study was conducted in accordance with the Declaration of Helsinki. Furthermore, the study was approved by the ethics committee of the University of Verona with anonymity, confidentiality, and allowance to leave the study at any point without any consequences being assured for the participants.

Measures

Running Performance

The running performance during each time-to-exhaustion (TTE) test was measured as the time the participants reached volitional exhaustion.

Metabolic Measures

Participants completed a CPET to volitional exhaustion on a treadmill (RunRace, Technogym, Gambettola, Italy) with continuous breath-by-breath respiratory gas exchange measurement to record their oxygen consumption ($\dot{V}O_2$, ml/min/kg). $\dot{V}O_2$ was measured using an online metabolic cart calibrated before each test (Quark C-PET; Cosmed Srl, Rome, Italy). Performers were required to wear a breathing mask, which was fitted individually. Heart rate (HR, bpm) was measured continuously using a chest belt by wireless telemetry (Cosmed HR monitor) which transmitted the HR signal to the spiroergometric system.

Blood Measures

The lactate profile (mmol/L) of participants was measured by taking blood samples from the earlobe. The blood samples were examined with an enzymatic-amperometric blood lactate analyzer (Biosen C-Line; EKF Diagnostics, Cardiff, United Kingdom) according to the manufacturer's instructions.

Ratings of Perceived Exertion (RPE)

The Borg CR-10 RPE scale (Borg, 1998) was administered to measure perceived exertion. Perceived exertion is proposed to complement physiological assessment in a wide range of areas, including exercise and sports. The Borg CR-10 RPE scale measures the perceived exertion on an interval using verbal anchors: 0 = *nothing at all*, 0.5 = *extremely weak*, 1 = *very weak*, 2 = *weak*, 3 = *moderate*, 5 = *strong*, 7 = *very strong*, 10 = *extremely strong*, • = *absolute maximum*. For 4, 6, 8, and 9 no verbal anchors are used. The score of 11 is assigned to *absolute maximum*.

Affect Grid

Russell et al. (1989) designed an affect grid to quickly assess core affect (i.e., arousal and hedonic tone) along the dimensions of sleepiness-energy and displeasure-pleasure. Following an explanation of the terms *arousal* and *hedonic tone*, the performer is asked to check a box within a 9 × 9 grid or to provide a verbal report that represents the perceived arousal and hedonic tone intensity at that moment. Hence, both the sleepiness-energy and the pleasure-displeasure dimensions could range from 1 to 9. Higher numbers indicate higher energy and higher pleasure levels, while lower numbers correspond to higher sleepiness and higher displeasure levels. This scale enables quick and low invasive assessment of one's introspective states during performance.

Manipulation Check

After the TTE tests the participants were asked to rate on a 10-point scale, ranging from 0 = *never* to 10 = *always*, the frequency they were able to focus attention externally or internally following the instructions provided them according to the experimental manipulations. The questions were: "*How often did you pay attention to the rhythm of the metronome, bellows, and ball?*" (low/high monitoring and external focus conditions), "*How often did you pay attention to the rhythm of the feet, breathing, and arms and shoulders?*" (low/high monitoring and internal focus conditions).

Procedure

The experimental protocol consisted of seven visits to the laboratory with intervisit intervals of 48 h. Collection of data occurred in an environmental controlled condition (temperature fixed at 20°C, no other people allowed in the laboratory, no music played). All trials were performed with the treadmill slope maintained at 1%.

Incremental Test

During the first visit the participants had the opportunity to familiarize with the experimental setting. They were instructed about the use of the Borg CR-10 RPE scale and the affect grid, and then completed a treadmill (RunRace, Technogym, Gambettola, Italy) cardiorespiratory incremental stress test. Breath-by-breath (Quark CPET, Cosmed, Rome, Italy) $\dot{V}O_2$ and carbon dioxide production, ventilation, and heart rate data were collected. After a 4 min of 8 km h^{-1} warm-up, the velocity was incremented by 0.1 km h^{-1} each 6 s up to voluntary exhaustion. Treadmill inclination was kept fixed at 1% throughout the test. Maximal oxygen consumption ($\dot{V}O_2max$) was obtained at the last 30 s of the test. Blood lactate concentration, from the earlobe, was measured at the third minute of recovery (Biosen C-Line, EKF Diagnostics, Cardiff, United Kingdom). In all tests, maximal heart rate was greater than 90% of age-predicted maximum value and respiratory quotient was greater than 1.10. The second ventilatory threshold (VT_2), also described as respiratory compensation point, was identified blindly by two operators at the simultaneous increasing of both ventilatory equivalents for O_2 ($\dot{V}E/\dot{V}O_2$) and for CO_2 ($\dot{V}E/\dot{V}CO_2$; Wasserman et al., 1994). Oxygen consumption (ml kg^{-1} min^{-1}), heart rate (bpm), and work velocity (km h^{-1}) at VT_2 were calculated.

Time-to-Exhaustion (TTE) Test at Individual Constant Load

During the second visit, participants performed a TTE test conducted without attentional manipulation conditions. In this baseline assessment, performers started with a 1-min resting period standing still on the treadmill, followed by a 4-min warm-up stage running at a constant individual speed calculated as the 50% of the individual $\dot{V}O_2max$. After 180 s run, the individual preferred running rate (PRR) was calculated as the number of steps on the treadmill in 1 min run at individual 105% of VT_2 measured at steady state condition. Participants were then asked to run until exhaustion at their constant individual speed calculated as the 105% of VT_2. During the following four visits to the laboratory, in which the attention focus was manipulated, the participants completed TTE tests running until exhaustion at a constant individual speed corresponding to the 105% of VT_2. The protocol of each TTE test was the same described for the second visit. TTE was considered as the maximum interval (sec) in which the participants could maintain the running intensity assigned until volitional exhaustion. During each test, individual PRR was set and controlled for each participant.

Participants were assigned in a counterbalanced order to one of the four attentional conditions each one occurring on a different day. The four conditions resulted from the interaction between conscious monitoring (low and high) and attention focus (external and internal; see **Table 1**). Consistent with the MAP model predictions (Bortoli et al., 2012; Robazza et al., 2016), low or high monitoring levels (either external or internal) were hypothesized to be associated with a Type 1 or a Type 2 performance state, respectively. In the external focus condition, a laptop and a slide projector were positioned in front of the treadmill to clearly project on a white wall three videos of a metronome, a bellows, and a ball. The projected videos were visible at 1.5 m from the participants' eye height. An amplifier and two audio speakers guaranteed a clear perception of the sound associated with the metronome, bellows, and ball moving rhythmically in synchrony with the individual PRR rhythm. Participants were requested to focus attention during running on the videos and the related sound. The projection of the metronome, bellows, and ball was alternated every 3 min or 1 min in the low or high monitoring conditions, respectively, until exhaustion. In the internal focus condition, participants were instructed to pay close attention to the rhythmic movement of feet, breathing, and arms and shoulders associated with running. Similar to the external focus condition, the internal focus on the rhythm of the different bodily parts were alternated every 3 min or 1 min until exhaustion. Reminders to pay close attention to the videos or to the physical sensations were systematically provided to performers. A follow up TTE test without manipulation of the attentional focus was conducted in a final visit to the laboratory 48 hr later.

Ratings of perceived exertion and affective states (arousal and hedonic tone) data were collected in the last 5 s of the 1-min resting period, in the last 5 s of the first minute of each TTE test, and in the last 5 s of every 3 min period throughout the entire test. During the last 30 s after the end of each TTE test, blood samples were taken from the earlobe of the participants to measure the blood lactate concentration. We collected breath-by-breath (Quark CPET; Cosmed, Rome, Italy) and calculated the mean steady state value during the last 30 s of the test for $\dot{V}O_2$, ventilation, and heart rate. Steady state blood lactate concentration, from the earlobe, was measured at the end of each trial (Biosen C-Line, EKF Diagnostics, Cardiff, United Kingdom). After a 4 min of 8 km h^{-1} warm-up, the running speed was maintained at 105% of second VT_2 velocity, with an inclination fixed at 1% until voluntary exhaustion. Steady state $\dot{V}O_2$ was calculated as the mean during the last 30 s of the test.

Data Analysis

Repeated-measures analysis of variance (RM-ANOVA) was performed to examine the effect of the experimental conditions (i.e., baseline, four experimental conditions, and follow up) on the study variables (i.e., performance, $\dot{V}O_2$, blood lactate levels, RPE, and perceived arousal and hedonic tone) across six visits to the laboratory and six data collections of each variable within a session. The six data values of each variable entered in the analysis corresponded to the 1-min resting period (baseline), isotimes 0% (first full minute), 25, 50, 75, and 100% (last completed minute) in the TTE test. The isotime at 100% was defined as the shortest TTE time attained by a performer in the four tests. The minute identified as 100% isotime was multiplied by 0.25, 0.5, and 0.75 to establish 25, 50, and 75% isotime values, respectively (see Blanchfield et al., 2014). RM-ANOVA was also conducted on the manipulation check data.

RESULTS

Descriptive statistics of study variables are reported in **Tables 2, 3**. In the RM-ANOVAs, the assumption of sphericity was violated, and thus the Greenhouse-Geisser correction was applied to the degrees of freedom for F statistic calculation. As can be seen from the results in **Table 4**, the only significant differences at $p < 0.01$ were found across the assessment phases (i.e., data collection within a session) for RPE, perceived arousal, and hedonic tone. The increasing levels of exertion through the task were accompanied by higher RPE, as well as lower ratings of perceived arousal (less energy) and hedonic tone (more displeasure), which indicate a worsening of the individual mental state during the TTE test. Significant differences were not observed either on experimental conditions or on the interaction between experimental conditions and assessment. Of note, manipulation check results indicate that performers were able to adhere satisfactorily to the experimental conditions given that mean ratings were between 7 and 8 (i.e., *much* and *very much*) on the 10-point scale.

TABLE 2 | Descriptive Statistics of Study Variables across Experimental Schedules.

Variable	Schedule	$M \pm SD$	% Change from baseline
Manipulation check	Low monitoring, external focus	7.81 ± 1.26	
	Low monitoring, internal focus	7.64 ± 1.07	
	High monitoring, external focus	8.09 ± 1.00	
	High monitoring, internal focus	7.41 ± 1.06	
Lactate (mmol/L)	Baseline	9.31 ± 3.07	
	Low monitoring, external focus	8.78 ± 2.60	−5.70
	Low monitoring, internal focus	9.16 ± 2.33	−1.68
	High monitoring, external focus	9.13 ± 2.37	−2.01
	High monitoring, internal focus	8.84 ± 2.44	−5.03
	Follow-up	8.50 ± 2.20	−8.72
Performance (sec)	Baseline	335.12 ± 147.43	
	Low monitoring, external focus	350.16 ± 150.71	4.49
	Low monitoring, internal focus	337.44 ± 126.54	0.69
	High monitoring, external focus	352.66 ± 120.19	5.23
	High monitoring, internal focus	356.19 ± 144.93	6.28
	Follow-up	345.00 ± 127.32	2.95

DISCUSSION

The purpose of the study was to establish whether low or high levels of external or internal conscious monitoring would influence performance in an endurance task. As expected, the four experimental conditions derived from the interplay between low/high conscious monitoring and external/internal attention focus did not yield significant results in the study variables (i.e., $\dot{V}O_2$, blood lactate levels, RPE, and perceived arousal and hedonic tone). Same performance levels (i.e., TTE) were also observed irrespective of whether participants used a high or low level of action monitoring through an external or internal focus of attention. Contrary to what was expected, the experimental conditions did not determine better performance compared to baseline and follow up. Also, significant results did not emerge across sessions in the other study variables. The lack of significant differences was probably due to the good physical activity level of participants who regularly engaged in endurance tasks, including running and cycling, during their leisure time. Experienced participants, acquainted with conditions of strain and fatigue and highly motivated toward endurance tasks, had most likely developed personal strategies to deal with endurance requirements.

Attentional focus in endurance sports has been found to largely affect performance (e.g., Brick et al., 2016a; McCormick et al., 2018; Robazza et al., 2018). Dealing effectively with task demands, physical exertion, and mental strain in high achievement, pressurized contexts, involves one's monitoring of both internal (e.g., bodily) sensations and external (e.g., environmental) stimuli (Carson and Collins, 2016; Gropel, 2016; Buchanan et al., 2018) to actively regulate the own pacing and strategy (Brick et al., 2014). Internal sensory monitoring (e.g., breathing, muscles soreness, fatigue), outward monitoring (e.g., other competitors, split times, route, mile markers, water stations), and active self-regulation (e.g., cadence, pacing, technique, strategy, muscle relaxation) are also emphasized in Brick et al.'s (2014) working model of attentional focus in endurance activity. Thus, results of the current study offer further support to the use of both internal and external attentional foci in endurance tasks. Notably, the study design required performers to monitor internal or external information while executing rather than directing attention to the control of automated processes. This design is in accordance with Schücker et al.'s (2014) classification of the attention focus on physical sensations helpful for performance, and a focus on

TABLE 3 | Descriptive Statistics (M ± SD) of Study Variables across Experimental Schedules and Six Data Collections.

Variable	Schedule	Baseline	Isotime				
			0%	25%	50%	75%	100%
$\dot{V}O_2$ (ml/min)	Baseline	453 ± 96	2478 ± 368	3478 ± 673	3800 ± 669	3935 ± 684	3944 ± 679
	Low, external	432 ± 115	2470 ± 340	3454 ± 614	3833 ± 657	3980 ± 680	4036 ± 657
	Low, internal	462 ± 112	2439 ± 323	3428 ± 616	3777 ± 646	3938 ± 664	3949 ± 649
	High, external	435 ± 126	2488 ± 400	3522 ± 629	3835 ± 637	3989 ± 658	4025 ± 650
	High, internal	456 ± 167	2455 ± 362	3472 ± 654	3829 ± 643	3978 ± 670	4011 ± 656
	Follow-up	467 ± 93	2446 ± 372	3479 ± 601	3837 ± 588	3977 ± 597	4038 ± 559
RPE	Baseline	1.38 ± 0.98	3.06 ± 0.86	4.78 ± 1.18	6.24 ± 1.50	8.58 ± 1.88	8.70 ± 1.49
	Low, external	1.25 ± 0.68	3.14 ± 1.00	4.84 ± 1.46	6.44 ± 1.47	8.52 ± 1.44	8.42 ± 1.44
	Low, internal	1.27 ± 0.78	3.26 ± 1.34	5.44 ± 3.47	6.54 ± 1.44	8.52 ± 1.56	8.58 ± 0.95
	High, external	1.28 ± 0.78	2.99 ± 0.97	4.68 ± 1.35	6.32 ± 1.88	8.55 ± 1.28	8.55 ± 1.25
	High, internal	1.14 ± 0.71	2.73 ± 0.89	4.37 ± 1.33	6.10 ± 1.66	8.27 ± 1.96	8.70 ± 1.64
	Follow-up	1.22 ± 0.76	2.90 ± 0.95	4.58 ± 1.27	6.31 ± 1.18	8.60 ± 1.25	8.68 ± 1.28
Sleepiness-energy (arousal)	Baseline	6.50 ± 1.52	5.83 ± 1.17	5.22 ± 1.26	4.60 ± 1.59	3.66 ± 2.13	3.66 ± 2.13
	Low, external	6.44 ± 1.34	5.84 ± 1.12	5.29 ± 1.24	4.55 ± 1.43	3.38 ± 1.84	4.13 ± 2.15
	Low, internal	6.44 ± 1.19	6.01 ± 1.20	5.43 ± 1.25	4.82 ± 1.61	3.69 ± 1.51	3.69 ± 1.91
	High, external	6.69 ± 1.12	6.15 ± 1.03	5.57 ± 1.27	4.99 ± 1.52	4.00 ± 2.00	3.66 ± 1.64
	High, internal	6.69 ± 1.38	6.20 ± 1.07	5.66 ± 1.04	4.91 ± 1.44	3.91 ± 2.01	3.59 ± 1.62
	Follow-up	6.41 ± 1.19	5.99 ± 1.03	5.52 ± 1.07	4.81 ± 1.31	3.66 ± 1.79	3.69 ± 1.77
Displeasure-pleasure (hedonic tone)	Baseline	5.47 ± 1.54	4.92 ± 1.49	4.26 ± 1.68	3.83 ± 1.64	2.78 ± 1.62	2.78 ± 1.62
	Low, external	5.88 ± 1.93	5.04 ± 1.85	4.55 ± 1.99	3.98 ± 1.97	3.00 ± 1.61	3.00 ± 1.85
	Low, internal	5.56 ± 1.68	5.04 ± 1.71	4.67 ± 3.05	3.72 ± 1.95	2.72 ± 1.49	2.78 ± 1.29
	High, external	5.56 ± 1.72	4.97 ± 1.70	4.42 ± 1.81	3.96 ± 1.79	3.06 ± 1.70	3.41 ± 1.85
	High, internal	6.00 ± 1.41	5.37 ± 1.37	4.55 ± 1.52	3.84 ± 1.61	3.59 ± 2.17	2.78 ± 1.54
	Follow-up	5.76 ± 1.50	5.44 ± 1.42	5.03 ± 1.62	4.61 ± 1.76	3.63 ± 1.91	3.66 ± 1.93

TABLE 4 | Analysis of Variance Results across Experimental Schedules and Six Data Collections (Assessment).

Variables Effects	*F*(df)	*p*	η_p^2	Power
Manipulation check				
Experimental schedules	3.472 (2.618, 81.159)	0.025	0.101	0.716
Lactate				
Experimental schedules	1.102 (3.872, 120.017)	0.358	0.034	0.332
Performance				
Experimental schedules	0.377 (2.687, 83.307)	0.748	0.012	0.118
$\dot{V}O_2$max				
Experimental schedules	1.368 (4.286, 132.861)	0.246	0.042	0.433
Assessment	839.287 (1.238, 38.388)	< 0.001	0.964	1.000
Experimental × assessment	1.158 (10.600, 328.609)	0.101	0.049	0.796
RPE				
Experimental schedules	0.918 (1.518, 44.016)	0.386	0.031	0.178
Assessment	227.224 (1.575, 45.669)	< 0.001	0.887	1.000
Experimental × assessment	1.196 (1.216, 35.271)	0.291	0.038	0.195
Sleepiness-energy (arousal)				
Experimental schedules	0.982 (3.719, 115.298)	0.416	0.031	0.292
Assessment	48.137 (1.157, 35.863)	< 0.001	0.608	1.000
Experimental × assessment	1.375 (7.851, 243.392)	0.209	0.042	0.615
Displeasure-pleasure (hedonic tone)				
Experimental schedules	2.324 (3.903, 120.998)	0.062	0.070	0.652
Assessment	92.649 (1.566, 48.559)	< 0.001	0.749	1.000
Experimental × assessment	1.236 (8.006, 248.178)	0.278	0.038	0.566

Greenhouse-Geisser correction was applied to the degrees of freedom (df); η_p^2 = partial eta squared.

automated processes hampering performance. Results can also be interpreted in light of the reinvestment theory (Masters, 1992; Masters and Maxwell, 2008) and explicit monitoring theory (Beilock and Carr, 2001; Beilock, 2011), which contend that directing attention on movement execution hinders automaticity. In these views, detrimental effects are contended to derive from a voluntary control of movement automatisms. On the other hand, beneficial effects of an internal focus are supposed to be in function of conscious monitoring, which involves awareness of the course of action without necessarily changing it (van Ginneken et al., 2017).

Results of our study can also be understood within the MAP model conceptualization (Bortoli et al., 2012; Robazza et al., 2016) inasmuch as different levels of conscious monitoring (low or high) of the core components of the action typify Type 1 and Type 2 functional states for performance. In particular, a low level of conscious monitoring characterizes a Type 1 state, while a high level of monitoring is a facet of a Type 2 state. Type 3 and Type 4 dysfunctional states, not examined in this study, are assumed to either involve excessive attention toward the execution of an automated action (Type 3) or wandering attention (Type 4). It is therefore critical for optimal performance to identify the core components of the action, especially when executing demanding tasks or strenuous activities, dealing with novel problems, fatigue, and unexpected events, or performing under competitive pressure. Under these circumstances, reinvesting attention in the task can be inevitable (Masters and Maxwell, 2008) and beneficial, as long as the athlete is able to direct attention on previously identified core components of the action (Hanin and Hanina, 2009; Hanin et al., 2016).

According to the MAP perspective (Bortoli et al., 2012; Robazza et al., 2016), core components are not those highly automated elements of the technique that are consistently executed in different conditions without conscious attentional control. Core components are instead conceived as fundamental actions or action-related behaviors that fluctuate in accuracy especially under challenging situations. Examples of core components are "grip" and "aiming" in shooting sports (Bortoli et al., 2012; Robazza et al., 2016), "elbow alignment" and "attention on target" in dart-throwing (Bertollo et al., 2013), "acceleration after the curve" and "braking modulation" in racecar driving (Filho et al., 2015). In a TTE, endurance cycling activity (Bertollo et al., 2015; di Fronso et al., 2018), external pacing focusing attention on metronome beats and internal pacing directing attention to feet rhythm while pedaling represented two core components of the task associated with Type 1 and Type 2 performance, respectively. In our study alike, we used external pacing (i.e., metronome, bellows, and ball moving rhythm) and internal pacing (i.e., feet, breathing, and arms/shoulders rhythm) as core components of the endurance task to attain Type 1 and Type 2 optimal performance states. However, previous studies did not establish whether different levels of external or internal monitoring of the core components of the action influence performance differently. Findings of the current study suggest that both external and internal foci of attention to specific action elements of a treadmill endurance task, which can be considered core components, have same effect on performance, regardless of the low or high levels of monitoring.

The MAP model conceptualization of different states associated with optimal performance is akin to other theoretical views (for a review, see Robazza and Ruiz, 2018). For example, the default-interventionist framework (Evans and Stanovich, 2013), within the dual-process theories, maintains that human behavior is governed by both automatic and controlled modes of processing (see Furley et al., 2015; Furley and Wood, 2016). Accordingly, Type 1 (default) autonomous processing is "intuitive," does not rely on working memory and controlled attention, and enables fast and effortless behavioral responses initiated in the presence of relevant triggering conditions. In contrast, Type 2 (interventionist) controlled processing relies on working memory capacity, involves intentional behavior, and is appropriate when facing novel problems or new challenges. Expert performers can move between the two types of processing to cope with pressure and adapt to the competitive demands. Toner et al. (2016) expressed similar positions while discussing the pre-reflective and reflective modes of functioning in the Colombetti (2011) taxonomy of bodily self-awareness. Toner et al. argued that "some performers may be perfectly used to *monitoring* and *controlling* certain aspects of their movement in order to maintain performance proficiency." (p. 308, italic added). Swann et al. (2016, 2017a,b) also proposed that superior performance can be reached both in a flow state (a condition of effortless attention and automatic experience) and a clutch state attitude (an effortful condition with deliberate focus on the task), and that athletes can alternate from one state to the other during performance. The MAP model conceptualization also fits with the attentional control theory (Eysenck et al., 2007; Eysenck and Wilson, 2016), which distinguishes performance effectiveness (i.e., quality of performance) from processing efficiency (i.e., resources expended in the achievement process). Framed within the MAP model, performance effectiveness typifies Type 2 effortful performance (top-down control), while processing efficiency underlies Type 1 effortless performance (bottom-up control; Bertollo et al., 2016).

CONCLUSION

Findings of our study have both theoretical and practical implications. Construed within the MAP model and other theoretical approaches, the results support the notion that internal and external monitoring in endurance sports can be equally effective and important for athletes to self-regulate pacing and deal with mental and physical strain (Brick et al., 2014). Our findings suggest this claim holds true regardless the levels of voluntary monitoring are low or high. Athletes should identify their most effective inward (e.g., breathing rhythm) and outward (e.g., mile markers) attentional foci, and be able to alternate between them to adjust pacing in function of their mental state, physical condition, and current situation. Switching among different low/high and internal/external monitoring strategies might complement other associative and dissociative psychological strategies (e.g., goal setting, imagery, self-talk;

McCormick et al., 2015, 2018) aimed to manage inner states and situational demands.

Some limitations of the study should be acknowledged for future research. Individual strategies to deal with the endurance task were not examined prior to the study. These may explain the lack of performance improvements across the intervention in comparison to the baseline. Investigating already developed personal strategies and preferences can provide information on how to develop applied interventions to suit individual needs. Moreover, the focus of the study was on functional task monitoring. To avoid excessive burden on the participants, dysfunctional attention toward the control of action or unrelated tasks was not included. Future studies may consider manipulating attention to ensure that participants experience all four performance states as conceptualized in the MAP model (Bortoli et al., 2012; Robazza et al., 2016) or related multiple states (MuSt; Robazza and Ruiz, 2018) perspectives. Finally, other limitations are that the investigation was conducted in the laboratory and that the cognitive effort induced using the contextual interference paradigm may not have been high. More ecologically valid studies can establish what kind of monitoring strategies are more effective and transferable to the field.

AUTHOR CONTRIBUTIONS

All authors listed have made a substantial, direct and intellectual contribution to the work, and approved it for publication.

REFERENCES

American College of Sports Medicine (2018). *ACSACSM's Guidelines for Exercise Testing and Prescription, 10th EdnM's Guidelines for Exercise Testing and Prescription*, 10th Edn. Philadelphia, PA: Wolters Kluwer Health.

Beilock, S. L. (2011). *Choke. The Secret to Performing Under Pressure*. London: Constable & Robinson.

Beilock, S. L., and Carr, T. H. (2001). On the fragility of skilled performance: what governs choking under pressure? *J. Exp. Psychol. Gen.* 130, 701–725. doi: 10.1037/0096-3445.130.4.701

Bertollo, M., Bortoli, L., Gramaccioni, G., Hanin, Y., Comani, S., and Robazza, C. (2013). Behavioural and psychophysiological correlates of athletic performance: a test of the multi-action plan model. *Appl. Psychophysiol. Biofeedback* 38, 91–99. doi: 10.1007/s10484-013-9211-z

Bertollo, M., di Fronso, S., Filho, E., Conforto, S., Schmid, M., Bortoli, L., et al. (2016). Proficient brain for optimal performance: the MAP model perspective. *PeerJ* 4:e2082. doi: 10.7717/peerj.2082

Bertollo, M., di Fronso, S., Filho, E., Lamberti, V., Ripari, P., Reis, V. M., et al. (2015). To focus or not to focus: is attention on the core components of action beneficial for cycling performance? *Sport Psychol.* 29, 110–119. doi: 10.1123/tsp.2014-0046

Blanchfield, A. W., Hardy, J., and Marcora, S. M. (2014). Non-conscious visual cues related to affect and action alter perception of effort and endurance performance. *Front. Hum. Neurosci.* 8:967. doi: 10.3389/fnhum.2014.00967

Boccia, G., Dardanello, D., Tarperi, C., Festa, L., La Torre, A., Pellegrini, B., et al. (2018). Women show similar central and peripheral fatigue to men after half-marathon. *Eur. J. Sport Sci.* 8, 695–704. doi: 10.1080/17461391.2018.1442500

Borg, G. (1998). *Borg's Perceived Exertion and Pain Scales*. Champaign, IL: Human Kinetics.

Bortoli, L., Bertollo, M., Hanin, Y., and Robazza, C. (2012). Striving for excellence: a multi-action plan intervention model for shooters. *Psychol. Sport Exerc.* 13, 693–701. doi: 10.1016/j.psychsport.2012.04.006

Brick, N., MacIntyre, T., and Campbell, M. (2014). Attentional focus in endurance activity: new paradigms and future directions. *Int. Rev. Sport Exerc. Psychol.* 7, 106–134. doi: 10.1080/1750984X.2014.885554

Brick, N. E., Campbell, M. J., Metcalfe, R. S., Mair, J. L., and Macintyre, T. E. (2016a). Altering pace control and pace regulation: attentional focus effects during running. *Med. Sci. Sports Exerc.* 48, 879–886. doi: 10.1249/mss.0000000000000843

Brick, N. E., MacIntyre, T. E., and Campbell, M. J. (2016b). Thinking and action: a cognitive perspective on self-regulation during endurance performance. *Front. Physiol.* 7:159. doi: 10.3389/fphys.2016.00159

Buchanan, J. J., Park, I., Chen, J., Mehta, R. K., McCulloch, A., Rhee, J., et al. (2018). Expert monitoring and verbal feedback as sources of performance pressure. *Acta Psychol.* 186, 39–46. doi: 10.1016/j.actpsy.2018.04.009

Carson, H. J., and Collins, D. (2016). The fourth dimension: a motoric perspective on the anxiety–performance relationship. *Int. Rev. Sport Exerc. Psychol.* 9, 1–21. doi: 10.1080/1750984X.2015.1072231

Colombetti, G. (2011). Varieties of pre-reflective self-awareness: foreground and background bodily feelings in emotion experience. *Inquiry* 54, 293–313. doi: 10.1080/0020174X.2011.575003

di Fronso, S., Tamburro, G., Robazza, C., Bortoli, L., Comani, S., and Bertollo, M. (2018). Focusing attention on muscle exertion increases EEG coherence in an endurance cycling task. *Front. Psychol.* 9:1249. doi: 10.3389/fpsyg.2018.01249

Evans, J. S. B. T., and Stanovich, K. E. (2013). Dual-process theories of higher cognition: advancing the debate. *Perspect. Psychol. Sci.* 8, 223–241. doi: 10.1177/1745691612460685

Eysenck, M. W., Derakshan, N., Santos, R., and Calvo, M. G. (2007). Anxiety and cognitive performance: attentional control theory. *Emotion* 7, 336–353. doi: 10.1037/1528-3542.7.2.336

Eysenck, M. W., and Wilson, M. R. (2016). "Sporting performance, pressure and cognition-Introducing attentional control theory: sport," in *An Introduction to Applied Cognitive Psychology*, 2nd Edn, eds D. Groome and M. W. Eysenck (New York, NY: Routledge), 329–350.

Farrow, D., and Buszard, T. (2017). "Exploring the applicability of the contextual interference effect in sports practice," in *Sport and the Brain: The Science of Preparing, Enduring and Winning (Part B)*, eds M. R. Wilson, V. Walsh, and B. Parkin (Cambridge, MA: Academic Press), 69–83.

Faul, F., Erdfelder, E., Lang, A.-G., and Buchner, A. (2007). G*Power 3: a flexible statistical power analysis program for the social, behavioral, and biomedical sciences. *Behav. Res. Methods* 39, 175–191. doi: 10.3758/BF03193146

Filho, E., Di Fronso, S., Mazzoni, C., Robazza, C., Bortoli, L., and Bertollo, M. (2015). My heart is racing! Psychophysiological dynamics of skilled racecar drivers. *J. Sports Sci.* 33, 945–959. doi: 10.1080/02640414.2014.977940

Furley, P., Schweizer, G., and Bertrams, A. (2015). The two modes of an athlete: dual-process theories in the field of sport. *Int. Rev. Sport Exerc. Psychol.* 8, 106–124. doi: 10.1080/1750984X.2015.1022203

Furley, P., and Wood, G. (2016). Working memory, attentional control, and expertise in sports: a review of current literature and directions for future research. *J. Appl. Res. Mem. Cogn.* 5, 415–425. doi: 10.1016/j.jarmac.2016.05.001

Gardner, F. L., and Moore, Z. E. (2007). *The Psychology of Enhancing Human Performance: The Mindfulness-Acceptance-Commitment (MAC) Approach*. New York, NY: Springer. doi: 10.1891/9780826103369

Gropel, P. (2016). Self-focused attention and motor skill failure: the moderating role of action orientation. *Sport Exerc. Perform. Psychol.* 5, 206–217. doi: 10.1037/spy0000059

Hanin, Y., and Hanina, M. (2009). Optimization of performance in top-level athletes: an action-focused coping approach. *Int. J. Sports Sci. Coach.* 4, 47–58. doi: 10.1260/1747-9541.4.1.47

Hanin, Y., Hanina, M., Šašek, H., and Kobilšek, A. (2016). Emotion-centered and action-centered coping in elite sport: task execution design approach. *Int. J. Sports Sci. Coach.* 11, 566–588. doi: 10.1177/1747954116654782

Lohse, K., and Sherwood, D. (2011). Defining the focus of attention: effects of attention on perceived exertion and fatigue. *Front. Psychol.* 2:332. doi: 10.3389/fpsyg.2011.00332

Malhotra, N., Poolton, J. M., Wilson, M. R., Uiga, L., and Masters, R. S. W. (2015). Examining movement-specific reinvestment and performance in demanding contexts. *J. Sport Exerc. Psychol.* 37, 327–338. doi: 10.1123/jsep.2014-0220

Marcora, S. M., and Staiano, W. (2010). The limit to exercise tolerance in humans: mind over muscle? *Eur. J. Appl. Physiol.* 109, 763–770. doi: 10.1007/s00421-010-1418-6

Marcora, S. M., Staiano, W., and Manning, V. (2009). Mental fatigue impairs physical performance in humans. *J. Appl. Physiol.* 106, 857–864. doi: 10.1152/japplphysiol.91324.2008

Martin, K., Meeusen, R., Thompson, K. G., Keegan, R., and Rattray, B. (2018). Mental fatigue impairs endurance performance: a physiological explanation. *Sports Med.* 48, 2041–2051. doi: 10.1007/s40279-018-0946-9

Masters, R., and Maxwell, J. (2008). The theory of reinvestment. *Int. Rev. Sport Exerc. Psychol.* 1, 160–183. doi: 10.1080/17509840802287218

Masters, R. S. W. (1992). Knowledge, knerves and know-how: the role of explicit versus implicit knowledge in the breakdown of a complex motor skill under pressure. *Br. J. Psychol.* 83, 343–358. doi: 10.1111/j.2044-8295.1992.tb02446.x

McCormick, A., Meijen, C., Anstiss, P. A., and Jones, H. S. (2018). Self-regulation in endurance sports: theory, research, and practice. *Int. Rev. Sport Exerc. Psychol.* doi: 10.1080/1750984X.2018.1469161 [Epub ahead of print].

McCormick, A., Meijen, C., and Marcora, S. (2015). Psychological determinants of whole-body endurance performance. *Sports Med.* 45, 997–1015. doi: 10.1007/s40279-015-0319-6

McMorris, T., Barwood, M., and Corbett, J. (2018). Central fatigue theory and endurance exercise: toward an interoceptive model. *Neurosci. Biobehav. Rev.* 93, 93–107. doi: 10.1016/j.neubiorev.2018.03.024

Morgan, W. P., and Pollock, M. L. (1977). Psychologic characterization of the elite distance runner. *Ann. N. Y. Acad. Sci.* 301, 382–403. doi: 10.1111/j.1749-6632.1977.tb38215.x

Patterson, J. T., and Lee, T. D. (2008). "Organizing practice: the interaction of repetition and cognitive effort for skilled performance," in *Developing Sport Expertise: Researchers and Coaches put Theory into Practice*, eds D. Farrow, J. Baker, and C. MacMahon (New York, NY: Routledge), 119–134.

Pedrinolla, A., Li Volti, G., Galvano, F., Schena, F., Perciavalle, V., and Di Corrado, D. (2018). Bioenergetics and psychological profile of an ultra endurance walker. *J. Sports Med. Phys. Fit.* 58, 549–554. doi: 10.23736/S0022-4707.17.07088-8

Robazza, C., Bertollo, M., Filho, E., Hanin, Y., and Bortoli, L. (2016). Perceived control and hedonic tone dynamics during performance in elite shooters. *Res. Q. Exerc. Sport* 87, 284–294. doi: 10.1080/02701367.2016.1185081

Robazza, C., Izzicupo, P., D'Amico, M. A., Ghinassi, B., Crippa, M. C., Di Cecco, V., et al. (2018). Psychophysiological responses of junior orienteers under competitive pressure. *PLoS One* 13:e0196273. doi: 10.1371/journal.pone.0196273

Robazza, C., and Ruiz, M. C. (2018). Emotional self-regulation in sport and performance. *Oxford Res. Encycl. Psychol.* doi: 10.1093/acrefore/9780190236557.013.154 [Epub ahead of print].

Russell, J. A., Weiss, A., and Mendelsohn, G. A. (1989). Affect grid: a single-item scale of pleasure and arousal. *J. Pers. Soc. Psychol.* 57, 493–502. doi: 10.1037/0022-3514.57.3.493

Schücker, L., Fleddermann, M., de Lussanet, M., Elischer, J., Böhmer, C., and Zentgraf, K. (2016a). Focusing attention on circular pedaling reduces movement economy in cycling. *Psychol. Sport Exerc.* 27, 9–17. doi: 10.1016/j.psychsport.2016.07.002

Schücker, L., Schmeing, L., and Hagemann, N. (2016b). Look around while running! Attentional focus effects in inexperienced runners. *Psychol. Sport Exerc.* 27, 205–212. doi: 10.1016/j.psychsport.2016.08.013

Schücker, L., Knopf, C., Strauss, B., and Hagemann, N. (2014). An internal focus of attention is not always as bad as its reputation: how specific aspects of internally focused attention do not hinder running efficiency. *J. Sport Exerc. Psychol.* 36, 233–243. doi: 10.1123/jsep.2013-0200

Smits, B. L. M., Pepping, G. J., and Hettinga, F. J. (2014). Pacing and decision making in sport and exercise: the roles of perception and action in the regulation of exercise intensity. *Sports Med.* 44, 763–775. doi: 10.1007/s40279-014-0163-0

Stevinson, C. D., and Biddle, S. J. H. (1998). Cognitive orientations in marathon running and "hitting the wall". *Br. J. Sports Med.* 32, 229–234. doi: 10.1136/bjsm.32.3.229

Stevinson, C. D., and Biddle, S. J. H. (1999). Cognitive strategies in running: a response to Masters and Ogles (1998). *Sport Psychol.* 13, 235–236. doi: 10.1123/tsp.13.2.235

Swann, C., Crust, L., Jackman, P., Vella, S. A., Allen, M. S., and Keegan, R. (2017a). Psychological states underlying excellent performance in sport: toward an integrated model of flow and clutch states. *J. Appl. Sport Psychol.* 29, 375–401. doi: 10.1080/10413200.2016.1272650

Swann, C., Crust, L., and Vella, S. A. (2017b). New directions in the psychology of optimal performance in sport: flow and clutch states. *Curr. Opin. Psychol.* 16, 48–53. doi: 10.1016/j.copsyc.2017.03.032

Swann, C., Keegan, R., Crust, L., and Piggott, D. (2016). Psychological states underlying excellent performance in professional golfers: "Letting it happen" vs. "making it happen". *Psychol. Sport Exerc.* 23, 101–113. doi: 10.1016/j.psychsport.2015.10.008

Toner, J., Montero, B. G., and Moran, A. (2016). Reflective and prereflective bodily awareness in skilled action. *Psychol. Conscious.* 3, 303–315. doi: 10.1037/cns0000090

van Ginneken, W. F., Poolton, J. M., Masters, R. S. W., Capio, C. M., Kal, E. C., and van der Kamp, J. (2017). Comparing the effects of conscious monitoring and conscious control on motor performance. *Psychol. Sport Exerc.* 30, 145–152. doi: 10.1016/j.psychsport.2017.03.001

Wasserman, K., Stringer, W. W., Casaburi, R., Koike, A., and Cooper, C. B. (1994). Determination of the anaerobic threshold by gas-exchange: biochemical considerations, methodology and physiological-effects. *Z. Kardiol.* 83(Suppl. 3), 1–12.

Wulf, G. (2007). Attentional focus and motor learning: a review of 10 years of research. *Bewegung Train.* 1, 4–14.

Wulf, G. (2013). Attentional focus and motor learning: a review of 15 years. *Int. Rev. Sport Exerc. Psychol.* 6, 77–104. doi: 10.1080/1750984x.2012.723728

Wulf, G., and Lewthwaite, R. (2016). Optimizing performance through intrinsic motivation and attention for learning: the OPTIMAL theory of motor learning. *Psychon. Bull. Rev.* 23, 1382–1414. doi: 10.3758/s13423-015-0999-9

Wulf, G., McNevin, N., and Shea, C. H. (2001). The automaticity of complex motor skill learning as a function of attentional focus. *Q. J. Exp. Psychol. A* 54, 1143–1154. doi: 10.1080/02724980143000118

Zhang, C.-Q., Si, G., Duan, Y., Lyu, Y., Keatley, D. A., and Chan, D. K. C. (2016). The effects of mindfulness training on beginners' skill acquisition in dart throwing: a randomized controlled trial. *Psychol. Sport Exerc.* 22, 279–285. doi: 10.1016/j.psychsport.2015.09.005

6

How Consistent are Challenge and Threat Evaluations?

Lee J. Moore[1], Paul Freeman[2], Adrian Hase[2], Emma Solomon-Moore[1] and Rachel Arnold[1]*

[1] *Department for Health, University of Bath, Bath, United Kingdom,* [2] *School of Sport, Rehabilitation, and Exercise Sciences, University of Essex, Colchester, United Kingdom*

Correspondence:
Lee J. Moore
L.J.Moore@bath.ac.uk

Viewing stressful situations as more of a challenge than a threat (i.e., coping resources match or exceed situational demands) has been associated with better performance and long-term health. However, to date, little research has examined if individuals have tendencies to evaluate all stressful situations as more of a challenge or threat. Thus, this study used generalizability analyses to investigate the consistency (or variability) of challenge and threat evaluations across potentially stressful situations. 1813 roller derby players (89.0% female; $M_{age} = 33$ years, $SD = 7$) read nine stressful vignettes (e.g., injury, non-selection, family illness), before completing self-report items assessing challenge and threat evaluations. Generalizability analyses revealed that the Athlete × Stressor interaction accounted for the greatest amount of variance in challenge and threat evaluations (51.9%), suggesting that athletes had idiosyncrasies in their tendency to view particular stressors as more of a challenge or threat. The Athlete (15.4%) and Stressor (21.9%) components also accounted for a significant amount of variance. While the Athlete component suggested some consistency in challenge and threat evaluations, and that differences existed between athletes in whether they tended to view stressors as more of a challenge or threat, the Stressor component indicated some agreement among the athletes in their tendency to view some stressors as more of a challenge or threat than others. The findings offer direct support for transactional stress theories, and have important implications for practitioners developing stress management interventions.

Keywords: cognitive appraisals, demand and resource evaluations, generalizability theory, roller derby, stressors, stress appraisals, stress management, variance partitioning approaches

INTRODUCTION

Sport is inherently stressful, with athletes required to cope with the multiple demands they face during competition (e.g., high pressure), day-to-day training (e.g., coach conflict), and their personal lives (e.g., family duties; Fletcher et al., 2006). The ability to cope with stress is highly sought-after, and is a psychological skill that characterizes world-class athletes (e.g., Olympians; Gould et al., 2002). As such, researchers continue to develop interventions that help athletes manage stress (e.g., mindfulness; see Rumbold et al., 2012; Randall et al., 2019 for reviews). To aid intervention development, researchers have tested models that explain how athletes evaluate stressful situations, and whether these evaluations, and subsequent responses, vary between athletes and across situations (e.g., model for coping with acute stress in sports; Anshel, 2001). One theory that has gained recent attention, and is the focus of this study, is the biopsychosocial model (BPSM) of challenge and threat states (Blascovich, 2008a).

Akin to other transactional stress theories (e.g., cognitive appraisal theory; Lazarus and Folkman, 1984), the BPSM states that when faced with a stressful situation, an athlete evaluates the demands of the situation and whether they possess the resources to cope with those demands (Blascovich, 2008a). If an athlete perceives that they have sufficient resources, they evaluate the situation as a challenge. However, if an athlete perceives that they lack the resources, they evaluate the situation as a threat (Blascovich, 2008a). The BPSM argues that these evaluations trigger distinct physiological responses (Seery, 2011). Specifically, inspired by the theory of physiological toughness (Dienstbier, 1989), a challenge evaluation initiates sympathetic-adrenomedullary activation and the release of catecholamines (e.g., adrenaline), resulting in dilation of the blood vessels and increased blood flow (marked by reduced total peripheral resistance and elevated cardiac output). Conversely, a threat evaluation triggers pituitary-adrenocortical activation and the release of cortisol, causing little change or constriction of the blood vessels and little change or decreased blood flow (marked by little change or elevated total peripheral resistance and little change or reduced cardiac output; Seery, 2011). Despite their discrete labels, challenge and threat are not conceptualized as dichotomous states but anchors of a bipolar continuum, meaning that relative rather than absolute differences in challenge and threat are often examined (e.g., situation evaluated as more or less of a challenge or threat; Seery, 2011).

The BPSM posits that a challenge state should lead to better performance than a threat state (Blascovich, 2008a). Research has supported this assertion (see Behnke and Kaczmarek, 2018; Hase et al., 2018 for reviews), demonstrating that athletes perform more optimally when they evaluate situations as more of a challenge (resources match or exceed demands; e.g., Moore et al., 2013), and respond to situations with cardiovascular reactivity more consistent with a challenge state (reduced total peripheral resistance and elevated cardiac output; e.g., Turner et al., 2013). Beyond their short-term effects on performance, challenge and threat states are also thought to impact long-term health (Blascovich, 2008b). Indeed, repeatedly evaluating stressful situations as a threat has been linked with poor mental health (e.g., depression), and frequently responding to situations with more threat-like cardiovascular reactivity has been associated with heart disease (Blascovich, 2008b). Despite these important outcomes, little research has explored the consistency (or variability) of challenge and threat, and whether individuals have tendencies to evaluate all stressful situations as more of a challenge or threat. This is surprising given that psychometric tools assessing individual differences in challenge and threat have recently emerged (Tomaka et al., 2018), and that while limited, evidence has hinted that threat evaluations are moderately to highly consistent across situations (e.g., Power and Hill, 2010).

One approach that could help elucidate the consistency (or variability) of challenge and threat evaluations is generalizability theory (Cronbach et al., 1972). Generalizability theory is a variance partitioning approach that is used to examine within-person variation, and specifically person × situation interactions, or differences between individuals in their perceptions and responses across the same situations (see Lakey, 2016 for a review). Generalizability theory has been applied to a range of psychosocial constructs to understand if these constructs are features of the person, situation, or person × situation interactions (e.g., social support; Lakey, 2010). For instance, Endler and Hunt (1966, 1969) applied generalizability theory to anxiety, asking participants to rate their anxiety in response to various situations (e.g., giving a speech, long car drive). Person effects accounted for 8% of variance in anxiety, suggesting some participants reported more anxiety than others across the situations. In addition, situation effects accounted for 7% of variance, implying that some situations evoked more anxiety than others, across all participants. Finally, person × situation interactions accounted for 17% of variance, suggesting idiosyncrasies in anxiety responses, and that participants reported different levels of anxiety across situations (e.g., some participants rated the speech as more anxiety-provoking than the long car drive, while others rated the drive as more anxiety-provoking). Thus, both person and situation effects explained small but meaningful proportions of variance in anxiety, and their interaction represented the largest variance component, explaining twice as much variance as the individual components. Despite its potential to improve our understanding of stress responses, generalizability theory has rarely been applied to this psychosocial construct, possibly due to the conceptual and analytical complexities associated with this approach (Lakey, 2016).

To the authors' knowledge, to date, only one study has used generalizability theory in the stress literature (Lucas et al., 2012). Lucas and colleagues found that the stress appraisals of police officers were primarily comprised of person × situation interactions (38–41% of variance), although the person and situation effects were also significant (14–15 and 18–19% of variance, respectively). The findings offered direct support for transactional theories (e.g., cognitive appraisal theory; Lazarus and Folkman, 1984), which conceptualize stress as a psychosocial construct that emerges from interactions between the individual and their environment. Furthermore, the findings had implications for stress management interventions, highlighting that to be effective, such interventions should move beyond solely individual- or environment-based approaches, and instead take a conjoint approach that considers who is encountering what particular stressors (e.g., cognitive-behavioral strategies that allow individuals to acquire new skills that they can use to cope with the stressors that they find uniquely stressful; Giga et al., 2003). Therefore, by illuminating the relative importance of different sources of variance in stress responses (person, situation, or person × situation effects), generalizability analyses can offer a direct test of theory and have important implications for the creation of stress management interventions.

Using generalizability theory, this study investigated the consistency (or variability) of challenge and threat evaluations across potentially stressful situations. Although the athlete (person) and stressor (situation) effects were expected to be significant, with a greater athlete effect suggesting that challenge and threat evaluations were relatively consistent across stressful situations, it was predicted that the athlete × stressor (person × situation) interaction effect would also be significant and account for the greatest amount of variance in challenge and threat evaluations. This interaction effect would reflect unique matches between athletes and stressors, or idiosyncrasies in the tendency for athletes to view certain stressors as more of a challenge or threat. The same pattern of significant effects were also expected when demand and resource evaluations were examined separately.

METHODS

Participants

Roller derby players were recruited via advertisements and a link to the study posted on publicly available internet message boards (e.g., Facebook), and by emailing teams and asking them to share the link. In total, the link was opened 2628 times, with 2176 participants partially completing the survey, however, 363 were missing challenge and threat evaluation data for all stressful vignettes. Thus, the final sample consisted of 1813 participants (140 males, 1625 females, 48 preferred to self-describe; demographic and sport-specific characteristics are summarized in **Table 1**). Participants were aged between 18 and 78 years (M_{age} = 33 years, *SD* = 7), and had been playing roller derby for between 0 (less than 1 year) and 14 years ($M_{experience}$ = 4 years, *SD* = 2). All participants provided written informed consent in line with the Declaration of Helsinki.

TABLE 1 | Demographic and sport-specific characteristics of the participants (*n* = 1813).

	n	%
Gender		
Male	140	7.7
Female	1625	89.6
Preferred to self-describe	48	2.7
Nationality		
European	902	49.8
North American	787	43.4
Australian	81	4.5
Other (South American, Asian etc.)	15	0.8
Did not report	28	1.5
Competitive level		
International	155	8.6
Advanced	577	31.8
Intermediate	758	41.8
Rookie	322	17.8
Did not report	1	0.1

Procedure and Measures

Following institutional ethical approval, an online survey was created using Qualtrics software. The survey took ~15 min to complete. In the first part, participants reported demographic and sport-specific information (age, gender, nationality, competitive level, and playing experience). In the second part, participants read nine vignettes, each describing a potentially stressful situation (e.g., 'deselection,' 'family illness'; see section "Stressful Vignettes"). After reading each vignette, participants completed four self-report items, two from the cognitive appraisal ratio (CAR; Tomaka et al., 1993), and two from the stressor appraisal scale (SAS; Schneider, 2008). Specifically, to assess evaluations of situational demands in response to each vignette, participants were asked "how demanding would you find this situation?" (CAR), and "how stressful would you find this situation?" (SAS). Furthermore, to assess evaluations of coping resources, participants were asked "how well would you be able to cope with the demands of this situation?" (CAR), and "how well do you think you could manage the demands imposed on you in this situation?" (SAS). All items were rated on six-point Likert scales anchored between 1 (*not at all*) and 6 (*extremely*). The items were then converted into two demand resource evaluation scores (DRES). The first DRES score, termed DRES-CAR, was calculated by subtracting the first demands item ("how demanding would you find this situation?") from the first resources item ("how well would you be able to cope with the demands of this situation?"). The second DRES score, labeled DRES-SAS, was calculated by subtracting the second demands item ("how stressful would you find this situation?") from the second resources item ("how well do you think you could manage the demands imposed on you in this situation?"). Both DRES scores ranged from −5 to +5, with positive values reflecting challenge evaluations (resources match or exceed demands), and negative values reflecting threat evaluations (demands exceed resources; as Moore et al., 2018).

Stressful Vignettes

Inspired by research highlighting the stressors commonly experienced in sport (e.g., Arnold and Fletcher, 2012a; Sarkar and Fletcher, 2014), two subsets of potentially stressful vignettes were created (as Lucas et al., 2012). Two separate subsets were used to reduce the length of the survey (36 vs. 72 items), and thus improve completion rates and sample size. Each subset contained nine vignettes, with three describing competitive stressors (e.g., 'underperforming'), three outlining organizational stressors (e.g., 'travel'), and three describing personal stressors (e.g., 'relationship problems'). A diverse set of stressors was selected to offer a better test of the consistency (or variability) of challenge and threat evaluations compared to a more uniform set of stressors (e.g., competitive only). All stressors were processive rather than systemic (i.e., required cognitive processing vs. purely physiological in nature; Anisman, 2014). Participants were randomly assigned to one of the two subsets by the Qualtrics survey, and the order in which the vignettes were presented within each subset was also randomized. The content and wording of each vignette was developed by the lead researcher and edited to improve sport-specificity by another member of the research team who was an experienced roller derby coach. Additionally, each vignette was scrutinized by two other coaches to ensure that the content was relevant, and the length, tone, and focus were appropriate. Each vignette is presented in full in **Table 2**.

Statistical Analyses

Consistent with previous generalizability theory research (e.g., Lakey et al., 2010; Lucas et al., 2012), variance components analyses with restricted maximum likelihood estimation were conducted separately for DRES, demand evaluations, and resource evaluations in IBM SPSS statistics software (version 22). For each outcome, the analysis had an 1813 (Athletes) × 18 (Stressors) × 2 (Items) × 2 (Subsets) design. Stressors and Items were within-participants factors, and Athletes and Subsets were between-participants factors. However, because the design was not fully crossed (i.e., Stressors and Athletes nested within Subsets), estimates of variance related to Stressors were adjusted accordingly (by specifying nested terms; e.g., Stressors [Subsets] and Athletes [Subsets]). The highest order interaction term was confounded with error and variance not attributable to any measured effect or component (Shavelson and Webb, 1991). The Stressor [Subsets], Athlete [Subsets], and the Athlete × Stressor were the key components of interest, but others were also estimated (Items, Subsets, Item × Stressor, Item × Athlete, Item × Subset, and Athlete × Subset). The significance of all estimated sources of variance was examined using 95% confidence intervals, where significant sources did not include or cross zero. The components were considered significantly different from one another if their 95% confidence intervals did not overlap (Field, 2013). Each raw variance component was converted into a percentage of total variance to provide a more meaningful measure of effect size.

RESULTS

Descriptive Statistics

The descriptive DRES, demand evaluation, and resource evaluation data for each vignette are presented in **Table 3**, grouped by subset. On average, participants evaluated the vignettes entitled 'outcome pressure,' 'officials,' 'spectators,' 'missing friends and family,' 'relationship problems,' 'expectations,' 'selection,' 'travel,' and 'financial issues' as more of a challenge (resources match or exceed demands). Conversely, participants evaluated the vignettes entitled 'inadequate preparation,' 'injury,' 'coach's personality and behavior,' 'balancing training and work,' 'underperforming,' 'self-presentation,' 'teammate attitude,' 'family illness,' and 'death of a friend' as more of a threat (demands exceed resources). Indeed, 'teammate attitude' and 'underperforming' were evaluated as most demanding, whereas 'missing friends and family' and 'travel' were rated as least demanding. Moreover, participants evaluated that they were most able to cope with 'missing friends and family' and 'expectations,' but least able to cope with 'teammate attitude' and 'death of a friend.'

Demand Resource Evaluation Score

The percentages and significance of variance components for DRES are presented in **Table 4**. The Athlete × Stressor component (interaction effect) accounted for the greatest amount of variance in DRES (51.9%), suggesting that athletes had different profiles of challenge and threat evaluations across the same stressors. This interaction component accounted for a significantly greater amount of variance in DRES than the Athlete (15.4%) and Stressor (21.9%) components, although these were also significant. The Athlete component (person effect) implied that the athletes differed in whether they tended to view the stressors as more of a challenge or threat, regardless of the characteristics of the stressors. The Stressor component (situation effect) suggested some agreement among the athletes in their tendency to view some stressors as more of a challenge or threat than others. The variance attributable to the Athlete and Stressor components did not differ significantly.

Demand and Resource Evaluations

The percentages and significance of variance components for demand and resource evaluations, analyzed separately, are presented in **Table 4**. The Athlete × Stressor components accounted for the greatest amount of variance in both demand and resource evaluations (46.5 and 52.6%, respectively), suggesting that athletes had idiosyncrasies in their evaluations of how demanding the different stressors were, and their resources to cope with the stressors. These interaction components accounted for significantly greater amounts of variance in demand and resource evaluations than the Athlete (14.6 and 19.9%, respectively) and Stressor (20.1 and 14.8%, respectively) components, although these were also significant. The Athlete components imply that the athletes differed in how demanding they tended to view the stressors and their resources to cope with the stressors, regardless of the specific stressor characteristics. Conversely, the Stressor components suggest some agreement among the athletes in their tendency to view some stressors as more or less demanding than others, and that they had the resources to cope with some stressors better than others. The variance attributable to the Athlete and Stressor components did not differ significantly for either demand or resource evaluations.

DISCUSSION

Repeatedly viewing stressful situations as a threat (situational demands exceed coping resources) has been linked to negative health outcomes (e.g., depression; Blascovich, 2008b). However, it is not well-known if individuals have tendencies to evaluate all stressful situations as more of a challenge or threat (Power and Hill, 2010). Thus, this study aimed to shed light on this issue using generalizability theory (Cronbach et al., 1972). The generalizability analyses revealed differences between the athletes in their tendency to view stressors as more of a challenge or threat (athlete component), as well as some agreement among the athletes in their propensity to view some stressors as more of a challenge or threat than others (stressor component). Crucially, the results predominately indicated that athletes had

TABLE 2 | The potentially stressful vignettes (or stressors) used in the study, grouped by subset.

Subset 1	
Inadequate preparation (C)	Due to factors outside of your control, you have arrived at the venue with only 20 min until the start of your game and first whistle. . .you feel under prepared as you have had no time to hydrate, warm-up, or test the floor. . .to make matters worse, you missed the team talk where the coach/captain talked tactics. . .
Injury (C)	You are about to play against a team known for being particularly aggressive and deliberately trying to injure their opponents. . .when you last played this team, one of your teammates suffered a serious injury, breaking their ankle. . .you know that if this happens to you, you will be unable to work. . .
Outcome Pressure (C)	It is moments until the last game of your competitive season and you are in the final of a roller derby tournament. . .if you win, you will be crowned champions, lift the trophy, and climb the rankings. . .however, if you lose, you will have failed, watch your opponents lift the trophy, and drop in the rankings. . .
Coach's personality and behavior (O)	A new coach has just joined your roller derby team and is now your bench manager during games. . .you do not like their personality, you think they are arrogant and get too angry. . .you are warming-up before an important game and the new coach is shouting at the team, accusing you and your teammates of being lazy. . .
Officials (O)	It is 15 min into the second half of a 'must-win' game. . .in the middle of a fiercely contested and intense jam, you hear a whistle from the referee who calls your number and gives you a penalty. . .when skating off, you realize that the referee has wrongly sent you to the penalty box, calling a 'cutting' penalty against you. . .
Spectators (O)	You are about to start a jam midway through the first half of an away game. . .there is a large and raucous crowd watching, most of which are supporting your opponents. . .the crowd are chanting loudly for your opponents, jeering at you and your teammates, calling penalties against you, and hassling the referees. . .
Balancing training and work (P)	You have been struggling to juggle work and derby recently. . .work has become harder and you have had to work more hours, and as a result you have been unable to train and practice your skills. . .it is now moments before the first whistle of an important game for your roller derby team. . .
Missing friends and family (P)	You are homesick, and missing your close friends and family. . .you have been away at a roller derby tournament which is several hours from home, and have been staying in a hotel with teammates the last two nights. . .you are now stood on the track waiting for the final game of the long, 2-day, tournament to begin. . .
Relationship problems (P)	Your family normally watch all of your roller derby games, home or away. . .however, you had a big argument with a family member last week and you have not spoken to them since, and they have not come to support you today. . .you have just warmed-up and your important game is about to start. . .
Subset 2	
Underperforming (C)	It is half-time in an important game and you are not playing very well. . .you have already had six visits to the penalty box and you know that if you are given one more penalty you will foul out of the game. . .you feel like you have let yourself and your teammates down with your awful performance. . .
Expectations (C)	You are just about to play against a team ranked far lower than you in the rankings. . .you are expecting your team to win by a huge margin and know you need to do so in order to move up in the rankings. . .personally, you are expecting to put in a brilliant performance and win one of the individual awards. . .
Self-presentation (C)	You have been selected to play for your roller derby team in an important game. . .just before the game is about to start, your coach/captain tells you that they will be assessing your skills and evaluating your performance. . .the coach/captain is considering promoting you to a higher team, rotation, or position. . .
Teammate attitude (O)	You have one teammate who thinks they are superior to you and has a bad attitude. . .you are returning to the bench after making a mistake which resulted in your team losing the last jam. . .when you get to the bench, this teammate shouts at you in front of the team, telling you how bad you are and what you need to do. . .
Selection (O)	Your team have qualified for an important roller derby tournament. . .you have attended every training session recently and have been playing the best derby since you started skating. . .just before the first game of this tournament, your coach tells you that you have been selected as reserve, and you will play very few jams. . .
Travel (O)	You have finally arrived at the venue of an important game your team cannot afford to lose. . .you had to wake-up very early to catch the team bus and then spent hours on the bus fighting through heavy traffic to get to the venue. . .on the bus, you had to sit next to a new teammate you have hardly spoken to before. . .
Family illness (P)	Your parents often come to watch and support you during your roller derby games, home or away. . .however, one of your parents has recently been diagnosed with a serious illness and so they are not there to watch you today. . .it is now seconds before the final game of the season and a game your team must win. . .
Death of a friend (P)	You have had an emotional and difficult few weeks leading up to an important game for your roller derby team. . .unfortunately, one of your best friends died recently in a sudden and tragic accident. . .you are now on the track moments before the first whistle of a crucial game for your roller derby team. . .
Financial issues (P)	The last couple of months have been challenging and difficult for you. . .a number of unexpected bills have left you struggling with your finances recently, plummeting you into large amounts of debt. . .you are now warming-up and practicing your skills before the final game of a large roller derby tournament. . .

C, competitive stressor; O, organizational stressor; P, personal stressor.

idiosyncrasies in their tendency to view particular stressors as more of a challenge or threat (athlete × stressor interaction), with the interaction component explaining twice as much variance as each of the individual components. The same pattern of results emerged when demand and resource evaluations were analyzed separately.

TABLE 3 | Mean (SD) demand resource evaluation score (DRES), demand evaluation, and resource evaluation data for the different potentially stressful vignettes (or stressors), grouped by subset (*n* = 1813).

	DRES (−5 to +5)		Demands (1 to 6)		Resources (1 to 6)	
	DRES-CAR	**DRES-SAS**	**CAR**	**SAS**	**CAR**	**SAS**
Subset 1 (*n* = 919)						
Inadequate preparation (C)	−0.81 (2.06)	−0.93 (2.04)	4.60 (1.27)	4.70 (1.28)	3.79 (1.11)	3.77 (1.10)
Injury (C)	−0.41 (2.13)	−0.41 (2.17)	4.35 (1.35)	4.34 (1.37)	3.93 (1.14)	3.93 (1.14)
Outcome pressure (C)	0.03 (1.78)	0.28 (1.86)	4.38 (1.35)	4.09 (1.33)	4.40 (0.95)	4.36 (0.95)
Coach's personality and behavior (O)	−1.21 (2.21)	−1.24 (2.21)	4.64 (1.33)	4.65 (1.34)	3.43 (1.26)	3.41 (1.24)
Officials (O)	1.21 (2.20)	1.06 (2.26)	3.32 (1.44)	3.42 (1.45)	4.54 (1.12)	4.48 (1.19)
Spectators (O)	1.12 (2.25)	1.20 (2.22)	3.35 (1.50)	3.22 (1.46)	4.46 (1.09)	4.42 (1.10)
Balancing training and work (P)	−0.19 (1.82)	−0.05 (1.92)	4.14 (1.23)	3.96 (1.27)	3.94 (1.00)	3.91 (0.99)
Missing friends and family (P)	2.17 (2.13)	2.50 (1.94)	2.73 (1.48)	2.35 (1.24)	4.90 (0.95)	4.86 (0.99)
Relationship problems (P)	1.35 (2.35)	1.29 (2.34)	3.11 (1.48)	3.15 (1.49)	4.46 (1.16)	4.43 (1.15)
Subset 1 Mean	0.36 (2.10)	0.41 (2.11)	3.84 (1.38)	3.77 (1.36)	4.21 (1.09)	4.17 (1.09)
Subset 2 (*n* = 894)						
Underperforming (C)	−1.26 (1.85)	−1.26 (1.90)	4.78 (1.13)	4.73 (1.16)	3.52 (1.13)	3.47 (1.11)
Expectations (C)	1.52 (2.06)	1.83 (2.00)	3.20 (1.46)	2.83 (1.33)	4.73 (0.97)	4.67 (1.01)
Self-presentation (C)	−0.12 (2.06)	0.04 (2.17)	4.32 (1.38)	4.13 (1.42)	4.20 (1.09)	4.17 (1.10)
Teammate attitude (O)	−1.41 (2.41)	−1.48 (2.45)	4.73 (1.41)	4.84 (1.36)	3.32 (1.43)	3.35 (1.45)
Selection (O)	0.59 (2.50)	0.49 (2.50)	3.42 (1.60)	3.58 (1.60)	4.00 (1.34)	4.07 (1.33)
Travel (O)	1.77 (2.41)	1.71 (2.38)	2.89 (1.56)	2.90 (1.55)	4.66 (1.13)	4.61 (1.13)
Family illness (P)	−0.08 (2.40)	0.06 (2.39)	4.02 (1.50)	3.92 (1.51)	3.95 (1.28)	3.98 (1.24)
Death of a friend (P)	−1.36 (2.40)	−1.08 (2.47)	4.69 (1.37)	4.43 (1.47)	3.33 (1.39)	3.35 (1.37)
Financial issues (P)	0.89 (2.20)	0.79 (2.25)	3.42 (1.47)	3.50 (1.51)	4.31 (1.11)	4.30 (1.08)
Subset 2 Mean	0.06 (2.26)	0.12 (2.28)	3.94 (1.43)	3.87 (1.43)	4.00 (1.21)	4.00 (1.20)

C, competitive stressor; O, organizational stressor; P, personal stressor; CAR, cognitive appraisal ratio; SAS, stressor appraisal scale.

The athlete component (person effect), or amount of variance in challenge and threat evaluations due to differences between athletes, was a significant, but also comparatively limited, source of variance. This result is congruent with previous research (e.g., Lucas et al., 2012), and has two contradictory implications. On one hand, the significant athlete component supports the notion that challenge and threat evaluations are, to some extent, relatively consistent across stressful situations, meaning that psychometric tools that assess individual differences in challenge and threat evaluations hold some merit (e.g., Tomaka et al., 2018). Indeed, such tools are likely to be useful for practitioners interested in selecting 'challenge responders' in high-pressure domains (e.g., medicine; Roberts et al., 2015), and researchers looking to monitor the long-term health of serial 'threat responders' (O'Donovan et al., 2012). On the other hand, the variance attributable to the athlete component was smaller than the other hypothesized components, which corroborates the often-cited concern that stress management interventions that overly rely on individual-based approaches, and ignore the specific environmental demands encountered by individuals, are less likely to be effective (only reflecting 'damage limitation'), despite their ease of implementation and widespread popularity (Giga et al., 2003). Indeed, these approaches shift responsibility from the organization to the individual (Cooper et al., 2001), and would need careful consideration before being implemented in elite sport given the obligations that sport organizations have to safeguard athlete welfare [see UK Government's, 2017; Duty of Care in Sport Review (Stevenson and Farmer, 2017)].

The stressor component (situation effect), or amount of variance in challenge and threat evaluations attributable to differences between stressors, was also a significant source of variance. Although sport- and sample-specific (i.e., female roller derby players), this result suggests that some stressors were more likely to be evaluated as a challenge (e.g., 'high expectations'), while others were more likely to be seen as a threat (e.g., 'negative coach behavior'), by all athletes. Interestingly, and in-keeping with prior research (e.g., Lucas et al., 2012), the stressor component was larger than the athlete component (albeit not significantly). This trend has implications for stress management interventions, and implies that interventions could be more effective if they focus on the environment rather than exclusively on the individual, an approach that is rarely adopted (Giga et al., 2003). For instance, armed with a list of stressors that athletes tend to evaluate as a threat (e.g., 'inadequate preparation,' 'disruptive teammate'), practitioners could change the environment by altering particular features of these stressors (e.g., frequency, intensity, duration; Arnold and Fletcher, 2012b), or by removing the stressors altogether. However, despite such environment-based interventions being able to impact more athletes and having longer-lasting effects (Arnold et al., 2017), these interventions can be disruptive and difficult to implement logistically (Cooper, 2015), especially given that some stressors

TABLE 4 | Percentages of variance and significance of DRES, demand evaluations, and resource evaluations.

Source	σ^2	% σ^2	95% CI
DRES			
Subset	0.00	0.00	N/A
Stressor (Subset)	1.36	21.89	(0.44, 2.27)*
Athlete (Subset)	0.95	15.37	(0.86, 1.04)*
Item	0.00	0.00	N/A
Athlete × Subset	0.00	0.00	N/A
Item × Subset	0.00	0.00	N/A
Athlete × Stressor	3.21	51.90	(3.13, 3.29)*
Stressor × Item	0.02	0.24	(0.00, 0.00)
Athlete × Item	0.05	0.81	(0.04, 0.06)*
Error	0.61	9.78	(0.59, 0.62)*
Demands			
Subset	0.00	0.00	N/A
Stressor (Subset)	0.50	20.07	(0.16, 0.84)*
Athlete (Subset)	0.36	14.58	(0.33, 0.40)*
Item	0.00	0.00	N/A
Athlete × Subset	0.00	0.00	N/A
Item × Subset	0.00	0.00	N/A
Athlete × Stressor	1.16	46.50	(1.13, 1.19)*
Stressor × Item	0.01	0.53	(0.00, 0.00)
Athlete × Item	0.04	1.70	(0.04, 0.05)*
Error	0.42	16.64	(0.40, 0.42)*
Resources			
Subset	0.00	0.00	N/A
Stressor (Subset)	0.23	14.76	(0.07, 0.39)*
Athlete (Subset)	0.31	19.94	(0.29, 0.34)*
Item	0.00	0.00	N/A
Athlete × Subset	0.00	0.00	N/A
Item × Subset	0.00	0.00	N/A
Athlete × Stressor	0.83	52.63	(0.80, 0.85)*
Stressor × Item	0.00	0.00	(0.00, 0.00)
Athlete × Item	0.01	0.50	(0.01, 0.01)*
Error	0.19	12.20	(0.19, 0.20)*

*Confidence intervals that do not cross zero indicate significant sources of variance (two-tailed $p < 0.05$). Components with a * indicate significant sources of variance. Parentheses in the source column indicate that a component is nested within subsets.*

are uncontrollable from a practitioner's perspective (e.g., 'travel disruptions'). In the case of such unpredictable stressors, "what if" planning might prove a more viable strategy than trying to alter or remove the stressor (Karageorghis and Terry, 2011). Indeed, some researchers have argued against 'sheltering' athletes from stressors, instead noting the benefits associated with experiencing, and learning from, stressors (Collins et al., 2016).

The athlete × stressor interaction accounted for the greatest amount of variance in challenge and threat evaluations, significantly more than the athlete and stressor components, which is in-line with previous research that has reported large person × situation interaction effects for other psychosocial constructs (e.g., anxiety, social support; Lakey, 2016). Furthermore, this result offers direct support for transactional stress theories (e.g., cognitive appraisal theory; Lazarus and Folkman, 1984), which state that stress-related perceptions result from an exchange between the person and their environment. Indeed, the findings illustrate that whether a stressor is evaluated as a challenge or threat largely depends on who, specifically, is considering what particular stressor (Lucas et al., 2012). That is, athletes have different profiles of challenge and threat evaluations across the same stressors. For example, while one athlete might evaluate non-selection as more of a threat than an official's poor decision, another might evaluate an official's erroneous decision as more of a threat than non-selection. Although the significant athlete and stressor components imply that stress management interventions that focus solely on the individual or environment might be effective, the large interaction suggests that interventions are more likely to be beneficial if they adopt a conjoint approach (Giga et al., 2003). For instance, practitioners could equip athletes with individualized coping strategies that they can use when faced with the stressors that they find uniquely threatening (e.g., arousal reappraisal; Jamieson et al., 2018), while also working with sport organizations to alter or remove the stressors that each athlete finds particularly threatening (e.g., make selection process more objective, transparent, fair). Indeed, this approach would ensure that athletes and sport organizations are jointly responsible for managing stress (Rumbold et al., 2018).

Despite its novel methodology and important implications, this study has several limitations. First, the data was collected from a predominately female sample and single sport. While focusing on one sport helped create more specific vignettes that could be considered by all participants, it restricted the number of male participants and limited the generalizability of the results. Research suggests that females may be more likely to evaluate stressful situations as a threat than males (e.g., Quigley et al., 2002), thus, future research should test whether the sources of variance in challenge and threat revealed in this study hold for male-dominated samples and other sports. Second, some participants failed to fully complete the survey (~17%), and therefore the results might have been influenced by non-completion bias (Mishra et al., 1993). Third, only self-report measures were used to assess challenge and threat. While this ensured data could be collected from a large athletic sample from all over the world, objective cardiovascular measures of challenge and threat are thought to be more accurate, unambiguous, and bias-free (Blascovich and Mendes, 2000; see Brimmell et al., 2018 for a recent application). Thus, future research should use generalizability analyses to uncover the consistency (or variability) of the cardiovascular markers of challenge and threat (total peripheral resistance and cardiac output reactivity), although this might be best achieved by asking participants to react to actual, rather than hypothetical, stressors. Indeed, the findings from such research could have important implications given that repeatedly reacting to stressful situations with a threat-like cardiovascular response has been linked to heart disease (Blascovich, 2008b).

To conclude, this study used generalizability theory to investigate the consistency (or variability) of challenge and threat evaluations across potentially stressful situations. The results revealed that the challenge and threat evaluations of athletes primarily comprised athlete × stressor interactions, suggesting that athletes had idiosyncrasies in their tendency to view certain stressors as a challenge or threat. The findings offer direct support for transactional stress theory, and imply that stress management interventions are more likely to be effective if they adopt a conjoint approach, equipping athletes with coping skills they can use when faced with the stressors they find particularly threatening, while simultaneously working with sport organizations to alter or remove these stressors.

ETHICS STATEMENT

This study was carried out in accordance with the code of ethics and conduct published by the British Psychological Society. The study protocol was approved by the Research Ethics Approval Committee for Health (REACH) at the University of Bath.

AUTHOR CONTRIBUTIONS

LM and ES-M led data collection, while PF and AH led data analysis. Finally, all authors contributed to the preparation of the study and writing of the manuscript.

REFERENCES

Anisman, H. (2014). *An Introduction to Stress and Health.* London: Sage.

Anshel, M. H. (2001). Qualitative validation of a model for coping with acute stress in sports. *J. Sport. Behav.* 24, 223–247.

Arnold, R., and Fletcher, D. (2012a). A research synthesis and taxonomic classification of the organizational stressors encountered by sport performers. *J. Sport. Exercise. Psy.* 34, 397–429. doi: 10.1123/jsep.34.3.397

Arnold, R., and Fletcher, D. (2012b). Psychometric issues in organizational stressor research: a review and implications for sport psychology. *Meas. Phys. Educ. Exercise. Sci.* 16, 81–100. doi: 10.1080/1091367X.2012.639608

Arnold, R., Fletcher, D., and Daniels, K. (2017). Organizational stressors, coping, and outcomes in competitive sport. *J. Sport. Sci.* 35, 694–703. doi: 10.1080/02640414.2016.1184299

Behnke, M., and Kaczmarek, L. D. (2018). Successful performance and cardiovascular markers of challenge and threat: a meta-analysis. *Int. J. Psychophysiol.* 130, 73–79. doi: 10.1016/j.ijpsycho.2018.04.007

Blascovich, J. (2008a). "Challenge and threat" in *Handbook of Approach and Avoidance Motivation,* ed. A.J. Elliot (New York, NY: Psychology Press), 431–445.

Blascovich, J. (2008b). "Challenge, threat, and health," in *Handbook of Motivation Science,* eds J. Y. Shah and W. L. Gardner (New York, NY: Guildford Press), 481–493.

Blascovich, J., and Mendes, W. B. (2000). "Challenge and threat appraisals: the role of affective cues," in *Feeling and Thinking: The Role of Affect in Social Cognition,* ed. J. P. Forgas (Paris: Cambridge University Press), 59–82.

Brimmell, J., Parker, J., Furley, P., and Moore, L. J. (2018). Nonverbal behavior accompanying challenge and threat states under pressure. *Psychol. Sport. Exercise.* 39, 90–94. doi: 10.1016/j.psychsport.2018.08.003

Collins, D. J., MacNamara, A., and McCarthy, N. (2016). Putting the bumps in the rocky road: Optimizing the pathway to excellence. *Front. Psychol.* 7:1482. doi: 10.3389/fpsyg.2016.01482

Cooper, C. L. (2015). "Stress management interventions: reflections," in *Derailed Organizational Interventions for Stress and Well-Being,* eds M. Karanika and C. Biron (Dordrecht: Springer), 271–273. doi: 10.1007/978-94-017-9867-9_31

Cooper, C. L., Dewe, P. J., and O'Driscoll, M. P. (2001). *Organizational Stress: A Review and Critique of Theory, Research, and Applications.* Thousand Oaks, CA: Sage Publications.

Cronbach, L. J., Gleser, G. C., Nanda, H., and Rajaratnam, N. (1972). *The Dependability of Behavioral Measurements: Theory of Generalizability for Scores and Profiles.* New York, NY: John Wiley & Sons.

Dienstbier, R. A. (1989). Arousal and physiological toughness: implications for mental and physical health. *Psychol. Rev.* 96, 84–100. doi: 10.1037/0033-295X.96.1.84

Endler, N. S., and Hunt, J. M. (1966). Sources of behavioral variance as measured by the S-R inventory of anxiousness. *Psychol. Bull.* 65, 336–346. doi: 10.1037/h0023309

Endler, N. S., and Hunt, J. M. (1969). Generalizability of contributions from sources of variance in the S-R inventories of anxiousness. *J. Pers.* 37, 1–24. doi: 10.1111/j.1467-6494.1969.tb01728

Field, A. (2013). *Discovering Statistics Using SPSS,* 4th Edn. Washington, DC: Sage.

Fletcher, D., Hanton, S., and Mellalieu, S. D. (2006). "An organizational stress review: conceptual and theoretical issues in competitive sport," in *Literature Reviews in Sport Psychology*, eds S. Hanton and S. D. Mellalieu (New York, NY: Nova Science), 321–374.

Giga, S. I., Cooper, C. L., and Faragher, B. (2003). The development of a framework for a comprehensive approach to stress management interventions at work. *Int. J. Stress. Manage.* 10, 280–296. doi: 10.1037/1072-5245.10.4.280

Gould, D., Dieffenbach, K., and Moffett, A. (2002). Psychological characteristics and their development in Olympic champions. *J. Appl. Sport Psychol.* 14, 172–204. doi: 10.1080/10413200290103482

Hase, A., O'Brien, J., Moore, L. J., and Freeman, P. (2018). The relationship between challenge and threat states and performance: a systematic review. *Sport. Exerc. Perform.* 8, 123–144. doi: 10.1037/spy0000132

Jamieson, J. P., Crum, A. J., Goyer, J. P., Marotta, M. E., and Akinola, M. (2018). Optimizing stress responses with reappraisal and mindset interventions: an integrated model. *Anxiety. Stress. Copin.* 31, 245–261. doi: 10.1080/10615806.2018.1442615

Karageorghis, C., and Terry, P. (2011). *Inside Sport Psychology*. Champaign, IL: Human Kinetics.

Lakey, B. (2010). "Social-clinical approaches to social support suggest new strategies for intervention," in *Social Psychological Foundations of Clinical Psychology*, eds J. E. Maddux and J. P. Tangney (New York, NY: Guilford Press), 177–194.

Lakey, B. (2016). Understanding the P×S aspect of within-person variation: a variance partitioning approach. *Front. Psychol.* 6:2004. doi: 10.3389/fpsyg.2015.02004

Lakey, B., Orehek, E., Hain, K., and van Vleet, M. (2010). Enacted support's links to negative affect and perceived support are more consistent with theory when social influences are isolated from trait influences. *Pers. Soc. Psychol. B.* 36, 132–142. doi: 10.1177/0146167209349375

Lazarus, R. S., and Folkman, S. (1984). *Stress, Appraisal, and Coping*. New York, NY: Springer.

Lucas, T., Weidner, N., and Janisse, J. (2012). Where does work stress come from? A generalizability analysis of stress in police officers. *Psychol. Health.* 27, 1426–1447. doi: 10.1080/08870446.2012.687738

Mishra, S. I., Dooley, D., Catalano, R., and Serxner, S. (1993). Telephone health surveys: potential bias from noncompletion. *Am. J. Public. Health.* 83, 94–99. doi: 10.2105/AJPH.83.1.94

Moore, L. J., Wilson, M. R., Vine, S. J., Coussens, A. H., and Freeman, P. (2013). Champ or chump? Challenge and threat states during pressurized competition. *J. Sport. Exercise. Psy.* 35, 551–562. doi: 10.1123/jsep.35.6.551

Moore, L. J., Young, T., Freeman, P., and Sarkar, M. (2018). Adverse life events, cardiovascular responses, and sports performance under pressure. *Scand. J. Med. Sci. Spor.* 28, 340–347. doi: 10.1111/sms.12928

O'Donovan, A., Tomiyama, A. J., Lin, J., Puterman, E., Adler, N. E., Kemeny, M., et al. (2012). Stress appraisals and cellular aging: a key role for anticipatory threat in the relationship between psychological stress and telomere length. *Brain. Behav. Immun.* 26, 573–579. doi: 10.1016/j.bbi.2012.01.007

Power, T. G., and Hill, L. G. (2010). Individual differences in appraisal of minor, potentially stressful events: a cluster analytic approach. *Cognition. Emotion.* 24, 1081–1094. doi: 10.1080/02699930903122463

Quigley, K. S., Barrett, L. F., and Weinstein, S. (2002). Cardiovascular patterns associated with threat and challenge appraisals: a within-subjects analysis. *Psychophysiology.* 39, 292–302. doi: 10.1017/S0048577201393046

Randall, R., Nielsen, K., and Houdmont, J. (2019). Process evaluation for stressor reduction interventions in sport. *J. Appl. Sport. Psychol.* 31, 47–64. doi: 10.1080/10413200.2018.1480544

Roberts, M. J., Gale, T. E., McGrath, J. S., and Wilson, M. R. (2015). Rising to the challenge: acute stress appraisals and selection centre performance in applicants to postgraduate specialty training in anaesthesia. *Adv. Health. Sci. Educ.* 21, 323–339. doi: 10.1007/s10459-015-9629-6

Rumbold, J., Fletcher, D., and Daniels, K. (2012). A systematic review of stress management interventions with sport performers. *Sport. Exercise. Perform.* 1, 173–193. doi: 10.1037/a0026628

Rumbold, J., Fletcher, D., and Daniels, K. (2018). Using a mixed method audit to inform organizational stress management interventions in sport. *Psychol. Sport. Exercise.* 35, 27–38. doi: 10.1016/j.psychsport.2017.10.010

Sarkar, M., and Fletcher, D. (2014). Psychological resilience in sport performers: a review of stressors and protective factors. *J. Sport. Sci.* 32, 1419–1434. doi: 10.1080/02640414.2014.901551

Schneider, T. R. (2008). Evaluations of stressful transactions: what's in an appraisal? *Stress. Health.* 24, 151–158. doi: 10.1002/smi.1176

Seery, M. D. (2011). Challenge or threat? Cardiovascular indexes of resilience and vulnerability to potential stress in humans. *Neurosci. Biobehav. R.* 35, 1603–1610. doi: 10.1016/j.neubiorev.2011.03.003

Shavelson, R. J., and Webb, N. M. (1991). *Generalizability Theory: A Primer*. Newbury Park: Sage.

Stevenson, D., and Farmer, P. (2017). *Thriving at Work: A Review of Mental Health and Employers*. Available at: https://www.gov.uk/government/publications/thriving-at-work-a-review-of-mental-health-and-employers (accessed April 8, 2019).

Tomaka, J., Blascovich, J., Kelsey, R. M., and Leitten, C. L. (1993). Subjective, physiological, and behavioral effects of threat and challenge appraisal. *J. Pers. Soc. Psychol.* 65, 248–260. doi: 10.1037/0022-3514.65.2.248

Tomaka, J., Palacios, R. L., Champion, C., and Monks, S. (2018). Development and validation of an instrument that assesses individual differences in threat and challenge appraisal. *J. Depression. Anxiety.* 7, 1–10. doi: 10.4172/2167-1044.1000313

Turner, M. J., Jones, M. V., Sheffield, D., Slater, M. J., Barker, J. B., and Bell, J. J. (2013). Who thrives under pressure? Predicting the performance of elite academy cricketers using the cardiovascular indicators of challenge and threat states. *J. Sport. Exerc. Psy.* 35, 387–397. doi: 10.1123/jsep.35.4.387

UK Government's (2017). *Duty of Care in Sport Review*. Available at: https://www.gov.uk/government/publications/duty-of-care-in-sport-review (accessed April 8, 2019).

7

Mindful Sensation Seeking: An Examination of the Protective Influence of Selected Personality Traits on Risk Sport-Specific Stress

Marie Ottilie Frenkel[1]*, Joana Brokelmann[2], Arne Nieuwenhuys[3,4], Robin-Bastian Heck[1], Christian Kasperk[5], Martin Stoffel[6] and Henning Plessner[1]

[1] Institute of Sports and Sports Sciences, Heidelberg University, Heidelberg, Germany, [2] Psychological Institute, Goethe University Frankfurt, Frankfurt, Germany, [3] Department of Exercise Sciences, The University of Auckland, Auckland, New Zealand, [4] Behavioural Science Institute, Radboud University, Nijmegen, Netherlands, [5] Department of Internal Medicine I and Clinical Chemistry, Steroid Laboratory, University Hospital Heidelberg, Heidelberg, Germany, [6] Institute of Medical Psychology, University Hospital Heidelberg, Heidelberg, Germany

***Correspondence:**
Marie Ottilie Frenkel
marie.frenkel@issw.uni-heidelberg.de

Stress often has a negative influence on sports performance. Stress-induced decreases in performance can be especially disastrous for risk sports athletes, who often put their life at risk when practicing their sport. Therefore, it is of great importance to identify protective factors in stressful situations in risk sports. On average, risk sports athletes score extremely high on the personality trait sensation seeking. At the same time, theoretical considerations about dispositional mindfulness suggest that mindful athletes can handle stress more effectively. The main goal of this experiment is to examine the influence of sensation seeking and mindfulness on the stress response to a risk sport-specific stressor. To induce stress, 88 male students completed the Heidelberg Risk Sport-Specific Stress Test (HRSST) which utilizes fear of falling as the stressful event during a climbing exercise. Psychological (anxiety) and physiological (cortisol) responses were measured at multiple time points before and after the HRSST to determine the severity of the stress response. In reaction to the stressor, a significant increase in self-reported state anxiety, but no significant increase in cortisol were observed. The mindfulness subscale *external observation* correlated positively with anxiety in the climbing wall, sensation seeking and the anxiety scales after the jump correlated negatively and sensation seeking predicted anxiety subscales after the jump in hierarchical regression analyses. However, mindfulness did not predict anxiety measures. Neither sensation seeking nor mindfulness correlated significantly with cortisol levels. The results suggest that high sensation seekers perceive a risk sport-specific stressor as less stressful. The missing physiological response might be explained by the Cross-Stressor-Adaptation-Hypothesis and particularities of the sample. Good internal observers might be especially aware of their need of stimulation and new experiences, which in turn might explain the higher experience-seeking scores.

Future studies should further examine the role of mindfulness in stressful situations and the interaction of its subscales with sensation seeking. The current experiment offers new possibilities for adjoining research fields at the interface between sports sciences, psychology and medicine: The findings can be transferred to high risk professions such as police officers, firefighters and military forces (e.g., for selection processes or for interventions).

Keywords: mindfulness, anxiety, cortisol, sensation seeking, risk sport-specific stress

INTRODUCTION

Athletes plunge from mountains only wearing a wingsuit, free climbers scale high rock faces without any form of protection, and surfers aim to ride huge waves before they break the shores. High risk sports athletes who practice those demanding activities frequently set their physical integrity at risk, making it crucial to deliver peak-performance. Typically, highly demanding situations induce distress and therefore threaten peak performance-delivery (Paulus et al., 2009; Röthlin et al., 2016). In contrast, however, some risk sports athletes are known to report positive rather than negative responses and emotions during task execution (Arijs et al., 2017; Frenkel et al., 2018b; Houge Mackenzie and Brymer, 2018), often resulting in peak performance. Why do some people report not being afraid in such extreme situations? Empirical studies point to specific personality traits that may influence stress and performance in (high risk) sports (Plessner et al., 2009; Allen et al., 2013; Röthlin et al., 2016). Pertinent to the current study, one of these traits – sensation seeking – is prevalent among risk sports athletes and seems to have stress-buffering and performance-facilitating effects (Anshel and Anderson, 2002; Ruedl et al., 2012; Frenkel et al., 2018b). In addition to being high in sensation seeking, narrative research indicates that risk sports athletes describe their strengths in risky situations in words that resemble mindful mindsets (Arijs et al., 2017; Houge Mackenzie and Brymer, 2018). Based on these data, an intriguing question is whether dispositional mindfulness may contribute to risk sports athletes' positive emotional responses and functioning in highly demanding situations. Building on existing narrative research, the aim of the present study is to provide an experimental examination of the protective influence of sensation seeking and mindfulness on risk sport-specific stress responses.

Stress

According to Lazarus and Folkman's (1984) transactional model of stress, stress results from the athlete's subjectively perceived discrepancy between the demands being placed by the environment and coping resources available in a particular situation. High risk sports athletes are often required to respond to situations which threaten their physical integrity or psychological well-being (Breivik, 1999b). In such circumstances, they usually have little opportunity to make corrective decisions, for example, deciding to interrupt a first free-solo ascent in rock climbing to try again later, or correcting errors and avoiding structures while flying in a wingsuit at a speed of over 200 mph. When an individual perceives environmental demands to outweigh their coping resources, a negative and unpleasant psychological state ensues, characterized by feelings of stress and anxiety (Lazarus, 2000). In this respect, anxiety is regarded as an aversive emotional and motivational state that arises when facing uncertainty or a perceived existential threat (Eysenck et al., 2007).

Critical incidents in high risk sports hold high levels of novelty, uncontrollability and personal threat of injury or death (Breivik, 1999b). Besides showing a psychological response (as indicated above), the human body also shows a physiological response to such situations (Campbell and Ehlert, 2012), including activation of the fast reacting sympathetic adrenomedullary system (SAM) – which triggers the release of adrenaline and noradrenaline – and the slower hypothalamic-pituitary-adrenal (HPA) axis, which triggers the release of cortisol from the adrenal cortex. Indeed, several studies have shown that critical incidents place high physiological demands on athletes. For example, although physiological response patterns were slightly inconsistent across studies, it has been found that athletes showed increases in subjective stress (e.g., self-reported anxiety) and salivary cortisol in response to various (sport-specific) experimental stress protocols (Lautenbach et al., 2014; Lautenbach, 2017; Frenkel et al., 2018b).

In general, both psychological and physiological stress responses are associated with impairments in cognitive performance (Eysenck et al., 2007) as well as with a decrease in sports performance (Lautenbach et al., 2014; Frenkel et al., 2018b; e.g., see Nieuwenhuys and Oudejans, 2012, 2017, for a review).

Sensation Seeking

With regard to high risk sports, one personality trait that may protect risk sports athletes from negative effects of stress is "sensation seeking" (Zuckerman, 1994, 1996). Indeed, risk sports athletes have been shown to score extremely high on measures of sensation seeking (Breivik, 1999b; Ruedl et al., 2012) which is defined as the "seeking of varied, novel, complex, and intense sensations and experiences and the willingness to take physical, social, legal, and financial risks for the sake of such experience" (Zuckerman, 1994, p. 27).

According to the psychobiological model of sensation seeking (Zuckerman, 1994, 1996), individuals differ in their optimal levels of physiological arousal and the stimulation required to establish a certain level of arousal. In contrast to low sensation seekers (LSS) – who feel better in less stimulating environments –, high sensation seekers (HSS) tend to have lower baseline levels of dopamine and norepinephrine, which leads these individuals to continuously seek new and intense sensations to maintain their optimal levels of arousal (Zuckerman, 2007).

In the context of the transactional model of stress (Lazarus and Folkman, 1984), HSS may be hypothesized to differ from LSS with respect to (a) their primary appraisal of the performance environment (e.g., lower perceived demands); (b) their perceived ability to cope (e.g., more resources) and, hence, may be expected to (c) show reduced psychological responses (e.g., lower levels of anxiety), as well as (d) reduced physiological responses (e.g., lower levels of salivary cortisol).

Indeed, with regards to (a), Franken et al. (1992) showed that HSS in comparison to LSS tended to judge risky and dangerous situations as less threatening and therefore postulate negative outcomes as less likely to occur. With regard to (b), empirical studies in sports are more scarce. Nevertheless, one study with high school athletes confirmed sensation seeking as a stress-resiliency factor, with HSS reporting better stress management coping skills than LSS (Smith et al., 1992). Regarding psychological responses (c), little is known about the relationship between sensation seeking and anxiety. Examining a sample of university students, Franken et al. (1992) found sensation seeking to be negatively correlated with anxiety. However, in a sample of parachute jumpers, only one out of four subscales of sensation seeking correlated negatively with state anxiety (Breivik et al., 1998) and – more recently – in a sample of 30 sports students, HSS did not show significantly lower anxiety than LSS in response to a high risk sport-specific stressor (Frenkel et al., 2018b). Finally, regarding physiological responses (d), high sensation seeking has been found to be related to lower baseline levels of cortisol (Shabani et al., 2011) and an attenuated cortisol response to stress (Couture et al., 2008), indicating that HSS might tolerate new, potentially stressful experiences better than LSS. Breivik (1999a) did not find a significant correlation between cortisol and sensation seeking in a sample of extreme sports athletes. However, in a recent experimental study, Frenkel et al. (2018b) confirmed that HSS showed lower levels of cortisol in response to a risk sport-specific stressor than LSS. Taken together, these data ("a," "b," "c," and "d") indicate that HSS appraise demanding performance environments more positively and exhibit psychological and physiological responses that allow them to perform better in stressful, high risk sports situations than LSS.

Mindfulness

In contrast to being reckless, risk sports athletes describe the use of internal strategies in risky situations that appear to reflect mindful mindsets (Arijs et al., 2017; Houge Mackenzie and Brymer, 2018): Including high present-moment awareness, high attunement with the environment, a simultaneous internal focus, as well as the use of deliberate value-guided action. Through well-tuned knowledge of their own physical and psychological capacities and limitations, risk sports athletes' actions are often guided by a "leave your ego at the door" mentality (Arijs et al., 2017, p. 7). Hence, in absence of (high levels of) anxiety – which often serves as a natural "brake" on behavior in LSS – HSS' mindful mindsets may allow them to make required corrective decisions when conditions are unsafe or suddenly turn aversive (such as the wind in the wrong direction for BASE jumpers).

Mindfulness is considered a specific kind of attention direction (Kabat-Zinn, 1994). Following an operational definition given by Bishop et al. (2004), mindfulness can be divided in two components: The process of continuous direction of attention and the inner attitude with which this process is carried out (openness, acceptance, self-support). A central feature of mindfulness is "centering" in the presence. Mindfulness directly impacts human behavior by interrupting automatized reaction patterns and by replacing them with flexible actions appropriate for the respective situation (Kabat-Zinn, 1994).

Different competing approaches attempt to explain positive mechanisms of trait mindfulness on well-being and health (Shapiro et al., 2006; Brown et al., 2007; Creswell and Lindsay, 2014; Creswell et al., 2019). Based on this work, and in context of the transactional model of stress (Lazarus and Folkman, 1984), highly mindful in contrast to lowly mindful individuals may be hypothesized to (a) show more favorable appraisals of their performance environment, (b) evaluate their coping resources more positively, and – hence – exhibit (c) reduced psychological responses (e.g., lower levels of anxiety), and (d) reduced physiological responses (e.g., lower levels of salivary cortisol).

Indeed, with regards to (a), the mindfulness stress buffering account (Creswell and Lindsay, 2014; Creswell et al., 2019) states that trait mindfulness mitigates stress assessment because stressors are observed with acceptance and equanimity which, in turn, buffers primary threat appraisals. In line with this assumption, Brown et al. (2012a) demonstrated that mindfulness may buffer attentional reactivity to threatening stimuli. Regarding (b), through the buffering of primary threat appraisals, mindfulness should facilitate positive secondary appraisals in favor of coping resources, decrease subsequent rumination, and increase effective coping strategies (Creswell and Lindsay, 2014). Mindful persons are found to possess better emotion-regulation abilities: Negative emotions are avoided less often (Shapiro et al., 2006). Moreover, as negative states are avoided only to a minor extent, a stronger voluntary exposition to negative emotions like anxiety takes place. As a result, a desensitization concerning anxiety responses occurs (Brown et al., 2007; Shapiro et al., 2006). In the context of sports, Josefsson et al. (2017) showed indirect effects of dispositional mindfulness on coping via rumination and emotion regulation. In line with these effects, regarding (c), research confirms that mindfulness is associated with reduced (i.e., less negative) psychological responses to stress. Outside the context of sports, research using different approaches (correlational, quasi-experimental, and laboratory studies) has shown that trait mindfulness is related to decreased levels of trait and state anxiety (e.g., Brown and Ryan, 2003; Arch and Craske, 2010). Within the sports context, Röthlin et al. (2016) showed that in elite athletes, trait mindfulness is negatively related to cognitive competitive trait anxiety, thereby helping them to perform better. Finally, regarding the physiological response to stress (d), the mindfulness stress buffering account (Creswell and Lindsay, 2014; Creswell et al., 2019) suggests that mindful individuals should exhibit increased activation of regulatory pathways in the prefrontal cortex, whilst reducing bottom-up stress-reactivity (e.g., HPA axis responses), thus inhibiting cortisol production and release from the adrenal cortex. Recent laboratory studies with healthy participants seem to confirm these assumptions (Arch and Craske, 2010; Brown et al., 2012b; Manigault et al., 2018). However, in the context of sports, there is a lack of experimental studies investigating the link between trait mindfulness and cortisol in response to a sport-specific stressor.

The Current Study

Integrating the literature, sensation seeking and trait mindfulness are described as personality characteristics that could potentially contribute to effective stress regulation and performance in demanding (high risk) sports situations (Kabat-Zinn et al., 1985; Smith et al., 1992; Breivik, 1999a; Röthlin et al., 2016; Frenkel et al., 2018b). However, there is a shortage of experimental studies in the context of sports and, to our knowledge, there is no research investigating the role of sensation seeking AND mindfulness within one study. Against this background – and based on Lazarus and Folkman's (1984) transactional model of stress –, the present experimental study investigates how sensation seeking and mindfulness affect individuals' psychological (anxiety) and physiological (cortisol) response to a sport-specific stressor and whether mindfulness can explain additional variance in the stress response beyond sensation seeking.

- Hypothesis (H) 1a and b: Sensation seeking is negatively associated with (a.) state anxiety and (b.) salivary cortisol, in response to the Heidelberg Risk Sport-Specific Stress Test (HRSST).
- H2a and b: Mindfulness is negatively associated with (a.) state anxiety and (b.) salivary cortisol, in response to the HRSST.
- H3a and b: Sensation seeking explains a significant proportion of variance in (a.) state anxiety and (b.) salivary cortisol, in response to the HRSST.
- H4a and b: Beyond sensation seeking, mindfulness explains a significant proportion of variance in the prediction of (a.) state anxiety and (b.) salivary cortisol, in response to the HRSST.

MATERIALS AND METHODS

Participants

During pre-selection, a sample of $N = 207$ male sports students of the Heidelberg University ($M = 22.9$, $SD = 3.3$) were screened for eligibility based on exclusion criteria that included sports habits and health condition. Participants were excluded from the study when they had more than 5 h of climbing experience ($n = 68$; to maximize the effectiveness of the stress induction; Ogden, 2012), or reported a particular fear of heights ($n = 17$), consumed medication containing cortisol ($n = 1$), or had injuries ($n = 14$). If none of the exclusion criteria were met, participants were invited for the experiment. Nineteen persons were not available or refused to participate.

Following the screening process, 88 male students, aged between 18 and 31 ($M = 22.5$, $SD = 2.8$), were deemed eligible and agreed to participate in this study. Two persons had to be excluded from the entire analyses because one participant did not jump and the other consumed branched amino acids and creatine during the experiment.

The most frequently reported types of sports in the sample (multiple answers allowed) were soccer (21.9%), fitness (12.5%), and weight training (10.2%). Concerning high risk sports, 13 persons had engaged in downhill mountain biking, three persons had done a bungee jump, three persons had engaged in different kinds of surfing activities and one person had done skydiving before. For medium risk sports, martial arts and American Football/rugby were mentioned by one participant, respectively, and skiing was reported by two participants. On average, the participants had 8.6 h of sports practice per week ($SD = 3.7$) and rated their fitness on average as 71.0 on a scale ranging from 1 to 100 ($SD = 18.3$). Participants gave written informed consent and were compensated for their participation (15 euros). The procedures were approved by the local Ethics Commission, a university board associated with the Faculty of Behavioural and Cultural Studies.

Design

This study is embedded in a bigger between-within-subject-design-study (Experiment 3 of Frenkel, 2018). In this study, participants were randomly assigned to an ego depletion vs. control group, while their stress parameters were assessed multiple times in the course of the investigation (see **Figure 1**). A state of ego depletion was induced using a 10-min copying task (Bertrams et al., 2010). Participants in the ego depletion group were instructed to copy a text about the history of the German city of Mannheim as fast and error-free as possible, while leaving out the letters "e" and "n". Because these two letters appear frequently in the German language, this variation of the copying task can be considered strenuous. Participants in the control group had to copy the text without leaving out any letters. They were also instructed to copy the text as fast and error-free as possible. Effects of the ego depletion are presented elsewhere (Frenkel, 2018). The analyses were conducted with both the experimental and the control group and the authors controlled for the influence of the experimental condition (see below).

Procedure

In this study, the psychological and physiological responses to a sport-specific stressor were tested at six measurement points (for an overview see **Figure 1**). To adequately represent the situational demands in risk sports, we conducted the HRSST (Frenkel et al., in press), which has been introduced as an innovative, externally valid and standardized stress induction protocol. This protocol uses a climbing task with a subsequent "jump into the rope" that leads to a fall of about 3 m to induce stress. Participants were asked not to consume caffeine, juices, food, nicotine or alcoholic beverages within 1 h prior to the experiment. In accordance with the recommendations of Kudielka et al. (2009), the effect of circadian hormone rhythms was minimized by holding testing time relatively constant and conducting all

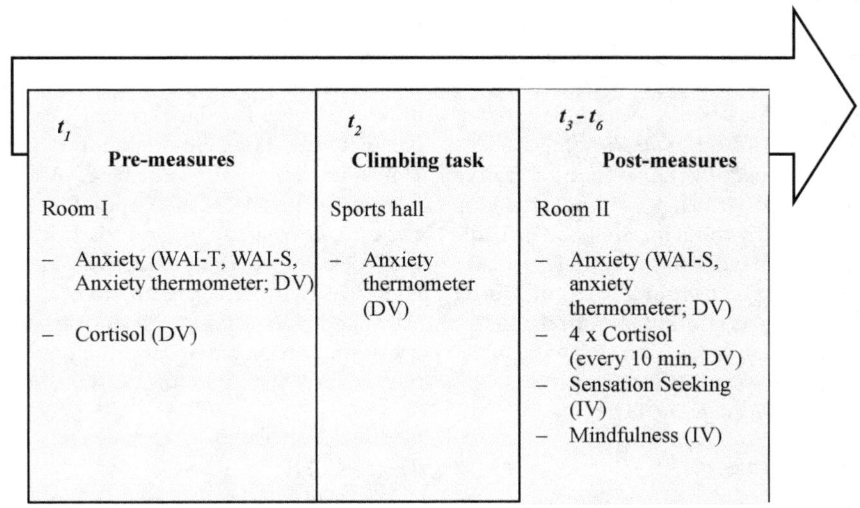

FIGURE 1 | Graphical summary of the procedure, measures, and measurement points. IV: independent variable, DV: dependent variable.

sessions in the afternoon (between 2 and 6 p.m.). Based on the idea that the stress induction and, consequently, the increase in cortisol are maximal for unpredictable tasks (Kirschbaum et al., 1993), baseline measurements before the HRSST were taken in a room outside the sports hall. This set-up ensured that participants did not develop any expectations about the upcoming climbing task. For reasons of standardization, the study followed a written protocol that described both the test procedure as well as the instructions given by the investigators.

At the first point of measurement (*t*1), participants filled out questionnaires for state and trait anxiety, the first salivary sample (baseline measurement) was taken and participants completed the copying task to manipulate their self-control strength. Then, participants were led to the sports hall where they put on a harness and received instructions for the HRSST: They were instructed to climb to the top of the wall top-rope secured (12 m). Having reached the top of the wall, participants reported their current anxiety state. Then the belayer explained that they had to "jump into the rope",[1] resulting in a fall of about 2–3 m. The instruction was to jump backward, not to touch the rope, and to land with both feet simultaneously on the wall. The participants were instructed to choose the moment of the jump themselves. The jump (or fall) was extended by the belayer by loosening the rope in the moment of the fall. If participants displayed at least three of five previously defined abort criterions at this point (i.e., shaking of the legs, slowdown and solidification of movements, cramping, loud and panting breathing and repeated asking), the study was stopped. After the jump, participants were lowered by the belayer.

Finally, the participants were led to the third room where the remaining measurements were taken. At the moment of the participant's jump into the rope, the investigator started a digital stopwatch (CASIO, HS-3V-1RET) so that, after the jump, four salivary samples could be taken with 10-min intervals (*t*3–*t*6). Moreover, at each time point, participants again filled out questionnaires regarding state anxiety (WAI-S; Ehrlenspiel et al., 2009). After the final measurement (i.e., at *t*6), participants completed questionnaires to assess both personality traits (e.g., Mindfulness: Kentucky Inventory for Mindfulness Skills Short; Höfling et al., 2011; Sensation Seeking: SSS-V; Zuckerman, 1994; German version: Beauducel et al., 2003). After the study, participants were thanked, compensated, and fully debriefed.

Measures

Predictors

Sensation seeking

Sensation seeking was assessed with the Sensation Seeking Scale V (SSS-V; Zuckerman, 1994, German version: Beauducel et al., 2003). The instrument consists of 40 items in a forced-choice format (e.g., "I would like to try to surf". vs. "I would not like to try to surf".) of which ten items can be allocated to one of the following for facets, respectively: 1. *Thrill and Adventure Seeking* (*TAS*): Search for danger and adventures, 2. *Experience Seeking* (*ES*): Search for experiences through a non-conformist lifestyle, 3. *Disinhibition* (*DIS*): Tendency for disinhibition in social situations, 4. *Boredom Susceptibility* (*BS*): Aversion to repetition and routines. Besides the separate scores for each facet, a total score varying between min = 0 and max = 40 can be calculated. Based on the current sample, the questionnaire showed satisfactory to good internal consistency, with values similar to those reported for the norm sample (i.e., total scale: $\alpha = 0.82$; subscales between 0.64 and 0.81; cf. Beauducel et al., 2003).

Mindfulness

Mindfulness was measured using the Kentucky Inventory for Mindfulness Skills Short (KIMS-D Short; German version:

[1] "Jumping into the rope" is a term belonging to "fall training". Jumping and falling often is experienced as exciting by beginners. This circumstance was used for stress induction.

Höfling et al., 2011). The 20 items of the short version are to be answered on a five-point Likert-type scale (ranging from 1 = *never or seldom* to 5 = *very often or always*) with participants rating to which extent the statements applied to them. The items can be allocated to the subscales *observation of external phenomena* (*obs-ext*), *observation of internal phenomena* (*obs-int*), *describing* (*des*), *acting mindfully* (*AM*) and *accepting without rating* (*AWR*; Höfling et al., 2011). An example item for the *AM* scale is "I judge whether my thoughts are good or bad". The five scales were combined to an index for mindfulness (in the following called mindfulness index). For mindfulness measured with the KIMS-D Short (Höfling et al., 2011), all reliabilities were satisfactory to good (i.e., $\alpha = 0.74$ for *observing* to $\alpha = 0.85$ for *describing*) and comparable to norm-values reported in the literature (i.e., $\alpha = 0.70$–0.89; Höfling et al., 2011).

Psychological Stress Response

State anxiety

Participants' psychological response to the stressor was assessed using two measures of state anxiety: Firstly, it was assessed at two measurement points (*t*1, *t*3), using the German questionnaire Wettkampf-Angst-Inventar-State (WAI-S; Ehrlenspiel et al., 2009). The WAI-S consists of 12 items (four-point scale, from 0 = "*not at all*" to 3 = "*extremely*") and the subscales *somatic anxiety* (*som*), *cognitive anxiety* (*cog*) and *confidence* (*conf*). An example item for the *somatic anxiety* subscale is "In the present moment... my heart throbs". The internal consistencies of the WAI-S were found to be clearly (at *t*1, before the stress induction) and slightly (at *t*3, after the stress induction) lower in the present sample (between $\alpha_{cog} = 0.52$ and $\alpha_{conf} = 0.79$), compared to the norm sample (Ehrlenspiel et al., 2009: between $\alpha_{cog} = 0.79$ and $\alpha_{conf} = 0.82$). Secondly, state anxiety was assessed at three measurement points (*t*1, *t*2, *t*3) using an anxiety thermometer (Houtman and Bakker, 1989). The anxiety thermometer captures the current feelings of anxiety by one item asking the question "How do you rate your current feelings of anxiety?" on a 10-cm visual analog scale, ranging from 0 = *no anxiety at all* to 10 = *extreme anxiety*. Houtman and Bakker (1989) report test-retest reliabilities of 0.60–0.70.

In this experiment, we applied two different measures of state anxiety at the same time. The questionnaire WAI-S permits with its three subscales a more detailed view of the facets of anxiety while at the same time taking more time to fill it out. The one-item anxiety thermometer promised a weaker reliability, but a better handling during the climbing task (see Nieuwenhuys et al., 2008).

Physiological Stress Response

Cortisol

The physiological stress response was assessed repeatedly using the cortisol concentration in saliva. Participants' samples were collected using Salivette Blue® Device (Sarstedt GmbH, Nümbrecht). Thereby, participants chewed on a synthetic swab for 1 min. As the cortisol peaks about 20 min after experiencing the stressor (the jump) (Kirschbaum and Hellhammer, 2000; Campbell and Ehlert, 2012), saliva samples were taken five times in 10-min intervals after the stress induction (10, 20, 30, and 40 min after the jump). The measurement point of interest was *t*4, 20 min after the jump. Additionally, the return to baseline levels could be assessed from the later measurement points. The saliva samples were stored at −20°C until analyses. The biochemical analysis of the samples was conducted by the steroid laboratory of the Steroid Laboratory, University Hospital Heidelberg. After thawing, the samples were centrifuged at 3000 rpm for 5 min which resulted in a clear supernatant of low viscosity. Salivary concentrations were determined using chemiluminescence immunoassay with high sensitivity (IBL International, Hamburg, Germany). The intra- and inter-assay coefficients for cortisol, which express the precision or repeatability of immunoassay test results, were good (i.e., below 8%; cf. Schultheiss and Stanton, 2009).

Control Variables

Trait anxiety

The control variable trait anxiety was measured with the German questionnaire Wettkampf-Angst-Inventar-Trait (WAI-T; Brand et al., 2009). The inventory consists of 12 items (four-point scale, from 0 = "*not at all*" to 3 = "*extremely*"). The 12 items can be allocated to the scales *somatic anxiety* (*som*), *cognitive anxiety* (*cog*) and *concentration difficulties* (*conc*). The items of the WAI-T are similar to those of the WAI-S, however, the introductory formulation "In the present moment..." is replaced by "Before sporting challenges...". In line with Smith et al.'s (1990) Sport Anxiety Scale – on which the WAI-T was based – and to optimize statistical power of our regression models, WAI-T subscales were combined to arrive at a single trait anxiety score for each individual (in the following called "WAI-T index").[2] In general, internal consistency of the WAI-T was acceptable to good (with αs between 0.60 and 0.82) and comparable to original values reported by Brand et al. (2009); i.e., with αs between 0.77 and 0.81).

Data Processing and Statistical Analyses

Initially, the data of all variables were analyzed to detect any missing and extreme values. Because missing values only occurred occasionally ($\leq 5\%$) and unsystematically, they were replaced using the *expectation maximization* (*EM*) method (Wirtz, 2004; Tabachnick and Fidell, 2007). Concerning cortisol, missing values were replaced using multiple imputations. Beforehand, necessary conditions were checked separately for each group using *missing-completely-at-random* (*MCAR*) tests (Tabachnick and Fidell, 2007). To identify extreme values, boxplots were created separately for experimental groups (depletion and non-depletion) and measurement points. *Tukey-far-out* was chosen as a criterion for extreme values: Values which are more than the triple interquartile range above/under the 75%/25% quartile were identified as extreme values (Tabachnick and Fidell, 2007). Concerning cortisol, the exclusion criterion

[2]"As a robustness check, all analyses were also performed with the WAI-T subscales as covariates. With regards to the associations between sensation seeking, mindfulness and our outcome measures, results for these analyses were highly similar to the reported analyses and showed the same significant and non-significant effects. Detailed analysis reports can be obtained from the first author upon request".

was a distance of ±3 SDs above/under the average group value (Adam and Kumari, 2009).

After the data had been prepared, it was checked for normal distribution as a necessary condition for the following arithmetical analyses. As the Kolmogorov–Smirnov test easily detects a violation of the normal distribution in big samples, additionally, histograms were used. If the Kolmogorov–Smirnov test was found to be significant, analyses were conducted nonetheless because of its high sensitivity and non-parametric relations were calculated on a descriptive statistical level additionally.

To identify the covariates, the dependent variables (i.e., state anxiety and cortisol) were correlated with possible covariates, including age, fitness, previous climbing experience, trait anxiety and experimental condition (ego depletion vs. no ego depletion). In addition, as a possible covariate for cortisol, starting time (time of day) was coded as a variable to control for the influence of the decrease in cortisol during the day. Beforehand, the covariate was adjusted for extreme values following the procedure described above.

Cortisol values were checked substantially and arithmetically for plausibility. To display the change in the response to the stressor, different characteristic values were calculated. Firstly, the increase from baseline to the jump was calculated by taking the difference between *t*1 and *t*4 (i.e., 20 min after the jump), after values had been approximated to the normal distribution using the box-cox-transformation (Miller and Plessow, 2013). In addition, two different versions of the *area under the curve* (AUC) were calculated, the *area under the curve with respect to ground* (AUCg) and the *area under the curve with respect to increase* (AUCi; Pruessner et al., 2003). The AUCg is considered as an indicator for the absolute cortisol concentration over time, mapping the total area of trapezes between the measurement points. For the AUCi, the area between the first measurement point (baseline) and the zero point is subtracted from AUCg. AUC_i thus represents the change in cortisol over time compared to the baseline. If the value is positive, an increase occurs. If the AUCi value is negative, cortisol decreases.

To test hypotheses 1 and 2, (partial) correlations between the independent and the dependent variables (while controlling for covariates) were calculated. The correlations are based on *z*-standardized variables.

To test hypotheses 3 and 4, hierarchical regressions were calculated, using SS and mindfulness (plus the covariates) as predictors and anxiety (WAI-S at *t*1 and *t*3, anxiety thermometer at *t*1, *t*2, and *t*3) and cortisol (AUCg, AUCi, increase and cortisol at *t*4) as criteria. Doing so, covariates were entered in step 1, followed by sensation seeking in step 2 and mindfulness in step 3. To increase the interpretability of the residues, predictors were grand-mean centered (Field, 2009). The covariates age and previous climbing experience (in hours) were not centered because a useful unit already existed.

The assessment of statistical significance followed conventional criteria. A probability of $p < 0.10$ was considered as marginally significant, of $p < 0.05$ as significant, of $p < 0.01$ as highly significant and of $p < 0.001$ as extremely significant. IBM SPSS Statistics 24 was used for all statistical analyses.

RESULTS

Data Preparation

Initially, the cortisol values were checked for plausibility: All values that were located outside the area that can be assessed for analyses using the assay (0.414–41.4 nmol/l) were excluded. This exclusion affected three participants for *t*1 and two participants for *t*3. Missing values were replaced using multiple imputation: This affected three participants for *t*1 and four participants for *t*3. In total, seven participants had to be excluded from the study because of content-related reasons or an extreme value at the third measurement point.

As there were no significant correlations between the experimental condition (ego depletion vs. no ego depletion) and the criteria (anxiety/cortisol), this potential covariate was not included into the regression analyses. Based on the significant correlations (see **Supplementary Material 1**), the covariates age, fitness state and climbing frequency as well as the WAI-T index were included in the respective analyses.

Time Course Analyses

To indicate the overall effectiveness of the stress manipulation (i.e., regardless of sensation seeking and mindfulness), differences in state anxiety and cortisol before and after the climb (see **Table 1**) were compared across all participants using paired *t*-tests. In response to the stressor, on a psychological level, anxiety (as indexed by the anxiety thermometer) increased significantly over time (baseline *t*1 compared to *t*2 on top of the climbing wall) by an average of 2.73 points [i.e., 10-point scale; $SD = 2.32$; $Min = -1$, $Max = 9$; $t(80) = -10.73$, $p < 0.001$; $d = 0.95$]. On a physiological level, salivary cortisol concentrations (*t*1 compared to *t*4) showed a slight but non-significant increase by an average of 0.79 nmol/l [$SD = 4.85$; $Min = -16.60$, $Max = 12.22$; $t(80) = -1.51$, $p = 0.13$; $d = 0.17$].

Correlations (Hypotheses 1 and 2)

As appears from **Table 2**, measures of sensation seeking (SS scale) and mindfulness (KIMS) were not significantly correlated, $r(82) = 0.11$, $p = 0.33$.

Regarding Hypothesis 1a, sensation seeking (SS total score) did not significantly correlate with any of the anxiety measures at baseline (i.e., *t*1; see **Table 3**). After the climb, however, sensation seeking was negatively correlated with the WAI-S somatic scale

TABLE 1 | Time course analysis.

Variables	*M* (*SD*) at *t*1	*M* (*SD*) at *t*2	*M* (*SD*) at *t*3	*M* (*SD*) at *t*4
WAI-S som	1.48 (0.44)	–	1.91 (0.49)	–
WAI-S cog	1.34 (0.36)	–	1.26 (0.33)	–
WAI-S conf	2.94 (0.48)	–	3.03 (0.62)	–
Anxiety thermometer	0.8 (0.8)	3.5 (2.4)	1.3 (1.6)	–
Salivary cortisol (in nmol/l)	9.42 (9.96)	–	–	10.21 (7.40)

WAI-S, Wettkampf-Angst-Inventar-State; WAI-S som, WAI-S somatic anxiety; WAI-S cog, WAI-S cognitive anxiety; WAI-S conf, WAI-S confidence.

TABLE 2 | (Partial) correlations of the independent variables.

Variables	1	2	3	4	5	6	7	8	9	10	11
1. SS total	–	0.67***	0.73***	0.74***	0.63***	0.11	0.23*	0.10	0.00	0.03	−0.05
2. SS BS	–	–	0.32**	0.38***	0.17	0.11	0.22*	0.09	0.03	0.01	−0.07
3. SS Dis	–	–	–	0.34**	0.22*	−0.03	0.13	−0.01	−0.11	−0.01	−0.06
4. SS ES	–	–	–	–	0.42***	0.17	0.20	0.14	0.04	0.00	0.06
5. SS TAS	–	–	–	–	–	0.08	0.08	0.08	0.06	0.09	−0.04
6. KIMS index	–	–	–	–	–	–	0.66***	0.53***	0.45***	0.47***	0.48***
7. KIMS obs-ext	–	–	–	–	–	–	–	0.52***	−0.09	−0.06	0.03
8. KIMS obs-int	–	–	–	–	–	–	–	–	−0.09	0.25*	0.08
9. KIMS des	–	–	–	–	–	–	–	–	–	0.09	0.31**
10. KIMS am	–	–	–	–	–	–	–	–	–	–	−0.05
11. KIMS awr	–	–	–	–	–	–	–	–	–	–	–

SS = Sensation Seeking; SS BS = SS Boredom-Susceptibility; SS Dis = SS Disinhibition; SS ES = SS Experience Seeking; SS TAS = SS Thrill-And-Adventure-Seeking; KIMS = Kentucky Inventory of Mindfulness Skills; KIMS obs-ext = KIMS observation-of-external-phenomena; KIMS obs-int = KIMS observation-of-internal-phenomena; KIMS des = KIMS describing; KIMS am = KIMS acting-mindfully; KIMS awr = KIMS accepting-without-rating. *$^{*}p < 0.05$. $^{**}p < 0.01$. $^{***}p < 0.001$.*

at $t3$ [$r(82) = -0.22, p = 0.01$] and with the WAI-S cognitive scale at $t3$ [$r(82) = -31, p = 0.01$]. No significant correlations of the SS total score were found with the WAI-S somatic scale at $t3$ as well as with the anxiety thermometer at $t2$ or $t3$. Regarding Hypothesis 1b, no relationship was observed between sensation seeking and cortisol responses (see **Table 3**).

Regarding Hypothesis 2a, mindfulness (KIMS index) was negatively correlated with one component of anxiety (i.e., WAI-S confidence scale) at baseline [i.e., $t1$; $r(92) = -22, p = 0.02$]. No other significant correlations were found. Regarding Hypothesis 2b, no relationship was observed between mindfulness and cortisol responses (see **Table 3**).

In addition to the above, various correlations were found between psychological and physiological responses (see **Table 4**): AUCi correlated significantly positively with the anxiety thermometer at $t1$ [$r(79) = 0.27, p = 0.02$] and the anxiety thermometer at $t2$ [$r(79) = 0.27, p = 0.02$]. The cortisol value at $t4$ [$r(79) = 0.27, p = 0.02$] and the increase in cortisol [$r(79) = 0.23$, $p = 0.04$] each displayed a significant positive correlation with the anxiety thermometer at $t2$. No significant associations were found between the remaining dependent variables (see **Table 4**). At a physiological data level, no significant relationship was found between AUCi and AUCg ($r = 0.10, p = 0.40$). The reason may be that, as argued by Pruessner et al. (2003), the variables mirror differential aspects of the physiological response. Moreover, AUCg was not correlated significantly with the increase in cortisol [$r(79) = 0.11, p = 0.33$] but displayed a significant positive correlation with the cortisol value at $t4$ [$r(79) = 0.84, p < 0.001$].

Hierarchical Regression Analyses (Hypotheses 3 and 4)

Regarding Hypothesis 3a, after controlling for covariates, sensation seeking (SS total score) did not predict any of the WAI-S anxiety measures at baseline (i.e., $t1$), but was found to be a marginally significant predictor of anxiety as measured with the anxiety thermometer (see **Table 5**). After the climb (i.e., at $t3$), sensation seeking (SS total score) again marginally predicted anxiety as measured with the anxiety thermometer and could explain 26.8% of the total variance in WAI-S somatic [$R^2 = 0.27$, $\Delta R^2 = 0.07$, $F(3,84) = 11.60$, $p < 0.001$] and 21.6% of the variance in WAI-S cognitive [$R^2 = 0.22$, $\Delta R^2 = 0.08$, $F(3,84) = 24.50$, $p < 0.001$]. For the confidence component, SS was found to be a marginally significant predictor (see **Table 5**). Regarding Hypothesis 3b, no significant associations were observed between sensation seeking (SS total score) and any of the physiological variables (i.e., AUCg, AUCi, increase in cortisol and cortisol at $t4$).

Regarding Hypothesis 4a, after controlling for covariates and sensation seeking, mindfulness (KIMS index) significantly predicted WAI-S confidence at baseline [$\beta = 0.13$, $t(83) = 2.11$, $p = 0.04$]. Together, the three predictors could explain 22.3% of the total variance [$R^2 = 0.22$, $\Delta R^2 = 0.04$, $F(3,84) = 8.03$, $p < 0.001$]. After the climb (i.e., at $t3$), mindfulness was found to be a marginally significant predictor of WAI-S confidence, but not for the two other components of the WAI-S (**Table 5**). Mindfulness did not predict anxiety as measured with the anxiety thermometers at any measurement point (see **Table 5**). Regarding Hypothesis 4b, no significant associations were observed between mindfulness (KIMS index) and any of the physiological variables (i.e., AUCg, AUCi, increase in cortisol and cortisol at $t4$).

DISCUSSION

The current study investigated whether sensation seeking and mindfulness affect individuals' psychological (anxiety) and physiological (cortisol) response to a sport-specific stressor: The HRSST. It was hypothesized that both sensation seeking and mindfulness would negatively correlate with anxiety (H1a and H2a) and cortisol (H1b and H2b), that sensation seeking would be a significant predictor of anxiety and cortisol in response to the HRSST (H3a and H3b), and that – beyond sensation seeking – mindfulness would explain additional variance in anxiety and cortisol (H4a and H4b).

TABLE 3 | (Partial) correlations of the independent variables with the psychological and physiological dependent variables.

Variables	WAI-S som $t1$	WAI-S cog $t1$	WAI-S conf $t1$	Anxiety thermometer $t1$	Anxiety thermometer $t2$	WAI-S som $t3$	WAI-S cog $t3$	WAI-S conf $t3$	Anxiety thermometer $t3$	AUC_g	AUC_i	Rise	Cortisol at $t4$
SS total	0.12	0.04	−0.06	−0.16	−0.17	−0.22*	−0.31**	0.15	0.00	−0.04	−0.02	−0.03	−0.04
BS	0.22*	−0.01	−0.06	−0.06	−0.15	−0.18	−0.11	−0.03	−0.11	0.06	−0.07	−0.07	−0.04
Dis	0.02	−0.03	−0.09	−0.13	−0.03	−0.02	−0.07	0.01	0.03	0.08	0.04	0.04	0.01
ES	0.02	−0.02	−0.11	−0.19	−0.22*	−0.10	−0.24*	0.19*	−0.08	−0.07	0.03	−0.004	−0.03
TAS	−0.02	0.19	−0.11	−0.19	−0.27*	−0.29*	−0.21	0.12	−0.26*	0.004	−0.07	−0.05	−0.09
KIMS index	−0.01	−0.11	−0.22*	−0.05	0.01	−0.04	−0.09	−0.16	0.01	−0.07	0.08	0.07	0.01
obs-ext	−0.12	−0.12	−0.05	−0.08	−0.25*	−0.20	−0.01	−0.14	−0.23*	0.09	−0.12	−0.12	−0.10
obs-int	0.12	−0.08	−0.03	−0.03	−0.08	−0.07	−0.05	−0.06	−0.27*	−0.01	−0.04	0.02	0.02
des	−0.08	−0.05	−0.32**	0.002	0.12	0.03	−0.07	−0.25*	0.24*	−0.07	0.20	0.13	0.08
am	−0.01	−0.09	−0.21	−0.05	−0.02	0.06	−0.09	−0.16	0.11	−0.11	−0.16	−0.09	−0.11
awr	0.02	0.08	−0.17	0.09	0.09	0.06	0.04	−0.13	0.13	−0.04	0.16	0.07	0.10

*SS = Sensation Seeking; SS DS = SS Boredom-Susceptibility; SS Dis = SS Disinhibition; SS ES = SS Experience Seeking; SS TAS = SS Thrill-And-Adventure-Seeking; KIMS = Kentucky Inventory of Mindfulness Skills; KIMS obs-ext = KIMS observation-of-external-phenomena; KIMS obs-int = KIMS-observation-of-internal-phenomena; KIMS des = KIMS describing; KIMS am = KIMS acting-mindfully; KIMS awr = KIM accepting-without-rating; WAI-S = Wettkampf-Angst-Inventar-State; WAI-S som = WAI-S somatic-anxiety; WAI-S cog = WAI-S cognitive anxiety; WAI-S conf = WAI-S confidence; AUC_g = Area under the curve with respect to ground; AUC_i = Area under the curve with respect to increase. *$p < 0.05$. **$p < 0.01$. ***$p < 0.001$.*

Psychological Response to the HRSST

Sensation Seeking

Our findings partly confirm hypotheses H1a and H3a that sensation seeking (SS) would be associated with and significantly predict participants' psychological response to the HRSST. At $t3$, we found a significant negative relationship between SS and two of the subscales of state anxiety (the somatic and the cognitive component). In the corresponding regression analyses (i.e., predicting both anxiety components at $t3$) – and after controlling for covariates – SS explained a significant proportion of variance, with individuals scoring high on SS exhibiting lower levels of anxiety. As became apparent from the analyses of subscales, the observed effects are likely driven by the TAS component and the ES component of SS (see **Table 3**). This observation is in line with a study conducted by Breivik (1999a), in which the difference in SS between high risk sports athletes and sport science students was also caused by TAS and ES. As such, TAS and ES appear to be essential components of SS and its effect on individuals' psychological response to risk-full sport situations. The current results are in line with the psychobiological multilevel theory (Zuckerman, 1994) and show that HSS differ from LSS in their psychological response to an unexpected stimulus, in this case the jump into the rope.

Contradicting H1a and H3a, SS was neither significantly associated with nor significantly predicted the confidence component of state anxiety. Whilst speculative, this may relate to the nature of the current task (i.e., a wall climb followed by a so-called jump in the rope), with which (a) participants had very little or no experience; and which (b), allowed participants little control over the course of action. Potentially, with higher levels of task experience or in tasks that allow more control, sensation seeking may also boost self-confidence and further contribute to the positive appraisal of high-risk performance environments that is characteristic of HSS. Future research aiming to investigate this matter may find Jones' (1995) control model of anxiety – which distinguishes between intensity and direction (i.e., positive vs. negative) of the anxiety response – to be a useful framework.

Matching the effects observed with the WAI-S (somatic and cognitive anxiety subscale), SS was found to explain a significant proportion of variance in participants' scores on the anxiety thermometer at $t3$. Unexpectedly, the effect of SS on anxiety thermometer scores at $t2$ failed to reach significance ($p = 0.11$, see **Table 5**). With the effect of SS on anxiety being generally small (see **Table 5**), one explanation for the absence of this effect may be that – being a one-item measure – the anxiety thermometer may simply not have been sensitive enough to detect a statistically significant difference. Indeed, *a posteriori* power analyses with G-Power (Faul et al., 2009) – based on the current sample and analyses and with effect sizes as reported in **Table 5** – indicate that statistical power for the anxiety thermometer at $t2$ was insufficient to detect a small effect (i.e., with power = 0.67), whereas power was sufficient (i.e., >0.85) for all other dependent variables.

Mindfulness

Our findings largely contradict hypotheses H2a and H4a in that mindfulness was neither significantly associated with nor significantly predicted anxiety in response to the HRSST.

TABLE 4 | (Partial) correlations of the psychological and physiological dependent variables.

Variables	1	2	3	4	5	6	7	8	9	10	11	12	13
1. WAI-S som *t1*	–	0.26*	0.08	0.28**	−0.01	0.21	0.23*	0.03	0.05	0.00	0.04	0.03	0.05
2. WAI-S cog *t1*	–	–	−0.22*	0.15	0.04	0.01	0.34**	0.49***	0.09	0.13	0.01	0.00	0.06
3. WAI-S conf *t1*	–	–	–	−0.28*	0.12	0.04	−0.17	0.49***	0.29**	0.16	−0.06	−0.06	0.03
4. Anxiety thermometer t_1	–	–	–	–	0.24*	0.21	0.26*	−0.21*	0.43*	0.04	0.27*	0.22	0.19
5. Anxiety thermometer t_2	–	–	–	–	–	0.49***	0.27**	0.01	0.61**	0.19	0.27*	0.23*	0.27*
6. WAI-S som *t3*	–	–	–	–	–	–	0.39***	−0.10	0.56**	−0.04	0.15	0.13	0.10
7. WAI-S cog *t3*	–	–	–	–	–	–	–	−0.38***	0.54**	−0.12	0.21	0.16	0.13
8. WAI-S conf *t3*	–	–	–	–	–	–	–	–	0.32**	0.11	−0.06	−0.08	−0.00
9. Anxiety thermometer t_3	–	–	–	–	–	–	–	–	–			0.35**	0.18
10. AUC_g	–	–	–	–	–	–	–	–	–	–	0.10	0.10	0.84***
11. AUC_i	–	–	–	–	–	–	–	–	–	–	–	0.88***	0.86***
12. rise *t1*–*t4*	–	–	–	–	–	–	–	–	–	–	–	–	0.89***
13. Cortisol *t4*	–	–	–	–	–	–	–	–	–	–	–	–	–

*WAI-S = Wettkampf-Angst-Inventar-State; WAI-S som = WAI-S somatic-anxiety; WAI-S cog = WAI-S cognitive anxiety; WAI-S conf = WAI-S confidence; AUC_g = area under the curve with respect to ground; AUC = area under the curve with respect to increase. *$p < 0.05$. **$p < 0.01$. ***$p < 0.001$.*

TABLE 5 | Hierarchical regressions of the dependent variables on SS and KIMS and the respective covariates.

Dependent variable	Covariate(s), independent variables	Standardized beta	Δ R^2	P	f^2
WAIS som *t1*	WAIT index	0.46***	0.22	0.00	0.28
	SS-total	0.02	0.00	0.85	0.00
	KIMS-index	0.01	0.00	0.94	0.00
WAIS cog *t1*	WAIT-index	0.49***	0.22	0.00	0.28
	SS-total	0.04	0.00	0.68	0.00
	KIMS-index	−0.06	0.01	0.47	0.01
WAIS conf *t1*	WAIT-index	0.26***	0.18	0.00	0.22
	SS-total	0.04	0.00	0.87	0.00
	KIMS-index	0.13*	0.04	0.04	0.04
Anxiety thermometer *t1*	WAIT-index	0.39***	0.13	0.00	0.15
	SS-total	−0.18	0.03	0.08	0.03
	KIMS-index	−0.00	0.00	0.98	0.00
Anxiety thermometer *t2*	Climbing	−0.25*	0.09	0.02	0.10
	SS-total	−0.17	0.03	0.11	0.03
	KIMS-index	−0.09	0.01	0.41	0.01
WAIS som *t3*	WAIT-index	0.44***	0.17	0.00	0.20
	Climbing	−0.17	0.05	0.09	0.05
	SS-total	−0.27**	0.07	0.01	0.08
	KIMS-index	−0.02	0.00	0.84	0.00
WAIS cog *t3*	WAIT-index	0.45***	0.15	0.00	0.18
	SS-total	−0.29**	0.08	0.00	0.09
	KIMS-index	−0.02	0.00	0.86	0.00
WAIS conf *t3*	WAIT-index	0.32**	0.12	0.00	0.14
	SS-total	−0.19	0.03	0.07	0.03
	KIMS-index	0.18	0.03	0.09	0.03
Anxiety thermometer *t3*	WAIT-index	0.40***	0.13	0.00	0.15
	Climbing	−0.18	0.06	0.08	0.06
	SS-total	−0.20	0.04	0.05	0.04
	KIMS-index	−0.09	0.01	0.37	0.01

*SS = Sensation Seeking; WAI-S = Wettkampf-Angst-Inventar-State; WAI-S som = WAI-S somatic-anxiety; WAI-S cog = WAI-S cognitive anxiety; WAI-S conf = WAI-S confidence; KIMS = Kentucky Inventory of Mindfulness Skills. *$p < 0.05$. **$p < 0.01$. ***$p < 0.001$. A posteriori power analyses: small ($f^2 = 0.02$), medium ($f^2 = 0.15$), large effects ($f^2 = 0.35$); α err prob < 0.05.*

The only significant associations that were observed regarded the WAI-S confidence subscale at baseline (see **Tables 3, 5**), indicating that mindful individuals tended to show slightly lower baseline levels of confidence. Note however, that baseline levels of confidence were generally positive and showed little between-subject variation (see **Table 1**). As such, the observed effect is likely to be of low clinical significance. Analyses of subscales (see **Table 3**) suggest that the observed effect is likely driven by the KIMS subscale "*describing*," which was negatively correlated with the confidence component of state anxiety at *t1* as well as at *t3*. Participants with a stronger tendency to (explicitly) describe phenomena in their surroundings reported lower confidence before and after the jump.

The general absence of significant effects regarding mindfulness may be explained by the correlational design of the current study and, potentially, insufficient variability in trait mindfulness (as measured with the KIMS), as well as the fact that the current study deliberately examined effects of mindfulness over and above effects of sensation seeking. As can be seen in **Table 5**, in case of significant effects, substantial variance in outcome measures was often explained by covariates (e.g., trait anxiety) and sensation seeking, leaving little room for mindfulness to make an additional impact. Still, narrative research from extreme sports (Brymer and Schweitzer, 2013; Arijs et al., 2017; Houge Mackenzie and Brymer, 2018) as well as theoretical explanations from other contexts than sports (Mindfulness Stress Buffering Account; Creswell and Lindsay, 2014; Creswell et al., 2019) suggest a link between trait mindfulness and state anxiety. Future studies are advised to consider effects across a broader range of mindfulness, either by contrasting extremes or by implementing tailored mindfulness interventions.

Physiological Response to the HRSST

Sensation Seeking

Our findings contradict hypotheses H1b and H3b, indicating no significant association between SS and salivary cortisol in response to the HRSST. This lack of association is surprising, as a previous study using the same stress induction protocol (Frenkel et al., 2018b) showed that HSS compared to LSS showed significantly smaller cortisol responses. In the broader literature, however, an apparent dissociation between physiological and psychological stress responses is not uncommon (Breivik, 1999a; Kudielka et al., 2009; Campbell and Ehlert, 2012). A review including 49 studies using the Trier Social Stress Test as a psychosocial stressor detected this mismatch in 75% of the studies (Campbell and Ehlert, 2012). This controversy of the results is explained, among others, by inter-individual differences in the degree of psycho-physiological correspondence, or possible mediating factors.

In explaining the observed null-finding, it is important to consider that the current sample consisted exclusively of highly fit and physically active sport science students, whose self-reported fitness level averaged around 70.98 (SD = 18.29) on a 0–100 scale. In line with the stressor adaptation hypothesis (CSA hypothesis; Sothmann et al., 1996), which suggests that adaptation to physical stress (e.g., following regular physical exercise) may transfer to include other stressors, several groups of researchers have found reduced psychological and physiological responses to psychological stress in physically active individuals (Klaperski et al., 2013; Zschucke et al., 2015). Matching these observations, the current study showed that – regardless of sensation seeking and mindfulness – increases in anxiety and salivary cortisol following the HRSST were small and, in case of cortisol, non-significant (see "*Time course analyses*" in the Results section). Addressing this issue, future studies on risk sport-specific stress which examine a highly physically active population, are advised to consider additional means to further intensify the stress protocol.

Mindfulness

Our findings contradict hypotheses H2b and H4b, indicating no significant associations between mindfulness and physiological stress response measured by salivary cortisol. As with sensation seeking, this null-finding is likely explained by the non-significant increase in cortisol following the HRSST. In addition to increasing the intensity of the stressor, future studies may consider to examine effects in the context of mindfulness- and acceptance-based interventions (e.g., Gardner and Moore, 2004, 2017; Birrer et al., 2012; Frenkel et al., 2018a; Josefsson et al., 2019) as opposed to examining (small) inter-individual differences in trait mindfulness. Although mindfulness training has a long standing tradition in applied sports psychology (Gardner and Moore, 2004, 2017), only few evidence based intervention studies have examined the effects of mindfulness practice on physiological and psychological performance surrogates or on performance outcomes in sports (Bühlmayer et al., 2017; Hoja et al., 2018). One intervention study that did investigate effects of a mindfulness intervention on HPA axis activation reported decreased salivary cortisol levels following mindfulness (John et al., 2011). In this regard, potential implications remain promising.

Potential, Limitations, and Outlook

To our knowledge, the current study is the first to examine the effects of sensation seeking and trait mindfulness on psychological and physiological responses to a standardized risk sport-specific stressor. A strength of the current study is the application of an experimentally controlled nature and external validity of the stressor, the HRSST, which allows robust examinations of stress responses and realistically mimics stressful situations in high risk sports. Results from the current study, as well as previous work (e.g., Frenkel et al., 2018b) indicate that the HRSST induces a consistent psychological response, which is characterized by robust increases in self-reported state anxiety. On the other hand, physiological responses to the HRSST have been more inconsistent. Salivary cortisol significantly increased after the HRSST in Frenkel et al.'s (2018b) initial validation study, but did not significantly increase in the current study. It is therefore important to further develop the paradigm so that an increase in cortisol can be reliably induced – also in highly fit and physically active populations. Potential considerations include prolonging the task or adding additional (external) stressors such as observation or evaluation.

Regarding the impact of sensation seeking and mindfulness, the current study employed a correlational design. While this informs about natural between-individual variability, stronger effects may be expected by considering extremes or – with regard to mindfulness – employing within-subject manipulations (e.g., mindfulness training; Bühlmayer et al., 2017; Hoja et al., 2018). Still, the current study identified sensation seeking as a significant predictor of individuals' psychological response to a risk sport-specific stressor (cf. Breivik, 1999a). Moving beyond the immediate context of high risk sports, this finding bears relevance for other high risk contexts and occupations, such as firefighting, policing or the military, where individuals are confronted with similar stressors and threats to their physical integrity (Neria et al., 2000; Nieuwenhuys and Oudejans, 2010, 2011; Meland et al., 2015; Nieuwenhuys et al., 2015; Giessing et al., 2019) and analyses of sensation seeking may potentially contribute to recruitment and selection processes (e.g., Landman et al., 2016).

In the current study, only male participants were included and – hence – potential gender-specific differences in sensation seeking, mindfulness and stress responses, were not taken into account. The decision to include only male participants was deliberate and driven by the fact that females' cortisol levels can be biased by the menstrual cycle and contraceptives (Kelly et al., 2008) as well as by the fact that climbing also depends on endurance and strength and that these domains differ between the sexes. In extrapolating the current findings to the wider population, these differences should be taken into account.

Building on the current findings, future studies may include a more detailed analysis of individuals' psychological response to stress and – in context of the appraisal process (Lazarus and Folkman, 1984) – clarify if the observed stress-buffering effects of sensation seeking are caused by the primary or secondary appraisal. In addition, and in light of recent work from clinical psychology (Engel-Yeger et al., 2016; Serafini et al., 2017), analyses of sensory processing patterns could be helpful to further characterize athletes and their vulnerability to stress. Finally, in order to forward understanding of high risk sports performance, it is important to replicate the current findings and contrast observations with those obtained among actual risk sport athletes (e.g., Breivik, 1999a).

CONCLUSION

In conclusion, the current study showed that the personality trait sensation seeking may act as a stress "buffer" and significantly reduces individuals' psychological response (i.e., self-perceived somatic and cognitive state anxiety) to an experimentally controlled, high risk sport-specific stressor. In contrast to our hypotheses, no additional anxiety-reducing effect was observed for trait mindfulness, and neither sensation seeking nor mindfulness could explain observed variance in individuals' physiological stress response (i.e., salivary cortisol). Because of the far-reaching negative consequences of stress, identifying protective factors to secure and improve the health and performance of people who are exposed to highly demanding and risky situations (e.g., in the context of work or sports) is of critical importance. With regards to the protective influence of sensation seeking and mindfulness, the current study takes a first step in addressing this issue.

ETHICS STATEMENT

The study's design was approved by the ethical committee of the Faculty of Behavioral and Cultural Studies of Heidelberg University.

AUTHOR CONTRIBUTIONS

This manuscript at hand was mutually developed. Each author contributed to the study planning, data analysis, and interpretation with an additional focus on their respective area of competence. All authors contributed crucially in drafting the aim of the study, concretizing the design, and finishing the manuscript, and examined and agreed to the submitted version of the manuscript. JB, R-BH, and MF conducted the experiments. JB was essentially responsible for the statistical analysis with the support of CK and MS. MF interpreted the data, wrote the first draft of the manuscript together with JB, managed the communication between all authors during the development of the manuscript, assumed responsibility for being the corresponding author, and for keeping the co-authors informed of the progress through the editorial review process, the contents of the reviews, and any revisions made.

ACKNOWLEDGMENTS

We gratefully acknowledge Dr. Ina Rehberger's fast laboratory analyses of the saliva samples and the contribution of her profound expertise. Special thanks to Friederike Uhlenbrock and Thomas Stoll for helping with the data collection in this study as well as to Laura Giessing and Friederike Uhlenbrock for their careful proofreading of the manuscript. We also thank the participating students. We acknowledge financial support by the Deutsche Forschungsgemeinschaft within the funding program Open Access Publishing, by the Baden-Württemberg Ministry of Science, Research and the Arts and by the Heidelberg University.

REFERENCES

Adam, E. K., and Kumari, M. (2009). Assessing salivary cortisol in large-scale, epidemiological research. *Psychoneuroendocrinology* 34, 1423–1436. doi: 10.1016/j.psyneuen.2009.06.011

Allen, M. S., Greenlees, I., and Jones, M. (2013). Personality in sport: a comprehensive review. *Int. Rev. Sport Exerc. Psychol.* 6, 184–208. doi: 10.1016/j.ynstr.2016.11.001

Anshel, M., and Anderson, D. (2002). Coping with acute stress in sport: linking athletes' coping style, coping strategies, affect, and motor performance. *Anxiety Stress Coping* 15, 193–209. doi: 10.1080/10615800290028486

Arch, J. J., and Craske, M. G. (2010). Laboratory stressors in clinically anxious and non-anxious individuals: the moderating role of mindfulness. *Behav. Res. Ther.* 48, 495–505. doi: 10.1016/j.brat.2010.02.005

Arijs, C., Chroni, S., Brymer, E., and Carless, D. (2017). 'Leave your ego at the door': a narrative investigation into effective wingsuit flying. *Front. Psychol.* 8:1985. doi: 10.3389/fpsyg.2017.01985

Beauducel, A., Strobel, A., and Brocke, B. (2003). Psychometrische eigenschaften und normen einer deutschsprachigen fassung der sensation seeking-skalen, form V [psychometric characteristics and norms of a german version of sensation seeking scales, form V]. *Diagnostica* 49, 61–72. doi: 10.1026//0012-1924.49.2.61

Bertrams, A., Englert, C., and Dickhäuser, O. (2010). Self-control strength in the relation between trait test anxiety and state anxiety. *J. Res. Pers.* 44, 738–741. doi: 10.1016/j.jrp.2010.09.005

Birrer, D., Röthlin, P., and Morgan, G. (2012). Mindfulness to enhance athletic performance: theoretical considerations and possible impact mechanisms. *Mindfulness* 3, 235–246. doi: 10.1007/s12671-012-0109-2

Bishop, S. R., Lau, M., Shapiro, S., Carlson, L., Anderson, N. D., and Carmody, J., et al. (2004). Mindfulness: a proposed operational definition. *Clin. Psychol. Sci. Pract.* 11, 230–241. doi: 10.1093/clipsy.bph077

Brand, R., Graf, K., and Ehrlenspiel, F. (2009). "Das wettkampfangst-inventar-trait" [The competitive anxiety inventory trait], in *Das Wettkampfangst-Inventar Manual [The Competitive Anxiety Inventory Manual]*, eds R. Brand, F. Ehrlenspiel, and K. Graf (Bonn: Bundesinstitut für Sportwissenschaft), 15–69.

Breivik, G. (1999a). *Empirical Studies of Risk Sport (Vol. B. 5)*. Oslo: Norges idrettshøgskole, Institutt for Samfunnsfag.

Breivik, G. (1999b). *Sensation Seeking in Sport*. Oslo: Norges Idrettshøgskole, Institutt for Samfunnsfag.

Breivik, G., Roth, W. T., and Jørgensen, P. E. (1998). Personality, psychological states and heart rate in novice and expert parachutists. *Pers. Indiv. Dif.* 25, 365–380. doi: 10.1016/S0191-8869(98)00058-0

Brown, K. W., Goodman, R. J., and Inzlicht, M. (2012a). Dispositional mindfulness and the attenuation of neural responses to emotional stimuli. *Soc. Cogn. Affect. Neurosci.* 8, 93–99. doi: 10.1093/scan/nss004

Brown, K. W., Weinstein, N., and Creswell, J. D. (2012b). Trait mindfulness modulates neuroendocrine and affective responses to social evaluative threat. *Psychoneuroendocrinology* 37, 2037–2041. doi: 10.1016/j.psyneuen.2012.04.003

Brown, K. W., and Ryan, R. M. (2003). The benefits of being present. *J. Pers. Soc. Psychol.* 84, 822–848. doi: 10.1037/0022-3514.84.4.822

Brown, K. W., Ryan, R. M., and Creswell, J. D. (2007). Mindfulness: theoretical foundations and evidence for its salutary effects. *Psychol. Inq.* 18, 211–237. doi: 10.1080/10478400701598298

Brymer, E., and Schweitzer, R. (2013). The search for freedom in extreme sports: a phenomenological exploration. *Psychol. Sport Exerc.* 14, 865–873. doi: 10.1016/

j.psychsport.2013.07.004

Bühlmayer, L., Birrer, D., Röthlin, P., Faude, O., and Donath, L. (2017). Effects of mindfulness practice on performance-relevant parameters and performance outcomes in sports: a meta-analytical review. *Sports Med.* 47, 2309–2321. doi: 10.1007/s40279-017-0752-9

Campbell, J., and Ehlert, U. (2012). Acute psychosocial stress: does the emotional stress response correspond with physiological responses? *Psychoneuroendocrinology* 37, 1111–1134. doi: 10.1016/j.psyneuen.2011.12.010

Couture, S., Brown, T. G., Ouimet, M. C., Gianoulakis, C., Tremblay, J., and Carbonneau, R. (2008). Hypothalamic-pituitary-adrenal axis response to stress in male DUI recidivists. *Accid. Anal. Prev.* 40, 246–253. doi: 10.1016/j.aap.2007.06.003

Creswell, J. D., and Lindsay, E. K. (2014). How does mindfulness training affect health? A mindfulness stress buffering account. *Curr. Dir. Psychol. Sci.* 23, 401–407. doi: 10.1177/0963721414547415

Creswell, J. D., Lindsay, E. K., Villalba, D. K., and Chin, B. (2019). Mindfulness training and physical health: mechanisms and outcomes. *Psychosom. Med.* 81, 224–232. doi: 10.1097/PSY.0000000000000675

Ehrlenspiel, F., Brand, R., and Graf, K. (2009). "Das wettkampfangst-inventar-state" [The competitive anxiety inventory state], in *Das Wettkampfangst-Inventar, Manual [The Competitive Anxiety Inventory, Manual]*, eds R. Brand, F. Ehrlenspiel, and K. Graf (Bonn: Bundesinstitut für Sportwissenschaft), 71–100.

Engel-Yeger, B., Muzio, C., Rinosi, G., Solano, P., Geoffroy, P. A., and Pompili, M., et al. (2016). Extreme sensory processing patterns and their relation with clinical conditions among individuals with major affective disorders. *Psychiatry Res.* 236, 112–118. doi: 10.1016/j.psychres.2015.12.022

Eysenck, M. W., Derakshan, N., Santos, R., and Calvo, M. G. (2007). Anxiety and cognitive performance: attentional control theory. *Emotion* 7, 336–353. doi: 10.1037/1528-3542.7.2.336

Faul, F., Erdfelder, E., Buchner, A., and Lang, A. G. (2009). Statistical power analyses using G*Power 3.1: tests for correlation and regression analyses. *Behav. Res. Methods* 41, 1149–1160. doi: 10.3758/BRM.41.4.1149

Field, A. (2009). *Discovering Statistics Using SPSS: (and Sex and Drugs and Rock 'n' Roll)* 3rd Edn. Los Angeles, CA: Sage Publications.

Franken, R. E., Gibson, K. J., and Rowland, G. (1992). Sensation seeking and the tendency to view the world as threatening. *Pers. Indiv. Dif.* 13, 31–38. doi: 10.1016/0191-8869(92)90214-A

Frenkel, M. O. (2018). *Der Einfluss Von Spezifischen Persönlichkeitsmerkmalen auf das Stresserleben im Sport [The Influence of Specific Personality Characteristics on the Stress Experience in Sport.]*, Unpublished habilitation thesis, Heidelberg University, Heidelberg.

Frenkel, M. O., Brokelmann, J., and Plessner, H. (2018a). Mental starke Kinder und Jugendliche durch Achtsamkeit? [Mentally though children and adolescents through mindfulness?]. *Leistungslust* 6, 28–32.

Frenkel, M. O., Heck, R. B., and Plessner, H. (2018b). Cortisol and behavioral reaction of low and high sensation seekers differ in responding to a sport-specific stressor. *Anxiety Stress Coping* 31, 580–593. doi: 10.1080/10615806.2018.1498277

Frenkel, M. O., Laborde, S., Rummel, J., Giessing, L., Kasperk, C., Plessner, H., et al. (in press). Heidelberg Risk Sport-Specific Stress Test: a paradigm to investigate the risk sport-specific psycho-physiological arousal. *Front. Psychol.*

Gardner, F. L., and Moore, Z. E. (2004). *A Mindfulness-Acceptance-Commitment-Based Approach to Athletic Performance Enhancement: Theoretical Considerations*. Orlando, FL: Elsevier Ltd.

Gardner, F. L., and Moore, Z. E. (2017). Mindfulness-based and acceptance-based interventions in sport and performance contexts. *Curr. Opin. Psychol.* 16, 180–184. doi: 10.1016/j.copsyc.2017.06.001

Giessing, L., Frenkel, M. O., Zinner, C., Rummel, J., Nieuwenhuys, A., Kasperk, C., et al. (2019). Effects of coping-related traits and psychophysiological stress responses on police recruits. Shooting behavior in reality-based scenarios. *Front. Psychol.* 10:1523. doi: 10.3389/fpsyg.2019.01523

Höfling, V., Ströhle, G., Michalak, J., and Heidenreich, T. (2011). A short version of the kentucky inventory of mindfulness skills. *J. Clin. Psychol.* 67, 639–645. doi: 10.1002/jclp.20778

Hoja, S., Zirkelbach, J., and Jansen, P. (2018). Achtsamkeit – Auch ein megatrend im leistungssport? [Mindfulness – Also a megatrend in competitive sport?]. *Sports Orthop. Traumatol.* 34, 38–44. doi: 10.1016/j.orthtr.2017.11.001

Houge Mackenzie, S., and Brymer, E. (2018). Conceptualizing adventurous nature sport: a positive psychology perspective. *Ann. Leis. Res.* 13, 1–13. doi: 10.1080/11745398.2018.1483733

Houtman, I. L. D., and Bakker, F. C. (1989). The anxiety thermometer: a validation study. *J. Pers. Assess.* 53, 575–583. doi: 10.1207/s15327752jpa5303_14

John, S., Verma, S. K., and Khanna, G. (2011). The effect of mindfulness meditation on HPA-axis in pre-competition stress in sports performance of elite shooters. *Natl. J. Integr. Res. Med.* 2, 15–21.

Jones, G. (1995). More than just a game: research developments and issues in competitive anxiety in sports. *Br. J. Psychol.* 86, 449–478. doi: 10.1111/j.2044-8295.1995.tb02565.x

Josefsson, T., Ivarsson, A., Gustafsson, H., Stenling, A., Lindwall, M., Tornberg, R., et al. (2019). Effects of mindfulness-acceptance-commitment (MAC) on sport- specific dispositional mindfulness, emotion regulation, and self-rated athletic performance in a multiple-sport population: an RCT study. *Mindfulness* 10:1518. doi: 10.1007/s12671-019-01098-7

Josefsson, T., Ivarsson, A., Lindwall, M., Gustafsson, H., Stenling, A., and Böröy, J., et al. (2017). Mindfulness mechanisms in sports: mediating effects of rumination and emotion regulation on sport-specific coping. *Mindfulness* 8, 1354–1363. doi: 10.1007/s12671-017-0711-4

Kabat-Zinn, J. (1994). *Wherever You Go, There You Are: Mindfulness Meditation in Everyday Life*. New York, NJ: Hyperion.

Kabat-Zinn, J., Beall, B., and Rippe, J. (1985). A systematic mental training program based on mindfulness meditation to optimize performance in collegiate and Olympic rowers. *Paper Presented at the World Congress in Sport Psychology*, Copenhagen.

Kelly, M. M., Tyrka, A. R., Anderson, G. M., Price, L. H., and Carpenter, L. L. (2008). Sex differences in emotional and physiological responses to the trier social stress test. *J. Behav. Ther. Exp. Psychiatry* 39, 87–98. doi: 10.1016/j.jbtep.2007.02.003

Kirschbaum, C., and Hellhammer, D. (2000). Salivary cortisol - An invaluable tool in studies of HPA function. *Psychoneuroendocrinology* 25:14. doi: 10.1016/S0306-4530(00)90086-6

Kirschbaum, C., Pirke, K. M., and Hellhammer, D. H. (1993). The 'Trier Social Stress Test'. A tool for investigating psychobiological stress responses in a laboratory setting. *Neuropsychobiology* 28, 76–81. doi: 10.1159/000119004

Klaperski, S., von Dawans, B., Heinrichs, M., and Fuchs, R. (2013). Does the level of physical exercise affect physiological and psychological responses to psychosocial stress in women? *Psychol. Sport Exerc.* 14, 266–274. doi: 10.1016/j.psychsport.2012.11.003

Kudielka, B. M., Hellhammer, D. H., and Wüst, S. (2009). Why do we respond so differently? Reviewing determinants of human salivary cortisol responses to challenge. *Psychoneuroendocrinology* 34, 2–18. doi: 10.1016/j.psyneuen.2008.10.004

Landman, A., Nieuwenhuys, A., and Oudejans, R. R. D. (2016). The impact of personality traits and professional experience on police officers' shooting performance under pressure. *Ergonomics* 59, 950–961.

Lautenbach, F. (2017). A laboratory study on attentional bias as an underlying mechanism affecting the link between cortisol and performance, leading to a discussion on the nature of the stressor (artificial vs. psychosocial). *Physiol. Behav.* 175, 9–15. doi: 10.1016/j.physbeh.2017.03.022

Lautenbach, F., Laborde, S., Achtzehn, S., and Raab, M. (2014). Preliminary evidence of salivary cortisol predicting performance in a controlled setting. *Psychoneuroendocrinology* 42, 218–224. doi: 10.1016/j.psyneuen.2014.01.011

Lazarus, R. S. (2000). How emotions influence performance in competitive sports. *Sport Psychol.* 14, 229–252. doi: 10.1123/tsp.14.3.229

Lazarus, R. S., and Folkman, S. (1984). *Stress, Appraisal, and Coping*. New York, NJ: Springer Publishing Company.

Manigault, A. W., Woody, A., Zoccola, P. M., and Dickerson, S. S. (2018). Trait mindfulness predicts the presence but not the magnitude of cortisol responses to acute stress. *Psychoneuroendocrinology* 90, 29–34. doi: 10.1016/j.psyneuen.2018.01.022

Meland, A., Ishimatsu, K., Pensgaard, A. M., Wagstaff, A., Fonne, V., and Garde, A. H., et al. (2015). Impact of mindfulness training on physiological measures of stress and objective measures of attention control in a military helicopter unit. *Int. J. Aviat. Psychol.* 25, 191–208. doi: 10.1080/10508414.2015.1162639

Miller, R., and Plessow, F. (2013). Transformation techniques for cross-sectional and longitudinal endocrine data: application to salivary cortisol concentrations. *Psychoneuroendocrinology* 38, 941–946. doi: 10.1016/j.psyneuen.2012.09.013

Neria, Y., Solomon, Z., Ginzburg, K., and Dekel, R. (2000). Sensation seeking, wartime performance, and long-term adjustment among Israeli war veterans. *Pers. Indiv. Dif.* 29, 921–932. doi: 10.1016/S0191-8869(99)00243-3

Nieuwenhuys, A., and Oudejans, R. R. D. (2010). Effects of anxiety on handgun shooting behavior of police officers: a pilot study. *Anxiety Stress Coping* 23, 225–233. doi: 10.1080/10615800902977494

Nieuwenhuys, A., and Oudejans, R. R. D. (2011). Training with anxiety: short- and long-term effects on police officers' shooting behavior under pressure. *Cogn. Process.* 12, 277–288. doi: 10.1007/s10339-011-0396-x

Nieuwenhuys, A., and Oudejans, R. R. D. (2012). Anxiety and perceptual-motor performance: toward an integrated model of concepts, mechanisms, and processes. *Psychol. Res.* 76, 747–759. doi: 10.1007/s00426-011-0384-x

Nieuwenhuys, A., and Oudejans, R. R. D. (2017). Anxiety and performance: perceptual-motor behavior in high-pressure contexts. *Curr. Opin. Psychol.* 16, 28–33. doi: 10.1016/j.copsyc.2017.03.019

Nieuwenhuys, A., Pijpers, J. R., Oudejans, R. R. D., and Bakker, F. C. (2008). The influence of anxiety on visual attention in climbing. *J. Sport Exerc. Psychol.* 30, 171–185. doi: 10.1123/jsep.30.2.171

Nieuwenhuys, A., Savelsbergh, G. J. P., and Oudejans, R. R. D. (2015). Persistence of threat-induced erros in police officers' shooting decisions. *Appl. Ergon.* 48, 263–272. doi: 10.1016/j.apergo.2014.12.006

Paulus, M. P., Potterat, E. G., Taylor, M. K., Van Orden, K. F., Bauman, J., and Momen, N., et al. (2009). A neuroscience approach to optimizing brain resources for human performance in extreme environments. *Neurosci. Biobehav. Rev.* 33, 1080–1088. doi: 10.1016/j.neubiorev.2009.05.003

Plessner, H., Unkelbach, C., Memmert, D., Baltes, A., and Kolb, A. (2009). Regulatory fit as a determinant of sport performance: how to succeed in a soccer penaltyshooting. *Psychol. Sport Exerc.* 10, 108–115. doi: 10.1016/j.psychsport.2008.02.001

Pruessner, J. C., Kirschbaum, C., Meinlschmid, G., and Hellhammer, D. H. (2003). Two formulas for computation of the area under the curve represent measures of total hormone concentration versus time-dependent change. *Psychoneuroendocrinology* 28, 916–931. doi: 10.1016/S0306-4530(02)00108-7

Röthlin, P., Horvath, S., Birrer, D., and Grosse Holtforth, M. (2016). Mindfulness promotes the ability to deliver performance in highly demanding situations. *Mindfulness* 7, 727–733. doi: 10.1007/s12671-016-0512-1

Ruedl, G., Abart, M., Ledochowski, L., Burtscher, M., and Kopp, M. (2012). Self-reported risk taking and risk compensation in skiers and snowboarders are associated with sensation seeking. *Accid. Anal. Prev.* 48, 292–296. doi: 10.1016/j.aap.2012.01.031

Schultheiss, O. C., and Stanton, S. J. (2009). "Assessment of salivary hormones", in *Methods in Social Neuroscience*, eds E. Harmon-Jones, and J. S. Beer (New York, NJ: Guilford Press), 17–44.

Serafini, G., Gonda, X., Canepa, G., Pompili, M., Rihmer, Z., Amore, M., et al. (2017). Extreme sensory processing patterns show a complex association with depression, and impulsivity, alexithymia, and hopelessness. *J. Affect. Disord.* 210, 249–257. doi: 10.1016/j.jad.2016.12.019

Shabani, S., Dehghani, M., Hedayati, M., and Rezaei, O. (2011). Relationship of serum serotonin and salivary cortisol with sensation seeking. *Int. J. Psychophysiol.* 81, 225–229. doi: 10.1016/j.ijpsycho.2011.06.015

Shapiro, S. L., Carlson, L. E., Astin, J. A., and Freedman, B. (2006). Mechanisms of mindfulness. *J. Clin. Psychol.* 62, 373–386. doi: 10.1002/jclp.20237

Smith, R., Ptacek, J., and Smoll, F. (1992). Sensation seeking, stress, and adolescent injuries: a test of stress-buffering, risk-taking, and coping skills hypotheses. *J. Pers. Soc. Psychol.* 62, 1016–1024. doi: 10.1037/00223514.62.6.1016

Sothmann, M. S., Buckworth, J., Claytor, R. P., Cox, R. H., White-Welkley, J. E., and Dishman, R. K. (1996). Exercise training and the cross-stressor adaptation hypothesis. *Exerc. Sport Sci. Rev.* 24, 267–288.

Tabachnick, B. G., and Fidell, L. S. (2007). *Using Multivariate Statistics*. Boston, MA: Pearson.

Wirtz, M. (2004). Über das problem fehlender Werte: wie der Einfluss fehlender informationen auf analyseergebnisse entdeckt und reduziert werden kann [about the problem of missing values: how to detect and reduce the influence of missing information on analyses results]. *Die Rehabilitation* 43, 109–115. doi: 10.1055/s-2003-814839

Zschucke, E., Renneberg, B., Dimeo, F., Wüstenberg, T., and Ströhle, A. (2015). The stress-buffering effect of acute exercise: evidence for HPA axis negative feedback. *Psychoneuroendocrinology* 51, 414–425. doi: 10.1016/j.psyneuen.2014.10.019

Zuckerman, M. (1994). *Behavioral Expressions and Biosocial Bases of Sensation Seeking*. Cambridge: Cambridge University Press.

Zuckerman, M. (1996). The psychobiological model for impulsive unsocialized sensation seeking: a comparative approach. *Neuropsychobiology* 34, 125–129. doi: 10.1159/000119303

Zuckerman, M. (2007). *Sensation Seeking and Risky Behavior*. Washington: American Psychological Association.

8

A Longitudinal Examination of Military Veterans' Invictus Games Stress Experiences

Gareth A. Roberts[1], Rachel Arnold[1], James E. Turner[1†], Martin Colclough[2] and James Bilzon[1†]*

[1] Department for Health, University of Bath, Bath, United Kingdom, [2] Help for Heroes Sports Recovery, Tidworth, United Kingdom

***Correspondence:**
Rachel Arnold
R.S.Arnold@bath.ac.uk
†ORCID:
James E. Turner
orcid.org/0000-0003-2427-1430
James Bilzon
orcid.org/0000-0002-6701-7603

This study explored patterns of change in stress variables (i.e., stressors, appraisals, emotions) encountered by wounded, injured, and sick military veterans in the build up to, during, and following an international sporting competition. The study also examined interactions between psychosocial variables and salivary biomarkers of stress and how these relate to veterans' health, well-being, illness, and performance. 40 Invictus Games (IG) athletes and a control group of 20 military veteran athletes completed questionnaires at seven time points over a 12-week period. Furthermore, participants provided morning and evening saliva samples at four time points to measure cortisol and secretory immunoglobulin A. Multilevel growth curve analyses revealed significant changes in growth trajectories of stress-related variables. For example, team and culture stressors and anger and dejection emotions significantly increased in the build up to competition, whilst challenge appraisals and excitement and happiness emotions significantly decreased over the same time-frame. A number of the stress related variables also predicted performance, well-being, and mental health. Specifically, organizational stressors and threat appraisals were found to negatively relate to performance, well-being, and mental health. Furthermore, whilst challenge appraisals and problem focused coping positively related to veterans' well-being, adopting emotion-focused and avoidance coping strategies negatively predicted well-being and mental health. Turning to emotions, experiencing anger, anxiety, and dejection negatively related to mental health, well-being and performance; whereas happiness and excitement displayed a positive relationship with these outcomes. The findings also highlighted that organizational stressor intensity was positively related to cortisol exposure at competition. To conclude, this study not only provides a novel, longitudinal, interdisciplinary insight into psychological and biological markers of the stress response as it relates to the performance, health, and well-being of military veterans, but also further contributes to theoretical understanding on the transactional nature of stress. Moreover, the findings significantly contribute to practice regarding how best to support this unique population in adaptively responding to and engaging with competitive sport.

Keywords: competition, cortisol, emotion, psychological stress, rehabilitation, sport

INTRODUCTION

Research conducted with military veterans illustrates that sport can provide significant physiological, psychological, and social benefits for recovery (Sporner et al., 2009; Caddick and Smith, 2014). To achieve these benefits, the Invictus Games (IG) were created to offer a large number of wounded, injured, or sick Armed Forces personnel and veterans the opportunity to compete in an international sport competition. Despite participation benefits, operating in such a demanding sporting environment can also produce undesirable outcomes (e.g., unpleasant emotions, performance dissatisfaction; Nicholls et al., 2012). Therefore, it is important to examine veterans' holistic experiences of high-level sport and the antecedents to both positive and negative outcomes, which have not been studied to date. Furthermore, the majority of research conducted on stress in sport, has been cross-sectional; thus inhibiting causal inferences and not accurately reflecting the dynamic nature of the stress process. As such, a transactional approach (cf. Lazarus and Folkman, 1984) can be adopted to underpin such enquiries. The transactional stress theory suggests that stressors arise from the environment the performer operates in, are mediated by the processes of perception, appraisal, and coping, and, as a consequence, result in positive or negative responses, feeling states, and outcomes (Fletcher et al., 2006, p. 333).

In line with transactional stress theory, environmental demands are often examined as the first component of the process, as they can indicate triggers of certain responses. Furthermore, in early definitions of stress (i.e., stimulus based; see Fletcher et al., 2006), the environmental conditions faced by individuals are emphasized. Research has identified three types of demands: competitive, organizational, and personal; with organizational-related demands found to be experienced and recalled more often than competitive-related demands (Hanton et al., 2005). Within sport, organizational stressors are defined as "the environmental demands associated primarily and directly with the organization within which an individual is operating" (Fletcher et al., 2006, p. 329). Organizational stressors can be prevalent and problematic for a range of sport performers who compete at various competitive levels (Arnold and Fletcher, 2012a; Fletcher et al., 2012a; Arnold et al., 2016a,b). Specifically, Arnold et al. (2016b) sampled elite athletes with a disability and identified 316 organizational stressors which were categorized into 31 concepts and four, previously conceptualized dimensions: leadership and personal issues (e.g., the coach's behavior and interactions), cultural and team issues (e.g., teammate's personality and attitudes), logistical and environmental issues (e.g., rules and regulations), and performance and personal issues (e.g., transitions). Further to this, organizational stressors have been linked to various outcomes including, emotions, motivation, well-being, performance, and burnout (Fletcher et al., 2012b; Tabei et al., 2012; Larner et al., 2016; Arnold et al., 2017, 2018; Bartholomew et al., 2017; Wagstaff et al., 2018). The samples recruited for this research on outcomes of organizational stressors, however, has typically been able-bodied sport performers with little attention afforded to the experiences of disabled sport performers. Furthermore, when examining the stress experienced by military veterans, the focus to date has tended to be on reported outcomes including post-traumatic stress disorder (PTSD), depression, and alcohol abuse (Fear et al., 2010; Murphy et al., 2016). Notwithstanding the importance of examining such consequences, research has suggested that veterans can encounter stressors directly associated with supporting organizations (cf. Weir et al., 2017), though this has been afforded limited attention to date. Organizational stressors are of particular interest in the current study considering the affiliation of the United Kingdom IG team to the military charity, Help for Heroes, whose Sports Recovery (HfHSR) team's mission is to support athletes pre, during, and post-competition.

After encountering a demand, such as the aforementioned organizational stressors, individuals make a cognitive evaluation on its meaning and significance in relation to their beliefs, values, goal commitments, and situational intentions (Lazarus and Folkman, 1984). This primary appraisal is informed by the individual's initial perception of whether a stressor is irrelevant, benign-positive, or stressful. A stressful encounter occurs when the situation is evaluated as significant to an individual's well-being and, subsequently, there are three possible appraisals: harm/loss, threat, or challenge (Fletcher et al., 2006). These cognitive appraisals can then determine whether individuals respond adaptively or maladaptively to motivated performance situations (cf. Blascovich, 2008), with research suggesting that challenge appraisals are considered more beneficial to performance than threat appraisals (Nicholls et al., 2011). If something is considered at stake, individuals will engage in secondary appraisal to evaluate the availability of coping resources (Lazarus, 2000). Research suggests that organizational stressors are predominantly appraised as harmful, with little perceived control, and few coping resources available (Didymus and Fletcher, 2014). In military settings, evidence suggests that appraisals are key, alongside coping strategies, to develop positive, mental health outcomes (Solomon et al., 1988). No research to date, however, has examined the appraisals made by military veterans during their sporting involvement.

According to the transactional theory of stress, emotions arise following the cognitive appraisal of a situation (Lazarus, 2000). In the sport setting, research has found associations between threat appraisals and the generation of unpleasant emotions (e.g., anger, anxiety), and between challenge appraisals and positive emotions (e.g., happiness, excitement) (Nicholls et al., 2011). The aforementioned emotions have also been found to be common responses to organizational stressors (Fletcher et al., 2012b). It is important to note, however, that given the lack of research conducted with military veterans, as well as the nature of military veterans' previous occupation and experience, it may be erroneous to assume that the patterns of stress, appraisal, and emotions will be similar to those observed in other populations (cf. Fletcher and Arnold, 2017). Additionally, the transactional stress process can be moderated by various personal and situational characteristics (Fletcher et al., 2006) which are yet to be explored with a military veteran population. When examining emotions in the military veteran population, exercise rehabilitation programs have been shown to help reduce negatively valenced emotions, as well as improve mood states (Otter and Currie, 2004). Literature could be advanced, however, to ascertain whether the same longitudinal effect exists for veterans who compete in sport. Turning to coping, sport research indicates that individuals should engage in task-orientated coping strategies in order to perform maximally, generate positive emotions, and improve physical and mental health (Nicholls et al., 2012). There is a need to examine, however, the ways in which veterans cope with sporting pressures, since the focus of military research to date has been around coping on a mission or within military occupations (Barnett et al., 2016).

Turning to the final component of the transactional stress theory, it would be beneficial to examine the impact of veterans' stress on psychological, behavioral, and immune and endocrine measurements. Research to date has investigated the impact of organizational stressors on psychosocial outcomes (e.g., performance, well-being) in a cross-sectional manner (see, for a review, Fletcher and Arnold, 2017), yet has not examined this longitudinally, nor their impact on immune and endocrine function. Chronic psychological stress can impair aspects of immune function, potentially increasing the chance of developing infections (Segerstrom and Miller, 2004; Pedersen et al., 2010). To explain this link, psychological stress influences immune function via alterations to the sympathetic-adrenal-medullary axis and the hypothalamic pituitary adrenal axis (Ader et al., 1995). Changes include abnormal sympathetic and parasympathetic stimulation of the immune system and alterations to the diurnal rhythm of the endocrine system; thus, changing overall exposure to hormones such as cortisol, which can impair immune function (Ader et al., 1995). Evidence shows that elite athletes and para-athletes report a high frequency of illness symptoms around the time of mass-participation sporting events (Derman et al., 2014; Bonini et al., 2015). A frequently cited explanation is that high volumes and intensities of exercise might impair aspects of immune function, increasing infection risk (Campbell and Turner, 2018). There is limited evidence to support this idea, and a more likely explanation is increased exposure to infections due to crowds (Choudhry et al., 2006; Campbell and Turner, 2018). If immunological alterations are evident, environmental stressors (e.g., sleep disruption, international flights), or indeed, psychological stress are most likely to be the factors affecting immune function (Taylor et al., 2015; Campbell and Turner, 2018). Thus, if psychological stress in the lead up to a sporting competition impairs immune function, then the chance of developing an infection due to attending a crowded mass-participation event could be exacerbated. One immune component that might be affected is secretory immunoglobulin-A (S-IgA), which provides a first line of defense against infections on mucosal surfaces (e.g., the lining of the mouth, nose, and airways). Previous studies have reported an inverse relationship between salivary S-IgA and symptoms of upper respiratory tract infections (URTIs; Neville et al., 2008; Mortatti et al., 2012) which coincide with increased levels of salivary cortisol (Cunniffe et al., 2011; Casto and Edwards, 2016) in athletes (ranging from novice to elite) at competition. It is often not examined in studies, however, whether psychological stress is driving immune function changes.

Based on the above review of extant literature, the primary purpose of this study is to examine the stress experiences of veterans in preparation for, during, and post the IG and to quantify how these change over time and in comparison to a control group not participating in high-level competition. A secondary purpose is to examine the relationships between stress (e.g., stressors, responses) and psychological, behavioral, and immune and endocrine measurements. In line with this latter outcome, a third purpose is to examine whether psychological stress is associated with changes in biomarkers of stress (i.e., salivary cortisol) potentially impacting immune function (i.e., salivary S-IgA) and symptoms of URTI.

MATERIALS AND METHODS

Participants

Forty participants were recruited from the 2016 United Kingdom IG Team (29 males, 11 females) who ranged in age from 24 to 51 years (M_{age} = 37.4 ± 8.6 years), and had served in either the British Army (n = 27), Royal Navy (n = 2), Royal Marines (n = 3), or Royal Air Force (n = 8) for an average of 12.7 ± 7.0 years. The IG group identified themselves as having various mental health issues (n = 3), or physical (n = 32), hearing (n = 1), visual (n = 1), or cognitive impairments (n = 1), or other injuries (n = 2); and reported that they had their injury/impairment for an average of 6.6 ± 5.2 years. Participants were competing at the Games in eight sports (e.g., Archery, Rowing, Powerlifting, Cycling, Swimming, Athletics, Wheelchair Basketball, and Wheelchair Rugby), with some veterans having never previously competed in their sport (n = 14), whereas others had competed from 3 months to 17 years (M_{years} = 4.6 ± 6.4), at standards ranging from club to international level.

Twenty military veterans who did not participate in the Games but still engaged in competitive sport were recruited as a control (CON) group (16 males, 4 females) who ranged in age from 24 to 62 (M_{age} = 42.5 ± 11.4). The CON group had served in either the British Army (n = 15), Royal Marines (n = 2), Royal Air Force (n = 2), or Royal Navy (n = 1) for an average of 15.5 ± 11.0 years. The veterans in the CON group identified themselves as having various mental health issues (n = 1), or physical (n = 10), hearing (n = 2), visual (n = 3), or cognitive impairments (n = 1), or other injuries (n = 3); and reported that they had their injury/impairment for an average of 8.1 ± 7.2 years. CON participants represented ten sports (e.g., Archery, Cycling) with some having never previously competed in their sport (n = 3), whereas others had competed for 6 months to 45 years (M_{years} = 6.5 ± 13.3 years), at standards ranging from club to international level. The comparison of the IG group and a relatively matched CON group affords an insight into the differences in the stress process encountered by those competing at an international sporting competition and those who are not. Additionally, usage of a control group means that the predominant factor for comparison when examining psychosocial and biomarker measures is the engagement with the IG, rather than alternative confounding factors.

Procedure

Following institutional ethical approval, military veterans who had been selected for the United Kingdom 2016 IG team were contacted by email about the study, as were military veterans who had not been selected (for the CON group). All veterans who expressed an interest in participating were contacted with further information before providing informed consent. Both groups were asked to complete questionnaires over seven time-points, which reflected competition milestones (e.g., post-selection at 6 weeks before Games, training camps at 1 and 3 weeks before the Games), with pre-competition time-points subsequently mirrored post-Games (e.g., final study time-points were 6 weeks, 3 weeks, and 1 week before the Games; during the Games; and 1 week, 3 weeks, and 6 weeks after the Games). Each questionnaire was selected for its use in previous transactional stress in sport research, and in total took approximately 30–40 min to complete. Data collection predominantly took place online, but paper questionnaires were available on request. The questionnaire packs at the first four time-points contained all seven psychological variable questionnaires detailed below, whilst the questionnaire packs at the remaining three time-points contained six questionnaires as the study only intended to examine the appraisals of stressors in the build up to and at the Games (i.e., not post the Games). Saliva samples were collected (30 min after waking and 30 min prior to sleep to rule out potential confounding by diurnal variation in biomarkers) 1 week before the Games; 24 h after landing in the United States (where the Games were held), 24 h before the first competitive event, and 1 week after the Games.

Measures

Stressors

The 23-item Organizational Stressor Indicator for Sports Performers (OSI-SP; Arnold et al., 2013) measured the organizational stressors that participants encountered during their participation in competitive sport over the past month. The five subscales on the OSI-SP are goals and development (six items; e.g., "my goals"), logistics and operations (nine items; e.g., "the training or competition venue"), team and culture (four items; e.g., "my teammates' attitudes"), coaching (two items; e.g., "my coach's personality"), and selection (two items; e.g., "how my team is selected"). For all items at all time points, the stem "In the past week, I have experienced pressures associated with. . ." was provided, to which the participants responded on three rating scales: frequency ("how often did this pressure place a demand on you?"; 0 = *never* to 5 = *always*), intensity ("how demanding was this pressure?"; 0 = *no demand* to 5 = *very high*), and duration ("how long did this pressure place a demand on you for?"; 0 = *no time* to 5 = *a very long time*). Organizational stressors were measured post-IG as athletes were still associated with HfHSR, who were still offering support to them. Arnold et al. (2013) have provided evidence to support the indicator's validity and reliability, with acceptable alpha values evident in the present study (α range = 0.76 to 0.91).

Appraisals

The 28-item Stress Appraisal Measure (SAM; Peacock and Wong, 1990) assessed the athletes' primary and secondary appraisals of the stressors they encountered at the time-points prior to the IG. Specifically, the SAM measures primary appraisals (threat, challenge, and centrality) and secondary appraisal (controllable-by self, by-others, and uncontrollable by anyone). For all items (e.g., "Does this situation make me feel anxious?"), participants were asked to respond in accordance with how they viewed the stressors at that moment in time, with all items rated on a five-point scale ranging from 1 (*not at all*) to 5 (*extremely*). Peacock and Wong (1990) reported acceptable reliability for the SAM, which was supported in this study (α range = 0.76 to 0.93).

Coping

Coping was assessed using the Modified COPE (MCOPE; Crocker and Graham, 1995). On this measure, 12 coping strategies are presented and participants were asked to indicate, on a five-point scale ranging from 1 (*not at all*) to 5 (*very much*), how much they used each strategy to cope with the pressures they experienced as part of their involvement in competitive sport over the past week. The strategies measured are classified into the higher-order functions of coping, with five categorized as problem-focused coping (e.g., item: "I work harder"), five as emotion-focused coping (e.g., item: "I talk about my feelings with someone"), and two as avoidance coping (e.g., item: "I act as though I am not having pressures"). Crocker and Graham (1995) reported that the alpha coefficients ranged from 0.62 to 0.92 and acceptable reliability was shown in the present study (α = 0.73 to 0.96).

Emotions

The 22-item Sport Emotion Questionnaire (SEQ; Jones et al., 2005) measured five emotions: anxiety (five items: nervous, anxious, tense, apprehensive, and uneasy), dejection (five items: unhappy, sad, upset, dejected, and disappointed), anger (four items: annoyed, irritated, furious, and angry), excitement (four items: enthusiastic, excited, energetic, and exhilarated), and happiness (four items: joyful, pleased, cheerful, and happy). Participants were asked to score the occurrence of items in relation to their involvement in competitive sport over the previous week on a five-point scale ranging from 0 (*not at all*) to 4 (*extremely*). The SEQ has been validated for usage of recalling retrospective emotions (cf. Arnold and Fletcher, 2015) as well as its original validation for pre-competition emotions. Jones et al. (2005) reported alpha coefficients ranging from 0.81 to 0.88 and excellent reliability was found in this study (α = 0.90 to 0.95).

Well-Being, Health, and Performance Outcomes

Notwithstanding the numerous available measures of well-being (Lundqvist, 2011), the 14-item Warwick-Edinburgh Mental Well-being Scale (WEMWBS; Tennant et al., 2007) was used to measure hedonic and eudaimonic aspects of psychological-well being, including positive affect, interpersonal relationships, and positive functioning. Reflecting on the previous week, participants were asked to respond to items (e.g., "I've been feeling useful") on a five-point scale ranging from 1 (*none of the time*) to 5 (*all of the time*). Tennant et al. (2007) reported excellent reliability for the WEMWBS (α = 0.91), as did this study (α = 0.95). The United Kingdom Short Form 12 Health Survey (United Kingdom SF-12; Ware et al., 1995) was used to measure components of mental health. The questionnaire asked participants to reflect back on the previous week, and a score of α = 0.76 showed acceptable internal consistency. Participants subjectively rated their athletic performance (cf. Pensgaard and Duda, 2003) by responding to the question "Please rate how well you consider your sport performance (including training and competitions) to have been over the past week" on a scale ranging from 0 (*very poor*) to 10 (*excellent*).

Salivary S-IgA and Cortisol

Participants were asked to refrain from eating, drinking, smoking, or brushing their teeth for 1 h prior to saliva sampling and to abstain from caffeine and alcohol for 24 h. To rule out potential confounding by diurnal variation in S-IgA and cortisol, participants were encouraged to collect saliva at roughly the same time in the morning and evening on each collection day (Gleeson et al., 2011). Furthermore, all participants were asked to declare all medication, including contraceptive pill usage. In view of the identified impact of exercise on cortisol responses (cf. Jacks et al., 2002), participants' physical activity patterns were measured using the Leisure Time Exercise Questionnaire (Godin and Shephard, 1985). Objective measures of physical activity (e.g., accelerometers) were not taken, given that participants were locked in to a similar defined behavioral pattern, which was largely determined by preparation for, travel to and performance at the Games. In view of this, it was deemed that there was minimal variability between participants that could have impacted on cortisol concentrations. Unstimulated saliva samples were collected over a 4-min period using the passive unstimulated drool/spitting method (Navazesh, 1993). Specifically, participants were asked to collect saliva on the floor of the mouth without stimulation by orofacial movement or swallowing before drooling/spitting into pre-weighed 15 mL centrifuge tubes at approximately 30-s intervals. Samples were stored at 4°C for up to 24 h, before being weighed to assess sample volume, and centrifuged for 10 min at 1500 × *g* to remove particulate matter. The supernatant was aliquoted, packaged, and transported back to the United Kingdom using dry ice. Samples remained frozen upon arrival and were stored at −80°C until analysis.

Secretory immunoglobulin-A and cortisol were measured using commercially available enzyme-linked immuno-sorbent assay (ELISA) kits according to the manufacturer's instructions (Salimetrics, Philadelphia, PA, United States). The inter- and intra-assay coefficients of variation for S-IgA were 14.96 and 5.64%, respectively. The inter- and intra-assay coefficients of variation for salivary cortisol were 3.79 and 5.12%, respectively. Average S-IgA secretion rate (μg/mL/min) and salivary cortisol concentrations (μg/mL) were calculated for each saliva sample. In addition to both of these measures and in line with research on diurnal rhythm (Li and Gleeson, 2004), secretion of S-IgA (μg/mL/min~15 h) and exposure to cortisol (μg/mL~15 h) over the course of the day was calculated by quantifying the area under the curve (AUCg) using the trapezoid method with respect to ground (Pruessner et al., 2003).

Symptoms of Upper Respiratory Tract Infections

Participants were required to complete a daily log in which they documented whether they felt they were suffering from a common cold or flu, and any signs/symptoms of URTI (e.g., sneezing, headache, and malaise). Participants were also instructed to code the severity of the symptom on a four-point scale from 0 (*none at all*) to 3 (*severe*). In accordance with the Jackson Score Questionnaire (Jackson et al., 1958), to be classified as a URTI, the symptoms had to last two or more days, and score greater than 14 (Predy et al., 2005).

Data Analyses

Using MPlus version 7.4 (Muthén and Muthén, 1998/2015), two-piece linear growth models [in a structural equation modeling (SEM) framework] were used to subdivide measurements into two meaningful time-periods: pre-Games (including competition) and post-Games (including competition). The flexibility of the piecewise growth model allows for the analyses of two distinct time-periods within a longer overall time-frame, without having to conform to assumptions that individual change follows a simple linear trend over the whole time-frame (Preacher et al., 2008). A SEM approach was adopted as it incorporates the observed repeated measures as multiple indicators in one or more latent factors to characterize the unobserved growth trajectories (cf. Curran et al., 2010). Time was centered on the competition time point [i.e., this time-point was labeled zero, with negative (pre-Games) and positive (post-Games) values the further from competition in either direction]; therefore the intercept represented the average score for the variable on the day of competition and the slopes represented the rate of change in the study variables before or after the competition. The intercept and slope coefficients were explored to establish the extent of between-person variation in the intercept and rates of change for all psychological variables (cf. Preacher et al., 2008). Following this, conditional latent growth models (LGMs) were used to determine whether between-person variation in the intercept or slope parameters could be predicted by IG attendance. To elaborate, the time-invariant covariate (TIC) was added to unconditional LGMs as a predictor variable to determine whether any differences existed between the IG and CON groups. Finally, unconditional LGMs with time-varying covariates (TVCs) were used to ascertain whether the veterans' stress (i.e., organizational stressors, appraisals, emotions) could predict outcome variables (i.e., performance, well-being, and health) at each time point.

RESULTS

All descriptive statistics for psychosocial measures are presented in **Table 1**.

TABLE 1 | Means and standard deviations for variables at all time points for IG group.

Variable	6 weeks prior		3 weeks prior		1 week prior		Invictus Games		1 week post		3 weeks post		6 weeks post	
	M	*SD*	*M*	*SD*	*M*	*SD*	*M*	*SD*	*M*	*SD*	*M*	*SD*	*M*	*SD*
Organizational Stressors Frequency	1.46	0.83	1.65	0.74	1.47	0.66	1.61	0.83	1.61	0.75	1.09	0.99	1.14	0.93
Goals and Development Frequency	2.22	1.15	2.49	1.27	2.23	1.32	2.16	1.24	2.06	1.20	1.57	1.87	1.75	1.73
Logistics and Operations Frequency	1.39	0.81	1.56	0.84	1.43	0.73	1.54	0.95	1.56	0.88	1.08	0.96	1.09	0.96
Team and Culture Frequency	1.24	1.22	1.55	0.96	1.52	0.82	1.89	1.34	1.54	0.89	1.03	0.51	0.98	0.51
Coaching Frequency	0.63	0.71	0.88	0.61	0.79	0.32	1.00	1.39	0.98	0.55	0.50	0.40	0.55	0.44
Selection Frequency	1.83	1.99	1.79	1.96	1.39	1.78	1.44	2.23	1.93	1.57	1.25	2.31	1.33	2.22
Organizational Stressors Intensity	1.68	1.31	1.85	1.03	1.60	0.94	1.72	0.97	1.85	2.24	1.11	1.11	1.18	1.06
Goals and Development Intensity	2.27	1.36	2.55	1.56	2.24	1.71	2.26	1.51	2.11	1.16	1.69	2.46	1.79	2.10
Logistics and Operations Intensity	1.44	0.97	1.68	1.04	1.53	0.89	1.69	1.06	1.49	0.86	1.03	0.89	1.09	0.98
Team and Culture Intensity	1.45	1.72	1.87	1.26	1.71	1.31	2.01	1.66	1.73	1.21	0.98	0.74	0.98	0.73
Coaching Intensity	1.16	2.21	1.23	1.21	1.09	0.86	1.14	1.49	1.03	0.70	0.38	0.21	0.50	0.35
Selection Intensity	2.05	2.27	1.93	2.52	1.41	1.65	1.50	2.45	1.89	1.74	1.37	2.87	1.42	2.72
Organizational Stressors Duration	1.59	1.08	1.71	0.98	1.62	0.79	1.70	0.95	1.77	2.17	1.12	1.17	1.17	1.11
Goals and Development Duration	2.19	1.27	2.42	1.39	2.37	1.35	2.36	1.48	2.06	1.20	1.69	2.49	1.84	2.19
Logistics and Operations Duration	1.47	0.96	1.60	1.02	1.58	0.84	1.69	1.03	1.50	0.91	1.11	1.01	1.12	1.03
Team and Culture Duration	1.34	1.38	1.70	1.32	1.69	0.91	1.95	1.48	1.60	1.03	0.99	0.79	1.00	0.81
Coaching Duration	0.94	1.78	1.11	1.32	1.05	0.95	0.98	0.10	0.94	0.49	0.43	0.31	0.47	0.43
Selection Duration	1.99	2.31	1.70	2.15	1.41	1.65	1.50	2.45	1.89	1.74	1.37	2.87	1.42	2.72
Appraisals														
Challenge	4.06	0.82	3.91	0.79	4.04	0.90	3.68	1.29	x	x	x	x	x	x
Threat	1.79	0.63	2.26	1.05	2.02	0.66	2.24	1.37	x	x	x	x	x	x
Centrality	3.24	1.01	2.94	1.42	3.17	1.20	3.24	1.57	x	x	x	x	x	x
Controllable-by-self	3.79	0.80	3.70	0.88	3.67	0.78	3.37	1.33	x	x	x	x	x	x
Controllable-by-others	3.59	1.18	3.76	1.04	3.61	0.95	3.41	1.72	x	x	x	x	x	x
Uncontrollable-by-anyone	1.54	0.45	1.89	1.05	1.59	0.48	1.96	0.83	x	x	x	x	x	x
Stressfulness	2.94	0.74	3.17	0.64	2.93	0.55	3.17	1.09	x	x	x	x	x	x
Emotions														
Anger	0.45	0.71	0.78	0.96	0.72	0.82	1.15	1.68	1.12	0.98	0.67	0.45	0.53	0.39
Anxiety	2.02	1.34	2.30	1.21	2.05	0.92	2.15	1.66	1.72	1.20	1.17	0.63	1.03	0.08
Dejection	0.49	0.88	0.62	0.87	0.71	1.17	1.19	2.03	1.28	1.23	0.64	0.27	0.59	0.25
Excitement	2.93	0.99	2.74	0.83	2.68	0.52	2.59	1.73	2.34	0.81	2.28	1.17	2.25	1.22
Happiness	2.81	1.16	2.51	1.13	2.46	0.66	2.57	1.50	2.42	1.02	2.50	1.22	2.47	1.20
Problem-focused Coping Strategies	3.46	0.84	3.51	0.72	3.57	0.64	3.65	0.65	3.24	0.60	2.80	0.77	2.89	0.97
SSSIR	3.40	0.86	3.30	0.55	3.36	0.53	3.17	0.61	2.73	0.68	2.45	0.65	2.53	0.75
Planning	3.43	1.33	3.45	1.10	3.68	1.03	3.56	1.22	3.51	0.90	3.05	1.27	3.11	1.62
Increasing Effort	3.85	1.29	4.13	0.69	3.91	0.92	4.06	1.04	3.73	0.84	3.32	1.17	3.35	1.22
Active Coping	3.76	1.23	3.76	1.15	3.80	0.96	3.96	0.98	3.46	0.84	3.35	1.44	3.38	1.49
Suppression of Competing Activities	2.86	1.39	2.91	1.26	3.08	0.68	3.52	0.99	2.76	0.97	1.84	0.64	2.09	1.03

(Continued)

TABLE 1 | Continued

Variable	6 weeks prior		3 weeks prior		1 week prior		Invictus Games		1 week post		3 weeks post		6 weeks post	
	M	*SD*	*M*	*SD*	*M*	*SD*	*M*	*SD*	*M*	*SD*	*M*	*SD*	*M*	*SD*
Emotion-focused Coping Strategies	2.23	0.45	2.47	0.34	2.45	0.73	2.77	0.80	2.27	0.50	1.91	0.23	1.93	0.27
SSSER	2.19	1.02	2.26	0.61	2.48	1.00	2.56	1.55	2.46	0.60	2.32	0.60	2.23	0.69
Venting Emotions	1.48	0.42	1.67	0.42	1.83	1.02	2.36	1.70	1.96	1.01	1.31	0.07	1.28	0.10
Wishful Thinking	2.51	0.65	2.71	0.79	2.56	0.91	3.08	1.44	2.08	1.06	1.96	0.38	1.90	0.33
Self-blame	2.81	1.55	2.93	1.31	2.74	1.35	2.94	1.70	2.68	1.32	2.23	1.37	2.33	1.54
Humor	2.18	1.08	2.76	1.26	2.65	1.38	2.91	1.45	2.21	1.39	1.73	0.65	1.92	0.92
Avoidance Coping Strategies	1.43	0.20	1.50	0.25	1.57	0.53	1.61	0.43	1.62	0.43	1.28	0.09	1.29	0.08
Denial	1.64	0.46	1.81	0.63	1.71	0.62	1.94	0.87	1.84	0.54	1.39	0.27	1.42	0.22
Behavioral Disengagement	1.21	0.24	1.19	0.09	1.43	0.67	1.26	0.40	1.39	0.55	1.17	0.13	1.17	0.14
Well-being	45.05	10.06	43.23	11.10	46.25	9.69	43.75	12.58	47.15	8.51	53.17	8.69	51.20	9.11
Mental Health	36.23	12.73	35.26	12.51	34.54	7.87	36.02	11.09	38.22	9.13	44.08	3.04	42.10	3.86
Subjective Performance	6.35	1.73	6.18	3.74	6.60	2.39	6.38	6.38	6.30	3.71	7.07	3.13	6.97	3.50

SSSIR, Seeking Social Support for Instrumental Reasons; SSSER, Seeking Social Support for Emotional Reasons; x, data not collected for this variable at these time points as questions were focused on the appraisals in relation to the upcoming Invictus Games.

Organizational Stressors

A significant increase ($p < 0.05$) was found in the frequency of team and culture stressors in the build-up to competition. The inter-individual variances in the intercept terms were shown to be significant for the majority of organizational stressors. From competition to the final, post-competition time-point, the frequency and intensity of team and culture stressors (frequency, $p < 0.01$; intensity, $p < 0.05$), and intensity of coaching stressors ($p < 0.05$) all significantly decreased. Including group as a TIC of organizational stressors (see **Figure 1**) revealed no significant influence at the intercept, although the IG group reported more intense team and culture stressors in the build-up to competition than those in the CON group ($p < 0.05$). Post-Games, the CON group reported significantly higher dimensions of team and culture stressors (frequency, $p < 0.05$; intensity, $p < 0.01$; duration, $p < 0.05$) as well as more intense logistics and operations stressors ($p < 0.05$). The inclusion of organizational stressors as a TVC in the well-being LGM revealed that the three dimensions of these demands (e.g., frequency, intensity, and duration) were negatively related to well-being at each time point ($p < 0.05$). There were significant negative effects of frequency and intensity of organizational stressors on performance for the day of competition ($p < 0.05$). Furthermore, all three dimensions of organizational stressors were negatively related to mental health at each time point in the build up to and at the Games ($p < 0.05$).

Appraisals

A significant decrease was found in challenge appraisals in the build-up to the Games ($p < 0.05$). Between-person variance was significant at the intercept for the appraisal of centrality ($p < 0.05$), and stressfulness ($p < 0.01$). Including group as a TIC of appraisals showed that in the build-up to competition, IG group participants appraised stressors encountered as uncontrollable-by-anyone more than those in the CON group ($p < 0.001$). Moreover, the CON group made challenge ($p < 0.01$) and centrality ($p < 0.05$) appraisals significantly more than the IG group at the competition time-point. The inclusion of appraisals as a TVC in a well-being LGM revealed that challenge appraisals were positively related to well-being at each time point in the build-up to and at the Games ($p < 0.01$), whilst threat appraisals were negatively related to well-being at each of the same time points ($p < 0.001$). The inclusion of appraisals as a TVC in a subjective performance LGM revealed that threat appraisals were negatively related to subjective performance at time points in the build up to and at the Games ($p < 0.05$). Threat appraisals were negatively related to mental health at all time points in the build up to the Games ($p < 0.001$).

Coping Strategies

Significant rates of growth (between time-points) were found for the use of seeking social support for emotional reasons ($p < 0.05$), suppression of competing activities ($p < 0.05$), venting of emotions ($p < 0.001$), and humor ($p < 0.001$) in the build-up to the Games. Between-person variance of the intercept terms were shown to be significant for the coping strategies of self-blame ($p < 0.05$), humor ($p < 0.01$), denial ($p < 0.01$), and wishful thinking ($p < 0.05$). Significant decreases in the use of humor and denial were found post-Games ($p < 0.05$). Including group as a TIC of coping strategies showed that in the build-up to the Games, the IG group employed the venting emotions coping strategy significantly more than the CON group ($p < 0.01$). At the competition time-point, the IG group used suppression of competing activities and increased effort coping strategies significantly more than the

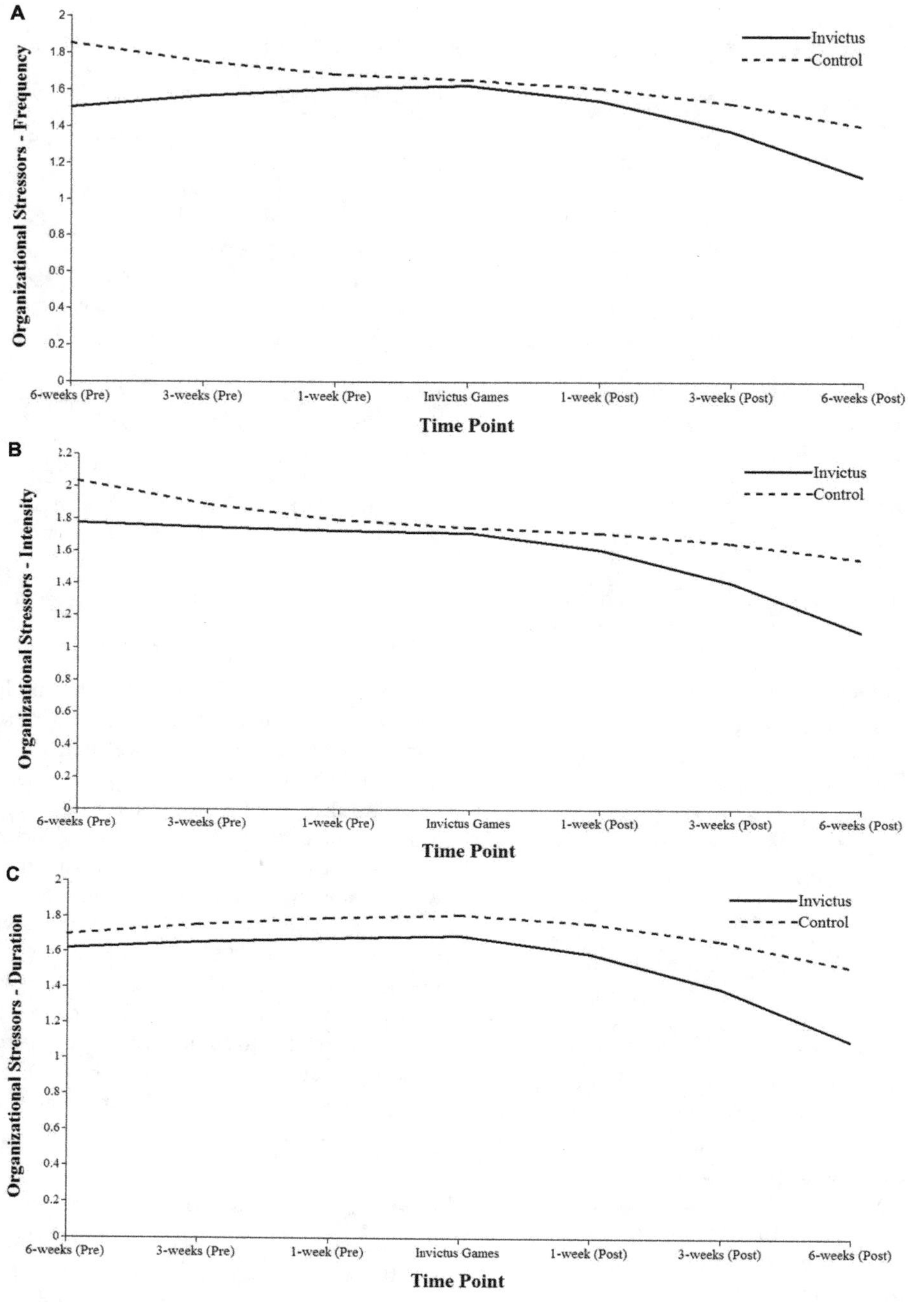

FIGURE 1 | Estimated growth curves for organizational stressor dimensions of frequency **(A)**, intensity **(B)**, and duration **(C)**. Athletes are split into the IG Group or CON Group.

CON group ($p < 0.01$); whereas those in the CON group used behavioral disengagement coping strategies significantly more than the IG group at this time-point ($p < 0.01$). When coping strategies were included as a TVC in a well-being LGM, problem-focused strategies were positively related to well-being at time-points 2 and 3 ($p < 0.05$). In contrast, emotion-focused and avoidance strategies were negatively related to well-being from time-point 3 to 7 ($p < 0.01$). Avoidance strategies were negatively related to mental health in the build up to and at the competition ($p < 0.001$).

Emotions

Anger and dejection showed significant rates of growth prior to competition ($p < 0.001$), whereas excitement and happiness decreased ($p < 0.05$). Between-person variance of the intercept terms were shown to be significant for anxiety ($p < 0.01$)

and anger ($p < 0.05$). In the post-competition period, anxiety decreased ($p < 0.05$). Including group as a TIC of emotions showed that in the build-up to the Games, the IG group reported anger ($p < 0.05$) and dejection ($p < 0.01$) significantly more than the CON group. Furthermore, at the competition time-point the IG group were significantly more anxious than the CON group ($p < 0.05$). The inclusion of emotions as a TVC in a well-being LGM showed that anger, anxiety, and dejection were negatively related to well-being in the build up to and at the Games ($p < 0.01$). Conversely, happiness and excitement were positively related to well-being at the same time points as well as post-competition ($p < 0.01$). The inclusion of emotions as a TVC in a performance LGM showed that anxiety and dejection were negatively related to performance in the build up to the Games ($p < 0.05$), whereas happiness was positively related to performance in the pre-competition period ($p < 0.05$). Anger, anxiety, and dejection were negatively related to mental health at each time-point in the build up to and at the Games ($p < 0.05$), whilst excitement and happiness were positively related to mental health ($p < 0.05$).

Salivary S-IgA and Cortisol

Table 2 displays descriptive statistics for salivary S-IgA and cortisol. There were no significant changes over time for secretion of S-IgA. Mean scores and between-person variance of the intercept terms were shown to be significant, indicating that S-IgA secretion on the day of competition varied across participants. The inclusion of group as a TIC revealed no significant differences between the IG and CON groups in S-IgA secretion rate (see **Figure 2**). The inclusion of all psychosocial variables as separate TVCs in S-IgA exposure across the day LGMs revealed no significant findings. There was a significant decrease in cortisol exposure over the course of the study period ($p < 0.05$). Between-person variance of the slope term was shown to be significant for cortisol exposure ($p < 0.05$) meaning that individuals varied in levels of cortisol throughout the study period. Including group as a TIC revealed no significant differences between the IG and CON groups in cortisol exposure (see **Figure 2**). The inclusion of organizational stressor dimensions as a TVC in the cortisol exposure across the day LGM revealed that intensity of organizational stressors was positively related to cortisol exposure on the day of competition ($p < 0.05$). The inclusion of all other stress variables as TVCs revealed non-significant findings.

Upper Respiratory Tract Infections

In line with the first criterion of classifying URTIs, that symptoms had to last two or more days and score greater than 14 (Predy et al., 2005), only one participant at the IG reported a cold over a period of 2 days. Using the second criterion of subjective self-report of a cold, only four participants at the IG reported a cold over an average of seven and a half days. Due to a small number of participants reporting URTIs, no further analyses were undertaken.

DISCUSSION

Research to date has not examined military veterans' holistic experiences of high-level sport and the antecedents to both positive and negative outcomes. Therefore, the primary purpose of this study was to examine the stress experiences of competitors in preparation for, during, and following the IG and how these experiences may alter over time and in comparison to a control group not participating in high-level competition. Furthermore, a secondary purpose of the study was to examine the relationships between veterans' stress (i.e., stressors, responses) and psychological, behavioral, and physiological (i.e., salivary measurements of immune and endocrine function) outcomes. The results provide the first longitudinal insight into how the dynamic stress process variables (e.g., stressors, appraisals, coping, and emotions) change over the extended period of a competitive sporting event and, importantly, the relationship between stress and military veterans' performance, well-being, and health. Contextualized within extant sport psychology literature and theory, these findings are in accordance with the transactional stress process (cf. Lazarus and Folkman, 1984) and can advance extant knowledge and understanding by advancing methodology from cross-sectional snapshots of stress-related variables to more robust examinations of how they can fluctuate over time and predict important outcomes.

This study showed that the organizational stressors encountered by IG participants changed over time. Specifically, team and culture stressors significantly increased in frequency in the build-up to the Games, before decreasing post-competition. These team and culture stressors, which refer to demands associated with attitudes and behavior in the team, may have increased because participants may not have previously encountered these types of stressor in a competitive sporting environment. Indeed, veterans may have reported more of these stressors due to either the new responsibilities they felt they had on their new team, or perhaps certain teammate attitudes that they may not have encountered previously. Furthermore, the increase in frequency and intensity of team and culture stressors may be explained by the increased amount of time athletes spent together when training and preparing for competition. Previous research examining military competitions (Sporner et al., 2009) has suggested that veterans look to their peers for support because they share similar experiences; the findings of this study suggest that this may have been difficult for some athletes, particularly if the stressor had been their teammates (cf. Arnold et al., 2018). Previous research has highlighted that the organizational stressors encountered by a sport performer can be associated at one time-point with negative emotions and performance dissatisfaction (Fletcher et al., 2012b; Arnold et al., 2013). Results from this study advance extant knowledge by finding that, over time, the dimensions of organizational stressors negatively relate to well-being, performance, and mental health in IG participants.

Appraisals are instrumental in the stress process and can provide insight into how a performer responds, and subsequently

TABLE 2 | Means and standard deviations for biomarkers of stress at all time points for all participants.

Variable	1 week prior		Post-flight		Invictus Games		1 week post	
	M	*SD*	*M*	*SD*	*M*	*SD*	*M*	*SD*
IG Group								
S-IgA Secretion Rate (μg/mL/min∼15 h)	715.97	824.32	830.53	804.61	595.16	500.61	707.56	518.62
Cortisol Concentration (μg/mL∼15 h)	4.26	6.21	5.44	5.53	5.63	6.31	2.41	1.37
URTI symptom severity	0.89	2.01	0.94	2.15	0.38	1.01	0.35	1.03
URTI symptom duration (days)	0.15	0.36	1.00	1.98	0.58	1.50	0.44	0.86
CON Group								
S-IgA Secretion Rate (μg/mL/min∼15 h)	529.12	207.69	583.54	318.09	687.16	452.66	628.74	330.21
Cortisol Concentration (μg/mL)	1.81	0.63	2.81	1.85	2.13	1.21	2.42	1.18
URTI symptom severity	0.00	0.00	0.00	0.00	0.00	0.00	0.00	0.00
URTI symptom duration (days)	0.00	0.00	0.00	0.00	0.00	0.00	0.00	0.00

S-IgA Secretion Rate (μg/mL/min∼15 h) refers to S-IgA exposure across the day and was calculated using AUCg; Cortisol concentration (μg/mL/min∼15 h) refers to cortisol exposure across the day and was calculated using AUCg; URTI symptom severity was calculated using total symptom scores across the study period and averaged across participants; URTI symptom duration was calculated using total days reported across the study period and averaged across participants.

adapts, to stressors in their sport. In contrast to extant literature (Cumming et al., 2017), the present study found that in the build-up to competition challenge appraisals significantly decreased. As organizational stressors (e.g., logistics and operations) typically relate to environmental factors often out of an athlete's control (i.e., controlled by the coach or organization), it is likely that athletes felt a lack of control and subsequent mastery of events, particularly close to competition which led to reductions in challenge appraisals. In support of the transactional stress approach, threat appraisals were shown to be negatively related to well-being and subjective performance in the build-up to the Games. This negative relationship is reflective of research in sport psychology where, across a number of sports, threat appraisals are considered maladaptive to performance (Nicholls et al., 2011). This study advances extant literature, however, by demonstrating this relationship over time and with a military veteran sample. This longitudinal focus is important as can provide insight into the temporal occurrence of and fluctuations in stressors and appraisals, and the sequence of events in the stress process (i.e., risk factors for particular health, well-being and performance outcomes). A negative relationship was also found between threat appraisals and mental health in the build-up to the Games. Work by Solomon et al. (1988) showed that military veterans who appraised situations as a threat and did not employ appropriate coping strategies had exacerbated PTSD symptoms. Considering the prevalence of PTSD in military veterans and the topicality of military veteran health (Caddick and Smith, 2014; HM Government, 2018), the findings of this study, highlighting the adaptive nature of challenge appraisals and maladaptive nature of threat appraisals for health and wellbeing, provides an important and significant advance for supporting individuals with such illnesses in a veteran population.

In the build-up to the Games, athletes who utilized problem-focused coping strategies reported higher levels of well-being. Nicholls et al. (2012) demonstrated similar findings among a non-military athlete population, who expressed more emotions that are positive when they engaged in problem-focused coping strategies. Conversely, emotion- and avoidance-focused strategies were negatively related to well-being over the same period. These findings support previous literature, which has demonstrated that not dealing with problems can negatively affect an athlete, regardless of age or level (Nicholls et al., 2012). Furthermore, this study advances previous military psychology literature (cf. Barnett et al., 2016) as it illustrates that avoidance-focused strategies adopted by veterans in the build-up to international sporting competitions are negatively related to mental health. This finding also has implications for practitioners encouraging military veterans to use sport as a form of recovery. Specifically, it is suggested that they look to support veterans with the development and implementation of problem-focused coping strategies in response to sporting demands, given the positive relationship found with well-being in this study and the recognized and topical importance of this outcome for military veterans' recovery journeys (Weir et al., 2017; Caddick and Smith, 2018; HM Government, 2018).

Negative emotions increased in the build-up to the Games and were negatively related to well-being, subjective performance, and mental health. To explain the heightened dejection reported in the build-up to the Games, it is likely that the IG participants lacked experience of international sporting competition; therefore, feelings of deficiency in terms of their performance may have arisen (cf. Jones et al., 2005). Conversely, athletes experiencing higher levels of positive emotions (e.g., happiness, enjoyment) reported higher well-being, subjective performance, and mental health prior to the Games. Positive emotions have been associated with sport and in particular, individuals appraising themselves as making progress toward a goal (Lazarus, 2000). This may explain the findings that positive emotions reported by military veterans were associated with well-being in the build-up to the Games, since participants were working toward the goal of competing at the IG.

The organizational stressor dimension of intensity was shown to be significantly, positively related to cortisol exposure on the day of competition. Previous research has demonstrated

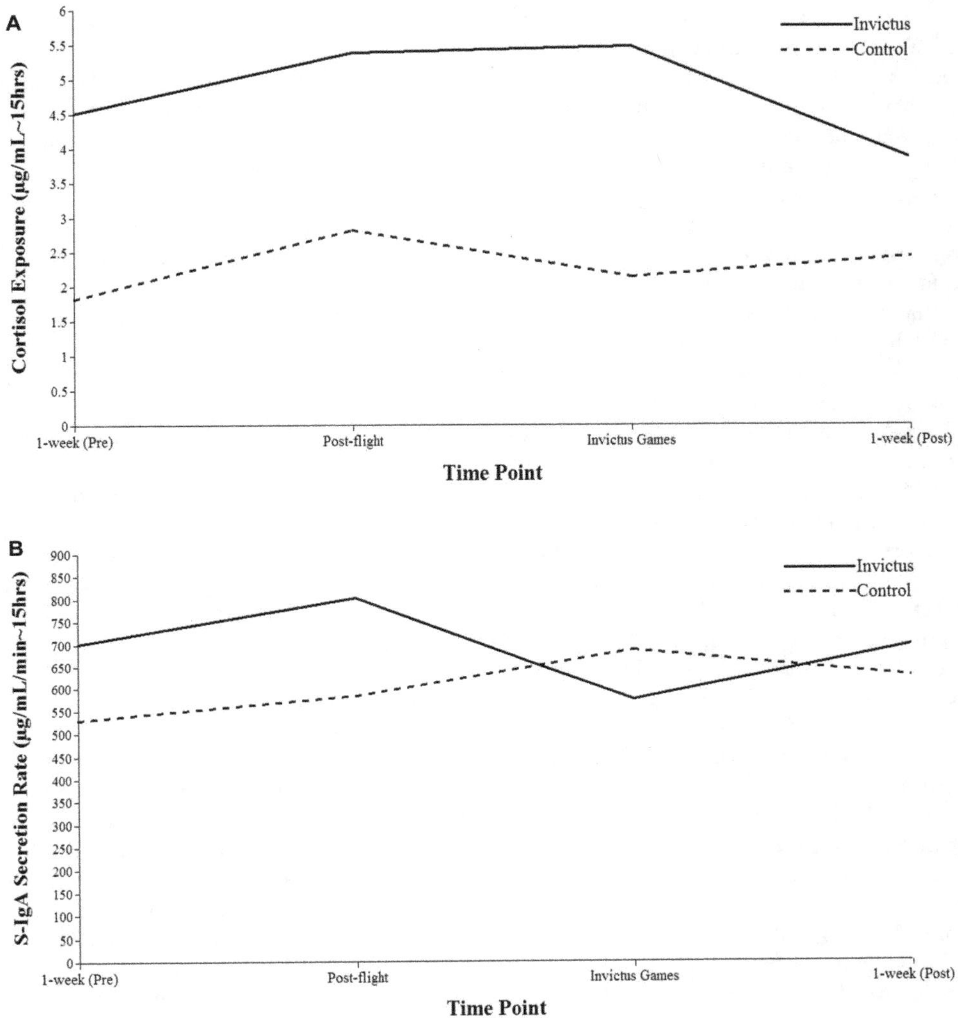

FIGURE 2 | Growth curves for biomarkers of stress: cortisol exposure **(A)** and salivary immunoglobulin A **(B)**. Athletes are split into the IG Group or CON Group.

increases in salivary cortisol concentration in response to competition (Casto and Edwards, 2016); however, this is the first study in sport to identify organizational stressors as a potential trigger of the salivary cortisol response. Indeed, it could be argued that this increased exposure to cortisol on the day of competition was in response to the intensity of stressors surrounding competition. Arguably, this rise in cortisol on the day of competition may have been a positive, appropriate, and adaptive response to prepare individuals for extreme physical exertions. Nevertheless, salivary cortisol exposure was shown to decrease over the course of the study. This is in contrast to previous research which has demonstrated anticipatory rises in cortisol prior to competition and even greater increases at competition, prior to an expected decrease post-competition (Casto and Edwards, 2016). Furthermore, previous research has shown that under conditions where participants appraise the situation as a threat, cortisol levels rise; though the effect of this physiological response may be moderated by important factors such as individual difference (Meggs et al., 2016). As previously mentioned, however, there was no significant change in threat appraisals observed prior to competition; therefore, although, challenge appraisal significantly decreased in the build-up to competition, it could be suggested that it is a threat appraisal increase (rather than challenge appraisal decrease) which is related to cortisol fluctuations. These relationships, however, require further investigation.

Although no significant changes were observed for S-IgA secretion across each day or between time-points, it is worth noting that S-IgA was, on average across IG participants, produced at the lowest levels on the day of competition. A potential explanation could be that elevated cortisol levels, due to organizational stressor intensity, suppressed S-IgA secretion. Thus, the findings of this study provide further weight to the argument that factors other than exercise *per se* might affect immune function (e.g., psychological stress or international travel; Campbell and Turner, 2018). Although few symptoms of URTIs were reported in the present study, the reduced S-IgA secretion could have potential longer-term implications for IG participants post-competition. For example, aspects of immune function appear to be impaired among individuals who have suffered physical and psychological injuries (Klokker et al., 1998; Neigh and Ali, 2016). Therefore, practitioners could consider monitoring biomarkers of stress, endocrine function, and immune competency, alongside psychological measures, to ensure that fully informed conclusions regarding an athlete's health and their ability to perform can be made (Taylor et al., 2015).

A key strength of this study is the population examined, since the diversity of previous life experiences and distinctiveness of military veterans who compete in sport can enrich sports psychology research, which has rarely sampled such individuals. The longitudinal study design employed is also a strength, since it has advanced sport psychology research from examining isolated components of the stress process cross-sectionally to a more theoretically informed transactional approach (cf. Lazarus, 2000). Advantages of this approach are that, compared to cross-sectional research designs, it has enabled changes over time to be established, recall bias in participants to be minimized, and stressors and responses (i.e., risk factors) to be related to particular outcomes with specific reference to their presence, timing, and dimensions. Furthermore, measuring salivary biomarkers of stress, endocrine function (i.e., cortisol), and immune competence (i.e., S-IgA) provides a holistic insight into stress in sport; thus, overcoming previously identified limitations of subjective measurements of stress (Arnold and Fletcher, 2012b). The assessment of both S-IgA and cortisol highlights the complex and dynamic response to stress and provides a novel insight into linking these measures to organizational stressors in particular. It must be noted, however, that the assessment of cortisol may have been affected in female athletes due to their menstrual cycle (Maki et al., 2015). The IG structure determined the relative timing of saliva samples, and as such, menstrual cycle effects on cortisol levels is unclear in this study and should be investigated further in the future. Although the sample in this study is a unique population, a limitation of this study was that it did not consider how stress varies as a result of injury characteristics and presence of comorbidities (e.g., PTSD). Examining these distinct characteristics will provide further insight into the specific experiences of military veterans. In line with the previous suggestion, a pertinent future research direction would also be to conduct research with a larger sample size, which will enable demographic and injury differences to be examined. It should also be highlighted that military veterans are predominantly male (Ministry of Defence, 2019) and this is reflected in this study's gender ratio. With an increasing presence of females in the military and as veterans (Lundberg et al., 2016), scholars are encouraged to examine in future investigations the potential differences between males and females' experiences of international sporting competition (cf. Lundberg et al., 2016). A further limitation is that the measures used provide snapshots in time of military veterans' stress and despite providing valuable insight, they do not provide depth and understanding of individuals' stress experiences. To address this, qualitative research methods would help to provide a deeper understanding of an individual's stress experience during international sports events.

Previous research has supported the notion that participation in high-level sport provides various benefits for military veterans (Brittain, 2012). Notwithstanding these benefits, the findings of this study have highlighted that elements of the psychological stress process reported in the build up to, during, and post international sports events can have negative consequences for psychological, behavioral, and immunological outcomes and should be carefully managed. Specifically, it is suggested based on this study's findings, that practitioners consider the development and implementation of stress management interventions which look to either reduce the presence or dimensions of demands (e.g., a primary stress management intervention focused on reducing the dimensions of team and culture stressors) or better support individual responses to them (e.g., a secondary stress management intervention; Cooper, 2015; Arnold et al., 2017). This secondary intervention could support military veterans in making challenge appraisals and reducing threat appraisals of the specific stressors encountered (cf. Jamieson et al., 2018) and enhancing their problem-focused coping by helping to develop strategies that deal with the stressor (e.g., planning, effort, and active coping). Furthermore, from an applied perspective, monitoring of S-IgA and cortisol in saliva as an indicator of immune and endocrine function in athletes could also be conducted to provide further insight into the potential biological consequences of stress. Findings from these biomarkers, alongside the psychosocial measures, imply that a holistic perspective is warranted toward athlete monitoring prior to and during competition as these factors can interact and impact upon an individual's functioning (see also Taylor et al., 2015).

To conclude, this is the first study to explore military veterans' holistic stress experiences during a sports competition period, as well as how this differs to veteran athletes who do not experience competition. The novel findings provide important advancements for research in the sports domain regarding fluctuations in components of the stress process over time (e.g., stressors, appraisals, coping, and emotions) and how these are associated with important outcomes (e.g., performance, health, and well-being). The novel, multidisciplinary findings of this study can enhance scholars and practitioners' awareness of the psychological and biological markers of the stress response, their interactions, and the relationship with the health and well-being of military veterans. Furthermore, the findings provide further weight to the argument that factors other than exercise *per se* might affect immune function (i.e., psychological stress; Campbell and Turner, 2018) and, for the first time in a sports context, have found that organizational stressors are a potential trigger of the salivary cortisol response. By understanding this study's findings, practitioners and organizations can help to proactively prevent organizational demands and aid individuals in optimally responding and adapting to encounters, which can ultimately, help to mitigate negative outcomes and proliferate the positive outcomes for military veterans participating in competitive sport.

ETHICS STATEMENT

This study was carried out in accordance with the APA ethical standards. This study was approved by the REACH ethics committee at the University of Bath. All participants gave written informed consent in accordance with the Declaration of Helsinki, and anonymity and confidentiality were assured.

AUTHOR CONTRIBUTIONS

All authors listed have made a substantial, direct and intellectual contribution to the work, and approved it for publication.

REFERENCES

Ader, R., Cohen, N., and Felten, D. (1995). Psychoneuroimmunology: interactions between the nervous system and the immune system. *Lancet* 345, 99–103. doi: 10.1016/S0140-6736(95)90066-7

Arnold, R., Edwards, T., and Rees, T. (2018). Organizational stressors, social support, and implications for subjective performance in high-level sport. *Psychol. Sport Exerc.* 39, 204–212. doi: 10.1016/j.psychsport.2018.08.010

Arnold, R., and Fletcher, D. (2012a). A research synthesis and taxonomic classification of the organizational stressors encountered by sport performers. *J. Sport Exerc. Psychol.* 34, 397–429. doi: 10.1123/jsep.34.3.397

Arnold, R., and Fletcher, D. (2012b). Psychometric issues in organizational stressor research: a review and implications for sport psychology. *Meas. Phys. Educ. Exerc. Sci.* 16, 81–100. doi: 10.1080/1091367X.2012.639608

Arnold, R., and Fletcher, D. (2015). Confirmatory factor analysis of the sport emotion questionnaire in organizational environments. *J. Sports Sci.* 33, 169–179. doi: 10.1080/02640414.2014.955520

Arnold, R., Fletcher, D., and Daniels, K. (2013). Development and validation of the organizational stressor indicator for sports performers (OSI-SP). *J. Sport Exerc. Psychol.* 35, 180–196. doi: 10.1123/jsep.35.2180

Arnold, R., Fletcher, D., and Daniels, K. (2016a). Demographic differences in sport performers' experiences of organizational stressors. *Scand. J. Med. Sci. Sports* 26, 348–358. doi: 10.1111/sms.12439

Arnold, R., Wagstaff, C., Steadman, L., and Pratt, Y. (2016b). The organizational stressors encountered by athletes with a disability. *J. Sports Sci.* 35, 1187–1196. doi: 10.1080/02640414.2016.1214285

Arnold, R., Fletcher, D., and Daniels, K. (2017). Organizational stressors, coping, and outcomes in competitive sport. *J. Sports Sci.* 35, 694–703. doi: 10.1080/02640414.2016.1184299

Barnett, T. M., Smith-Osborne, A., and Barnett-Braddock, F. (2016). Systematic review of veterans' coping strategies: how can rural veterans improve their quality of life? *Contemp. Rural Soc. Work* 8, 37–62.

Bartholomew, K. J., Arnold, R., Hampson, R. J., and Fletcher, D. (2017). Organizational stressors and basic psychological needs: the mediating role of athletes' appraisal mechanisms. *Scand. J. Med. Sci. Sports* 27, 2127–2139. doi: 10.1111/sms.12851

Blascovich, J. (2008). "Challenge and threat," in *Handbook of Approach and Avoidance Motivation*, ed. A. J. Elliot (New York, NY: Psychology Press), 431–445.

Bonini, M., Gramiccioni, C., Fioretti, D., Ruckert, B., Rinaldi, M., Akdis, C., et al. (2015). Asthma, allergy and the Olympics: a 12-year survey in elite athletes. *Curr. Opin. Allergy Clin. Immunol.* 15, 184–192. doi: 10.1097/ACI.0000000000000149

Brittain, I. (2012). The paralympic games: from a rehabilitation exercise to elite sport (and back again?). *Int. J. Ther. Rehabil.* 19, 526–530. doi: 10.12968/itjr.2012.19.9.526

Caddick, N., and Smith, B. (2014). The impact of sport and physical activity on the well-being of combat veterans: a systematic review. *Psychol. Sport Exerc.* 15, 9–18. doi: 10.1016/j.psychsport.2013.09.011

Caddick, N., and Smith, B. (2018). Exercise is medicine for mental health in military veterans: a qualitative commentary. *Qual. Res. Sport Exerc. Health* 10, 429–440. doi: 10.1080/2159676X.2017.1333033

Campbell, J. P., and Turner, J. E. (2018). Debunking the myth of exercise-induced immune suppression: redefining the impact of exercise on immunological health across the lifespan. *Front. Immunol.* 9:648. doi: 10.3389/fimmu.2018.00648

Casto, K. V., and Edwards, D. A. (2016). Before, during, and after: how phases of competition differentially affect testosterone, cortisol, and estradiol levels in women athletes. *Adapt. Hum. Behav. Physiol.* 2, 11–25. doi: 10.1007/s40750-015-0028-2

Choudhry, A. J., Al Mudaimegh, K. S., Turkistani, A. M., and Al Hamdan, N. A. (2006). Hajj-associated acute respiratory infection among hajjis from Riyadh. *East Mediterr. Health J.* 12, 300–309.

Cooper, C. L. (2015). "Stress management interventions: reflections," in *Derailed Organizational Interventions for Stress and Well-Being*, eds M. Karanika, and C. Biron (Dordrecht: Springer), 271–273. doi: 10.1007/978-94-017-9867-9_31

Crocker, P. R. E., and Graham, T. R. (1995). Coping by competitive athletes with performance stress: gender differences and relationships with affect. *Sport Psychol.* 9, 325–338. doi: 10.1123/tsp.9.3.325

Cumming, S. J. D., Turner, M., and Jones, M. (2017). Longitudinal changes in elite rowers' challenge and threat appraisals of pressure situations. *Sport Psychol.* 31, 217–226. doi: 10.1123/tsp.2016-0087

Cunniffe, B., Griffiths, H., Proctor, W., Davies, B., Baker, J. S., and Jones, K. P. (2011). Mucosal immunity and illness incidence in elite rugby union players across a season. *Med. Sci. Sports Exerc.* 43, 388–397. doi: 10.1249/MSS.0b013e3181ef9d6b

Curran, P. J., Obeidat, K., and Losardo, D. (2010). Twelve frequently asked questions about growth curve modeling. *J. Cogn. Dev.* 11, 121–136. doi: 10.1080/15248371003699969

Derman, W., Schwellnus, M., and Jordan, E. (2014). Clinical characteristics of 385 illnesses of athletes with impairment reported on the WEB-IISS system during the London 2012 paralympic games. *PM R* 6(8 Suppl.), 23–30. doi: 10.1016/j.pmrj.2014.05.016

Didymus, F. F., and Fletcher, D. (2014). Swimmers' experiences of organizational stress: exploring the role of cognitive appraisal and coping behaviors. *J. Clin. Sport Psychol.* 8, 159–183. doi: 10.1123/jcsp.2014-0020

Fear, N. T., Jones, M., Murphy, D., Hull, L., Iversen, A. C., Coker, B., et al. (2010). What are the consequences of deployment to Iraq and Afghanistan on the mental health of the UK armed forces? A cohort study. *Lancet* 375, 22–28. doi: 10.1016/S0140-6736(10)60672-1

Fletcher, D., and Arnold, R. (2017). "Stress in sport: the role of the organizational environment," in *An Organizational Psychology of Sport: Key Issues and Practical Applications*, ed. C. R. D. Wagstaff (Abingdon: Routledge), 83–100.

Fletcher, D., Hanton, S., and Mellalieu, S. D. (2006). "An organizational stress review: conceptual and theoretical issues in competitive sport," in *Literature Reviews in Sport Psychology*, eds S. Hanton, and S. D. Mellalieu (Hauppauge, NY: Nova Science Publishers), 321–373.

Fletcher, D., Hanton, S., Mellalieu, S. D., and Neil, R. (2012a). A conceptual framework of organizational stressors in sport performers. *Scand. J. Med. Sci. Sports* 22, 545–557. doi: 10.1111/j.1600-0838.2010.01242.x

Fletcher, D., Hanton, S., and Wagstaff, C. R. D. (2012b). Performers' responses to stressors encountered in sport organizations. *J. Sports Sci.* 30, 349–358. doi: 10.1080/02640414.2011.633545

Gleeson, M., Bishop, N. C., Oliveira, M., McCauley, T., and Tauler, P. (2011). Sex differences in immune variables and respiratory infection incidence in an athletic population. *Exerc. Immunol. Rev.* 17, 122–135.

Godin, G., and Shephard, R. J. (1985). A simple method to assess exercise behavior in the community. *Can. J. Appl. Sport Sci.* 10, 141–146.

Hanton, S., Fletcher, D., and Coughlan, G. (2005). Stress in elite sport performers: a comparative study of competitive and organizational stressors. *J. Sports Sci.* 23, 1129–1141. doi: 10.1080/02640410500131480

HM Government, (2018). *The Strategy for Our Veterans – UK Government Consultation Paper*. Available at: https://assets.publishing.service.gov.uk/government/uploads/system/uploads/attachment_data/file/755933/Strategy_for_our_Veterans_UK_Gov_Consultation_FINAL_12.11.18_web.pdf (accessed July 17, 2019).

Jacks, D. E., Sowash, J., Anning, J., McGloughlin, T., and Andres, F. (2002). Effect of exercise at three exercise intensities on salivary cortisol. *J. Strength Cond. Res.* 16, 286–289. doi: 10.1519/00124278-200205000-00018

Jackson, G. G., Dowling, H. F., Spiesman, I. G., and Boand, A. V. (1958). Transmission of the common cold to volunteers under controlled conditions. I. The common cold as a clinical entity. *Arch. Intern. Med.* 101, 267–278. doi: 10.1001/archinte.1958.00260140099015

Jamieson, J. P., Crum, A. J., Goyer, J. P., Marotta, M. E., and Akinola, M. (2018). Optimizing stress responses with reappraisal and mindset interventions: an integrated model. *Anxiety Stress Coping* 31, 245–261. doi: 10.1080/10615806.2018.1442615

Jones, M. V., Lane, A. M., Bray, S. R., Uphill, M., and Catlin, J. (2005). Development and validation of the sport emotion questionnaire. *J. Sport Exerc. Psychol.* 27, 407–431. doi: 10.13072/midss.117

Klokker, M., Mohr, T., Kjaer, M., Galbo, H., and Pedersen, B. K. (1998). The natural killer cell response to exercise in spinal cord injured individuals. *Eur. J. Appl. Physiol.* 79, 106–109. doi: 10.1007/s004210050481

Larner, R. J., Wagstaff, C. R. D., Thelwell, R. C., and Corbett, J. (2016). A multi-study examination of organizational stresors, emotional labor, burnout, and turnover in sport organizations. *Scand. J. Med. Sci. Sports.* 27, 2103–2115. doi: 10.1111/sms.12833

Lazarus, R. S. (2000). How emotions influence performance in competitive sports. *Sport Psychol.* 14, 229–252. doi: 10.1123/tsp.14.3.229

Lazarus, R. S., and Folkman, S. (1984). *Stress, Appraisal, and Coping*. New York, NY: Springer Publications Company.

Li, T.-L., and Gleeson, M. (2004). The effect of single and repeated bouts of prolonged cycling and circadian variation on saliva flow rate, immunoglobulin A and α-amylase responses. *J. Sports Sci.* 22, 1015–1024. doi: 10.1080/02640410410001716733

Lundberg, N., Taniguchi, S., McGovern, R., and Smith, S. (2016). Female veterans' involvement in outdoor sports and recreation. *J. Leis. Res.* 48, 413–430. doi: 10.18666/JLR-2016-V48-I5-6897

Lundqvist, C. (2011). Well-being in competitive sports – The feel-good factor? A review of conceptual considerations of well-being. *Int. Rev. Sport Exerc. Psychol.* 4, 109–127. doi: 10.1080/1750984X.2011.584067

Maki, P. M., Mordecai, K. L., Rubin, L. H., Sundermann, E., Savarese, A., Eatough, E., et al. (2015). Menstrual cycle effects on cortisol responsivity and emotional retrieval following a psychosocial stressor. *Horm. Behav.* 74, 201–208. doi: 10.1016/j.yhbeh.2015.06.023

Meggs, J., Golby, J., Mallett, C. J., Gucciardi, D. F., and Polman, R. C. (2016). The cortisol awakening response and resilience in elite swimmers. *Int. J. Sports Med.* 37, 169–174. doi: 10.1055/s-0035-1559773

Ministry of Defence, (2019). *Annual Population Survey: UK Armed Forces Veterans residing in Great Britain, 2017*. Available at: https://assets.publishing.service.gov.uk/government/uploads/system/uploads/attachment_data/file/774937/20190128_-_APS_2017_Statistical_Bulletin_-_OS.pdf (accessed July 17, 2019).

Mortatti, A. L., Moreira, A., Aoki, M. S., Crewther, B. T., Castagna, C., de Arruda, A. F. S., et al. (2012). Effect of competition on salivary cortisol, immunoglobulin A, and upper respiratory tract infections in elite young soccer players. *J. Strength Cond. Res.* 26, 1396–1401. doi: 10.1519/JSC.0b013e31822e7b63

Murphy, D., Spencer-Harper, L., Carson, C., Palmer, E., Hill, K., Sorfleet, N., et al. (2016). Long-term responses to treatment in UK veterans with military-related PTSD: an observational study. *BMJ Open* 6, 1–8. doi: 10.1136/bmjopen-2016-011667

Muthén, L. K., and Muthén, B. O. (1998/2015). *Mplus User's Guide*, Seventh Edn. Los Angeles, CA: Muthén and Muthén.

Navazesh, M. (1993). Methods for collecting saliva. *Ann. N. Y. Acad. Sci.* 694, 72–77. doi: 10.1111/j.1749-6632.1993.tb18343.x

Neigh, G. N., and Ali, F. F. (2016). Co-Morbidity of PTSD and immune system dysfunction: opportunities for treatment. *Curr. Opin. Pharmacol.* 29, 104–110. doi: 10.1016/j.coph.2016.07.011

Neville, V., Gleeson, M., and Folland, J. P. (2008). Salivary IgA as a risk factor for upper respiratory infections in elite professional athletes. *Med. Sci. Sports Exerc.* 40, 1228–1236. doi: 10.1249/MSS.0b013e31816be9c3

Nicholls, A. R., Levy, A. R., Jones, L., Rengamani, M., and Polman, R. C. J. (2011). An exploration of the two-factor schematization of relational meaning and emotions among professional rugby union players. *Int. J. Sport Exerc. Psychol.* 9, 78–91. doi: 10.1080/1612197X.2011.563128

Nicholls, A. R., Polman, R., and Levy, A. (2012). A path analysis of stress appraisals, emotions, coping, and performance satisfaction among athletes. *Psychol. Sport Exerc.* 13, 263–270. doi: 10.1016/j.psychsport.2011.12.003

Otter, L., and Currie, J. (2004). A long time getting home: vietnam veterans' experiences in a community exercise rehabilitation programme. *Disabil. Rehabil.* 26, 27–34. doi: 10.1080/09638280410001645067

Peacock, E. J., and Wong, P. T. P. (1990). The stress appraisal measure (SAM): a multidimensional approach to cognitive appraisal. *Stress Med.* 6, 227–236. doi: 10.1002/smi.2460060308

Pedersen, A., Zachariae, R., and Bovbjerg, D. H. (2010). Influence of psychological stress on upper respiratory infection – A meta-analysis of prospective studies. *Psychosom. Med.* 72, 823–832. doi: 10.1097/PSY.0b013e3181f1d003

Pensgaard, A. M., and Duda, J. L. (2003). Sydney 2000: the interplay between emotions, coping, and the performance of Olympic-level athletes. *Sport Psychol.* 17, 253–267. doi: 10.1123/tsp.17.3.253

Preacher, K. J., Wichman, A. L., MacCullum, R., and Briggs, N. E. (2008). *Latent Growth Curve Modeling*. Thousand Oaks, CA: Sage Publications.

Predy, G. N., Goel, V., Lovlin, R., Donner, A., Stitt, L., and Basu, T. K. (2005). Efficacy of an extract of North American ginseng containing poly-furanosyl-saccharides for preventing upper respiratory tract infections: a randomized controlled trial. *CMAJ* 173, 1043–1048. doi: 10.1503/cmaj.1041470

Pruessner, J. C., Kirschbaum, C., Meinlschmid, G., and Hellhammer, D. H. (2003). Two formulas for the computation of the area under the curve represent measures of total hormone concentration versus time-dependent change. *Psychoneuroendocrinology* 28, 916–931. doi: 10.1016/S0306-4530(02)00108-7

Segerstrom, S. C., and Miller, G. E. (2004). Psychological stress and the human immune system: a meta-analytic study of 30 years of inquiry. *Psychol. Bull.* 130, 601–630. doi: 10.1037/0033-2909.130.4.601

Solomon, Z., Mikulincer, M., and Avitzur, E. (1988). Coping, locus of control, social support, and combat-related posttraumatic stress disorder: a prospective study. *J. Pers. Soc. Psychol.* 55, 279–285. doi: 10.1037/0022-3514.55.2.279

Sporner, M. L., Fitzgerald, S. G., Dicianno, B. E., Collins, D., Teodorski, E., Pasquina, P. F., et al. (2009). Psychosocial impact of participation in the National Veterans wheelchair games and winter sports clinic. *Disabil. Rehabil.* 31, 410–418. doi: 10.1080/09638280802030923

Tabei, Y., Fletcher, D., and Goodger, K. (2012). The relationship between organizational stressors and athlete burnout in soccer players. *J. Clin. Psychol.* 6, 146–165. doi: 10.1123/jcsp.6.2.146

Taylor, I. M., Turner, J. E., Gleeson, M., and Hough, J. (2015). Negative psychological experiences and saliva secretory immunoglobulin a in field hockey players. *J. Appl. Sport Psychol.* 27, 67–78. doi: 10.1080/10413200.2014.949907

Tennant, R., Hiller, L., Fishwick, R., Platt, S., Joseph, S., Weich, S., et al. (2007). The Warwick-Edinburgh mental well-being scale (WEMWBS): development and UK validation. *Health Qual. Life Outcomes.* 5:63. doi: 10.1186/1477-7525-5-63

Wagstaff, C. R. D., Hings, R., Larner, R., and Fletcher, D. (2018). Psychological resilience's moderation of the relationship between the frequency of organizational stressors and burnout in athletes and coaches. *Sport Psychol.* 32, 178–188. doi: 10.1123/tsp.2016-0068

Ware, J. E., Kosinski, M., and Keller, S. D. (1995). A 12-item short-form health survey. Construction of scales and preliminary tests of reliability and validity. *Med. Care* 34, 220–233. doi: 10.1097/00005650-199603000-00003

Weir, B., Cunningham, M., Abraham, L., and Allanson-Oddy, C. (2017). Military veteran engagement with mental health and well-being services: a qualitative study of the role of the peer support worker. *J. Ment. Health* doi: 10.1080/09638237.2017.1370640 [Epub ahead of print].

9

Emotional Intelligence (EI) Training Adapted to the International Preparation Constraints in Rugby: Influence of EI Trainer Status on EI Training Effectiveness

Mickaël Campo[1,2], Sylvain Laborde[3,4], Guillaume Martinent[5], Benoît Louvet[6] and Michel Nicolas[1]*

[1]Laboratory of Psychology, Psy-DREPI (EA7458), Faculty of Sport Sciences, Université Bourgogne Franche-Comté (UBFC), Dijon, France, [2]Department d'Accompagnement Mental à la Performance, Fédération Française de Rugby (FFR), Marcoussis, France, [3]Department of Performance Psychology, German Sport University Cologne, Cologne, Germany, [4]CESAMS (EA4260), UFR STAPS, Normandie Université, Caen, France, [5]L-VIS (EA 7428), Faculty of Sports Sciences, Université Claude Bernard Lyon 1, Lyon, France, [6]CETAPS (EA 3832), Faculty of Sports Sciences, Normandie Université, Rouen, France

***Correspondence:**
Mickaël Campo
mickael.campo@u-bourgogne.fr

Given the positive influence of emotional intelligence (EI) on sports performance, particular attention should be paid on how to improve it. Following promising results, previous research concluding that it was possible to improve EI *via* specific training programs also raised considerable debates. Indeed, previous EI training programs were very time-consuming for participants. This lessens consequently their suitability with the schedule constraints of elite sport. While, in the absence of sport psychologists, numerous coaches or physiologists try to work with players to improve their emotional competences, the aim of this study was to investigate the effectiveness of EI training programs fitting the schedule constraints of elite team sports, provided by three different EI trainers: the team's coach, the team's physiotherapist, and an expert in sport psychology. Young elite rugby union players ($N = 96$) participated in this study. Based on schedule constraints imposed by the head coach of the French u18 rugby union national team, the program consisted in three 1 h group-based EI training sessions occurring the last 3 days before a game (1 per day). Linear mixed-effects models showed that despite the constraining organizational challenge imposed by the coach, the intervention helped the players to increase some emotional competences at the trait level. Furthermore, a pairwise analysis showed that the type of emotional competencies developed depended on the status of the EI trainers. These findings highlight the suitability of a group-based approach in the training-week structure. They also point the way to EI improvement in a short period of time. Moreover, the specific influences of the EI trainer's status on players' EI development invite coaches and researchers to jointly combine their efforts in order to increase the EI training opportunities and to maximize the effects of their interventions. Together, these preliminary results provide first evidence facilitating the integration of such work in the preparation periods during international seasons.

Keywords: emotional intelligence, training, coaching, team sports, rugby, performance, elite sport, coach-athlete relationship

INTRODUCTION

Emotions play a key role in sport performance (e.g., Lane et al., 2010; Laborde et al., 2013; Doron and Martinent, 2017; Martinent and Nicolas, 2017; Campo et al., 2018; Martinent et al., 2018), and rugby is no exception (Campo et al., 2012). Indeed, recent studies showed the influence of individual (Campo et al., 2016a), group-based (i.e., emotion as member of a group) and team-referent emotions (i.e., emotions of the group as a whole; Campo et al., 2019), as well as the importance of interpersonal emotion regulation processes (Campo et al., 2017). Therefore, the influence of emotional intelligence (EI) on rugby performance may occur *via* its effects at the individual and team levels (Meyer and Zizzi, 2007; Laborde et al., 2016; Kopp and Jekauc, 2018).

Indeed, although the influence of emotions have often been considered as states, it is also acknowledged that athletes should develop stable emotional competences, such as the ability to regulate ones' own emotions (Lazarus, 2000). This trait perspective has received increased attention with the concept of EI, that is, how individual deals with their own and others' emotions through five main emotional competences: identification, expression, understanding, regulation, and use (Petrides, 2009; Brasseur et al., 2013). Interestingly, previous research has shown that it is possible to train EI, as indicated by a recent meta-analysis (Hodzic et al., 2017) and a systematic review (Kotsou et al., 2019). EI training programs have already been tested in sports and in rugby in particular (Campo et al., 2016b). However, some limitations appeared in implementing such programs in regards with the organizational constraints of elite sports in terms of duration and feasibility. The current study aimed at addressing this issue by investigating the tripartite model (Mikolajczak, 2009), which considers three levels: the knowledge level (i.e., what people know about emotions), the ability level (i.e., what people can do regarding emotions), and the trait level (i.e., what people actually do on an everyday basis regarding emotions). Basically, EI training suggests that acting on the knowledge and ability levels would provoke changes at the trait level (Campo et al., 2015, 2017; Hodzic et al., 2017; Laborde et al., 2017a, 2018a; Kotsou et al., 2019).

EI training has already been implemented in sports teams, like in cricket (Crombie et al., 2011) and in netball (Barlow and Banks, 2014). In rugby, an EI training program has been specifically elaborated by Campo et al. (2017) comprising four individual intervention sessions lasting from 45 to 90 min, one session every 5 weeks, over one season. This EI training program was based on trait emotional intelligence theory (Petrides, 2009), and integrated aspects linked to appraisal theories (Lazarus, 1999) and the individual zone of optimal functioning in sport (Hanin, 2000). Together, those EI training programs were able to increase EI to some extent (Crombie et al., 2011; Campo et al., 2016b) or influence aspects related to emotions, such as self-efficacy and anxiety (Barlow and Banks, 2014). However, EI training programs could be usually seen as very time-consuming and not adapted to the schedule constraints of elite athletes. The current study aimed to address this gap.

Furthermore, given the frequent absence of permanent sport psychologists within the staff of elite rugby teams, mental work with players is frequently provided by the coach or the physiologist. Thus, beyond the schedule constraints, working with elite athletes in team sports raises the question of the members of a staff who deliver such intervention. For instance, we can suggest that whether the person has or has not an influence on the selection process (e.g., coach vs. physiotherapist) or whether the person is considered by the players as being an expert in sport psychology (e.g., the sport psychologist vs. other staff members) may influence the effectiveness of the EI training program. Indeed, participants' engagement and commitment into an EI program may be contingent on their interaction with the person providing the intervention, in terms of personality traits (Cuperman and Ickes, 2009), but also in terms of the relationship with the person, which may be influenced by the status. But surprisingly, the influence of the status of the person delivering the intervention on the intervention effectiveness has been so far under-researched (Allen and Laborde, 2014). In a recent meta-analysis, Brown and Fletcher (2017) indicated that the type of provider is a perplexing issue when considering the effects of psychological interventions on sport performance. Among the very few studies addressing this topic, the type of provider accounted for some of the variation in the observed effect. Interestingly, the effects of coach-delivered interventions were higher than those provided by qualified practitioners. Given this issue still needs to be investigated, the second aim of this study was thus to clarify this influence.

To sum up, the aim of this study was to investigate the effectiveness of an EI training program fitting the schedule constraints of international rugby players and included within the training week preceding a competition like usual technical or physical conditioning sessions. The second aim of this study was to investigate whether the status of the person delivering the intervention influenced its effectiveness. First, it was hypothesized that regardless of the person delivering the intervention, the current EI training increased players' emotional competences (based on Campo et al., 2017). In the second hypothesis, it was postulated that, compared with a rugby coach or a physiologist, the current EI training is more effective when the person delivering the intervention is an expert in sport psychology.

MATERIALS AND METHODS

Participants

Ninety-six male 17 years old elite rugby union players were involved in this study. The players were randomly assigned within four groups: a control group (GC, $n = 23$); a first experimental group (G1, $n = 23$) in which the intervention was delivered by the first author which is an expert in sport psychology and in rugby; a second experimental group (G2, $n = 24$) in which the intervention was delivered by a the head coach of the u18 French team (rugby coach for 36 years at the young international levels and at the professional level);

and a third experimental group (G3, n = 22) in which the intervention was delivered by a member of the medical staff of the French team (physiologist for 10 years, working with rugby teams at the professional and young international levels).

Measure

In this study, we used the Profile of Emotional Competences (PEC; Brasseur et al., 2013), which contains 50 items assessing five core emotional competencies separately, distinctly for one's own and others' emotions. It thus provides 10 subscores (identification of one's emotions, identification of others' emotions, understanding of one's emotions, understanding of others' emotions, expression of one's emotions, listening to others' emotions, regulation of one's emotions, regulation of others' emotions, use of one's emotions, and use of others' emotions). In line with the trait conceptualization of emotional intelligence (Petrides, 2009), this tool clearly posits the fact that emotional intelligence and/or competence can be trained and developed (Brasseur et al., 2013). Athletes were asked to indicate the extent to which they agreed with statements regarding their intrapersonal and interpersonal emotional competences on 5-point Likert scale ranging from strongly disagree to strongly agree. Reliability analysis performed on the four samples indicated very good internal consistency of the subscales (>0.86) as well as for the total score (>0.86). To the best of our knowledge, this study is one of the first studies using this instrument in the sport context. Previous studies relying on the PEC have been conducted in the general population (Mikolajczak and Van Bellegem, 2017).

Procedure

The challenge of this present work was to build an EI training program adapted to the constraints imposed by the players' availability during a usual 1-week preparation period preceding international games. Although approval from an ethics committee was not required for this non-invasive study as per applicable institutional guidelines and regulations, we sought to obtain an approval by a consortium of independent researchers in the humanities and in sport sciences verifying that the study procedures followed international ethical guidelines for research (World Medical Association Declaration of Helsinki, 2013).

As shown in **Figure 1**, the first stage consisted in contacting the head coach of the u18 French national rugby union team to ask him to freely schedule EI training sessions during the week preceding a game organized to select players for the two u18 French Rugby union teams. The head coach proposed to the authors to build a training program based on three 1-h sessions conducted during the three consecutive last days before the competition (1 session per day). The second stage consisted in a 3-h session to train the head coach and the team's physiologist so as they were able to deliver the training program with players. Finally, at the beginning of the training camp, we met with the participants to provide them with information about the study. Players who agreed to participate in the study provided written informed consent.

The EI training was developed on the basis of the work by Campo et al. (2015, 2016b), adapted to the imposed organizational constraints. The two first sessions focused on the intrapersonal emotional competencies, while the last session aimed at improving interpersonal ones. Particularly, the program was conducted with examples, illustrations, videos, and exercises taken from the rugby context to facilitate the appropriation of the contents relating to emotional competences. Each session was implemented with half of the team and then again with the other half according to the rugby training schedule. That is, when the back players participated in the EI session, the forward players participated in a rugby training session, and vice versa. At the same time, the control group participated in three 1-h sessions during which the players followed video analyses of u18 competitions with a game analyst without any feedback related to emotional competences.

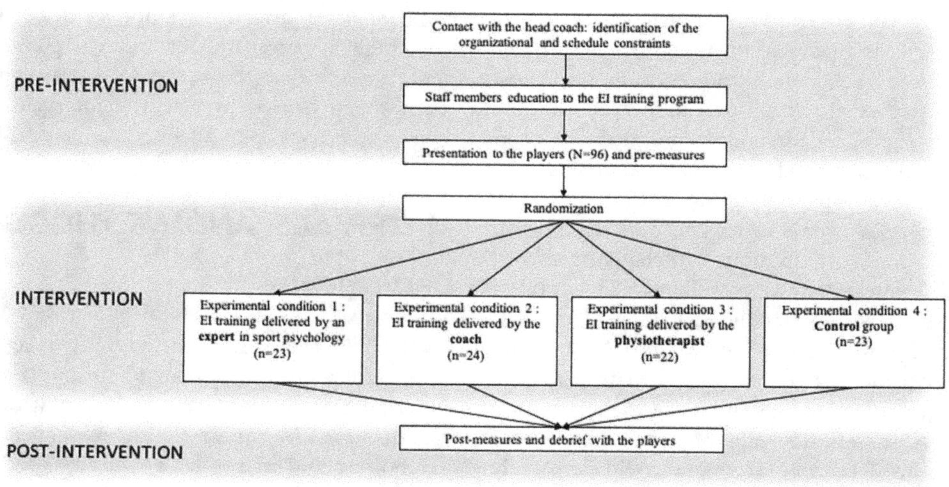

FIGURE 1 | Flow chart of the experimental protocol.

At the end of the three EI training sessions, the participants completed the same measure of emotional competences.

Data Analysis

To assess the influence of the intervention and that of the person delivering the intervention, every 10 subscales and the global score of emotional competences were successively modeled by the same linear mixed-effects model (LMEM, Pinheiro and Bates, 2000) process. Particularly, two piecewise LMEMs were used to model changes in emotional competences. First, we compared the control group with experimental groups in the same models. Subjects were a random effect. Condition (control vs. experimental), linear time, and their interactions were considered as fixed effects. Second, in order to carefully detail the effect of the person providing the intervention, the analysis strategy consisted in pairwise comparisons considering each every experimental group to the control group. Subjects were a random effect. Condition (control vs. expert, control vs. coach, and control vs. physiologist), linear time, and their interactions were considered as fixed effects.

A descending selection algorithm was employed. Removal was based on likelihood ratio tests at the 5% threshold, respecting marginality restrictions (Venables and Ripley, 2002, p. 172). The final resulting model was interpreted using coefficients for each independent variable in the model, corresponding t statistics, degrees of freedom, p using the alpha level, and relative effect sizes (ES). All calculations were made using the R 3.4.3 software and packages: nlme and car.

RESULTS

Global Effect of the Intervention

The comparison between the experimental condition (i.e., EI training groups) and the control group showed that the intervention had significant positive effects on emotional competences. Particularly, the LME models showed that the EI training program helped the players belonging with the experimental condition to better express [$\beta = +0.33$, $t(80) = 2.01$, $p = 0.048$, ES = 0.28] and regulate their own emotions [$\beta = +0.39$, $t(80) = 2.15$, $p = 0.035$, ES = 0.21]. It could be also noted that the models showed a negative single effect of Time regarding the identification of others' emotions [$\beta = -0.16$, $t(82) = -2.61$, $p = 0.011$, ES = 0.21]. No other significant or marginal effect has been found on the other emotional competences or on the global score.

Specific Effect of the Intervention Considering the Characteristics of the "Trainer"

When EI training was implemented by the expert in sport psychology, LME models revealed a significant interaction positive effect of Condition by Time for regulation of own emotions [$\beta = +0.07$, $t(40) = 2.21$, $p = 0.033$, ES = 0.10]. A simple negative effect of Condition was also found for this competence ($p = 0.008$).

When EI training was implemented by the coach, LME models revealed a marginal positive interaction effect of condition by time for the expression of own emotions [$\beta = +0.06$, $t(38) = 1.96$, $p = 0.055$, ES = 0.09]. A simple negative effect of the Condition was also found for this competence ($p = 0.015$).

When EI training was implemented by the physiologist, LME models revealed a positive interaction effect of condition by time for the use of others' emotions [$\beta = 0.08$, $t(37)$, $p = 0.033$, ES = 0.15]. A simple negative effect of Condition was also found for this same competence ($p = 0.002$).

DISCUSSION

The aim of this study was to investigate the influence of EI trainer status on EI training effectiveness, regarding a short-term EI training program realized during a training camp before a competition. We first hypothesized that the current EI training would improve emotional competences in comparison to the control condition. This hypothesis was partially validated, with EI training specifically improving expressing and regulating one's own emotions. Further, we hypothesized that, in comparison to a coach or physiologist, the EI training would trigger more improvements in emotional competences when the person delivering the intervention was an expert in sport psychology. Our findings did not support this hypothesis, as a positive effect was found on specific emotional competences for each experimental group.

Regarding our main hypothesis, only two (identification of own's emotions and expressing one's emotions) of the 10 emotional competences measured by the PEC (Brasseur et al., 2013) were shown to increase after the intervention. These results are in line with previous EI training research realized with rugby players (Campo et al., 2017), where improvements were shown only on some EI subscales (social competence, emotion perception, and emotion management). This can be explained by several factors, the main one being the duration of the EI intervention, which lasted less longer than interventions that have been shown to improve global EI (Hodzic et al., 2017; Kotsou et al., 2019). Longer interventions usually target the different emotional competences with more depth and potentially include follow-up (e.g., with emails) that help to integrate the elements learned. In addition, we have to acknowledge that measuring the effects of this intervention only with the PEC was finally non-optimal given the imposed time constraints of this protocol that limited evolutions at the trait level. Accordingly, these findings can already be seen as promising, given we were able to observe positive changes at the trait level within 1 week. Future studies should consider assessing the effectiveness of EI training not only at the trait level but also at the ability level, given this is what has primarily been trained during the current EI training based on the tripartite model (Mikolajczak, 2009).

With the benefit of the hindsight, a closer look to the context is required to better understand our findings. National teams are composed by players coming from different clubs. Except for the year of the World Rugby Cup, international seasons include only few matches played intermittently during the year. Most of the time, staff of national teams has 1 or 2 weeks only with international players to prepare a game. This implies great training structure constraints as coaches have to include different physical conditioning sessions and train the players to perform well in the different areas of their game plan. Moreover, while psychological resources are more and more often considered as a key factor of performance in rugby (Mellalieu et al., 2008; Campo et al., 2012; Campo and Djaït, 2016), mental training is not always shared among coaches as a trainable performance area and is still considered as being the "private preserve" of experts in sport psychology, implying consequently other additional organizational constraints. This observation has already been reported by Campo et al. (2015, 2016b) who explained that their individual EI training program was not adapted to the on-the-ground realities if it is expected to train all team members. The EI training program of Campo et al. (2017) was particularly time-consuming, which alters players' compliance, increase the risk of players' withdrawal and ultimately, the overall expected effects on performance. Therefore, the present study addressed this issue by testing the effects of an EI training program adapted to the schedule constraints imposed by the head coach of a national rugby union team. In addition, we sought to know whether a trained member of the staff may help players to increase their emotional competences. The current research demonstrated that it is possible to develop players' emotional competences during a preparation competitive week without altering the technical and physical training habits.

Of course, these results should be also considered in the light of different other variables that may have influenced the observed evolutions. For instance, it is important to keep in mind that sport performance is a holistic process involving transactional relationships between physiological and psychological parameters. Thus, while some studies showed an influence of EI on physiological variables (Laborde et al., 2011, 2014, 2017b, 2018b), it should be also noted that other research have provided evidence about the effect of genetic substrates in the management of the sport stress situations (e.g., Petito et al., 2016). In addition, the weak experience at the elite level of our population raises the question of the adaptive changes in young athletes. Indeed, different studies showed differences in abilities to cope with stressful situation according to the experience and age (e.g., Brummer et al., 2013). Therefore, we invite researchers to have these perspectives in mind for future research testing the effectiveness of EI training programs.

Moreover, our findings invite to question the influence of the important constraints the head coach imposed for this study specifically. Indeed, learning processes require a familiarization time with the training program and a period of time to acquire the knowledge and facilitate the use of the tools taught. Because of the scheduling constraints (i.e., one 1-h session per day during the last 3 days of the week before the game), the players had not enough time to put into practice what they learn during the IE training sessions. Moreover, the program comprised two sessions on intrapersonal emotional competencies, while only one was devoted to improve players' interpersonal emotional competencies. Therefore, future studies may consider designing longer EI trainings including one more session on interpersonal emotional competencies and lasting one or two "rest-days" between sessions, giving players the possibility to put their emotional competences into practice (intersession work). Increasing EI training program length and content should help to close the gap with EI training programs that have been shown to be effective in the literature (Hodzic et al., 2017; Kotsou et al., 2019).

Despite these limitations, the current study had several strengths. This is the first in sports to investigate the effects of the trainer delivering the EI training program. Indeed, while it is commonly accepted that such psychological intervention should be implemented by an expert in sport psychology, there is a lack of knowledge in the current EI literature on whether a person trained to deliver an EI training protocol may be also effective in improving players' emotional competences. This echoes the quality of the relationship between practitioners and players. In the sport setting, it is largely accepted that the coach has a specific proximal relationship with the players. Previous research showed that the coach has a significant influence on athletes' psychological states (e.g., to such extent that some academics metaphorically explained this influence by claiming that "the coach is the "first" mental trainer of the players and the team," Campo and Djaït, 2016, p. 3). So, it could be expected that the coach, by using the same language as the players, and with his/her status may strengthen the players' involvement in the training program. The same could be expected from the physiotherapist, who is also often involved in providing social support to the players. In the current study, the expert in sport psychology was able to improve players' emotional regulation competences; the coach improved the players' capacities to express their emotions, while the physiologist improved their competences to use others' emotions. Therefore, our findings showed for the first time that the effects of the EI training were influenced by the person who delivered the program. This result presents a particular interest in highlighting the importance of the concept of working alliance, established in the field of therapy and counseling research (Hersoug et al., 2001; McKenna and Davis, 2009) and consisting in a close relationship between coach and coachee, here, athletes. The importance of proximity between coach and athletes has already been highlighted by different academics in the field of performance (e.g., Jowett and Poczwardowski, 2007) and should now be furthered in that of IE in sports.

From an applied perspective, our findings open new venues in implementing mental training in sport, by highlighting the suitability of a group-based approach in the training-week structure and demonstrating positive effects in a short-time period. Moreover, the fact that a coach previously trained to deliver EI training may be able to develop emotional competences in his/her players is encouraging, given a staff member may be more autonomous in providing this kind training in a constantly changing schedule. While mobilizing at the same time almost 100 elite players in four homogenous experimental groups may be considered as a strength of an IE intervention study in the context of sport (Laborde et al., 2016), we also acknowledge that the few number of participants is also a limitation to well support and generalize the findings. Therefore, we invite future researchers to test with a wider sample these preliminary results. By the meantime, they provide first evidence suggesting the integration of EI trainings in the preparation periods during international seasons.

ETHICS STATEMENT

In the university of MC in which the experiment was carried out, no ethical board existed for non-invasive studies. Nonetheless, to ensure a high ethical standard for our research, we presented the study to a panel of independent researchers in the field of the humanities. This consortium informed us that this study respected the international ethical guideline of the World Medical Association Declaration of Helsinki (2013). This has been noted as follows in the manuscript: "Following approval by a consortium of independent researchers in the humanities and in sport sciences verifying that the study procedures followed international ethical guidelines for research (World Medical Association Declaration of Helsinki, 2013), [...]. Players who agreed to participate in the study provided informed consent."

AUTHOR CONTRIBUTIONS

MC led the project, analyzed the data, and wrote this manuscript. SL participated actively in the writing of the manuscript and contributed in the elaboration of the protocol. GM participated in the data analysis strategy, the elaboration of the protocol and contributed in the manuscript. BL and MN contributed equally in the manuscript and in the elaboration of the protocol.

ACKNOWLEDGMENTS

We thank Cyrinus Bio-Akanni Elegbede from the Plateforme Universitaire de Données de Dijon (PUDD, University of Burgundy) for the support in controlling the data analysis strategy used in this project. We also thank all the members of the French Rugby Union who participated in the organization of this protocol.

REFERENCES

Allen, M. S., and Laborde, S. (2014). The role of personality in sport and physical activity. *Curr. Dir. Psychol. Sci.* 23, 460–465. doi: 10.1177/0963721414550705

Barlow, A., and Banks, A. P. (2014). Using emotional intelligence in coaching high-performance athletes: a randomised controlled trial. *Coaching* 7, 132–139. doi: 10.1080/17521882.2014.939679

Brasseur, S., Grégoire, J., Bourdu, R., and Mikolajczak, M. (2013). The profile of emotional competence (PEC): development and validation of a self-reported measure that fits dimensions of emotional competence theory. *PLoS One* 8, 1–8. doi: 10.1371/journal.pone.0062635

Brown, D. J., and Fletcher, D. (2017). Effects of psychological and psychosocial interventions on sport performance: a meta-analysis. *Sports Med.* 47, 77–99. doi: 10.1007/s40279-016-0552-7

Brummer, L., Stopa, L., and Bucks, R. (2013). The influence of age on emotion regulation strategies and psychological distress. *Behav. Cogn. Psychother.* 42, 668–681. doi: 10.1017/s1352465813000453

Campo, M., Champely, S., Lane, A. M., Rosnet, E., Ferrand, C., and Louvet, B. (2016a). Emotions and performance in rugby. *J. Sport Health Sci.* doi: 10.1016/j.jshs.2016.05.007

Campo, M., Champely, S., Louvet, B., Ferrand, C., Rosnet, E., Pauketat, J., et al. (2019). Group-based emotions: evidence for emotion-performance relationships in team sports. *Res. Q. Exerc. Sport.* 90, 54–63. doi: 10.1080/02701367.2018.1563274

Campo, M., and Djaït, R. (2016). *La dimension mentale en rugby—Quels outils au service de l'entraîneur pour former et accompagner les joueurs?* Bruxelles: Editions De Boeck.

Campo, M., Laborde, S., and Mosley, E. (2016b). Emotional intelligence training in team sports. *J. Individ. Differ.* 37, 152–158. doi: 10.1027/1614-0001/a000201

Campo, M., Laborde, S., and Weckemann, S. (2015). "Emotional intelligence training: implications for performance and health" in *Advances in psychology research.* ed. A. M. Colombus (New York: Nova Publishers), 75–92.

Campo, M., Martinent, G., Pellet, J., Boulanger, J., Louvet, B., and Nicolas, M. (2018). Emotion-performance relationships in team sport: the role of personal and social identities. *Int. J. Sports Sci. Coach.* 13, 629–635. doi: 10.1177/1747954118785256

Campo, M., Mellalieu, S., Ferrand, C., Martinent, G., and Rosnet, E. (2012). Emotions in team contact sports: a systematic review. *Sport Psychol.* 26, 62–97. doi: 10.1123/tsp.26.1.62

Campo, M., Sanchez, X., Ferrand, C., Rosnet, E., Friesen, A. P., and Lane, A. M. (2017). Interpersonal emotion regulation in team sport: mechanisms and reasons to regulate teammates' emotions examined. *Int. J. Sport Exercise Psychol.* 15, 379–394. doi: 10.1080/1612197x.2015.1114501

Crombie, D., Lombard, C., and Noakes, T. D. (2011). Increasing emotional intelligence in cricketers: an intervention study. *Int. J. Sports Sci. Coach.* 6, 69–86. doi: 10.1260/1747-9541.6.1.69

Cuperman, R., and Ickes, W. (2009). Big five predictors of behavior and perceptions in initial dyadic interactions: personality similarity helps extraverts and introverts, but hurts "disagreeables". *J. Pers. Soc. Psychol.* 97, 667–684. doi: 10.1037/a0015741

Doron, J., and Martinent, G. (2017). Appraisal, coping, emotion, and performance during elite fencing matches: a random coefficient regression model approach. *Scand. J. Med. Sci. Sports* 27, 1015–1025. doi: 10.1111/sms.12711

Hanin, Y. (2000). *Emotions in sport.* Champaign, IL: Human Kinetics.

Hersoug, A. G., Høglend, P., Monsen, J. T., and Havik, O. E. (2001). Quality of working alliance in psychotherapy: Therapist variables and patient/therapist similarity as predictors. *J. Psychother.* 10, 205–216.

Hodzic, S., Scharfen, J., Ripoll, P., Holling, H., and Zenasni, F. (2017). How efficient are emotional intelligence trainings: a meta-analysis. *Emot. Rev.* 10, 138–148. doi: 10.1177/1754073917708613

Jowett, S., and Poczwardowski, A. (2007). "Understanding the coach-athlete relationship" in *Social psychology in sport.* eds. S. Jowett, and D. Lavallee (Champaign, IL: Human Kinetics), 4–14.

Kopp, A., and Jekauc, D. (2018). The influence of emotional intelligence on performance in competitive sports: a meta-analytical investigation. *Sports* 6:175. doi: 10.3390/sports6040175

Kotsou, I., Mikolajczak, M., Heeren, A., Grégoire, J., and Leys, C. (2019). Improving emotional intelligence: a systematic review of existing work and future challenges. *Emot. Rev.* 11, 151–165. doi: 10.1177/1754073917735902

Laborde, S., Brüll, A., Weber, J., and Anders, L. S. (2011). Trait emotional intelligence in sports: a protective role against stress through heart rate variability? *Personal. Individ. Differ.* 51, 23–27. doi: 10.1016/j.paid.2011.03.003

Laborde, S., Dosseville, F., and Allen, M. S. (2016). Emotional intelligence in sport and exercise: a systematic review. *Scand. J. Med. Sci. Sports* 26, 862–874. doi: 10.1111/sms.12510

Laborde, S., Dosseville, F., and Raab, M. (2013). Introduction, comprehensive approach, and vision for the future. [special issue] emotions and decision making in sports. *Int. J. Sport & Exercise Psychol.* 11, 143–150. doi: 10.1080/1612197X.2013.773686

Laborde, S., Furley, P., Musculus, L., and Ackermann, S. (2017a). *Emotionale Intelligenz im sport (emotional intelligence in sports).* Aachen, Germany: Meyer & Meyer.

Laborde, S., Lautenbach, F., Allen, M. S., Herbert, C., and Achtzehn, S. (2014). The role of trait emotional intelligence in emotion regulation and performance

McKenna, D. D., and Davis, S. L. (2009). Hidden in plain sight: the active ingredients of executive coaching. *Ind. Organ. Psychol.* 2, 244–260. doi: 10.1111/j.1754-9434.2009.01143.x

Mellalieu, S. D., Hanton, S., and Shearer, D. A. (2008). Hearts in the fire, heads in the fridge: a qualitative investigation into the temporal patterning of the precompetitive psychological response in elite performers. *J. Sports Sci.* 26, 811–824. doi: 10.1080/02640410701790787

Meyer, B. B., and Zizzi, S. J. (2007). "Emotional intelligence in sport: conceptual, methodological, and applied issues" in *Mood and human performance: Conceptual, measurement, and applied issues*. ed. A. M. Lane (London, England: Nova Science), 131–152.

Mikolajczak, M. (2009). Going beyond the ability-trait debate: the three-level model of emotional intelligence an unifying view: the three-level model of EI. *E-J. Appl. Psychol.* 5, 25–31.

Mikolajczak, M., and Van Bellegem, S. (2017). Increasing emotional intelligence to decrease healthcare expenditures: how profitable would it be? *Personal. Individ. Differ.* 116, 343–347. doi: 10.1016/j.paid.2017.05.014

Petito, A., Altamura, M., Iuso, S., Padalino, F. A., Sessa, F., D'Andrea, G., et al. (2016). The relationship between personality traits, the 5HTT polymorphisms, and the occurrence of anxiety and depressive symptoms in elite athletes. *PLoS One* 11:e0156601. doi: 10.1371/journal.pone.0156601

Petrides, K. V. (2009). *Technical manual for the trait emotional intelligence questionnaire (TEIQue)*. London, England: London Psychometric Laboratory.

Pinheiro, J., and Bates, D. (2000). "Linear mixed-effects models: basic concepts and examples" in *Mixed-effects models in S and S-plus*. eds. J. C. Pinheiro, and D. M. Bates (New York: Springer-Verlag), 1–56.

Venables, W. N., and Ripley, B. D. (2002). *Modern applied statistics with S*. New York: Springer-Verlag.

World Medical Association Declaration of Helsinki (2013). *JAMA*. 310:2191. doi: 10.1001/jama.2013.281053

under pressure. *Personal. Individ. Differ.* 57, 43–47. doi: 10.1016/J.Paid.2013.09.013

Laborde, S., Mosley, E., Ackermann, S., Mrsic, A., and Dosseville, F. (2018a). "Emotional intelligence in sports and physical activity: an intervention focus" in *Emotional intelligence in education: Integrating research with practice*. eds. K. V. Keefer, J. D. A. Parker, and D. H. Saklofske (Cham: Springer International Publishing), 289–320.

Laborde, S., Mosley, E., and Dosseville, F. (2018b). Commentary: emotional intelligence impact on half marathon finish times. *Front. Psychol.* 9:2593. doi: 10.3389/fpsyg.2018.02593

Laborde, S., Mosley, E., and Thayer, J. F. (2017b). Heart rate variability and cardiac vagal tone in psychophysiological research-recommendations for experiment planning, data analysis, and data reporting. *Front. Physiol.* 8:213. doi: 10.3389/fpsyg.2017.00213

Lane, A. M., Devonport, T. J., Soos, I., Karsai, I., Leibinger, E., and Hamar, P. (2010). Emotional intelligence and emotions associated with optimal and dysfunctional athletic performance. *J. Sports Sci. Med.* 9, 388–392.

Lazarus, R. S. (1999). *Stress and emotion: A new synthesis*. New York, NY: Springer.

Lazarus, R. S. (2000). How emotions influence performance in competitive sports. *Sport Psychol.* 14, 229–252. doi: 10.1123/tsp.14.3.229

Martinent, G., Gareau, A., Lienhart, N., Nicaise, V., and Guillet-Descas, E. (2018). Emotion profiles and their motivational antecedents among adolescent athletes in intensive training settings. *Psychol. Sport Exerc.* 35, 198–206. doi: 10.1016/j.psychsport.2018.01.001

Martinent, G., and Nicolas, M. (2017). Athletes' affective profiles within competition situations: a two-wave study. *Sport Exerc. Perform. Psychol.* 6, 143–157. doi: 10.1037/spy0000085

10

Coach-Created Motivational Climate and Athletes' Adaptation to Psychological Stress: Temporal Motivation-Emotion Interplay

Montse C. Ruiz[1], Claudio Robazza[2], Asko Tolvanen[3], Saara Haapanen[1] and Joan L. Duda[4]*

[1] Faculty of Sport and Health Sciences, University of Jyväskylä, Jyväskylä, Finland, [2] BIND-Behavioral Imaging and Neural Dynamics Center, Department of Medicine and Aging Sciences, Università degli Studi G. d'Annunzio Chieti e Pescara, Chieti, Italy, [3] Faculty of Education and Psychology, University of Jyväskylä, Jyväskylä, Finland, [4] School of Sport, Exercise and Rehabilitation Sciences, University of Birmingham, Birmingham, United Kingdom

***Correspondence:**
Claudio Robazza
c.robazza@unich.it

This two-wave study investigated the temporal interplay between motivation and the intensity and reported impact of athletes' emotions in training settings. In total, 217 athletes completed self-report measures of motivational climate, motivation regulations, emotional states (i.e., pleasant states, anger, and anxiety) experienced before practice at two time points during a 3-month period. Latent change score modeling revealed significantly negative paths from task-involving climate at time 1 to the latent change in the intensity of dysfunctional anxiety and anger, and significantly positive paths from ego-involving climate at time 1 to the latent change in dysfunctional anger (i.e., intensity and reported impact). The paths from controlled motivation at time 1 to the latent change in the intensity of dysfunctional anxiety and vice versa were significantly positive. The path from controlled motivation at time 1 to the latent change in the intensity of functional anger was significantly positive, but not vice versa. In addition, the paths from dysfunctional anger (i.e., intensity and reported impact) at time 1 to the latent change in motivation regulations were significant, but not vice versa. Overall, evidence provided suggested that the temporal interplay of motivation and emotions is contingent on the specific emotions. The findings highlight the role of coach-created motivational climate and the importance of identifying high levels of controlled motivation to help athletes better adapt to psychological stress.

Keywords: feelings, psychobiosocial states, IZOF model, achievement goal theory, self-determination theory, structural equation modeling

INTRODUCTION

The focus of existing sport emotion literature has been on the prediction of performance (Beedie et al., 2000; Woodman et al., 2009) or the strategies athletes use to regulate their emotions in order to enhance performance (Lane et al., 2012; Wagstaff, 2014). The antecedents of performance related emotions in sport, however, have received less research attention. The purpose of this study was to examine the social environmental antecedents of and the interplay between emotions and motivation. Understanding these antecedents can provide useful information to coaches and practitioners to help athletes enhance their adaptation to psychological stress related to their performance in high achievement settings.

Theorists and research evidence suggest that the social environment and individual variables influence the way people think, feel, and behave (Nicholls, 1989; Deci and Ryan, 2000; Lazarus, 2000). Two prominent theoretical frameworks used in the study of motivation are achievement goal theory (AGT; Nicholls, 1989), and self-determination theory (SDT; Deci and Ryan, 1985, 2000; Ryan and Deci, 2017). These theories have been applied to examine the intrapersonal motivational and emotional consequences of the social environment in the sporting context.

According to AGT, a task-involving climate is defined by situations where the coach focuses on skill improvement, individual progress, and encourages cooperation with others, and in which every individual has an important role in the team. In contrast, an ego-involving climate involves the use of normative-based evaluation, emphasis on competition, and social comparison between participants. In line with SDT, individuals' motivation varies in their degree of self-determination. For example athletes experience autonomous motivation when their reasons for engagement in sport are volitional or intrinsic, while controlled motivation is experienced when the reasons for engagement are pressured either internally or externally. These reasons for engagement lie on a continuum from intrinsic to extrinsic motivation. The most autonomous form of motivation is intrinsic motivation, which occurs when athletes derive a sense of enjoyment and satisfaction from participating in sport. In contrast, extrinsic motivation involves participation that is contingent upon specific reward or outcomes. For instance, integrated regulation, which is the most autonomous form of extrinsic motivation, occurs when athletes view participation in sport as personally important and assimilated with their own self. Identified regulation occurs when the outcome of a sport is personally valued. Introjected regulation is reflected when athletes engage in a sport to reduce feelings of shame or guilt. The most controlled form of motivation is external regulation, which is manifested when athletes engage in an activity for purely instrumental reasons, such as obtaining reward or satisfying an external demand, while a lack in motivation has been referred to as amotivation (Deci and Ryan, 1985; Ryan and Deci, 2000, 2017). Researchers have typically examined autonomous motivation as comprised by intrinsic motivation, integrated regulation, and identified regulation, while introjected regulation and external regulation were indicators of controlled motivation (Lonsdale et al., 2008; Langan et al., 2016).

The vast majority of research in this area has placed motivational climate as the antecedent of intrapersonal variables. However, the examination of the temporal sequence of intrapersonal variables, such as athletes' motivation and emotions as predictors or determinants, remains unexplored. According to both AGT and SDT, much of the variance in individuals' motivation and quality of involvement derives from the interaction with significant others, such as the coaches within sport contexts. Research evidence indicates that perceptions of a task-involving climate are related to a more functional/adaptive motivational pattern, intrinsic motivation, and achievement striving in sport, while the opposite has been found for an ego-involving climate (for review, see Harwood et al., 2015). Overall, research has generally revealed that a task-involving climate is related to athletes' intrinsic motivation and need satisfaction (Reinboth and Duda, 2006; Vazou et al., 2006; Álvarez et al., 2012; for an overview see Duda and Balaguer, 2007). A task-involving climate has also been found to be a positive predictor of more self-determined styles of motivation (Standage et al., 2003; Kipp and Amorose, 2008). In contrast, an ego-involving climate has been related to feelings of pressure, antisocial behavior, the belief of ability as determinant of success, and dropping out in sport (Sarrazin et al., 2002; Bortoli et al., 2012). This maladaptive motivational pattern reflects a lack of adaptation to psychological stress. An ego-involving climate was also found to positively predict extrinsic motivation and amotivation (Bortoli et al., 2015; Jaakkola et al., 2017).

Regarding the relationships between the social environment created by coaches and athletes' emotional responses, research has shown that perceptions of a task-involving motivational climate significantly predicted pleasant states in soccer players (Bortoli et al., 2012) and enjoyment in young hockey players (Jaakkola et al., 2016). In contrast, perceptions of an ego-involving climate were predictors of unpleasant states, anxiety, worry, and decreased enjoyment (Vazou et al., 2006; Cumming et al., 2007; Bortoli et al., 2012). A systematic review of 39 studies (Harwood et al., 2015) indicates a moderate positive correlation between perceived task-involving motivational climate and pleasant affect, while an overall small, negative correlation was found between an ego-involving motivational climate and pleasant states.

The vast majority of research exploring the relationships between motivational climate, motivation, and emotions is cross-sectional in nature. Thus, the direction of causality in these relationships remains unexamined. Previous research in this area has examined the consequences of the social motivational context investigating two possible sequences. The first sequence considers that motivational climate dimensions serve as antecedents of variability in motivation regulations, which in turn, trigger different emotions. The second sequence assumes that emotion is a mediator in the relationship, and thus, motivation is positioned at the end of the sequence. AGT and SDT postulate that the social environment and achievement goals have emotional, cognitive, and behavioral consequences (Deci and Ryan, 1985; Nicholls, 1989; Ames, 1992; Duda and Balaguer, 2007; Ryan and Deci, 2017). Motivational climate and motivation (especially a task-involving climate, and autonomous motivation) are assumed to influence performance with emotion mediating this relationship. Also in line with the first sequence (motivational climate > motivation > emotion), Lazarus (2000) placed importance on causal cognitive, motivational, and relational aspects in the initiation and maintenance of emotions. He stated that individuals' emotions result from appraisals about the personal significance of the interaction with others and the environment, and options for coping with situational demands. Emotions would, thus, be placed at the end of the sequence. The second sequence (motivational climate > emotion > motivation) has been mainly tested within physical education settings and youth sport (Bortoli et al., 2009, 2011, 2012, 2014). The main focus in such contexts is typically on the creation of an environment that would enhance pleasant states (e.g., enjoyment), which are believed to increase the motivation to be involved in the activity.

Both sequences, however, have been examined separately. Moreover, most previous studies have involved school or college participants, with a few studies recruiting high-performing athletes, young athletes in particular. In addition, the vast majority of studies have been limited to the examination of one dimension of emotions, intensity. Another important dimension in the sporting context is the functional impact on performance. A very few studies have considered this dimension, which has been for the most part only assumed by researchers. For example, Bortoli et al. (2014) implied pleasant states as functional states and unpleasant states as dysfunctional; however, athletes' perceptions of the functional impact on performance were not assessed.

Traditionally, athletes' emotions have been studied using either a global affect approach, which emphasizes dimensions such as hedonic tone and activation (Watson and Tellegen, 1985), or a discrete emotion approach, which considers emotion as distinct entities (e.g., anxiety, anger) triggered by the person's appraisal of their interaction with the environment (Lazarus, 2000). One sport-specific theoretical framework concerned with the study of emotions is the individual zones of optimal functioning (IZOF) model (Hanin, 2000, 2007). The IZOF model, which combines global affect and discrete emotion perspectives, conceptualizes emotions within the framework of two interrelated factors, hedonic tone (i.e., pleasure–displeasure), and performance functionality (i.e., functional-dysfunctional effects). This categorization results in a range of pleasant and unpleasant, functional and dysfunctional emotional experiences. Extensive empirical evidence supports this conceptualization (for reviews, see Ruiz et al., 2017b; Robazza and Ruiz, 2018). Most IZOF-based research, however, has focused on the emotion-performance relationship disregarding the study of the antecedents of emotional states.

A study examining the interplay between motivational climate, motivation, and the intensity and functional impact of athletes' emotions revealed that task-involving climate was a positive predictor of autonomous motivation and perceived functional anger, and a negative predictor of the intensity of anxiety and dysfunctional anger (Ruiz et al., 2017a). An ego-involving climate was a positive predictor of controlled motivation, the intensity and perceived impact of functional anger, and the intensity of dysfunctional anger. Such study involved data assessed at one moment in time, which did not allow for the examination of the mediating role of motivation versus emotions in the motivational climate–outcome relationship.

Current Study and Hypotheses

To our knowledge, no study has yet examined the relationship between pleasant and stress-related (i.e., anxiety and anger) emotions and motivation over time prior to practice. The time-lagged design of the present study allows addressing this gap in the literature, which has been for the most part relying on cross-sectional designs. The purpose of the current investigation was to examine the change over time in the interplay between perceptions of the motivational climate, motivation regulations, and emotional states in competitive athletes. Specifically, we used a 3-month, two-wave repeated measures design to examine the relationship between athletes' perceptions of the task- and ego-involving features of the motivational climate, autonomous and controlled motivations, and functional/dysfunctional and pleasant/unpleasant emotional states. A second aim of the study was to determine the temporal ordering of athletes' emotions on motivation regulations. We tested the following four hypotheses: (a) H_0: athletes' motivation regulations do not predict changes in emotions, and emotions do not predict changes in motivation regulations; (b) H_1: emotions predict changes in motivation regulations—pleasant emotions positively predict autonomous motivation and negatively predict controlled motivation, whereas unpleasant emotions positively predict controlled motivation and negatively predict autonomous motivation; (c) H_2: motivation regulations predict changes in emotions—autonomous motivation positively predicts pleasant emotions and negatively predicts unpleasant emotions, whereas controlled motivation positively predicts unpleasant emotions and negatively predicts pleasant emotions; and (d) H_3: emotions and motivation regulations have a reciprocal relationship—motivation regulation predicts changes in emotions, and emotions predict changes in motivation regulations.

MATERIALS AND METHODS

Participants

The participants were 217 Finnish athletes (126 men, 91 women, M_{age} = 21.24 year, SD = 4.53). One hundred and sixty-one competed in team sports (e.g., ice hockey, soccer, floorball, and volleyball), and 56 in individual sports (e.g., swimming, karate, and track and field). One hundred and twenty-five were national level competitors and 92 were international level athletes having achieved good results in European or World Championships. The participants' mean sport experience was 10.53 years (SD = 3.84), and they had trained an average of 14.15 h per week (SD = 5.05). Approximately two-thirds (60.45%, n = 359) of time 1 participants also responded to the questionnaire at time 2.

Measures

Motivational Climate

A Finnish version of the Perceived Motivational Climate in Sport Questionnaire-2 (PMCSQ-2; Newton et al., 2000) was used to measure athletes' perceptions of their motivational climate in terms of task- and ego-involving. Task-involving climate items (e.g., "the focus is to improve each game/practice") reflect perceptions that the athlete has an important role on the team, and that co-operative learning and effort/improvement are encouraged. Ego-involving items (e.g., "players/athletes are afraid to make mistakes") reflect feelings of intra-team rivalry among players/athletes on the team, perceptions that mistakes are punished, and that coach recognition is reserved for the most talented athletes. Each item was rated on a 5-point Likert scale ranging from 1 (*strongly disagree*) to 5 (*strongly agree*). The Finnish version of the PMCSQ-2 revealed acceptable internal consistency as administered to 494 athletes (283 men, 211 women) with $\alpha = 0.87$ for both task-involving and ego-involving climates (Ruiz et al., 2017a).

Motivation Regulations

A Finnish version of the Behavior Regulation in Sport Questionnaire (BRSQ; Lonsdale et al., 2008) was used to assess athletes' motivation regulations. The BRSQ comprises six 4-item subscales that measure intrinsic motivation (e.g., "because I enjoy it"), integrated regulation (e.g., "because it's a part of who I am"), identified regulation (e.g., "because the benefits of sport are important to me"), introjected regulation (e.g., "because I would feel ashamed if I quit"), external regulation (e.g., "because people push me to play") and amotivation (e.g., "but I question why I continue"). Each item was assessed on a 7-point Likert type scale ranging from 1 (*not at all true*) to 7 (*very true*). In this study, mean scores were calculated for autonomous and controlled styles of motivation. Adequate internal reliability of the BRSQ has been reported with $\alpha = 0.87$ for autonomous motivation, $\alpha = 0.90$ for controlled motivation, and $\alpha = 0.78$ for amotivation (Ruiz et al., 2017a).

Emotional Experiences

Eight emotional modality items from psychobiosocial states scales (Robazza et al., 2016; Ruiz et al., 2016, 2018) were used to assess athletes' emotional experiences. Each item includes 3–4 descriptors per row and is categorized as functionally helpful or harmful for performance with two items assessing: (a) functional pleasant states ("enthusiastic, confident, carefree, joyful"), and (b) functional anger ("fighting spirit, fierce, aggressive"); and two items measuring: (c) dysfunctional anxiety ("worried, apprehensive, concerned, troubled"); and (d) dysfunctional anger ("furious, resentful, irritated, annoyed"). First, athletes were asked to select one word answering the question "how do you feel right now in relation to your forthcoming performance?" Second, they rated the intensity on a scale ranging from 0 (*nothing at all*) to 4 (*very much*). Third, athletes rated the anticipated or perceived functional impact on performance on a scale ranging from +3 (*very helpful*) to −3 (*very harmful*).

Procedure

Following approval from the local university ethics committee, data collection occurred at two time points during a 3-month period. The participants were recruited via training centers, sport schools, and clubs in five cities in Northern, Central, and Southern parts of Finland. Written consent was obtained from all participants after having explained them the purpose of the study, emphasized voluntary participation, and assured confidentiality of the results. Athletes under 18 gave their assent and a guardian provided written consent. The questionnaires were administered either individually or in small groups, in a quiet place, close to the participants training facilities. To ensure that participants had experience and awareness of the motivational aspects of the coach-created environment, data collection took place a few weeks after the beginning of the season, 30 min prior to a practice session. Participants responded to the questionnaires at time 1 (T1) and 3 months later (T2). Questionnaire administration took approximately 30 min.

Data Analysis

Prior to conducting the main analysis, data were screened for inputting errors, distribution, and multivariate outliers (Tabachnick and Fidell, 2013). Twelve participants were identified as outliers (Mahalanobis distance larger than $\chi^2[18] = 51.179$) and were removed from further analyses. Intra-class correlations (ICC) were calculated to examine the need to conduct multilevel analysis. Statistically significant ICC were only found for task-involving climate, thus, single level analyses were conducted. Descriptive statistics, variable intercorrelations and Cronbach's α coefficients were calculated. Structural equation modeling was conducted with Mplus 8.2 (Muthén and Muthén, 2017) using the missing-data function and adjusting for non-normality with the robust full information maximum likelihood estimator. Confirmatory factor analysis was conducted for the full measurement model at both T1 and T2. As the main analysis, latent change score modeling was used to examine the relationship between perceptions of the motivational climate, motivation relations, and athlete's emotions (intensity and functional impact). Latent change score modeling, also called latent difference score modeling, is conducted within the framework of structural equation modeling that combines features from cross-lagged regression modeling and latent growth curves (Ferrer and McArdle, 2003; McArdle and Prindle, 2008; McArdle, 2009). In latent change score model the focus is on describing a variable Y at a time t defining ΔY_t as the change in Y from $t - 1$ to t (McArdle, 2009). The coefficients relating Y_t and Y_{t-1} are constrained to 1 and there is no error terms in the equation for Y_t, thus Y_t is directly the sum of Y_{t-1} and ΔY_t, where ΔY_t can be used as a latent variable. Latent difference scores were calculated separately for task-involving climate, autonomous motivation regulations, and reported intensity and impact of each of the following emotions: functional pleasant states, anxiety, functional and dysfunctional anger. On the other hand, latent difference scores were calculated for ego-involving climate, controlled motivation regulations, and the intensity and reported impact of anxiety, functional anger, and dysfunctional anger (see **Figure 1**).

The fit of the path models was evaluated considering the comparative fit index (CFI), the Tucker-Lewis Index (TLI), the standardized root mean square residual (SRMR), and the root mean square error of approximation (RMSEA). As recommended by Hu and Bentler (1999), a good model fit is inferred when values of CFI and TLI are close to 0.95, the SRMR is close to 0.08, and the RMSEA is close to 0.06. The null hypothesis (H_0) would be supported if the regression coefficients β_{10} or β_{11} (see **Figure 1**) were non-significantly different from zero. If coefficient β_{10}, but not coefficient β_{11}, was significant, H_1 (motivational regulations predict changes in emotions) would be supported. If coefficient β_{11}, but not coefficient β_{10}, was

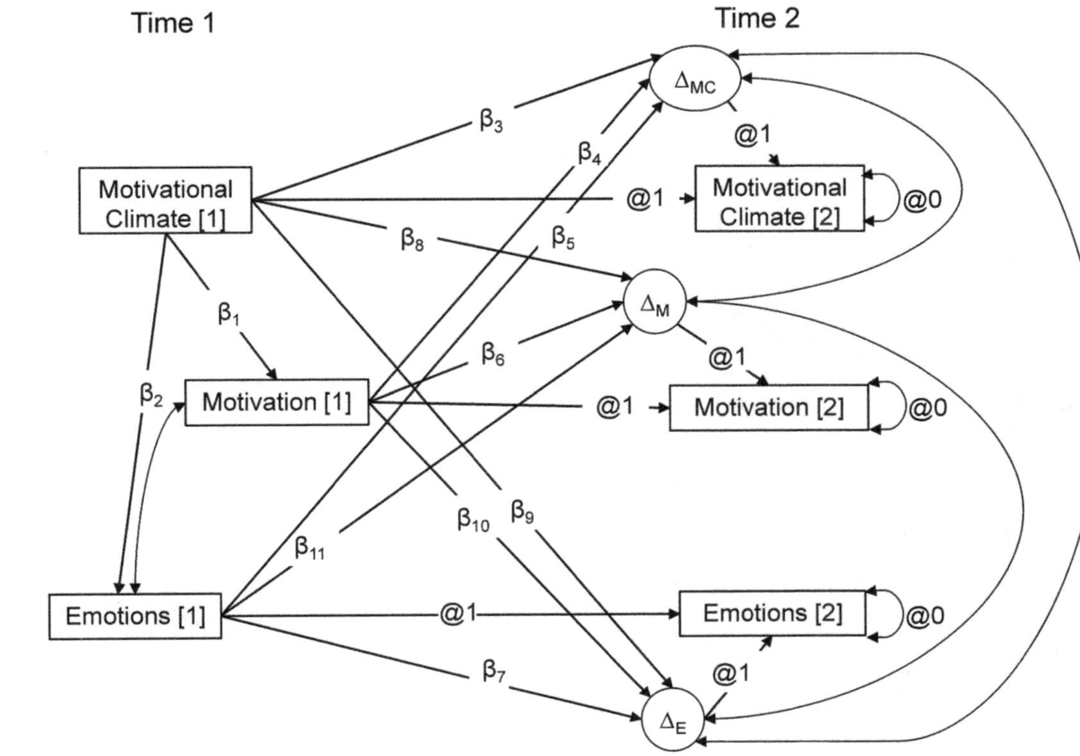

FIGURE 1 | Hypothesized latent change score model of motivational climate, motivation regulations, and emotions. Δ represents latent change score.

significant, then H_2 (emotions predict changes in motivational regulations) would be supported. Finally, if both coefficients β_{10} and β_{11} were significant, then H_3 (reciprocal effects) would be supported. Effect sizes were interpreted following Cohen's (1988) guidelines, whereby values of 0.2 are considered small, 0.5 are moderate, and 0.8 are large.

RESULTS

Descriptive Statistics and Correlations

The athletes reported moderate to high values for perceptions of a task-involving climate, autonomous motivation, intensity and perceived impact of functional pleasant states, and low values for ego-involving climate, controlled motivation, intensity and perceived impact of dysfunctional anger, and dysfunctional anxiety at both time points (**Table 1**). Cronbach's α coefficients and ω values for the scales were acceptable (all $\alpha > 0.868$, and $\omega > 0.882$) deeming the scales reliable (McNeish, 2018).

As shown in **Table 2**, and following Zhu (2012) criteria, positive low correlations were observed between perceptions of a task-involving climate and autonomous motivation, and between perceptions of an ego-involving climate and controlled motivation at both times. Positive low correlations were also observed between task-involving climate and the perceived impact of functional anger, while an ego-involving climate was positively correlated with the intensity and perceived impact of dysfunctional anger. Weak or no correlations were found between the intensity and the perceived impact of athletes' emotions.

Confirmatory Factor Analysis

Following recommendations by Little et al. (2002) and to improve the ratio of variable to sample size, we created construct-specific parcels. Specifically, six parcels were created following the theoretical structure of motivational climate

TABLE 1 | Descriptive statistics and Cronbach's alphas (α) and composite reliability (ω) of study variables.

	T1			T2		
Variable (range)	*M*	*SD*	α/ω	*M*	*SD*	α/ω
(1) Task climate (1–5)	4.01	0.50	0.889 /0.892	3.93	0.57	0.925 /0.925
(2) Ego climate (1–5)	2.58	0.61	0.880 /0.884	2.70	0.63	0.892 /0.899
(3) Autonomous motivation (1–7)	5.55	0.76	0.868 /0.882	5.55	0.80	0.888 /0.896
(4) Controlled motivation (1–7)	2.07	0.99	0.883 /0.885	2.20	1.03	0.883 /0 884
(5) Pleasant$^{+\text{intensity}}$ (0–4)	2.55	0.69	*	2.51	0.86	*
(6) Anxiety$^{-\text{intensity}}$ (0–4)	1.03	0.98	*	1.10	1.12	*
(7) Anger$^{+\text{intensity}}$ (0–4)	1.74	1.09	*	1.78	1.07	*
(8) Anger$^{-\text{intensity}}$ (0–4)	0.86	1.02	*	1.04	1.10	*
(9) Pleasant$^{+\text{impact}}$ (−3/+3)	1.70	1.29	*	1.72	1.37	*
(10) Anxiety$^{-\text{impact}}$ (−3/+3)	−1.36	1.17	*	−1.51	1.19	*
(11) Anger$^{+\text{impact}}$ (−3/+3)	2.03	1.21	*	1.98	1.23	*
(12) Anger$^{-\text{impact}}$ (−3/+3)	−0.83	1.29	*	−0.90	1.40	*

*N = 205. T1 = Time 1; T2 = Time 2 (three months later). *Individual items.*

TABLE 2 | Bivariate correlations of the study variables in Time 1 and Time 2.

	1	2	3	4	5	6	7	8	9	10	11	12	13	14	15	16	17	18	19	20	21	22	23
Time 1																							
(1) TC																							
(2) EC	−0.37																						
(3) AM	0.36	−0.12																					
(4) CM	−0.07	0.23	0.03																				
(5) $P^{+\text{intensity}}$	0.08	−0.08	0.19	−0.03																			
(6) $Ax^{-}-^{\text{intensity}}$	−0.21	0.19	−0.01	0.17	−0.15																		
(7) $Ag^{+\text{intensity}}$	0.07	0.12	0.18	−0.12	0.19	0.18																	
(8) $Ag^{-}-^{\text{intensity}}$	−0.22	0.21	−0.09	0.17	−0.14	0.46	0.14																
(9) $P^{+\text{impact}}$	0.11	−0.08	0.23	−0.12	0.11	0.01	0.23	−0.07															
(10) $Ax^{-}-^{\text{impact}}$	−0.06	0.08	−0.17	−0.11	0.01	−0.01	0.07	−0.05	−0.07														
(11) $Ag^{+\text{impact}}$	0.28	−0.07	0.20	−0.07	0.06	−0.03	0.24	−0.05	0.41	−0.10													
(12) $Ag^{-\text{impact}}$	−0.14	0.14	−0.08	−0.02	0.02	−0.09	−0.13	0.00	−0.05	0.34	−0.09												
Time 2																							
(13) TC	0.68	−0.29	0.26	−0.03	0.11	−0.05	0.07	−0.14	0.16	−0.07	0.30	−0.16											
(14) EC	−0.30	0.69	−0.09	0.18	−0.02	0.18	0.10	0.25	−0.07	0.13	−0.19	0.07	−0.44										
(15) AM	0.39	−0.14	0.75	0.03	0.13	0.00	0.14	−0.01	0.15	−0.18	0.20	−0.12	0.34	−0.13									
(16) CM	−0.18	0.26	0.05	0.76	−0.06	0.26	−0.11	0.22	−0.03	−0.06	−0.11	0.12	−0.16	0.29	−0.05								
(17) $P^{+\text{intensity}}$	0.06	−0.08	0.04	0.13	0.23	−0.04	0.03	0.04	0.15	−0.11	0.14	−0.08	0.10	−0.08	0.21	0.12							
(18) $Ax^{-\text{intensity}}$	−0.19	0.12	−0.01	0.21	−0.02	0.27	−0.02	0.18	0.06	−0.14	−0.08	0.08	−0.19	0.20	−0.02	0.29	−0.17						
(19) $Ag^{+\text{intensity}}$	−0.02	0.03	0.01	0.11	0.16	0.09	0.30	0.15	0.13	−0.02	0.06	0.07	−0.10	0.17	0.02	0.14	0.31	0.04					
(20) $Ag^{-\text{intensity}}$	−0.17	0.22	0.03	0.09	0.00	0.25	0.06	0.29	−0.04	0.04	−0.12	0.07	−0.19	0.32	0.00	0.24	−0.12	0.45	0.10				
(21) $P^{+\text{impact}}$	0.11	−0.20	0.16	0.04	0.01	0.06	−0.03	−0.01	0.21	−0.16	0.16	−0.13	0.15	−0.16	0.08	0.08	0.34	−0.11	0.21	−0.09			
(22) $Ax^{-\text{impact}}$	−0.17	0.18	−0.18	0.08	0.01	−0.02	−0.11	0.08	−0.18	0.39	−0.22	0.26	−0.09	0.12	−0.22	0.12	−0.12	0.02	−0.11	0.09	−0.10		
(23) $Ag^{+\text{impact}}$	0.14	−0.07	0.12	0.05	0.05	0.01	0.10	0.06	0.28	−0.16	0.35	−0.05	0.12	−0.05	0.16	−0.04	0.17	−0.08	0.32	−0.13	0.25	−0.21	
(24) $Ag^{-\text{impact}}$	−0.16	0.24	0.03	0.10	0.00	0.02	−0.04	0.05	−0.03	0.26	0.02	0.50	−0.18	0.14	−0.10	0.18	−0.17	0.01	−0.08	0.05	−0.15	0.22	−0.06

Bivariate correlations of 0.13 and above are significant at $p < 0.05$; bivariate correlations of 0.18 and above are significant at $p < 0.01$; TC, task-involving climate; EC, ego-involving climate; AM, autonomous motivation; CM, controlled motivation; P, pleasant states; Ag, anger; Ax, anxiety; +, functional; –, dysfunctional.

(Newton et al., 2000). Three parcels were defined for task-involving climate by calculating the sums of the items representing the second-order dimensions of cooperative learning, important role, and effort/improvement. The remaining items representing punishment for mistakes, unequal recognition, and intra-team member rivalry were assigned to the three parcels defined for ego-involving climate. In line with SDT (Deci and Ryan, 1985) conceptualization and Ryan and Connell's (1989) suggestion, four parcels were defined for autonomous motivation by calculating the sums of items representing intrinsic motivation, integrated regulation, and identified regulation. The remaining items representing introjected regulation and external regulation were allocated to four parcels for controlled motivation. Amotivation was excluded from the analysis because we were interested in the quality of motivation rather than the quantity of motivation. Overall, acceptable model fit was obtained for the full measurement model representing perceived motivational climate, motivation regulations, functional emotions, and dysfunctional emotions at T1, $\chi^2/df = 8.436$, RMSEA = 0.057, CFI = 0.924, TLI = 0.909, SRMR = 0.065, and at T2, $\chi^2/df = 8.7653$, RMSEA = 0.043, CFI = 0.958, TLI = 0.950, SRMR = 0.068.

Structural Equation Modeling

A total of 14 structural models were tested to examine the temporal ordering of motivation regulations and the intensity and perceived impact of emotions. Specifically, four models were estimated including paths relating task-involving climate and autonomous motivation with the intensity of functional pleasant states, dysfunctional anxiety, functional anger, and dysfunctional anger separately (Models 1–4). Three other models included paths relating ego-involving climate and controlled motivation with the intensity of dysfunctional anxiety, functional anger, and dysfunctional anger (Models 5–7). Similarly, seven models were tested to examine the relationships with impact ratings of emotions (Models 8–14). All models were saturated. In regards to emotion intensity, one additional path was included in the model from dysfunctional anger intensity to the latent difference score of ego-involving climate (M7). We also added a path going from functional anger impact ratings to the latent difference score of ego-involving climate (M13).

Overall, a task-involving climate was a positive predictor of autonomous motivation at T1 (see **Table 3**, M1–M4 and M8–M11, β_1) and of the latent change in autonomous motivation at T2 (M1–M4 and M8–M11, β_8). A task-involving climate was a negative predictor of the intensity of anxiety and dysfunctional anger at T1 (M2-β_2 and M4-β_2), and the latent change in these emotions at T2 (M2-β_9 and M4-β_9), while it positively predicted the reported impact of functional anger at T1 (M10-β_2), but not the change in this emotion at T2 (M10-β_9). An ego-involving climate positively predicted controlled motivation at T1 (M5–M7 and M12–M14, β_1) and the latent difference in controlled motivation at T2, but only for the path including the intensity of functional anger (M6-β_8). Ego-involving climate was a positive predictor of the intensity of anxiety at T1 (M5-β_2), the intensity and reported impact of dysfunctional anger at T1 (M7-β_2 and M14-β_2, respectively), and latent change in the intensity and reported impact of dysfunctional anger at T2 (M7-β_9 and M14-β_9, respectively). Effect sizes for these reported significant paths were low.

TABLE 3 | Standardized path coefficients for relationships between motivational climate (MC), motivation regulations (M), and emotions (E).

			MC_1-M_1	MC_1-E_1	MC_1-ΔMC	M_1-ΔMC	E_1-ΔMC	M_1-ΔM	E_1-ΔE	MC_1-ΔM	MC_1-ΔE	M_1-ΔE	E_1-ΔM
Model			(β_1)	(β_2)	(β_3)	(β_4)	(β_5)	(β_6)	(β_7)	(β_8)	(β_9)	(β_{10})	(β_{11})
M1 TC	AM	P^{+int}	0.36***	0.08	−0.27***	0.02	0.07	−0.35***	−0.51***	0.21**	0.05	−0.02	−0.03
M2 TC	AM	Ax^{-int}	0.36***	−0.21**	−0.24***	0.02	0.13	−0.35***	−0.56***	0.22**	−0.13*	0.04	0.05
M3 TC	AM	Ag^{+int}	0.36***	0.07	−0.27***	0.03	0.03	−0.35***	−0.59***	0.21**	−0.02	−0.03	0.00
M4 TC	AM	Ag^{-int}	0.36***	−0.22**	−0.27***	0.03	0.02	−0.35***	−0.57***	0.23**	−0.13*	0.10	0.13*
M5 EC	CM	Ax^{-int}	0.23***	0.19**	−0.37***	0.02	0.06	−0.34***	−0.56***	0.10	0.03	0.14*	0.18*
M6 EC	CM	Ag^{+int}	0.23***	0.12	−0.37***	0.03	0.03	−0.33***	−0.59***	0.14*	−0.04	0.13*	−0.05
M7 EC	CM	Ag^{-int}	0.23***	0.21**	−0.39***	0.00	0.14	−0.33***	−0.58***	0.11	0.14*	0.01	0.12
M8 TC	AM	P^{+pi}	0.36***	0.11	−0.27***	0.01	0.11	−0.34***	−0.63***	0.21**	0.05	0.08	−0.06
M9 TC	AM	Ax^{-pi}	0.36***	−0.06	−0.27***	0.02	0.04	−0.36***	−0.55***	0.21**	−0.12	−0.07	−0.08
M10 TC	AM	Ag^{+pi}	0.36***	0.28***	−0.31***	0.01	0.16	−0.36***	−0.58***	0.20**	0.03	0.03	0.04
M11 TC	AM	Ag^{-pi}	0.36***	−0.14	−0.28***	0.03	−0.09	−0.35***	−0.45***	0.20**	−0.14	0.12	−0.07
M12 EC	CM	Ax^{-pi}	0.23***	0.08	−0.37***	0.04	0.09	−0.32***	−0.54***	0.13	0.12	0.08	0.02
M13 EC	CM	Ag^{+pi}	0.23***	−0.07	−0.37***	0.01	0.18	−0.32***	−0.56***	0.13	−0.06	0.08	−0.08
M14 EC	CM	Ag^{-pi}	0.23***	0.14*	−0.36***	0.02	−0.03	−0.31***	−0.46***	0.10	0.16**	0.08	0.20**

*Δ, latent change score between Time 1 and Time 2 (three months later). TC, task-involving climate; EC, ego-involving climate; AM, autonomous motivation; CM, controlled motivation; P, pleasant states; Ag, anger; Ax, anxiety; +, functional; −, dysfunctional; int, intensity; pi, perceived impact. *$p < 0.05$; **$p < 0.01$; ***$p < 0.001$.*

As can be observed in **Table 3**, the path from the reported intensity of dysfunctional anger at T1 to the latent change in autonomous motivation at T2 (M4-β_{11}) was significant and positive, but the coefficient from autonomous motivation at T1 to the latent change in dysfunctional anger at T2 (M4-β_{10}) was non-significant. Also, the path from the reported impact of dysfunctional anger at T1 to the latent change in controlled motivation (M14-β_{11}) was significant and positive, but β_{10} was non-significant. These findings regarding the intensity and perceived impact of dysfunctional anger would support H_1 (emotion predicts changes in motivational regulations). The path from controlled motivation at T1 to the latent change in the intensity of functional anger at T2 (M6-β_{10}) was significant, but not β_{11}, supporting H_2 (motivational regulations predict changes in emotions). Finally, the path from controlled motivation at T1 to the latent change in reported intensity of anxiety at T2 (M5-β_{10}) and the path from the intensity of anxiety at T1 to the latent change in controlled motivation at T2 (M5-β_{11}) were significant and positive, thus providing support for H_3 (reciprocal effects). Effect sizes for these reported significant paths were also low.

DISCUSSION

The current study examined the relationship between athletes' perceptions of their motivational climate, motivation regulations, intensity, and reported functional impact of pleasant and stress-related emotions over time. We expected that perceptions of task-involving climate would positively predict athletes' autonomous motivation and functional emotions, and that this relationship would hold over time. In contrast, an ego-involving climate was expected to be a positive predictor of controlled motivation and dysfunctional emotions. A main aim of this study involved testing the temporal ordering of athletes' emotions and motivation regulations by investigating two different sequences. The first sequence examined the mediating role of motivation regulations in the motivational climate and emotion relationships, while the second sequence placed emotions as mediators of the motivational climate and motivation regulations relationship.

The results indicated moderately high positive correlations in the reported scores of perceived motivational climate across time. These findings concur with empirical evidence from a previous longitudinal study examining the perceptions of football players about their motivational climate at the beginning and at the end of the season (Sage and Kavussanu, 2008). A slightly lower stability was found in the Sage and Kavussanu's study. However, their study included other variables (i.e., goal orientations and moral behaviors), which may have suppressed the magnitude of the values. In addition, the timeframe in their study was relatively longer including data from the beginning to the end of the season, which may also have allowed for other aspects (e.g., performance outcome) to influence the perceptions of the motivational climate. Moderately high positive correlations were also found in the participants' reported motivation regulations. This finding is in line with the Lonsdale and Hodge's (2011) study results on elite level athletes assessed over a 4-month period. However, in regards to athletes' emotional states, low positive correlations were found for the emotion intensity. These results concur with Hanin's (2000) assumption about intra-individual variability of emotion intensity as well as with Lazarus (2000) conceptualization of emotions as individuals' responses to a transaction with the environment that unfolds over time. Empirical support for variability in emotional intensity has derived from studies assessing the intensity of anxiety 1 h prior to four meets (Turner and Raglin, 1996) or a range of feeling states 15 min prior a fight in 10 competitions across the entire season (Robazza et al., 2004). In regards to the functional impact, positive low correlations were reported in the case of stress-related emotions, with the exception of dysfunctional anger where a moderate correlation was found across times ($r = 0.50$). These results indicate that meta-experiences reflecting athletes' awareness of the impact, preferences, or attitudes toward emotions (Hanin, 2004) are more stable than emotional states.

As expected, significant positive paths were found from the perceptions of a task-involving climate to the changes in athletes' autonomous motivation (**Table 3**), although effect size was low. However, partial support was obtained for the hypothesized link between ego-involving climate and the change in controlled motivation, as only one significant positive path was found with the intensity of functional anger included in the model, but not in the case of other emotions. Negative significant paths were found between task-involving climate and the change in intensity of dysfunctional anxiety and dysfunctional anger. In contrast, significant positive paths were found for ego-involving climate and the change in intensity and reported impact of dysfunctional anger. Notably, small effect sizes of significant paths were observed. These findings indicate that the perceptions of a motivational climate have a carryover effect on athletes' emotional experiences, especially on anger and anxiety. The results are in line with AGT (Nicholls, 1989) and SDT (Deci and Ryan, 1985, 2000; Ryan and Deci, 2017) assumptions that a task-involving climate is associated with a more adaptive achievement pattern while an ego-involving climate is associated with a more maladaptive pattern. Taken together, these results confirm our hypothesis regarding the stability of the interplay between motivational climate, motivation, and emotions supporting the notion that the social situation created by significant others influences goal involvement and how participants interpret their experiences.

Our findings showed that the relationship between athletes' quality of motivation and emotions varied depending on the type of motivation and emotions assessed. Specifically, the first hypothesis (emotions predict changes in motivation regulations) was supported by the significant links found between the intensity of dysfunctional anger and the change score in autonomous motivation, and between dysfunctional perceptions of anger and the change score for controlled motivation. The links in the opposite directions were non-significant. The second hypothesis (motivation regulations predict changes in emotions) was partially supported by a significant path from controlled motivation to the change score in intensity of functional anger, while a non-significant link was found in the opposite direction. The third hypothesis (reciprocal relationship between emotions and motivation regulations) was supported by significant paths between controlled motivation and the change score of the intensity of anxiety in both directions. Taken together, the results suggest that the interplay between motivation and emotions is contingent of the specific emotions. Different findings were observed regarding the intensity and functional impact of emotions. Thus, the findings also provide support for the assessment of both intensity and functional impact of emotions. However, effect sizes were low, thus, overall findings should be interpreted with caution.

The notion that motivation determines emotions is supported by several theorists. For instance, in addition to AGT (Nicholls, 1989) and SDT (Deci and Ryan, 2000; Ryan and Deci, 2017), in the contextual motivation sequence proposed within the hierarchical model (Vallerand, 1997) it is assumed that motivation determines behavior, emotions, and thoughts. Also Lazarus (2000) cognitive-motivational-relational theory of emotion conceptualizes emotion as an organized psychophysiological reaction reflecting person-environment relationships. Emotions are the results of an individual's appraisal of a situation in terms of goal relevance and congruence. According to Lazarus, the function of emotions is to facilitate adaptation. Similarly, the IZOF model (Hanin, 2000, 2007) assumes that emotions are triggered by person's appraisals of the probability of achieving relevant goals, and the interaction of both functional and dysfunctional emotions influences performance.

Previous research, with young participants in particular, has also examined emotions as both antecedents and consequences of motivation. For instance, Blanchard et al. (2009) found that self-determined motivation predicted higher intensity levels of positive emotions in young basketball players. In addition, intervention studies have provided evidence for the influence of motivation in the individuals' pleasant emotional experiences such as enjoyment (Smith et al., 2007; MacPhail et al., 2008). In contrast, in the Bortoli et al. (2014) study, pleasant and unpleasant states were included as mediators in the relationship between motivational climate and motivation regulations.

Our results indicate that only in the instance of controlled motivation and the intensity of anxiety there were significant paths indicating a reciprocal relationship. This may support the notion that emotions and motivation are complex phenomena. Lazarus (1999) suggested using a systems theory approach whereby each subsystem would be comprised of several variables, and thus, it would be possible to assume that sometimes one may act as an independent variable and at other times as an outcome variable. According to a systems theory approach, in the IZOF model emotions are conceptualized as core components of a psychobiosocial state, which can be manifested in several interrelated modalities including emotional and motivational aspects (for descriptions, see Hanin, 2010; Ruiz et al., 2016). Based on our results, significant emotion-motivation relationships emerged on the reported data on anxiety and anger, but not on pleasant experiences.

Strengths, Limitations, and Future Research Directions

This study was one of the first to explore the sequential interplay between the quality of motivation and performance related emotions in sport. The repeated measures design allowed the examination of two alternative sequences in which motivational climate would serve as antecedents of: (1) the variability in motivation regulations, which would result in different emotions; or (2) different emotions, which would be antecedents of the quality of motivation. Overall, results indicate that emotions and motivation are intertwined: specific emotions predicted different types of motivation and, at the same time, motivation regulations predicted specific emotions.

The study has some limitations that should to be addressed in the future. First, because of the relatively small sample size, we estimated the models for each emotion separately. Previous studies have used a composite index for motivation (Lonsdale and Hodge, 2011). However, because emotions reflect different meanings we opted for separate analysis on the relationship between autonomous/controlled motivation and different emotions. Future research should attempt to replicate the present findings with a larger sample to allow for the estimation of a model including all study variables. Effect sizes obtained in the study were relatively small, thus, larger sample studies are warranted in the replication of these findings. Second, we used repeated measures at two time points across 3 months. This allowed us to examine inter-individual variability in intra-individual patterns of change over time. However, future research could include a larger number of measurement points, which would provide a more reliable assessment and information about individual trajectories, thereby shedding more light into the understanding of the interplay of motivational and emotional variables across time. A final limitation of the study is the use of a correlational design. Thus, future experimental research where some of the studied variables are manipulated would allow for a direct test of the proposed models, providing a better understanding of the nature of the motivation and emotion relationship. Another important avenue for future research would be the examination of the role of athletes' basic psychological needs satisfaction as potential mediators in this relationship.

Practical Implications

The study has important practical implications. Findings support the notion that coaches need to promote a task-involving motivational climate to attain long lasting positive effects on autonomous motivation. They also need to decrease dysfunctional anxiety and anger to enhance the athletes' adaptation to psychological stress associated with performance in high achievement contexts. Coaches should also be mindful that an ego-involving climate could have negative long-term effects by triggering controlled motivation and dysfunctional stress-related emotions. Sport psychology practitioners should help athletes become aware of the personal reasons to participate in sport, their emotional experiences, and the interplay between motivation and emotions. Sport psychology interventions could focus on an early identification of athletes presenting high levels of controlled motivation or dysfunctional anxiety, in order to prevent maladaptive responses to psychological stress and their negative long-term effects.

ETHICS STATEMENT

This study was carried out in accordance with 'the ethical principles of research in the humanities and social and behavioral sciences and proposals for ethical review' drafted by the National Advisory Board on Research Ethics in Finland (TENK). The University of Jyväskylä Ethical Committee approved the research protocol. In accordance with the Declaration of Helsinki, all participants gave written informed consent, after anonymity and confidentiality was assured.

AUTHOR CONTRIBUTIONS

All authors listed have made a substantial, direct and intellectual contribution to the work, and approved it for publication.

REFERENCES

Álvarez, M. S., Balaguer, I., Castillo, I., and Duda, J. L. (2012). The coach created motivational climate, young athletes' well-being, and intentions to continue participation. *J. Clin. Sport Psychol.* 6, 166–179. doi: 10.1123/jcsp.6.2.166

Ames, C. (1992). "Achievement goals, motivational climate, and motivational processes," in *Motivation in Sport and Exercise*, ed. G. C. Roberts (Champaign, IL: Human Kinetics), 161–176.

Beedie, C., Terry, P., and Lane, A. (2000). The profile of mood states and athletic performance: two meta-analyses. *J. Appl. Sport Psychol.* 12, 49–68. doi: 10.1080/10413200008404213

Blanchard, D., Amiot, C., Perreault, S., and Vallerand, R. (2009). Cohesiveness, coach's interpersonal style and psychological needs: their effects on self-determination and athletes' subjective well-being. *Psychol. Sport Exerc.* 10, 545–551. doi: 10.1016/j.psychsport.2009.02.005

Bortoli, L., Bertollo, M., Comani, S., and Robazza, C. (2011). Competence, achievement goals, motivational climate, and pleasant psychobiosocial states in youth sport. *J. Sports Sci.* 29, 171–180. doi: 10.1080/02640414.2010.530675

Bortoli, L., Bertollo, M., Filho, E., and Robazza, C. (2014). Do psychobiosocial states mediate the relationship between perceived motivational climate and individual motivation in youngsters? *J. Sports Sci.* 32, 572–582. doi: 10.1080/02640414.2013.843017

Bortoli, L., Bertollo, M., and Robazza, C. (2009). Dispositional goal orientations, motivational climate, and psychobiosocial states in youth sport. *Pers. Individ. Differ.* 47, 18–24. doi: 10.1016/j.paid.2009.01.042

Bortoli, L., Bertollo, M., Vitali, F., Filho, E., and Robazza, C. (2015). The effects of motivational climate interventions on psychobiosocial states in high school physical education. *Res. Q. Exerc. Sport* 86, 196–204. doi: 10.1080/02701367.2014.999189

Bortoli, L., Messina, G., Zorba, M., and Robazza, C. (2012). Contextual and individual influences on antisocial behaviour and psychobiosocial states of youth soccer players. *Psychol. Sport Exerc.* 13, 397–406. doi: 10.1016/j.psychsport.2012.01.001

Cohen, J. (1988). *Statistical Power Analysis for the Behavioral Sciences*, 2nd Edn. New York, NY: Psychology Press.

Cumming, S., Smoll, F., Smith, R., and Grossbard, J. (2007). Is winning everything? The relative contributions of motivational climate and won-lost percentage in youth sports. *J. Appl. Sport Psychol.* 19, 322–336. doi: 10.1080/10413200701342640

Deci, E. L., and Ryan, R. M. (1985). *Intrinsic Motivation and Self-determination in Human Behavior*. New York, NY: Plenum Publishing Co. doi: 10.1007/978-1-4899-2271-7

Deci, E. L., and Ryan, R. M. (2000). The "what" and "why" of goal pursuits: human needs and the self-determination of behavior. *Psychol. Inq.* 11, 227–268. doi: 10.1207/s15327965pli1104_01

Duda, J. L., and Balaguer, I. (2007). "Coach-created motivational climate," in *Social Psychology in Sport*, eds S. Jowett and D. Lavalle (Champaign, IL: Human Kinetics), 117–130.

Ferrer, E., and McArdle, J. (2003). Alternative structural models for multivariate longitudinal data analysis. *Struct. Equ. Modeling* 10, 493–524. doi: 10.1207/S15328007SEM1004_1

Hanin, Y. L. (2004). "Emotion in sport: an individualized approach," in *Encyclopedia of Applied Psychology*, Vol. 1, ed. C. D. Spielberger (Oxford: Elsevier Academic Press), 739–750. doi: 10.1016/B0-12-657410-3/00611-5

Hanin, Y. L. (2007). "Emotions in sport: current issues and perspectives," in *Handbook of Sport Psychology*, 3rd Edn, eds G. Tenenbaum and R. C. Eklund (Hoboken, NJ: John Wiley & Sons), 31–58.

Hanin, Y. L. (2010). "Coping with anxiety in sport," in *Coping in Sport: Theory, Methods, and Related Constructs*, ed. A. Nicholls (Hauppauge, NY: Nova Science), 159–175.

Hanin, Y. L. (ed.) (2000). *Emotions in Sport*. Champaign, IL: Human Kinetics.

Harwood, C. G., Keegan, R. J., Smith, J. M. J., and Raine, A. S. (2015). A systematic review of the intrapersonal correlates of motivational climate perceptions in sport and physical activity. *Psychol. Sport Exerc.* 18, 9–25. doi: 10.1016/j.psychsport.2014.11.005

Hu, L., and Bentler, P. M. (1999). Cutoff criteria for fit indexes in covariance structure analysis: conventional criteria versus new alternatives. *Struct. Equ. Modeling* 6, 1–55. doi: 10.1080/10705519909540118

Jaakkola, J., Ntoumanis, N., and Liukkonen, J. (2016). Motivational climate, goal orientation, perceived sport ability, and enjoyment within Finnish junior ice hockey players. *Scand. J. Med. Sci. Sports* 26, 109–115. doi: 10.1111/sms.12410

Jaakkola, T., Yli-Piipari, S., Barkouris, V., and Liukkonen, J. (2017). Relationships among perceived motivational climate, motivational regulations, enjoyment, and PA participation among Finnish physical education students. *Int. J. Sport Exerc. Psychol.* 15, 273–290. doi: 10.1080/1612197X.2015.1100209

Kipp, L., and Amorose, A. J. (2008). Perceived motivational climate and self determined motivation in female high school athletes. *J. Sport Behav.* 2, 108–129.

Lane, A. M., Beedie, C. J., Jones, M. V., Uphill, M., and Devonport, T. J. (2012). The BASES expert statement on emotion regulation in sport. *J. Sports Sci.* 30, 1189–1195. doi: 10.1080/02640414.2012.693621

Langan, E., Hodge, K., McGowan, S., Carney, S., Saunders, V., and Lonsdale, C. (2016). The influence of controlled motivation alongside autonomous motivation: maladaptive, buffering, or additive effects? *Int. J. Sport Exerc. Psychol.* 14, 57–71. doi: 10.1080/1612197X.2015.1016084

Lazarus, R. S. (1999). *Stress and Emotion: A New Synthesis*. New York, NY: Springer Publishing Company, Inc.

Lazarus, R. S. (2000). How emotions influence performance in competitive sports. *Sport Psychol.* 14, 229–252. doi: 10.1123/tsp.14.3.229

Little, T. D., Cunningham, W. A., Shahar, G., and Widaman, K. F. (2002). To parcel or not to parcel: exploring the question, weighing the merits. *Struct. Equ. Modeling* 9, 151–173. doi: 10.1207/S15328007SEM0902_1

Lonsdale, C., and Hodge, K. (2011). Temporal ordering of motivational quality and athlete burnout in elite sport. *Med. Sci. Sports Exerc.* 43, 913–921. doi: 10.1249/MSS.0b013e3181ff56c6

Lonsdale, C., Hodge, K., and Rose, E. A. (2008). The development of the behavioral regulation in sport questionnaire (BRSQ): instrument development and initial validity evidence. *J. Sport Exerc. Psychol.* 30, 323–335. doi: 10.1123/jsep.30.3.323

MacPhail, A., Gorely, T., Kirk, D., and Kinchin, G. (2008). Children's experiences of fun and enjoyment during a season of sport education. *Res. Q. Exerc. Sport* 79, 344–355. doi: 10.1080/02701367.2008.10599498

McArdle, J. J. (2009). Latent variable modeling of differences and changes with longitudinal data. *Annu. Rev. Psychol.* 60, 577–605. doi: 10.1146/annurev.psych.60.110707.163612

McArdle, J. J., and Prindle, J. J. (2008). A latent change score analysis of a randomized clinical trial in reasoning training. *Psychol. Aging* 23, 702–719. doi: 10.1037/a0014349

McNeish, D. (2018). Thanks coefficient alpha, we'll take it from here. *Psychol. Methods* 23, 412–433. doi: 10.1037/met0000144

Muthén, L. K., and Muthén, B. O. (2017). *Mplus User's Guide*, 8th Edn. Los Angeles, CA: Muthén & Muthén.

Newton, M., Duda, J. L., and Yin, Z. (2000). Examination of the psychometric properties of the perceived motivational climate in sport questionnaire-2 in a sample of female athletes. *J. Sports Sci.* 18, 275–290. doi: 10.1080/026404100365018

Nicholls, J. G. (1989). *The Competitive Ethos and Democratic Education*. London, UK: Harvard University Press.

Reinboth, M., and Duda, J. (2006). Perceived motivational climate, need satisfaction and indices of well-being in team sports: a longitudinal perspective. *Psychol. Sport Exerc.* 7, 269–286. doi: 10.1016/j.psychsport.2005.06.002

Robazza, C., Bertollo, M., Ruiz, M. C., and Bortoli, L. (2016). Measuring psychobiosocial states in sport: initial validation of a trait measure. *PLoS One* 11:e0167448. doi: 10.1371/journal.pone.0167448

Robazza, C., Bortoli, L., and Hanin, Y. L. (2004). Precompetition emotions, bodily symptoms, and task-specific qualities as predictors of performance in high-level karate athletes. *J. Appl. Sport Psychol.* 16, 151–165. doi: 10.1080/10413200490437679

Robazza, C., and Ruiz, M. C. (2018). Emotional self-regulation in sport and performance. *Oxford Res. Encycl. Psychol.* doi: 10.1093/acrefore/9780190236557.013.154 [Epub ahead of print].

Ruiz, M., Robazza, C., Tolvanen, A., and Hanin, J. (2018). The psychobiosocial states scale (PBS-S): factor structure and reliability. *Eur. J. Psychol. Assess.* doi: 10.1027/1015-5759/a000454 [Epub ahead of print].

Ruiz, M. C., Haapanen, S., Tolvanen, A., Robazza, C., and Duda, J. (2017a). Predicting athletes' functional and dysfunctional emotions: the role of the motivational climate and motivation regulations. *J. Sports Sci.* 35, 1598–1606. doi: 10.1080/02640414.2016.1225975

Ruiz, M. C., Hanin, Y. L., and Robazza, C. (2016). Assessment of performance-related experiences: an individualized approach. *Sport Psychol.* 30, 201–218. doi: 10.1123/tsp.2015-0035

Ruiz, M. C., Raglin, J., and Hanin, Y. L. (2017b). The individual zones of optimal functioning (IZOF) model (1978– 2014): historical overview of its development and use. *Int. J. Sport Exerc. Psychol.* 15, 41–63. doi: 10.1080/1612197X.2015.1041545

Ryan, R. M., and Connell, J. P. (1989). Perceived locus of causality and internalization: examining reasons for acting in two domains. *J. Pers. Soc. Psychol.* 57, 749–761. doi: 10.1037/0022-3514.57.5.749

Ryan, R. M., and Deci, E. L. (2000). Self-determination theory and the facilitation of intrinsic motivation, social development, and well being. *Am. Psychol.* 55, 68–78. doi: 10.1037/0003-066X.55.1.68

Ryan, R. M., and Deci, E. L. (2017). *Self-Determination Theory: Basic Psychological Needs in Motivation, Development, and Wellness*. New York, NY: The Guilford Press.

Sage, L., and Kavussanu, M. (2008). Goal orientations, motivational climate, and prosocial and antisocial behaviour in youth football: exploring their temporal stability and reciprocal relationships. *J. Sports Sci.* 26, 717–732. doi: 10.1080/02640410701769716

Sarrazin, P., Vallerand, R., Guillet, E., Pelletier, L., and Cury, F. (2002). Motivation and dropout in female handballers: a 21-month prospective study. *Eur. J. Soc. Psychol.* 32, 395–418. doi: 10.1002/ejsp.98

Smith, R. E., Smoll, F. L., and Cumming, S. P. (2007). Effects of a motivational climate intervention for coaches on young athletes' sport performance anxiety. *J. Sport Exerc. Psychol.* 29, 39–59. doi: 10.1123/jsep.29.1.39

Standage, M., Duda, J. L., and Ntoumanis, N. (2003). Predicting motivational regulations in physical education: the interplay between dispositional goal orientations, motivational climate and perceived competence. *J. Sports Sci.* 21, 631–647. doi: 10.1080/0264041031000101962

Tabachnick, B. G., and Fidell, L. S. (2013). *Using Multivariate Statistics*, 6th Edn. Boston, MA: Pearson Education.

Turner, P. E., and Raglin, J. S. (1996). Variability in precompetition anxiety and performance in college track and field athletes. *Med. Sci. Sports Exerc.* 28, 378–385. doi: 10.1097/00005768-199603000-00014

Vallerand, R. J. (1997). "Toward a hierarchical model of intrinsic and extrinsic motivation," in *Advances in Experimental Social Psychology*, Vol. 29, ed. M. P. Zanna (New York, NY: Academic Press), 271–360. doi: 10.1016/S0065-2601(08)60019-2

Vazou, S., Ntoumanis, N., and Duda, J. (2006). Predicting young athletes' motivational indices as a function of their perceptions of the coach- and peer-created climate. *Psychol. Sport Exerc.* 7, 215–233. doi: 10.1016/j.psychsport.2005.08.007

Wagstaff, C. (2014). Emotion regulation and sport performance. *J. Sport Exerc. Psychol.* 36, 401–412. doi: 10.1123/jsep.2013-0257

Watson, D., and Tellegen, A. (1985). Toward a consensual structure of mood. *Psychol. Bull.* 98, 219–235. doi: 10.1037/0033-2909.98.2.219

Woodman, T., Davis, P., Hardy, L., Callow, N., Glasscock, I., and Yuill-Proctor, J. (2009). Emotions and sport performance: an exploration of happiness, hope, and anger. *J. Sport Exerc. Psychol.* 31, 169–188. doi: 10.1123/jsep.31.2.169

Zhu, W. (2012). Sadly, the earth is still round ($p < 0.05$). *J. Sport Health Sci.* 1, 9–11. doi: 10.1016/j.jshs.2012.02.002

11

Can Preinjury Adversity affect Postinjury Responses?

Ross Wadey[1]*, Lynne Evans[2], Sheldon Hanton[2], Mustafa Sarkar[3] and Helen Oliver[2]

[1]Faculty of Sport, Health, and Applied Sciences, St Mary's University, Twickenham, United Kingdom, [2]School of Sport and Health Sciences, Cardiff Metropolitan University, Cardiff, United Kingdom, [3]School of Science and Technology, Nottingham Trent University, Nottingham, United Kingdom

***Correspondence:**
Ross Wadey
ross.wadey@stmarys.ac.uk

Informed by and drawing on both the integrated model of response to sport injury (Wiese-Bjornstal et al., 1998) and the biopsychosocial model of challenge and threat states (Blascovich, 2008), this multi-study paper examined whether preinjury adversity affected postinjury responses over a 5-year time period. Study 1 employed a prospective, repeated measures methodological design. Non-injured participants ($N = 846$) from multiple sites and sports completed a measure of adversity (Petrie, 1992); 143 subsequently became injured and completed a measure of coping (Carver et al., 1989) and psychological responses (Evans et al., 2008) at injury onset, rehabilitation, and return to sport. MANOVAs identified significant differences between groups categorized as low, moderate, and high preinjury adversity at each time phase. Specifically, in contrast to low or high preinjury adversity groups, injured athletes with moderate preinjury adversity experienced less negative psychological responses and used more problem- and emotion-focused coping strategies. Study 2 aimed to provide an in-depth understanding of *why* groups differed in their responses over time, and *how* preinjury adversity affected these responses. A purposeful sample of injured athletes from each of the three groups were identified and interviewed ($N = 18$). Using thematic analysis, nine themes were identified that illustrated that injured athletes with moderate preinjury adversity responded more positively to injury over time in comparison to other groups. Those with high preinjury adversities were excessively overwhelmed to the point that they were unable to cope with injury, while those with low preinjury adversities had not developed the coping abilities and resources needed to cope postinjury. Practical implications and future research directions are discussed.

Keywords: coping, emotions, recovery, rehabilitation, stress, trauma

INTRODUCTION

For over 20 years, two models have been at the forefront of research into the psychology of sport injury: Williams and Andersen's (1998) multicomponent theoretical model of stress and injury and Wiese-Bjornstal et al.'s (1998) integrated model of psychological response to the sport injury and rehabilitation process. Underpinned by Williams and Andersen's model, several preinjury factors have been found to predict injury including personality traits (e.g., hardiness, optimism), adversity (e.g., major negative life events, daily hassles), and coping resources (for a review, see Ivarsson et al., 2017). Postinjury, and consistent with Wiese-Bjornstal et al.'s model, research has also supported the effect of a number of personal and situational factors on athletes' emotional (e.g., anger, anxiety, guilt, relief) and behavioral responses (e.g., adherence, behavioral coping), and recovery outcomes (e.g., functional performance, readiness to return to sport). However, to date, researchers have largely overlooked the importance of drawing on both models to gain a more complete and comprehensive understanding of the injury process.

According to Wiese-Bjornstal et al.'s (1998) integrated model, preinjury factors that predispose athletes to injury can continue to exert their effects postinjury by influencing injured athletes' emotional and behavioral responses, and ultimately their recovery outcomes. Indeed, as early as 1995, Wiese-Bjornstal, Smith, and LaMott stated that it would be remiss to think that factors affecting athletes preinjury would simply disappear postinjury. For example, the strain of dealing with a relationship breakdown preinjury was suggested by Wiese-Bjornstal et al. (1995) to likely further compound the strain of dealing with the injury. To date, however, very few empirical studies have examined preinjury *and* postinjury factors; rather, researchers have focused on either preinjury *or* postinjury factors (for notable exceptions, see Albinson and Petrie, 2003; Wadey et al., 2012, 2013). In one of the few studies, Albinson and Petrie examined the effect of a number of preinjury factors (i.e., preinjury adversity, social support satisfaction, and dispositional optimism) on postinjury responses (i.e., appraisals, mood disturbance). Using a prospective methodological design, preinjury measures were completed preseason and postinjury measures were completed 1, 4, and 7 days after injury occurrence. From the 84 Division I-A university football players who completed the preinjury measures, 13 subsequently became injured. Findings identified a positive and significant correlation ($r = 0.64$) between preinjury adversity (i.e., major negative life events) and greater postinjury mood disturbance 1 day after injury occurrence. This finding supported Wiese-Bjornstal et al.'s integrated model and the importance of accounting for preinjury factors when examining postinjury responses.

It is important to recognize that the study by Albinson and Petrie (2003) was not without its limitations. As observed by the authors' themselves, the sample size was small for a quantitative study ($N = 13$) and sport-specific, reducing statistical power and the potential scope of findings across sports, and they did not account for postinjury responses beyond rehabilitation. According to Albinson and Petrie, to overcome these limitations, researchers should employ multi-site and multisport data collection strategies and account for postinjury responses beyond injury rehabilitation. Another important limitation, and one that researchers need to address, relates to the potential mechanisms underpinning the relationship between preinjury adversity and postinjury mood disturbance. To elaborate, whilst Albinson and Petrie's finding about the relationship between preinjury adversity and postinjury mood disturbance was intuitively appealing, the authors did not aim to account for, nor seek to explain, the factors and processes underpinning and informing it. Further, Wiese-Bjornstal et al.'s (1998) model offers no theoretical explanation for this relationship because of its descriptive nature rather than theoretical explanation. One theoretical framework that could be used to this end is the biopsychosocial model (BPSM) of challenge and threat states (Blascovich, 2008).

The BPSM (Blascovich, 2008) hypothesizes that prior to a task, individuals will evaluate the demands of the task (i.e., demand evaluation) and whether they possess the necessary resources to cope effectively (i.e., resource evaluation). When an individual evaluates he or she has sufficient resources to meet the demands of the task, a challenge state occurs. In contrast, when an individual evaluates they do not possess the resources required to meet the demands of the task, a threat state occurs (Seery, 2011). The BPSM proposes that these evaluations trigger distinct cardiovascular responses (Blascovich, 2008). To elaborate, a challenge state results in sympathetic-adrenomedullary activation, which releases catecholamines that dilate the blood vessels, and increase cardiac activity and oxygenated blood flow to the brain and muscles. A threat state also results in pituitary-adrenocortical activation, which releases cortisol that inhibits dilation of the blood vessels and reduces cardiac activity, resulting in less blood flow. Consequently, compared to a threat state, a challenge state is marked by relatively higher cardiac output and lower total peripheral resistance (i.e., net constriction vs. dilation in the arterial system; Seery, 2011).

Over the past decade, research has shown a challenge state to facilitate, whereas a threat state to hinder, performance (Hase et al., 2019). Aligned with this research, the BPSM has been used to investigate the relationship between prior adversity and subsequent responses (Seery et al., 2010a,b, 2013). In one such study, Seery et al. (2013) investigated participants' histories of adversity before a computer-based navigation task. A curvilinear relationship was identified, with a moderate number of adverse life events related to a cardiovascular response more reflective of a challenge state compared to no or a high number of events. In the only study to investigate this assertion in a sport context, Moore et al. (2018) explored the relationship between nonsporting adverse events and cardiovascular responses to, and performance during, a pressurized sporting task. Participants who reported a moderate number of adverse life events displayed cardiovascular responses more reflective of a challenge state compared to those who reported a lower or higher number of events. In addition, participants with a moderate history of adverse events outperformed those who reported a lower or higher number of events. Thus, this contradicts the perspective that adversity increases the risk of future psychological concerns (Turner and Lloyd, 1995). Rather, the findings suggest that exposure to some negative adversity may have a "silver lining." Specifically, they may benefit individuals during future challenging situations by helping individuals to view such situations as less demanding and/or by enhancing their ability to cope. However, among the limitations of the studies in this area to date are the cross-sectional nature of research designs, a focus on laboratory-based experiments, and the investigation of a limited number of outcomes (e.g., cardiovascular responses, performance). To the best of our knowledge, no research has longitudinally examined the relationship between adverse life events and subsequent responses during and after the experience of a commonplace sporting challenge such as injury. The purpose of this study is to address this oversight by investigating whether preinjury adversity affects postinjury responses (i.e., psychological responses and coping strategies).

STUDY 1

Study 1 aimed to extend previous research by providing a 5-year prospective, repeated measures examination of the relationship between preinjury adversity and postinjury responses (i.e., emotional responses and coping strategies). Informed by and drawing on both the integrated model of response to sport injury (Wiese-Bjornstal et al., 1998), the biopsychosocial model of challenge and threat states (Blascovich, 2008), and associated research (e.g., Moore et al., 2018), the following four hypotheses were proposed: (1) injured athletes with a moderate number of preinjury adverse life events would experience less postinjury negative psychological responses at injury onset, rehabilitation, and return to sport compared to injured athletes with a low or high number of preinjury adverse life events; (2) injured athletes with a moderate number of preinjury adverse life events would experience more intense postinjury positive psychological responses at injury onset, rehabilitation, and return to sport compared to injured athletes with a low or high number of preinjury adverse life events; (3) injured athletes with a moderate number of preinjury adverse life events would use more postinjury problem-focused and emotion-focused coping strategies at injury onset, rehabilitation, and return to sport compared to injured athletes with a low or high number of preinjury adverse life events; and (4) injured athletes with a moderate number of preinjury adverse life events would use less postinjury avoidance coping strategies at injury onset, rehabilitation, and return to sport compared to injured athletes with a low or high number of preinjury adverse life events.

Method

Research Design

Scholars have questioned the methodological rigor of research in the psychology of sport injury (e.g., Petrie and Falkstein, 1998; Brewer, 2010). Responding to calls for future research to utilize rigorous methodological designs that have multiple data collection points to account for the temporal nature of recovery (viz. Evans et al., 2006), this study employed a prospective, repeated measures design that aligned with the purpose of the study.

Participants

The participants[1] (N = 846) were drawn from six Universities and represented eight team and 18 individual sports and competitive levels that ranged from recreational to international standards of performance. Mean age was 20 (SD = 2.11 years) and 481 were males and 365 were females. Participants' injury status was monitored for 5 years and 143 subsequently became injured. All injuries were diagnosed by a medically qualified practitioner and included fractures, dislocations, strains, and sprains of different body parts. The resulting time loss from training and competition ranged from 14 to 393 days (M days = 41; SD = 50). The injured participants represented team and individual sports from recreational to international standards of competition. Mean age was 19 (SD = 1.21 years) and 76 were males and 67 were females.

Measures

Preinjury Adversity

The Life Events Survey for Collegiate Athletes (LESCA) was used to measure negative major life events (Petrie, 1992). The LESCA comprises 69 major life events (e.g., death of a close family member, breaking up with partner, failing an important exam, not attaining personal goals in sport, major mistakes in actual competition, being dropped from the team). Participants rated the perceived impact and desirability of each event they had encountered in the last 24 months on an 8-point Likert scale, anchored at −4 (*extremely negative*) and +4 (*extremely positive*). Petrie (1992) reported 1-week test-retest reliabilities ranging from 0.76 to 0.84, and 8-week test-retest reliabilities ranging from 0.48 to 0.72 for the LESCA. Petrie also provided strong evidence of predictive, discriminant, and convergent validity. Only the negative major life events score was used in this study. Participants were divided into low, moderate, and high preinjury adversity groups based on percentile scores. The rationale for this approach was threefold: (1) it aligned with the study's theoretical underpinning (i.e., biopsychosocial model of challenge and threat states; Blascovich, 2008), (2) it was congruent with our hypotheses, and (3) it has been adopted in previous empirical research (e.g., Moore et al., 2018).

Postinjury Coping Strategies

A situation-specific version of the Coping Orientation to Problems Experienced (COPE; Carver et al., 1989) scale was used postinjury to assess coping at injury onset, rehabilitation, and return to sport. The COPE comprises 52 items and 13 different coping strategies (four items per strategy). Participants responded to each item on a 4-point Likert scale, from 1 (*I am not doing this at all*) to 4 (*I am doing this a lot*). Cronbach's alpha coefficients ranged from 0.52 to 0.90 in this study. Consistent with conceptual models of coping (Hoar et al., 2006) and empirical findings (Stowell et al., 2001; Litman, 2006), the 13 coping strategies were summated into three higher order factors: (1) *problem-focused coping* (i.e., positive reinterpretation and growth, planning, active coping, suppression of competing activities, restraint coping, and acceptance); (2) *emotion-focused coping* (i.e., seeking social support for emotional reasons, focus on and venting of emotions, and seeking social support for instrumental reasons); and (3) *avoidance coping* (i.e., behavioral disengagement, denial, and mental disengagement). The strategy *turning to religion* was excluded from the study on the basis that researchers have demonstrated its failure to load onto any factors (Stowell et al., 2001; Litman, 2006).

[1]694 participants were drawn from a previously published study (Wadey et al., 2012); however, the relationship between major life events and postinjury responses was not examined in this study. Furthermore, the current study recruited an additional 170 participants.

Postinjury Psychological Responses
The Psychological Responses to Sport Injury Inventory (PRSII) was used to measure athletes' postinjury psychological responses (Evans et al., 2008). It consists of six subscales: devastation, dispirited, reorganization, feeling cheated, restlessness, and isolation. Each subscale has four items, apart from Reorganization which consists of three items. Participants indicated the extent to which each statement reflected how they presently feel on a 5-point Likert scale anchored at 1 (*strongly disagree*) and 5 (*strongly agree*). Each subscale score ranges from a low of 4 to a high of 20. For Reorganization, this equates to a low of 3 and a high of 15. Evans et al. (2008) provided evidence of content and predictive validity.

Procedure

Ethical approval for this study was sought and granted by the first author's University Research Ethics Committee. Asymptomatic participants (i.e., non-injured and engaging in full participation in sport) were then recruited by approaching key stakeholders (e.g., coaches, lecturers) at recognized sports institutions within the United Kingdom that had large cohorts of competitive athletes. The key stakeholders granted permission that the first author could contact their athletes to request their participation in the study. Group sessions were then undertaken at each institution to explain the aim and scope of the study. Given the longitudinal nature of the study (i.e., 5-year time span), some athletes declined to participate because they were either moving to a new country or ceasing their participation in sport. The athletes who agreed to participate provided written informed consent. Participation was entirely voluntary, and the performers were not compensated in anyway. Participants subsequently completed a demographic information sheet and a preinjury major life event measure (i.e., LESCA), which took 15 min to complete. These were completed online to avoid missing data, according to the standardized instructions recommended by Petrie (1992).

The authors monitored and recorded the injury status of the original sample for a period of 5 years by contacting them and key stakeholders (e.g., coaches, physiotherapists) on a weekly basis after scheduled training sessions or competitions. Consistent with Wadey et al. (2012), an injury was defined as a medical problem resulting from sport participation that prevented normal training and competition for a minimum period of 2 weeks. Minor scrapes and bruises that may require certain modifications (e.g., strapping or protective garments) for training and competition purposes were not classified as injuries. The rationale for not including injuries less than 2 weeks was because this study was interested in postinjury responses at different times phases of recovery (i.e., injury onset, rehabilitation, and return to sport), which injuries of a minimal of 2 weeks' time loss allowed for (cf. Wadey et al., 2012). Our decision not to focus only on more severe injuries (e.g., a minimum of 6 weeks and beyond; Bianco et al., 1999) was predicated on the need to maximize sample size to increase statistical power. Sample size is a perennial problem with injury research (Cupal, 1998).

If an athlete became injured, they completed the PRSII and COPE at three time points: (1) in the first week of their injury occurrence (i.e., Time 1), (2) midway through their rehabilitation (i.e., Time 2), and (3) in the first week of their return to full training (i.e., Time 3). Questionnaires took 20 min to complete. During the first time point, four other details were also recorded: (1) date of injury occurrence; (2) type and location of the injury; (3) who diagnosed the injury; and (4) estimated duration for recovery (i.e., the approximated number of weeks the athlete would be injured and unable to participate in normal training and competition). The latter information was used to estimate the subsequent two time points for postinjury measure completion (i.e., rehabilitation and return to competitive sport), which was monitored and confirmed by the first author as the participants' rehabilitation progress unfolded. Postinjury measures included standardized instructions from Evans et al. (2008) and Carver et al. (1989) and were counterbalanced (i.e., ordered randomly).

Data Analysis

Data analysis involved three stages. First, data screening procedures were conducted. Second, preliminary analyses were conducted to examine possible differences between groups (i.e., low, moderate, and high preinjury adversity) for demographic factors (i.e., age, sex, and injury severity). These preliminary analyses were used to identify potential covariates. Third, one-way multivariate analysis of variance (MANOVA) was used to explore differences between groups (i.e., low, moderate, and high preinjury adversity) for dependent variables (i.e., coping strategies and psychological responses) at Time 1 (injury onset), Time 2 (rehabilitation), or Time 3 (return to sport). Due to the independent variable having three levels, follow-up one-way analysis of variance (ANOVA) was conducted to identify where significant differences lay. Data analysis was performed using SPSS 21.0 for Windows.

Results

Preliminary Analyses

Three preliminary analyses were conducted to examine differences between groups (i.e., low, moderate, and high adversity) for age, injury severity, and sex. A one-way between-groups analysis of variance (ANOVA) identified no significant difference between groups for age [$F(2, 140) = 2.3$, $p = 0.103$] or injury severity [$F(2, 140) = 0.1$, $p = 0.990$]. Using a Pearson's chi-squared test, it was identified that there was no statistically significant association between sex and adversity groups, $\chi(1) = 2.270$, $p = 0.321$. Demographics therefore were not controlled for in the main analysis.

Injury Onset

A one-way MANOVA identified a statistically significant difference at injury onset between groups, $F(18, 264) = 4.32$, $p < 0.001$; Wilks' Lambda = 0.61, $\eta^2 = 0.23$. Using a Bonferroni-adjusted alpha level of 0.005 for the multiple analyses, one-way ANOVAs indicated a significant difference for the following five dependent variables: dispirited, $F(2, 140) = 13.8$, $p < 0.001$, $\eta^2 = 0.23$. *Post hoc* comparisons (Tukey's HSD test) indicated that the high preinjury adversity group ($M = 13.38$, SD = 3.01) was significantly more dispirited than the low ($M = 11.44$,

SD = 2.29) and moderate groups (M = 10.45, SD = 2.83); Devastation, $F(2, 140) = 15.6$, $p < 0.001$, $\eta^2 = 0.18$. *Post hoc* comparisons indicated that the high (M = 13.16, SD = 2.55) and low preinjury adversity group (M = 12.09, SD = 1.87) reported significantly more devastation than the moderate group (M = 10.55, SD = 2.48); problem-focused coping, $F(2, 140) = 10.6$, $p < 0.001$, $\eta^2 = 0.13$. *Post hoc* comparisons indicated that the moderate preinjury adversity group (M = 54.28, SD = 9.94) reported significantly more problem-focused coping than the high (M = 45.11, SD = 12.62) and low groups (M = 44.69, SD = 12.82); emotion-focused coping, $F(2, 140) = 9.3$, $p < 0.001$, $\eta^2 = 0.18$. *Post hoc* comparisons indicated that the moderate preinjury adversity group (M = 26.74, SD = 8.81) reported significantly more emotion-focused coping than the high (M = 21.33, SD = 6.99) and low groups (M = 20.89, SD = 6.32); and avoidance coping, $F(2, 140) = 17.4$, $p < 0.001$, $\eta^2 = 0.20$. *Post hoc* comparisons indicated that the moderate preinjury adversity group (M = 18.47, SD = 4.34) reported significantly less avoidance coping than the high (M = 27.29, SD = 9.91) and low groups (M = 23.98, SD = 7.68). There were no significant differences between groups at injury onset for restlessness, reorganization, isolation, or feeling cheated.

Rehabilitation

A one-way MANOVA identified a statistically significant difference at rehabilitation between groups, $F(18, 264) = 5.38$, $p < 0.001$; Wilks' Lambda = 0.54, $\eta^2 = 0.27$. Using a Bonferroni-adjusted alpha level of 0.005 for the multiple analyses, one-way ANOVAs indicated a significant difference for the following dependent variables: dispirited, $F(2, 140) = 14.5$, $p < 0.001$, $\eta^2 = 0.17$. *Post hoc* comparisons indicated that the high preinjury adversity group (M = 10.87, SD = 2.61) was significantly more dispirited than the low (M = 8.27, SD = 2.79) and moderate groups (M = 8.26, SD = 2.66); devastation, $F(2, 140) = 12.87$, $p < 0.001$, $\eta^2 = 0.15$. *Post hoc* comparisons indicated that the high (M = 9.44, SD = 2.93) and low preinjury adversity groups (M = 9.00, SD = 2.36) reported significantly more devastation than the moderate group (M = 7.21, SD = 1.69); reorganization, $F(2, 140) = 17.6$, $p < 0.01$, $\eta^2 = 0.20$. *Post hoc* comparisons indicated that the moderate group (M = 10.39, SD = 2.26) reported significantly more reorganization than the high (M = 7.98, SD = 1.97) and low groups (M = 8.78, SD = 1.91); restlessness, $F(2, 140) = 14.0$, $p < 0.001$, $\eta^2 = 0.17$. *Post hoc* comparisons indicated that the high preinjury adversity group (M = 10.42, SD = 3.01) reported significantly more restlessness than the low (M = 7.80, SD = 2.36) and moderate groups (M = 8.08, SD = 2.43); problem-focused coping, $F(2, 140) = 12.7$, $p < 0.001$, $\eta^2 = 0.15$. *Post hoc* comparisons indicated that the moderate preinjury adversity group (M = 58.32, SD = 12.0) reported significantly more problem-focused coping than the high (M = 46.27, SD = 14.24) and low groups (M = 46.91, SD = 14.26); emotion-focused coping, $F(2, 140) = 8.9$, $p < 0.001$, $\eta^2 = 0.11$. *Post hoc* comparisons indicated that the moderate preinjury adversity group (M = 27.66, SD = 9.55) reported significantly more emotion-focused coping than the high (M = 23.11, SD = 6.25) and low groups (M = 21.35, SD = 6.39); and avoidance coping, $F(2, 140) = 17.4$, $p < 0.001$, $\eta^2 = 0.20$. *Post hoc* comparisons indicated that the moderate preinjury adversity group (M = 18.47, SD = 4.34) reported significantly less avoidance coping than the high (M = 27.29, SD = 9.91) and low groups (M = 23.98, SD = 7.68). There were no significant differences between groups at rehabilitation for isolation or feeling cheated.

Return to Sport

A one-way MANOVA identified a statistically significant difference at return to sport between groups, $F(18, 264) = 4.53$, $p < 0.001$; Wilks' Lambda = 0.58, $\eta^2 = 0.24$. Using a Bonferroni-adjusted alpha level of 0.005 for the multiple analyses, one-way ANOVAs indicated a significant difference for the following dependent variables: reorganization, $F(2, 140) = 10.7$, $p < 0.001$, $\eta^2 = 0.13$. *Post hoc* comparisons indicated that the moderate group (M = 11.57, SD = 1.67) reported significantly more reorganization than the high (M = 9.64, SD = 2.39) and low groups (M = 10.13, SD = 2.40); restlessness, $F(2, 140) = 10.8$, $p < 0.001$, $\eta^2 = 0.13$. *Post hoc* comparisons indicated that the high (M = 10.58, SD = 3.80) and low (M = 9.93, SD = 3.67) preinjury adversity groups reported significantly more restlessness than the moderate group (M = 7.79, SD = 1.67); problem-focused coping, $F(2, 140) = 11.33$, $p < 0.001$, $\eta^2 = 0.14$. *Post hoc* comparisons indicated that the high (M = 58.13, SD = 10.6) and moderate preinjury adversity groups (M = 57.19, SD = 13.32) reported significantly more problem-focused coping than the low group (M = 46.56, SD = 14.51); avoidance coping, $F(2, 140) = 10.8$, $p < 0.001$, $\eta^2 = 0.12$. *Post hoc* comparisons indicated that the high (M = 18.93, SD = 3.19) and moderate preinjury adversity groups (M = 19.62, SD = 3.19) reported significantly less avoidance coping than the low group (M = 23.77, SD = 8.36). There were no significant differences between groups at return to sport for dispirited, devastation, feeling cheated, isolation, and emotion-focused coping.

Discussion

Aligned with the study's hypotheses, this study found that athletes with moderate preinjury adversity responded more adaptively postinjury over time than those with lower or higher preinjury negative adverse events. By adaptively, we mean athletes with moderate preinjury adversity not only responded with lower negatively toned psychological responses (i.e., feelings of devastation, dispiritedness, and restlessness) and used less maladaptive coping strategies (e.g., denial, mental disengagement), but they also experienced more positively toned psychological responses (i.e., reorganization) and used greater problem- and emotion-focused coping strategies (e.g., planning, active coping, focus on and venting of emotions) than those with lower or higher preinjury adversity. Findings support Endler and Hunt (1966) and Endler and Magnusson (1976) work on person-situation interactions and Wiese-Bjornstal et al.'s (1998) integrated model, which proposes that preinjury factors affect postinjury responses. However, this model does not stipulate the nature of the relationship between prior adverse life events and subsequent responses to sport injury. Extending the integrated model and associated research (Albinson and Petrie, 2003), the present findings support the notion that exposure to a moderate number of adverse events may have a "silver lining" and may benefit athletes during a future adverse situation such as a sport-related injury – helping them to experience less maladaptive and more adaptive responses in light of prior adversities (cf. Moore et al., 2018).

This study also significantly extends the broader literature on adversity in other fields of research. Indeed, research on the consequences of adversity has long been defined by its traditional focus on the negative effects to health and well-being (e.g., Turner and Lloyd, 1995). The predominant and fundamental assumption of such research is that there is a negative linear dose-response relationship between the extent of adversity experienced and health and well-being. However, the current findings challenge this assumption and provide evidence that adverse experiences may not always be detrimental. Rather, past adverse experiences (e.g., preinjury adversity) can aid future coping with adversity (i.e., sport-related injury). That said, what the current study was not able to explain was *how* moderate preinjury adversity is associated with more adaptive functioning when compared with those lower or higher preinjury adversity. According to the BPSM (Blascovich, 2008), our findings could be explained by those with a moderate preinjury adversity evaluating injury as a challenge because of their prior adversities. In contrast, those with lower or higher prior adversities might evaluate injury as a threat rather than a challenge. To elaborate, Holtge et al. (2018) recently hypothesized higher prior adversities may overwhelm an individual to the point that they are unable to cope with the adversity, whereas a moderate amount of adversity might be sufficiently challenging so that an individual can not only successfully cope, but also learn and improve their coping skills and resources for subsequent exposures to adversity. However, these hypotheses (and others) warrant more research attention to help explain these observed effects.

STUDY 2

Building upon the findings from Study 1, Study 2 aimed to provide an in-depth understanding of *why* groups (i.e., low, moderate, and high preinjury adversity) differed in their responses at each time phase (i.e., injury onset, rehabilitation, and return to sport) and *how* preinjury adversity affected these responses. Specifically, it enabled us to explore how preinjury adversity affected athletes' responses to injury; why do athletes with moderate preinjury adversity respond adaptively postinjury and why do athletes with low or high preinjury adversity respond less adaptively postinjury? Given the richness and complexity required to answer these questions, an ideographic rather than nomothetic methodological design was employed using qualitative inquiry. Considering the research questions were not focused on developing theory (i.e., grounded theory), examining "how" stories are told (i.e., narrative inquiry), exploring conscious experience of everyday life (i.e., phenomenology), or understanding culture (i.e., ethnography), a qualitative tradition was not employed. Rather, this study relied on qualitative methods of data collection to address the participants' perceptions of *why* and *how* their prior adversities affected their postinjury responses. Several recent reviews illustrate how qualitative methods can achieve these aims (e.g., Culver et al., 2012).

Method

Participants

From the injured athletes (N = 143) in Study 1, a two-step procedure was used for Study 2 to select a purposeful sample. Participants' preinjury major life event scores were used to identify participants who experienced low, moderate, and high preinjury adversity. Those who scored below the 20th percentile were classified as low, those between the 40th and 60th percentile as moderate, and those above the 80% percentile as high. Maximum variation sampling was then used to purposefully sample participants from the three groupings (i.e., low, moderate, and high) to account for predetermined characteristics that would help to offer novel insights into the findings of Study 1, specifically, sex, sport type, competitive level, and severity of injury. This resulted in each group comprising males and females, participants from team and individual sports and different standards of competition, (e.g., recreation, club, regional, national, and international), in addition to injuries that varied in severity. Eighteen injured athletes were contacted, informed about, and invited to participate in the qualitative study; all agreed and provided written informed consent. Of the participants who represented high (N = 6), low (N = 6), and moderate (N = 6) preinjury adversity groups, nine were males and nine were females, who ranged from 21 to 59 years of age (M_{age} = 25.4; SD = 9.65). They represented team and individual sports and ranged from club to international levels of performance. At the time of the study, all participants had returned to competition.

Interview Guide and Timelining

A semi-structured interview guide developed specifically for this study enhanced the quality of the interviewing process by providing a framework for participants to discuss their experiences while offering the flexibility and freedom for them to share their unique insights, into areas of interest pertinent to the study (Sparkes and Smith, 2014). The interview guide comprised three sections. The first section focused on the participants' general sporting involvement and the role that injury had played throughout their sporting careers. The aim of this section was to establish rapport with the participants. The second section focused on discussing each of the negative adversities reported in the preinjury questionnaire. Questions included: "Can you tell me more about this event?"; "What (if anything) led up to this event?"; "What impact (if any) did the event have on you?" During this section, the participants were also asked if they had experienced any adversities between completing the preinjury questionnaire and the onset of their injury.

During the second section, to facilitate the interview, timelining was used to visually represent the temporal order of the negative adverse events and how the participants made sense of their experiences over time. The participant drew a temporal graph and plotted the negative events as they unfolded (Sheridan et al., 2011). According to Kolar et al. (2015), timelines can enhance the quality of data collected during interviews by building rapport through actively engaging with the participants.

The third and final section of the interview focused on the effect of preinjury adversities on postinjury responses. This section had three subsections: injury onset, rehabilitation, and return to sport. Example questions included: "Do you think any of the preinjury adversities we've discussed impacted your injury experience at this stage of recovery? If so, how? If not, why?" During this stage of the interview, the participants' quantitative findings from Study 1 were also drawn upon, where appropriate, to facilitate reflection. The interviewer concluded the interview inviting additional insights from the participants.

Procedure

Ethical approval for this study was sought and granted by the first and second author's University Research Ethics Committee. Interviews were conducted face to face by the first and fifth authors in a mutually convenient location. Although the participants were asked the same questions in the same way, each participant's response determined the sequencing of the questions. This approach was intended to foster a more open communication with participants (Sparkes and Smith, 2014). Elaboration (e.g., "Could you please explain that in more detail?") and clarification (e.g., "I'm not sure exactly what you meant, could you please go over that again?") probes were used throughout to elicit more in-depth information and ensure understanding (Sparkes and Smith, 2014). Interviews, which lasted between 80 and 180 min (M = 130; SD = 32), were recorded in their entirety and transcribed verbatim. This resulted in over 300 pages of single-spaced transcribed text.

Data Analysis and Methodological Rigor

Thematic analysis was conducted by the first author (Braun et al., 2016). The process of analysis initially involved the first author immersing himself in the data by transcribing the data and (re)reading the transcripts multiple times. Initial codes were derived by highlighting interesting features across the entire dataset. Data relevant to each code was subsequently collated and combined to form overarching themes, a process that involved thinking about the relationships between the codes and themes. This involved, for example, exploring horizontal (i.e., themes across the dataset) and vertical (i.e., how themes develop upon one another) patterns within the dataset. To facilitate the process, visual representation (i.e., a thematic map) was used to illustrate the themes and enable the first author to think critically about how the themes related to one another both *horizontally* and *vertically* (Clarke et al., 2017). Themes were then reviewed in relation to the coded extracts, the story they each told, the entire dataset, and the overall story the themes told about the participants' experiences in relation to the research question.

Throughout this iterative process, a reflexive journal (i.e., introspective reflexivity) was kept by the first author to situate the previous findings from Study 1, his own personal identities, and to explore the surprises and undoings in the research process (i.e., unexpected turns in the research), with himself ultimately becoming the site of analysis and the subject of critique (McGannon and Metz, 2010). These reflections were also shared with the co-authors (i.e., intersubjective reflexivity) at regular intervals. The first author presented his interpretations of the data to them on a regular basis and provided written summaries of the findings for evaluation to enhance the study's methodological rigor (Smith and McGannon, 2017). The co-authors provided a "sounding board" to encourage reflection upon, and exploration of, alternative interpretations and explanations of the data. As part of this process of critical dialogue, the first author was required to make a defendable case about his interpretations. The production of the final report involved ensuring the write up provided a concise, coherent, logical, non-repetitive, and thought-provoking account of the data, with vivid and compelling example extracts (Braun et al., 2016). In addition, participant reflections on our analytical interpretations were sought (Smith and McGannon, 2017), a process that involved sharing and dialoguing with the participants about the study findings and provided opportunities for additional insight.

Results

Nine themes were identified in the data that described *how* preinjury adversity affected postinjury responses within each of the three groups and *why* there were differences between them. The results are presented for each group separately (i.e., low, moderate, and high preinjury adversity) and the themes within each group are described in temporal order to align with the vertical thematic analysis. Three themes per group: low (i.e., "Caught in the headlights," "Not knowing where to turn," and "Feeling vulnerable"); moderate (i.e., "Looking back to look forward," "Another challenge to overcome," and "Coping, recovery, and growth"); and high preinjury adversity (i.e., "The final straw," "Drained resources," and "Seeking professional help"). Each theme is now described with illustrative verbatim quotations.

Low Preinjury Adversity

Caught in the Headlights

This theme was defined as the injured athletes' shock of being injured and their inability to cognitively process the injury and its short- and long-term implications. Indeed, injury onset was reported to be an overwhelming experience for these athletes, with too many thoughts and emotions to process. One athlete reported, "I just was taken back by it all. I was just in shock that I was injured. There was just so much to get my head around. I didn't know whether I was coming or going." Another athlete reported how her reaction was due to having minimal experiences with adversity:

> What's the expression, "A deer caught in the headlights." I was so shocked that I was injured and, nervous. What have I done? How am I going to get about? When am I going to return? I found it so stressful at the

> time … The thing is I have not experienced much stress in my life; this was all a new experience for me and I found it tough, really tough. I do not know how to deal with stress.

Not Knowing Where to Turn
This theme was defined as the injured athletes' inability to cope during their rehabilitation from having minimal prior adversities to develop coping abilities and resources. That is, they either lacked coping abilities, used maladaptive coping strategies, and/or did not know how to mobilize their coping resources during rehabilitation. Indeed, the athletes reported continually feeling "lost," "distressed," "uncertain," "confused," "at a crossroads," and "not knowing where to turn for help." One participant reported:

> I really struggled during the rehabilitation. I was distraught. I was in pain. I was angry. I was depressed. And I did not know how to deal with these feelings. I've never experienced them before… I've got lots of friends and family. But, I did not know how to ask others for help. And I did not know who to ask for help. I felt very alone.

One athlete reported using an avoidance coping strategy to manage his negative thoughts and feelings during his rehabilitation. Despite having a short-term desired effect, this strategy proved to be ineffective in the longer term. He reported:

> I got really depressed, for a good few months I would say. I was in this, bubble. Every day I'd wake up and I'd have the same brace on my knee and I would say, "Same as yesterday then." Things were not moving forward. I started gambling, a lot. I missed the buzz of playing rugby (union), so I started to gamble. I gambled every single day for about 3 h. I enjoyed the buzz, it gave me something to do, and it took my thoughts away from the injury… Then, it got out of hand. I became addicted and even more depressed. I needed someone to tell me to step being an idiot.

Feeling Vulnerable
This theme was defined as the injured athletes' reflections upon their return to sport and their ability to cope well. They labeled themselves as "poor copers" and felt vulnerable to future adversity. Looking back, the athletes reported that recovery was a stressful experience, an experience they would not want to reencounter. One athlete reported, "I just can't cope with stress. Some people can, but clearly, I can't. I guess you could say I'm a poor coper." One athlete explained:

> I am concerned for the future. I mean, this was my first real experience of stress and I did not handle it well. I guess I've lived quite a sheltered life until now. I do not know if I could handle any more stress. This experience has really shaken me. It's alarmed me. I cannot deal with tough situations. Even sitting here with you now, I feel nervous about any future stresses. I do not know, perhaps I'm not tough enough to make it in sport.

Moderate Preinjury Adversity

Looking Back to Look Forward
This theme was defined as the injured athletes' recalling the lessons learnt from their prior adversities and how they could apply them to their current situation. To contextualize this theme, the athletes at injury onset did initially report negative thoughts such as catastrophizing and negative affective states (e.g., depressed, anxious, angry, frustrated). However, they reported over time how they were able to reflect on previous adverse events to regulate these thoughts and feelings, which also reminded them of their personals values and what was important in life. This theme was starkly illustrated by one athlete who reflected on the death of his father to help him rationalize his thoughts and feelings:

> I lost my dad. He was in a car with one of my uncles. My uncle was speeding, it was raining, and the car flipped over. A lorry hit the car and my dad died. That's the biggest thing that has ever happened to me in my life. It made me grow up fast … It's the moments in life when I need advice, like getting injured, when I really miss him. That's when it hits you. I got a tattoo 2 years ago, just to remember him. He always used to say, "Together we are strong." It's kind of a buffer when I'm feeling down … My dad was always the best person for calming me down. He was as 'cool as a cucumber.' But I've learnt to do this myself now. I can remember all the things he used to say to me. In that way, he's never really gone, has he? I've become calmer, a more relaxed person. I do not get angry about the little things. Crap happens all the time. You cannot let it bog you down. And I think when I was injured, I started thinking how would dad deal with this? And that played a big part in helping me to come to my senses. It gives me perspective on life really. All I've done is hurt my shoulder. I think because other bigger things have happened in my life, I think injury does not seem a big deal any more.

Another Challenge to Overcome
This theme was defined as the injured athletes' appraising injury as a challenge to overcome. Rather than being overwhelmed by the injury experience, these athletes reported injury as an opportunity for growth, development, and mastery. By reflecting upon and recalling the lessons learnt from past and current adverse situations (e.g., loss of parent, parent diagnosed with cancer, miscarriage, friend experiencing a spinal cord injury), the athletes believed they had the coping abilities and resources to deal with the injury. This belief led them to focus on their recovery and how they could keep moving forward rather than dwelling on the past. One athlete reported:

> What I've learned from past events is that you have got to be positive and not dwell on stuff too much. Focus on the things you can do rather than thinking about the

> things you cannot do. Yes, I may initially think it's the end of the world and anticipate the worst but from going through bigger stuff [prior adversities] I soon realise I'm over reacting. I know I can overcome it. You've got to put it in perspective and think about how you can make the most out of it. Regardless of whether I'm injured or not, I will fill up my time. That's my way of coping. How can I make the most of this injury? Could it lead to positive outcomes? It's just another challenge in life to overcome.

Coping, Recovery, and Growth

This theme was defined as the injured athletes' successful coping efforts to promote their psychological and physical recovery and to ultimately grow from the experience. From experiencing past and current negative adverse events, the athletes reported that they had developed an understanding of how they react to stressful situations and of their coping resources from prior adversities. That is, they knew who to seek support from (and who not to seek support from), to accept support offered from others rather than turning them away, to be proactive rather than reactive, to tell others what support they need rather than letting others determine their support needs, and to not over rely on or tax their resources too much. One athlete reported:

> The big thing I've learnt from previous events is to talk about how I am feeling. I used to keep my feelings to myself, which made me short tempered and get in to lots of arguments. You can walk around angry all day and hate everyone, but where does that get you? If you just bottle it up it just comes out in other ways. If anything, it'll make you feel worse and then you will not want to do you physiotherapy. You're not going to want to get better. I've learnt that I need to talk to my family and get everything off my chest. And they also remind me of previous events I've faced. I remember talking to my mum about my injury and she reminded me of my friend who became paralysed playing sport. So, my injury wasn't really the end of the world.

This refined knowledge of themselves and understanding of their coping abilities and resources enabled the athletes to cope with the challenges of rehabilitation and to successfully recover and return to sport. Furthermore, the athletes reported that they learned a great deal from their injury experience. One athlete reported, "Every adverse situation will teach you something. I've learnt a lot from the events I've experienced in the past, just like I have with this injury." It was reported that the injury experience reminded them of their values, how mobilizing their social support network had strengthened them, and how they felt more resilient having overcome another stressful experience.

High Preinjury Adversity

The Final Straw

This theme was defined as how the athletes' injury was the latest in a series of undesirable events that made them feel that they could not cope with their current situation any longer. The injury was described as the "final straw" and "too much" for them to handle and that they could not keep "spinning the plates" any longer. One participant reported the difficulty with juggling too many adverse life events:

> At the same time as the injury, I was dealing with the loss of my father from cancer and we had also just bought a house and we were trying to sell ours. Our buyer pulled out 2 days before completion, and it was just, like everything was going wrong. It, kind of snowballed. It was a really crap time. Not only was my body under a lot of stress, but I was mentally exhausted too. That was a low point and a rough time to go through.

The athletes reported being overwhelmed by what was happening and the only immediate coping strategy reported being used during injury onset was mental disengagement. One athlete reported, "I just denied I was injured and got on the cross-trainer. I needed to vent my feelings, but my injury just got worse." Another athlete expressed:

> Denial, that was my strategy. I would be like, I am not thinking about the injury. It's a strategy, but it's bad one because you do not confess to what's going on and you kind of kid yourself. I put myself in a bubble. And I did not accept anything that was going on … I would just bury myself in other things and try and shut it out.

Drained Resources

This theme was defined as venting one's emotions, ineffective support exchanges, and burdening one's coping resources. Following the denial of their injury and other adverse situations, the athletes reported during their rehabilitation that their anger and frustrations "boiled" over and they vented onto those in their immediate social network (i.e., family, friends). One athlete reported, "I just couldn't deny it any longer. It got to the point where I couldn't suppress my feelings any longer." Because many of their friends and family were unaware of the athletes' injury and other past and current adverse events, these revelations came as a shock to them and made for difficult conversations. One athlete reported:

> I remember just offloading everything on to my friend. She was taken back by it. She could not keep up with what I was saying. To be honest, I did not really know what I was saying either. I was talking rubbish. I could see she felt uncomfortable and did not know how to respond to me. I just walked off in the end and said not to worry about it, and that I'll try and figure it out.

These ineffective support exchanges continued as the athletes reported feeling in a "catch-22." On the one hand, the athletes reported that they did not know what they were thinking and feeling because not only had they not processed the events, but they also had too many events to process. Consequently, they wanted to disclose to others to help process the events and thereby better understand themselves and to let others help them. On the other hand, they found it difficult to articulate all the events and their impact on others, which left members of their support network feeling frustrated from being unable to help. This "catch-22" caused frictions within relationships and led the providers to withdraw their support. One athlete explained: "I had burdened them too much. I could tell they were getting fed up with me. I was getting fed up with me too. I didn't know where to turn next."

Seeking Professional Help

This theme was defined as seeking help from external sources from taxing their resources and developing symptoms of mental illness (i.e., depression, distress, anxiety). The athletes reported that during the later stages of their rehabilitation and return to competitive sport that they had to seek help from others outside of their social support network. This included support from sport psychologists, psychologists, and/or counselors. One athlete reported, "It got to the point where I needed professional help. I made an appointment with my doctor and he connected me with a psychologist." At the time of the interviews for this study, many of the athletes reported that they were still receiving professional help. One reported:

> I'm still trying to come to terms with all the stuff that's happened to me, the injury as well. I just could not keep denying it. I needed help. It took me a while to be ready to "open the doors" to how the events have impacted me. Working my way through everything with a psychologist is really helping me to better understand what I'm going through. It's a horrible process but it's giving me some perspective.

Discussion

This study aimed to provide an in-depth understanding of *why* groups (i.e., low, moderate, and high preinjury adversity) differed in their responses over time (i.e., injury onset, rehabilitation, and return to sport) and *how* preinjury adversity affected these responses. Three themes were identified for each of the three groups. For the low preinjury adversity group, the three themes were: "Caught in the headlights," "Not knowing where to turn," and "Feeling vulnerable." These findings provide empirical support for Holtge et al.'s (2018) suggestion that those individuals who experience no or minimal adversities may not develop coping abilities and resources to manage future exposure to adversity. Indeed, the participants reported being overwhelmed when they become injured and that they could not cope. Interestingly, and extending Holtge et al.'s (2018) suggestions in their recent review, this experience also led the participants to report that they felt vulnerable to future adversity. These findings provide somewhat of a dilemma for professional practice. On the one hand, there are increasing recommendations in the literature that to improve the well-being of those involved in sport we should embark on interventions to reduce the likelihood of experiencing adversity (e.g., Randall et al., 2018). These types of interventions are proactive and preventative and based on the assumption that the most effective way to combat the strain experienced by athletes in sport is to eliminate or at least reduce the quantity, frequency, and/or intensity of adverse events. On the other hand, it has been speculated that "talent needs trauma" (Collins and MacNamara, 2012) and the current findings suggest that minimal exposure to adversity does not stimulate the development of coping abilities and resources. Therefore, while not encouraging the experience of negative adverse events, our findings suggest that practitioners should avoid "sheltering" athletes from stressful demands and instead, if suitable, appropriately and progressively optimize the adversities they encounter. In other professions where individuals are required to act under pressure (e.g., police, fire service), exposing individuals to stimulated adversity has facilitated better performance in future stressful scenarios (e.g., Robertson et al., 2015). How best to support athletes who have experienced none or minimal adversity warrants future research.

For the moderate preinjury adversity group, the three themes were: "Looking back to look forward," "Another challenge to overcome," and "Coping, recovery, and growth." To expand, the participants reported they had personally developed from experiential learning with previous adverse situations, which enabled them to view injury as less demanding, believe they can cope given their prior adversities, and evaluate it as a challenge to overcome. From a BPSM perspective (Blascovich, 2008), divergent responses to a pressurized task (e.g., sport injury) are likely due to the differences in how individuals evaluate the task. When resources are judged to match or exceed demands, an individual evaluates a situation as a challenge. When demands are deemed to outweigh resources, an individual evaluates the situation as a threat. This aligns with the present findings, given that the participants had developed their coping abilities and resources from previously experiencing adverse events and as a result they evaluated that they had the resources to cope with their injury. Not only does this finding highlight the importance of injured athletes' evaluations (cf. Wiese-Bjornstal et al., 1998) and that fostering a challenge state is pivotal to explaining how athletes respond to and recover from injury (cf. Blascovich, 2008), it also reinforces the importance of reflective practice (Ghaye and Ghaye, 1998). Injured athletes should reflect on their prior adverse experiences (and their current injury) as a means of harnessing self-awareness of how they have personally grown from the experience, which aligns with recent research on growth following adversity (Howells et al., 2017) and sport-injury related growth (Roy-Davis et al., 2017).

The concept of growth following adversity in sport is gaining increased research attention. Examples of the types of adversities that have been examined in the sport and performance psychology literature include deselection (Neely et al., 2018); performance slumps, coach conflicts, bullying, eating disorders, and sexual abuse (Tamminen et al., 2013); and repeated non-selection and significant sporting failure (Sarkar et al., 2015). While these adversities have been identified to have negative consequences, the studies have also shown that adversity is not entirely debilitative; it can also bring about positive change, broadly conceptualized as *growth following adversity.* Howells et al.'s (2017) recent systematic review suggested that indicators of growth can be collapsed across three categories: intrapersonal (e.g., new life philosophy, heightened resilience), interpersonal (e.g., less judgmental, increased pro-social behavior), and physical (e.g., superior performance, enhanced body awareness). Yet, while some researchers have examined growth across adversities, others have focused on specific types such as sport-related injuries. Conceptualized as a context-specific form of growth following adversity, Roy-Davis et al. (2017) proposed the term *sport injury-related growth* to reflect the growth that can result from sport injury. Relating back to the current study, the findings support both these conceptualizations. That is, participants reported experiencing growth following various types of preinjury sporting (e.g., major mistakes in actual competition) and nonsporting adversities (e.g., death of a close family member) as well as sport injury specifically. Furthermore, our findings also extend this research by illustrating growth from prior adversities can influence future adverse events. Future research should continue to examine the experience of growth across sporting and nonsporting adversities to further understand the complexity of the phenomenon (cf. Hardy et al., 2017).

For the high preinjury adversity group, the three themes were: "The final straw," "Drained resources," and "Seeking professional help." The participants reported how their injury was the latest in a series of adverse events that made them feel that they could not cope with their current situation any longer. This finding provides empirical support for Holtge et al.'s (2018) suggestion that a high number of adversities may excessively overwhelm the individual to the point that they are unable to cope with the adversity. The participants reported that they did initially try and cope using avoidance strategies (i.e., mental disengagement), which did prove effective in the short term. This supports the findings of Carson and Polman (2010) who identified that avoidance coping strategies postinjury can facilitate control of short-term emotional states. However, our findings suggest that avoidance coping is ineffective in the long term because it can lead to emotional outbursts to others in the athletes' support network, which can tax the resources of their support providers (cf. Rook, 1992). This finding extends the psychology of sport injury literature. For some time now, social support has been proposed to be a positive way of coping postinjury (for a review, see Bianco and Eklund, 2001). However, it is important to acknowledge that support exchanges can lead to maladaptive responses for the support provider. An important practical recommendation moving forward therefore is that it is not only important to support injured athletes, but it is also critical to monitor and support their social support networks (cf. Wadey et al., 2018). On a final note, the participants in the high preinjury adversity group did report seeking professional help. Clearly, future researchers need to identify interventions that can be used to minimize the damaging consequences of adversity to help athletes cope more effectively with reduced well-being. Examples may include performer assistance programs, clinical counseling, and educational coping programs. Given the rise in mental health concerns in elite athletes (e.g., Souter et al., 2018), this warrants more immediate future research attention.

As with all studies, this study has several limitations that must be acknowledged and accounted for by future researchers to extend this study. First, this study only assessed preinjury adversity once. Given that participants' appraisal of the desirability of the adversity might have altered over time, future researchers should aim to measure preinjury variables on multiple occasions. Second, there was a time lag between preinjury measures and injury occurrence and this differed between participants. During this time lag, participants may have encountered other adversities and experiences that could have influenced postinjury responses. Third, other preinjury variables were not accounted for that could have explained postinjury findings. For example, the differences in postinjury responses between groups might reflect differences in other personal variables such as mood and the types of experienced adversity rather than the injury *per se*. To account for this in future research, researchers could consider accounting for other preinjury variables, such as mood states as a potential moderating variable. Lastly, the injured samples in this study were heterogeneous in that they differed in the type and severity of injury. This diversity creates challenges for researchers who aim to compare responses across participants at specific time points (e.g., rehabilitation). Future researchers could address this by using more homogenous samples, particularly in relation to injury type (cf. King et al., 2018).

CONCLUSION

The studies herein make an important contribution to the psychology of sport injury literature in at least three ways. First, this study is novel in that it is one of the very few studies to integrate preinjury and postinjury factors to help better understand and explain athletes' responses to injury. Future researchers should continue to examine the interrelationships within the sport injury process (i.e., preinjury to postinjury and back again) to advance this field of research. Second, this study extends our theoretical understanding. Whilst Wiese-Bjornstal et al.'s (1998) integrated model is arguably the dominant model in this field of research, which does hypothesize that preinjury factors may affect postinjury responses, it is descriptive rather than explanatory. The present findings demonstrate that a moderate preinjury adversity can positively influence postinjury responses, whereas higher preinjury adversities can excessively overwhelm the injured athlete and lower preinjury adversities do not challenge the athlete to stimulate the development of coping abilities and resources to enable them to cope with future adversity (e.g., sport injury). It is important, therefore, that future researchers examining adversity not only examine its negative impact, but also understand it can have a "silver lining" and benefit athletes during future adverse situations (Howells et al., 2017). Finally, this study heeded recommendation in the literature (viz. Petrie and Falkstein, 1998; Brewer, 2010) to adopt a rigorous methodology to investigate athletes' responses to injury (i.e., a prospective, repeated measures, multi-study, multi-method methodological design). In agreement with Brewer (2010), we hope other researchers strive, "... to conduct investigations of the calibre needed to thoroughly examine the role of psychological factors in sport injury rehabilitation outcomes" (p. 57).

ETHICS STATEMENT

This study was carried out in accordance with the recommendations of St Mary's University's Research Ethics Committee with written consent from all subjects. All subjects gave written informed consent in accordance with the Declaration of Helsinki. The protocol was approved by St Mary's University's Research Ethics Committee.

AUTHOR CONTRIBUTIONS

RW contributed to research design, data collection, data analysis, and write up. LE and SH contributed to research design and editing of the manuscript. MS contributed to write up and editing of the manuscript. HO contributed to data collection and editing of the manuscript.

REFERENCES

Albinson, C. B., and Petrie, T. A. (2003). Cognitive appraisals, stress and coping: preinjury and postinjury factors influencing psychological adjustment to sport injury. *J. Sport Rehabil.* 12, 306–322. doi: 10.1123/jsr.12.4.306

Bianco, T., and Eklund, R. C. (2001). Conceptual considerations for social support research in sport and exercise settings: the case of sport injury. *J. Sport Exerc. Psychol.* 23, 85–107. doi: 10.1123/jsep.23.2.85

Bianco, T., Malo, S., and Orlick, T. (1999). Sport injury and illness: elite skiers describe their experiences. *Res. Q. Exerc. Sport* 70, 157–169. doi: 10.1080/02701367.1999.10608033

Blascovich, J. (2008). "Challenge and threat" in *Handbook of approach and avoidance motivation*. ed. A. J. Elloit (New York, NY: Psychology Press), 431–445.

Braun, V., Clarke, V., and Weate, P. (2016). "Using thematic analysis in sport and exercise research" in *Routledge handbook of qualitative research methods in sport and exercise*. eds. B. Smith and A. Sparkes (London: Routledge), 191–205.

Brewer, B. W. (2010). The role of psychological factors in sport injury rehabilitation outcomes. *Int. Rev. Sport Exerc. Psychol.* 3, 40–61. doi: 10.1080/17509840903301207

Carson, F., and Polman, R. C. (2010). The facilitative nature of avoidance coping within sport injury rehabilitation. *Scand. J. Med. Sci. Sports* 20, 235–240. doi: 10.1111/j.1600-0838.2009.00890.x

Carver, C. S., Scheier, M. F., and Weintraub, J. K. (1989). Assessing coping strategies: a theoretically based approach. *J. Pers. Individ. Dif.* 56, 267–283. doi: 10.1037/0022-3514.56.2.267

Clarke, V., Hayfield, N., Moller, N., and Tischner, I. (2017). "Once upon a time ... Qualitative story completion methods" in *Collecting qualitative data: A practical guide to textual, media, and virtual techniques*. eds. V. Braun, V. Clarke, and D. Grey (United Kingdom, UK: Cambridge University Press).

Collins, D., and MacNamara, A. (2012). The rocky road to the top: why talent needs trauma. *Sports Med.* 42, 907–914. doi: 10.2165/11635140-000000000-00000

Culver, D. M., Gilbert, W., and Sparkes, A. (2012). Qualitative research in sport psychology journals: the next decade 2000–2009 and beyond. *Sport Psychol.* 26, 261–281. doi: 10.1123/tsp.26.2.261

Cupal, D. D. (1998). Psychological interventions in sport injury prevention and rehabilitation. *J. Appl. Sport Psychol.* 10, 103–123. doi: 10.1080/10413209808406380

Endler, N. S., and Hunt, J. M. (1966). Sources of behavioral variance as measured by the S-R inventory of anxiousness. *Psychol. Bull.* 65, 336–346. doi: 10.1037/h0023309

Endler, N. S., and Magnusson, D. (1976). Toward an interactional psychology of personality. *Psychol. Bull.* 83, 956–974. doi: 10.1037/0033-2909.83.5.956

Evans, L., Hardy, L., Mitchell, I., and Rees, T. (2008). The development of a measure of psychological responses to sport injury. *J. Sport Rehabil.* 16, 21–37. doi: 10.1123/jsr.17.1.21

Evans, L., Mitchell, I., and Jones, S. (2006). "Psychological responses to sport injury: A review of current research" in *Literature reviews in sport psychology*. eds. S. Hanton and S. D. Mellalieu (Hauppage, New York: Nova Science), 289–319.

Ghaye, A., and Ghaye, K. (1998). *Teaching and learning through critical reflective practice*. (London: David Fulton).

Hardy, L., Barlow, M., Evans, L., Rees, T., Woodman, T., and Warr, C. (2017). Great British medallist: psychosocial biographies of super-elite and elite athletes from Olympic sports. *Prog. Brain Res.* 232, 1–119. doi: 10.1016/bs.pbr.2017.03.004

Hase, A., O'Brien, J., Moore, L., and Freeman, P. (2019). The relationship between challenge and threat states and performance: A systematic review. Sport, Exercise, and Performance Psychology [Epub ahead of print].

Hoar, S. D., Kowalski, K. C., Gaudreau, P., and Crocker, P. R. E. (2006). "A review of coping in sport" in *Literature reviews in sport psychology*. eds. S. Hanton and S. D. Mellalieu (New York: Nova Science), 47–90.

Holtge, J., McGee, S. L., Maercker, A., and Thoma, M. V. (2018). A salutogenic perspective on adverse experiences: a curvilinear relationship of adversity and well-being. *Eur. J. Health Psychol.* 25, 53–69. doi: 10.1027/2512-8442/a000011

Howells, K., Sarkar, M., and Fletcher, D. (2017). "Can athletes benefit from difficulty. A systematic review of growth following adversity in competitive sport" in *Sport and the brain: The science of preparing, enduring, and winning (pp. 117–159). Progress in Brain Research*. eds. M. R. Wilson and B. Parkin (Academic Press).

Ivarsson, A., Johnson, U., Andersen, M. B., Tranaeus, U., Stenling, A., and Lindwall, M. (2017). Psychosocial factors and sport injuries: meta-analyses for prediction and prevention. *Sports Med.* 47, 353–365. doi: 10.1007/s40279-016-0578-x

King, E., Richter, C., Franklyn-Miller, A., Daniels, K., Wadey, R., Jackson, M., et al. (2018). Biomechanical but not timed performance asymmetries persist between limbs 9 months after ACL reconstruction during planned and unplanned change of direction. *J. Biomech.* 16, 93–103. doi: 10.1016/j.jbiomech.2018.09.021

Kolar, K., Ahmad, F., Chan, L., and Erickson, P. G. (2015). Timeline mapping in qualitative interviews: a study of resilience with marginalized groups. *Int. J. Qual. Methods* 14, 13–32. doi: 10.1177/160940691501400302

Litman, J. A. (2006). The COPE inventory: dimensionality and relationships with approach- and avoidance-motives and positive and negative traits. *Personal. Individ. Differ.* 41, 273–284. doi: 10.1016/j.paid.2005.11.032

McGannon, K. R., and Metz, J. L. (2010). "Through the funhouse mirror: understanding access and (un)expected selves through confessional tales" in *Contemporary sport psychology*. ed. R. J. Schinke (Hauppauge, NY: Nova Science Publishers), 153–170.

Moore, L. J., Young, T., Freeman, P., and Sarker, M. (2018). Adverse life events, cardiovascular responses, and sport performance under pressure. *Scand. J. Med. Sci. Sports* 28, 340–347. doi: 10.1111/sms.12928

Neely, K. C., Dunn, J. G. H., McHugh, T. F., and Holt, N. L. (2018). Female athletes' experiences of positive growth following deselection in sport. *J. Sport Exerc. Psychol.* 40, 173–185. doi: 10.1123/jsep.2017-0136

Petrie, T. (1992). Psychosocial antecedents of athletic injury: the effects of life stress and social support on female collegiate gymnasts. *J. Behav. Med.* 18, 127–138. doi: 10.1080/08964289.1992.9936963

Petrie, T., and Falkstein, D. L. (1998). Methodological, measurement, and statistical issues in research n sport injury prediction. *J. Appl. Sport Psychol.* 10, 26–45. doi: 10.1080/10413209808406376

Smith, B., and McGannon, K. (2017). Developing rigor in qualitative research: problems and opportunities within sport and exercise psychology. *Int. Rev. Sport Exerc. Psychol.* 11, 1–21. doi: 10.1080/1750984X.2017.1317357

Souter, G., Lewis, R., and Serrant, L. (2018). Men, mental health and elite sport: a narrative review. *Sports Med.* 57, 1–8. doi: 10.1186/s40798-018-0175-7

Sparkes, A., and Smith, B. (2014). *Qualitative research methods in sport, exercise and health: From process to product.* (London, UK: Routledge).

Stowell, J. R., Kiecolt-Glaser, J. K., and Glaser, R. (2001). Perceived stress and cellular immunity: when coping count. *J. Behav. Med.* 24, 323–339. doi: 10.1023/A:1010630801589

Tamminen, K. A., Holt, N. L., and Neely, K. C. (2013). Exploring adversity and the potential for growth among elite female athletes. *Psychol. Sport Exerc.* 14, 28–36. doi: 10.1016/j.psychsport.2012.07.002

Turner, R. J., and Lloyd, D. A. (1995). Lifetime traumas and mental health: the significant of cumulative adversity. *J. Health Soc. Behav.* 36, 360–375. doi: 10.2307/2137325

Wadey, R., Day, M., Cavallerio, F., and Martinelli, L. (2018). "The multilevel model of sport injury: can coaches impact and be impacted by injury?" in *Professional advances in sports coaching: Research and practice.* eds. R. Thelwell and M. Dicks (New York, NY: Routledge).

Wadey, R., Evans, L., Hanton, S., and Neil, R. (2012). An examination of hardiness throughout the sport injury process: a qualitative follow-up study. *Br. J. Health Psychol.* 17, 872–893. doi: 10.1111/j.2044-8287.2012.02084.x

Wadey, R., Evans, L., Hanton, S., and Neil, R. (2013). The effect of dispositional optimism pre- and post-injury. *Med. Sci. Sports Exerc.* 45, 387–394. doi: 10.1249/MSS.0b013e31826ea8e3

Wiese-Bjornstal, D. M., Smith, A. M., and LaMott, E. E. (1995). A model of psychologic response to athletic injury and rehabilitation. *Athl. Train. Sports Health Care Perspect.* 1, 17–30.

Wiese-Bjornstal, D. M., Smith, A. M., Shaffer, S. M., and Morrey, M. A. (1998). An integrated model of response to sport injury: psychological and sociological dimensions. *J. Appl. Sport Psychol.* 10, 46–69. doi: 10.1080/10413209808406377

Williams, J. M., and Andersen, M. B. (1998). Psychosocial antecedents of sport injury: review and critique of the stress and injury model. *J. Appl. Sport Psychol.* 10, 5–25. doi: 10.1080/10413209808406375

Randall, R., Nielsen, K., and Houdmont, J. (2018). Process evaluation for stressor reduction interventions in sport. *J. Appl. Sport Psychol.* 31, 47–64. doi: 10.1080/10413200.2018.1480544

Robertson, I. T., Cooper, C. L., Sarkar, M., and Curran, T. (2015). Resilience training in the workplace from 2003 to 2014: a systematic review. *J. Occup. Organ. Psychol.* 88, 533–562. doi: 10.1111/joop.12120

Rook, K. S. (1992). "Detrimental aspects of social relationships: taking stock of an emerging literature" in *The series in clinical and community psychology. The meaning and measurement of social support.* eds. H. O. F. Veiel and U. Baumann (Washington, DC, US: Hemisphere Publishing Corp), 157–169.

Roy-Davis, K., Wadey, R., and Evans, L. (2017). A grounded theory of sport injury-related growth. *Sport Exerc. Perform. Psychol.* 6, 35–52. doi: 10.1037/spy0000080

Sarkar, M., Fletcher, D., and Brown, D. (2015). What doesn't kill me: adversity-related experiences are vital in the development of superior Olympic performance. *J. Sci. Med. Sport* 18, 475–479. doi: 10.1016/j.jsams.2014.06.010

Seery, M. D. (2011). Challenge or threat. Cardiovascular indexes of resilience and vulnerability to potential stress in humans. *Neurosci. Biobehav. Rev.* 35, 1603–1610. doi: 10.1016/j.neubiorev.2011.03.003

Seery, M. D., Holman, E. A., and Silver, R. C. (2010a). Whatever does not kill us: cumulative lifetime adversity, vulnerability, and resilience. *J. Pers. Soc. Psychol.* 99, 1025–1041. doi: 10.1037/a0021344

Seery, M. D., Leo, R. J., Holman, E. A., and Silver, R. C. (2010b). Lifetime exposure to adversity predicts functional impairment and healthcare utilization among individuals with chronic back pain. *Pain* 150, 507–515. doi: 10.1016/j.pain.2010.06.007

Seery, M. D., Leo, R. J., Lupien, S. P., Kondrak, C. L., and Almonte, J. L. (2013). An upside to adversity? Moderate cumulative lifetime adversity is associated with resilient responses in the face of controlled stressors. *Psychol. Sci.* 24, 1181–1189. doi: 10.1177/0956797612469210

Sheridan, J., Chamberlain, K., and Dupuis, A. (2011). Timelining: visualizing experience. *Qual. Res.* 11, 552–569. doi: 10.1177/1468794111413235

12

Self-Compassion and Psycho-Physiological Recovery from Recalled Sport Failure

Laura A. Ceccarelli[1], Ryan J. Giuliano[1], Cheryl M. Glazebrook[2] and Shaelyn M. Strachan[2]*

[1] Department of Psychology, University of Manitoba, Winnipeg, MB, Canada, [2] Faculty of Kinesiology and Recreation Management, University of Manitoba, Winnipeg, MB, Canada

***Correspondence:**
Laura A. Ceccarelli
umceccal@myumanitoba.ca

Failure inherent to high-performance sport can precipitate emotional distress that can impair athletes' performance and physical and mental health. Identifying factors that allow athletes to manage failure to sustain their health is critical. Self-compassion, treating oneself kindly in response to failure, may help athletes manage failure; it buffers against negative affective psychological responses, yet athletes often fear self-compassion. It is unknown whether the benefits of self-compassion extend to athletes' physiological responses to failure and whether fear of self-compassion has an influence on psychological and physiological responses to failure, beyond self-compassion. The purpose of this study was to examine the influence of self-compassion on athletes' psychological and physiological responses when recalling a sport failure and determine if fear of self-compassion exerted unique effects, beyond self-compassion. Participants ($n = 91$; M age = 21) were university or national-level athletes. In this laboratory-based, observational study, athletes were connected to a multi-modal biofeedback system to measure physiological responding at baseline, during a stress induction (imagining a past performance failure), and during a recovery period. Physiological responding was assessed according to athletes' high-frequency heart rate variability (HRV), indexing parasympathetic nervous system activity, during the stress induction and recovery phase. Next, to assess psychological reactivity, athletes completed a series of scales (behavioral reactions, thoughts, and emotions). Regression analyses revealed that self-compassion predicted athletes' HRV reactivity to the stress induction ($\beta = 0.30$, $p < 0.05$). There was no relationship between self-compassion and HRV recovery. Further, self-compassion predicted adaptive behavioral reactions ($\beta = 0.46$, $p < 0.01$), and negatively predicted maladaptive thoughts ($\beta = -0.34$, $p < 0.01$) and negative affect ($\beta = -0.39$, $p < 0.01$). Fear of self-compassion explained additional variance in some maladaptive thoughts and behavioral reactions. Results suggest that self-compassion promotes adaptive physiological and psychological responses in athletes relative to a recalled sport failure and may have implications for performance enhancement, recovery and health outcomes. Further, addressing athletes' fears of self-compassion may also be important in promoting optimal psychological recovery.

Keywords: self-compassion, heart rate variability, sport, recovery, athletes, performance failure

INTRODUCTION

Failure is common among high-performance athletes who pursue challenging goals and must maintain high performance standards (Smith et al., 2006; Davis et al., 2007). These failures can be challenging for athletes to accept and cope with given the pressures they feel to perform well, combined with the significant investment of time and energy required to participate in elite sport. Further, athletes are harshly criticized when they fail to meet performance expectations, and often endure the consequences of failing to meet expectations (i.e., lost playing time; withdrawn financial support) (Davis and Sime, 2005; Bauman, 2016). Though failure is common for athletes, the criticism and consequences that athletes experience when they fail, combined with the pressures and expectations to be "mentally tough" in the face of challenges (Hammond et al., 2013; Bauman, 2016) make experiencing and coping with failure challenging for athletes. These failure experiences may contribute to poor mental health among athletes (Davis et al., 2007; Hammond et al., 2013; Mosewich et al., 2014). Indeed, many athletes report feeling a diminished sense of self and emotional distress following performance failure (Davis et al., 2007; Sagar et al., 2007; Sutherland et al., 2014) and these failures can precipitate depressive symptoms, anger and decreased vigor (Jones and Sheffield, 2008; Hammond et al., 2013).

The emotional distress that athletes report following failure often takes the form of self-criticism, self-blame, obsession and rumination (Mosewich et al., 2013; Ferguson et al., 2014). Many athletes believe this way of relating to themselves is necessary for success in elite sport and without it, they will become complacent and fail to reach their potential (Sutherland et al., 2014; Rodriguez and Ebbeck, 2015). However, researchers suggest this response to failure can actually be counter-productive; responding to failure with self-criticism and harsh self-punishment undermines self-regulation, emotional recovery, stress management and performance (Powers et al., 2009; Tenenbaum et al., 2013; Ferguson et al., 2015) and is positively associated with emotional reactivity, avoidance and fear of failure (Sagar et al., 2007; Powers et al., 2009). Further, this response pattern increases athletes' vulnerability to psychological distress and psychopathology (Powers et al., 2009; Hammond et al., 2013; Tenenbaum et al., 2013). Frequent failure experiences combined with these self-critical and ruminative tendencies that athletes endorse in response to failure may contribute to athletes experiencing equal or greater instances of mental health concerns than the general population (Reardon and Factor, 2010; Hammond et al., 2013). Given that athletes' mental health issues are often discounted, overlooked or go undetected, the estimates likely under-represent the true state of mental health problems among athletes (Reardon and Factor, 2010).

There may also be physiological costs when athletes are self-critical about their failures. The autonomic nervous system plays an integral role in responding and adapting to changing stimuli in the environment. While the sympathetic branch of the autonomic nervous system is implicated in "fight-or-flight" responses and active mobilization, the parasympathetic branch has been implicated in so-called "rest-and-digest" processes that promote long-term health and restoration of the body (Thayer and Sternberg, 2006; Porges, 2007; Thayer et al., 2012). The relative activity of these systems can depend upon whether or not we perceive our environment as safe, such that parasympathetic activity is notably increased for organisms who perceive their environment to be safe (Thayer and Lane, 2000; Porges, 2007). The parasympathetic nervous system can be measured via high-frequency heart rate variability (HRV), the variation in beat-to-beat intervals of the heart at relatively short cycles (0.15 to 0.40 Hz in adults; Porges, 2007). Commonly referred to as respiratory sinus arrhythmia, HRV has been utilized for the assessment of parasympathetic activity at rest and in response to environmental challenges, with the parasympathetic branch acting to inhibit or slow heart rate during moments of regulation. When stressed, the parasympathetic branch releases its inhibitory influences on the heart, decreasing HRV and accelerating heart rate, as the sympathetic nervous system drives an excitatory and "locked in" or inflexible state (Porges, 2007; Thayer and Lane, 2009; Thayer et al., 2012). This inflexible state is typically less adaptable in terms of range of behaviors than when HRV is high. Such states characterized by low HRV are commonly reported in association with emotional arousal or dysregulation, negativity bias (the tendency to be overly attentive to negative or threatening stimuli) and an increased likelihood of disease and mortality (Thayer and Sternberg, 2006; Porges, 2007; Thayer and Lane, 2009). Sustained activation of the body's stress response (i.e., persisting low HRV) can be brought on by ruminative thinking, obsession or self-criticism (McEwen and Wingfield, 2003; Gilbert, 2014), which can be detrimental to physical and mental health and can undermine performance (e.g., inhibits coordination, decision making, response time, and automatic skill execution; Davis and Sime, 2005; Bertollo et al., 2013; Tenenbaum et al., 2013). Thus, by examining a physiological marker of the parasympathetic nervous system, we can gain an understanding of the body's state of responsiveness to environmental demands and well-being.

Performance failures cause significant distress for high-performance athletes (Davis and Sime, 2005; Hammond et al., 2013; Bauman, 2016). The stress that athletes feel when they encounter failure is compounded by their tendencies to respond to failure with harsh self-criticism, judgment, and rumination, which are psychologically and physically costly (Juster et al., 2010; Gilbert, 2014). Thus, in order to optimize the health and performance of athletes it is important for researchers and practitioners to identify factors that effectively regulate psychological and physiological reactions to stressful experiences, such as sport performance failure (Juster et al., 2010; Dupee et al., 2015). Self-compassion may represent one such factor. Self-compassion involves treating oneself with care and concern in times of struggle and consists of three integrated components (Neff, 2003a). The first, self-kindness versus self-judgment, involves alleviating one's own suffering through self-care and concern versus harsh self-criticism. Next, mindfulness versus over identification, entails an open and balanced view of one's emotions without avoiding them or over-identifying with them. Finally, common humanity versus isolation, is the acceptance that failure is a shared human experience rather than an isolated experience (Neff, 2003a).

Researchers theorize that self-compassion can provide people with the emotional safety in times of failure that allows them to see their shortcomings in an open and balanced way, without feeling threatened, or the need to avoid difficult emotions as a means of coping (Neff et al., 2005; Allen and Leary, 2010). Indeed, in the face of set-backs self-compassion is positively associated with individuals' accurate self-appraisals and low levels of avoidance, negative affect and rumination (Neff et al., 2005; Leary et al., 2007; Breines and Chen, 2012). Further, self-compassion is positively associated with personal initiative and taking an approach (vs. avoidance) orientation to problems (Neff et al., 2005, 2007; Zhang and Chen, 2016). There is experimental evidence that inducing a self-compassionate state leads people to take more responsibility for their role in negative events, to view shortcomings as changeable and to be motivated to change when compared to control participants (Breines and Chen, 2012; Zhang and Chen, 2016). Thus, it is not surprising that self-compassion is positively related to emotional coping skills, and ability to repair negative emotional states (Neff, 2003b, Neff et al., 2005; Arimitsu and Hofmann, 2015).

In addition to the psychological benefits of self-compassion (Barnard and Curry, 2011), self-compassion may promote adaptive physiological regulation in response to failure. When people respond to failure with self-criticism, they may activate similar affect pathways, in this case a threat-defense system, as when they are being attacked by another person or experience a threatening event (Gilbert and Irons, 2005; Gilbert et al., 2006; Gilbert, 2014). This activation of the stress response can occur because the brain and nervous system respond similarly to internally generated images as to external stimuli (Gilbert, 2014). Sustaining this activation of the body's threat response can increase one's vulnerability to developing psychopathology and illness (McEwen and Wingfield, 2003; Thayer and Sternberg, 2006; Juster et al., 2010; Karatsoreos and McEwen, 2011; Gilbert, 2014). Responding to failures with self-compassion, rather than self-criticism, appears to encourage adaptive physiological processes, in particular increases in parasympathetic nervous system activity as indexed by high-frequency HRV (Rockliff et al., 2008; Arch et al., 2014; Svendsen et al., 2016). Both dispositional (Breines et al., 2015) and increased (Arch et al., 2014) levels of self-compassion are associated with adaptive autonomic reactivity following a laboratory acute stressor, seen as reduced sympathetic and increased parasympathetic nervous system activity. Relatedly, experimentally inducing a compassionate state using compassion-focused imagery increases participants' HRV, suggesting that self-compassion could stimulate a soothing affect system in the body via the parasympathetic nervous system (Rockliff et al., 2008). The impact of compassion on elevated parasympathetic activity has been replicated multiple times, including four studies demonstrating that a compassion induction elevates participants' HRV relative to a variety of control group contexts (Stellar et al., 2015).

Self-compassion may support well-being through promoting both adaptive psychological and physiological responses to failure that could be helpful to athletes as they cope with failure in the context of competitive sport. Researchers have examined the psychological benefits of self-compassion among female athletes and found that self-compassion negatively associated with guilt and shame, body consciousness, fear of failure, fear of negative evaluation (Mosewich et al., 2011) and predicted favorable performance evaluations (Killham et al., 2017). Not surprisingly, self-compassion positively related to psychological well-being, positivity, initiative and perseverance and negatively related to passivity, anxiety, negative affect and avoidance coping in response to emotionally challenging sport scenarios among female collegiate athletes (Ferguson et al., 2014, 2015; Reis et al., 2015). Researchers provide experimental support that self-compassion can promote healthy psychological responses to failure; a self-compassion intervention reduced female athletes' self-criticism, rumination and concern over mistakes, and these results were maintained at a 4-week follow-up (Mosewich et al., 2013). While there is emerging support that self-compassion can promote adaptive psychological responses to failure, whether self-compassion offers *physiological* benefits to athletes has not been explored.

Despite the benefits of self-compassion in sport, athletes remain hesitant to adopt this approach, as doing so would be contradictory to the (supposed) formula for success of mental toughness and self-criticism when they fail (Sutherland et al., 2014; Rodriguez and Ebbeck, 2015). Indeed, the mindset that self-criticism is necessary for success has persisted in competitive sport (Sutherland et al., 2014). Moreover, athletes are expected to be "mentally tough" when they fail and failing to do so would be considered a sign of weakness (Reardon and Factor, 2010; Bauman, 2016). These prevalent beliefs and expectations make athletes fearful that being honest about the emotional distress that they feel when they fail and being gentler with themselves would lead to stigmatization or being seen as incapable (Sagar et al., 2007; Reardon and Factor, 2010; Hammond et al., 2013; Bauman, 2016). That is to say that athletes may not only show low levels of self-compassion, but they may actively *resist* or fear adopting a self-compassionate perspective. When attempting to implement Compassion-Focused Therapy among individuals with high self-criticism, Gilbert and Procter (2006) discerned that when trying to offer oneself compassion, many people are met with resistance and fear. Gilbert et al. (2011) defined this construct as fear of self-compassion, or the experience of difficulty or unpleasantness when extending kindness and understanding to oneself during times of distress (e.g., when we make a mistake or things go wrong in life). People high in fear of self-compassion experience self-compassion as threatening and actively resist this experience (Gilbert and Procter, 2006; Gilbert et al., 2011). Fear of self-compassion is a related but distinct construct from self-compassion (Gilbert et al., 2011; Joeng and Turner, 2015; Kelly et al., 2013) that positively associates with maladaptive psychological characteristics (i.e., feelings of inadequacy, self-hatred and self-criticism), a threat-defense response to compassionate experiences (i.e., low HRV and high cortisol; Rockliff et al., 2008), and impaired mental health (Gilbert et al., 2011; Joeng and Turner, 2015).

Fear of self-compassion is relevant to athletes given that it is amplified in highly competitive and evaluative environments, such as competitive sport (Gilbert et al., 2011; Mosewich et al., 2011; Gilbert, 2014). Competitive environments emphasize dynamics of inferiority and superiority, where individuals feel a need to be accepted and attain and sustain dominance which amplifies fears of subordination and exclusion (Gilbert, 2014). Indeed, people fear that by adopting self-compassion, they will become weak, lose their self-criticism and their standards will drop (Gilbert et al., 2011). Self-reported findings from athletes mirror these concerns and suggest they are fearful of adopting self-compassion because they will become complacent or be viewed negatively by others (Mosewich et al., 2014; Sutherland et al., 2014), despite the negative psychological consequences that are associated with this resistance in times of failure (Ferguson et al., 2015). Research examining the role of fear of self-compassion among athletes remains limited to a few studies, and researchers need to replicate and more fully understand the role of fear of self-compassion as it relates to self-compassion in sport. For example, whether fear of self-compassion acts as a barrier to effective psychological and physiological regulation beyond the effects of self-compassion is unknown.

Our primary purpose in the present study was to explore previously supported associations between self-compassion and psychological responses to failure among athletes and to provide a preliminary exploration of associations between self-compassion and physiological responses to failure. A secondary purpose was to determine if fear of self-compassion accounted for any additional variance in study outcomes beyond the effects of self-compassion.

MATERIALS AND METHODS

Design and Participants

We conducted a power analysis using G*Power (Erdfelder et al., 1996), based on an alpha level of 0.05, a power level of 0.95, and an effect size of 0.20 and determined that we required sample size of 90 participants. A total of 91 athletes completed this laboratory-based, observational study. Eligibility criteria included being currently selected to compete in their sport at a university or national level, free from psychological or physical conditions or medications that may alter their stress response, and the ability to recall a recent distressing sport failure or setback that they remembered well. Eligibility was completed online by 142 people; 24 were ineligible. From the 118 remaining eligible people, 27 did not complete baseline measures, stopped responding, or were unavailable for the laboratory session. Participants who completed the study and were included in the analyses were 91 adult athletes (*M* age = 21.4; *SD* = 3.47; range: 18 to 40) who were primarily single (94.4%), Caucasian (76.9%), university students (92%), with slightly more participation from females (58%) and represented a variety of sports with the most participation from track and field athletes (20.9%). Participants had spent an average of 4.19 years competing at their current level in sport (*SD* = 4.15) and were highly involved in their sport (*M* weekly training hours in competitive season = 15; *SD* = 5.78; *M* weekly training hours in the off-season = 9; *SD* = 5.43). A summary of participant characteristics can be found in **Table 1**.

TABLE 1 | Participant characteristics.

Characteristic	N	%
Ethnicity		
Caucasian	70	77
African	5	6
Aboriginal	4	4
Asian	2	2
Latin American	1	1
East Indian	1	1
Philippine	1	1
Other	7	8
Marital Status	85	93
Single	3	3
Common Law	2	2
Other		
Sport Type		
Track and Field	20	22
Volleyball	18	20
Hockey	17	19
Soccer	8	9
Football	6	7
Basketball	4	4
Swimming	3	3
Cross Country	3	3
Rowing	3	3
Racquetball	2	2
Badminton	2	2
Ringette	2	2
Curling	1	1
Figure Skating	1	1
Rugby	1	1
Gender		
Female	53	58
Male	38	42

Baseline Measures

Demographics

Participants reported their age, gender, marital status, current sport, sport history, year in sport at a university or national level and university major.

Self-Compassion

Self-compassion was assessed using the 26-item Self-Compassion Scale (Neff, 2003b). Participants responded on a five-point Likert scale ranging from 1 (*almost never*) to 5 (*almost always*). Six subscales assess the three facets of self-compassion and their opposing facets: mindfulness (over-identification), self-kindness (self-criticism) and common humanity (isolation). Negatively worded items were reverse scored. Means of each subscale were created and combined to create a grand self-compassion mean (Neff, 2003b). Higher scores on this scale indicate higher levels of self-compassion. The Self-Compassion Scale has good test-retest reliability, discriminant and concurrent validity and good internal consistency reliability (α = 0.92) and scale items have been found to be reliable among athletic samples (α = 0.87; Mosewich et al., 2011) including the present sample (α = 0.91).

Fear of Self-Compassion

Fear of self-compassion was assessed using the 15-item Fear of Self-Compassion Scale (Gilbert et al., 2011); participants rated their agreement with statements on a five-point scale: 0 (*don't agree at all*) to 4 (*completely agree*). Items were summed to represent and overall score. Higher scores indicate higher levels of the construct. Items of the Fear of Self-Compassion Scale show good internal consistency (α = 0.85, 0.95; Gilbert et al., 2011; Kelly et al., 2013), including within the present sample (α = 0.89) and the scale has been used previously with athletic samples (Ferguson et al., 2015).

Imagery Ability

Given that imagery ability may impact participants' reactivity during the stress induction (Kwekkeboom, 2000), imagery ability was included as a possible control variable in this study. The Motivational General-Arousal (MG-A) subscale of the Motivational Imagery Ability Measure for Sport (MIAMS), was chosen in order to assess participant's ability to generate emotional experiences associated with sport (e.g., anxiety) using imagery (Gregg and Hall, 2006). This subscale assesses participants ease of forming the image, and intensity of the emotional experience generated by the image. To complete this scale, participants were asked to generate images associated with four different sport scenarios (e.g., feeling anxious before a sporting competition), and rate the ease of forming the image (four-items) and the emotional experience (four-items) created by the image on scale from 1 (*no emotion*) to 7 (*very strong emotion*). Emotion and ease were assessed separately (Gregg and Hall, 2006). The MG-A subscale of the MIAMS has shown acceptable reliability (α = 0.74 emotion; α = 0.73 ease), including within the present sample (α = 0.70 emotion; α = 0.69 ease) among athletic samples.

Self-Esteem

The 10-item Rosenberg self-esteem scale (RSES; Rosenberg, 1965) assessed self-esteem. Participants indicated the extent to which they agreed with each statement on a scale from 1 (*strongly disagree*) to 4 (*strongly agree*). Negatively worded items were reverse scored, and scores from all 10 items were summed. Higher scores represent higher levels of self-esteem. The scale shows good predictive, concurrent, construct validity and scale items were internally consistent in other (α = 0.87; Rosenberg, 1965) and in the present sample (α = 0.82). The scale shows acceptable psychometric properties when used with athletic samples (e.g., Mosewich et al., 2011) and has been used previously as a control variable alongside self-compassion (Mosewich et al., 2011).

Laboratory Measures

High-Frequency Heart Rate Variability

Participants' HRV was assessed in the frequency-domain according to the natural log of the total power of the high-frequency band (0.15–40 Hz) (Task Force of The European Society of Cardiology and The North American Society of Pacing and Electrophysiology, 1996) using a ProComp Infiniti (Thought Technology, Montreal, QC, Canada) multi-modal biofeedback system. This system is suitable for assessing physiological markers such as high-frequency HRV (e.g., Shaw et al., 2012; Heathers et al., 2014). Data was assessed by measuring participant's blood volume pulse using a photo-plethysmograph sensor on the palmer surface of the non-dominant index finger at a sampling rate of 2048 Hz (Combatalade, 2010; Shaw et al., 2012). This method is considered a reliable and valid method of assessing HRV in typically developing samples (Heathers et al., 2014). Recordings were utilized from three, 120-s phases: Before (baseline assessment), during (reactivity) and following stress induction (recovery). Recordings longer than 60 s have been demonstrated to show good reliability for assessing HRV in athletes (Esco and Flatt, 2014).

Emotional Difficulty

A single item had athletes rate how "emotionally difficult" the scenario was for them on a scale from 1 (*not at all*) to 6 (*extremely*) which has been used in past research with athletes (Ferguson et al., 2015; Reis et al., 2015). The item served as a manipulation check to ensure that the recalled sport scenarios were distressing for the athlete at the time that they occurred.

Image Quality

Athletes rated the extent to which the generated failure image was easy to generate, arousing, clear, meaningful, emotional, and useful (six-items) on a scale from 1 (*not at all easy to form*) to 7 (*very easy to form*). A mean score was computed from the sum of six items to assess overall image quality. This manipulation check ensured the effectiveness of the stress induction. This measure was developed based on recommendations from imagery researchers (see Lang, 1979; Gregg and Hall, 2006; Hammond et al., 2012).

Assessment of Outcomes

Psychological Responses to Failure Scenarios

Participants failure-related behavioral reactions, thoughts and emotions were assessed as an indicator of athletes' psychological reactivity. While there are no psychometric properties for these measures, they have been used in studies conducted among university students (Leary et al., 2007) and athletes (Reis et al., 2015).

Behavioral reactions

Using a scale range of 1 (*not at all*) to 6 (*extremely*), participants rated how much they reacted in each of nine ways (e.g., "I took steps to fix the problem or made plans to do so") at the time of the sport failure.

Thoughts

Participants rated the extent to which each of the six thoughts about the failure scenario were relevant for them on a scale ranging from 1 (*I did not think this thought at all*) to 5 (*I kept thinking about this thought*). All individual thought items were analyzed as is consistent with past research (see Leary et al., 2007; Reis et al., 2015).

Emotions

Participants rated the extent to which they felt 16 emotions on a scale from 1 (*not at all*) to 6 (*extremely*), at the time that the failure took place. The 16 terms were divided into four subscales: sad (four items: sad, dejected, down, and depressed), anxious (four items: nervous, worried, anxious, and fearful), angry (four items: irritated, angry, hostile, and mad), and self-conscious (four items: embarrassed, humiliated, guilty, and ashamed). Scores from individual terms within each of the four subscales (i.e., sadness, anxiety, anger, and self-conscious emotions) were summed to create subscale scores, (Leary et al., 2007; Reis et al., 2015).

Physiological Reactivity

Reactivity was assessed according to recommendations (Laborde et al., 2018) to compute a difference score (i.e., stress induction – baseline) to quantify changes in participants' mean value of HRV during the stress induction (120-s) relative to participant's individual baseline values (120-s).

Physiological Recovery

Following recommendations (Laborde et al., 2018), the mean value of participants' HRV during recovery (120-s) was subtracted from their mean value of HRV during the stress induction (120-s).

Procedures

Recruitment, Eligibility and Baseline Assessment

Upon attaining institutional ethics approval, we recruited participants from two Canadian universities and a national sport center, through requests to teams, posters, and word of mouth. We emailed interested participants the online eligibility survey. Eligible participants provided informed consent and completed the baseline survey online which included measures of self-compassion, self-esteem, fear of self-compassion and demographics.

Laboratory Session

Two days prior to a scheduled laboratory session, participants were briefed regarding pre-laboratory session eligibility criteria. Participants were asked to ensure that they were free from substances (e.g., alcohol, drugs, or medications) or physical conditions (e.g., concussion, lack of/poor sleep, or illness) that may impact their body's physical responses to stress (Svendsen et al., 2016; Laborde et al., 2017), in order to ensure that their physiological data was as reliable as possible. Participants were asked to reschedule their session if they did not meet the pre-laboratory session criteria. The first author conducted sessions at laboratories at the universities and the sports center. After a brief orientation to study procedures, the researcher connected the participant to the equipment used to record physiological responses (ProComp Infiniti, Thought Technology, Montreal, QC, Canada).

The researcher then instructed the participant to remain calm and relaxed for a 2-min acclimation period, followed by a 2-min baseline assessment of physiology. A 2-min acclimation period is considered acceptable in order to alleviate participants' anxieties or nerves and to help them to feel comfortable with being connected to the physiological recording equipment (Heathers et al., 2014; Laborde et al., 2017). The instructions for the acclimation and baseline assessments were to sit comfortably and relaxed with both of their feet flat on the floor, hands on their thighs and palms facing up (Laborde et al., 2017). Participants were told to remain as still as possible, as movement may interfere with the recording. Next, participants underwent a stress induction. To induce a stress response, participants were asked to imagine a recent sport failure or setback with their eyes closed, for 2 min, using a guided imagery script read aloud by the researcher. Participants were instructed to remain seated with their eyes closed and provided the same instructions that were delivered during the baseline recording (feet flat on the floor, hands on their thighs and palms facing up) and were again instructed to remain as still as possible. The imagery script was read aloud to prompt participants to image their past failure for the entire 2-min period. Prompts were provided followed by brief pauses to allow participants to generate their images. The imagery script provided prompts to promote elaboration of participant's images and the emotion associated with their failure experience. Further, providing ongoing prompts helped to ensure that participants were thinking about the failure scenario for the duration of the stress induction. The imagery script was developed based on imagery best practice (Lang, 1979; Hammond et al., 2012) and by consulting with a sports imagery expert. The imagery script was pilot tested prior to commencing data collection to ensure it extended for the duration of the 2-min time frame. Moreover, the same researcher (the first author) read and followed the rehearsed script for all participants to provide uniform delivery. The imagery script for the stress induction was as follows:

> *Remember a time when you failed... Maybe you made a costly mistake, failed to meet an important goal, or experienced a setback in your sport progress...... Imagine this experience....... In your mind, really try to take yourself back to this experience...... Remember your expectations leading up to this... Remember the pressures that you felt... Imagine what you were looking forward to and your hopes... Then remember the situation unfolding as it did... Remember where you were, what your surroundings looked like, who was there.........Take yourself back to the stressful situation in as much detail as possible............... Really focus on the feelings that you had...... Disappointment, anger, frustration, despair... Try to remember those feelings in as much detail as possible...... Really allow yourself to feel them... Remember the changes in your body......tension, anxiousness, uneasiness....... Imagine this scenario in as much detail as possible...... Even after this moment or situation had passed, notice any feelings that remain: tension, regret, uneasiness......... Really try to take yourself back to the feelings and emotions that you experienced........... Now, please take a deep breath and gently open your eyes.*

The stress induction was followed by a 2-min recovery period where participants were instructed to relax their body and their mind with their eyes open. The researcher then disconnected the participant from the equipment and the participant completed the psychological laboratory measures (see section "Laboratory Measures" in "Materials and Methods"). The researcher then debriefed participants by providing a detailed explanation of the study's purposes and how they could access the results and then thanked the participant for their time.

RESULTS

Data Management and Preliminary Analyses

Artifacts from physiological data were removed using visual inspection and manually corrected to ensure accurate placement of individual heart beats (Combatalade, 2010). We followed recommendations for cleaning and preparing the physiological and psychological data (Pallant, 2007; Tabachnick and Fidell, 2013).

Correlational analyses (Pearson product moment correlations) showed that main study outcomes were correlated in the expected directions. Self-compassion was negatively associated with fear of self-compassion and self-esteem and fear of self-compassion was associated with self-esteem (see **Table 2**).

We considered covariates used in past research: age, gender; (Corrales et al., 2012) and imagery ability (Kwekkeboom, 2000; Gregg and Hall, 2006). We also considered emotional difficulty of the recalled failure and time since the failure as covariates given the possibility that they may influence study outcomes. We included these variables as covariates if they were correlated with the outcome variable (Tabachnick and Fidell, 2013) as determined by Pearson product moment correlations. When we included the aforementioned variables in our analyses, none had an effect on our outcome variables. Finally, given the associations between self-esteem and self-compassion, and the past precedent and recommendation to control for self-esteem when assessing self-compassion (Neff, 2003a), self-esteem was automatically included as a covariate in all analyses.

Note that all analyses reported herein were replicated with respiration rate included as a covariate. In all cases, respiration rate had no effect on the pattern of results reported. Thus, we excluded respiration rate from analyses reported here.

Recalled Performance Failures

Repeated measures analysis of variance (ANOVA) analyses of high-frequency HRV were conducted across three timepoints (baseline, stressor and recovery) to ensure that our stress induction produced the expected changes in participants' HRV. This analysis revealed a main effect of Time, $F(1, 90) = 5.30$, $p < 0.05$). A pairwise comparison revealed that the stress induction (failure recollection) produced significant reductions in HRV from baseline to stressor ($p < 0.001$) in the expected direction (*M* decrease = 39%), which is consistent with a stress response. Moreover, additional pairwise comparisons showed that the differences in HRV approached the conventional level of significance between baseline and recovery ($p = 0.07$) and stressor to recovery ($p = 0.07$). The reduction in HRV during a stressor is consistent with differences observed in other studies that have utilized a standard laboratory stressor (Arch et al., 2014; Wawrzyniak et al., 2016) and greater than reductions observed during personally relevant, stressful imagery task (Levine et al., 2016). Participants reported that they were able to easily generate their failure images ($M = 5.26$ out of 7, $SD = 1.24$), and these images were clear ($M = 5.63$ out of 7, $SD = 1.17$), emotional ($M = 4.60$ out of 7, $SD = 0.99$) and meaningful ($M = 5.20$ out of 7, $SD = 1.10$). Further, participants reported that during the imagery task, they felt the emotions of the image ($M = 4.70$ out of 7, $SD = 1.10$) and used the image ($M = 5.25$ out of 7, $SD = 0.96$) for the duration of the task. Our participants showed slightly higher ease of imaging compared to participants in a study by Williams et al. (2017); $M = 4.05$ out of 7 in stress condition who used a similar scale to assess participant's ease of imaging a stressful imaging task. Consideration of participants' physiological and self-reported responses suggest that the imagery induction successfully induced a stress response in the expected directions.

TABLE 2 | Descriptive statistics and correlations of main variables

Measure	1	2	3	4	5	*M*	*SD*	α
(1) Self-compassion	–					3.10	0.56	0.91
(2) Fear of self-compassion	−0.48**	–				17.91	9.49	0.89
(3) Self-esteem	−0.61**	0.50**	–			19.80	4.44	0.82

*$p < 0.05$, **$p < 0.01$.

Main Analyses

Hierarchical linear regression analyses were conducted in order to test three research questions. Self-esteem was included as a covariate in Step 1 of all analyses. The first hypothesis was partially supported; self-compassion was positively related to participants' HRV reactivity during the stress induction, but it was not related to HRV during the recovery phase. The addition of self-compassion in Step 2 accounted for an additional 5.7% variance in participants' HRV reactivity during the stress induction [$F(1, 88) = 8.18$, $R^2 = 0.06$, R^2 *change* $= 0.06$, $p < 0.05$], beyond the effects of self-esteem. That is, high levels of self-compassion were positively associated with parasympathetic nervous system activity during the stressor (high-frequency HRV). The size of this effect was small ($f^2 = 0.06$). Inspection of the beta values revealed that only self-compassion (*beta* $= 0.30$, $p = 0.02$) accounted for participants' HRV during the stress induction. A visual depiction of these data is presented in **Figure 1**.

Hierarchical regression analyses were conducted for all psychological outcomes of interest (i.e., behavioral reactions, thoughts, and emotions), with self-esteem entered in Step 1, followed by the main variable, self-compassion in Step 2. For behavioral reactions, combining eight of the nine items produced acceptable reliability ($\alpha = 0.78$) so we analyzed these items as a composite "behavioral equanimity" measure. Six thought items and four emotion subscales (sad, anxious, angry, and self-conscious) were entered separately as the outcome variables in a series of hierarchical regression analyses. Results supported our second hypothesis that self-compassion was associated with all three aspects of psychological reactivity (i.e., behavioral equanimity, maladaptive thoughts, and negative affect), in the

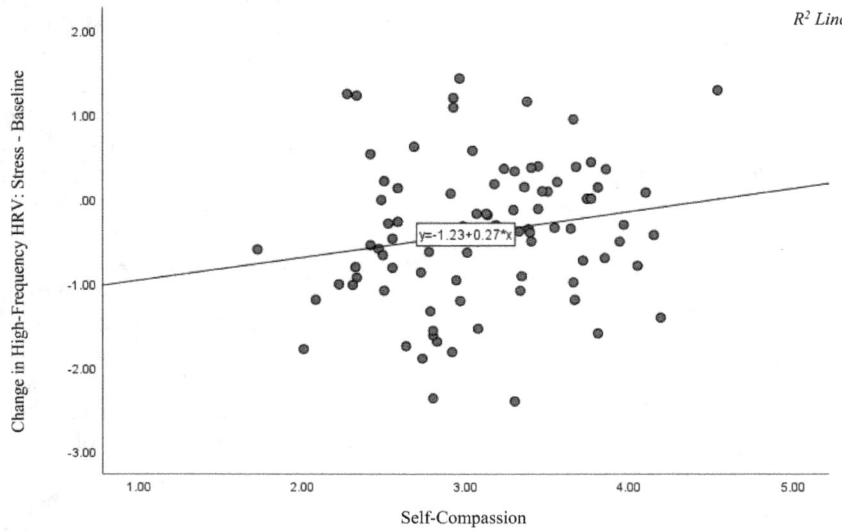

FIGURE 1 | Difference Score of High-Frequency HRV for Stressor – Baseline and Self-Compassion. This figure depicts the change scores in participants' high-frequency HRV from the stress induction subtracted from their baseline scores relative to their self-compassion scores. Self-compassion was positively related to parasympathetic nervous system activity (high-frequency HRV) during the stressor (*p* = 0.02).

expected directions (see **Tables 2–4**), beyond the effects of self-esteem. Self-compassion was related to behavioral equanimity [$F(1, 88) = 15.1$, $R^2 = 0.21$, R^2 *change* = 0.13, $p < 0.01$) and had unique effects on this outcome (*beta* = 0.46, $p < 0.01$), such that the effects of self-esteem were no longer significant (*beta* = 0.03, $p = 0.82$). This was considered to be a medium sized effect ($f^2 = 0.27$). Self-compassion related to one adaptive thought ("This is no worse than what other people go through") and negatively related to maladaptive thoughts and emotions (see **Tables 3, 4**). Of note, with some thought items (e.g., thinking "I'm a loser," "my life is really screwed up" and "I have bigger problems than most people do"), self-compassion and self-esteem had opposite effects; self-esteem was positively associated while self-compassion was negatively associated with these maladaptive thoughts.

Related to our third hypothesis, fear of self-compassion did not associate with participants' physiological responses. However, the addition of fear of self-compassion in Step 3 accounted for unique variance in one of the six thought items, when controlling for self-esteem and self-compassion, and approached the conventional level of significance for two additional thought items and behavioral equanimity. For the item "Everyone has a bad day now and then," the model that included fear of self-compassion accounted for an additional 4.7% of the variance in the outcome beyond self-esteem and self-compassion [$F(1, 87) = 4.45$, $R^2 = 0.08$, R^2 *change* = 0.05, $p < 0.05$). The size of this effect was small ($f^2 = 0.10$). Inspection of the beta values showed that fear of self-compassion was negatively associated with this outcome (*beta* = −0.26, $p = 0.04$), and exerted the opposite effect of self-compassion (*beta* = 0.11, $p = 0.42$). Further, the model that included fear of self-compassion in Step 3 approached the conventional level of significance for the thought item "In comparison to other people, my life is really screwed up" [$F(1, 87) = 3.10$, $R^2 = 0.20$, R^2 *change* = 0.03, *beta* = 0.20, $p = 0.08$], and exerted the opposite effect from self-compassion (*beta* = −0.28, $p = 0.03$). Additionally, the model that included the addition of fear of self-compassion approached the conventional level of significance for behavioral equanimity (*beta* = −0.19, $p = 0.09$).

DISCUSSION

The primary purpose of the present study was to examine the relationship between self-compassion and athletes' physiological and psychological responses to a recalled sport failure, and further, to determine if fear of self-compassion accounts for unique variance in these outcomes beyond self-compassion. Self-compassion related to participants' physiological response to a sport failure in terms of their HRV during recollection of a previous failure: participants with greater self-compassion showed a more regulated autonomic profile as indexed by greater parasympathetic nervous system activity. Self-compassion also associated with athletes' adaptive psychological reactions to their recalled sport failure. Fear of self-compassion did not account for any unique variance in physiological responses beyond self-compassion, but accounted for unique variance in some psychological responses, beyond self-compassion.

Self-Compassion and Physiological Reactivity

Self-compassion related to dampened physiological reactivity, in the form of blunted HRV withdrawal, during the stress induction. Consistent with other studies showing that compassion is positively related to parasympathetic nervous system activity, self-compassion appeared to dampen athletes' physiological

TABLE 3 | Results from hierarchical regression analyses: thoughts.

Thought item		β	R^2	ΔR^2	f^2
"I seem to have bigger problems than most people do"	Step 1		0.04		
	Self-esteem	0.20			
	Step 2		0.10*	0.06*	0.11
	Self-esteem	0.01			
	Self-compassion	−0.31*			
"In comparison o other people, my life is really screwed up"	Step 1		0.10**		
	Self-esteem	0.32**			
	Step 2		0.17**	0.07**	0.20
	Self-esteem	11			
	Self-compassion	−0.34**			
"Why do these things always happen to me?"	Step 1	−0.00	0.04		
	Self-esteem	0.19			
	Step 2		0.10*	0.06*	0.11
	Self-esteem	−0.00			
	Self-compassion	−0.31*			
"Everyone has a bad day now and then"	Step 1		0.02		
	Self-esteem	−0.12			
	Step 2		0.04	0.02	
	Self-esteem	−0.01			
	Self-compassion	0.18			
"I'm a loser"	Step 1		0.13**		
	Self-esteem	0.36**			
	Step 2		0.24**	0.11**	0.32
	Self-esteem	0.11			
	Self-compassion	−0.43**			
"This is no worse than what other people go through"	Step 1		0.01		
	Self-esteem	0.09			
	Step 2		0.05	0.04*	
	Self-esteem	0.25			
	Self-compassion	0.26*			

*$p < 0.05$, **$p < 0.01$.

responding to the stress induction and was associated with higher HRV during the reactivity measurement.

This finding is consistent with other research where HRV was influenced by self-compassion in laboratory settings (Arch et al., 2014; Breines et al., 2015) and related to responses that reflect self-compassion such as adaptive cognitive processing, emotional regulation and behavioral responses to changing demands (Thayer et al., 2009, 2012). We are the first, to our knowledge, to show this relationship among athletes recalling a sport failure and we have reason to suggest the possibility that because of this association, self-compassion may offer a physiological resource to athletes when they encounter stress. Rather than prevent the experience of stress, self-compassion may promote willingness to confront and soothe oneself during stressful times. In line with this explanation, self-compassion has been positively associated with the ability to accept, tolerate and experience negative emotions rather than avoid or suppress those feelings (Neff et al., 2005, 2007; Allen and Leary, 2010; Diedrich et al., 2014) and has been negatively associated with avoidance, thought suppression and rumination (Neff et al., 2005, 2007; Barnard and Curry, 2011), which can have deteriorating effects on our physiological systems (Gilbert, 2014). Responding to experiences of stress with self-compassion rather than harsh self-criticism and judgment appears to have a soothing effect on the affect system and creates an adaptive physiological profile during stress (Arch et al., 2014; Gilbert, 2014; Breines et al., 2015). Consistent with these findings, our results showed that self-compassion was associated with higher parasympathetic tone during a stressor.

Indeed, the regulation of HRV has implications for well-being (Porges, 2007; Thayer et al., 2012), health (Thayer and Sternberg, 2006) and performance (Wawrzyniak et al., 2016; Williams et al., 2016) that may be beneficial to athletes. For example, sustained low or dysregulated HRV predicts behavioral risk factors (inhibition and risk aversion; Porges, 2007; Thayer et al., 2012) and psychological risk factors (negativity bias and poor emotional regulation; Thayer and Lane, 2009; Thayer et al., 2012) for psychopathology and adverse health (e.g., glucose dysregulation, inflammation and disrupted hypothalamic-pituitary axis function; Thayer and Sternberg, 2006; Thayer and Lane, 2009; Juster et al., 2010; Thayer et al., 2012). Further, withdrawal of parasympathetic tone during a

TABLE 4 | Results from hierarchical regression analyses: emotions.

Emotion subscale		β	R^2	ΔR^2	f^2
Anxious	Step 1		0.02		
	Self-esteem	0.15			
	Step 2		0.08*	0.06*	0.10
	Self-esteem	−0.04			
	Self-compassion	−0.31*			
Angry	Step 1		0.02		
	Self-esteem	0.13			
	Step 2		0.09*	0.07*	0.10
	Self-esteem	−0.07			
	Self-compassion	−0.33**			
Sad	Step 1		0.11**		
	Self-esteem	0.33**			
	Step 2		0.16*	0.05*	0.20
	Self-esteem	0.15			
	Self-compassion	−0.29*			
Self-conscious	Step 1		0.03		
	Self-esteem	0.15			
	Step 2		0.12**	0.09**	0.14
	Self-esteem	−0.09			
	Self-compassion	−0.39**			

*$p < 0.05$, **$p < 0.01$.*

stressor is associated with longer reaction times and lowered accuracy (Wawrzyniak et al., 2016; Williams et al., 2016), both of which have implications for sport performance. Though we did not test this in this study, our findings suggest that adopting self-compassion should facilitate optimal health and performance for athletes when they encounter performance stressors, given its association with high HRV (Arch et al., 2014). Researchers should employ experimental designs in future research to test this possibility.

Self-Compassion and Physiological Recovery

Self-compassion was not related to athletes' physiological recovery, in the form of HRV during recovery from the stress induction relative to baseline levels. It is possible that recovery from the stress induction is a longer process than could be measured in a 2-min recovery period immediately following the stressor. Consistent with this, prior studies suggest that HRV recovery takes approximately five to 10 min, whether the stressor is psychological (Ulrich et al., 1991) or physical (Seiler et al., 2007). However, other researchers have shown that utilizing a recording time longer than 60 s of HRV data were reliable among collegiate athletes (Esco and Flatt, 2014). Additionally, the timeframe that we used (2-min stress induction and recovery periods) may better reflect the demands of many sport contexts, where athletes are required to rapidly respond to failures compared to longer recording periods of 5 min or more. As suggested below, future studies should examine a longer induction and recovery procedure, to unpack physiological dynamics related to reactivity and recovery from stress.

Self-Compassion and Psychological Reactions

In our study, self-compassion was also positively associated with adaptive *psychological* reactions to a past performance failure or setback in terms of behavioral equanimity, as well as many indicators of adaptive thoughts and low negative affect. Our findings replicate those of other researchers examining self-compassion among athletes (Mosewich et al., 2013; Ferguson et al., 2015; Reis et al., 2015) and general samples (Leary et al., 2007; Arimitsu and Hofmann, 2015) who have shown that being self-compassionate protects against negative affect and promotes equanimous thoughts and actions. Researchers argue that, in the face of hard times, self-compassion promotes a balanced awareness of, and reduction in difficult emotions, a desire to soothe the self rather than ruminate about and over-identify with failure, connection with others, and motivation to think and behave in ways that sustain well-being (Neff, 2003a; Allen and Leary, 2010; Barnard and Curry, 2011; Terry and Leary, 2011). Ours' and others' findings (Mosewich et al., 2013; Ferguson et al., 2015; Reis et al., 2015) suggest that self-compassion is positively associated with this adaptive psychological responding to failure in athlete populations. However, relatively few studies have examined self-compassion among athletes and researchers need to continue this line of investigation in order to more fully understand the role of self-compassion when dealing with performance failure (e.g., prospective and experimental designs; examinations of mediators and moderators).

Results from our study support others that suggest that self-compassion is positively associated with adaptive psychological reactions to sport (Reis et al., 2015) and exercise failures (Semenchuk et al., 2018), beyond the effects of self-esteem. We found that for some items (e.g., thinking "I'm a loser," "my life is really screwed up" and "I have bigger problems than most people do"), self-compassion and self-esteem had opposite effects; self-esteem was positively associated while self-compassion was negatively associated with these maladaptive thoughts. According to Neff (2003b), a drawback of self-esteem is that maintaining high self-esteem involves an increased reliance on showing/feeling superiority over others and meeting performance standards. Thus, Neff and others propose that the beneficial effects of self-esteem can break down when performance standards are not met Neff (2003b), for instance in the case of performance failure, and can lead to negative psychological outcomes (e.g., negative affect and displacing responsibility; Leary et al., 2007; Neff and Vonk, 2009). Self-compassion, alternatively, allows individuals to face and experience negative feelings associated with failure, and turn those feelings into positive experiences of kindness, learning and understanding, and it promotes acceptance of responsibility without dismissal, blame to others or harsh self-judgment (Neff, 2003b; Neff and Vonk, 2009). That is, self-compassion permits individuals to maintain positive feelings toward the self, even when performance standards are not met. Our results and other's results are consistent with Neff (2003b) arguments that suggest targeting self-compassion may be a more useful approach than self-esteem when dealing with failure. Thus, while both self-esteem and self-compassion can have value for athletes, a growing body of research suggests that in some instances, self-compassion may be a more useful resource than self-esteem – and one of those instances may be when athletes must manage difficult experiences associated with sport such as failure.

Fear of Self-Compassion

Despite the benefits associated with self-compassion for athletes (Mosewich et al., 2013; Ferguson et al., 2015; Reis et al., 2015), athletes are hesitant to adopt this approach (Ferguson et al., 2014; Sutherland et al., 2014) because they fear that being self-compassionate will lead to poor performance. Contrary to these other findings, we found that athletes are not overly fearful of self-compassion (M = 17.91; scale range = 0–60) compared to highly self-critical samples (Kelly et al., 2013; M = 32.85) and scored similarly to another athletic sample (Ferguson et al., 2015; M = 15.18). However, we did find that fear of self-compassion was positively associated with some negative psychological reactions (e.g., "In comparison to other people, my life is really screwed up") and negatively associated with positive psychological thoughts (e.g., thinking "everyone has a bad day now and then") and behavioral reactions to a sport failure beyond self-compassion. These results are consistent with other's (e.g., Ferguson et al., 2015) and challenge athletes' assertions that self-criticism is necessary for growth and improvement in sport (Ferguson et al., 2014; Rodriguez and Ebbeck, 2015). Moreover, fear of self-compassion did not explain any of the variance in physiological responding beyond self-compassion. Given that fear of self-compassion involves an active resistance to extending compassion toward the self (Gilbert et al., 2011), it may be that fear of self-compassion's relationship with physiological, and possibly psychological, responses is more apparent when the opportunity to be self-compassionate is made salient (e.g., Rockliff et al., 2008), which was not the case in this study. Therefore, fear of self-compassion may be more relevant in an intervention or experimental induction where athletes are taught or urged to put self-compassion in place in response to a failure. Further investigation is needed in order to understand when and how fear of self-compassion is distinct and dominant relative to self-compassion.

Strengths and Limitations

Our study had a number of strengths. First, we followed a well-controlled, laboratory scenario which is appropriate for early stages of research (Czajkowski et al., 2015). Further, the stress induction (imagery task) was informed by imagery best practice and developed in consultation with an expert in the field of sports imagery. The effectiveness of the stress induction was confirmed by physiological changes and additional self-reported manipulation checks.

A limitation of this study is the reliance on recalled stimuli, to ensure personal relevance, to induce changes in physiological state rather than an immediate stimulus (e.g., a novel laboratory stressor or a real-life failure situation). In the future, researchers should examine whether self-compassion associates with adaptive physiological responding to standardized laboratory stressors or, seek out practical ways of assessing responses to more recent failures than assessed presently. Additionally, due to our use of 2-min recording intervals, our results should be considered tentative. Although some researchers suggest that recording times as short as 1 min can be considered reliable when assessing HRV (Esco and Flatt, 2014; Laborde et al., 2017), future studies should utilize longer recording times in order to understand the time course of the effect that we observed. It is possible that a longer induction and recovery protocol would enable better identification of HRV reactivity and recovery dynamics resulting from the imagery task. It should also be noted that here we used photoplethysmography as a proxy for electrocardiogram activity, and although these two measures may diverge under conditions of acute stress (Schäfer and Vagedes, 2013), photoplethysmography has been demonstrated to reliably assess acute stress reactivity (Charlton et al., 2018). Future studies are needed to determine whether the stress reactivity effects reported here would be more pronounced in electrocardiogram-derived measures of HRV. Finally, although there are theoretical connections between HRV, self-compassion and performance, performance was not assessed directly. As such, the relationship between self-compassion and performance is still unclear and is an important direction for future research.

CONCLUSION

We found physiological support, in the case of high frequency HRV, to complement existing self-reported findings that self-compassion promotes adaptive emotional regulation and psychological reactivity to failure and stress, among athletes. Athletes with higher levels of self-compassion showed adaptive psychological and physiological responses relative to a recalled sport failure compared to those lower in self-compassion. This is encouraging given that individual's stress responses may be consistent and easily replicated across contexts and stimuli (Andreassi, 2007). It is promising that self-compassion emerged as a protective factor for athletes' parasympathetic reactivity during a stressor, suggesting that athletes with more self-compassion are better able to maintain calming influences on their physiological state. However, given that this is the first study to show this relationship among athletes, our results are preliminary and should be interpreted with caution. More research should be conducted in order to replicate our findings and to more fully understand the relationship between self-compassion and physiological reactivity when dealing with stress. Nonetheless, these findings provide evidence that self-compassion is relevant and beneficial for athletes and offer additional support for the ability of self-compassion to impact physiological responding to stress. Based on our results we suggest that athletes can benefit from developing self-compassion, but care should also be taken to address athletes' apprehension and resistance to adopting this approach when they fail.

ETHICS STATEMENT

This study was carried out in accordance with the recommendations of the "University of Manitoba Research Ethics and Compliance committee." All subjects provided their informed consent online accordance with the Declaration of Helsinki. The protocol was approved by the "University of Manitoba Research Ethics and Compliance committee."

AUTHOR CONTRIBUTIONS

LC and SS developed the design of the study. LC conducted the laboratory sessions and surveyed the data collection, organized the database and carried out the statistical analyses for the psychological variables, and wrote the first draft of the manuscript. LC, RG, and CG organized the physiological data and conducted the data analyses for the physiological variables. All authors contributed to the manuscript revision, and read and approved the submitted version.

ACKNOWLEDGMENTS

We would like to offer special thanks to Dr. Melanie Gregg for sharing her expertise and consultation. We would also like to thank the many athletes and coaches who supported us in conducting this project.

REFERENCES

Allen, A., and Leary, M. (2010). Self-compassion, stress, and coping. *Soc. Pers. Psychol. Compass* 4, 107–118. doi: 10.1111/j.1751-9004.2009.00246.x

Andreassi, J. L. (2007). *Psychophysiology: Human Behavior and physiological Response*. Mahwah, NJ: Erlbaum.

Arch, J., Brown, K., Dean, D., Landy, L., Brown, K., and Laudenslager, M. (2014). Self-compassion training modulates alpha-amylase, heart rate variability, and subjective responses to social evaluative threat in women. *Psychoneuroendocrinology* 42, 49–58. doi: 10.1016/j.psyneuen.2013.12.018

Arimitsu, K., and Hofmann, S. (2015). Effects of compassionate thinking on negative emotions. *Cogn. Emot.* 31, 160–167. doi: 10.1080/02699931.2015.1078292

Barnard, L., and Curry, J. (2011). Self-compassion: conceptualization, correlates, & interventions. *Rev. Gen. Psychol.* 15, 289–303.

Bauman, J. (2016). The stigma of mental health in athletes: are mental toughness and mental health seen as contradictory in elite sport? *Br. J. Sports Med.* 50, 135–136. doi: 10.1136/bjsports-2015-095570

Bertollo, M., Bortoli, L., Gramacioni, G., Hanin, Y., Comani, S., and Robazza, C. (2013). Behavioural and physiological correlates of athletic performance: a test of the multi-action plan model. *Appl. Psychophysiol. Biofeedback* 38, 91–99. doi: 10.1007/s10484-013-9211-z

Breines, J., and Chen, S. (2012). Self-compassion increases self-improvement motivation. *Pers. Soc. Psychol. Bull.* 38, 1133–1143. doi: 10.1177/0146167212445599

Breines, J., McInnis, C., Kuras, Y., Thoma, M., Gianferante, D., Hanlin, L., et al. (2015). Self-compassionate young adults show lower salivary alpha-amylase responses to repeated psychosocial stress. *Self Identity* 14, 390–402. doi: 10.1080/15298868.2015.1005659

Charlton, P. H., Celka, P., Farukh, B., Chowienczyk, P., and Alastruey, J. (2018). Assessing mental stress from the photoplethysmogram: a numerical study. *Physiol. Meas.* 39:054001. doi: 10.1088/1361-6579/aabe6a

Combatalade, D. (2010). *Basics of Heart Rate Variability Applied to Psychophysiology*. Montreal, QC: Thought Technology Ltd.

Corrales, M., Torres, B., Esquivel, A., Salazar, M., and Orellana, J. (2012). Normal values of heart rate variability at rest in a young, healthy and active mexican population. *Health* 4, 377–385. doi: 10.4236/health.2012.47060

Czajkowski, S. M., Powell, L. H., Adler, N., Narr-King, S., Reynolds, K. D., Hunter, C. M., et al. (2015). From ideas to efficacy: the ORBIT model for developing behavioral treatments for chronic diseases. *Health Psychol. Open* 34, 971–982. doi: 10.1037/hea0000161

Davis, H., Liotti, M., Ngan, E., Woodward, T., Van Snellenberg, J., van Anders, S., et al. (2007). fMRI BOLD signal changes in elite swimmers while viewing videos of personal failure. *Brain Imaging Behav.* 2, 84–93. doi: 10.1007/s11682-007-9016-x

Davis, P., and Sime, W. (2005). Toward a psychology of performance: sport psychology principles dealing with anxiety. *Int. J. Stress Manag.* 12, 363–378. doi: 10.1037/1072-5245.12.4.363

Diedrich, A., Grant, M., Hofmann, S., Hiller, W., and Berking, M. (2014). Self-compassion as an emotion regulation strategy in major depressive disorder. *Behav. Res. Ther.* 58, 43–51. doi: 10.1016/j.brat.2014.05.006

Dupee, M., Werthner, P., and Forneris, T. (2015). A preliminary study on the relationship between athletes' ability to self-regulate and world ranking. *Biofeedback* 42, 57–63. doi: 10.5298/1081-5937-43.2.01

Erdfelder, E., Faul, F., and Buchner, A. (1996). GPOWER: a general power analysis program. *Behav. Res. Methods Instr. Comput.* 28, 1–11. doi: 10.3758/bf03203630

Esco, M. R., and Flatt, A. A. (2014). Ultra-short-term heart rate variability indexes at rest and post-exercise in athletes: evaluating the agreement with accepted recommendations. *J. Sports Sci. Med.* 13, 535–541.

Ferguson, L., Kowalski, K., Mack, D., and Sabiston, C. (2014). Exploring self-compassion and eudaimonic well-being in young women athletes. *J. Sport Exerc. Psychol.* 36, 203–216. doi: 10.1123/jsep.2013-0096

Ferguson, L., Kowalski, K., Mack, D., and Sabiston, C. (2015). Self-compassion and eudaimonic well-being during emotionally difficult times in sport. *J. Happiness Stud.* 16, 1263–1280. doi: 10.1007/s10902-014-9558-8

Gilbert, P. (2014). The origins and nature of compassion focused therapy. *Br. J. Clin. Psychol.* 53, 6–41. doi: 10.1111/bjc.12043

Gilbert, P., Baldwin, M., Irons, C., Baccus, J., and Palmer, M. (2006). Self-criticism and self-warmth: an imagery study exploring their relation to depression. *J. Cogn. Psychother. Int. Q.* 20, 183–200. doi: 10.1891/088983906780639817

Gilbert, P., and Irons, C. (2005). "Focused therapies for shame and self-attacking, using cognitive, behavioural, emotional, imagery and compassionate mind training," in *Compassion: Conceptualisations, Research and Use in Psychotherapy*, ed. P. Gilbert (Lane: Brunner-Routledge), 263–325.

Gilbert, P., McEwan, K., Matos, M., and Rivis, A. (2011). Fear of compassion: development of three self-report measures. *Psychol. Psychother.* 84, 239–255. doi: 10.1348/147608310x526511

Gilbert, P., and Procter, S. (2006). Compassionate mind training for people with high shame and self-criticism: overview and pilot study of a group therapy approach. *Clin. Psychol. Psychother.* 13, 353–379. doi: 10.1002/cpp.507

Gregg, M., and Hall, C. (2006). Measurement of motivational imagery abilities in sport. *J. Sports Sci.* 24, 961–971. doi: 10.1080/02640410500386167

Hammond, T., Gialloreto, C., Kubas, H., and Davis, H. (2013). The prevalence of failure-based depression among elite athletes. *Clin. J. Sports Med.* 23, 273–277. doi: 10.1097/JSM.0b013e318287b870

Hammond, T., Gregg, M., Hrycaiko, D., Mactavish, J., and Leslie-Toogood, A. (2012). The effects of a motivational-general mastery imagery intervention on the imagery ability and sport confidence of inter-collegiate golfers. *J. Imagery Res. Sport Phys. Activ.* 7, 1–20.

Heathers, J., Fink, E., Kuhnert, R.-L., and de Rosnay, M. (2014). Blood volume pulse (BVP) derived vagal tone (VT) between 5 and 7 years of age: a methodological investigation of measurement and longitudinal stability. *Dev. Psychobiol.* 56, 23–35. doi: 10.1002/dev.21088

Joeng, J., and Turner, S. (2015). Mediators between self-criticism and depression: fear of compassion, self-compassion, and importance to others. *J. Counsel. Psychol.* 62, 453–463. doi: 10.1037/cou0000071

Jones, M., and Sheffield, D. (2008). The impact of game outcome on the wellbeing of athletes. *Int. J. Sport Exerc. Psychol.* 5, 54–65. doi: 10.1080/1612197x.2008.9671812

Juster, R., McEwen, B., and Lupien, S. (2010). Allostatic load biomarkers of chronic stress and impact on health and cognition. *Neurosci. Biobehav. Rev.* 35, 2–16. doi: 10.1016/j.neubiorev.2009.10.002

Karatsoreos, I., and McEwen, B. (2011). Psychobiological allostasis: resistance, resilience and vulnerability. *Trends Cogn. Sci.* 15, 576–584. doi: 10.1016/j.tics.2011.10.005

Kelly, A. C., Carter, J. C., Zuroff, D. C., and Borairi, S. (2013). Self-compassion and fear of self-compassion interact to predict response to eating disorders treatment: a preliminary investigation. *Psychother. Res.* 23, 252–264. doi: 10.1080/10503307.2012.717310

Killham, M., Mosewich, A., Mack, D., Gunnell, K., and Ferguson, L. (2017). Women athletes' self-compassion, self-criticism, and perceived sport performance. *Sport Exerc. Perform. Psychol.* 7, 297–307. doi: 10.1037/spy0000127

Kwekkeboom, K. (2000). Measuring imagery ability: psychometric testing of the imaging ability questionnaire. *Res. Nurs. Health* 23, 301–309. doi: 10.1002/1098-240x(200008)23:4<301::aid-nur6>3.0.co;2-0

Laborde, S., Mosley, E., and Mertgen, A. (2018). Vagal tank theory: the three Rs-resting, reactivity and recovery. *Front. Psychol.* 12:458. doi: 10.3389/fnins.2018.00458

Laborde, S., Mosley, E., and Thayer, J. (2017). Heart rate variability and cardiac vagal tone in psychophysiological research- recommendations for experiment planning, data analysis, and data reporting. *Front. Psychol.* 8:213. doi: 10.3389/fpsyg.2017.00213

Lang, P. (1979). A bio-informational theory of emotional imagery. *Psychophysiology* 16, 495–512. doi: 10.1111/j.1469-8986.1979.tb01511.x

Leary, M., Tate, E., Adams, C., Allen, A., and Hancock, J. (2007). Self-compassion and reactions to unpleasant self-relevant events: the implications of treating oneself kindly. *J. Pers. Soc. Psychol.* 92, 887–904. doi: 10.1037/0022-3514.92.5.887

Levine, J., Flemming, R., Piedmont, J., Cain, S., and Chen, W.-J. (2016). Heart rate variability and generalized anxiety disorder during laboratory-induced worry and aversive imagery. *J. Affect. Disord.* 205, 207–215. doi: 10.1016/j.jad.2016.07.019

McEwen, B., and Wingfield, J. (2003). The concept of allostasis in biology and biomedicine. *Hormones Behav.* 43, 2–15. doi: 10.1016/s0018-506x(02)00024-7

Mosewich, A., Crocker, P., and Kowalski, K. (2014). Managing injury and other setbacks in sport: experiences of (and resources for) high-performance women athletes. *Qual. Res. Sport Exerc. Health* 6, 182–204. doi: 10.1080/2159676x.2013.766810

Mosewich, A., Crocker, P., Kowalski, K., and DeLongis, A. (2013). Applying self-compassion in sport: an intervention with women athletes. *J. Sport Exerc. Psychol.* 35, 514–524. doi: 10.1123/jsep.35.5.514

Mosewich, A., Kowalski, K., Sabiston, C., Sedgwick, W., and Tracy, J. (2011). Self-compassion: a potential resource for young women athletes. *J. Sport Exerc. Psychol.* 33, 103–123. doi: 10.1123/jsep.33.1.103

Neff, K. (2003a). Self-compassion: an alternative conceptualization of a healthy attitude toward oneself. *Self Identity* 2, 85–101. doi: 10.1080/15298860309032

Neff, K. (2003b). The development and validation of a scale to measure self-compassion. *Self Identity* 2, 223–250. doi: 10.1080/15298860309027

Neff, K., Hsieh, Y., and Dejitterat, K. (2005). Self-compassion, achievement goals, and coping with academic failure. *Self Identity* 4, 263–287. doi: 10.1080/13576500444000317

Neff, K., Rude, S., and Kirkpatrick, K. (2007). An examination of self-compassion in relation to positive psychological functioning and personality traits. *J. Res. Pers.* 41, 908–916. doi: 10.1016/j.jrp.2006.08.002

Neff, K., and Vonk, R. (2009). Self-compassion versus global self-esteem: two different ways of relating to oneself. *J. Pers.* 77, 23–50. doi: 10.1111/j.1467-6494.2008.00537.x

Pallant, J. (2007). *SPSS Survival Manual: A Step by Step Guide to Data Analysis Using SPSS*, 3rd Edn. Milton Keynes: Open University Press.

Porges, S. (2007). The polyvagal perspective. *Biol. Psychol.* 74, 116–143. doi: 10.1016/j.biopsycho.2006.06.009

Powers, T., Koestner, R., Lacaille, N., Kwan, L., and Zuroff, D. (2009). Self-criticism, motivation and goal progress of athletes and musicians: a prospective study. *Pers. Individ. Differ.* 47, 279–283. doi: 10.1016/j.paid.2009.03.012

Reardon, C., and Factor, R. (2010). Sport psychiatry: a systematic review of diagnosis and medical treatment of mental illness in athletes. *Sports Med.* 961–980. doi: 10.2165/11536580-000000000-00000

Reis, N., Kowalski, K., Ferguson, L., Sabiston, C., Sedgwick, W., and Crocker, P. (2015). Self-compassion and women athletes' responses to emotionally difficult sport situations: a brief induction. *Psychol. Sport Exerc.* 16, 18–25. doi: 10.1016/j.psychsport.2014.08.011

Rockliff, H., Gilbert, P., McEwan, K., Lightman, S., and Glover, D. (2008). A pilot exploration of heart rate variability and salivary cortisol responses to compassion-focused imagery. *Clin. Neuropsychiatry* 5, 132–139.

Rodriguez, M., and Ebbeck, V. (2015). Implementing self-compassion strategies with female college gymnasts. *J. Sport Psychol. Action* 6, 44–53. doi: 10.1080/21520704.2014.991052

Rosenberg, M. (1965). *Society and the Adolescent Self-Image*. Princeton, NJ: Princeton University Press. 40,

Sagar, S., Lavallee, D., and Spray, C. (2007). Why young athletes fear failure: consequences of failure. *J. Sports Sci.* 25, 1171–1184. doi: 10.1080/02640410601040093

Schäfer, A., and Vagedes, J. (2013). How accurate is pulse rate variability as an estimate of heart rate variability: a review on studies comparing photoplethysmographic technology with an electrocardiogram. *Int. J. Cardiol.* 166, 15–29. doi: 10.1016/j.ijcard.2012.03.119

Seiler, S., Haugen, O., and Kuffel, E. (2007). Autonomic recovery after exercise in trained athletes: intensity and duration effects. *Med. Sci. Sports Exerc.* 1366–1373. doi: 10.1249/mss.0b013e318060f17d

Semenchuk, B., Fortier, M., and Strachan, S. M. (2018). Self-compassion and self-regulation of exercise: reactions to recalled exercise setbacks. *J. Sport Exerc.* 31–39. doi: 10.1123/jsep.2017-0242

Shaw, L., Zaichkowsky, L., and Wilson, V. (2012). Setting the balance: using biofeedback and neurofeedback with gymnasts. *J. Clin. Sport Psychol.* 6, 47–66. doi: 10.1123/jcsp.6.1.47

Smith, S., Kass, S., Rotunda, R., and Schneider, S. (2006). If at first you don't succeed: effects of failure on general and task-specific self-efficacy and performance. *N. Am. J. Psychol.* 8, 171–182.

Stellar, J. E., Cohen, A., Oveis, C., and Keltner, D. (2015). Affective and physiological responses to the suffering of others: compassion and vagal activity. *J. Pers. Soc. Psychol.* 108, 572–585. doi: 10.1037/pspi0000010 39,

Sutherland, L., Kowalski, K., Ferguson, L., Sabiston, C., Sedgwick, W., and Crocker, P. (2014). Narratives of young women athletes' experiences of emotional pain and self-compassion. *Qual. Res. Sport Exerc. Health* 6, 499–516. doi: 10.1080/2159676x.2014.888587

Svendsen, J., Osnes, B., Binder, P., Dundas, I., Visted, E., Nordby, H., et al. (2016). Trait self-compassion reflects emotional flexibility through an association with high vagally mediated heart rate variability. *Mindfulness* 7, 1103–1113. doi: 10.1007/s12671-016-0549-1

Tabachnick, B. G., and Fidell, L. S. (2013). *Using Multivariate Statistics*, 6th Edn. Boston, MA: Allyn and Bacon.

Task Force of The European Society of Cardiology and The North American Society of Pacing and Electrophysiology (1996). Heart rate variability: standards of measurement, physiological interpretation, and clinical use. *Eur. Heart J.* 17, 354–381.

Tenenbaum, G., Basevitch, I., Gershgoren, L., and Filho, E. (2013). Emotions-decision-making in sport: theoretical conceptualization and experimental evidence. *Int. J. Sport Exerc. Psychol.* 11, 151–168. doi: 10.1080/1612197x.2013.773687

Terry, M., and Leary, M. (2011). Self-compassion, self-regulation, and health. *Self Identity* 10, 352–362. doi: 10.1080/15298868.2011.558404

Thayer, J., Ahs, F., Fredrikson, M., Sollers, J., and Wager, T. (2012). A meta-analysis of heart rate variability and neuroimaging studies: implications for heart rate variability as a marker of stress and health. *Neurosci. Biobehav. Rev.* 36, 747–756. doi: 10.1016/j.neubiorev.2011.11.009

Thayer, J., Hansen, A., Saus-Rose, E., and Johnsen, B. (2009). Heart rate variability, prefrontal neural function, and cognitive performance. the neurovisceral

Wawrzyniak, A., Hamer, M., Steptoe, A., and Endrighi, R. (2016). Decreased reaction time variability is associated with greater cardiovascular responses to acute stress. *Psychophysiology* 53, 739–748. doi: 10.1111/psyp.12617

Williams, D., Thayer, J., and Koenig, J. (2016). Resting cardiac vagal tone predicts intraindividual reaction time variability during an attention task in a sample of young and healthy adults. *Psychophysiology* 53, 1843–1851. doi: 10.1111/psyp.12739

Williams, S. E., Veldhuijzen van Zanten, J. J. C. S., Trotman, G. P., Quinton, M. L., and Ginty, A. T. (2017). Challenge and threat imagery manipulates heart rate and anxiety responses to stress. *Int. J. Psychophysiol.* 117, 111–118. doi: 10.1016/j.ijpsycho.2017.04.011

Zhang, J., and Chen, S. (2016). Self-compassion promotes personal improvement from regret experiences via acceptance. *Pers. Soc. Psychol. Bull.* 42, 244–258. doi: 10.1177/0146167215623271

integration perspective on self-regulation, adaptation and health. *Ann. Behav. Med.* 37, 141–153. doi: 10.1007/s12160-009-9101-z

Thayer, J., and Lane, R. (2000). A model of neurovisceral integration in emotion regulation and dysregulation. *J. Affect. Disord.* 61, 201–216. doi: 10.1016/s0165-0327(00)00338-4

Thayer, J., and Lane, R. (2009). Claude bernard and the heart-brain connection: further elaboration on a model of neurovisceral integration. *Neurosci. Biobehav. Rev.* 33, 81–88. doi: 10.1016/j.neubiorev.2008.08.004

Thayer, J., and Sternberg, E. (2006). Beyond heart rate variability: vagal regulation of allostatic systems. *Ann. N. Y. Acad. Sci.* 1088, 361–362.

Ulrich, R. S., Simons, R. F., Losito, B. D., Fiorito, E., Miles, M. A., and Zelson, M. (1991). Stress recovery during exposure to natural and urban environments. *J. Environ. Psychol.* 11, 201–230. doi: 10.1016/s0272-4944(05)80184-7

13

Competition Stress Leads to a Blunting of the Cortisol Awakening Response in Elite Rowers

Douglas MacDonald[1,2] *and Mark A. Wetherell*[1*]

[1]*Psychobiology Research Group, Department of Psychology, Northumbria University, Newcastle upon Tyne, United Kingdom,* [2]*Scottish Canoe Association, Edinburgh, United Kingdom*

Correspondence:
Mark A. Wetherell
mark.wetherell@northumbria.ac.uk

Background: Anticipation of forthcoming demands is often met with biological up-regulation, for example, levels of the stress hormone cortisol are typically elevated immediately prior to an anticipated event. Similarly, the cortisol awakening response (CAR), a surge in cortisol in the period following waking, is elevated on days of anticipated demand and this is viewed as an adaptive response in the preparation for challenge. This study assessed the effects of competition as an anticipated challenge in elite rowers.

Methods: Elite rowers ($N = 8$) were assessed during two training and two competition weekends. Each assessment involved the measurement of self-reported competitive (cognitive and somatic) anxiety and salivary diurnal cortisol across 2 days representing a preparation day prior to either a training or competition day. Competitive anxiety was measured each morning and saliva samples were provided immediately upon waking and 30 min post waking (CAR) and before bed.

Results: Self-reported cognitive and somatic anxiety levels were significantly greater during the competition phase compared with training. Additionally, levels of cognitive anxiety were greater on the day of competition compared with the preparation day. CAR magnitude was significantly reduced during the competition phase compared with training; however, there were no differences between preparation and event days.

Conclusions: Reduced or blunted CARs are typically observed in chronically stressed populations and are characteristic of burnout and fatigue. While an increased CAR during competition may represent an adaptive response to challenge, blunted CARs and the concomitant increases in competitive anxiety observed here indicate maladaptive responding during a period where maximized functioning is critical.

Keywords: stress, anticipation, competition, rowers, cortisol awakening response

INTRODUCTION

The anticipation of forthcoming demand is ubiquitous in competitive sport and the period prior to competition is typically accompanied by changes in mood, in particular, increases in competition anxiety. This manifests as cognitive anxiety, characterized by a lack of concentration, disrupted attention, and ruminations about performance, and as somatic anxiety, characterized by self-perceptions of how arousal has affected the body (Martens et al., 1990a). Situations in which an individual anticipates a requirement to react or respond are typically met with increased biological activity, in particular, increases in neuroendocrine and cardiovascular activity, and this biological up-regulation serves to prepare the individual for the forthcoming perceived demand.

For forthcoming events where demand is likely, it is therefore adaptive for resources to be mobilized before the event is encountered in order that the appropriate response can be initiated immediately. This is especially the case where there is a need for rapid responses, and activation of two key physiological systems, the sympathetic-adrenal-medullary (SAM) and hypothalamic-pituitary-adrenal (HPA) axis provide resource to deal with the presenting situation (Hare et al., 2013). For example, activation of the SAM axis leads sprinters to demonstrate cardiovascular up-regulation before the starter's gun (McArdle et al., 1967; Inui, 1987) and this facilitates immediate physical exertion at the start of the race. Cortisol, secreted by the HPA axis, is an energizing hormone responsible for mobilizing activities directed toward responding to demand or threat. When faced with a demanding situation, acute up-regulation of cortisol increases the release of glucose and stimulates the sympathetic nervous system providing resource to deal with the threat and maintain homeostasis (Wetherell et al., 2006). Accordingly, higher levels of cortisol have been observed immediately before and during competition compared with practice rounds in golf (McKay et al., 1997), and immediately before a judo competition compared with resting days (Salvador et al., 2003). A recent review concluded that cortisol levels are elevated in athletes prior to competition and that levels are greatest when sampled closer to the start of competition (van Paridon et al., 2017). This may provide evidence of an adaptive role for biological up-regulation to enable resources immediately prior to demand.

The nature of this up-regulation, however, depends upon how the forthcoming event is perceived. The Theory of Challenge and Threat States in Athletes (TCTSA: Jones et al., 2009) demonstrates how this may manifest in the context of sporting competitions. That is, whether forthcoming competition is perceived as a challenge or a threat determines whether athletes respond positively or negatively, respectively. Moreover, this perception can lead to distinct patterns of biological up-regulation. Specifically, perceptions of challenge typically lead to activation of the SAM axis, subsequent increases in cardiac activity and reductions in peripheral vascular resistance, which serve to mobilize resources to facilitate coping. Perceptions of threat, however, are associated with SAM and HPA activation, leading to corticosteroid release without corresponding reductions in vascular resistance. This pattern of responding is not facilitative for coping and has negative consequences in terms of emotions and performance (Jones et al., 2009). The TCTSA therefore suggests that biological up-regulation is determined by the perception of the event, and that this can lead to adaptive or maladaptive psychobiological responding depending on whether the event is perceived as a challenge or a threat.

In addition to changes in response to acute threat, the secretion of cortisol follows a marked diurnal profile characterized by a rapid increase in the 30–45 min immediately following awakening (cortisol awakening response, CAR) and a decline across the day toward lowest levels around midnight (Stalder et al., 2016). Deviations from this typical increase following awakening are characteristic of neuroendocrine dysregulation and associated negative consequences for health and well-being. For example, reduced CARs, typically described as blunted, are associated with fatigue, burnout, and exhaustion (Chida and Steptoe, 2009).

Although in sporting contexts, acute HPA activation is typically associated with perceived threat, there is now increasing evidence that the secretion of cortisol during the CAR period is an adaptive response that plays a role in the preparation for forthcoming demands (Fries et al., 2009; Clow et al., 2010). Increased CARs have been observed during periods of greater uncertainty and workload (Brant et al., 2010); on workdays characterized by greater feelings of stress (Kunz-Ebrecht et al., 2004); and in teachers on the day of an assessed observation (Wolfram et al., 2013). CARs of greater magnitudes have also been observed on the day of a manipulated social and cognitively demanding stressors in ambulatory (Wetherell et al., 2015) and controlled sleep laboratory conditions (Elder et al., 2018). Increased cortisol secretion has also been observed on the days of competitive sports. Elevated levels of cortisol were observed in the morning of dancing (Rohleder et al., 2007), motorcycling, and tennis (Filaire et al., 2007, 2009) competitions, compared with control days, and in the evenings during a 3-day soccer competition compared with sampling prior to the competition (Aizawa et al., 2006). In contrast, no change in cortisol secretion in the hour following awakening was observed 3–7 days prior to and on the day of a martial arts competition (Strahler et al., 2010) suggesting possible adaptation of the HPA axis in the lead up to competition.

Given the potential role of the CAR as a marker of anticipation of forthcoming demand, it may provide a novel insight into the impact of forthcoming competition on neuroendocrine functioning. The current study is therefore the first to assess both the acute and prolonged impact of competition on the CAR. Specifically, the study followed a crew of eight male elite rowers across consecutive weekends of training and competition, assessing competition anxiety and cortisol indices on the day before (preparation) and the day of (participation) a competitive event. It was predicted that levels of competition anxiety will be greater during competition compared with training weekends and on competition days compared with preparation days. Based on studies suggesting that the CAR has an adaptive role in preparing for forthcoming demand, it is predicted that greater CARs will be observed during competition compared with training weekends and on competition days compared with the preparation days.

MATERIALS AND METHODS

Participants

All recruitment and study procedures were granted ethical approval from the Faculty Ethics Committee in line with relevant regulatory bodies. Eight male university rowers (range: 19–23 years; M_{age} = 20.62, SD = 1.30) participated in the study. All participants were part of an elite rowing program and were competing at national or international level. Throughout the testing period, the athletes trained under the same program and competed as a team. None of the participants were taking drugs or medication and had no known history of endocrine disorders. Prior to the last weekend of testing, one rower developed an injury which made him unable to compete in the last race and his data from the final weekend are excluded from analyses.

Measures

Salivary Cortisol

The researcher met with all rowers and their coach to detail the requirements of the protocol, engage them with the study goals, and explain saliva collections procedures. Participants collected their own saliva using Salivettes (Sarstedt, Germany). All samples were frozen (−20°C) and assayed using the enzyme-linked immunosorbant assay method (Salimetrics-Europe, UK; intra and inter-assay coefficients <10%). Cortisol values are reported in nmol/L.

Competitive Anxiety

The Competitive State Anxiety Inventory (CSAI-2, Martens et al., 1990b) was used to record self-reported levels of cognitive and somatic anxiety. The CSAI-2 comprises 27 items rated on a 4-point Likert scale with higher scores indicating higher levels of each state. It is a well-established tool for the assessment of competition anxiety across a wide variety of sporting contexts and has been previously used, alongside the measurement of cortisol, to differentiate practice and competition in sport (McKay et al., 1997).

Protocol

Testing took place over 4 consecutive weekends during April and May, incorporating 2 weeks at the end of the training season and the first 2 weeks of the competition season. Each weekend comprised 2 days of testing: during training weekends, these comprised typical training, and during competition weekends, comprised a preparation day (the day before competition), and a participation day (the day of competition). On each testing day, rowers provided three cortisol samples: immediately upon awakening; 30 min following awakening; and before bed. The CSAI-2 was completed each day following the provision of the 30-min sample and prior to training or competition. Training weekends comprised a 5- to 10-km run followed by a 16-km row on day one, and two 10- to 12-km high-intensity rows followed by one 16-km low-intensity session on day two. The first competition weekend was the British Universities' competition, which comprised eight crews racing in heats, semi-finals and finals (depending on success). The second weekend was the annual inter-varsity race which comprised two crews in a single head-to-head race.

Treatment of Data

The dependent variables of awakening cortisol, CAR, levels of cortisol prior to bed, cognitive anxiety, and cognitive anxiety were assessed using ANOVAs with repeated measures for each independent variable: Phase (Training versus Competition); Weekend (Practice 1, Practice 2, Competition 1, Competition 2); and Day (Preparation versus Participation). The CAR was calculated by subtracting cortisol levels at awakening from levels at 30 min post waking. All data used in analyses are provided in **Data Sheet 1**.

RESULTS

There were no significant differences in levels of cortisol at awakening or prior to bed between phases, weekends, or days of testing ($p > 0.05$). The phase x day interaction demonstrated higher levels of cortisol at awakening on competition days compared with training days; however, this was not significant ($p = 0.06$, $\eta^2 = 0.41$).

There was a statistically significant difference in the CAR between phases [$F(1,6) = 20.1$, $p = 0.004$, $\eta^2 = 0.77$] where CAR magnitude was greater during the training phase compared with the competition phase. There were no significant differences in the CAR between weekends or days of testing. **Figure 1** presents mean diurnal cortisol profiles on each day of testing across the practice and competition weekends. The CAR is represented as the change from levels at awakening to levels at 30 min post awakening.

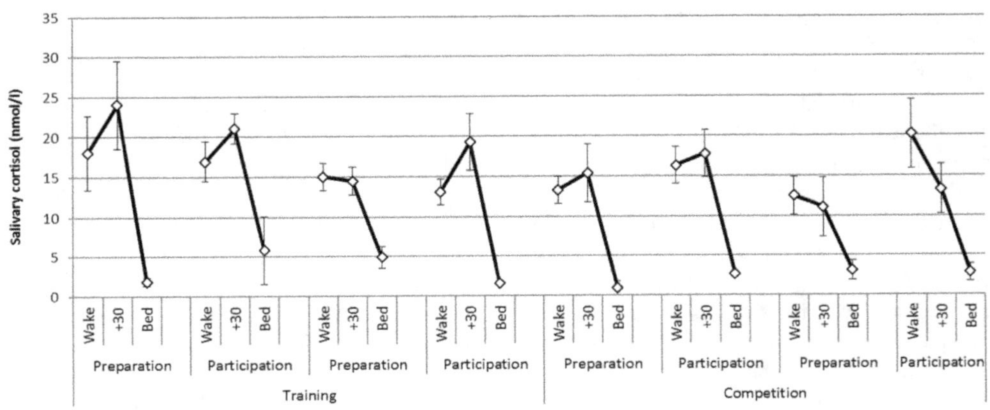

FIGURE 1 | Mean (S.E) diurnal (awakening, +30 min, bed) cortisol profiles on each day of testing across the training and competition weekends.

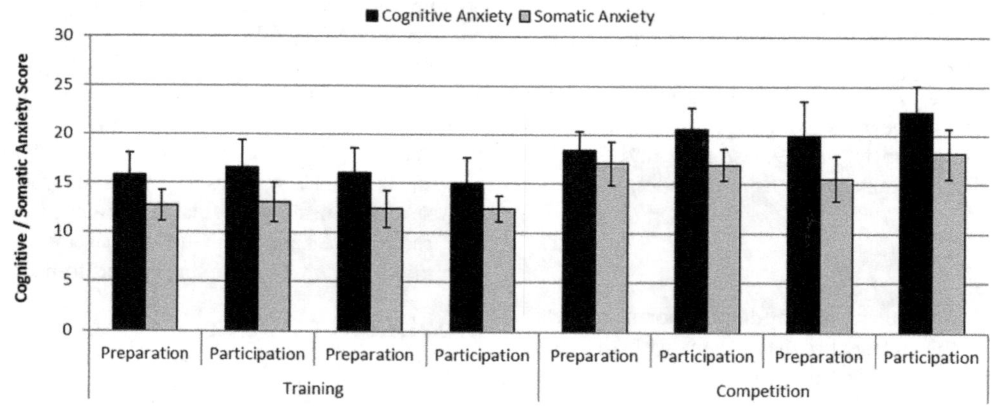

FIGURE 2 | Mean (S.E) self-reported levels of cognitive anxiety and somatic anxiety on each day of testing across the training and competition weekends.

There were statistically significant differences in cognitive anxiety [F (1,6) = 8.13, p = 0.029, η^2 = 0.58] and somatic anxiety [F (1,6) = 7.87, p = 0.031, η^2 = 0.57] between phases where anxiety levels were greater during the competition phase compared with the practice phase. Additionally, there was a significant effect of Day on cognitive anxiety [F (1,6) = 20.61, p = 0.004, η^2 = 0.78] where anxiety levels were greater on the participation day compared with the preparation day. **Figure 2** shows mean self-reported levels of cognitive and somatic anxiety on each day of testing across the practice and competition weekends.

DISCUSSION

In line with predictions, rowers reported significantly greater levels of cognitive and somatic anxiety during competition compared with training, and greater levels of cognitive anxiety on the participation day compared with the preparation day. There were no differences in the CAR between participation and preparation days, but there were significant differences between competition and training. Contrary to prediction, however, greater CARs were not observed during competition, but were significantly blunted during competition compared with training.

Evidence in sporting and non-sporting contexts suggests an adaptive role for increased CARs in preparation for forthcoming demand. In support, increased cortisol has been reported on the mornings of competition compared with control days. In the current study, the magnitude of the CAR, however, was not greater during competition weekends or on the day of competition. This finding is similar to those of Strahler et al. (2010) who observed no increases in the CAR in martial artists in the week-long lead up to a competition, suggesting that elite athletes become accustomed to competitive environments and show neuroendocrine habituation. Reduced psychobiological reactivity to acute stress has also been observed in elite athletes compared with non-trained controls (Rimmele et al., 2007). Adaptation is therefore one explanation for the current findings. That is, elite athletes demonstrate reduced stress responsiveness either as a positive function of repeated exercise or habituation to competition (Strahler et al., 2010).

However, unlike the martial artists, the CARs observed during the competition phase in the current study were not unchanged, but were significantly blunted compared with those during training. Furthermore, the competition phase and day of competition were accompanied by significantly greater levels of competition anxiety. Although no change in neuroendocrine reactivity in response to competition may be indicative of adaptation to competitive stress, the blunted responding and increased anxiety observed during the competition phase are more typical of chronic stress. Outside of sporting contexts, reduced CARs are signatures of fatigue, exhaustion, and burnout (Chida and Steptoe, 2009) and blunted CARs are typical in conditions of chronic stress, for example, in students experiencing academic stress (Lovell et al., 2011; Duan et al., 2013); informal caregivers (Mortensen et al., 2019); parents of children who display problem behaviors (Lovell et al., 2013); and following early life adversity (Mangold et al., 2010; Raffington et al., 2018). Blunted CARs have also been associated with impaired cortisol recovery following acute laboratory stress, demonstrating a link between deficits in these preparatory responses (Dienes et al., 2019). As increased training volume and competition can lead to higher levels of burnout, somatic stress, and reduced stress recovery in rowers (Jürimäe et al., 2002; Purge et al., 2005), the blunted CARs during the competition phase may therefore reflect burnout and exhaustion. The CAR is considered an adaptive response to prepare for forthcoming demands; a blunted CAR during competition is, therefore, not optimal in terms of performance and health. Indeed, it is suggested that training and competition loads that are too great can have a detrimental impact on performance (Purge et al., 2005). Moreover, blunted CARs are linked to a range of psychiatric and physical conditions (c.f. Fries et al., 2009), and prolonged hypo-responding is a risk factor for morbidity (Phillips et al., 2013). The follow-up period in the current study did not extend beyond the final competition weekend and, as such, longer term HPA activity and health status are unknown. As these rowers are young and healthy, a return to typical diurnal secretion of cortisol and a reduction in anxiety is expected; however, this is reliant on adequate recovery. Over-training, in the absence of adequate recovery can to lead to a plethora of negative health outcomes through physiological dysregulation. Such periods have been associated with a blunting of the CAR (Cadegiani and Kater, 2017) and higher levels of morning cortisol following a 4-week period of overload training in rowers (Smith et al., 2011), and this is exacerbated in the presence of psychosocial stressors (Meeusen et al., 2013). There is no specific marker of over-training in rowers, and in their review, Mäestu and Colleagues (2005) advocate an individualized approach to understanding impact of over-training in athletes. As sustained HPA dysregulation accompanied by high levels of anxiety places rowers at greater risk of psychological and physical morbidity, measurement of the CAR may provide a useful tool for assessing physical functioning during training and competition.

These findings should be considered in light of limitations. First, the sample size was dictated by the opportunity to sample a single crew of elite athletes; the current findings therefore warrant further investigation in a larger equivalent sample. Second, there were no objective measures of waking and sample provision and therefore protocol adherence is not known. This was, however, an extremely motivated cohort with strict training regimes which would necessitate typical waking times during the testing periods. Further, strategies which aim to increase the motivation to participate are associated with improved adherence. As such, in line with guidelines (Stalder et al., 2016), the researchers personally engaged the participants and their coach with the research goals, ascertained participant understanding of the procedures, and expressed the importance of adherence. Third, although there were no statistically significant differences between the weekends within each phase, there were differences in the nature of the two competitions. The first was the British Universities' competition comprising eight crews, while the second was the inter-varsity race between two rival universities. Both competitions were significant events for the participating rowers; however, the importance of winning is far greater in an event with two teams. Furthermore, anecdotally, the inter-varsity race, between two local rival crews, attracts larger crowds that are closer to the crews, and is typically perceived as a higher stakes competition where reputation and pride are under more intense scrutiny. Critical social evaluation is a pertinent stressor that leads to HPA activation in acute situations (Dickerson and Kemeny, 2004). Indeed, in the context of competitive ballroom dancing, cortisol responses are greatest when being socially evaluated by judges, and these increases are over and above those attributed to the physical strain of exercise observed during training. Although no measures of perceptions of social evaluation were recorded in the current study, it is interesting to note that levels of cognitive and somatic anxiety, and awakening cortisol, were highest on the day characterized by greater social evaluation. Furthermore, in support of the notion that increased competition stress can have a detrimental impact on performance (Purge et al., 2005), and a blunting of the CAR is a maladaptive response in terms of preparation for demand, the crew lost this inter-varsity competition. It should be noted, however, that the perceived importance of each competition to the rowers was not formally ascertained. Finally, the CSAI-2 was used to assess perceived levels of cognitive and somatic anxiety prior to competition. Although frequently used to assess competition anxiety across a wide range of sporting contexts, concerns have been raised regarding its ability to distinguish between affective states (Jones and Uphill, 2004). For example, the same somatic symptoms can be attributed to excitement and fear (Kerr, 1997) leading to potential ambiguity in the meaning of the somatic anxiety sub-scale. Further, high scores on the cognitive anxiety sub-scale may not reflect cognitive anxiety per se, but moreover may reflect recognition of forthcoming challenge and the need to activate coping resources (Lane et al., 1999). Given the observation of blunted CARs and their association with fatigue, exhaustion, and burnout in non-sporting contexts, it is likely that, in these rowers, high scores represent higher levels of somatic and cognitive anxiety; however, the precise attribution of these perceptions is not known.

Notwithstanding these limitations, this study demonstrates clear differences in competition anxiety and HPA axis function between periods of training and competition in elite rowers. The observed increased anxiety and blunted CARs are not optimal for psychological and physical well-being or performance, and this warrants further investigation in a larger sample in order to consider strategies to facilitate more adaptive responding in elite rowers during competition.

ETHICS STATEMENT

This study was carried out in accordance with the recommendations of the "British Psychological Society" with written informed consent from all subjects. All subjects gave written informed consent in accordance with the Declaration of Helsinki. The protocol was approved by the Department of Psychology Ethics Committee at Northumbria University Newcastle.

AUTHOR CONTRIBUTIONS

MW designed and helped to execute the study, analyzed and interpreted data, and wrote the manuscript. DM designed and executed the study, recruited participants, analyzed and interpreted data, and contributed to the manuscript.

REFERENCES

Aizawa, K., Nakahori, C., Akimoto, T., Kimura, F., Hayashi, K., Kono, I., et al. (2006). Changes of pituitary, adrenal and gonadal hormones during competition among female soccer players. *J. Sports Med. Phys. Fitness* 46, 322–327.

Brant, H., Wetherell, M. A., Lightman, S. L., Crown, A. L., and Vedhara, K. (2010). Discrepancies between physiological and self-report measures of stress in pre-registration doctors at the beginning and the end of a clinical rotation. *Stress, the International Journal on the Biology of Stress* 13, 155–162.

Cadegiani, F. A., and Kater, C. E. (2017). Hypothalamic-pituitary-adrenal (HPA) axis functioning in overtraining syndrome: findings from endocrine and metabolic responses on overtraining syndrome. *Sports Med. Open* 3:45. doi: 10.1186/s40798-017-0113-0

Chida, Y., and Steptoe, A. (2009). Cortisol awakening response and psychosocial factors: a systematic review and meta-analysis. *Biol. Psychol.* 80, 265–278. doi: 10.1016/j.biopsycho.2008.10.004

Clow, A., Hucklebridge, F., Stalder, T., Evans, P., and Thorn, L. (2010). The cortisol awakening response: more than a measure of HPA axis function. *Neurosci. Biobehav. Rev.* 35, 97–103. doi: 10.1016/j.neubiorev.2009.12.011

Dickerson, S. S., and Kemeny, M. E. (2004). Acute stressors and cortisol responses: a theoretical integration and synthesis of laboratory research. *Psychol. Bull.* 130, 355–391. doi: 10.1037/0033-2909.130.3.355

Dienes, K., Gartland, N., and Ferguson, E. (2019). The relationship between the cortisol awakening response and cortisol reactivity to a laboratory stressor. *Br. J. Health Psychol.* 24, 265–281. doi: 10.1111/bjhp.12352

Duan, H., Yuan, Y., Zhang, L., Qin, S., Zhang, K., Buchanan, T. W., et al. (2013). Chronic stress exposure decreases the cortisol awakening response in healthy young men. *Stress* 16, 630–637. doi: 10.3109/10253890.2013.840579

Elder, G. J., Barclay, N. L., Wetherell, M. A., and Ellis, J. G. (2018). Anticipated next day demand affects the magnitude of the cortisol awakening response but not subjective or objective sleep. *J. Sleep Res.* 27, 47–55. doi: 10.1111/jsr.12569

Filaire, E., Alix, D., Ferrand, C., and Verger, M. (2009). Psychophysiological stress in tennis players during the first single match of a tournament. *Psychoneuroendocrinology* 34, 150–157. doi: 10.1016/j.psyneuen.2008.08.022

Filaire, E., Filaire, M., and Le Scanff, C. (2007). Salivary cortisol, heart rate and blood lactate during a qualifying trial and an official race in motorcycling competition. *J. Sports Med. Phys. Fitness* 7, 413–417.

Fries, E., Dettenborn, L., and Kirschbaum, C. (2009). The cortisol awakening response (CAR): facts and future directions. *Int. J. Psychophysiol.* 72, 67–73. doi: 10.1016/j.ijpsycho.2008.03.014

Hare, O. A., Wetherell, M. A., and Smith, M. A. (2013). State anxiety and cortisol reactivity to skydiving in novice versus experienced skydivers. *Physiol. Behav.* 118, 40–44. doi: 10.1016/j.physbeh.2013.05.011

Inui, N. (1987). Anticipatory cardiac responses to two running events. *J. Hum. Ergol.* 16, 19–29.

Jones, M., Meijen, C., McCarthy, P. J., and Sheffield, D. (2009). A theory of challenge and threat states in athletes. *Int. J. Sport Exercise Psychol.* 2, 161–180. doi: 10.1080/17509840902829331

Jones, M. V., and Uphill, M. (2004). Responses to the competitive state anxiety Inventory-2 (d) by athletes in anxious and excited scenarios. *Psychol. Sport Exerc.* 5, 201–212. doi: 10.1016/S1469-0292(02)00054-7

Jürimäe, J., Mäestu, J., Purge, P., Jürimäe, T., and Sööt, T. (2002). Relations among heavy training stress, mood state, and performance for male junior rowers. *Percept. Mot. Skills* 95, 520–526. doi: 10.2466/PMS.95.6.520-526

Kerr, J. H. (1997). *Motivation and emotion in sport.* East Sussex: Psychology Press.

Kunz-Ebrecht, S. R., Kirschbaum, C., Marmot, M., and Steptoe, A. (2004). Differences in cortisol awakening response on work days and weekends in women and men from the Whitehall II cohort. *Psychoneuroendocrinology* 29, 516–528. doi: 10.1016/S0306-4530(03)00072-6

Lane, A. M., Sewell, D. F., Terry, P. C., Bartram, D., and Neti, M. S. (1999). Confirmatory factor analysis of the competitive state anxiety Inventory-2. *J. Sports Sci.* 17, 505–512. doi: 10.1080/026404199365812

Lovell, B., Moss, M., and Wetherell, M. A. (2011). Perceived stress, common health complaints and diurnal patterns of cortisol secretion in young, otherwise healthy individuals. *Horm. Behav.* 60, 301–305. doi: 10.1016/j.yhbeh.2011.06.007

Lovell, B., Moss, M., and Wetherell, M. A. (2013). The psychophysiological and health corollaries of child problem behaviours in caregivers of children with autism and ADHD. *J. Intellect. Disabil. Res.* 59, 150–157. doi: 10.1111/jir.12081

Mangold, D., Wand, G., Javors, M., and Mintz, J. (2010). Acculturation, childhood trauma and the cortisol awakening response in Mexican-American adults. *Horm. Behav.* 58, 637–646. doi: 10.1016/j.yhbeh.2010.06.010

Martens, R., Vealey, R. S., and Burton, D. (1990a). *Competitive anxiety in sport.* Champaign, IL: Human Kinetics.

Martens, R., Vealey, R. S., Burton, D., Bump, L., and Smith, D. E. (1990b). "Development and validation of the Competitive Sports Anxiety Inventory 2" in *Competitive Anxiety in Sport.* eds. R. Martens, R. S. Vealey and D. Burton (Champaign, IL: Human Kinetics), 117–178.

McArdle, W. D., Foglia, G. F., and Patti, A. V. (1967). Telemetered cardiac response to selected running events. *J. Appl. Physiol.* 23, 566–570. doi: 10.1152/jappl.1967.23.4.566

McKay, J. M., Selig, S. E., Carlson, J. S., and Morris, T. (1997). Psychophysiological stress in elite golfers during practice and competition. *Aust. J. Sci. Med. Sport* 29, 55–61.

Meeusen, R., Duclos, M., Foster, C., Fry, A., Gleeson, M., Nieman, D., et al. (2013). European College of Sport Science, American College of Sports Medicine. Prevention, diagnosis, and treatment of the overtraining syndrome: joint consensus statement of the European College of Sport Science and the American College of Sports Medicine. *Med. Sci. Sports Exerc.* 45, 186–205. doi: 10.1249/MSS.0b013e318279a10a

Mortensen, J., Dich, N., Clark, A. J., Ramlau-Hansen, C. H., Head, J., Kivimäki, M., et al. (2019). Informal caregiving and diurnal patterns of salivary cortisol: results from the Whitehall II cohort study. *Psychoneuroendocrinology* 100, 41–47. doi: 10.1016/j.psyneuen.2018.09.030

Phillips, A. A., Ginty, A. T., and Hughes, B. M. (2013). The other side of the coin: blunted cardiovascular and cortisol reactivity are associated with negative health outcomes. *Int. J. Psychophysiol.* 90, 1–7. doi: 10.1016/j.ijpsycho.2013.02.002

Purge, P., Jürimäe, J., and Jürimäe, T. (2005). Changes in recovery stress state and performance in elute rowers during preparation for major competitions. *Percept. Mot. Skills* 101, 375–381. doi: 10.2466/PMS.101.6.375-381

Raffington, L., Prindle, J., Keresztes, A., Binder, J., Heim, C., and Shing, Y. L. (2018). Blunted cortisol stress reactivity in low-income children related to lower memory function. *Psychoneuroendocrinology* 100, 41–47. doi: 10.1016/j.psyneuen.2018.02.002

Rimmele, U., Zellweger, B. C., Marti, B., Seiler, R., Mohiyeddini, C., Ehlert, U., et al. (2007). Trained men show lower cortisol, heart rate and psychological responses to psychosocial stress compared with untrained men. *Psychoneuroendocrinology* 32, 627–635. doi: 10.1016/j.psyneuen.2007.04.005

Rohleder, N., Beulen, E. S., Chen, E., Wolf, J. M., and Kirschbaum, C. (2007). Stress on the dance floor: the cortisol stress response to social-evaluative threat in competitive ballroom dancers. *Personal. Soc. Psychol. Bull.* 33, 69–84. doi: 10.1177/0146167206293986

Salvador, A., Suay, F., Gonzalez-Bono, E., and Serrano, M. A. (2003). Anticipatory cortisol, testosterone and psychological responses to judo competition in young men. *Psychoneuroendocrinology* 28, 364–375. doi: 10.1016/S0306-4530(02)00028-8

Smith, T. B., Hopkins, W. G., and Low, T. E. (2011). Are there useful physiological or psychological markers for monitoring overload training in elite rowers? *Int. J. Sports Physiol. Perform.* 6, 469–484. doi: 10.1123/ijspp.6.4.469

Stalder, T., Kirschbaum, C., Kudielka, B. L., Adam, E. K., Pruessner, J. C., Wüst, S., et al. (2016). Assessment of the cortisol awakening response: expert consensus guidelines. *Psychoneuroendocrinology* 63, 414–432. doi: 10.1016/j.psyneuen.2015.10.010

Strahler, K., Ehrlenspiel, F., Heene, M., and Brand, R. (2010). Competitive anxiety and cortisol awakening response in the week leading up to a compeition. *Psychol. Sport Exerc.* 11, 148–154. doi: 10.1016/j.psychsport.2009.10.003

van Paridon, K. N., Timmis, M. A., Nevison, C. M., and Bristow, M. (2017). The anticipatory stress response to sport competition; a systematic review with meta-analysis of cortisol reactivity. *BMC Open Sport Exercise Med.* 3:e000261. doi: 10.1136/bmjsem-2017-000261

Wetherell, M. A., Crown, A. L., Lightman, S. L., Miles, J. N. V., Kaye, J., and Vedhara, K. (2006). The four-dimensional stress test: psychological, sympathetic-adrenal-medullary, parasympathetic and hypothalamic-pituitary-adrenal responses following inhalation of 35% CO2. *Psychoneuroendocrinology* 31, 736–747. doi: 10.1016/j.psyneuen.2006.02.005

Wetherell, M. A., Lovell, B., and Smith, M. A. (2015). The effects of an anticipated challenge on diurnal cortisol secretion. *Stress Int. J. Biol. Stress* 18, 42–48. doi: 10.3109/10253890.2014.993967

Wolfram, M., Belingrath, S., Feurehahn, N., and Kudielka, B. M. (2013). Cortisol responses to naturalistic and laboratory stress in student teachers: comparison with a non-stress control day. *Stress. Health* 29, 143–149. doi: 10.1002/smi.2439

14

Alpine Ski Coaches' and Athletes' Perceptions of Factors Influencing Adaptation to Stress in the Classroom and on the Slopes

Paul Davis[1], Anton Halvarsson[1], Wictor Lundström[1] and Carolina Lundqvist[2]*

[1] *Department of Psychology, Umeå University, Umeå, Sweden,* [2] *Department of Behavioural Sciences and Learning, Linköping University, Linköping, Sweden*

Correspondence:
Paul Davis
paul.davis@umu.se

Research examining the student-athlete experience proposes a number of factors that can be both sources of stress and/or support. The dual career pathway offers a number of potential positive outcomes including psychological, social, and financial benefits; however, challenges including time management, fatigue, and restricted social activities are well documented. In consideration of the multidimensional student-athlete experience and the numerous factors that influence the complexity of potential stress, a mixed methods research study design was used in the study. First, data collected from surveys completed by 173 elite junior alpine skiers were analyzed to identify the degree to which athletes report experiencing stress associated with specific aspects pertaining to training, life, and organizational factors. These factors were then explored through semi-structured interviews with six coaches at the associated national elite sport schools. Taken collectively, athletes' reports of psychophysiological training stress on the Multidimensional Training Distress Scale were low. Scores on the college student-athletes' life stress scale revealed very low levels of general life stress; although the subscales associated with "performance demand" and "academic requirements" scored marginally higher. Scores on the Organizational Stressor Indicator for Sport Performers indicated low levels of organizational stress. The interviews with coaches elucidated the underlying factors potentially influencing athletes' positive adaptations to stress as they reported programming a number of strategies to reduce negative outcomes. Coaches aimed to teach athletes self-awareness and regulation strategies through the use of the training diaries and ongoing communication to promote positive adaptation to stress. A number of coaches also worked with sport psychology consultants to optimize athletes' training and study situations. Traditionally, research has noted high levels of stress in student-athletes due to co-occurring demands (school & sport); however, the data in the present study suggests that optimizing support mechanisms across domains can promote positive adaptations to potential sources of stress.

Keywords: emotions, coping, mixed methods, dual career athletes, student athlete

INTRODUCTION

Research examining the experience of adolescent student-athletes proposes that individuals aiming to achieve high levels of success within both sport and academic domains are prone to increased stress as a result of combined performance demands (Stambulova and Wylleman, 2015; Kristiansen, 2017). The perceived pressure of striving within the intertwined domains has been shown to contribute to reports of symptoms associated with burnout and mental health issues (Sorkkila et al., 2017b, 2018a). An athlete's ability to adapt to the stressful situation of the dual career pathway (i.e., combining sport and education, sport and work) may be influenced by the contributing factors and support mechanisms that comprise their environment (Stambulova et al., 2015). In particular, within the student-athlete's environment coaches have been identified as both a potential source of pressure as well as a support (Ronkainen et al., 2018). Further, the role of the coach is to promote athletes' positive adaptations to the demands of training and competition with the aim of maximizing performance outcomes; their perspective of athletes' development within the dual career pathway is particularly relevant (Gledhill and Harwood, 2015). Therefore, the purpose of the present study was to examine Swedish elite alpine skiers' reports of academic and sport related psychological stress in combination with coaches' perspectives of related factors influencing athletes' adaptations to stress.

Extensive research investigating the dual career pathway has highlighted problematic aspects derived from the combination of high level sport competition and academic study (see Stambulova and Wylleman, 2015 for a review). Historically, the responsibility for determining how best to navigate the co-occurring demands of academics and sport largely fell upon the athlete (Kristiansen, 2017). In the 1970s the Swedish Sports Confederation acknowledged both the risks and benefits for athletes pursuing a dual career pathway, and identified the need for student-athletes to be able to train and study in an educational environment that could support their sporting aspirations as well as develop academic skills. Subsequently, the first National Elite Sport Schools were established to support athletes in optimizing their holistic health and high performance (Stambulova et al., 2015). Currently, there are 51 National Elite Sport Schools across Sweden supporting about 1200 athletes competing in 30 sports[1]; 11 elite sport schools admit athletes competing in alpine skiing. The role of the sport schools in the development of adolescent student-athletes is particularly important as they are generally attended by individuals 16–19 years old; this age group of athletes are typically approaching or commencing the transition from junior to senior competition, and/or considering the difficult decision of withdrawing from participation in elite level competition (Pummell et al., 2008; Stambulova and Wylleman, 2014). The implications of this transition phase can be particularly impactful upon an athlete's identity as well as his/her adaptation to the stress underlying these formative years in adolescence (Brewer et al., 1993; López et al., 2015b; Gustafsson et al., 2018).

Adolescence has been identified as a key stage in which strategies promoting positive adaptation to stress and resilience can be developed (Gerber et al., 2013; White and Bennie, 2015). Extensive empirical research in sport suggests that athletes displaying high levels of sporting success and general wellbeing are those that can adapt when confronted with adversities and stressors (Fletcher and Sarkar, 2013; Galli and Gonzalez, 2014; Drew and Matthews, 2018). Multiple decades of research activity has sought to identify potential stressors within the athlete environment (Scanlan et al., 1991; Woodman and Hardy, 2001; McKay et al., 2008). Taken collectively, the findings across this research has led to the categorization of stressors into those that are associated with competitive performance, organizational factors, and personal life beyond the sport context (Fletcher et al., 2006; Sarkar and Fletcher, 2013). Adolescent student-athletes in particular, face an intensification of these potential stressors across domains as they enter a phase of increasing elite competition as well as escalating academic demands (Stambulova et al., 2015; Kristiansen, 2017). Moreover, their strategies to adapt to these stressors are in development as they gain increasing experience and feedback of their efficacy (Holt et al., 2005; Galli and Vealey, 2008; White and Bennie, 2015).

A number of psychological protective factors against the negative effects of stress have also been identified (Sarkar and Fletcher, 2013). In particular, the social support an athlete perceives is identified as being particularly influential to stress adaptation (Rosenfeld et al., 1989; Kerdijk et al., 2016; Hagiwara et al., 2017). Teammates, family, and coaches have been identified as being sources of social support for young elite athletes when dealing with competition and organizational stress (Kristiansen and Roberts, 2010). Coaches in particular can influence athletes' stress appraisals and adaptation, as well as performance outcomes and general health (Arnold et al., 2017; Dixon et al., 2017; Davis et al., 2018). Specifically, the quality of the coach-athlete relationship has been observed to be associated with stress appraisals and athlete wellbeing (Davis and Jowett, 2014; Nicholls et al., 2016). Coaches can promote athletes' development of resilience and positive adaptation to stress through the provision of social support as well as facilitating the development of emotion regulation strategies and functional skills to cope with stressors (Turner and Jones, 2014; Davis and Davis, 2016; Lu et al., 2016).

Typically high performance coaches operate within either a club setting or national team program separate from the sport school (Ronkainen et al., 2018). However, in Swedish National Elite Sport High Schools coaches are often hired as staff at the school and have the opportunity to act as a link for athletes between the domains of sport and academics (Stambulova et al., 2015). The opportunity for coaches to gain greater proximity to athletes' academic setting has the potential to increase coaches' awareness of the holistic experience of student-athletes; subsequently, this knowledge may influence both their coaching behaviors as well as the quality of their relationship with the athletes. Ultimately, this may also optimize student-athletes' stress adaptation and promote both high performance and health.

In consideration of the significant role of coaches in student-athletes' stress adaptation, the central research question in

[1] http://www.svenskidrott.se/elitidrottpagymnasiet/

the present study aimed to explore the underlying factors that influence student-athletes' experience of academic and sport related stress. In particular, to gain a comprehensive understanding of the context shaping student-athletes' reports of academic and sport related psychological stress, qualitative interviews with coaches were compared with athletes' scores on validated multidimensional stress scales using a mixed methods research design.

MATERIALS AND METHODS

Extensive research investigating the dual career pathway in sport has previously used research designs that predominantly focus solely upon student-athletes' perceptions of a range of variables associated with health and performance (see Stambulova and Wylleman, 2019). Although both qualitative and quantitative methods have been used widely across the study of dual career athletes, very limited studies have used mixed methods research (MMR; e.g., Sorkkila et al., 2018b) and to our knowledge no studies have combined data collected from a variety of participants (e.g., athletes and coaches). In consideration of the present study's research question, as well as the multidimensionality of student-athletes' experience of stress and the role of significant others (i.e., coaches) potentially impacting upon the complexity of their stress, a MMR study design was used. Bryman et al. (2008) highlight the following criteria in judging the quality of a study and the decision to use MMR: relevance to research questions; transparency; a rationale for using mixed methods research; and the need for integration of mixed methods findings. Specific to the domain of sport, the use of MMR offers many benefits for sport psychology research (Moran et al., 2011) including the ability to offset weaknesses and provide stronger inferences, triangulation, and completeness (Hagger and Chatzisarantis, 2011; Horn, 2011). Although, Sparkes (2015) and Smith and McGannon (2018) note potential challenges with the use of MMR in sport and exercise psychology research (e.g., problematic assumptions and integrating findings), if these issues are considered throughout the research process the integration of research techniques may provide a thorough investigation of a phenomenon of interest (Teddlie and Tashakkori, 2012). These techniques can be typified by both focused descriptive cross-sectional data collection to identify relationships between multiple factors (Gratton and Jones, 2010), in combination with follow-up approaches aiming to collect rich, descriptive data depicting complex experiences and perspectives (Silverman, 2006). The present study collected quantitative survey responses from student-athletes to analyze their experience of psychological stress, in combination with semi-structured interviews devised by the researchers to explore coaches' perceptions of athletes' experiences and associated factors (Kvale and Brinkmann, 2009). The findings from the quantitative and qualitative data were subsequently integrated through a process of comparing and contrasting analyses to provide a more comprehensive understanding of stress adaptation within the dual career pathway of adolescent alpine athletes (Creswell and Tashakkori, 2007).

Participants

A sample of 173 junior alpine skiers (78 male, 93 female, 2 did not respond) was recruited from the eleven national elite sports high schools in Sweden that admit alpine skiers. The athletes' mean age was 17.5 (*SD* = 1.15); they reported an average skiing experience of 12.78 years (*SD* = 2.89) and trained on average 13.42 h per week (*SD* = 4.07). The athletes were at various stages of their studies: 58 (34%) first, 51 (29%) second, 38 (22%) third, and 26 (15%) final year of study.

To explore factors related to the student-athletes' experiences of psychological stress a purposive sampling technique was adopted (Flick, 2008) to recruit a sample of six coaches (five male, one female), that were each employed at a different national sport high school from which the alpine skiers were recruited. The mean age of the coaches was 46.25 (*SD* = 6.55); they reported being involved in coaching alpine skiing an average of 14.00 years (*SD* = 2.71). The present study was appraised and approved by Umeå University's Coaching Program review panel for student research, the panel is responsible for evaluating ethical aspects of the research; additional ethical scrutiny was deemed not to be required as per applicable institutional and national guidelines and regulations. Principals at each of the participating national elite sports high schools reviewed the ethical considerations of the study prior to approving the commencement of data collection.

Measures

Multi-Component Training Distress Scale

The Multi-component training distress scale (MTDS; Main and Grove, 2009) is a multidimensional questionnaire consisting of 22 items that aim to assess symptoms concerning training distress. It includes six subscales in total; four subscales are measured in terms of their frequency: "depressed mood," "perceived vigor," "perceived stress" and "general fatigue" scored on a five-point Likert scale ranging from "*never*" (0) to "*very often*" (4). The subscale perceived vigor is scored positively, with higher scores reflecting greater frequency of experiencing higher levels of energy. The remaining two subscales are measured in terms of their intensity: "physical symptoms," "sleep disturbance" scored on a five-point Likert scale ranging from "*not at all*" (0) to "*extreme amount*" (4). The MTDS has acceptable reliability and evidence of construct validity; in the present study the overall internal consistency was α = 0.84. More specifically, the individual subscales demonstrated the following Cronbach's α: depressed mood = 0.84, perceived vigor = 0.76, physical symptoms = 0.50, sleep disturbances = 0.87, perceived stress = 0.81, fatigue = 0.80.

College Student-Athletes' Life Stress Scale

The college student-athletes' life stress scale (CSALSS; Lu et al., 2012) is designed to capture the current state of stress among intercollegiate student-athletes. It is comprised of 24 items that reflect potential stressors respondents may encounter in their everyday life and in sports. The scale includes eight subscales divided into two categories; sport-specific stressors (i.e., "sports injury," "performance demand," "coach relationships," "training adaptation") and general life stressors (i.e., "interpersonal relationship," "romantic relationship," "family relationship," "academic requirements"). The CSALSS presents potential answers in terms of their frequency scored on a six-point Likert scale ranging from 1 (*never*) to 6 (*always*). The CSALSS examines sport-specific stressors and general life stressors and has reported Cronbach's α of its eight factors ranging from 0.72 to 0.86, with the reliability for all items being 0.88. The scale has been subject to further tests for discriminant and concurrent validity and report standard psychometric results (Lu et al., 2012). The CSALSS demonstrated good internal consistency with Cronbach's α = 0.82 for sport-specific stress and 0.83 for general life stress in the present study. More specifically, the individual subscales demonstrated the following Cronbach's α: sports injury = 0.82, performance demands = 0.60, coach relationships = 0.80, training adaptation = 0.67, interpersonal relationships = 0.86, romantic relationships = 0.62, family relationships = 0.81, academic requirements = 0.72.

Organizational Stressor Indicator for Sport Performers

The Organizational Stressor Indicator for Sport Performers (OSI-SP; Arnold et al., 2013) was developed to comprehensively measure the organizational pressures that sport performers may encounter. The OSI-SP consists of 23 items with five subscales: "goals and development," "logistics and operations," "team and culture," "coaching," and "selection." Each of the subscales are evaluated in terms of their frequency, intensity, and duration. Items on the OSI-SP are scored on a six-point Likert scale ranging from 0 (*never*) to 5 (*always*). The OSI-SP has been validated through a series of studies, with support provided for its internal consistency (Cronbach's alpha coefficients ranged from 0.75 to 0.85 for the frequency scales, 0.71 to 0.83 for the intensity scales, and 0.74 to 0.83 for the duration scales), content, concurrent, discriminant, and factorial validity (Arnold et al., 2013). In the present study the frequency aspect of the dimensions were measured; Arnold et al. (2013) state that researchers requiring a shorter version of the indicator would benefit using the frequency scale alone. Regarding internal consistency, in the present study the five subscales of OSI-SP demonstrated the following Cronbach's α: goals and development = 0.81, logistics and operation = 0.89, team and culture = 0.86, coaching = 0.89, selection = 0.43. In consideration of the low Cronbach's α for the "selection" subscale we inspected the two items comprising the subscale (i.e., "*how my team is selected*" and "*selection of my team for competition*") and determined that they were not entirely relevant for these athletes as their selection to the team was established upon admission to the high school; therefore the subscale was not included in subsequent analyses.

The process of back-translation (Brislin, 1970) was used to translate all of original questionnaires from English into Swedish. Specifically, a bilingual individual first translated the English version of each scale into Swedish and then another bilingual individual independently translated the Swedish version back to English to compare it with the original versions for confirmation of clarity and accuracy. Revisions to the Swedish versions were discussed and final versions were agreed following the process of inter-translator reliability.

Procedure

Initial discussions and a subsequent study proposal outlining the purpose of the present study were exchanged between the authors of the study and the Swedish Ski Association. Upon receiving an indication of support from the Ski Association, coaches at all of the National Elite Sports High Schools were verbally informed about the purpose of the study at the Swedish National Junior Championships. Emails were then sent to principals and head coaches at each school to update and inform them about the protocol of the study. All 11 schools replied by phone or email with approval and contact information of an individual at the school to support data collection; the total number of student-athletes at the schools with the potential to participate was 296, subsequently this number of questionnaires was sent across the schools.

The participating athletes completed the questionnaire in a classroom setting or a training session under the supervision of a teacher or coach. Prior to completing the questionnaire, athletes were provided information sheets about the nature of the study. They were informed participation was voluntary and that they could skip any questions they did not want to answer or discontinue their participation at any time. After the participants had signed the consent form and completed the questionnaires they placed their questionnaires and consent form in two separate envelopes to ensure their completed responses were kept separate from their names and any potentially identifying information. The sealed envelopes were then mailed to the research team. The data collection occurred toward the end of the competitive season with approximately 6 weeks of events remaining.

Following the analysis of the questionnaire data, it was determined that greater understanding of the alpine athletes' dual-career context was required and that qualitative data collected from an alternative source (i.e., coaches) would be relevant in exploring the research question as well as support the rationale for using MMR (Bryman et al., 2008). The qualitative interviews were developed upon reflection of the findings from the athletes' responses and in review of research literature of the student-athlete experience. More specifically, coaches' perceptions of the potential sources of stress and the support mechanisms that were present within the context of the National Elite Sports High Schools were explored. Therefore, the questions comprising the interview guide were grouped into three sections: (i) perceptions of stress as it relates to student-athlete performance and wellbeing; (ii) sources of stress relating to performance and life in general; (iii) strategies/support systems targeting student-athlete stress. The interviews were semi-structured and contained primarily open-ended questions aimed at encouraging insightful responses. Initially, introductory questions were asked allowing the participant to discuss their general perceptions/personal definition of psychological stress. Questions progressed to be more specific in nature by asking participants to outline the implications of psychological stress on student-athletes' performance and wellbeing, contributing factors, and sources of support.[2]

[2]The interview guides are available from the first author upon request.

Coaches at the schools where athletes completed the questionnaires were contacted via email and/or telephone and provided information about the research plan to conduct interviews to follow up the questionnaires and were asked if they would be interest in taking part in the study. Those who responded with a confirmation of intention to participate were subsequently contacted to arrange for the completion of the interview. The second author conducted all the interviews as he possesses experience of alpine ski coaching and was able to share experiences from the sport to develop rapport with the coaches.

Prior to commencing the interview, each participant provided his/her consent to be recorded and was reminded that participation in the study was voluntary. The confidentiality of the coaches was assured by the author conducting the interviews. The interviews took place over a 2-week period and were conducted individually over the telephone. The participants were told they would be interviewed about their perceptions of student-athletes' experiences of stress related to school and performance, as well as potential sources of stress and support. When required, follow up questions were used to encourage further discussion or if participants did not fully understand the question. The interviews ranged in time from 15 to 35 min and were simultaneously recorded on two digital audio recorders. The interviews were conducted in Swedish and subsequently transcribed verbatim; transcripts were checked by the interviewer to ensure accuracy.

Data Analysis

First, to examine student-athletes' experience of psychological stress, responses to questionnaires were analyzed to identify potential factors that were highlighted by the athletes. Descriptive statistics and bivariate correlations are reported to identify the degree to which athletes reported experiencing stress associated with these factors. In conjunction with the quantitative data analyses of athletes' reports, coaches' perceptions of the factors influencing student-athletes' psychological stress were analyzed. The transcripts from the interviews with the coaches underwent coding and were scrutinized using inductive content analysis.

Coding

A variety of approaches to analyzing qualitative data has been used within sport psychology research exploring psychological stress; in the present study, a conventional content analysis procedure was selected for use to analyze, organize, and articulate the responses of participants. Inductive content analysis was used to assist with the development and interpretation of categories from each of the interview transcripts (Hsieh and Shannon, 2005). This technique was identified as being applicable as it permitted perceptions of specific factors associated with sources of stress to be acknowledged (e.g., organizational stress); categorizing the coaches' responses also helped differentiate the multidimensional aspects of the dual-career pathway (e.g., academic and sport demands).

The initial stage of the coding process was open coding, this allows researchers to engage the data in the transcripts and promote the identification of raw-data quotes related to student-athletes' psychological stress (Hsieh and Shannon, 2005). The first and second authors read through the transcripts independently; they produced notes to each segment to facilitate subsequent reviews and enable the coding of chunks of data regardless of the context. Quotes which characterized common themes were collated and labeled as categories prior to being pooled and identified as higher order categories (Aronson, 1995). In sum, categories were structured into general dimensions promoting the development of a comprehensive overview of participants' collective perceptions to be established (Patton, 2002; Vaismoradi et al., 2016). Two members of the research team undertook the process of coding and established the higher order themes independently; these themes were debated extensively and agreed upon amongst the research team. Further, colleagues of the investigators acted as critical friends (Sparkes and Smith, 2014) and offered a critical perspective of the proposed themes that were identified from the analysis process.

RESULTS

The present study sought to examine the psychological stress of student-athletes studying at National Elite Sport High Schools in Sweden and competing in alpine skiing; underlying factors associated with athletes' adaptation to stress were also explored. First, data collected from a survey were analyzed to identify the degree to which athletes reported experiencing stress associated with specific aspects pertaining to training, life, and organizational factors. These factors were then explored through semi-structured interviews undertaken with coaches at the high schools to elucidate their influence upon stress adaptation within the dual career pathway of adolescent alpine athletes.

To examine the extent to which athletes reported symptoms of psychophysiological stress related to training, scores on the MTDS were scrutinized. Taken collectively, athletes' reports of training distress were generally low (see **Table 1**, for descriptives) with most of the subscales' (i.e., depressed mood, physical symptoms, sleep disturbance, perceived stress) mean score positioned between the range of "*a little bit*" and "*moderate amount*;" the only exception was general fatigue (M = 2.44; SD = 0.82) scoring between "*moderate amount*" and "*quite a bit*." Athletes also reported higher scores on the positively oriented subscale perceived vigor (M = 2.51; SD = 0.68) indicting they frequently experienced higher levels of energy and feeling alert.

Scores on the MTDS were then compared with measures of sport specific stressors on the CSALSS (i.e., sports injury, performance demand, coach relationships, training adaptation), again athletes' reported very low levels of stress with mean scores between "*never*" and "*rarely*" for the factors of coach relationships and training adaptation. The subscales associated with sports injury and performance demand, scored marginally higher with the mean scores between the range of "*rarely*" and "*sometimes*" (see **Table 1**, for descriptives). General fatigue scores on the MTDS were correlated with measures of sports injury $r = 0.219$, $p < 0.01$ and performance demand $r = 0.304$, $p < 0.01$; although sleep disturbance was noted as being most strongly associated with general fatigue $r = 0.486$, $p < 0.01$. In consideration of athletes' scores on the OSI-SP, the subscales of

TABLE 1 | Descriptive statistics, correlations for multi-component training distress scale, college student-athlete life stress scale, and organizational stressor indicator for sport performers.

	1	2	3	4	5	6	7	8	9	10	11	12	13	14	15	16	17	18
1. Stress	1																	
2. Depressed mood	0.591**	1																
3. Vigor	−0.188*	−0.270**	1															
4. Physical symptoms	0.204**	0.265**	0.065	1														
5. Sleep disturbance	0.459**	0.555**	−0.173*	0.289**	1													
6. Fatigue	0.457**	0.434**	−0.358**	0.242**	0.486**	1												
7. Injury	0.253**	0.408**	−0.001	0.365**	0.291**	0.219**	1											
8. Performance demands	0.523**	0.532**	−0.060	0.335**	0.317**	0.304**	0.423**	1										
9. Coach relationship	0.371*	0.321**	−0.229**	0.117	0.174*	0.310**	0.107	0.386**	1									
10. Training adaptation	0.478**	0.509**	−0.218**	0.253**	0.303**	0.416**	0.280**	0.532**	0.659**	1								
11. Interpersonal relationship	0.345**	0.548**	−0.133	0.165*	0.158*	0.164*	0.216**	0.459**	0.421**	0.486**	1							
12. Romantic relationship	0.215**	0.447**	−0.083	0.131	0.067	0.279**	0.216**	0.369**	0.363**	0.451**	0.575**	1						
13. Family relationship	0.358**	0.465**	−0.171*	0.187*	0.291**	0.366**	0.197*	0.390**	0.239**	0.387**	0.412**	0.252**	1					
14. Academic requirements	0.467**	0.408**	−0.070	0.227**	0.257**	0.404**	0.220**	0.437**	0.246**	0.403**	0.255**	0.304**	0.382**	1				
15. Goals and development	0.544**	0.542**	−0.108	0.389**	0.419**	0.319**	0.643**	0.737**	0.362**	0.504**	0.319**	0.250**	0.393**	0.443**	1			
16. Logistics operations	0.492**	0.509**	−0.064	0.394**	0.311**	0.397**	0.308**	0.485**	0.439**	0.498**	0.430**	0.460**	0.399**	0.414**	0.549**	1		
17. Team and culture	0.507**	0.507**	−0.156*	0.328**	0.416**	0.246**	0.252**	0.474**	0.481**	0.452**	0.536**	0.264**	0.391**	0.311**	0.479**	0.570**	1	
18. Coaching	0.382**	0.382**	−0.251**	0.027	0.131	0.283**	0.079	0.266**	0.812**	0.603**	0.326**	0.277**	0.216**	0.243**	0.306**	0.346**	0.461**	1
M	1.96	1.16	2.51	1.53	1.05	2.44	2.32	2.46	1.86	1.99	1.73	1.64	1.72	2.50	1.74	0.84	1.10	0.78
SD	0.81	0.82	0.68	0.71	1.03	0.82	1.32	0.94	0.96	0.88	0.98	0.81	0.94	0.99	1.02	0.66	1.04	1.07

*N = 173; *p < 0.05; **p < 0.01. Range of scores for: "depressed mood", "perceived vigor", "perceived stress" "general fatigue" is 0 to 4 representing frequency; "physical symptoms", "sleep disturbance" is 0 to 4 representing intensity; "sports injury", "performance demand", "coach relationships", "training adaptation", "interpersonal relationship", "romantic relationship", "family relationship", "academic requirements" is 1 to 6 representing frequency; "goals and development", "logistics and operations", "team and culture", "coaching" is 0 to 5 representing frequency.*

goals and development and team and culture were on the low end of the six point range between "*rarely*" and "*sometimes*," whilst the subscales of logistics and coaching were in the range between "*never*" and "*rarely*" (see **Table 1**, for descriptives).

Athletes' reports of general life stressors were also examined using scores on the CSLASS relating to the subscales identified as interpersonal relationship, romantic relationship, family relationship, and academic requirements (see **Table 1**, for descriptives). Scores indicating the frequency that athletes experienced these stressors were very low with means ranging between "*never*" and "*always*" for all of the subscales except academic requirements (M = 2.50; SD = 0.99) in the range between "*rarely*" and "*sometimes*." It may be noted that academic requirements was the highest scoring source of stress of all the measures recorded, and was most strongly correlated with reports of perceived stress on the MTDS $r = 0.467$, $p < 0.01$. Overall, the analyses of athletes' responses to the various assessments indicated that they perceived relatively low levels of stress.

To gain a comprehensive understanding of the context shaping student-athletes' reports of academic and sport related psychological stress, qualitative interviews with coaches were undertaken to collect data exploring the conditions influencing athletes' scores on the stress scales. In particular, the factors influencing athletes' overall experience of stress were elucidated by the interviews with the coaches as they identified that athletes' expected themselves to perform to a high level in both sport and academic study (see **Table 2** for higher order themes and categories). Further, multiple coaches outlined that athletes' previous experience of being "high achievers" in sport and academia guided expectations and evaluations of success. "There are many that are high achievers in elementary school and then they come here and want to continue on the same level and have very good results" (P1).

TABLE 2 | Summary of higher order themes and categories pertaining to coaches' perceptions of factors influencing athletes' stress adaptation.

Higher order themes	Categories	Subcategories
Sources of stress	Appraisals and expectations of performance	Athletes' previous levels of success Athletes' personal sport goals Athletes' comparison with teammates Parents' expectations
	Academic requirements	Conflict between balancing sport and academic demands Athletes' personal standards and goals
	Limited resources	Time management Costs of competition
	Friends and Family	Over-involvement Challenge of independent living Fear of missing out/feeling isolated
Support mechanisms	Friends and Family	Recovery outside of sport Investment in talent development
	Teammates	Empathy Affiliation
	Coaches	Monitoring of athletes Connection and communication Programming of training
	School	Flexibility Support staff and services Sport focused educational environment

Coaches also differentiated the sources of stress athletes experienced; they noted that the stress had varying implications for performance and wellbeing depending on its initial source. In particular, it was suggested that stress may facilitate sport performance if athletes were able to understand its origin and regulate its intensity; for example, fear arising from the anticipation of a challenging course could enhance an athlete's concentration and promote greater investment in preparation, "The nervousness itself is a type of additional resource. And it's something they should learn to manage and use for something positive. You get a focus and you get a certain rise of adrenaline that you can use" (P1).

Alternatively, coaches viewed academic stress as being largely negative for athlete wellbeing. Collectively, the coaches outlined a number of factors contributing to academic stress; in particular, time management was a challenge when the time athlete's spent traveling and training was difficult to balance with academic requirements. Coach number 3 outlined how the issue of balancing time allocated between sport and studies is exacerbated when athletes are attempting to make the national team and choosing to attend an increased number of competitions in order to gain FIS points:

> In our sport there is a stress about being selected for a junior national team and it is of course a great advantage to join a junior team; you get skis, you get clothes, you get everything possible, and a lot of training. It's obviously a great advantage to be accepted there and it also comes as a stress. You can compete 100 times in 1 year or you can compete 25 and then the question is what is best (strategy to make the team). Plan 25 competitions or leave it up to fate all the time and hope that some time it will work.

The financial cost associated with traveling was also noted by three coaches as a potential stressor for the athlete and their family. Investing in the athletes' pursuit of elite level sporting success placed a burden on the family in terms of costs as well as time spent traveling to competitions. On a related note, three coaches reported that some parents contribute to athletes' stress by being too involved. "Committed parents who are behind their children and helping in a healthy way, as I see it, are the ones who are in the background. While those that go 'all-in' and plan competitions and are involved in training and everything else, that can be wrong" (P3). However, family and friends at home (outside of the high school) could also provide support to athletes; sincere and non-judgmental interest in the athlete's development was appreciated by the coaches. Moreover, family and friends may offer an outlet for recovery by providing a space for athletes that was not connected directly with skiing or training. ". . .it can be nice to spend time with people who don't ask about how much you squat or how fast you ran 3000 meters . . .." (P4). Although, one coach suggested that the potential for feelings associated with a "fear of missing out" can arise when athletes are aware of challenges managing social relationships via connections with friends on social media.

Athletes' relationships within sport were also influential to their accounts of psychological stress. Multiple coaches provided details about how relationships between teammates were largely positive as the understanding of the shared experience lead to feelings of empathy being exchanged. However, two coaches did note that when athletes compared themselves with teammates' rates of development, it could be a source of stress, "They should not compare their results but they do it all the time" (P2).

All of the coaches predominantly viewed themselves as being supportive in athletes' positive adaptations to stress. The coaches reported programming a number of strategies to reduce the negative effects of stress. First, they spoke about the importance of monitoring levels of stress through communication with the athlete. Frequently "checking in" was noted as being central to understanding the athlete experience; although, varying levels of frequency and formality were reported across the coaches' interviews. Most schools scheduled meetings at least twice an academic term (e.g., beginning and middle), with some schools scheduling meetings to occur monthly or once a week. Three coaches also mentioned less formal opportunities for gaining status updates from athletes when seeing them at the school or time spent together at training, "Usually you can take the lift up with someone to check how it is going" (P2).

Remote forms of monitoring athletes' adaptation to psychosocial and training factors were also outlined by coaches; training diaries were used at some of the schools. At one school first year students were encouraged to keep a journal of their general thoughts and experiences, then in the second year it was more structured and obligatory. Other schools used online training logs that were shared between athletes and coaches and provided a basis for follow up discussions. "Usually once every week or every second week I will take a look in the training journal to check if they are OK and doing what they are supposed to be doing" (P6).

Through the use of the training diaries and ongoing communication, coaches aimed to teach athletes self-awareness and regulation strategies to promote positive adaptation to stress associated with training and competition demands. Coaches also adopted more pro-active roles in optimizing recovery and preventing negative adaptations, "...many are very, very ambitious and sometimes our role might be to put on the 'brakes' more than to apply the 'gas'" (P3). The programming of training sessions was often based upon consideration of athletes' academic requirements; specifically, four coaches outlined limiting training sessions in order to offer time for academic demands. For example, it was a common practice at multiple schools for coaches to avoid training on the Monday following a weekend competition in order for students to catch up on the school work they likely missed on the preceding Friday due to travel arrangements.

The elite sport high schools also attempted to support the student-athletes by offering flexible schedules for classes and assessments that complemented competition schedules. Further, mental health support services were available at all of the schools; however, these provisions were only initiated in severe cases, and coaches suggested that this was not required very often. Two coaches commented that their school had mental coaches that engaged with the athletes to varying degrees. These mental coaches often worked across all the sports offered at the school "I think it is very good, that we have been given the opportunity to have a mental coach; that we can cooperate and help each other" (P2). Although the alpine coaches noted that the mental coach's effectiveness was enhanced when he/she possessed sport specific knowledge. In terms of more sport specific support, one school offered mentors from the skiing community to the athletes in order to provide an additional support mechanism in preventing negative adaptation to stress. "An athlete should be able to check with their training mentor to check where they are heading, this can help them feel secure" (P3).

GENERAL DISCUSSION

Previous research highlights that student-athletes are typically extremely motivated to excel in both education and sport (Lupo et al., 2015; Stambulova et al., 2015; Ryba et al., 2017) and coaches in the present study suggest that the alpine athletes they work with also expect themselves to be successful in both domains. However, athletes' scores across the measures of the sport and life stress indicate they were not experiencing particularly high levels of stress. As a source of stress, academic requirements scored highest; although athletes' reports indicate that stress related to demands at school were not frequently a cause for concern. Research by López et al. (2015a) of Spanish student-athletes highlights that the most significant barrier to studying is time management. Time management was also reported by coaches in the present study as being a challenge for the athletes; therefore, time management skills appear to be an important skill to teach student-athletes at an early stage in the dual career process.

In the present study, coaches outlined that time spent traveling to competitions has implications that extend beyond the athlete to include their family. Research examining stress in youth sport identifies that the time and money spent in high level sport participation can have a negative impact upon the wellness of both the athletes and the parents due to excessive investment (Harwood and Knight, 2009). The alpine student-athletes indicated that their family and romantic relationships were not frequently a source of stress; coaches also outlined how friends outside of sport were a source of support in providing an outlet for alternative interests and recovery. Related research with data collected from sport parents suggests, however, that maintaining these relationships can be difficult for talented young athletes (Elliott et al., 2018). In consideration of the positive effects of friendships outside of sport found in the present study, and the difficulties in maintaining these relationships reported in previous research, it appears important to support athletes' development of social skills and efforts in nurturing important social connections.

Relationships within sport between teammates were also noted to be influential to athletes' stress adaptation. Coaches suggested that teammates for the most part were supportive of each other, and empathy associated with shared experiences helped athletes' stress management. Athletes indicated that the team and culture surrounding them was not a frequent source of stress. Research investigating the availability of social support from teammates has been shown to be associated with lower risk of burnout and enhanced self-determined motivation (DeFreese and Smith, 2013; Appleby et al., 2018). This is particularly important for coaches, sport psychology practitioners, and sport schools to note as research indicates that athletes' performance expectations in the domains of sport and school can influence their risk for burnout (Sorkkila et al., 2017a, 2018b).

A central finding taken from the integration of the quantitative and qualitative data analysis was the role of the coach in athletes' stress adaptation and the underlying mechanisms of developing and maintaining a high quality coach-athlete relationships. Athletes' scores on the measure of coaches as a source of organizational stress were the lowest recorded on the scale. In review of the interviews with the coaches it was apparent that extensive efforts were made on the part of coaches to connect with their athletes through a range of communication strategies. Research suggests that effective communication between a coach and athlete can optimize the coach-athlete relationship and assist in protecting athletes from negative implications of stress (e.g., exhaustion; Rhind and Jowett, 2011; Davis and Davis, 2016; Lu et al., 2016; Davis et al., 2018). In addition to regular face to face communication across a number of venues (e.g., chairlift, school hallway) coaches used remote communication tools to collect information from the athletes. The collection of subjective self-ratings (e.g., stress, mental fatigue, motivation) has been shown to be important information in monitoring athletes' training load to optimize performance and prevent injury (Coyne et al., 2018). Further, feedback from athletes was integrated with information regarding other factors influencing athletes' wellbeing (e.g., academic demands), and coaches reported adjusting training protocols accordingly. Sorkkila et al. (2018b) interviews with Finnish athletes highlight that athletes appreciate adaptations to training schedules in consideration of academic demands as well as competitive seasons.

The flexibility of academic and training schedules was one feature of the National Elite Sport Schools that appeared to benefit athletes' stress adaptation. Further coaches noted the provision of mental health support services and mental skills coaches within the schools acted as support mechanisms for athletes. However, a lack of sport specific knowledge on the part of the psychological support could be a barrier to their effectiveness. To obtain a successful support provision, the importance of applied sport psychology practitioners to thoroughly learn about the sport and its conditions is well documented (e.g., Ravizza, 1988; Gould et al., 1991; Pain and Harwood, 2004). Sport specific support can also be sought through the use of mentors and their effectiveness is well established within other areas of sport (e.g., women coaches; Vinson et al., 2016), and many North American sport programs use mentors extensively with student-athletes (e.g., Perna et al., 1996; Hoffmann and Loughead, 2016); however, their use in European academic-sport programs to promote athletes' health and high performance has not been as well documented or evaluated.

The present mixed methods research study not only provided an overview of various psychological stress symptoms reported by elite adolescent alpine student-athletes, it also offered unique insight from the coaches responsible for working with the athletes in their sport and academic development. Thus, the results contribute not only to an understanding of various stressors that may be present when adolescents attend national elite sport schools but also various efforts (e.g., support by mentors and practical arrangements) that may facilitate the combination of sport and studies. Importantly, the results in this study indicate that the combination of academic study and sport does not automatically induce high levels of stress among young athletes. Rather, the thoughtful efforts of the coaches to support and care for the athletes and the overall structure and support resources the sports program itself includes seem to be of great importance to young athletes' stress experiences. A comprehensive understanding of different supportive factors in the environment and personal strategies that young athletes may need to successfully develop both in school and in sport also helps to customize and increase relevant support to this young population. This project is the first to focus specifically on student-athletes competing in the sport of alpine skiing, as well as recruit coaches directly employed at the elite sport high schools.

The study does, however, have a number of limitations that warrant discussion. Specifically, the cross-sectional data does not permit conclusions regarding causation to be determined. Longitudinal research would enhance knowledge derived from the present study and enable researchers to observe changes in stress adaptation and fluctuations of the impact of specific factors over time. Moreover, longitudinal research incorporating objective measures of stress reactivity (e.g., biomarkers; Blume et al., 2018) would supplement self-report data. One challenge to longitudinal data is the attrition of participants; the present study may also have suffered indirectly from this issue as those student-athletes that were potentially overwhelmed with stress may have been absent at the time of data collection and/or dropped out of the school earlier in the course of their studies. That said, the interviews with the coaches offered the opportunity for those students that may have dropped out from the program to be represented from the coaches' perspectives. The contributing factors influencing student-athlete drop out are difficult to capture with traditional approaches to data collection undertaken at the schools. Future research investigating stress adaptation in sport would be enhanced by collecting data from individuals that choose to withdraw from the stressful situation. Additionally, collecting data from multiple sources (e.g., coaches, parents) that were involved with the athlete's experience may elucidate the factors influencing stress adaptation.

Extensive research attention has been paid to the dual career pathway and advanced understanding of the student-athlete experience. Further research is required with alternative research designs and methods using a variety of data sources to gain greater insight from key stakeholders. Developing a more comprehensive understanding of the factors underlying stress adaption will enhance both the performance and holistic health of the student-athlete. The National Elite Sport Schools in Sweden were originally implemented to facilitate the combination of school and high-level sport. Thus, the aim was thereby to contribute to a positive and helpful overall solution for young athletes who wished to strive to reach the elite sport level in their sports. Contrary to this original aim, a traditional assumption in sport psychology research is that the combination of academic study and high-level sport may also involve challenges that could make athletes vulnerable to increased levels of stress (cf. Stambulova and Wylleman, 2015; Sallen et al., 2018). In the present study, the stress levels reported by the athletes were nevertheless relatively low in intensity. Thus, the data in the present study do not support the assumption of increased stress levels among student-athletes. Importantly, what has been less considered in previous research is the consideration of various levels of psychosocial resources student-athletes possess, their level of resilience, as well as the possibility of increased maturity and personal development that attending a national elite sport school may also plausibly contribute. In light of this consideration, instead of a unilateral search of reported stress experiences based on common assumptions, which may also increase the risk of confirmation-bias, future research would be well served by paying attention to potential psychosocial resources and supportive systems within the school-sport environment which may act to counteract stress and potentially promote psychological growth among student-athletes. The present study contributes to the literature with a first step toward such an approach in which the focus was to explore both reported stress experiences, as well as contextually supportive factors in the student-athlete life-situation.

ETHICS STATEMENT

This study was carried out in accordance with the recommendations of "Tränarprogrammet/Coaching Program review committee for Student Research at Umeå University" with written informed consent from all subjects. All subjects gave written informed consent in accordance with the Declaration of Helsinki. The protocol was approved by the Tränarprogrammet/Coaching Program review committee for Student Research at Umeå University as well as each of the participating schools.

AUTHOR CONTRIBUTIONS

PD designed the study, analyzed the data, and prepared the manuscript. AH designed the study, collected and analyzed the data, and reviewed the manuscript. WL designed the study, collected and analyzed the data. CL designed aspects of the study, consulted on the analyses and wrote sections as well as reviewed the manuscript.

REFERENCES

Appleby, R., Davis, P., Davis, L., and Gustafsson, H. (2018). Examining perceptions of teammates' burnout and training hours in athlete burnout. *J. Clin. Sport Psychol.* 12, 316–332. doi: 10.1123/jcsp.2017-0037

Arnold, R., Fletcher, D., and Daniels, K. (2013). Development and validation of the organizational stressor indicator for sport performers (OSI-SP). *J. Sport Exerc. Psychol.* 35, 180–196. doi: 10.1123/jsep.35.2.180

Arnold, R., Fletcher, D., and Daniels, K. (2017). Organisational stressors, coping, and outcomes in competitive sport. *J. Sports Sci.* 35, 694–703. doi: 10.1080/02640414.2016.1184299

Aronson, J. (1995). A pragmatic view of thematic analysis. *Qualitat. Rep.* 2, 1–3.

Blume, K., Körber, N., Hoffmann, D., and Wolfarth, B. (2018). Training load, immune status, and clinical outcomes in young athletes: a controlled, prospective, longitudinal study. *Front. Physiol.* 9:120. doi: 10.3389/fphys.2018.00120

Brewer, B. W., Van Raalte, J. L., and Linder, D. E. (1993). Athletic identity: hercules' muscles or achilles' heel? *Int. J. Sport Psychol.* 24, 237–254.

Brislin, R. W. (1970). Back-translation for cross-cultural research. *J. Cross. Cult. Psychol.* 1, 185–216. doi: 10.1177/135910457000100301

Bryman, A., Becker, S., and Sempik, J. (2008). Quality criteria for quantitative, qualitative and mixed methods research: a view from social policy. *Int. J. Soc. Res. Methodol.* 11, 261–276. doi: 10.1136/bmjopen-2015-010034

Coyne, J. O., Haff, G. G., Coutts, A. J., Newton, R. U., and Nimphius, S. (2018). The current state of subjective training load monitoring—a practical perspective and call to action. *Sports Med. Open* 4:58. doi: 10.1186/s40798-018-0172-x

Creswell, J., and Tashakkori, A. (2007). Editorial: developing publishable mixed methods manuscripts. *J. Mixed Methods Res.* 1, 107–111. doi: 10.1177/1558689806298644

Davis, L., Appleby, R., Davis, P., Wetherell, M., and Gustafsson, H. (2018). The role of coach-athlete relationship quality in team sport athletes' psychophysiological exhaustion: implications for physical and cognitive performance. *J. Sports Sci.* 36, 1985–1992. doi: 10.1080/02640414.2018.1429176

Davis, L., and Jowett, S. (2014). Coach–athlete attachment and the quality of the coach–athlete relationship: implications for athlete's well-being. *J. Sports Sci.* 32, 1454–1464. doi: 10.1080/02640414.2014.898183

Davis, P. A., and Davis, L. (2016). "Emotions and emotion regulation in coaching," in *The Psychology of Effective Coaching and Management*, ed. P. A. Davis (New York, NY: Nova Science Publishers Inc.), 285–306.

DeFreese, J. D., and Smith, A. L. (2013). Teammate social support, burnout, and self-determined motivation in collegiate athletes. *Psychol. Sport Exerc.* 14, 258–265. doi: 10.1016/j.psychsport.2012.10.009

Dixon, M., Turner, M. J., and Gillman, J. (2017). Examining the relationships between challenge and threat cognitive appraisals and coaching behaviours in football coaches. *J. Sports Sci.* 35, 2446–2452. doi: 10.1080/02640414.2016.1273538

Drew, B., and Matthews, J. (2018). The prevalence of depressive and anxiety symptoms in student-athletes and the relationship with resilience and help-seeking behavior. *J. Clin. Sport Psychol.* 1, 1–32. doi: 10.1123/jcsp.2017-0043

Elliott, S., Drummond, M. J., and Knight, C. (2018). The experiences of being a talented youth athlete: lessons for parents. *J. Appl. Sport Psychol.* 30, 437–455. doi: 10.1080/10413200.2017.1382019

Fletcher, D., Hanton, S., and Mellalieu, S. D. (2006). "An organizational stress review: Conceptual and theoretical issues in competitive sport," in *Literature Reviews in Sport Psychology*, eds S. Hanton and S. D. Mellalieu (Hauppauge, NY: Nova Science), 321–374.

Fletcher, D., and Sarkar, M. (2013). Psychological resilience: a review and critique of definitions, concepts, and theory. *Eur. Psychol.* 18:12. doi: 10.1027/1016-9040/a000124

Flick, U. (2008). *Designing Qualitative Research.* London: Sage.

Galli, N., and Gonzalez, S. P. (2014). Psychological resilience in sport: a review of the literature and implications for research and practice. *Int. J. Sport Exerc. Psychol.* 13, 243–257. doi: 10.1080/1612197X.2014.946947

Galli, N., and Vealey, R. S. (2008). "Bouncing back" from adversity: Athletes' experiences of resilience. *Sport Psychol.* 22, 316–335. doi: 10.1123/tsp.22.3.316

Gerber, M., Kalak, N., Lemola, S., Clough, P. J., Perry, J. L., Pühse, U., et al. (2013). Are adolescents with high mental toughness levels more resilient against stress? *Stress Health* 29, 164–171. doi: 10.1002/smi.2447

Gledhill, A., and Harwood, C. (2015). A holistic perspective on career development in UK female soccer players: a negative case analysis. *Psychol. Sport Exerc.* 21, 65–77. doi: 10.1016/j.psychsport.2015.04.003

Gould, D., Tammen, V., Murphy, S., and May, J. (1991). An evaluation of US Olympic sport psychology consultant effectiveness. *Sport Psychol.* 5, 111–127. doi: 10.1123/tsp.5.2.111

Gratton, C., and Jones, I. (2010). *Research Methods for Sports Studies.* London: Routledge.

Gustafsson, H., Martinent, G., Isoard-Gautheur, S., Hassmén, P., and Guillet-Descas, E. (2018). Performance based self-esteem and athlete-identity in athlete burnout: a person-centered approach. *Psychol. Sport Exerc.* 38, 56–60. doi: 10.1016/j.psychsport.2018.05.017

Hagger, M. S., and Chatzisarantis, N. L. (2011). Never the twain shall meet? Quantitative psychological researchers' perspectives on qualitative research. *Qualitat. Res. Sport Exerc. Health* 3, 266–277. doi: 10.1080/2159676x.2011.607185

Hagiwara, G., Iwatsuki, T., Isogai, H., Van Raalte, J. L., and Brewer, B. W. (2017). Relationships among sports helplessness, depression, and social support in American college student-athletes. *J. Phys. Educ. Sport* 17, 753.

Harwood, C., and Knight, C. (2009). Stress in youth sport: a developmental investigation of tennis parents. *Psychol. Sport Exerc.* 10, 447–456. doi: 10.1016/j.psychsport.2009.01.005

Hoffmann, M. D., and Loughead, T. M. (2016). A comparison of well-peer mentored and non-peer mentored athletes' perceptions of satisfaction. *J. Sports Sci.* 34, 450–458. doi: 10.1080/02640414.2015.1057517

Holt, N. L., Hoar, S., and Fraser, S. N. (2005). How does coping change with development? A review of childhood and adolescence sport coping research. *Eur. J. Sport Sci.* 5, 25–39. doi: 10.1080/17461390500076915

Horn, T. S. (2011). Multiple pathways to knowledge generation: qualitative and quantitative research approaches in sport and exercise psychology. *Qualitat. Res. Sport Exerc. Health* 3, 291–304. doi: 10.1080/2159676x.2011.607181

Hsieh, H. F., and Shannon, S. E. (2005). Three approaches to qualitative content analysis. *Qualitat. Health Res.* 15, 1277–1288. doi: 10.1177/1049732305276687

Kerdijk, C., van der Kamp, J., and Polman, R. (2016). The influence of the social environment context in stress and coping in sport. *Front. Psychol.* 7:875. doi: 10.3389/fpsyg.2016.00875

Kristiansen, E. (2017). Walking the line: how young athletes balance academic studies and sport in international competition. *Sport Soc.* 20, 47–65. doi: 10.1080/17430437.2015.1124563

Kristiansen, E., and Roberts, G. C. (2010). Young elite athletes and social support: coping with competitive and organizational stress in "Olympic" competition. *Scand. J. Med. Sci. Sports* 20, 686–695. doi: 10.1111/j.1600-0838.2009.00950.x

Kvale, S., and Brinkmann, S. (2009). *Interviews: Learning the Craft of Qualitative Research.* California: SAGE.

López, D. S., Barriopedro, M., and Conde, E. (2015a). Supporting dual career in Spain: elite athletes' barriers to study. *Psychol. Sport Exerc.* 21, 57–64. doi: 10.1016/j.psychsport.2015.04.012

López, D. S., Barriopedro, M., and Sanz, I. (2015b). Dual career motivation and identity on elite athletes. *Rev. Psicol. Deporte* 24, 55–57.

Lu, F. J., Hsu, Y. W., Chan, Y. S., Cheen, J. R., and Kao, K. T. (2012). Assessing college student-athletes' life stress: initial measurement development and validation. *Meas. Phys. Educ. Exerc. Sci.* 16, 254–267. doi: 10.1080/1091367x.2012.693371

Lu, F. J., Lee, W. P., Chang, Y. K., Chou, C. C., Hsu, Y. W., Lin, J. H., et al. (2016). Interaction of athletes' resilience and coaches' social support on the stress-burnout relationship: a conjunctive moderation perspective. *Psychol. Sport Exerc.* 22, 202–209. doi: 10.1016/j.psychsport.2015.08.005

Lupo, C., Guidotti, F., Goncalves, C. E., Moreira, L., Doupona Topic, M., Bellardini, H., et al. (2015). Motivation towards dual career of European student-athletes. *Eur. J. Sport Sci.* 15, 151–160. doi: 10.1080/17461391.2014.940557

Main, L., and Grove, J. R. (2009). A multi-component assessment model for monitoring training distress among athletes. *Eur. J. Sport Sci.* 9, 195–202. doi: 10.1080/17461390902818260

McKay, J., Niven, A. G., Lavallee, D., and White, A. (2008). Sources of strain among UK elite athletes. *Sport Psycholog.* 22, 143–163. doi: 10.1123/tsp.22.2.143

Moran, A. P., Matthews, J. J., and Kirby, K. (2011). Whatever happened to the third paradigm? Exploring mixed methods research designs in sport and exercise psychology. *Qualitat. Res. Sport Exerc. Health* 3, 362–369. doi: 10.1080/2159676x.2011.607843

Nicholls, A. R., Levy, A. R., Jones, L., Meir, R., Radcliffe, J. N., and Perry, J. L. (2016). Committed relationships and enhanced threat levels: perceptions of coach behavior, the coach–athlete relationship, stress appraisals, and coping among athletes. *Int. J. Sports Sci. Coach.* 11, 16–26. doi: 10.1177/1747954115624825

Pain, M. A., and Harwood, C. G. (2004). Knowledge and perceptions of sport psychology within English soccer. *J. Sports Sci.* 22, 813–826. doi: 10.1080/02640410410001716670

Patton, M. Q. (2002). *Qualitative Research and Evaluation Methods.* Thousand Oaks, CA: Sage.

Perna, F. M., Zaichkowsky, L., and Bocknek, G. (1996). The association of mentoring with psychosocial development among male athletes at termination of college career. *J. Appl. Sport Psychol.* 8, 76–88. doi: 10.1080/10413209608406309

Pummell, B., Harwood, C., and Lavallee, D. (2008). Jumping to the next level: a qualitative examination of within-career transition in adolescent event riders. *Psychol. Sport Exerc.* 9, 427–447. doi: 10.1016/j.psychsport.2007.07.004

Ravizza, K. (1988). Gaining entry with athletic personnel for season long consulting. *Sport Psycholog.* 4, 330–340.

Rhind, D., and Jowett, S. (2011). "Working with coach–athlete relationships: their quality and maintenance," in *Professional Practice in Sport Psychology: A Review*, eds S. Mellalieu and S. Hanton (London, UK: Routledge), 219–248.

Ronkainen, N. J., Ryba, T. V., Littlewood, M., and Selänne, H. (2018). 'School, family and then hockey!' Coaches' views on dual career in ice hockey. *Int. J. Sports Sci. Coach.* 13, 38–45. doi: 10.1177/1747954117712190

Rosenfeld, L. B., Richman, J. M., and Hardy, C. J. (1989). Examining social support networks among athletes: description and relationship to stress. *Sport Psycholog.* 3, 23–33. doi: 10.1123/tsp.3.1.23

Ryba, T. V., Stambulova, N. B., Selänne, H., Aunola, K., and Nurmi, J. E. (2017). "Sport has always been first for me" but "all my free time is spent doing homework": dual career styles in late adolescence. *Psychol. Sport Exerc.* 33, 131–140. doi: 10.1016/j.psychsport.2017.08.011

Sallen, J., Hemming, K., and Richartz, A. (2018). Facilitating dual careers by improving resistance to cronic stress: effects of an intervention program for elite student athletes. *Eur. J. Sport Sci.* 18, 112–122. doi: 10.1080/17461391.2017.1407363

Sarkar, M., and Fletcher, D. (2013). How should we measure psychological resilience in sport performers? *Meas. Phys. Educ. Exerc. Sci.* 17, 264–280. doi: 10.1080/1091367X.2013.805141

Scanlan, T. K., Stein, G. L., and Ravizza, K. (1991). An in-depth study of former elite figure skaters: III. Sources of stress. *J. Sport Exerc. Psychol.* 1, 102–120. doi: 10.1123/jsep.13.2.103

Silverman, D. (2006). *Interpreting Qualitative Data*, 3rd Edn. London: Sage.

Smith, B., and McGannon, K. R. (2018). Developing rigor in qualitative research: problems and opportunities within sport and exercise psychology. *Int. Rev. Sport Exerc. Psychol.* 11, 101–121. doi: 10.1080/1750984x.2017.1317357

Sorkkila, M., Aunola, K., and Ryba, T. V. (2017a). A person-oriented approach to sport and school burnout in adolescent student-athletes: the role of individual and parental expectations. *Psychol. Sport Exerc.* 28, 58–67. doi: 10.1016/j.psychsport.2016.10.004

Sorkkila, M., Ryba, T. V., Aunola, K., Selänne, H., and Salmela-Aro, K. (2017b). Sportburnout inventory–dual career form for student-athletes: assessing validity and reliability in a finnish sample of adolescent athletes. *J. Sport Health Sci.* (in press). doi: 10.1016/j.jshs.2017.10.006

Sorkkila, M., Aunola, K., Salmela-Aro, K., Tolvanen, A., and Ryba, T. V. (2018a). The co-developmental dynamic of sport and school burnout among student-athletes: the role of achievement goals. *Scand. J. Med. Sci. Sports* 28, 1731–1742. doi: 10.1111/sms.13073

Sorkkila, M., Ryba, T. V., Selänne, H., and Aunola, K. (2018b). Development of school and sport burnout in adolescent student-athletes: a longitudinal mixed-methods study. *J. Res. Adolesc.* doi: 10.1111/jora.12453 [Epub ahead of print].

Sparkes, A. C. (2015). Developing mixed methods research in sport and exercise psychology: critical reflections on five points of controversy. *Psychol. Sport Exerc.* 16, 49–59. doi: 10.1016/j.psychsport.2014.08.014

Sparkes, A. C., and Smith, B. (2014). *Qualitative Research Methods in Sport, Exercise and Health: From Process to Product.* New York, NY: Routledge.

Stambulova, N., and Wylleman, P. (2014). "Athletes' career development and transitions," in *Routledge Companion to Sport and Exercise Psychology*, eds A. Papaioannou and D. Hackfort (New York, NY: Routledge).

Stambulova, N. B., Engström, C., Franck, A., Linner, L., and Lindahl, K. (2015). Searching for an optimal balance: dual career experiences of Swedish adolescent athletes. *Psychol. Sport Exerc.* 21, 4–14. doi: 10.1016/j.psychsport.2014.08.009

Stambulova, N. B., and Wylleman, P. (2015). Special issue: dual career development and transitions. *Psychol. Sport Exerc.* 21, 1–134.

Stambulova, N. B., and Wylleman, P. (2019). Psychology of athletes' dual careers: a state-of-the-art critical review of the European discourse. *Psychol. Sport Exerc.* 42, 72–88. doi: 10.1016/j.psychsport.2018.11.013

Teddlie, C., and Tashakkori, A. (2012). Common "core" characteristics of mixed methods research: a review of critical issues and call for greater convergence. *Am. Behav. Sci.* 56, 774–788. doi: 10.1177/0002764211433795

Turner, M. J., and Jones, M. (2014). "Stress, emotions, and athletes' positive adaptation to sport: Contributions from a transactional perspective," in *Positive Human Functioning From a Multidimensional Perspective*, eds A. R. Gomes, R. Resende, and A. Albuquerque (New York, NY: Nova Science Publishers Inc.), 143–162.

Vaismoradi, M., Jones, J., Turunen, H., and Snelgrove, S. (2016). Theme development in qualitative content analysis and thematic analysis. *J. Nurs. Educ. Pract.* 6, 100–110. doi: 10.5430/jnep.v6n5p100

Vinson, D., Christian, P., Jones, V., Williams, C., and Peters, D. M. (2016). Exploring how well UK coach education meets the needs of women sports coaches. *Int. Sport Coach. J.* 3, 287–302. doi: 10.1123/iscj.2016-0004

White, R. L., and Bennie, A. (2015). Resilience in youth sport: a qualitative investigation of gymnastics coach and athlete perceptions. *Int. J. Sports Sci. Coach.* 10, 379–393. doi: 10.1260/1747-9541.10.2-3.379

Woodman, T., and Hardy, L. (2001). A case study of organizational stress in elite sport. *J. Appl. Sport Psychol.* 13, 207–238. doi: 10.1111/j.1600-0838.2012.01521.x

15

Taking Action or Thinking About it? State Orientation and Rumination are Correlated in Athletes

*Alena Kröhler and Stefan Berti**

Department of Clinical Psychology and Neuropsychology, Institute for Psychology, Johannes Gutenberg-University Mainz, Mainz, Germany

***Correspondence:**
Stefan Berti
berti@uni-mainz.de

Athletic performance in competitive sports relies heavily on the ability to cope effectively with stressful situations. In contrast, some athletes report that their thoughts revolve around the future or past and not around the actual demands during competitions. In those specific stressful situations, the lack of focus like an unintended fixation on repetitive cognitions can have fatal consequences with regard to the performance. Especially when competitors are close in their athletic capabilities, differences in effectively coping with stress and mental stability may decide about winning and losing. One established factor of performing effectively under pressure is the individual tendency to either focus on taking action (i.e., action orientation) or on focusing on the own emotions (i.e., state orientation). It is widely acknowledged that state-oriented athletes have disadvantages in performing under stress. Moreover, the action control theory claims that state orientation is related to ruminative cognitions, which itself is assumed to impair performance in the long term. We tested this hypothesis in 157 competitive athletes from different sports (including individual and team sports). Regression analysis demonstrates a substantial correlation of failure-related action orientation (i.e., state orientation) with different measures of rumination (including general, clinically relevant, and competition-related rumination). In addition, general (i.e., content independent) rumination also correlated substantially with a rumination scale adapted specifically to sports-related competition. These results suggest (1) that a sports and competition-related ruminative mechanism exists and (2) that ruminative cognitions are related to the cognitive basis of state orientation. While our study does not allow for a causal interpretation, it provides an additional approach to investigate mental factors underlying inter-individual differences in athletic performance under stress and pressure.

Keywords: rumination, action control theory, state orientation, action orientation, failure-related behavioral adaptation, competitive sports, competition-related rumination, competitive athletes

INTRODUCTION

Competitive athletes distinguished themselves through conscious permanent acting under stressful conditions ascribable to their special environment, the participation in competitions, and the immediate consequences of their actions. In general, those situations require a high degree of immediate and long-term self-regulatory capabilities. Therefore, successful athletes were attributed to problem-focused, resilient coping-strategies (Henkel and Schneider, 2014). However, in the high demanding domain of competitive sports, inter-individual differences in the competence of adaption to stressful situations are observable and can have an enormous positive or negative impact on the athletic behavior and performance, especially throughout a competitive season or in the period of a training camp (Filho et al., 2013, 2015; Kölling et al., 2015). One theory that is well established in this context is the *action control theory* (Beckmann and Kossok, 2018), which was originally developed by Kuhl (1983, 1994a) and represents one of the most prominent theories in the context of volition. In essence, this theory assumes that regulation becomes necessary if conflicts between competing action tendencies occur (Beckmann and Kossok, 2018). Take, for instance, a soccer player who has to decide how to act after playing a bad pass during an attack: there might be different options for taking immediate action (like tackling an opponent to regain the ball or running back to support the defense) but it is also possible to focus on the lost (i.e., by cursing the conditions or the teammates or feeling guilty or incompetent). According to the theory of action control, in such situations, volitional processes are influenced by individual differences in action orientation. In detail, the theory distinguishes between action and state orientation, two extremes on a continuous scale describing the likelihood whether people respond with action-taking when situational demands are increasing. Action-oriented individuals distinguish themselves through solving problems intuitively in adverse conditions (e.g., bad weather, broken equipment, and poor field or arena conditions), rapid acting without excessively thinking about the source or the person responsible, and developing different possibilities to act in demanding situations (Kuhl and Kazén, 2003). They typically act in high demanding situations as efficiently or even better as in comparable relaxing situations (Koole and Jostmann, 2004; Koole et al., 2012). Athletes with an action orientation can also handle failures in high demanding situations more efficiently and draw the attention to forthcoming challenges.

In contrast, athletes with a tendency to state orientation are focused on their emotions and thoughts. An unintended fixation on the own situation is mostly the consequence, which is why they do not solve problems easily and refocus on the actual task (Kuhl and Kazén, 2003; Koole et al., 2012). Moreover, state-oriented athletes think a lot about their goals but fail to take immediate action. This behavior, therefore, could inhibit the readiness and the implementation of action (Dibbelt and Kuhl, 1994). Finally, in the theory of action orientation, ruminative cognitions are described as the most immediate and conscious consequence of a dispositional state orientation (Kuhl, 1994a).

A number of studies tested whether these hypothesized differences of action- and state-oriented individuals comply in the context of competitive sports. The previous findings pointed mainly in the same direction, suggesting disadvantages of state-oriented athletes compared to action-oriented athletes in different aspects that are relevant for athletic performance particularly in stressful situations. Two studies found differences in the level of action orientation and risk-taking behavior in the sense of measuring accuracy and time of the individual decision-making process (Stiensmeier-Pelster et al., 1989; Raab and Johnson, 2004). Further studies with different experimental paradigms showed differences in depletion of self-control resources (Gröpel et al., 2014) and in the efficiency of intention initiation (Kazén et al., 2008). This picture is generally supported by a review of Koole et al. (2005) who provided a summary of disruptive effects of stress on state-oriented individuals. In addition, Koole et al. (2005) described also potential positive effects of state orientation. In detail, state orientation can be adaptive (1) through external support, (2) in dangerous, unpredictable environments and (3) in interpersonal relationships. This applies to sports, too: for instance, Beckmann and Kazén (1994) reported inverse effects of state orientation in the sense of a positive consequence by maximum power. This shows that state orientation does not necessarily exhibit only negative effects on sport performance (see also Beckmann and Kossok, 2018, for a summary of advantages and disadvantages of the individual action orientation). However, the majority of studies demonstrated the disadvantage of state orientation in sports performance and the question arises whether this effect is related to the higher tendency of state-oriented persons to focus on thoughts and the assumed higher level of rumination (Kuhl, 1994a).

The effect of rumination on athletic behavior and performance has frequently been stated but was only rarely explicitly investigated. Only a few studies examined the mediating role of rumination indirectly in the process of athletic performance: one study with 305 competitive athletes examined the relationship between anger rumination and athlete aggression based on the Anger Rumination Scale (Maxwell, 2004). Results revealed a significant correlation between anger rumination and the athletes' reported aggressive behavior. However, a direct relation of rumination and the athletes' performance was not investigated. A study by Scott et al. (2002) confirmed a negative correlation between an overall measure of rumination (Scott-McIntosh Rumination Inventory; Scott and McIntosh, 1999) and a composite of measure of athletic performance of tennis players. The main limitation of this study was the small sample size (N = 10), which did not advocate a broad generalization. Roy et al. (2016) investigated the relation between rumination and performance in soccer and field hockey players using the Ruminative Response Scale (RRS; Treynor et al., 2003). They found an expertise effect mirrored in lower reflective rumination in athletes (professionals and nonprofessionals) compared with non-athletes. Furthermore, Roy et al. (2016) assumed that low scores on the RRS are associated with a longer career at a higher level in soccer players. Here, the level of expertise (professional vs. nonprofessional players) and the duration of a successful sports career defined the athletes' performance. This suggests that at least success over the long term is correlated with rumination. However, a recent study also suggests that the achievement of short- and mid-term sports-specific goals is related to rumination (see Kröhler and Berti, 2017).

The aim of the study was to investigate the assumed relation between action orientation and rumination (see Kuhl, 1983, 1994a). As summarized above, the action control theory claims that rumination is an effect of a lower action orientation (i.e., higher state orientation) under stress. As both, the individual degree of action orientation as well as rumination, show associations with sports performance, it remains open whether a correlation of state orientation and rumination really exists in athletes. Therefore, we tested whether state orientation in the context of failure is correlated with rumination in general. The action control theory does not limit the theoretical claim to a specific situation, which implies that such a correlation should be observable in this highly selective population, too. In contrast, competitive athletes are highly trained in performing under pressure (i.e., in highly competitive situations) and, therefore, might exhibit competences in coping especially with potential or actual failures, which would result in increased stress in a normal population. From this point of view, athletes may not demonstrate a correlation between their levels of action orientation and rumination (i.e., on the trait level). However, even if athletes acquired specific competences in performing under stress, it remains open whether these competences are effective in general or in competitive situations only.

To date, different scales exists to measure action or state orientation either in general (Kuhl, 1994b) or in sports-related (Beckmann and Wenhold, 2009) context. Both measurements, the general Action Control Scale (ACS-90; Kuhl, 1994b; German Version: HAKEMP-90; Kuhl, 1990) and the sports-specific measure of action orientation in competitive sports (German: *Handlungsorientierung im Sport*; HOSP; Beckmann and Wenhold, 2009), consist of three subscales, namely (1) action orientation subsequent to failure scale (German: *Handlungsorientierung nach Misserfolg*; HOM), (2) prospective and decision-related action orientation scale (German: *Handlungsorientierung bei Entscheidungs- und Handlungsplanung*; HOP), and (3) action orientation during (successful) performance of activities (German: *Handlungsorientierung bei Tätigkeitsausführung*; HOT). Here we focus on the first subscale (HOM), which describes the capability to suppress failures and refocus on the following task immediately. With regard to rumination, we applied rumination questionnaires from three different contexts: clinically relevant rumination (RRQ, König, 2012), rumination in general (PTQ, Ehring et al., 2011), and competition-related rumination (modified from Krys et al., 2018).

We expect a relationship between HOM and rumination because the action control theory assumes that higher failure-related action orientation is associated with lower individual rumination. To test this hypothesis, we first conduct a correlational analysis. In addition, we investigate this relationship by applying linear robust regression analysis to quantify the potential association.

MATERIALS AND METHODS

Subjects and Procedure

Within a period of 3 months (October–December 2016), athletes from different sports, including team sports as well as individual sports, participated in an online study voluntarily. We conducted the study in compliance with the Declaration of Helsinki (World Medical Association, 2013). The online instruction contained information about the nature and the procedure of the study and all participants gave consent before completing the questionnaires. The participants received no incentives for completion of the survey. For athletes under the age of 18, we obtained additional consent from the legally authorized representatives. The participants completed the action orientation subsequent to failure scale (HOM, Beckmann and Wenhold, 2009), the Perseverative Thinking Questionnaire (PTQ; Ehring et al., 2011), the Rumination scale from the Rumination-Reflection Questionnaire (RRQ; König, 2012) and a competition-related rumination scale (KSR-WK; modified from Krys et al., 2018). In addition to these, the participants filled out biographical and sports-related questions as well as other questionnaires, which were unrelated to the present study. We describe the utilized questionnaires below.

Overall, 210 athletes participated in our online survey. Criteria for selecting the subjects for our analysis were as follows: athletes between 15 and 30 years of age corresponding to the athletic high-performance age (Willimczik et al., 2006; Conzelmann, 2017) and a background in competitive sports. The final sample of athletes who met these criteria was 157 (female: n = 80, male: n = 77). Mean age was 21.57 years (SD = 3.63). The athletes averaged 10.00 h (SD = 5.60) of discipline-specific training in 4.46 training sessions (SD = 2.54) and 2.54 additional sessions (SD = 1.99; e.g., weight or athletic training) per week. The averaged participation in competitions per year was 13.40 (SD = 8.02). Besides, 32 athletes were already part of the junior national team and 16 athletes were part of the senior national team in their sports. Ten of these 48 athletes were in the junior as well as in the senior national team of their sports. According to the categorization of Beckmann and Wenhold (2009), the sample was assigned into six different sport categories and two performance levels (see **Table 1**). Depending on the organizational form of the disciplines (leagues or squads system), the sample was divided into two performance levels: performance level 1 includes all athletes belonging to highest to the third highest national level (comparable with A- to C-squad or First German Bundesliga as well as participations in German/European/World Championships or

TABLE 1 | Distribution of athletes separated in sport categories, gender and performance level.

Sport category	Performance level 1		Performance level 2		
	Female	Male	Female	Male	Sum
Ball sports-individual	1	1	3	2	7
Ball sports-team	7	5	13	23	48
Endurance sports-individual	24	25	19	15	83
Coordinative-compositional	6	2	5	0	13
Martial arts	0	2	1	2	5
Target focus	1	0	0	0	1
Sum	39	35	41	42	157

Examples: ball sports-individual = (table) tennis; ball sports-team = basketball, football; conditioning-individual = swimming, athletics; coordinative-compositional = rhythmic gymnastics, snowboard; martial arts = boxing, taekwondo; target focus = billiard, sport shooting.

Olympic Games; $n = 74$). Performance level 2 includes all athletes belonging to the fourth highest or subjacent level (comparable with D-squad, Second German Bundesliga or below as well as participation in German Junior or regional championships; $n = 83$).

Measures

Failure-Related Action Orientation

We measured the failure-related action orientation with the German action orientation in sports questionnaire (HOSP, Beckmann and Wenhold, 2009). The HOSP is a standardized self-evaluation assessment with 36 items, consisting of three scales: action orientation subsequent to failure, decision-related action orientation, and action orientation during performance. Each scale consists of 12 items, which describe a particular situation. Each item has two alternative answers (A or B), one of which is indicative of action orientation and the other of state orientation. For the present study, only the action orientation subsequent to failure scale is relevant (HOM). The HOM measures the athletes' ability to cope with failures and focus again on new demands. For athletes with lower values on this scale compared to those with higher values, it is difficult to cope with failures. They fight intensively with the setback, by what they may affect the execution of following tasks. For instance: "If I miss a clear chance of winning ..." then A: "it sticks in my mind during the rest of the competition" (state orientation), or B: "I forget this failed attempt and concentrate on the next chance" (action orientation) [translations from the German original by AK].

Athletes earn one point for choosing the action-oriented answer. The sum of the action-oriented answers for each scale is between 0 and 12. The following applies: the higher the characteristics in the action orientation subsequent to failure scale, the higher the action orientation in this context.

Perseverative Thinking

The German version of the Perseverative Thinking Questionnaire (PTQ; Ehring et al., 2011) is a questionnaire independent from content for measuring repetitive negative thoughts. The PTQ consists of 15 items and is rated on a 5-point Likert scale, ranging from "0" (never) to "4" (almost always). In each case, three items correspond to a process characteristic of repetitive negative thinking, building one subscale: (1a) repetitive (e.g., "The same thoughts keep going through my mind again and again"), (1b) intrusive (e.g., "Thoughts come to my mind without me wanting them to"), (1c) difficult to disengage from (e.g., "I can't stop dwelling on them"), (2) unproductive (e.g., "I keep asking myself questions without finding an answer"), (3) capturing mental capacity (e.g., "My thought prevent me from focusing on other things"; all items are taken from the English original).

The PTQ provides three scores for the particular subscales as well as a general PTQ score, which is the sum of the three subscales' scores. Here, we report the general PTQ score. The internal consistency (Cronbach's alpha: α) for the entire PTQ is $\alpha = 0.95$ for the original and $\alpha = 0.94$ for the present sample. Therefore, the analysis of the internal consistency in the present sample supports previous findings.

Rumination

Trapnell and Campbell (1999) developed the Rumination-Reflection Questionnaire (RRQ), for differentiating rumination and reflection, two relevant factors of private dispositional self-focus. The original version comprises 24 items in two scales: 12 items for rumination as well as for reflection. In the present study, we utilized the German version (König, 2012) and applied only the Rumination scale. This scale measures the self-attentiveness motivated by perceived threats, losses, or injustices to the self (Trapnell and Campbell, 1999). For instance, "Often I'm playing back over in my mind how I acted in a past situation." Athletes rate the different statements on a 5-point Likert scale presenting the level of agreement ranging from "1" (strongly disagree) to "5" (strongly agree). The value of the items 6, 9, and 10 should be reversed. The individual test score can be calculated by adding up all values of the 12 items. Therefore, the scores are ranging between 12 and 60, and the higher the scores the higher the individual level of rumination. The internal consistency for the original sample is $\alpha = 0.90$ (Trapnell and Campbell, 1999) and for the present sample $\alpha = 0.88$.

Competition-Related Rumination

We used a questionnaire from Krys et al. (2018) for measuring the handling with difficulties in the context of a competition. The original version contains eight items according to learning-related difficulties during the preparation for a statistic exam (for instance, "I can't stop thinking about learning-related problems"). The original questionnaire was developed in the way that the problem-related context is changeable. Therefore, we modified the items (Krys et al., 2018) to competition-related problems (KSR-WK); e.g., "I can't stop thinking about competition-related problems." Athletes respond on a 5-point Likert scale, ranging from "1" (does not apply at all) to "5" (fully applies).

The individual test score can be calculated by adding up all values of the eight items. Therefore, the scores are ranging between 8 and 40 and; again, the higher the scores the higher the individual level of rumination. The internal consistency for the original sample lies between $\alpha = 0.91$ and $\alpha = 0.94$ (Krys et al., 2018) and for the present sample $\alpha = 0.92$.

Data Analysis

We analyzed the relationship between failure-related action orientation and rumination by means of three single robust regression models. In doing so, failure-related action orientation represents the independent variable and the scales of PTQ, RRQ and KSR-WK represent the dependent variable for each single regression model. Beforehand, we checked the requirements for the application of regression analyses. We generated Q-Q plots for testing the assumption of normal distribution (Kabacoff, 2015), conducted analyses for testing the independence of the predictor variable including the standard errors (Durbin-Watson Test; Field et al., 2012) as well as the multi-collinearity of all used variables (VIF: variance inflation factor; Field et al., 2012). Except the normal distribution, all requirements for regression analyses were fulfilled. In addition, we analyzed outliers and influential cases using Cook's distance, leverage values, and the proportion of co-variances (Field et al., 2012). While there were no outliers in the data, Cook's distance revealed the existence of influential cases. These could have a considerable impact of the constant and the gradient of the regression model. We decided not to exclude the influential cases from further calculation. Instead, we applied robust regression analyses with a MM-estimation (a kind of maximum-likelihood estimation; Susanti and Pratiwi, 2014). This method uses a criterion, which is less vulnerable for influential cases. It has also a high breakdown value (general measurement of the proportion of influential cases, which are edited before influencing the regression model; Susanti and Pratiwi, 2014). Hence, the robust method is more appropriate in calculating regressions. Moreover, it is possible to conduct the regression analyses with all observed cases by restricting the effect of influential cases *via* Cook's distance and high leverage values at the same time.

RESULTS

Table 2 sums up the descriptive statistics among the study variables for all competitive athletes (N = 157).

The results of the correlational analysis revealed significant associations between failure-related action orientation (HOM) and the three rumination scales (PTQ, RRQ, KSR-WK; $p < 0.05$; alpha corrected with Holm, see **Figure 1**). **Figure 2** demonstrates that there is a substantial, inter-individual variation in all three rumination measures in the participating athletes but the robust regression analyses indicated that failure-related action orientation significantly predicts rumination (see **Table 3**). In addition, we determined the power of our regression analyses (G*Power 3.1.; Faul et al., 2009) with the sample size N = 157, an alpha level α = 0.001, and the obtained medium effect sizes; this analyses revealed a power of 0.9998 for the PTQ regression (f^2 = 0.30), 0.9997 for the RRQ regression (f^2 = 0.28), and 0.9999 for the KSR-WK regression (f^2 = 0.32).

DISCUSSION

Our study demonstrates in competitive athletes a direct relationship of rumination and action orientation after failure. This supports the claims of the action control theory (Kuhl, 1983, 1994a) and does suggest an expansion to context-specific situations (here, competitive sports). The correlational analyses show middle to strong association between failure-related action orientation and all three rumination scales. Findings of the regression analyses support our hypothesis, in the way that failure-related action orientation is a significant predictor for rumination as reflected in a general, a clinically oriented as well as a competition-related measure. It is worth noting that the explained variance in the regression analyses is about 20% for all three rumination measures. On the one hand, this indicates that a general "ruminative" factor is shared by these different measures and that this aspect of rumination indeed is linked to action control (as assumed by Kuhl, 1983, 1994a). On the other hand, this leaves a lot of variability in the data, which is not explained by individual level of action orientation. While this might be attributed to different specific characteristics of rumination captured by these particular scales (e.g., well-being in a clinical context vs. negative outcome in the context of a competition), this may also suggest that neither of the applied rumination scales is already suitable for a competitive athletes' population. However, the correlation between the competition-related rumination (KSR-WK) and the general rumination scale (PTQ) indicates that the applied variant of the KSR-WK (Krys et al., 2018) does tap rumination in a specific context. Both variables share a common variance of nearly 40%, indicating that besides the general factor an independent competitive specific factor emerged.

In general, our findings are in line with previous studies (e.g., Beckmann and Trux, 1991; Beckmann and Kazén, 1994) and indicated that rumination might be a relevant factor for individual requirements in competitive sports. As the aim of coaches in competitive sports is to help athletes to gain their optimal performance, additional information about athletes' disposition in relevant mental factors may allow coaches to adapt to the individual needs of their athletes. For instance, in team sports, the knowledge about the athletes' level of action or state orientation could be beneficial when selecting playing positions or deciding ball allocation strategies depending on different gaming situations. This is suggested by a study of Beckmann and Trux (1991), who showed that key players in high-performance professional sports tend to be state oriented rather than action oriented, whereas the strikers were mainly action oriented. Beckmann and Kossok (2018) suggested applying the knowledge of athletes' dispositions in order to selectively introduce them to different disciplines or positions in which their personal dispositions might promise particular success. Therefore, from the perspective of applied sports psychology, the concept of rumination offers a number of potential applications. For instance, athletes and coaches typically perceived ruminative thoughts (especially with negative content) as a limiting factor for gaining high performance. One aim could be to identify athletes with a predisposition toward extensive rumination especially in younger ages. It is also promising to support young talents in their ability to control repetitive disruptive thoughts, because many athletes perform suboptimally in pressure situations despite a high motivation to succeed (Baumeister and Showers, 1986). Well-known moderators for suboptimal performance in pressure situations

TABLE 2 | Descriptive statistics among the study variables for all competitive athletes (N = 157).

	M	*SD*	*SE*	Median	Skew	Kurtosis	95% CI
HOM	6.35	3.12	0.25	6	−.0.09	−0.83	[5.86, 6.84]
PTQ	25.5	10.66	0.85	24	0.52	0.52	[23.82, 27.18]
RRQ	37.07	9.02	0.72	38	−0.06	−0.39	[35.65, 38.49]
KSR-WK	19.37	7.11	0.57	19	0.51	−0.36	[18.25, 20.49]

M, mean; SD, standard deviation; SE, standard error of mean; 95% CI, 95% confidence intervals.

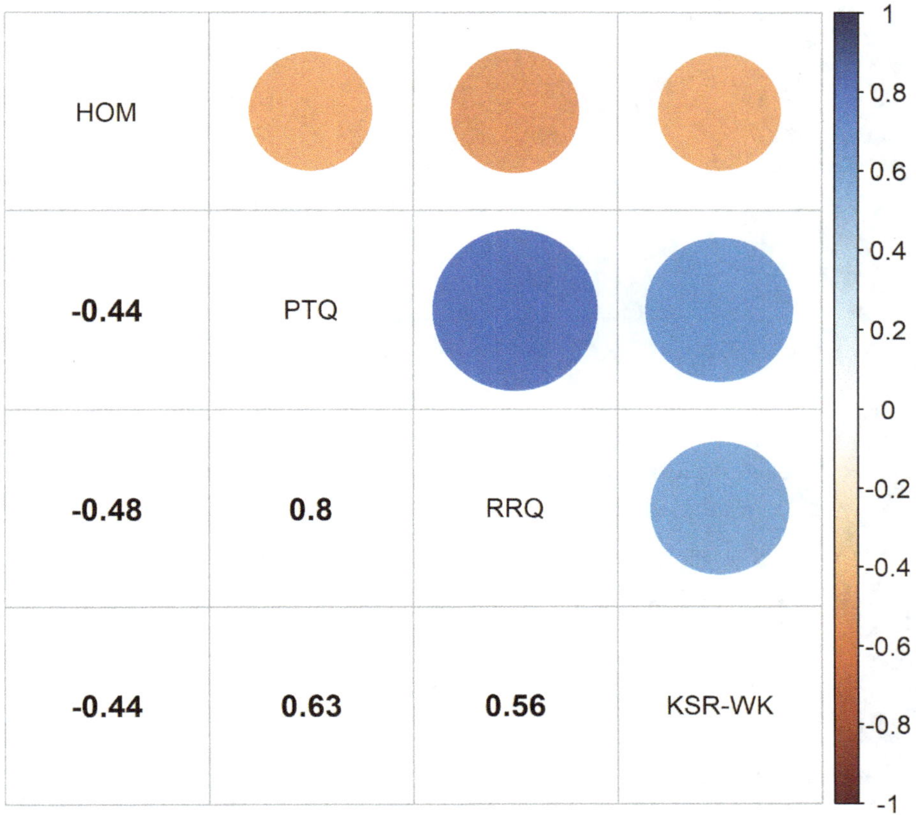

FIGURE 1 | Summary of the Pearson correlations coefficients (*r*) between action orientation subsequent to failure scale and three rumination scales. The diagonal depicts the individual scales used in this study. The arrays under the diagonal depict the correlational coefficients of the particular scales (all *p*'s < 0.05 [Holm corrected *p*'s for multiple comparisons]; all *df*'s = 155). The arrays above the diagonal illustrate these values in a symbolic way with the size of the circles specifying the extent of the parameter value (values between 0 and 1) and the color of the circles depicting the direction of the parameter value (positive or negative; see color scale at the right).

(choking under pressure) are among others trait anxiety, reinvestment, and perfectionism, which are all closely related to rumination (Flett et al., 2002; Nolen-Hoeksema et al., 2008; Kinrade et al., 2010). To this end, early identification of the individual dispositional rumination at the beginning of a sports career might enable a more effective support by application of treatments to avoid rumination (and thereby potential stress) in the long run. For instance, Roy et al. (2016) report a relationship between a successful sports career and a low reflective rumination style. Existing therapeutic interventions related to rumination (see Broderick, 2005; Nolen-Hoeksema et al., 2008; Watkins, 2008; Van Aalderen et al., 2012; Querstret and Cropley, 2013) therefore, might be adapted to the non-clinical group of athletes on the one hand. On the other hand, recent studies (Birrer et al., 2012; Mosewich et al., 2013; Josefsson et al., 2017) deal with rumination-related interventions in competitive sports. Contents of these interventions focused mainly on self-compassion (Mosewich et al., 2013) and mindfulness (Josefsson et al., 2017). Results already show an improved regulation of maladaptive thoughts, feelings, and behavior and therefore provide a promising approach for future research.

Study Limitations and Future Directions

Our study revealed correlations between failure-related action orientation and rumination in three different contexts in competitive athletes. However, the time of survey was far away from the actual competition or a special failure-related situation. Therefore, we only received information about individual traits and cannot rule out that the obtained correlations are modulated by the experience of an upcoming or actual competition. This limits also our current understanding of whether the action orientation and rumination link is more of a trait or state. One future direction is to survey athletes immediately after the competition or a failure-related situation. For instance, ambulatory assessment with an event-based design could provide a promising approach: within a defined period, athletes could complete a short questionnaire related to action orientation and rumination immediately after the experience. This could also serve as an interesting starting point in gaining more information about differences in individual action orientation and the consequences of it. An open question is whether there is a direct link between failure-related action orientation and individual rumination. Due to the cross-sectional design (only one measurement), the results are only correlational in nature.

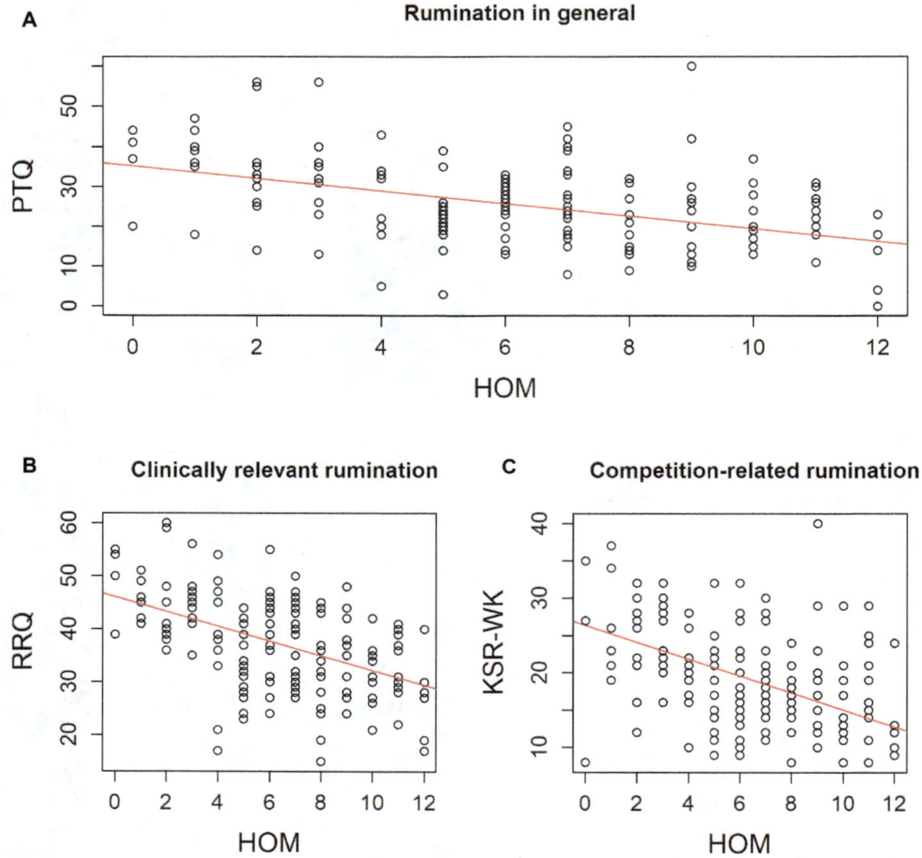

FIGURE 2 | Scatterplots of failure-related action orientation (HOM; range 0–12) and rumination (*N* = 157). In detail, HOM is plotted with **(A)** rumination in general (PTQ; range 0–60), **(B)** clinically relevant rumination (RRQ; range 12–60), and **(C)** competition-related rumination (KSR-WK; range 8–40). The regression lines are based on robust linear regressions of HOM with the respective rumination measure (for details see text).

TABLE 3 | Characteristics of the single robust regression analyses with failure-related action orientation as predictor and three rumination scales as criterion.

Criterion	Predictor	*B*	*SE B*	β	*p*	R^2_{adj}
PTQ	HOM	−1.57	0.24	−0.46	<0.001	0.23
RRQ	HOM	−1.25	0.17	−0.48	<0.001	0.22
KSR-WK	HOM	−1.13	0.19	−0.50	<0.001	0.24

In other words, additional research is required to investigate whether the relation of failure-related action orientation and rumination is replicable and generalizable in a broader population.

CONCLUSION

The action control theory by Kuhl (1983, 1994a) claimed a link of rumination and state orientation and, therefore, provides a theoretical framework for examination of the negative effect of both on athletic performance. Here we demonstrate that this hypothesis in general holds in a very specialized population, namely competitive athletes. This suggests that both, the action control theory and the theoretical considerations related to rumination may offer further routes of investigating the nature of individual performance variations in athletes under stress, e.g., in the context of a competition.

ETHICS STATEMENT

The study was conducted in accordance with the Declaration of Helsinki and the Ethical Code of the German Society for Psychology (DGPs) and all subjects gave written informed consent prior to their participation in the study. In the case of our selection of participants (all healthy persons) and our study design the local ethics committee at the Institute for Psychology do not ask for an approvement.

AUTHOR CONTRIBUTIONS

AK and SB contributed with the conception and design of the study. AK collected the data and performed the statistical analysis, and AK and SB wrote the manuscript.

ACKNOWLEDGMENTS

We would like to thank all clubs and sports organizations for cooperating with us and all athletes, who participated in our study.

REFERENCES

Baumeister, R. F., and Showers, C. J. (1986). A review of paradoxical performance effects: choking under pressure in sports and mental tests. *Eur. J. Soc. Psychol.* 16, 361–383. doi: 10.1002/ejsp.2420160405

Beckmann, J., and Kazén, M. (1994). "Action and state orientation and the performance of top athletes" in *Volition and personality. Action versus state orientation.* eds. J. Kuhl, and J. Beckmann (Seattle, WA: Hogrefe & Huber), 439–451.

Beckmann, J., and Kossok, T. (2018). "Motivation and volition in sports" in *Motivation and action.* eds. J. Heckhausen, and H. Heckhausen (Heidelberg, Berlin: Springer), 853–889.

Beckmann, J., and Trux, J. (1991). Wen lasse ich wo spielen? Persönlichkeitseigenschaften und die Eignung für bestimmte Positionen in Sportspielmannschaften [Personality traits and the selection of athlets for tactical positions in team sports]. *Sportpsychologie* 5, 18–21.

Beckmann, J., and Wenhold, F. (2009). *Handlungsorientierung im Sport [Action orientation in Sports] (HOSP), Manual.* (Köln: Strauß).

Birrer, D., Röthlin, P., and Morgan, G. (2012). Mindfulness to enhance athletic performance: theoretical considerations and possible impact mechanisms. *Mindfulness* 3, 235–246. doi: 10.1007/s12671-012-0109-2

Broderick, P. C. (2005). Mindfulness and coping with dysphoric mood: contrasts with rumination and distraction. *Cogn. Ther. Res.* 29, 501–510. doi: 10.1007/s10608-005-3888-0

Conzelmann, A. (2017). "Wettkampfleistung im Alter [Competition performance over the lifespan]" in *Handbuch Trainingswissenschaft-Trainingslehre.* eds. K. Hottenrott, and I. Seidel (Hofmann: Schorndorf), 352–355.

Dibbelt, S., and Kuhl, J. (1994). "Volitional processes in decision making: personality and situational determinants" in *Volition and personality: action versus state orientation.* eds. J. Kuhl, and J. Beckmann (Seattle: Hogrefe & Huber Publisher), 177–194.

Ehring, T., Zetsche, U., Weidacker, K., Wahl, K., Schönfeld, S., and Ehlers, A. (2011). The Perseverative Thinking Questionnaire (PTQ): validation of a content-independent measure of repetitive negative thinking. *J. Behav. Ther. Exp. Psychiatry* 42, 225–232. doi: 10.1016/j.jbtep.2010.12.003

Faul, F., Erdfelder, E., Buchner, A., and Lang, A. G. (2009). Statistical power analyses using G*Power 3.1: tests for correlation and regression analyses. *Behav. Res. Methods* 41, 1149–1160. doi: 10.3758/brm.41.4.1149

Field, A., Miles, J., and Field, Z. (2012). *Discovering statistics using R.* (London: Sage Publication Ltd).

Filho, E., di Fronso, S., Forzini, F., Agostini, T., Bortoli, L., Robazza, C., et al. (2013). Stress/recovery balance during the Girobio: profile of highly trained road cyclists. *Sport Sci. Health* 9, 107–112. doi: 10.1007/s11332-013-0153-x

Filho, E., di Fronso, S., Forzini, F., Murgia, M., Agostini, T., Bortoli, L., et al. (2015). Athletic performance and recovery-stress factors in cycling: an ever changing balance. *Eur. J. Sport Sci.* 15, 671–680. doi: 10.1080/17461391.2015.1048746

Flett, G. L., Madorsky, D., Hewitt, P. L., and Heisel, M. J. (2002). Perfectionism cognitions, rumination, and psychological distress. *J. Ration. Emot. Cogn. Behav. Ther.* 20, 33–47. doi: 10.1023/a:1015128904007

Gröpel, P., Baumeister, R., and Beckmann, J. (2014). Action versus state orientation and self-control performance after depletion. *Pers. Soc. Psychol. Bull.* 40, 476–487. doi: 10.1177/0146167213516636

Henkel, K., and Schneider, F. (2014). Psychische Erkrankungen bei Leistungssportlern [Mental illness in competitive athletes]. *Sports Orthop. Traumatol.* 30, 339–345. doi: 10.1016/j.orthtr.2014.09.003

Josefsson, T., Ivarsson, A., Lindwall, M., Gustafsson, H., Stenling, A., Böröy, J., et al. (2017). Mindfulness mechanisms in sports: mediating effects of rumination and emotion regulation on sport-specific coping. *Mindfulness* 8, 1354–1363. doi: 10.1007/s12671-017-0711-4

Kabacoff, R. I. (2015). *R in action. Data analysis and graphics with R.* (New York: Manning).

Kazén, M., Kaschel, R., and Kuhl, J. (2008). Individual differences in intention initiation under demanding conditions: interactive effects of state vs. action orientation and enactment difficulty. *J. Res. Pers.* 42, 693–715. doi: 10.1016/j.jrp.2007.09.005

Kinrade, N. P., Jackson, R. C., Ashford, K. J., and Bishop, D. T. (2010). Development and validation of the decision-specific reinvestment scale. *J. Sports Sci.* 28, 1127–1135. doi: 10.1080/02640414.2010.499439

Kölling, S., Hitzschke, B., Holst, T., Ferrauti, A., Meyer, T., Pfeiffer, M., et al. (2015). Validity of the Acute Recovery and Stress Scale: training monitoring of the German junior national field hockey team. *Int. J. Sports Sci. Coach.* 10, 529–542. doi: 10.1260/1747-9541.10.2-3.529

König, D. (2012). *Deutsche Version der Skala Rumination aus dem Rumination-Reflection Questionnaire (RRQ) [German version of the Rumination subscale from the Rumination-Reflection Questionnaire (RRQ)].* Retrieved from: http://dk.akis.at/RRQ_Rumination.pdf

Koole, S. L., and Jostmann, N. B. (2004). Getting a grip on your feelings: effects of action orientation and external demands on intuitive affect regulation. *J. Personal. Soc. Psychol.* 87, 974–990. doi: 10.1037/0022-3514.87.6.974

Koole, S. L., Jostmann, N. B., and Baumann, N. (2012). Do demanding conditions help or hurt self-regulation? *Soc. Personal. Psychol. Compass* 6, 328–346. doi: 10.1111/j.1751-9004.2012.00425.x

Koole, S. L., Kuhl, J., Jostmann, N. B., and Vohs, K. D. (2005). "On the hidden benefits of state orientation: can people prosper without efficient affect regulation skills" in *On building, defending and regulating the self: A psychological perspective.* 217–243.

Kröhler, A., and Berti, S. (2017). Rumination im Zusammenhang mit dem Erreichen selbst gesetzter Ziele bei leistungssportlich-orientierten Schwimmern [Rumination in the context of individual goal achievement in performance-oriented swimmers]. *Z. Sportpsychol.* 24, 161–166. doi: 10.1026/1612-5010/a000200

Krys, S., Otte, K.-P., and Knipfer, K. (2018). *Student' psychological distress and academic performance in higher education: A longitudinal examination of the role of rumination.* Manuscript submitted for publication.

Kuhl, J. (1983). *Motivation, Konflikt und Handlungskontrolle [Motivation, conflict and action orientation].* (Berlin: Springer), 251–301.

Kuhl, J. (1990). *Der Fragebogen zur Erfassung von Handlungs- versus Lageorientierung* (HAKEMP-90) *[Questionnaire for action vs. state orientation].* Unpublished manuscript, (University Osnabrück).

Kuhl, J. (1994a). "A theory of action and state orientation" in *Volition and personality: Action versus state orientation.* eds. J. Kuhl, and J. Beckmann (Göttingen: Hogrefe & Huber), 9–46.

Kuhl, J. (1994b). "Action versus state orientation: psychometric properties of the Action Control Scale (ACS-90)" in *Volition and personality: Action versus state orientation.* eds. J. Kuhl, and J. Beckmann (Göttingen: Hogrefe & Huber), 47–59.

Kuhl, J., and Kazén, M. (2003). "Handlungs- und Lageorientierung: Wie lernt man, seine Gefühle zu steuern [Action and state orientation: how can we learn to control emotions]" in *Diagnostik von Motivation und Selbstkonzept.* eds. J. Stiensmeier-Pelster, and F. Rheinberg (Göttingen: Hogrefe), 201–219.

Maxwell, J. P. (2004). Anger rumination: an antecedent of athlete aggression? *Psychol. Sport Exerc.* 5, 279–289. doi: 10.1016/s1469-0292(03)00007-4

Mosewich, A. D., Crocker, P. R., Kowalski, K. C., and DeLongis, A. (2013). Applying self-compassion in sport: an intervention with women athletes. *J. Sport Exerc. Psychol.* 35, 514–524. doi: 10.1123/jsep.35.5.514

Nolen-Hoeksema, S., Wisco, B. E., and Lyubomirsky, S. (2008). Rethinking rumination. *Perspect. Psychol. Sci.* 3, 400–424. doi: 10.1111/j.1745-6924.2008.00088

Querstret, D., and Cropley, M. (2013). Assessing treatments used to reduce rumination and/or worry: a systematic review. *Clin. Psychol. Rev.* 33, 996–1009. doi: 10.1016/j.cpr.2013.08.004

Raab, M., and Johnson, J. G. (2004). Individual differences of action orientation for risk taking in sports. *Res. Q. Exerc. Sport* 75, 326–336. doi: 10.1080/02701367.2004.10609164

Roy, M. M., Memmert, D., Frees, A., Radzevick, J., Pretz, J., and Noël, B. (2016). Rumination and performance in dynamic, team sport. *Front. Psychol.* 6:2016. doi: 10.3389/fpsyg.2015.02016

Scott, V., and McIntosh, W. (1999). The development of a trait measure of ruminative thought. *Pers. Individ. Dif.* 26, 1045–1056. doi: 10.1016/s0191-8869(98)00208-6

Scott, V. B. Jr., Stiles, K. B., Raines, D. B., and Koth, A. W. (2002). Mood, rumination, and mood awareness in the athletic performance of collegiate tennis players. *N. Am. J. Psychol.* 4, 457–468.

Stiensmeier-Pelster, J., John, M., Stulik, A., and Schürmann, M. (1989). Die Wahl von Entscheidungsstrategien: Der Einfluß von Handlungs-und Lageorientierung und die Bedeutung psychologischer Kosten [Choosing between different decision-making strategies: the influence of action and state orientation and the impact of mental costs]. *Z. Exp. Angew. Psychol.* 36.

Susanti, Y., and Pratiwi, H. (2014). M estimation, S estimation, and MM estimation in robust regression. *Int. J. Pure Appl. Math.* 91, 349–360. doi: 10.12732/ijpam.v91i3.7

Trapnell, P. D., and Campbell, J. D. (1999). Private self-consciousness and the five-factor model of personality: distinguishing rumination from reflection. *J. Personal. Soc. Psychol.* 76, 284–304. doi: 10.1037/0022-3514.76.2.284

Treynor, W., Gonzalez, R., and Nolen-Hoeksema, S. (2003). Rumination reconsidered: a psychometric analysis. *Cogn. Ther. Res.* 27, 247–259. doi: 10.1023/A:1023910315561

Van Aalderen, J. R., Donders, A. R. T., Giommi, F., Spinhoven, P., Barendregt, H. P., and Speckens, A. E. M. (2012). The efficacy of mindfulness-based cognitive therapy in recurrent depressed patients with and without a current depressive episode: a randomized controlled trial. *Psychol. Med.* 42, 989–1001. doi: 10.1017/s0033291711002054

Watkins, E. (2008). Constructive and unconstructive repetitive thought. *Psychol. Bull.* 134, 163–206. doi: 10.1037/0033-2909.134.2.163

Willimczik, K., Voelcker-Rehage, C., and Wiertz, O. (2006). Sportmotorische Entwicklung über die Lebensspanne [Lifespan development of motor skills: empirical findings on a theoretical concept]. *Zeitschrift für Sportpsychol.* 13, 10–22. doi: 10.1026/1612-5010.13.1.10

World Medical Association (2013). World Medical Association Declaration of Helsinki: ethical principles for medical research involving human subjects. *JAMA* 310, 2191–2194. doi: 10.1001/jama.2013.281053

16

Perceived and Received Dimensional Support: Main and Stress-Buffering Effects on Dimensions of Burnout

Chris Hartley* and Pete Coffee

Faculty of Health Sciences and Sport, University of Stirling, Stirling, United Kingdom

Correspondence:
Chris Hartley
Christopher.hartley@stir.ac.uk

Social support is an adaptive resource associated with lower levels of burnout in sport. The effects of social support on burnout have typically been demonstrated through (1) a main effects model (direct negative associations between social support and burnout) and (2) a stress-buffering model (social support buffering the negative effects of stress on burnout). While both models provide insights into functional adaptations to burnout and stress in sport, evidence for significant main and stress-buffering effects are inconsistent. Reasons for this is include: (1) testing of a singular perspective of support in empirical research, and (2) a lack of specificity when analyzing social support and burnout (e.g., adoption of global-level analyses). To address this, the purpose of the study was to test differing perspectives of social support (perceived availability of support and received support) in regards to the main and stress-buffering effects of dimensions of social support (emotional, esteem, informational, and tangible) on dimensions of burnout (reduced sense of accomplishment, devaluation, emotional and physical exhaustion). Cross-sectional data were collected from 222 athletes. Moderated hierarchical regression analyses revealed that: (1) higher levels of stress were associated with higher levels of burnout (all dimensions); (2) higher levels of perceived availability of support were associated with lower levels of reduced sense of accomplishment and devaluation (with the exception of perceived availability of emotional support upon devaluation), and (3) perceived availability of emotional support buffered the negative effects of high stress upon devaluation. There were no significant main or interactive effects for any dimensions of received support. The significant interaction suggests that higher levels of perceived availability of emotional support may result in a functional adaptation to higher stress such that individuals may be protected from higher levels of devaluation of sport.

Keywords: perceived availability of support, received support, stress, sport psychology, moderation

INTRODUCTION

Sport participation commonly involves exposure to a range of stressors (Fletcher et al., 2006; Sarkar and Fletcher, 2014). Yet the experience of stress has the potential to lead to burnout and negatively impact upon the psychological wellbeing of athletes (Udry et al., 1997; Gustafsson et al., 2017). While social support has the potential to protect athletes from deleterious adaptations to stress (e.g., from burnout: DeFreese and Smith, 2014; Lu et al., 2016), a lack of differentiated investigations have prevented researchers from developing a more nuanced understanding of how these constructs are related to one another. Such understanding would inform the design of theory-led interventions. As such, the purpose of the present study was to test differing perspectives of social support (perceived availability of support and received support) in regards to the main and stress-buffering effects of dimensions of social support (emotional, esteem, informational, and tangible) on dimensions of burnout (reduced sense of accomplishment, devaluation, emotional, and physical exhaustion).

There is an abundance of evidence demonstrating the beneficial effects of socially supportive relationships in sport (Holt and Hoar, 2006; Rees and Freeman, 2007; Lu et al., 2016). Social support has been positively associated with objective performance outcome (Freeman and Rees, 2008, 2009; Rees and Freeman, 2009, 2010), Olympic performance (Gould et al., 2002), challenge appraisals (Freeman and Rees, 2009), flow (Bakker et al., 2011), and self-confidence (Holt and Hoar, 2006; Rees and Freeman, 2007; Freeman et al., 2011), as well as lower risks for injury (Carson and Polman, 2012) and burnout (Freeman et al., 2011; DeFreese and Smith, 2013, 2014; Lu et al., 2016). Social support encompasses both structural (i.e., number and type of relationships) and functional components of interpersonal relationships (Cohen et al., 2000; Vangelisti, 2009). Functional components refer to the particular functions and purposes served by structural relationships, and there is general agreement that functional support can be categorized into dimensions of emotional support (i.e., providing a sense of comfort, security, and being loved and cared for), esteem support (i.e., bolstering ones' esteem and sense of competence), informational support (i.e., advice and guidance), and tangible support (i.e., concrete instrumental assistance; Rees and Hardy, 2000; Freeman et al., 2011).

Functional support, and the respective dimensions of support, are often further divided into two perspectives of support: perceived availability of support (perceived support) and received support (Vangelisti, 2009; Lakey, 2010). Perceived support refers to the subjective perception of support being available from one's friends, family, team-mates and coaches who may provide assistance, if needed (Rees and Freeman, 2010). Received support, on the other hand, refers to support actually received—the specific helping and supportive actions provided by friends, family, team-mates, and coaches (Bianco and Eklund, 2001; Rees and Freeman, 2010). Perceived and received support are considered distinct constructs (Dunkel-Schetter and Bennett, 1990), sharing as little as 12% common variance (Haber et al., 2007) and demonstrating different relationships with outcome variables (Rees and Freeman, 2007; Freeman and Rees, 2008; Uchino, 2009). Conceptualizing social support as a complex construct (perspectives: perceived, received) and multivariate (dimensions: emotional, esteem, informational, and tangible) is relevant to concerns over matching the most appropriate dimensions and perspectives of social support to the particular demands of sport-related outcomes such as burnout (Cutrona and Russell, 1990; Berg and Upchurch, 2007).

Dimensions and perspectives of social support may be particularly salient factors in protecting against stress and reducing burnout in sport (Eklund and Defreese, 2015; Gustafsson et al., 2017). In line with the psychological stress perspective (Cohen et al., 1997), individuals exposed to the demands of the sport environment might frequently encounter sport-related stressors and experience prolonged stress (Smith, 1986; Gustafsson et al., 2008). In this regard, burnout is a deleterious adaptation to stress (Raedeke et al., 2002; Ntoumanis et al., 2012). Recent reviews defined the experience of burnout as being characterized by distinct indicators, namely physical and psychological exhaustion, and a reduced sense of accomplishment and value toward sport (Eklund and Defreese, 2015; Gustafsson et al., 2017).

While stress is considered to be a key antecedent to the formation of burnout dimensions (alongside other contributing factors; Raedeke, 1997; Gustafsson et al., 2017), exposure to stressors does not necessarily lead to the experience of stress and formation of burnout, as social factors may protect against them (DeFreese and Smith, 2013). Specifically, perceived support is theorized to influence individuals' perceived capabilities and resources to cope with stressors, thereby affecting both primary and secondary stress-appraisals (Lazarus and Folkman, 1984; Freeman and Rees, 2009). Received support is theorized to intervene in response to stress experienced (e.g., through moderating coping behaviors), which may have implications for dimensions of burnout (Cohen et al., 2000; Bianco and Eklund, 2001). Indeed, social support is typically associated with lower levels of burnout dimensions (DeFreese and Smith, 2013, 2014), and may be considered an effective resource for protecting against the deleterious effects of stress and dimensions of burnout in sport (Freeman et al., 2011; Lu et al., 2016).

There have been investigations into the relative impact of specific dimensions of social support upon global burnout (e.g., Lu et al., 2016), and there have been comparisons made between perceived and received support at a global level upon dimensions of burnout (e.g., DeFreese and Smith, 2013, 2014). However, there are limitations to using global measures. Global measures of social support and burnout ignore the possibility that certain dimensions of support might be more strongly associated with certain dimensions of burnout (DeFreese and Smith, 2013; Freeman et al., 2014; Lu et al., 2016), and there may be discrepancies in the magnitude of these contributions.

Indeed, the development of burnout is a highly individualistic experience (Gould et al., 1997; Gustafsson et al., 2007), with longitudinal evidence suggesting individual dimensions of burnout may not develop in tandem (Isoard-Gautheu et al., 2015). For example, Lundkvist et al. (2018) found that exhaustion negatively predicted devaluation across a 6-month period (after which this association faded within an 18-month sample), and argued that several models outlining the proposed development of burnout indices appear to be problematic in sport contexts. There are also theoretical grounds for expecting discrepancies in the presence and magnitude of dimensional associations between social support and burnout, as certain dimensions of support might allow for functional adaptations to certain outcomes (Cutrona and Russell, 1990). For example, certain dimensions of support might exclusively foster specific types of coping behavior in response to deleterious adaptations to stress (such as burnout; Cohen and Wills, 1985). This can only be investigated using dimensional measures of social support and, to our knowledge, Freeman et al. (2011) have been the only researchers to investigate the main effects of specific dimensions of support upon specific dimensions of burnout in sport. Freeman et al. (2011) reported that esteem support was the only significant predictor for reduced sense of accomplishment, and informational support was the only significant predictor for devaluation and for emotional and physical exhaustion. These results suggest there may indeed be discrepancies in the presence and magnitude of associations between dimensions of social support and dimensions of burnout.

Two principal models typically guide social support research: (1) the main effects model, and (2) the stress-buffering model (Cohen and Wills, 1985; Cohen et al., 2000). The main effects model proposes social support to have a direct effect on outcomes irrespective of whether individuals are under high or low levels of stress; the stress-buffering model proposes social support to be related to outcomes as a function of stress (Cohen et al., 2000; Rees and Freeman, 2007; Freeman and Rees, 2010). Although perceived support is theorized to act primarily through the main effects model and received support through the stress-buffering model (Bianco and Eklund, 2001), researchers have often found evidence to the contrary. For example, perceived support has been found to buffer the deleterious effects of stress upon outcomes (Rees and Hardy, 2004; Freeman and Rees, 2010), and researchers have cited that there is only limited evidence for received support buffering the deleterious effects of stress upon outcomes (Rees and Freeman, 2007; Rees et al., 2007; Mitchell et al., 2014). Furthermore, it seems only two studies have directly investigated the stress-buffering effects of social support in relation to burnout in sport – yet these studies only investigated dimensional stress-buffering effects of received support upon global burnout (Lu et al., 2016), and global stress-buffering of social support upon dimensions of burnout (DeFreese and Smith, 2014). In short, our understanding of the dimensional operationalization of social support upon burnout through main and stress-buffering models remains unclear (Rueger et al., 2016).

A comparison of main and stress-buffering effects for perceived versus received support warrants a further consideration with regards to method of analyses. When perceived and received support are examined separately, both tend to be associated with main and stress-buffering effects, however, when examined together different effects tend to be observed (Rees and Freeman, 2007; Freeman and Rees, 2008). It has been suggested that although perceived and received support are considered separate constructs (Wethington and Kessler, 1986; Dunkel-Schetter and Bennett, 1990; Helgeson, 1993), they may potentially influence each other and be conceptually related under certain circumstances (Uchino, 2009). Considering this, it is advisable to simultaneously examine the differential impact of perceived and received support dimensions upon outcomes, as it might provide an indication as to which perspective of support exerts greater and/or unique effects upon outcomes and under what conditions (Dunkel-Schetter and Bennett, 1990; Bianco and Eklund, 2001; Rees and Freeman, 2007; Freeman and Rees, 2010).

The purpose of the present study was to test differing perspectives of social support (perceived availability of support and received support) in regards to the main and stress-buffering effects of dimensions of social support (emotional, esteem, informational, and tangible) on dimensions of burnout (reduced sense of accomplishment, devaluation, emotional and physical exhaustion). Considering the dearth of evidence upon which to postulate fully differentiated hypotheses in line with this purpose (e.g., DeFreese and Smith, 2013; DeFreese and Smith, 2014; Lu et al., 2016), we hypothesized the following: (1) higher levels of stress would be associated with higher levels of burnout dimensions; (2) there would be differences observed between perceived and received dimensional main effects of support on dimensions of burnout; and, (3) there would be differences observed between perceived and received support dimensional stress-buffering effects on dimensions of burnout.

MATERIALS AND METHODS

Participants

Participants were 222 athletes (122 male; mean age of 25.93 years, SD = 10.11 years), partaking in a range of 54 different sports (the most frequent of which were cycling, rugby, and soccer). The competitive levels of participants ranged from recreational (n = 58), club (n = 52), regional (n = 57), national (n = 36), to international (n = 19) standard.

Procedure

The study was approved by a University Ethics Committee and all participants provided informed consent. An online questionnaire was constructed and disseminated opportunistically through online portals, with all questionnaire sections randomized and counter-balanced to control for order-effects.

Measures

Stress

Participants were asked to indicate the degree of stress experienced by completing a 4-item measure representing four sources of sport-specific stress commonly drawn upon within the literature (e.g., Freeman and Rees, 2008, 2010): high performance concerns from others, injury concerns, stamina/fitness concerns, and doubts about current form. This approach to assessing specific stress experienced resulting from each stressor is in line with the psychological stress perspective (Cohen et al., 1997; Freeman and Rees, 2008), which focuses on whether individuals experience context-specific stress (as opposed to general stress) and not merely whether they encountered particular sport-related stressors. As developed by Freeman and Rees (2008, 2010), and given that there may be individual differences in the extent and timeliness of stress reactions (Lazarus and Folkman, 1984), the stem for each item was: "Please indicate how stressed you felt as a result of the following situations over the past two weeks." Participants were given 2 weeks to consider their stress experienced to ensure applicability to a range of athletes and timings across different sports and to gather an estimation of levels of stress. Participants were required to respond on a 5-point Likert scale ranging from 1 (*not at all*) to 5 (*a lot*). Item responses were summed to reduce the number of models and aid clarity of interpretation by creating a total score of stress (α = 0.77).

Perceived Support

The 16-item Perceived Available Support in Sport Questionnaire (the PASS-Q; Freeman et al., 2011) was used to assess perceived support. The PASS-Q has demonstrated good reliability and validity indices across independent samples (Freeman et al., 2011; Boat and Taylor, 2015). The stem for the PASS-Q is: "Please indicate to what extent you have these types of support available to you." Participants were required to respond on a 5-point Likert scale, ranging from 0 (*not at all*) to 4 (*extremely*). In line with the established factorial structure of the PASS-Q, dimensional item responses were averaged to create subscale (dimensional) scores for emotional (α = 0.90), esteem (α = 0.92), informational (α = 0.91), and tangible perceived support (α = 0.85).

Received Support

The 22-item Athletes' Received Support Questionnaire (the ARSQ; Freeman et al., 2014) was used to assess received support. The ARSQ has demonstrated good reliability and validity indices across independent samples (Freeman et al., 2014). The stem for the ARSQ is: "Please indicate the frequency with which you received each type of support during the last week." Participants were required to respond on a 5-point frequency scale, ranging from 0 (*not at all*) to 4 (*seven or more times*). In line with the established factorial structure of the ARSQ, dimensional item responses were averaged to create subscale scores for emotional (α = 0.89), esteem (α = 0.90), informational (α = 0.92), and tangible received support (α = 0.92).

Burnout

Dimensions of athlete burnout were assessed using the 15-item Athlete Burnout Questionnaire (ABQ; Raedeke and Smith, 2001), which has demonstrated good construct and structural validity in independent samples (Cresswell and Eklund, 2006; Raedeke and Smith, 2009; Gerber et al., 2018). The stem for the ABQ is: "Please indicate the extent to which you are currently experiencing each feeling." Participants were required to respond on a 5-point Likert scale, ranging from 0 (*almost never*) to 4 (*almost always*). In line with the established factorial structure of the ABQ, dimensional item responses were averaged to provide subscale scores for reduced sense of accomplishment (α = 0.79), devaluation (α = 0.81), and emotional and physical exhaustion (α = 0.90).

Analyses

The data were screened for outliers, indices of non-normality, and missing values, of which there were none. In order to compare, simultaneously, the main and stress-buffering potential for each dimension of perceived and received support upon dimensions of burnout, moderated hierarchical regression analyses were performed using a three-step process within the enter-method of regression (Cohen and Wills, 1985; Freeman and Rees, 2008). First, stress was entered at Step 1. Second, respective dimensions of perceived and received support (e.g., emotional perceived support and emotional received support) were entered at Step 2. Finally, the product terms for each support and stress (e.g., stress × emotional perceived support and stress × emotional received support) were entered at Step 3. Prior to analyses, all independent variables (stress, dimensions of perceived support, and dimensions of received support) were mean-centred (Jaccard et al., 1990). The significance of increments in explained variance in dimensions of burnout over and above that accounted for by the already-entered variables was assessed at each step.

RESULTS

Descriptives and bivariate correlations between all variables in the study are presented in **Table 1**. Stress was positively associated with all dimensions of burnout, and higher levels of perceived and received support were associated with lower levels of reduced sense of accomplishment and devaluation (except for the non-significant association between received tangible support and devaluation).

Main and Stress-Buffering Effects for Dimensions of Perceived and Received Support Upon Dimensions of Burnout

Results from moderated hierarchical regression analyses are presented in **Table 2**. At Step 1, there were significant positive main effects for stress upon reduced sense of accomplishment (Cohen's $F^2 = 0.03$, a small effect), devaluation (Cohen's $F2 = 0.08$, a small effect), and emotional and physical exhaustion (Cohen's $F^2 = 0.20$, a medium effect). In summary, higher levels of stress were associated with higher levels on dimensions of burnout.

At Step 2, there were, with the exception of a non-significant effect of perceived emotional support upon devaluation, significant negative main effects for all dimensions of perceived support upon reduced sense of accomplishment (Cohen's F^2 ranging between 0.14 and 0.23, representing medium effects) and devaluation (Cohen's F^2 = ranging between 0.05 and 0.06, representing small effects). For all significant effects, higher levels of support were associated with lower levels of burnout. There were no significant main effects for perceived support upon emotional and physical exhaustion, and there were no significant main effects for any dimensions of received support upon any dimensions of burnout.

Finally, at Step 3 the interaction of stress x perceived emotional support explained significant additional variance in devaluation, F (2,217) = 8.12**, $b = -0.17$**, $SE = 0.07$ [−0.30, −0.04], Cohen's $F^2 = 0.03$ (a small effect; the interaction is depicted in **Figure 1A**). The relationship between stress and devaluation was significantly different from zero at low ($t = 5.10$, $p < 0.01$) but not at high levels of perceived emotional support ($t = 0.99$, $p = 0.33$). Specifically, the relationship between stress and devaluation differed significantly from zero at levels of perceived emotional support less than 0.82 standard deviations above the mean (the simple slopes analysis is depicted in **Figure 1B**). The interaction was consistent with a stress-buffering explanation: higher levels of perceived emotional support negated the deleterious effects of higher levels of stress on devaluation (rather than burnout).

TABLE 1 | Means, standard deviations, and bivariate correlations for study variables.

	Variable	1	2	3	4	5	6	7	8	9	10	11	12
1	Reduced Sense of Accomplishment												
2	Devaluation	0.47**											
3	Emotional and physical exhaustion	0.23**	0.44**										
4	Stress	0.18**	0.27**	0.41**									
5	Perceived Emotional Support	−0.35**	−0.24**	0.01	−0.11								
6	Perceived Esteem Support	−0.43**	−0.23**	−0.04	−0.01	0.78**							
7	Perceived Informational Support	−0.40**	−0.25**	−0.04	−0.01	0.55**	0.77**						
8	Perceived Tangible Support	−0.38**	−0.25**	0.06	−0.06	0.70**	0.75**	0.72**					
9	Received Emotional Support	−0.22**	−0.15*	0.09	0.17*	0.54**	0.53**	0.41**	0.54**				
10	Received Esteem Support	−0.32**	−0.19**	0.05	0.04	0.49**	0.64**	0.54**	0.60**	0.84**			
11	Received Informational Support	−0.28**	−0.16*	0.09	0.14*	0.42**	0.56**	0.61**	0.59**	0.72**	0.77**		
12	Received Tangible Support	−0.26**	−0.10	0.12	0.10	0.43**	0.51**	0.52**	0.67**	0.67**	0.67**	0.84**	
	M	2.58	2.31	2.49	2.75	2.60	2.70	2.70	2.37	2.16	2.41	1.96	1.82
	SD	0.74	0.90	0.91	0.96	1.00	0.95	0.98	1.03	1.13	1.05	1.07	1.19

N = 222; $^*p < 0.05$; $^{**}p < 0.01$.

TABLE 2 | Moderated hierarchical regression results.

			Dependent Variable								
			RSA			DEV			EXH		
Dimension of support		Step	ΔR^2	*F*	B	ΔR^2	*F*	B	ΔR^2	*F*	B
Emotional	1	Stress	0.03**	7.13	0.13**	0.07**	17.78	0.25**	0.17**	44.35	0.37**
	2	Perceived Support	0.12**	12.55	−0.21**	0.06**	10.85	−0.13	< 0.01	14.99	0.06
		Received Support			−0.07			−0.11			−0.01
	3	Stress × PS	< 0.01	7.72	< 0.01	0.03*	8.12	−0.17*	< 0.01	9.08	−0.05
		Stress × RS			0.05			0.01			0.01
Esteem	1	Stress	0.03**	7.13	0.13**	0.07**	17.78	0.25**	0.17**	44.35	0.37**
	2	Perceived Support	0.19**	20.76	−0.27**	0.06**	11.17	−0.15*	0.01	15.27	−0.08
		Received Support			−0.07			−0.09			0.08
	3	Stress × PS	0.01	12.95	−0.05	< 0.01	6.88	−0.07	0.01	9.39	−0.08
		Stress × RS			0.08			0.01			0.03
Informational	1	Stress	0.03**	7.13	0.13**	0.07**	17.78	0.25**	0.17**	44.35	0.37**
	2	Perceived Support	0.16**	17.67	−0.25**	0.06**	11.67	−0.17*	0.01	15.23	−0.08
		Received Support			−0.08			−0.08			0.08
	3	Stress × PS	< 0.01	10.81	−0.07	< 0.01	7.00	−0.04	0.01	9.50	−0.10
		Stress × RS			0.05			0.03			0.08
Tangible	1	Stress	0.03**	7.13	0.13**	0.07**	17.78	0.25**	0.17**	44.35	0.37**
	2	Perceived Support	0.14**	14.63	−0.25**	0.05**	10.77	−0.24**	0.01	15.45	0.05
		Received Support			−0.04			0.04			0.04
	3	Stress × PS	0.01	9.16	−0.08	0.01	7.08	−0.13	0.01	9.80	−0.12
		Stress × RS			0.08			0.07			0.06

N = 222; $^*p < 0.05$; $^{**}p < 0.01$; RSA, reduced sense of accomplishment; DEV, devaluation of sport; EXH, emotional and physical exhaustion; PS, perceived support; RS, received support. All variables standardized except for products. Products were formed from preceding (standardized) variables.

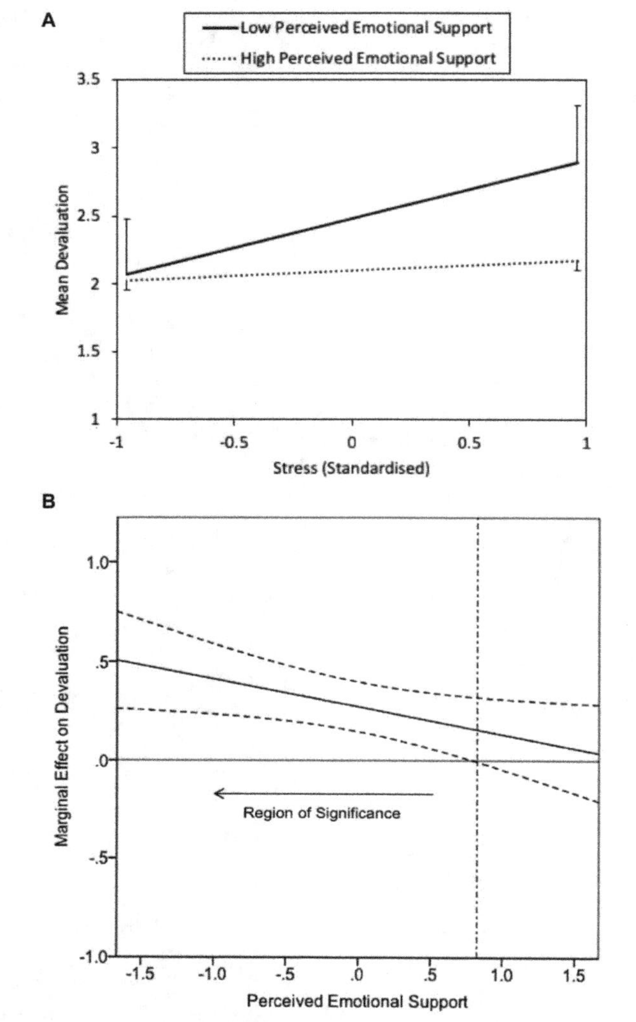

FIGURE 1 | The interactive relationship between stress and perceived emotional support upon devaluation **(A)**, with simple slopes analysis **(B)**.

DISCUSSION

The purpose of the present study was to test differing perspectives of social support (perceived availability of support and received support) in regards to the main and stress-buffering effects of dimensions of social support (emotional, esteem, informational, and tangible) on dimensions of burnout (reduced sense of accomplishment, devaluation, emotional and physical exhaustion). Hypothesis 1 was supported. Stress had deleterious relationships with all dimensions of burnout, such that higher levels of stress were associated with higher levels of dimensions of burnout. These results support stress-based models of burnout (Eklund and Defreese, 2015; Gustafsson et al., 2017). Hypotheses 2 was partially supported. Differences were observed between the dimensional main effects for perceived versus received support upon dimensions of burnout. Finally, Hypothesis 3 was supported. Differences were observed between the dimensional stress-buffering effects for perceived versus received support upon dimensions of burnout.

With regards to Hypothesis 2, higher levels of perceived availability of support were associated with lower levels of reduced sense of accomplishment and devaluation (with the exception of perceived availability of emotional support upon devaluation). No effects for received support on dimensions of burnout were observed. Although we did not hypothesize directional differences to exist between these fully differentiated measures, these findings are similar to previously found associations between global (DeFreese and Smith, 2013) and dimensional social support (Freeman et al., 2011) with dimensions of burnout. The observed differences between the independent main effects for perspectives of social support when entered simultaneously upon dimensions of burnout suggest that, compared to received support, perceived support was more strongly associated with dimensions of burnout. These findings are in line with global-level social support research that demonstrates (1) higher levels of perceived support are associated with lower levels of burnout (Bianco and Eklund, 2001; Freeman et al., 2011), and (2) received support is less consistently associated with outcome variables (Rees and Hardy, 2004; Rees and Freeman, 2007; Freeman and Rees, 2008, 2009; Lakey, 2010; Boat and Taylor, 2015) such as dimensions of burnout (DeFreese and Smith, 2013, 2014).

Empirical evidence from the extant literature reports discrepancies in the magnitude of perceived support's contributions to specific dimensions of burnout (e.g., DeFreese and Smith, 2013). Our findings support this. All perceived support dimensions had medium associations with reduced sense of accomplishment and small associations with devaluation (with the exception of perceived emotional support), however, no perceived support dimensions were associated with emotional and physical exhaustion. The medium association between perceived support and reduced sense of accomplishment suggests that knowing that different dimensions of supportive acts are available if needed might combat feelings of inefficacy and the tendency to evaluate oneself negatively in terms of performance capabilities. The small association between perceived support and devaluation suggests that knowing that different dimensions of supportive acts are available if needed might bolster ones' concern for performance quality and encourage a more positive attitude toward sport participation (Eklund and Defreese, 2015; Gustafsson et al., 2017). In contrast, there was an absence of an association between perceived support and exhaustion. Considering that physical exhaustion is a natural part of sport, it may be worthwhile exploring if the relevance of perceived support depends on whether exhaustion is driven primarily by physical (perceived support perhaps of little relevance) or psychological (perceived support perhaps of greater relevance) causes (DeFreese and Smith, 2013).

Further to our second hypothesis, the only difference observed between dimensions of perceived support and dimensions of burnout was an absence of an association between perceived emotional support and devaluation (perceived esteem, informational, and tangible support were associated with devaluation). This dimensional difference suggests that merely increasing levels of perceived social support in a global manner may not translate directly into beneficial outcomes. Further, providing unsatisfactory forms of support may fail to result in beneficial sport-related outcomes. For example, in our study, increasing levels of perceived emotional support did not result in beneficial adaptations for devaluation. Similarly, Freeman and Rees (2009) found that the only significant dimension of perceived support associated with enhanced performance was esteem support, which was shown to have both positive associations with challenge appraisals (through perceptions of situational control), and negative associations with threat appraisals. This supports Cohen and Wills (1985) theorizing that emotional and esteem support could be most useful in a range of achievement contexts, while informational and tangible support may be more effective in particular situations (Cohen and Wills, 1985). Indeed, specific associations have been found between certain dimensions of social support and other sport-related outcomes such as self-confidence (Freeman et al., 2011), burnout (dimensionally and globally; Freeman et al., 2011; Lu et al., 2016), and performance (Rees et al., 2007).

With regards to Hypothesis 3, only perceived emotional support buffered the deleterious association of stress upon devaluation. No dimensions of received support buffered the deleterious association of stress upon burnout dimensions. The observed differences between the independent stress-buffering effects for perspectives of social support when entered simultaneously upon dimensions of burnout are in line with previous research that reports that, compared to received support, perceived support is more consistently associated with stress-buffering (Rees and Hardy, 2004; Rees et al., 2007, 2010; Freeman and Rees, 2010; Mitchell et al., 2014). Perceived support, compared to received support, may also be more consistently related to beneficial outcomes. Perhaps the consistent perceived availability of support over time may lead to the formation of "trait-like" support profiles. In turn, this may facilitate persistent perceptions of support resource availability and control in individuals during times of stress (compared to received support which may be more context-dependent; Freeman and Rees, 2009; Uchino, 2009). Conversely, as seen in instances where social support fails to be beneficial (or even harmful; Schwarzer and Leppin, 1991; Reynolds and Perrin, 2004; Brock and Lawrence, 2009; Kellezi and Reicher, 2012), received support may unintentionally undermine recipients' perceptions of competency or autonomy, potentially triggering experiences of stress and/or feelings of embarrassment (e.g., Bolger and Amarel, 2007; Hassell et al., 2010). Consistent with a resiliency perspective (Sarkar and Fletcher, 2014), perceived support may thus allow for more functional adaptations to stress and dimensions of burnout, as knowing that support is available if needed may increase ones' perceived social resources and abilities to cope (Lazarus and Folkman, 1984; Bianco and Eklund, 2001), thereby resulting in more challenge and less threat-based stress appraisals (Freeman and Rees, 2009). As such, perceived support may result in more functional adaptations to dimensions of burnout by reducing the experience of stress (Gustafsson et al., 2017), as well as improving one's concern for performance quality and/or encouraging a more positive attitude toward sport participation (i.e., reducing devaluation; Raedeke et al., 2002).

Further to our third hypothesis, the only difference observed between dimensions of perceived support and dimensions of burnout was perceived emotional support buffering the deleterious association of stress on devaluation (perceived esteem, informational, and tangible support did not exhibit any stress buffering effects on any dimensions of burnout). This is only somewhat in line with previous findings, as Freeman and Rees (2010) found stress-buffering effects for perceived emotional, esteem and informational support dimensions upon self-confidence. Furthermore, our study found that no dimensions of received support buffered the deleterious associations of stress upon burnout dimensions. Although this is in line with evidence showing that received support dimensions may fail to exhibit stress-buffering effects upon global burnout (Lu et al., 2016), this contrasts with evidence showing global received support to exhibit stress-buffering effects upon self-confidence and performance (Rees and Freeman, 2007; Freeman and Rees, 2008). While the dimensional stress-buffering effect observed in this study provides empirical evidence for a stress-buffering effect in sport more generally, it highlights the importance of adopting multivariate conceptualizations of social support and outcomes, such as burnout (Lakey and Cronin, 2008; Rueger et al., 2016; Lundkvist et al., 2018). Indeed, it could be that knowing emotional support is available if needed, particularly during times of high levels of stress, may lead to the ideal sort of emotion-focused coping (e.g., Cutrona and Russell, 1990) needed when an athlete feels a detached and cynical attitude toward their performance quality and/or sport (Rees and Hardy, 2004). It may, therefore, be that merely increasing levels of social support irrespective of an athlete's social support or burnout-related needs may not translate directly into functional adaptations to stress (i.e., stress-buffering), and there may even be risks associated with providing unsatisfactory forms of support (i.e., resulting in deleterious adaptations to stress; Freeman and Rees, 2008).

The present study has several strengths. First, questionnaires developed in social and health psychology (e.g., SSQ; Sarason et al., 1987) have often been used in sport, and their utility in sport has been questioned as they do not necessarily reflect the specific forms of support that athletes require (Rees et al., 1999; Holt and Hoar, 2006). Therefore, our use of dimensional social support and burnout measures derived for the sport context (e.g., Raedeke and Smith, 2001; Freeman et al., 2011, 2014) reduces concerns over measurement error (Dunkel-Schetter and Bennett, 1990; Gerber et al., 2018), together with providing more sensitive tests for moderation (Uchino et al., 2012; Rueger et al., 2016). Second, to the best of our knowledge, our study is the first to investigate both main and stress buffering effects while using recommended multivariate conceptualizations of both social support and burnout (e.g., Freeman et al., 2011, 2014; Lundkvist et al., 2018). Fully differentiated investigations allow researchersk to determine the relative impact of different perspectives of support (i.e., received versus perceived) and specific supportivek acts (i.e., dimensions) upon adaptations to stress and other sport-related outcomes (Freeman and Rees, 2010; Hassell et al., 2010). Developing a more nuanced understanding of *how* different perspectives and dimensions of social support (and other contributing factors) influence functional adaptations to stress and other sport-related outcomes highlights an important area for future research. Such investigations will advance our understanding of stress and athlete psychological functioning more generally, and inform the design of interventions focussed on specific perspectives and dimensions of supportive acts (Freeman and Rees, 2009; Thoits, 2011).

Some limitations of the present study should also be noted. First, the use of a cross-sectional design prevents any causal inferences from being made. Second, while dimensional investigations into perceived versus received support and burnout allows for evaluations of the effects of specific support perspectives and specific supportive acts (i.e., dimensions; Cutrona and Russell, 1990; Raedeke and Smith, 2009), it does have several disadvantages: (1) it reduces parsimony for determining the differences between perspectives and dimensions of support (Rees and Freeman, 2007), and; (2) running multiple stress-buffering models may increase the risk of Type 1 Error (although this number of models is similar to those computed in previous social support research; DeFreese and Smith, 2014). Relatedly, an examination of gendered effects were beyond the scope of the current study. There is some evidence that a non-significant (Lai and Wiggins, 2003) to small gendered effect may exist for both work (Purvanova and Muros, 2010) and sport related burnout (Cremades and Wiggins, 2008 Isoard-Gautheu et al., 2015), and this may be an interesting avenue for future research to explore. Furthermore, due to the range of sports and athletes recruited, participants may have been at different stages of their competitive seasons and/or been injured, and it is therefore possible that our interpretation of the analysis could have been influenced had such demographic data been collected (Cresswell and Eklund, 2005; Quested and Duda, 2011). Future research may consider incorporating such variables in analyses.

Considering the above, more research is needed into the underlying mechanisms of why and under what conditions certain perspectives and/or dimensions of social support are more strongly associated with stress and particular dimensions of burnout. For example, Lu et al. (2016) found that under conditions of low stress, athletes with higher (lower) levels of resilience but low (high) levels of informational support were less prone to global burnout than those who were low in both resilience and informational social support. This suggests that single moderators may fail to fully capture the complexity of social support's stress-buffering effects (Smith et al., 1990). It is reasonable, therefore, to think that specific perspectives and/or dimensions of social support may interact in a conjunctive manner (Smith et al., 1990) with other socio-contextual moderators to influence the stress-burnout relationship. To provide an example, Social Identity Theory (Tajfel and Turner, 1979; Turner et al., 1987) posits the experience of sport-related stress and social support to be bound-up within the social dynamics of group life (Rees et al., 2015), both in terms of accentuating or alleviating the effects of stress (Lazarus and Folkman, 1984) and social support (Turner, 1991; Rees et al., 2013).

CONCLUSION

In conclusion, the findings from the present study highlight the unique differences observed between differing perspectives of social support (perceived availability of support and received support) in regards to the main and stress-buffering effects of dimensions of social support (emotional, esteem, informational, and tangible) on dimensions of burnout (reduced sense of accomplishment, devaluation, emotional and physical exhaustion). Our findings help address an important gap in the literature by showing that higher levels of perceived availability of emotional support may result in a functional adaptation to higher stress such that individuals may be protected from higher levels of devaluation of sport.

ETHICS STATEMENT

This study was carried out in accordance with the recommendations of the University of Stirling's Research Proposal Ethics Checklist (General University Ethics Panel), with written informed consent from all subjects. All subjects gave written informed consent in accordance with the Declaration of Helsinki. The protocol was approved by the University of Stirling's General University Ethics Panel.

AUTHOR CONTRIBUTIONS

Both authors contributed equally to the design, data collection, analysis and writing of this manuscript.

REFERENCES

Bakker, A. B., Oerlemans, W., Demerouti, E., Slot, B. B., and Ali, D. M. (2011). Flow and performance: a study among talented Dutch soccer players. *Psychol. Sport Exerc.* 12, 442–450. doi: 10.1016/j.psychsport.2011.02.003

Berg, C. A., and Upchurch, R. (2007). A developmental-contextual model of couples coping with chronic illness across the lifespan. *Psychol. Bull.* 133, 920–954. doi: 10.1037/0033-2909.133.6.920

Bianco, T., and Eklund, R. C. (2001). Conceptual considerations for social support research in sport and exercise settings: the case of sport injury. *J. Sport Exerc. Psychol.* 23, 85–107. doi: 10.1123/jsep.23.2.85

Bolger, N., and Amarel, D. (2007). Effects of social support visibility on adjustment to stress: experimental evidence. *J. Pers. Soc. Psychol.* 92, 458–475. doi: 10.1037/0022-3514.92.3.458

Brock, R. L., and Lawrence, E. (2009). Too much of a good thing: underprovision versus overprovision of partner support. *J. Family Psychol.* 23, 181–192. doi: 10.1037/a0015402

Boat, R., and Taylor, I. M. (2015). Patterns of change in psychological variables leading up to competition in superior versus inferior performers. *J. Sport Exerc. Psychol.* 37, 244–256. doi: 10.1123/jsep.2014-0216

Carson, F., and Polman, R. (2012). Experiences of professional rugby union players returning to competition following anterior cruciate ligament reconstruction. *Phys. Ther. Sport* 13, 35–40. doi: 10.1016/j.ptsp.2010.10.007

Cohen, S., Gottlieb, B. H., and Underwood, L. G. (2000). "Social relationships and health," in *Social Support Measurement and Intervention: A Guide for Health and Social Scientists*, eds S. Cohen, L. G. Underwood, and B. H. Gottlieb (New York, NY: Oxford University Press), 3–25.

Cohen, S., Kessler, R. C., and Underwood-Gordon, L. G. (1997). "Strategies for measuring stress in studies of psychiatric and physical disorders," in *Measuring Stress: A Guide for Health and Social Scientists*, eds S. Cohen, R. C. Kessler, and L. G. Underwood-Gordon (Oxford: Oxford University Press), 3–26.

Cohen, S., and Wills, T. A. (1985). Stress, social support and the buffering hypothesis. *Psychol. Bull.* 98, 310–357. doi: 10.1037//0033-2909.98.2.310

Cremades, J., and Wiggins, M. (2008). *Direction and Intensity of Trait Anxiety as Predictors of Burnout Among Collegiate Athletes.* Available at: http://www.athleticinsight.com/Vol10Iss2/TraitAnxiety.htm (accessed June 12, 2019).

Cresswell, S. L., and Eklund, R. C. (2005). Changes in athlete burnout and motivation over a 12-week league tournament. *Med. Sci. Sports Exerc.* 37, 1957–1966. doi: 10.1249/01.mss.0000176304.14675.32

Cresswell, S. L., and Eklund, R. C. (2006). The convergent and discriminant validity of burnout measures in sport: a multi-trait/multi-method analysis. *J. Sports Sci.* 24, 209–220. doi: 10.1080/02640410500131431

Cutrona, C. E., and Russell, D. W. (1990). "Type of social support and specific stress: toward a theory of optimal matching," in *Social Support: An Interactional View*, eds B. R. Sarason SUFFIXI, G. Sarason, and G. R. Pierce (New York, NY: Wiley), 319–336.

DeFreese, J. D., and Smith, A. L. (2013). Teammate social support, burnout, and self-determined motivation in collegiate athletes. *Psychol. Sport Exerc.* 14, 258–265. doi: 10.1016/j.psychsport.2012.10.009

DeFreese, J. D., and Smith, A. L. (2014). Athlete social support, negative social interactions and psychological health across a competitive sport season. *J. Sport Exerc. Psychol.* 36, 619–630. doi: 10.1123/jsep.2014-0040

Dunkel-Schetter, C., and Bennett, T. L. (1990). "Differentiating the cognitive and behavioral aspects of social support," in *Social Support: An Interactional View*, eds B. R. Sarason SUFFIXI, G. Sarason, and G. R. Pierce (New York, NY: Wiley), 267–296.

Eklund, R. C., and Defreese, J. D. (2015). Athlete burnout: what we know, what we could know, and how we can find out more. *Int. . Appl. Sci.* 27, 63–75. doi: 10.24985/ijass.2015.27.2.63

Fletcher, D., Hanton, S., and Mellalieu, S. (2006). "An organizational stress review: Conceptual and theoretical issues in competitive sport," in *Literature Reviews in Sport Psychology*, eds S. Hanton and S. D. Mellalieu (Hauppage, NY: Nova Science), 321–375.

Freeman, P., Coffee, P., Moll, T., Rees, T., and Sammy, N. (2014). The ARSQ: the athletes' received support questionnaire. *J. Sport Exerc. Psychol.* 36, 189–202. doi: 10.1123/jsep.2013-0080

Freeman, P., Coffee, P., and Rees, T. (2011). The PASS-Q: the perceived available support in sport questionnaire. *J. Sport Exerc. Psychol.* 33, 54–74. doi: 10.1123/jsep.33.1.54

Freeman, P., and Rees, T. (2008). The effects of perceived and received support on objective performance outcome. *Eur. J. Sport Sci.* 8, 359–368. doi: 10.1080/17461390802261439

Freeman, P., and Rees, T. (2009). How does perceived support lead to better performance? An examination of potential mechanisms. *J. Appl. Sport Psychol.* 21, 429–441. doi: 10.1080/10413200903222913

Freeman, P., and Rees, T. (2010). Perceived social support from team-mates: direct and stress-buffering effects on self-confidence. *Eur. J. Sport Sci.* 10, 59–67. doi: 10.1080/17461390903049998

Gerber, M., Gustafsson, H., Seelig, H., Kellmann, M., Ludyga, S., Colledge, F., et al. (2018). Usefulness of the Athlete Burnout Questionnaire (ABQ) as a screening tool for the detection of clinically relevant burnout symptoms among young elite athletes. *Psychol. Sport Exerc.* 39, 104–113. doi: 10.1016/j.psychsport.2018.08.005

Gould, D., Greenleaf, C., Chung, Y., and Guinan, D. (2002). A survey of U.S. Atlanta and Nagano Olympians: variables perceived to influence performance. *Res. Q. Exerc. Sport* 73, 175–186. doi: 10.1080/02701367.2002.10609006

Gould, D., Udry, E., Tuffey, S., and Loehr, J. (1997). Burnout in competitive junior tennis players: III. individual differences in the burnout experience. *Sport Psychol.* 11, 257–276. doi: 10.1123/tsp.11.3.257

Gustafsson, H., DeFreese, J. D., and Madigan, D. J. (2017). Athlete burnout: review and recommendations. *Curr. Opin. Psychol.* 16, 109–113. doi: 10.1016/j.copsyc.2017.05.002

Gustafsson, H., Hassmen, P., Kenta, G., and Johansson, M. (2008). A qualitative analysis of burnout in elite Swedish athletes. *Psychol. Sport Exerc.* 9, 800–816. doi: 10.1016/j.psychsport.2007.11.004

Gustafsson, H., Kenttä, G., Hassmén, P., Lundqvist, C., and Durand-Bush, N. (2007). The process of burnout: a multiple case study of three elite endurance athletes. *Int. J. Sport Psychol.* 38, 388–416.

Haber, M., Cohen, J., Lucas, T., and Baltes, B. (2007). The relationship between self?-reported received and perceived social support. *Am. J. Commun. Psychol.* 39, 133–144. doi: 10.1007/s10464-007-9100-9

Hassell, K., Sabiston, C. M., and Bloom, G. A. (2010). Exploring the multiple dimensions of social support among elite female adolescent swimmers. *Int. J. Sport Psychol.* 41, 340–359.

Helgeson, V. S. (1993). Two important distinctions in social support: kind of support and perceived versus received. *J. Appl. Soc. Psychol.* 23, 825–845. doi: 10.1111/j.1559-1816.1993.tb01008.x

Holt, N. L., and Hoar, S. D. (2006). "The multidimensional construct of social support," in *Literature Reviews in Sport Psychology*, eds S. Hanton and S. D. Mellalieu (New York, NY: Nova Science), 1–27.

Isoard-Gautheu, S., Guillet-Descas, E., Gaudreau, P., and Chanal, J. (2015). Development of burnout perceptions during adolescence among high-level athletes: a developmental and gendered perspective. *J. Sport Exerc. Psychol.* 37, 436–448. doi: 10.1123/jsep.2014-0251

Jaccard, J., Turrisi, R., and Wan, C. K. (1990). *Interaction Effects in Multiple Regression.* Newbury Park, CA: Sage.

Kellezi, B., and Reicher, S. D. (2012). "Social cure or social curse? The psychological impact of extreme events during the Kosovo conflict," in *The Social Cure*, eds J. Jetten, C. Haslam, and S. A. Haslam (London: Psychology Press).

Lai, C., and Wiggins, M. (2003). Burnout perceptions over time in NCAA Division I soccer players. *Int. Sports J.* 7, 120–127.

Lakey, B. (2010). "Basic research in social support suggests new strategies for intervention," in *Social Psychological Foundations of Clinical Psychology*, eds J. E. Maddux and P. Tangey (New York, NY: Guildford Publications), 177–194.

Lakey, B., and Cronin, A. (2008). "Low social support and major depression: Research, theory and methodological issues," in *Risk Factors for Depression*, eds K. S. Dobson and D. Dozois (San Diego: Academic Press), 385–408. doi: 10.1016/b978-0-08-045078-0.00017-4

Lazarus, R. S., and Folkman, S. (1984). *Stress Appraisal and Coping.* New York, NY: Springer.

Lu, F. J. H., Lee, W. P., Chang, Y., Chou, C., Hsu, Y., Lin, J., et al. (2016). Interaction of athletes' resilience and coaches' social support on the stress-burnout relationship: a conjunctive moderation perspective. *Psychol. Sport Exerc.* 22, 202–209. doi: 10.1016/j.psychsport.2015.08.005

Lundkvist, E., Gustafsson, H., Davis, P. A., Holmström, S., Lemyre, N., and Ivarsson, A. (2018). The temporal relations across burnout dimensions in athletes. *Scand. J. Med. Sci. Sports* 28, 1215–1226. doi: 10.1111/sms.13000

Mitchell, I., Evans, L., Rees, T., and Hardy, L. (2014). Stressors, social support and the buffering hypothesis: effects on psychological responses of injured athletes. *Br. J. Health Psychol.* 19, 486–508. doi: 10.1111/bjhp.12046

Ntoumanis, N., Taylor, I. M., and Thøgersen-Ntoumani, C. (2012). A longitudinal examination of coach and peer motivational climates in youth sport: implications for moral attitudes, well-being, and behavioral investment. *Dev. Psychol.* 48, 213–223. doi: 10.1037/a0024934

Purvanova, R. K., and Muros, J. P. (2010). Gender differences in burnout: a meta-analysis. *J. Vocat. Behav.* 77, 168–185. doi: 10.1016/j.jvb.2010.04.006

Quested, E., and Duda, J. L. (2011). Antecedents of burnout among elite dancers: a longitudinal test of basic needs theory. *Psychol. Sport Exerc.* 12, 159–167. doi: 10.1016/j.psychsport.2010.09.003

Raedeke, T. D. (1997). Is athlete burnout more than stress? A commitment perspective. *J. Sport Exerc. Psychol.* 19, 396–417. doi: 10.1123/jsep.19.4.396

Raedeke, T. D., Lunney, K., and Venables, K. (2002). Understanding athlete burnout: coach perspectives. *J. Sport Behav.* 25, 181–206. doi: 10.1177/0033294117698465

Raedeke, T. D., and Smith, A. L. (2001). Development and preliminary validation of an athlete burnout measure. *J. Sport Exerc. Psychol.* 23, 281–306. doi: 10.1123/jsep.23.4.281

Raedeke, T. D., and Smith, A. L. (2009). *The Athlete Burnout Questionnaire Manual.* Morgantown, WV: West Virginia University.

Rees, T., and Freeman, P. (2007). The effects of perceived and received support on self-confidence. *J. Sports Sci.* 25, 1057–1065. doi: 10.1080/02640410600982279

Rees, T., and Freeman, P. (2009). Social support moderates the relationship between stressors and task performance through self-efficacy. *J. Soc. Clin. Psychol.* 28, 244–263. doi: 10.1521/jscp.2009.28.2.244

Rees, T., and Freeman, P. (2010). Social support and performance in a golf-putting experiment. *Sport Psychol.* 24, 333–348. doi: 10.1123/tsp.24.3.333

Rees, T., and Hardy, L. (2000). An investigation of the social support experiences of high-level sports performers. *Sport Psychol.* 14, 327–347. doi: 10.1123/tsp.14.4.327

Rees, T., and Hardy, L. (2004). Matching social support with stressors: effects on factors underlying performance in tennis. *Psychol. Sport Exerc.* 5, 319–337. doi: 10.1016/S1469-0292(03)00018-9

Rees, T., Hardy, L., and Freeman, P. (2007). Stressors, social support, and effects upon performance in golf. *J. Sports Sci.* 25, 33–42. doi: 10.1080/02640410600702974

Rees, T., Haslam, S. A., Coffee, P., and Lavallee, D. (2015). A social identity approach to sport psychology: principles, practise and prospects. *Sports Med.* 45, 1083–1096. doi: 10.1007/s40279-015-0345-4

Rees, T., Ingledew, D. K., and Hardy, L. (1999). Social support dimensions and components of performance in tennis. *J. Sports Sci.* 17, 421–429. doi: 10.1080/026404199365948

Rees, T., Mitchell, I., Evans, L., and Hardy, L. (2010). Stressors, social support and psychological responses to sport injury in high and low-performance standard participants. *Psychol. Sport Exerc.* 11, 505–512. doi: 10.1016/j.psychsport.2010.07.002

Rees, T., Salvatore, J., Coffee, P., Haslam, S. A., Sargent, A., and Dobson, T. (2013). Reversing downward performance spirals. *J. Exp. Soc. Psychol.* 49, 400–403. doi: 10.1016/j.jesp.2012.12.013

Reynolds, J. S., and Perrin, N. A. (2004). Mismatches in social support and psychosocial adjustment to breast cancer. *Health Psychol.* 23, 425–430. doi: 10.1037/0278-6133.23.4.425

Rueger, S. Y., Malecki, C. K., Pyun, Y., Aycock, C., and Coyle, S. (2016). A meta-analytical review of the association between perceived social support and depression in childhood and adolescence. *Psychol. Bull.* 142, 1017–1067. doi: 10.1037/bul0000058

Sarason, I. G., Sarason, B. R., Shearin, E. N., and Pierce, G. R. (1987). A brief measure of social support: practical and theoretical implications. *J. Soc. Pers. Relat.* 4, 497–510. doi: 10.1177/0265407587044007

Sarkar, M., and Fletcher, D. (2014). Psychological resilience in sport performers: a review of stressors and protective factors. *J. Sports Sci.* 32, 1419–1434. doi: 10.1080/02640414.2014.901551

Schwarzer, R., and Leppin, A. (1991). Social support and health: a theoretical and empirical overview. *J. Soc. Pers. Relat.* 8, 99–127. doi: 10.1177/0265407591081005

Smith, R. E. (1986). Toward a cognitive-affective model of athletic burnout. *J. Sport Psychol.* 8, 36–50. doi: 10.1123/jsp.8.1.36

Smith, R. E., Smoll, F. L., and Ptacek, J. T. (1990). Conjunctive moderator variables in vulnerability and resiliency research: life stress, social support, and coping skills, and adolescent sport injuries. *J. Pers. Soc. Psychol.* 58, 360–370. doi: 10.1037//0022-3514.58.2.360

Tajfel, H., and Turner, J. C. (1979). "An integrative theory of intergroup conflict," in *The Social Psychology of Intergroup Relations*, eds W. G. Austin and S. Worchel (Monterey, CA: Brooks-Cole), 33–47.

Thoits, P. A. (2011). Mechanisms linking social ties and support to physical and mental health. *J. Health Soc. Behav.* 52, 145–161. doi: 10.1177/0022146510395592

Turner, J. C. (1991). *Social Influence.* Pacific Grove, CA: Brooks-Cole.

Turner, J. C., Hogg, M. A., Oakes, P. J., Reicher, S. D., and Wetherell, M. S. (1987). *Rediscovering the Social Group: A Self-Categorization Theory.* Oxford: Blackwell.

Uchino, B. N. (2009). Understanding the links between social support and physical health: a lifespan perspective with emphasis on the separability of perceived and received support. *Perspect. Psychol. Sci.* 4, 236–255. doi: 10.1111/j.1745-6924.2009.01122.x

Uchino, B. N., Bowen, K., Carlisle, M., and Birmingham, W. (2012). What are the psychological pathways linking social support to health outcomes? A visit with the "ghosts" of research past, present, and future. *Soc. Sci. Med.* 74, 949–957. doi: 10.1016/j.socscimed.2011.11.023

Udry, E., Gould, D., Bridges, D., and Tuffey, S. (1997). People helping people? Examining the social ties of athletes coping with burnout and injury stress. *J. Sport Exerc. Psychol.* 19, 368–395. doi: 10.1123/jsep.19.4.368

Vangelisti, A. L. (2009). Challenges in conceptualizing social support. *J. Soc. Pers. Relat.* 26, 39–51. doi: 10.1177/0265407509105520

Wethington, E., and Kessler, R. C. (1986). Perceived support, received support, and adjustment to stressful life events. *J. Health Soc. Behav.* 27, 78–89. doi: 10.2307/2136504

17

Effects of a Mental Health Intervention in Athletes

Stephen Shannon[1,2*], Donncha Hanna[3,4], Tandy Haughey[1], Gerard Leavey[5], Conor McGeown[1] and Gavin Breslin[1,2]

[1] Sport and Exercise Sciences Research Institute, Ulster University, Newtownabbey, United Kingdom, [2] Institute of Mental Health Sciences, Ulster University, Derry, United Kingdom, [3] School of Psychology, Queen's University Belfast, Belfast, United Kingdom, [4] Centre for Evidence and Social Innovation, Queen's University Belfast, Belfast, United Kingdom, [5] Bamford Centre for Mental Health and Wellbeing, School of Psychology, Ulster University, Coleraine, United Kingdom

***Correspondence:**
Stephen Shannon
s.shannon@ulster.ac.uk

Introduction: Many sport associations have responded to mental health issues in sport through the inclusion of self-management programs, such as mindfulness training, which may improve well-being through increasing one's competence in self-regulating stressors. Yet, the mechanisms accounting such changes lack a theoretical basis, particularly in athletes.

Aim: To determine the effect of a mental health intervention comprising a mindfulness program for promoting well-being, reducing stress, and increasing competence in mental health self-management. This is the first study among athletes to test the mechanisms of change in a mindfulness program using Self-Determination Theory (SDT).

Methods: A 2 (groups) × 2 (time-point) non-randomized controlled trial was conducted, and between-groups baseline differences were firstly assessed. Two competing regression models assessing singular and serial indirect mediating mechanisms were conducted, in which mindfulness (Model 1) and competence satisfaction (Model 2) were both tested as primary and secondary mediators predicting change scores in stress and well-being. Demographic variables (i.e., gender, age) were controlled for in the analyses.

Results: Two hundred and thirty-eight student athletes (mean age = 20.47 years, $SD = 3.30$, 57.6% = males) participated, with 108 in the intervention group who received an instructional workshop, and a home-directed mindfulness program comprising daily meditation sessions. No baseline differences were found between intervention and control groups. In Model 1, mindfulness was not directly enhanced by the intervention, subsequently resulting in no indirect effects on competence, stress and well-being. In Model 2, the intervention was directly related to positive changes in competence ($\beta = 0.39$, $p < 0.05$), subsequently resulting in indirect effects on mindfulness awareness ($\beta = 0.07$, $p < 0.05$), stress ($\beta = -0.06$, $p < 0.05$), and well-being ($\beta = 0.05$, $p < 0.05$). In addition, serial indirect effects for the intervention on stress were present through competence and mindfulness awareness in sequence ($\beta = -0.02$, $p < 0.05$), and; on well-being through competence, mindfulness awareness, and stress in sequence ($\beta = 0.01$, $p < 0.05$; $R^2 = 0.54$).

Conclusion: Mindfulness-based mental health interventions may be effective at reducing stress and promoting well-being in athletes, with the caveat that attention is given to the inclusion of mental health competence promotion in program design. However, it remains unclear whether increasing mindfulness itself can exert additional salutary effects. Our findings have an important bearing on how mindfulness programs are developed within athlete mental health interventions.

Keywords: health psychology, sport, mediation, well-being, needs satisfaction

INTRODUCTION

Well-being is defined as a state of optimal functioning (Ryan and Deci, 2017) and a key component of a two-continua model of mental health (Keyes, 2005). As a theoretical construct, well-being is characterized by psychological (i.e., a sense of purpose, realizing one's potential), emotional (i.e., positive affective states, reduced negative affect) and social (i.e., relationships) dimensions (Keyes, 2005). Stress, inversely related to well-being (Keyes, 2005; Huppert, 2009; Diener et al., 2018), occurs when one feels overwhelmed or unable to cope as a result of pressures (Mental Health Foundation, 2018), and hence requires a preventative and treatment response. Student-athletes (or collegiate athletes) are prone to stress because of co-existing academic, social and sporting demands (Wilson and Pritchard, 2005; Bennett, 2007). For example, student-athletes report pressure to achieve in both academic and sporting pursuits, a constrained social life, relationship difficulties and examination pressures (Gavrilova et al., 2017). Student-athletes have higher clinical and sub-clinical risks for behavioral mental health problems (e.g., substance misuse, eating disorders, gambling) compared to non-athletes (Moreland et al., 2018). Moreover, student-athletes are at least as, or more likely, to experience mood disorders compared to non-athletes (Donohue et al., 2018). Furthermore, due to the physical, and often aggressive nature of sport, student-athletes can incur physical injury, and experience emotional and physical fatigue from competition and over-training (Putukian, 2016). Athletes may also experience performance pressures from coaches, teammates and spectators, and often strive to succeed at the expense of personal well-being (Abedalhafiz et al., 2010; Breslin et al., 2018b). When left untreated, such stressors can manifest in impaired functioning (Moreland et al., 2018), highlighting the need for mental health self-management interventions.

Mental health self-management refers to monitoring how one's mental health is impacting upon daily functioning, and utilization of strategies that protect and promote mental health (Wolf, 1996). Many student-athletes report that they do not have the skills, or resources, to self-manage mental health, resulting in maladaptive coping strategies (e.g., substance misuse) (Eisenberg et al., 2007; Hunt and Eisenberg, 2010). Mindfulness is an example of a self-management strategy available to athletes (Noetel et al., 2017). Mindfulness is defined as a mental state characterized by an awareness of present events and experiences (Brown and Ryan, 2003), achieved mainly through meditative practices (Sappington and Longshore, 2015). Although mindfulness has traditionally been guided by practitioners in group-based or individual therapies (Langley, 2013), recently, mindfulness programs have become widely available through auditory meditative guidance in smartphone applications (Howells et al., 2016).

In sport, most mindfulness interventions intend to improve performance-related outcomes (e.g., improving psychological flow during performance) rather than mental health (Sappington and Longshore, 2015; Noetel et al., 2017). While mindfulness intervention studies for improving mental health outcomes among athletes are promising (e.g., Vidic et al., 2017; Glass et al., 2018), so far, none have examined the theoretical mechanisms of change that may explain the benefits experienced. To ascertain how changes occur during mindfulness programs, theoretical constructs are modeled to assess the indirect effect of a treatment (X) on an outcome (Y) through one or more mediators (M) (Kok et al., 2004).

Relevant to the monitoring and ability components of the mental health self-management construct (Wolf, 1996), it is proposed that when one perceives mental health competence, one can cope adaptively, regulate stress and experience a positive sense of well-being (Gustafsson and Skoog, 2012). Self-Determination Theory (SDT) (Ryan and Deci, 2000) posits that competence, an innate psychological need and feeling a sense of effectiveness in one's environment, is essential for optimal well-being. Of the three core psychological needs in SDT (i.e., competence, autonomy, relatedness) competence has been shown to have clear theoretical links with self-management, and indeed, a comprehensive body of research indicates that competence satisfaction is robustly related to positive mental health (Ryan and Deci, 2017). Models of SDT (Vallerand, 1997) outline that psychological needs exist and influence each other at three levels, i.e., situational (here and now), contextual (specific domains) and global (day-to-day). At the contextual level of mental health, researchers have shown that competence is linked to enhanced well-being (Mikolajczak et al., 2015) and reduced stress (Jex et al., 2001). Moreover, validated health domain measures of competence have been developed from a SDT perspective (Williams and Deci, 1996). Hence, given the clear theoretical links, mental health competence can be operationalized in a self-management intervention aiming to promote well-being.

In SDT, Ryan and Deci (2000) outline that needs-support (i.e., provision of choice, positive feedback, and caring dialogue) from intervention instructors has important implications for participants' needs satisfaction, which ultimately aides in the initiation of health behavior change (e.g., mindfulness practices, exercise) and well-being. Indeed, from an interpersonal perspective, health interventions delivered in a needs-supportive environment have been shown to improve participants' perceived autonomy-support, which subsequently resulted in improved needs satisfaction and well-being (Shannon et al., 2018). However, beyond such social-contextual factors, individuals can also draw upon internal psychological skills processes to satisfy their needs and well-being, such as one's ability to be mindful of present events and experiences (Weinstein and Ryan, 2011; Ryan and Deci, 2017). In other words, through having an improved awareness and attention of the present moment, a person can reflectively self-manage the thoughts, and ultimately regulate feelings and basic needs satisfaction (Schultz and Ryan, 2015).

While SDT research on interpersonal predictors of needs satisfaction is extensive (Ryan and Deci, 2017), a small but growing number of studies show that mindfulness is related to competence satisfaction, and consequent mental health outcomes (Chang et al., 2018). In a temporal sense, it has been proposed that competence satisfaction is a corollary of mindfulness, such that mindful states provide individuals with a greater awareness of ongoing events, and subsequent purposive selection of need-satisfying experiences (Campbell et al., 2016; Campbell et al., 2017). In support of this hypothesis, correlational studies (Schultz et al., 2015; Chang et al., 2018) have shown that mindfulness is positively related to competence satisfaction which indirectly predicted stress reductions and improvements in well-being. However, it has also been shown that competence satisfaction is a precursor to mindfulness, and predicted improvements in employee well-being through mindfulness (Olafsen, 2017). With this view, it is proposed that competence satisfaction can be thought of as a resource that enables a person to be mindful, which therein provides individuals with an awareness that supports positive psychological well-being. Indeed, Brown et al. (2007) have emphasized that most research has taken the perspective of mindfulness as a facilitative factor of needs satisfaction, yet it is equally probable that psychological needs satisfaction cultivates mindful states.

Therefore, the temporal nature of the competence–mindfulness relationship remains unclear and requires further theoretical assessment (Brown et al., 2007; Creswell, 2017), and has yet to be rigorously assessed through an intervention study using SDT. Testing these questions has important theoretical and practical implications for the way in which mental health interventions with a mindfulness component are designed. Hence, the inclusion of SDT constructs in the analyses of a mindfulness intervention are warranted to contribute to current theoretical understanding of the mechanisms of change in mindfulness interventions. As such, the aim of this study was to determine whether a mental health intervention could improve well-being through reducing stress, and enhancing mindfulness and mental health competence.

Study Hypotheses and Models Tested

The intervention was analyzed through two competing regression models comprising theoretically driven hypotheses. In both Models 1 and 2, well-being was designated as the dependent variable (*Y*), with participation in the intervention as the independent variable (*X*). To test the temporal relationship between competence satisfaction and mindfulness, in Model 1, mindfulness was designated as the primary mediator (*M1*), competence satisfaction (i.e., in self-managing mental health) was designated as mediator 2 (*M2*), and stress as mediator 3 (*M3*) (see **Figure 1**). The intervention was hypothesized to directly increase mindfulness (Hypothesis 1; H1), was in turn hypothesized to mediate the effects of the intervention on competence satisfaction (Hypothesis 2; H2). Considering stress has been inversely related to both mindfulness and competence, the intervention was hypothesized to indirectly effect stress through mindfulness (Hypothesis 3; H3), and through mindfulness and competence in sequence (Hypothesis 4; H4). Lastly, the intervention's effects on well-being were hypothesized to be indirectly influenced through a combination of singular (i.e., intervention > mindfulness > well-being), double (i.e., intervention > mindfulness > competence > well-being; intervention > mindfulness > stress > well-being), and triple (i.e., intervention > mindfulness > competence > stress > well-being) sequential mediating pathways (Hypothesis 5; H5). In Model 2, competence satisfaction was designated the primary mediator (*M1*), while mindfulness was designated as mediator 2 (*M2*), and stress as mediator 3 (*M3*). We explored all of the above hypotheses, assuming the same direction of relationships.

MATERIALS AND METHODS

Design, Inclusion Criteria, Recruitment Setting and Procedure

Ethical approval was granted by Ulster University (January 2017). All participants provided informed consent prior to their involvement. A mixed 2 (groups) × 2 (time-points) non-randomized controlled trial was conducted and reported using the Transparent Reporting of Evaluations with Non-randomized Designs (TREND) statement (Des Jarlais et al., 2004). It was not possible to implement a waiting-list controlled randomized design due to several foreseen practical considerations. These included; limited human resources to deliver the workshop across multiple university courses, and; student-athletes' unavailability beyond the specified study time period because of travel, academic and work commitments. However, efforts were made to reduce the potential for contamination, as outlined below.

Inclusion criteria was based on participants responding "yes" to the following survey question consistent with the definition of sport, "are you an athlete involved in a structured, competitive physical activity?" (Rejeski and Brawley, 1988), resulting in 238 in the final sample, and exclusion of 58 non-athletes. Intervention participants were recruited by a verbal presentations which supplemented content from sport and exercise psychology modules in three academic sport courses. No academic course credit was received for engagement with the intervention, and participation was voluntary. Control participants were recruited by the research team through a range of sport centers and sports clubs, and selected university courses that did not comprise intervention participants. From March to April 2018, trained researchers led survey data collection under quiet classroom conditions, and participants completed the survey through online

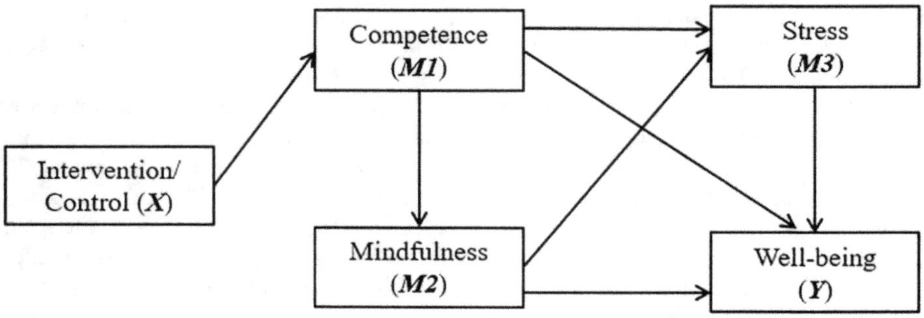

Note: competence and mindfulness were both tested as mediator 1 in the two competing regression models; direct and indirect hypothesised effects were tested through Hayes PROCESS macro for SPSS, in addition to direct and indirect effects on each mediator.

FIGURE 1 | Hypothesized competing regression models assessing the effect of a mental health intervention (*X*) on well-being (*Y*), through mental health competence/mindfulness (*M1*), mental health competence/mindfulness (*M2*) and stress (*M3*).

computer devices at baseline (Time 1), and two-weeks following the intervention (Time 2). The survey included descriptive items on the participants' gender, sport, and age.

Intervention

The State of Mind Ireland (Lawlor et al., 2015; Breslin et al., 2018a, 2019) intervention is a mental health awareness intervention, comprising an instructional workshop on mental health and mindfulness, and home-directed mindfulness training program. The intervention workshop took place in a seminar classroom on university campuses. Workshops lasted approximately 90 min (see **Table 2**), wherein each workshop comprised an average of 49 participants. The SOMI program was delivered by a psychiatrist and a student counselor with extensive course delivery experience. To ensure further available mental health support, the intervention deliverers consistently signposted participants to freely available clinical help at the university.

The workshop content was designed around SDT principles (Stone et al., 2009), to the extent that the activities and tutor delivery-style were provided through a needs-supportive environment[1] that acknowledged participant input through open-ended questions, included regular positive instructional feedback, and empathetic and caring communication (e.g., use of the word "may" instead of "should" when providing instructions). For instance, the workshop introduced mental health as a positive concept, and asked participants to reflect on common stressors, and discuss their knowledge of mindfulness as a mental health self-management tool. Participants viewed vignettes of prominent athlete meditators, and then feedback on how a mindful state may improve participants' competence to manage stressors, and promote mental health both in sport and university life contexts.

The second half of the workshop comprised instructions on the mindfulness mobile application that was designed by an online healthcare company specializing in meditation. The application included fourteen daily sessions comprising auditory and visual guidance, such as mindful body scanning for physical sensations, counting inhalations and exhalations, and noting thoughts and feelings. As part of the workshop participants engaged in a one minute-long guided taster session. Using needs-supportive communication, the workshop deliverers encouraged the participants to complete the daily sessions as much as possible during the a two-week period, with the application allowing for self-selection of the session durations (i.e., 5, 10, 15 or 20 min in length). Further positive instructional reminders were sent to participants through email and SMS acknowledging the challenges of mindfulness training, and encouragement to continue with the program. To assess adherence to the sessions, at follow-up the intervention participants reported on how many mindfulness sessions they completed by answering a single questionnaire item ranging from none through to 14.

Outcomes

Mindfulness

Mindfulness was measured using Brown and Ryan (2003) Mindfulness Attention Awareness Scale (MAAS), a 15-item questionnaire designed to assess attention to, and awareness of, day-to-day experiences. All items were scored on a 6-point Likert scale ranging from "almost always" (1), to "almost never" (6), with higher scores reflecting better mindfulness. The MAAS is a valid and reliable measure, with several studies showing a unidimensional factor structure (Brown and Ryan, 2003; MacKillop and Anderson, 2007) and a Cronbach's alpha = 0.88. An example item from the MAAS is: "I could be experiencing some emotion and not be conscious of it until some time later."

Competence Satisfaction

The Perceived Competence Scale (PCS; Williams and Deci, 1996) was adapted and used to measure the participants' competence

[1]Both deliverers were trained in leading the workshops through an autonomy-supportive style, and training was adapted from previous interventions using SDT in the physical activity domain (Shannon et al., 2018).

with respect to self-managing mental health. All four items were scored on a 7-point Likert scale, with higher scores indicating higher competence. An example item includes: "I feel confident in my ability to manage my mental health." The PCS is a valid and reliable tool for measuring domain-level competence (Williams et al., 1998), with a Cronbach's alpha = 0.94 within the present study.

Stress

Stress was measured using the 10-item Perceived Stress Scale (PSS) (Cohen et al., 1994). The PSS assesses the appraisal of stress in day-to-day experiences and demonstrates excellent psychometric properties, with a unidimensional structure (Roberti et al., 2006; Lee, 2012). Each item assessed on a 5-point Likert scale ranging from 0 ("never") to 4 ("very often"), with lower scores representing less stress. Cronbach's alpha = 0.83 within the present sample.

Well-Being

Well-being was measured using the 14-item Warwick-Edinburgh Mental Well-being Scale (WEMWBS) a validated and reliable instrument used to measure both hedonic (e.g., happiness and life satisfaction), social (e.g., relationship), and eudemonic (e.g., self-actualization) components of well-being through a unidimensional factor structure (Tennant et al., 2007). Items were anchored on a 5-point Likert scale ranging from "none of the time" (1), to "all of the time" (5). Higher scores indicate better well-being. Cronbach's alpha = 0.90.

Data Management and Analyses

Data Management

The Statistical Package for Social Sciences (SPSS, version 24) was used for all analyses. On each independent scale, Little's Missing Completely at Random (MCAR; Little, 1988) was used to assess if responses were missing in random order. Analyses revealed that the data were missing at random ($p > 0.05$), warranting use of the Expectation Maximisation (EM) algorithm for estimating missing values. EM was conducted on each individual scale, using inter-correlated items as predictors, which assumes a logical theoretical structure within the items (Field, 2013).

Data Analyses

Descriptive percentage statistics were calculated for gender (i.e., male or female), sport type and sessions completed by the intervention group. Mean and standard deviation scores were for each study outcome at their corresponding time points (baseline and two-weeks follow-up), categorized by intervention and control group. To ascertain if the intervention and control groups differed on any of the demographic variables or study outcomes at baseline, a series of independent samples *t*-tests, and a chi-square test (i.e., for gender) were conducted, with alpha significance set to $p < 0.05$.

All outcome variables were standardized as *z*-scores and difference scores were calculated by subtracting baseline scores from the post-intervention scores. Skewness values ranged from −0.217 to 0.980, while kurtosis values ranged from 0.355 to 1.67. Multicollinearity was not present as all variance inflation factors were below 1.17, and the variables were thus deemed acceptable for regression analyses. All variables were imputed into Hayes (2017) PROCESS macro for SPSS to test the study hypotheses (see section "Study Hypotheses and Models Tested"). In Model 1 (see **Figure 1**), the intervention (*X*; intervention group coded as 1; control coded as 0) was regressed onto the mindfulness (*M1*), competence (*M2*), stress (*M3*), and well-being (*Y*) difference scores, whereas in Model 2 (see **Figure 1**), competence replaced mindfulness as *M1*. Gender and age were regressed onto the dependent variable as covariates in both models. Effects on the dependent variable and mediators were inspected through the singular and serial pathways indicated in the study hypotheses. Given the scoring format of the PSS, each of the relationships predicting stress were assumed to be negative.

Model 6 was used in Hayes' (2017) PROCESS Macro, wherein the effect of *X* on *Y*, and the effect of *X* on the Mediators (i.e., *M1, M2, M3*), was determined through a number of statistical criterion: (i) non-significant (i.e., no relationship); (ii) direct with non-mediation (i.e., mediators do not exert an influence on the relationship); (iii) full mediation (i.e., direct effect is not significant when controlling for mediators' effect); (iv) partial mediation (i.e., direct effect is significant even when controlling for mediators' effects) or, (v) indirect (i.e., no direct effect, but *X* exerts an indirect effect on *M2, M3* and *Y* when in sequence with mediators; Hayes, 2009). All effects were examined using a bootstrapping technique, with 10000 samples (Byrne, 2001). Effects were determined statistically significant if confidence intervals did not cross zero (Field, 2013; Hayes, 2017). Completely standardized beta (β) coefficient values were used to assess relationships attributable to the intervention. Moreover, R^2 values were included for the total variance predicted in the model on the difference scores.

RESULTS

Participant Demographic and Baseline Analysis

Two hundred and thirty eight student-athletes took part, with 108 in the intervention group, and 130 in the control group. The most commonly reported sports the athletes participated in included: Gaelic Football and Hurling (42%), Soccer (22.5%), Rugby (5.8%), Hockey (5.1%), Basketball (3.6%), Netball (2.9%), and others (18.1%; e.g., Athletics, Combat sports). The mean age of the sample was 20.47 years (*SD* = 3.30), 57.6% were males and 42.4% were females. Regarding demographic differences, the chi-square test revealed that there were no significant gender differences between intervention and control groups ($p > 0.05$). However, the control group had a significantly higher ($p < 0.05$) mean average age (21.39, *SD* = 3.97) than the intervention group (19.45, *SD* = 1.76).

At baseline, a series of independent samples *t*-tests revealed that the intervention and controlled groups did not significantly differ on any of the study outcomes (all $p > 0.05$). Descriptive statistics for the study outcomes are presented in **Table 1**, showing mean scores for each scale at each time-point, categorized by either intervention or control groups. With regard

TABLE 1 | Mean scores and standard deviations for scales, categorized for intervention and control participants at baseline and follow-up timepoints.

Variables	*Intervention M (SD)*	*Control M (SD)*
Mindfulness awareness Baseline	54.11 (13.01)	55.58 (10.90)
Two-week follow-up	60.02 (9.82)	60.36 (5.77)
Competence satisfaction Baseline	21.21 (5.11)	22.97 (4.60)
Two-week follow-up	23.21 (3.00)	23.29 (1.49)
Stress Baseline	18.26 (5.39)	18.07 (5.96)
Two-weeks follow-up	16.75 (3.58)	16.50 (2.26)
Well-being Baseline	43.74 (7.20)	45.41 (8.14)
Two-week follow-up	47.36 (5.60)	47.86 (3.89)

to adherence, on average the intervention group participated in 3.70 (*SD* = 2.78) mindfulness sessions, with 21.90% reporting engagement with one session, 12.38% at two sessions, and 11.43% at three sessions. Less than 2% of the intervention group reported completing the full available 14 sessions.

Main Results

Model 1

Results of Model 1 confirmed that in comparison to the control group, the intervention did not significantly enhance changes in the primary mediator of mindfulness (H1). Moreover, the intervention did not indirectly effect changes in competence satisfaction difference scores through mindfulness (H2), or stress through singular (i.e., mindfulness) or double (i.e., mindfulness > stress) sequential pathways (H3 and H4). Lastly, the intervention did not indirectly effect changes in well-being through any of the specified singular, double, or triple mediating pathways tested (H5). Overall, despite the mindfulness practices inherent within the program, the intervention did not exert any direct changes on mindfulness. Further, as the primary mediator, mindfulness did not exert any indirect effects on competence, stress or well-being difference scores. Lastly, as covariates gender and age did not significantly predict well-being.

Model 2

When replacing mindfulness with competence as the primary mediator (*M1*) in Model 2, analyses revealed support for H1 such that, in comparison to the control group, the intervention predicted a direct effect on changes in competence satisfaction difference scores (H1; β = 0.39, 95% CI's = 0.13 to −0.64, $p < 0.05$). Further support was revealed for H2, H3, and H4, to the extent that indirect effects were found for the intervention on mindfulness through competence satisfaction (H2; β = 0.07, 95% CI's = 0.03 to −0.13, $p < 0.05$); on stress through competence satisfaction (H3; β = −0.06, 95% CI's = −0.11 to −0.02, $p < 0.05$), and; on stress through competence satisfaction and mindfulness in sequence (H4; β = −0.02, 95% CI's = −0.04 to −0.00, $p < 0.05$). In respect of H5, the intervention indirectly effected changes in well-being difference scores through competence satisfaction (β = 0.05, 95% CI's = 0.02 to 0.10, $p < 0.05$); through competence satisfaction and mindfulness in sequence (β = 0.02, 95% CI's = 0.01 to 0.04, $p < 0.05$); through competence satisfaction and stress in sequence (β = 0.03, 95% CI's = 0.01 to 0.06, $p < 0.05$), and; through competence satisfaction, mindfulness, and stress in sequence (β = 0.01, 95% CI's = 0.00 to 0.002, $p < 0.05$). Factoring in all of the variables in the models resulted in a significant proportion of variance predicted for changes in well-being difference scores (R^2 = 0.54), in addition to stress (R^2 = 0.17), mindfulness, (R^2 = 0.14) and competence (R^2 = 0.04). Similar to Model 1, as covariates gender and age did not significantly predict the dependent variable well-being. See **Figure 2** for a visual description of Model 2, including significant beta coefficient values.

DISCUSSION

This study was in response to calls that mental health awareness interventions should be theory-based and when requested be available to student athletes to effectively manage academic, social and sporting stressors (Breslin et al., 2017; Moreland et al., 2018; Shannon et al., 2019). In Model 1, the intervention did not directly affect the primary mediator of mindfulness, exerting no indirect effects on the study outcomes. However in Model 2, the intervention was effective at directly improving changes in competence satisfaction (H1), which subsequently resulted in indirect effects on mindfulness (H2), stress (H3 and H4) and well-being (H5), through SDT mechanisms reflective of competence satisfaction (Ryan and Deci, 2017).

Thus, despite the inclusion of mindfulness practices in the program, the intervention was not effective at directly increasing mindfulness itself, and the positive effects on mindfulness, stress and well-being were all indirectly realized through competence satisfaction (see **Figure 2** above). Overall, results indicate that while the enhancement of mindfulness itself does carry some of the responsibility for mindfulness interventions' effects, as evidenced in indirect effects in H4 and H5 (Brown et al., 2007), the act of engaging with mindfulness training can also foster perceptions of competence in mental health self-management, which may be beneficial to stress regulation and well-being promotion (Ryan and Deci, 2017). However, effect sizes were generally small, and as such, we now discuss findings

TABLE 2 | Core content of the mental health workshop and mindfulness application.

Intervention component	Key themes	Tasks
Mental health workshop part 1	Introduction to mental health concepts (i.e., stress, mindfulness)	Group-based and participant-led discussions on positive framing of mental health and mindfulness as a tool.
Mental health workshop part 2	Instructions and how to use the mindfulness application.	One-minute taster meditation, download and try-out of the application.
Home-directed mindfulness program	Non-judgmental awareness of the present moment	Guided practices including counting breaths, body scanning and noting thoughts and feelings.

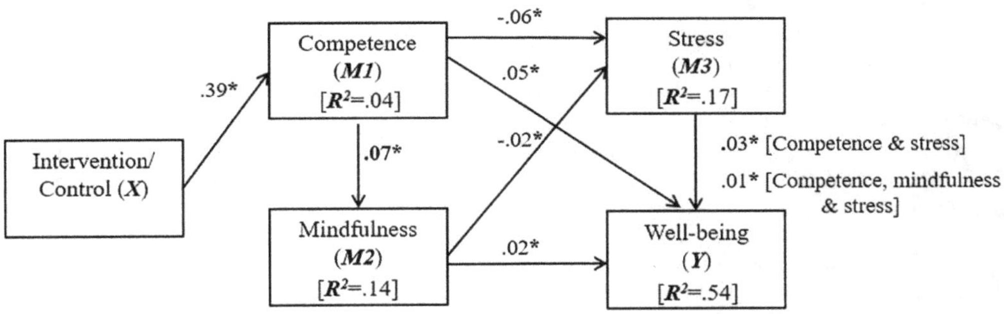

FIGURE 2 | Model 2 showing direct and indirect effects of the mindfulness-based mobile application (*X*) on competence satisfaction (*M1*), mindfulness (*M2*), stress (*M3*), and well-being (*Y*). For visual clarity only significant paths attributable to the intervention were included; $*p < 0.05$.

with a view of advancing mental health interventions for the athlete population.

Model 1

The intervention's effects were modeled through SDT using both mindfulness and competence satisfaction as primary and secondary mediators. This approach enabled an empirical inquiry into the mechanisms of change in the program, specifically the temporal nature of the relationship between competence and mindfulness, and their salutary effects, which is considered a crucial step in developing a theoretical underpinning for mental health promotion through mindfulness (Sedlmeier et al., 2018). In Model 1, there was a lack of support for a direct intervention effect on mindfulness changes scores (H1), as measured by the MAAS (Brown and Ryan, 2003). It is likely that the relatively low combined engagement with the program (i.e., on average the intervention participants completed 3.70 sessions) and short duration of the intervention (i.e., 2 weeks) and sessions (i.e., session durations ranged from an optional five through to 20 min) was not a sufficient enough dose to exert direct changes on one's daily awareness (Creswell, 2017). Indeed, a meta-analyses of 72 mindfulness-based interventions (Visted et al., 2015) reported that approximately 50% have not reported a significant increase in self-reported mindfulness. While some evidence indicates that improvement in mindfulness skills (e.g., counting accuracy of breaths during tasks) are possible during short interventions (Rosenkranz et al., 2019), authors (Cayoun, 2011; Creswell, 2017) have proposed that better adherence to mindfulness programs predicts one's capacity to achieve heightened mindful states.

To this end, the present intervention may benefit from formative sustainability research that accounts for contextual factors such as the service structure (i.e., how and when the intervention is delivered) and population characteristics (i.e., whether athletes scoring low on well-being may require a longer intervention) (Shelton et al., 2018). Also from a program fidelity perspective, it would have been useful to know the precise amount of time the participants spent meditating (i.e., session length was optional), and moreover, it is possible that the present intervention had effects on additional dimensions of mindfulness not measured by the MAAS. These include non-judgmental reflection and reaction, observation, and descriptions of current experiences, which are assessed in the Five-Factor Mindfulness Questionnaire (FFMQ; Baer et al., 2006). Despite the null findings in Model 1, there were indirect effects present in Model 2, which are of theoretical and practical value to mental health interventions.

Model 2 Theoretical Implications

Specifically, the finding that improvements in mindfulness difference scores were indirectly predicted by the intervention's direct effect on competence satisfaction (H1), suggests that the act of engaging with mindfulness practices and instructions can facilitate improved perceptions of competence in mental health self-management, which in turn, produces the conditions that enable one to be mindful and focus on the present (Olafsen, 2017). While SDT hypotheses (Brown et al., 2007) and extant studies (Chang et al., 2015, 2018; Schultz et al., 2015; Campbell et al., 2016; Campbell et al., 2017) propose that the mindfulness construct may precede competence satisfaction, the effects present in Model 2 show support to the contrary. Yet, it should be noted that the null direct effect of the intervention on mindfulness precludes our ability to examine the precise temporal nature of this relationship. Indeed, it may be that there is a bi-directional association between mindfulness and competence satisfaction.

The indirect effects found for the intervention on reducing stress difference scores through competence satisfaction (H3), and competence satisfaction and mindfulness in sequence (H4), supports evidence that mindfulness-based interventions can reduce stress through self-regulatory mechanisms (Gu et al., 2015; Vidic et al., 2017). Specifically findings are theoretically aligned with a SDT perspective (Ryan and Deci, 2017) that the manner in which one appraises and is aware of mental health challenges is crucial, to the extent that improved competence satisfaction can result in better self-regulation of environmental stressors (Weinstein and Ryan, 2011). Indeed, research studies have shown that competence independently predicts reduced stress and improved well-being (Jex et al., 2001; Mikolajczak et al., 2015), and the present intervention's effect support, respectively, a positive direct, and inverse indirect, relationship with competence and stress through mindfulness-based programs.

Given student-athletes experience multiple social, academic and sporting stressors, and often report a lack of ability in self-regulating stressors (Moreland et al., 2018), improving competence through provision of mindfulness training may be of value. Such efforts may be aided by longer-lasting interventions that provide sufficient time to directly improve mindfulness skills (Cayoun, 2011), and from a theoretical perspective, may help disentangle the temporal relationship between competence satisfaction and mindfulness.

Supporting H5, competence, mindfulness and stress indirectly predicted the interventions positive effects on well-being difference scores, as measured by the WEMWBS (Tennant et al., 2007). The specific skills taught to the participants through the mindfulness program, including improving awareness of the concept of mindfulness, and the relationship between thoughts, breathing and attention, may have improved student-athlete's well-being through the key medium of competence needs satisfaction (Brown and Ryan, 2003; Weinstein and Ryan, 2011). It is well acknowledged that competence satisfaction is robustly related to improved well-being (Ryan and Deci, 2017), however, this is the first methodologically rigorous mindfulness-based study to test such indirect mechanisms through statistical mediation analyses among athletes.

Mindfulness and stress both accompanied the intervention's indirect effects on well-being through competence, supporting the view that mindfulness-based programs can help individuals feel effective at self-regulating the stressors that are predictive of mental health (Creswell, 2017). Indeed, inclusion of the mediators alongside the intervention and control group resulted in a significant proportion of variance explained for well-being difference scores in the model (R^2 = 0.54). What was not considered in model 2, was the intervention's effects on distinct eudemonic, hedonic and social well-being constructs (Keyes, 2005), and additional mental health domain-specific measures of autonomy and relatedness. Although the WEMWBS (Tennant et al., 2007) items do tap into such components, its unidimensional structure permits the examination of precise pathways. Hence, it may be worth including multi-dimensional mental well-being measures in future studies, such as the mental health continuum (Keyes, 2002) that has recently been applied to mental health in sport (Uphill et al., 2016), and further mental health domain measures of autonomy and relatedness.

Generalizability and Limitations

The key contribution of this study was the inclusion of SDT to test the mechanisms of change in a mindfulness-based mental health intervention among athletes. While this research showed support for indirect mechanisms which are of theoretical and practical value (Creswell, 2017), effect sizes were generally small, and the study is also not without its limitations. These include: the lack of a long-term follow-up period which prevents determining whether effects extended beyond two-weeks; a lack of randomization to groups; a relatively small level of adherence to the full mindfulness program, and; a full testing of SDT components (i.e., autonomy and relatedness satisfaction for mental health). A further and longer-lasting SDT-based mindfulness intervention is warranted that accounts for these limitations. From a practical standpoint, researchers have suggested better adherence to mental health interventions when athletes feel the program is aligned, and sensitive to the nuances of sports performance culture (Gavrilova et al., 2017). Such examples do exist, such the Mindfulness-Acceptance-Commitment Program (MACP; Gardner and Moore, 2004), which has been linked to both positive sporting and mental health outcomes (Gardner and Moore, 2007; Gross et al., 2016; Zhang et al., 2016), and may be aided by application of SDT and online modalities. When utilizing such approaches, researchers and practitioners may be cautious of the remaining open-questions regarding potential risks of online mindfulness interventions, in addition to financial and technological barriers (Creswell, 2017). From a measurement perspective, further research could apply multicomponent measures of mindfulness (see, Baer et al., 2006) and develop mental health domain-specific autonomy and relatedness scales. In this vein, researchers may consider good practice in psychometrics (Hagger and Chatzisarantis, 2009). Further interventions may also consider program fidelity aspects, such as the length, duration and participant adherence to the mindfulness sessions, in addition to training deliverers in SDT principles, as conducted in the present study (see Shannon et al., 2018 for an example of needs-supportive teacher training). Various level of sport participation among the athletes (e.g., elite, semi-elite, amateur), current mental health levels (e.g., flourishing, moderate or languishing mental health, see Keyes, 2002), and past participant experience in mental health self-management training (e.g., CBT) may also be considered.

CONCLUSION

Psychological well-being is facilitated by an awareness of and ability to self-regulate stressors (Weinstein and Ryan, 2011). As student-athletes frequently report the presence of multifaceted sporting, academic and social stressors (Moreland et al., 2018), the present study sought to examine the efficacy of a mental health intervention for reducing stress and promoting well-being, whilst also contributing to theoretical understanding of the mechanisms of change in mindfulness interventions. Support was found for the competence-promoting processes in the intervention, to the extent that the act of engaging with mindfulness practices can foster perceptions of competence in mental health self-management, which exerted indirect intervention effects on mindfulness, stress regulation, and ultimately, psychological well-being. Overall, we propose that mindfulness-based mental health interventions may offer a way to promote mental health among athletes, with the caveat that attention is given to the promotion of competence in such programs. However, effects were generally small, and there are a number of remaining theoretical and practical questions to addressed. Specifically, as the present intervention was not effective at directly increasing mindfulness, the temporal association between competence satisfaction and mindfulness, and their salutary effects, remains open for further assessment. From a practical viewpoint, we suggest that longer-lasting programs tailored for sports culture are warranted (Gavrilova et al., 2017), in which those involved in program design control for intervention accessibility and sustainability, adherence, duration and intensity of mindfulness sessions, in addition to theoretical application by deliverers and potential risks (Creswell, 2017). Moreover, future programs may consider theoretically driven mindfulness interventions in all aspects of design and analyses that are conducted through a longitudinal experimental design, in which allocation to groups is randomized. To conclude, a mindfulness-based mental health intervention was associated with reduced stress, and improved well-being among athletes through SDT mechanisms reflective of competence satisfaction.

ETHICS STATEMENT

This study was carried out in accordance with Ulster University ethical guidance. All subjects gave written informed consent in accordance with the Declaration of Helsinki. The protocol was approved by the Sport and Exercise Sciences Research Institute filter committee.

AUTHOR CONTRIBUTIONS

SS and GB designed the study. SS, TH, and CM collected the data. DN and ML delivered the intervention. SS, DH, and GB analyzed the data. All authors contributed to the final drafting of the manuscript.

ACKNOWLEDGMENTS

We would like to thank the student-athletes that volunteered to participate in this study. We would like to acknowledge the late Dr. Martin Lawlor, as co-founder of the State of Mind Ireland program and advocate of mental health for his contributions to program delivery and training. Drew Neill from the Student Support at Ulster University, and Dr. Martin Lawlor from the Health Executive, Cork, delivered the intervention. Lastly, we would like to thank Caoimhín Ó Seanáin for his help in proofreading the article.

REFERENCES

Abedalhafiz, A., Altahayneh, Z., and Al-Haliq, M. (2010). Sources of stress and coping styles among student-athletes in Jordan universities. *Procedia Soc. Behav. Sci.* 5, 1911–1917. doi: 10.1016/j.sbspro.2010.07.387

Baer, R. A., Smith, G. T., Hopkins, J., Krietemeyer, J., and Toney, L. (2006). Using self-report assessment methods to explore facets of mindfulness. *Assessment* 13, 27–45. doi: 10.1177/1073191105283504

Bennett, G. (2007). The role of a clinical psychologist in a division I athletics program. *J. Clin. Sport Psychol.* 1, 261–269. doi: 10.1123/jcsp.1.3.261

Breslin, G., Haughey, T., O'Brien, W., Caulfield, L., Robertson, A., and Lawlor, M. (2018a). Increasing athlete knowledge of mental health and intentions to seek help: the state of mind ireland (SOMI) pilot program. *J. Clin. Sport Psychol.* 12, 39–56.

Breslin, G., Shannon S., Ferguson, K., Devlin, S., Haughey, T., and Prentice, G. (2018b). Predicting athlete mental health stigma using the theory of reasoned action framework *J. Clin. Sport Psychol.* 13, 103–115.

Breslin, G., Haughey, T. J., Shannon, S., Neill, D., and Lawlor, M. (2019). "The state of mind ireland programme for student athletes," in *Mental Health and Well-being Interventions in Sport: Research, Theory and Practice*, Vol. 2019, eds G. Breslin, and G. Leavey (Abingdon: Routledge), 63–74.

Breslin, G., Shannon, S., Haughey, T., Donnelly, P., and Leavey, G. (2017). A systematic review of interventions to increase awareness of mental health and well-being in athletes, coaches and officials. *Syst. Rev.* 6:177. doi: 10.1186/s13643-017-0568-6

Brown, K. W., and Ryan, R. M. (2003). The benefits of being present: mindfulness and its role in psychological well-being. *J. Pers. Soc. Psychol.* 84, 822–448.

Brown, K. W., Ryan, R. M., and Creswell, J. D. (2007). Mindfulness: theoretical foundations and evidence for its salutary effects. *Psychol. Inquiry* 18, 211–237. doi: 10.1080/10478400701598298

Byrne, B. M. (2001). Structural equation modeling with AMOS, EQS, and LISREL: comparative approaches to testing for the factorial validity of a measuring instrument. *Int. J Test.* 1, 55–86. doi: 10.1207/s15327574ijt0101_4

Campbell, R., Tobback, E., Delesie, L., Vogelaers, D., Mariman, A., and Vansteenkiste, M. (2017). Basic psychological need experiences, fatigue, and sleep in individuals with unexplained chronic fatigue. *Stress Health* 33, 645–655. doi: 10.1002/smi.2751

Campbell, R., Vansteenkiste, M., Delesie, L., Soenens, B., Tobback, E., Vogelaers, D., et al. (2016). The role of basic psychological need satisfaction, sleep, and mindfulness in the health-related quality of life of people living with HIV. *J. Health Psychol.* 24, 535–545. doi: 10.1177/1359105316678305

Cayoun, B. A. (2011). *Mindfulness-Integrated CBT: Principles And practice.* Hoboken: John Wiley & Sons.

Chang, J. H., Huang, C. L., and Lin, Y. C. (2015). Mindfulness, basic psychological needs fulfillment, and well-being. *J. Happ. Stud.* 16, 1149–1162. doi: 10.1016/j.cpr.2010.03.001

Chang, W. H., Chang, J. H., and Chen, L. H. (2018). mindfulness enhances change in athletes' well-being: the mediating role of basic psychological needs fulfillment. *Mindfulness* 9, 815–823. doi: 10.1007/s12671-017-0821-z

Cohen, S., Kamarck, T., and Mermelstein, R. (1994). "Perceived stress scale," in *Measuring Stress: A Guide for Health and Social Scientists*, eds S. Cohen, R. C. Kessler, and L. Underwood Gordo (Oxford: Oxford University Press), 235–283.

Creswell, J. D. (2017). Mindfulness interventions. *Annu. Rev. Psychol.* 68, 491–516. doi: 10.1146/annurev-psych-042716-051139

Des Jarlais, D. C., Lyles, C., Crepaz, N., and Trend Group, (2004). Improving the reporting quality of nonrandomized evaluations of behavioral and public health interventions: the TREND statement. *Am. J. Public Health* 94, 361–366. doi: 10.2105/ajph.94.3.361

Diener, E., Lucas, R. E., and Oishi, S. (2018). Advances and open questions in the science of subjective well-being. *Collabra Psychol.* 4:15. doi: 10.1525/collabra.115

Donohue, B., Gavrilova, Y., Galante, M., Gavrilova, E., Loughran, T., Scott, J., et al. (2018). Controlled evaluation of an optimization approach to mental health and sport performance. *J. Clin. Sport Psychol.*. 12, 1–42.

Eisenberg, D., Golberstein, E., and Gollust, S. E. (2007). Help-seeking and access to mental health care in a university student population. *Med. Care* 45, 594–601. doi: 10.1097/mlr.0b013e31803bb4c1

Field, A. (2013). *Discovering Statistics using IBM SPSS Statistics.* Housand Oaks: Sage.

Gardner, F. L., and Moore, Z. E. (2004). A mindfulness-acceptance-commitment-based approach to athletic performance enhancement: theoretical considerations. *Behav. Therapy.* 35, 707–723. doi: 10.1016/s0005-7894(04)80016-9

Gardner, F. L., and Moore, Z. E. (2007). *The Psychology of Enhancing Human Performance: The Mindfulness-Acceptance-Commitment (MAC) Approach.* New York, NY: Springer Publishing Company.

Gavrilova, Y., Donohue, B., and Galante, M. (2017). Mental health and sport performance programming in athletes who present without pathology: a case examination supporting optimization. *Clin. Case Stud.* 16, 234–253. doi: 10.1177/1534650116689302

Glass, C. R., Spears, C. A., Perskaudas, R., and Kaufman, K. A. (2018). Mindful sport performance enhancement: randomized controlled trial of a mental training program with collegiate athletes. *J. Clin. Sport Psychol.* (in press).

Gross, M., Moore, Z. E., Gardner, F. L., Wolanin, A. T., Pess, R., and Marks, D. R. (2016). An empirical examination comparing the mindfulness-acceptance-commitment approach and psychological skills training for the mental health and sport performance of female student athletes. *Int. J. Sport Exerc. Psychol.* 1–21.

Gu, J., Strauss, C., Bond, R., and Cavanagh, K. (2015). How do mindfulness-based cognitive therapy and mindfulness-based stress reduction improve mental health and wellbeing? *Syst. Rev. Meta Anal. Med. Stud. Clin. Psychol. Rev.* 37, 1–12. doi: 10.1016/j.cpr.2015.01.006

Gustafsson, H., and Skoog, T. (2012). The mediational role of perceived stress in the relation between optimism and burnout in competitive athletes. *Anxiety Stress Coping* 25, 183–199. doi: 10.1080/10615806.2011.594045

Hagger, M. S., and Chatzisarantis, N. L. (2009). Assumptions in research in sport and exercise psychology. *Psychol. Sport Exercise* 10, 511–519. doi: 10.1016/j.psychsport.2009.01.004

Hayes, A. F. (2009). Beyond baron and kenny: statistical mediation analysis in the new millennium. *Commun. Monogr.* 76, 408–420. doi: 10.1080/03637750903310360

Hayes, A. F. (2017). *Introduction to Mediation, Moderation, and Conditional Process Analysis: A Regression-Based Approach.* London: Guilford Publications.

Howells, A., Ivtzan, I., and Eiroa-Orosa, F. J. (2016). Putting the 'app'in happiness: a randomised controlled trial of a smartphone-based mindfulness intervention to enhance wellbeing. *J. Happiness Stud.* 17, 163–185. doi: 10.1007/s10902-014-9589-1

Hunt, J., and Eisenberg, D. (2010). Mental health problems and help-seeking behavior among college students. *J. Adolesc. Health* 46, 3–10. doi: 10.1016/j.jadohealth.2009.08.008

Huppert, F. A. (2009). Psychological well-being: evidence regarding its causes and consequences. *Appl. Psychol.: Health Well Being* 1, 137–164. doi: 10.1111/j.1758-0854.2009.01008.x

Jex, S. M., Bliese, P. D., Buzzell, S., and Primeau, J. (2001). The impact of self-efficacy on stressor–strain relations: coping style as an explanatory mechanism. *J. Appl. Psychol.* 86, 401–409. doi: 10.1037/0021-9010.86.3.401

Keyes, C. L. (2002). The mental health continuum: from languishing to flourishing in life. *J. Health Soc. Behav.* 43, 207–222.

Keyes, C. L. (2005). Mental illness and/or mental health? Investigating axioms of the complete state model of health. *J. Consult. Clin. Psychol.* 73, 539–548. doi: 10.1037/0022-006x.73.3.539

Kok, G., Schaalma, H., Ruiter, R. A., Van Empelen, P., and Brug, J. (2004). Intervention mapping: protocol for applying health psychology theory to prevention programmes. *J. Health Psychol.* 9, 85–98. doi: 10.1177/1359105304038379

Langley, M. (2013). *The Mindfulness Workbook.* London,: Hodder and Stoughton.

Lawlor, M., Rae, M., Kelly, N., and Moriarty, P. (2015). *"State of mind Ireland: Towards a skills for life passport," in Proceedings of the CRSI Conference.* Retrieved from: www.stateofmindireland.com/crsi/resources (accessed January, 2019).

Lee, E. H. (2012). Review of the psychometric evidence of the perceived stress scale. *Asian Nurs. Res.* 6, 121–127. doi: 10.1016/j.anr.2012.08.004

Little, R. J. (1988). A test of missing completely at random for multivariate data with missing values. *J. Am. Statist. Assoc.* 83, 1198–1202. doi: 10.1080/01621459.1988.10478722

MacKillop, J., and Anderson, E. J. (2007). Further psychometric validation of the mindful attention awareness scale (MAAS). *J. Psychopathol. Behav. Assess.* 29, 289–293. doi: 10.1007/s10862-007-9045-1

Mental Health Foundation (2018). *Stress: are we coping?* Available at: https://www.mentalhealth.org.uk/a-to-z/s/stress (accessed February 2019).

Mikolajczak, M., Avalosse, H., Vancorenland, S., Verniest, R., Callens, M., Van Broeck, N., et al. (2015). A nationally representative study of emotional competence and health. *Emotion* 15, 653–751. doi: 10.1037/emo0000034

Moreland, J. J., Coxe, K. A., and Yang, J. (2018). Collegiate athletes' mental health services utilization: A systematic review of conceptualizations, operationalizations, facilitators, and barriers. *J. Sport Health Sci.* 7, 58–69. doi: 10.1016/j.jshs.2017.04.009

Noetel, M., Ciarrochi, J., Van Zanden, B., and Lonsdale, C. (2017). Mindfulness and acceptance approaches to sporting performance enhancement: a systematic review. *Int. Rev. Sport Exercise Psychol.* 1, 1–37.

Olafsen, A. H. (2017). The implications of need-satisfying work climates on state mindfulness in a longitudinal analysis of work outcomes. *Motiv. Emot.* 41, 22–37. doi: 10.1007/s11031-016-9592-4

Putukian, M. (2016). The psychological response to injury in student athletes: a narrative review with a focus on mental health. *Br. J. Sports Med.* 50, 145–148. doi: 10.1136/bjsports-2015-095586

Rejeski, W. J., and Brawley, L. R. (1988). Defining the boundaries of sport psychology. *Sport Psychol.* 2, 231–242. doi: 10.1123/tsp.2.3.23

Roberti, J. W., Harrington, L. N., and Storch, E. A. (2006). Further psychometric support for the 10-item version of the perceived stress scale. *J. College Couns.* 9, 135–147. doi: 10.1002/j.2161-1882.2006.tb00100.x

Rosenkranz, M. A., Dunne, J. D., and Davidson, R. J. (2019). The next generation of mindfulness-based intervention research: what have we learned and where are we headed? *Curr. Opin. Psychol.* 28, 179–183. doi: 10.1016/j.copsyc.2018.12.022

Ryan, R. M., and Deci, E. L. (2000). Self-determination theory and the facilitation of intrinsic motivation, social development, and well-being. *Am. Psychol.* 55, 68. doi: 10.1037//0003-066x.55.1.68

Ryan, R. M., and Deci, E. L. (2017). *Self-determination theory: Basic psychological needs in motivation, development, and wellness.* York, NY: Guilford Publications.

Sappington, R., and Longshore, K. (2015). Systematically reviewing the efficacy of mindfulness-based interventions for enhanced athletic performance. *J. Clin. Sport Psychol.* 9, 232–262. doi: 10.1123/jcsp.2014-0017

Schultz, P. P., and Ryan, R. M. (2015). "The "why," "what," and "how" of healthy self-regulation: Mindfulness and well-being from a self-determination theory perspective," in *Handbook of Mindfulness and Self-Regulation*, eds B. D. Ostafin, M. D. Robinson, and B. P. Meier (New York, NY: Springer), 81–94.

Schultz, P. P., Ryan, R. M., Niemiec, C. P., Legate, N., and Williams, G. C. (2015). Mindfulness, work climate, and psychological need satisfaction in employee well-being. *Mindfulness* 6, 971–985. doi: 10.1007/s12671-014-0338-7

Sedlmeier, P., Losse, C., and Quasten, L. C. (2018). Psychological effects of meditation for healthy practitioners: an update. *Mindfulness* 9, 371–387. doi: 10.1007/s12671-017-0780-4

Shannon, S., Brennan, D., Hanna, D., Younger, Z., Hassan, J., and Breslin, G. (2018). The effect of a school-based intervention on physical activity and well-being: a non-randomised controlled trial with children of low socio-economic status. *Sports Med. Open* 4:16. doi: 10.1186/s40798-018-0129-0

Shannon, S., Breslin, G., Haughey, T., Sarju, N., Neill, D., Lawlor, M., et al. (2019). Predicting student-athlete and non-athletes' intentions to self-manage mental health: testing an integrated behaviour change model. *Men. Health Prev.* 13, 92–99. doi: 10.1016/j.mhp.2019.01.006

Shelton, R. C., Cooper, B. R., and Stirman, S. W. (2018). The sustainability of evidence-based interventions and practices in public health and health care. *Annu. Rev. Public Health* 39, 55–76. doi: 10.1146/annurev-publhealth-040617-014731

Stone, D. N., Deci, E. L., and Ryan, R. M. (2009). Beyond talk: creating autonomous motivation through self-determination theory. *J. Gen. Manag.* 34, 75–91. doi: 10.1177/030630700903400305

Tennant, R., Hiller, L., Fishwick, R., Platt, S., Joseph, S., Weich, S., et al. (2007). The Warwick-Edinburgh mental well-being scale (WEMWBS): development and UK validation. *Health Q. Life Outcomes* 5:63. doi: 10.1186/1477-7525-5-63

Uphill, M. A., Sly, D., and Swain, J. (2016). An exploration of Keyes' two-continuum model of mental health in athletes: resilience, mental illness and performance. *J. Sport Exercise Psychol.* 38, S266–S267.

Vallerand, R. J. (1997). Toward a hierarchical model of intrinsic and extrinsic motivation. *Adv. Exp. Soc. psychol.* 29, 271–360. doi: 10.1016/S0065-2601(08)60019-2

Vidic, Z., St. Martin, M., and Oxhandler, R. (2017).). Mindfulness Intervention with a US women's NCAA division I basketball team: impact on stress, athletic coping skills and perceptions of intervention. *Sport Psychol.* 31, 147–159. doi: 10.1123/tsp.2016-0077

Williams, G. C., Freedman, Z. R., and Deci, E. L. (1998). Supporting autonomy to motivate patients with diabetes for glucose control. *Diabetes Care* 21, 1644–1651. doi: 10.2337/diacare.21.10.1644

Wilson, G. S., and Pritchard, M. (2005). Comparing sources of stress in college student athletes and non-athletes. *Athl. Insight* 7, 1–8.

Wolf, H. (1996). *Self-management and Mental health, in Bährer-Kohler, S. (*2012). Social determinants and mental health. Hauppauge, NY: Nova Science Publishers.

Zhang, C. Q., Si, G., Chung, P. K., and Gucciardi, D. F. (2016). Mindfulness and burnout in elite junior athletes: the mediating role of experiential avoidance. *J. Appl. Sport Psychol.* 28, 437–451. doi: 10.1080/10413200.2016.1162223

Visted, E., Vøllestad, J., Nielsen, M. B., and Nielsen, G. H. (2015). The impact of group-based mindfulness training on self-reported mindfulness: a systematic review and meta-analysis. *Mindfulness* 6, 501–522. doi: 10.1002/14651858.CD010806.pub2

Weinstein, N., and Ryan, R. M. (2011). A self-determination theory approach to understanding stress incursion and responses. *Stress Health* 27, 4–17. doi: 10.1002/smi.1368

Williams, G. C., and Deci, E. L. (1996). Internalization of biopsychosocial values by medical students: a test of self-determination theory. *J. Pers. Soc. Psychol.* 70, 767–779. doi: 10.1037//0022-3514.70.4.767

18

Influence of Slow-Paced Breathing on Inhibition after Physical Exertion

Sylvain Laborde[1,2], Theresa Lentes[1], Thomas J. Hosang[3], Uirassu Borges[1], Emma Mosley[4] and Fabrice Dosseville[5,6]*

Department of Performance Psychology, German Sport University Cologne, Cologne, Germany, [2] Normandie Université, UFR STAPS, EA 4260, Cesams, Caen, France, [3] Experimental Psychology Unit, Department of Psychology, Helmut Schmidt University, Hamburg, Germany, [4] Southampton Solent University, Southampton, United Kingdom, [5] Normandie Université, UMR-S 1075 COMETE, Caen, France, [6] INSERM, UMR-S 1075 COMETE, Caen, France

Correspondence:
Sylvain Laborde
s.laborde@dshs-koeln.de

This research aims to investigate whether slow-paced breathing (SPB) improves adaptation to psychological stress, and specifically inhibition, when it is performed before or after physical exertion (PE). According to the resonance model, SPB is expected to increase cardiac vagal activity (CVA). Further, according to the neurovisceral integration model, CVA is positively linked to executive cognitive performance, and would thus play a role in the adaptation to psychological stress. We hypothesized that SPB, in comparison to a control condition, will induce a better adaptation to psychological stress, measured via better inhibitory performance. Two within-subject experiments were conducted with athletes: in the first experiment (N = 60) SPB (or control – neutral TV documentary) was realized before PE ("relax before PE"), and in the second experiment (N = 60) SPB (or the watching TV control) was realized after PE ("relax after PE"). PE consisted of 5 min Burpees, a physical exercise involving the whole body. In both experiments the adaptation to psychological stress was investigated with a Stroop task, a measure of inhibition, which followed PE. Perceived stress increased during PE (partial η^2 = 0.63) and during the Stroop task (partial η^2 = 0.08), and decreased during relaxation (partial η^2 = 0.15), however, no effect of condition was found. At the physiological level PE significantly increased HR, RF, and decreased CVA [operationalized in this research via the root mean square of successive differences (RMSSD)] in both experiments. Further, the number of errors in the incongruent category (Stroop interference accuracy) was found to be lower in the SPB condition in comparison to the control condition, however, these results were not mediated by RMSSD. Additionally, the Stroop interference [reaction times (RTs)] was found to be lower overall in "relax before PE," however, no effect was found regarding SPB and Stroop interference (RTs). Overall, our results suggest that SPB realized before or after PE has a positive effect regarding adaptation to psychological stress and specifically inhibition, however, the underlying mechanisms require further investigation.

Keywords: acute exercise, physical activity, executive function, cognition, heart rate variability

INTRODUCTION

Executive functions underpin goal-directed behavior and are essential for self-control (Miyake et al., 2000; Diamond, 2013; Kotabe and Hofmann, 2015). Executive functions may be hindered by factors such as stress (e.g., Arnsten, 2009), fatigue (Kurzban et al., 2013; Inzlicht et al., 2014; Schmit and Brisswalter, 2018), and pressure (e.g., Laborde et al., 2014). The aim of this paper is to investigate the influence of a relaxation method [slow-paced breathing (SPB)], to prevent inhibition failure during psychological stress following physical exertion (PE).

Several neurological mechanisms have been identified in the literature to explain the influence of perceived stress (PS; e.g., Archer et al., 2018), mental fatigue (e.g., Guo et al., 2018) or physical fatigue (e.g., Tanaka et al., 2013) on inhibition failure. In this research, we focus on the role of the autonomic nervous system, and more specifically of its parasympathetic branch. The neurovisceral integration model (Thayer et al., 2009; Smith et al., 2017) assumes that similar structures are involved in the regulation of executive performance and cardiac functioning. The functional organization of these structures is depicted by the central autonomic network (Benarroch, 1993), the output of this network being cardiac vagal activity (CVA), the activity of the vagus nerve which regulates cardiac functioning (Thayer et al., 2009; Laborde et al., 2017b). Based on this functional organization, the neurovisceral integration model (Thayer et al., 2009; Smith et al., 2017) assumes that the effectiveness of the central autonomic network is reflected in CVA and can be indexed via heart rate variability (HRV), the time interval between adjacent heartbeats (Malik, 1996; Berntson et al., 1997). Specifically, the neurovisceral integration model assumes that a higher resting CVA is linked to better executive functioning (Wendt et al., 2015; Albinet et al., 2016; Spangler and Friedman, 2017; Spangler et al., 2018). In this paper, we operationalize CVA with the RMSSD (Malik, 1996; Berntson et al., 1997), which has been found to be less affected by respiratory influences than other HRV variables suggested to index CVA (Hill et al., 2009). Given that CVA reflects self-regulation and higher levels of CVA promote better executive performance (Thayer et al., 2009), it serves as a valuable measure when assessing performance under both physiological and psychological stress.

Psychological stress occurs when an individual perceives that personal or environmental demands tax or exceed his or her adaptive abilities (Lazarus and Folkman, 1984). Even if psychological stress can be considered as an idiosyncratic phenomena, given it will differ across individuals and situations, a common method of inducing stress is using tasks taxing executive functions. In addition, putting an emphasis on performing well helps to represent a situation which differs markedly from resting states in terms of psychological demands placed on the individual. For example, the Color Word Stroop Test (CWST; Stroop, 1935), a classical cognitive test to investigate inhibition (Diamond, 2013), has been used to create psychological stress (e.g., Vazan et al., 2017), and was found to increase biological markers of stress (e.g., Brugnera et al., 2018). In the CWST, an inhibitory interference occurs when the processing of a stimulus feature affects the simultaneous processing of another attribute of the same stimulus (Stroop, 1935). Many variations exist, but the basic experimental paradigm depicted in the CWST is the use of color words printed either in the same color for the congruent category (for example, "BLUE" printed in blue color) or in a different color for the incongruent category (for example, "BLUE" printed in red). The participant has then to name the color in which the word is printed. The accuracy (number of errors) and reaction times (RTs) are measured to investigate the Stroop test performance (Stroop, 1935; Scarpina and Tagini, 2017). Better performance in this test reflects better inhibitory control which directly reflects the processing of incongruent stimuli in comparison to congruent stimuli. This differential processing constitutes the basis of the so-called Stroop interference, although a high heterogeneity to calculate the Stroop interference is reported in the literature (Scarpina and Tagini, 2017). Inhibition is primarily displayed by the error rate (accuracy) (McDowd et al., 1995), which represents as well an index of the ability to maintain the task's goal temporarily in a highly retrievable state (Kane and Engle, 2003). Assessing RTs may also be useful to uncover other processes linked to inhibition (Scarpina and Tagini, 2017).

The CWST and its variations (which we refer to thereafter as "Stroop tests") have already been investigated with HRV (Hoshikawa and Yamamoto, 1997; Prinsloo et al., 2011; Satish et al., 2015; Subramanya and Telles, 2015; Vazan et al., 2017; Zeki Al Hazzouri et al., 2017), however, only limited studies exist examining Stroop performance related to CVA (Johnsen et al., 2003; Subramanya and Telles, 2015; Albinet et al., 2016). In several studies, the Stroop test has been used with the mere purpose to create psychological stress (Hoshikawa and Yamamoto, 1997; Satish et al., 2015; Vazan et al., 2017), and no link with inhibition performance has been established. In other studies, although Stroop performance has been investigated with HRV, it has not been directly related to CVA indices (Prinsloo et al., 2011; Zeki Al Hazzouri et al., 2017). Among the studies linking Stroop performance and CVA, Johnsen et al. (2003) found that patients with dental fear having a higher resting CVA had shorter RTs to the incongruent color words and to the threat words compared to patients with lower resting CVA. However, Stroop interference accuracy (number of errors) was not measured, which does not provide a holistic representation of inhibition (McDowd et al., 1995). Albinet et al. (2016) showed that CVA improvements linked to a 5-months aquaerobics training program in older adults were linked to improvements on the Stroop interference accuracy (lower number of errors). Those two studies would be in line with the assumptions of the neurovisceral integration model (Thayer et al., 2009). On the contrary, Subramanya and Telles (2015) found that Stroop performance was better (less errors in the incongruent condition) with a decrease in high-frequency HRV, which usually depicts CVA when breathing patterns are comprised between 9 and 24 (Berntson et al., 1997), and increases in low-frequency HRV. However, these results were observed following a cyclic meditation condition involving slow body movements and slow breathing patterns, so there may have been some confounding effects of the experimental manipulation, and we can also speculate that in this case low-frequency HRV may have been mainly vagally driven. In summary, limited studies have linked Stroop performance to CVA, investigating either only RTs or accuracy (number of errors). Our research aims to address this gap and link CVA to both Stroop performance RTs and accuracy (number of errors).

When considering the effects of PE on Stroop performance, one should distinguish the timing of the Stroop test. During exercise cognitive performance is usually impaired and improves after exercise (Lambourne and Tomporowski, 2010), unless exhaustion is reached (Schmit et al., 2015). After acute exercise, RT on the Stroop interference is shorter after PE in comparison to a resting control condition (Alves et al., 2012), or in comparison to before PE (Johnson et al., 2016), regardless of the fitness level of the participants (Chang et al., 2014). Improvements on the Stroop interference accuracy (number of correct answers) after acute exercise were found (Peruyero et al., 2017), however, some mixed findings were also reported (Vincent and Hall, 2017). Improved cognitive performance after acute exercise is usually linked to an increase in physiological arousal (Chang et al., 2014). In line with the inverted-U hypothesis, moderate arousal is linked to optimal cognitive performance, while if arousal levels are either too low or too high cognitive performance is impaired (Ploughman, 2008; Kashihara et al., 2009). Acute effects of physical activity on Stroop performance are explained in particular via increased brain-derived neurotrophic factor (Griffin et al., 2011) and brain activation in the left dorsolateral prefrontal cortex (Yanagisawa et al., 2010), but do not seem to be related to changes in cerebral blood flow (Ogoh et al., 2014). At present, we are not aware of any research linking acute physical fatigue, Stroop performance, and CVA, and our research aims to address this gap.

Physical exertion will induce a drop in CVA, due to the activation of the sympathetic nervous system and the inhibition of the parasympathetic nervous system (Goldsmith et al., 2000; Iellamo, 2001; Winsley, 2002; Aubert et al., 2003; Stanley et al., 2013; Michael et al., 2017). Stopping PE induces a parasympathetic reactivation, which speed and magnitude depends on the fitness level of the individual (Stanley et al., 2013; Romero et al., 2017). If we follow the assumptions of the neurovisceral integration model (Thayer et al., 2009), the fact cognitive performance is decreased during exercise but improved after exercise (Lambourne and Tomporowski, 2010) may be linked to the parasympathetic deactivation observed during PE and reactivation after PE. Importantly, it may be possible to influence the speed and magnitude of CVA recovery after PE via specific strategies. Indeed, many factors were found to influence CVA (Laborde et al., 2018b), and some of them will be particularly adapted for athletes (Laborde et al., 2018c). Among those, we focus in this research on SPB.

Slow-paced breathing is a breathing technique with controlled inhalation and exhalation times ("paced"), realized at a slower pace, around 6 cycles per minute (cpm) than spontaneous breathing, which is usually comprised between 12 and 20 cpm in adults (Sherwood, 2006; Tortora and Derrickson, 2014). The pacing is usually realized via a visual, audio, or kinesthetic pacer (e.g., Allen and Friedman, 2012). According to the resonance model (Lehrer and Gevirtz, 2014), four processes play a role to understand the effects of SPB at 6 cpm: (1) the phase relationship between heart rate (HR) oscillations and breathing at 6 cpm; (2) the phase relationship between HR and blood pressure oscillations at 6 cpm; (3) the activity of the baroreflex; and (4) the resonance characteristics of the cardiovascular system. Combined, those processes are expected to strengthen homeostasis in the baroreceptor (Vaschillo et al., 2002, 2006; Lehrer et al., 2006), which results in improving gas exchanges at the level of alveoli and in increasing vagal afferences (Lehrer and Gevirtz, 2014). Evidence has already been found for both acute (Laborde et al., 2017a) and chronic (Laborde et al., 2019) increases in CVA (i.e., vagal efferent activity) following SPB interventions.

Slow-paced breathing has already been shown to improve cognitive functioning, with inhibition and working memory (Prinsloo et al., 2011). Prinsloo et al. (2011) investigated a modified Stroop test, combining the classical inhibition component (i.e., naming the ink in which a word corresponding to another color is printed) to a working memory component, asking participants to remember how many control white squares appeared on the screen. Participants were allocated either to a SPB condition with biofeedback (seeing live the effects of SPB on their HRV via a device) or to a control condition where they were breathing spontaneously, for 10 min. Results showed no differences between conditions on the Stroop test inhibition component (number of errors), however, the working memory performance of the SPB group was better when compared to the control group. Limitations of this study were a reduced sample size ($N = 18$ in a between-subjects design), the fact that inhibition and working memory were mixed in the modified Stroop test, which did not allow for drawing clear conclusions about the specific executive functions targeted, and finally the link between Stroop performance and CVA was not investigated. To conclude, research investigating the effects of SPB on inhibition is still required.

In summary, based on the research gaps identified in the literature, the aim of this research was to investigate the influence of a short-term SPB technique (in comparison to a watching TV control condition) on adaptation to psychological stress characterized via inhibition performance, before (Experiment 1) and after (Experiment 2) PE. The overall research was conceived as a mixed-model design, both experiments were conducted as within-subject designs (i.e., meaning participants take part in both the SPB and the control conditions of the same experiment), however, participants of Experiment 1 were not participating to Experiment 2, corresponding to the between-subject part. The within-subject part is always recommended in experiments involving HRV to limit inter-individual differences (Quintana and Heathers, 2014; Laborde et al., 2017b), however, given participating in four experimental sessions may have created some habituation effect, we split our research in two experiments, so that each participant was participating to two experimental sessions. At the subjective level, we expected PE and the CWST to increase the level of PS given both activities may lead the individual to perceive that demands of the task tax or exceed current adaptive abilities, while the relaxation moment would decrease the level of PS (Lazarus and Folkman, 1984; Lehrer and Gevirtz, 2014; Conway and Rubin, 2016). Further, we expected the SPB condition to show larger effect sizes than the control condition, based on its relaxing effects (Lehrer and Gevirtz, 2014). Further, at the physiological level, we expect PE to increase HR and RF and decrease RMSSD, reflecting cardiovascular and respiratory adaptations to acute exercise (Stanley et al., 2013). Regarding our main hypothesis, based on the neurovisceral integration model (Thayer et al., 2009) and on the resonance model (Lehrer and Gevirtz, 2014), we hypothesize that in both experiments, SPB will improve inhibition (Stroop interference) in terms of accuracy (number of errors) and RTs. The improvement in Stroop interference will be mediated by resting RMSSD before starting the Stroop test.

MATERIALS AND METHODS

Participants

In order to determine our sample size, we utilized previous research combining SPB and inhibition (Prinsloo et al., 2011). The study of Prinsloo et al. (2011) did not find any effect of SPB on inhibition and was likely underpowered ($N = 18$ for a between-subject design).[1] Based on this previous work, we computed an *a priori* power analysis with G*Power (Faul et al., 2007) based on a small effect size, for a repeated-measures ANOVA with a within-between interaction, with a power of 0.80 and an alpha level of 0.05, which gave us a total sample size of 120. A total of $N = 60$ participants (35 men, 25 women, mean age = 25.57 years old, age range = 19–40, BMI: $M = 23.62$, $SD = 2.52$) took part in Experiment 1, where the relaxation condition (SPB vs. watching TV control) was realized before physical PE. We refer thereafter to this first experiment as "relax before PE." Similarly, a total of $N = 60$ participants took part in Experiment 2 (38 men, 22 women, Mean age = 24.87 years old, age range = 18–41, BMI: $M = 22.86$, $SD = 2.29$), where the relaxation condition (SPB vs. watching TV control) was realized after PE. We refer thereafter to this second experiment as "relax after PE." Exclusion criteria were self-reported cardiovascular diseases, and other chronic diseases that might influence breathing or HR patterns, such as asthma, diabetes, psychiatric, and neurological diseases (Laborde et al., 2017b) or being color-blind, making them ineligible to complete the CWST. Participants were students at the German Sport University. The protocol of the study was approved by the Ethics committee of the German Sport University (N° 175/2016).

Material and Measures

Cardiac Vagal Activity

Cardiac vagal activity was operationalized via HRV and more specifically with RMSSD. An electrocardiography (ECG) device (Faros 180°, Mega Electronics, Kuopio, Finland) was used during the experiment to assess HRV, with a sampling rate of 500 Hz. We used two disposable ECG pre-gelled electrodes (Ambu L-00-S/25, Ambu GmbH, Bad Nauheim, Germany). The negative electrode was placed in the right infraclavicular fossa (just below the right clavicle) while the positive electrode was placed on the left side of the chest, below the pectoral muscle in the left anterior axillary line. The Faros device was taped to the participants' chest in order to avoid moving too much while the participant was performing PE. From ECG recordings we extracted RMSSD with Kubios© (University of Eastern Finland, Kuopio, Finland). The full ECG recording was inspected visually, and artifacts were corrected manually (Laborde et al., 2017b). As recommended by Laborde et al. (2017b), respiratory frequency (RF) was also taken into account. RF was computed via the ECG derived respiration algorithm of Kubios© (Tarvainen et al., 2014).

Perceived Stress

A visual analog scale (VAS) was used to measure PS (Lesage and Berjot, 2011). Participants were asked "How stressed do you feel right now?" and they responded by marking a cross on a 100 mm line with two anchors ("not at all stressed" to "very much stressed").

Physical Exertion – Burpees

Physical exertion was achieved with a modified version of the Burpee test (Podstawski et al., 2013). The Burpee test was named after the American physiologist Royal H. Burpee (1940), and was originally designed to measure agility and coordination. Burpees are physical exercises involving the whole body and requires no additional equipment. The following version of the Burpee was performed,[2] with these instructions: (1) start from a standing position; (2) bend over and place both hands firmly on the ground in front of the feet; (3) kick (or step) both feet back into a push-up position and lower the entire body to the ground (this is not a push-up); (4) the chest and thighs need to make full contact with the ground; (5) then extend the arms, lifting the chest and jump (or step) both feet in toward the chest; and (6) stand, jump (opening the hips fully), and clap hands behind the head while in the air.

Slow-Paced Breathing

Similar to previous research (Laborde et al., 2017a), the SPB exercise was conducted with a video showing a little ball moving up and down at the rate of 6 cpm. Participants having to inhale continuously through the nose while the ball was going up, and exhale continuously with pursed lips when the ball was going down. The video used was the same used in Laborde et al. (2017a), displaying a 3 × 5-min SPB exercise, with a 1-min break between each unit, corresponding to a total of 17-min. Exhalation (5.5 s) was slightly longer than inhalation (4.5 s), because a prolonged exhalation contributed to larger beat-to-beat heart fluctuations compared to prolonged inhalation, and therefore induce higher CVA (Strauss-Blasche et al., 2000).

TV Neutral Documentary

The control condition (CON) used a TV documentary about world travel destinations, this was shown to the participants for the same duration as the SPB exercise (17 min). This TV documentary was found to be subjectively emotionally neutral in a previous pilot study.

[1] No precise *a posteriori* power calculation could be performed, given exact descriptive statistics related to Stroop accuracy could not be extracted from the study.

[2] https://www.youtube.com/watch?v=X60BcsO_wE (retrieved on April 3, 2019).

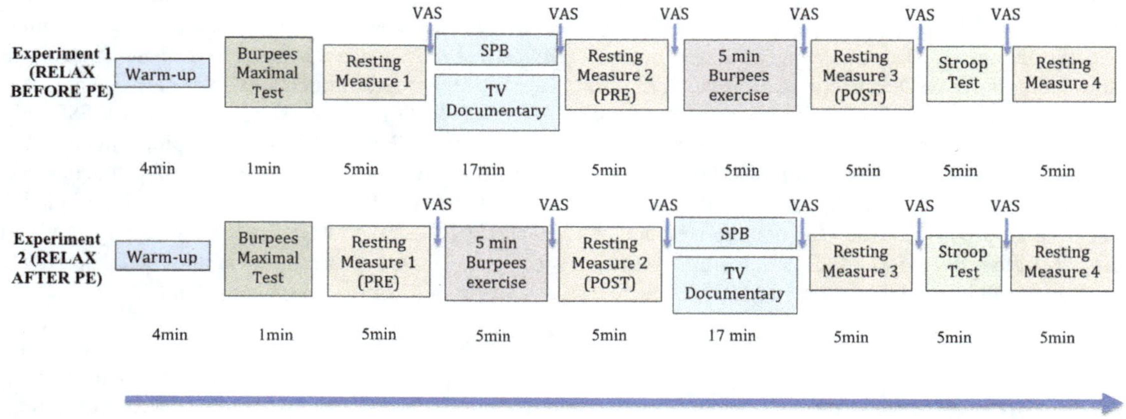

FIGURE 1 | Experimental protocol. "Relax before PE": experiment in which the relaxation moment (either slow-paced breathing or watching the TV documentary) took place before the 5 min Burpees exercise; "Relax after PE": experiment in which the relaxation moment (either slow-paced breathing or watching the TV documentary) took place after the 5 min Burpees exercise. For the manipulation check of the Burpee exercise, "PRE" refers to the 5 min resting measure realized before PE (so resting measure 1 for "relax before PE" and resting measure 2 for "relax after PE"), while "POST" refers to the 5 min resting measure realized after PE (so resting measure 2 for "relax before PE" and resting measure 3 for "relax after PE"). VAS: Visual Analog Scale (perceived stress).

Inhibition Performance (Measured With the Stroop Interference)

We used the computerized version of the CWST with verbal responding available in the Inquisit library,[3] and ran this with the Inquisit software (Inquisit 5 [Computer Software], 2016). We used a 15-in. flat-screen monitor (1,280 × 960 pixels at 60 Hz) at a viewing distance of 60 cm. Words appeared in 28-pt Arial font in the middle of a white screen. Three types of stimuli were used: colored square (congruent control stimuli), colored words displayed with the color corresponding to the word (congruent stimuli, for example the word "green" is displayed in the color green), and colored words displayed with an inconsistent color (incongruent stimuli, for example the word "green" is displayed in the color red). Participants were asked to name the color in which the word was written as fast and as accurately as possible, while ignoring the written meaning of the word. A headset mounted microphone recorded the verbal answers. A familiarization was realized with 20 trials. For the test, participants completed 84 trials (4 colors – red, green, blue, black) × 3 color stimulus congruency (congruent, incongruent, control squares) × 7 repetitions = 84 trials. Stimuli stayed on screen until response, latencies were measured from onset of stimuli. The intertrial interval was of 200 ms, and the error feedback (a red cross) of 400 ms.

Procedure

Participants were recruited via flyers on the campus of the local University and via posts on social networks groups linked to the local University. For each experiment, there were two testing sessions involved (lasting around 90 min each, see **Figure 1** for full description). The experimental order of the sessions was counterbalanced. The two sessions were separated by 1 week, to keep learning effects to a minimum, and took place at the same time of the day, given this parameter may influence HRV (van Eekelen et al., 2004) and performance (Folkard, 1990; Laborde et al., 2018a). Participants were either taking part in Experiment 1 or Experiment 2, they could not participate to both. They were asked to wear sports clothes to take part in the experiment. Prior to the testing sessions, participants were instructed not to drink or eat anything but water during the 2 h before the experiment, or take part in any strenuous exercise or drink alcohol for the 24 h prior testing (Laborde et al., 2017b). Both experiments were the same in their conception, the only aspect that differed was whether the relaxation moment was taking place before (Experiment 1) or after (Experiment 2) PE.

Upon arrival to the laboratory, participants were asked to fill out an informed consent form and a demographic questionnaire regarding variables potentially influencing HRV (Laborde et al., 2017b). At the beginning of the SPB condition, participants also received a short video introduction on how to perform the technique correctly, which was checked by the experimenter. Then participants were asked to perform a warm up[4] for 4 min involving squats, lunges, leg swings, jumping jacks, press up's, and squat thrusts. The warm up was chosen in agreement with an expert strength and conditioning coach from the German Sport University who was part of the research team. To prepare the PE (5 min Burpees exercise), participants had to perform five trials Burpees, so that the experimenter could check whether they were performed correctly. Then participants had to do a maximal Burpees test for 1 min, with the instruction to perform as many technically correct Burpees as they could. We then calculated 70% of this maximal number, and this gave the number of Burpees for the participants to realize during the 5 min Burpees exercise. For example, if the participant performed a maximal number of 20

[3]https://www.millisecond.com/download/library/stroop/ (retrieved on April 3, 2019).

[4]https://www.youtube.com/watch?v=HDfvWrGUkC8 (retrieved on April 3, 2019).

Burpees, 70% × 20 = 14, for the 5 min Burpees exercise he/she would have then to perform 14 Burpees each minute for 5 min. During the 5 min Burpees exercise, the realization of the Burpees was paced by the experimenter, giving a signal as a time marker to perform each Burpee, so the participant could better distribute his/her effort along the 5 min. The value of 70% was chosen based on a pilot study realized with 10 participants, where 70% was found to be an achievable compromise between achievability and degree of exhaustion, which had to be higher than 17 on the Borg Scale of Perceived Exertion (Borg, 1982). The 1 min Burpees maximal test was realized at the beginning of each session, given we wanted to account for potential differences in daily fitness level. The number of Burpees to be realized during the 5 min Burpees exercise was then based on the maximal number of Burpees achieved during the 1 min Burpees test at the beginning of the same session.

The relaxation task (either SPB or watching TV control) was placed either before (Experiment 1) or after (Experiment 2) PE. Finally participants had to perform the Stroop test, that lasted between 4 and 5 min. Between each block of the sessions, a HRV resting measure of 5 min was taken, based on the Task Force recommendation (Malik, 1996). HR and RF were derived from this HRV measurement. The HRV resting measure was realized in a sitting position with eyes closed, knees at 90°, hands on the thighs. At the end of the second testing session, participants were debriefed and thanked.

Data Analysis

Due to technical problems, the ECG data of the last 13 participants of Experiment 2 were lost, therefore the sample size of Experiment 2 was reduced to $N = 47$. Regarding the HRV data, RMSSD was extracted from the Kubios output. RF (respiratory cycles per minute) was calculated multiplying the EDR (ECG derived respiration) value obtained via the Kubios algorithm by 60.

For the Stroop test, the number of incorrect answers was retrieved for the congruent colored squares, as well as for the congruent and incongruent stimuli. Regarding response times, we analyzed only those of the correct answers. Then we used two filters (see Lautenbach et al., 2016). In the first filter, trials with response times lower than 200 ms and higher than 3000 ms were excluded in order to account for extreme results (see Putman and Berling, 2011). The second filter then screened for RTs higher or lower than two standard deviations from the mean, which were also removed to account for outliers (see Dresler et al., 2009).

The VAS data and the Stroop performance data were normally distributed and homoscedastic. The physiological data (HRV, HR, RF) were not normally distributed, thus a log-transform (Log 10) was used to achieve normal distribution (Laborde et al., 2017b), and data were homoscedastic. Regarding the physiological data, we ran the analyses with the log-transformed values, however, we indicate as descriptive values the raw data, given they make more sense for the reader. For RMSSD, we controlled as well for the influence of covariates that have been linked to variations in CVA, such as RF, age, gender, smoking status, and BMI.

For the manipulation check related to PS, we ran three successive repeated-measures ANOVA for the relaxation technique, the 5 min Burpees exercise, and the Stroop task. We had time (before vs. after), condition (SPB vs. CON) as within-subject independent variable, and relaxation moment ("relax before PE" or "relax after PE") as between-subject independent variable.

For the physiological manipulation check related to the 5 min Burpees exercise, "PRE" refers to the 5 min resting measure realized before PE (so resting measure 1 for "relax before PE" and resting measure 2 for "relax after PE"), while "POST" refers to the 5 min resting measure realized after PE (so resting measure 2 for "relax before PE" and resting measure 3 for "relax after PE"). As manipulation check, we wanted to ensure that PE was leading to physiological changes usually seen with acute exercise, meaning we expected a main effect of time ("PRE PE" vs. "POST PE") on HR (increase), RMSSD (decrease), and RF (increase), based on classical cardiorespiratory effects observed with PE (Stanley et al., 2013; Menz et al., 2016; Mlynczak and Krysztofiak, 2019). We investigated this manipulation check hypothesis running three repeated-measures ANOVA, with condition (SPB vs. CON), time (PRE vs. POST) as within-subject independent variables and relaxation moment ("relax before PE" or "relax after PE") as between-subject independent variables, with HR, RF, and RMSSD as dependent variables. Regarding RMSSD, in order to control for the potential effect of covariates, a linear mixed model analysis was conducted with age, gender, smoking status, BMI, and RF as covariates. The linear mixed model analysis allows to take into account time-varying covariates, in this case RF, which is not possible with the linear general model repeated-measures analysis module of SPSS. Given our hypothesis related to the manipulation check concerned only the main effect of time, we only report this result for clarity matters. Further, in order to ensure that changes are not due to a different amount of Burpees realized, the number of Burpees performed during the 5 min Burpees exercise will be checked via a repeated-measures ANOVA, with condition (SPB vs. CON) as within-subject independent variable and relaxation moment ("relax before PE" or "relax after PE") as between-subject independent variable.

Regarding our main working hypothesis, we ran a repeated-measures ANOVA with condition (SPB vs. CON) as within-subject independent variable, and relaxation moment ("relax before PE" or "relax after PE") as between-subject independent variable. Errors (error rate to incongruent stimuli, reflecting Stroop interference accuracy) and RTs (incongruent stimuli-congruent stimuli) were used as dependent variables for the Stroop interference, and RMSSD to infer CVA. Regarding errors in the Stroop task, we decided not to take into account errors made with congruent stimuli in the calculation, given they were none. Interactions were investigated with further t-tests either paired or independent according to the analysis, with Bonferroni correction regarding the significance level. Regarding RMSSD, similar to the previous analysis related to PE, a linear mixed model analysis was further conducted with age, gender, smoking status, BMI, and RF as covariates.

Finally, in case a significant effect of SPB on Stroop interference (errors and/or RTs) was found, potential mediation via RMSSD was performed via the PROCESS 3.3 dialog box developed by Hayes (2013). This custom dialog tests the total, direct, and indirect effect of an independent variable on a dependent variable through a proposed mediator and allows

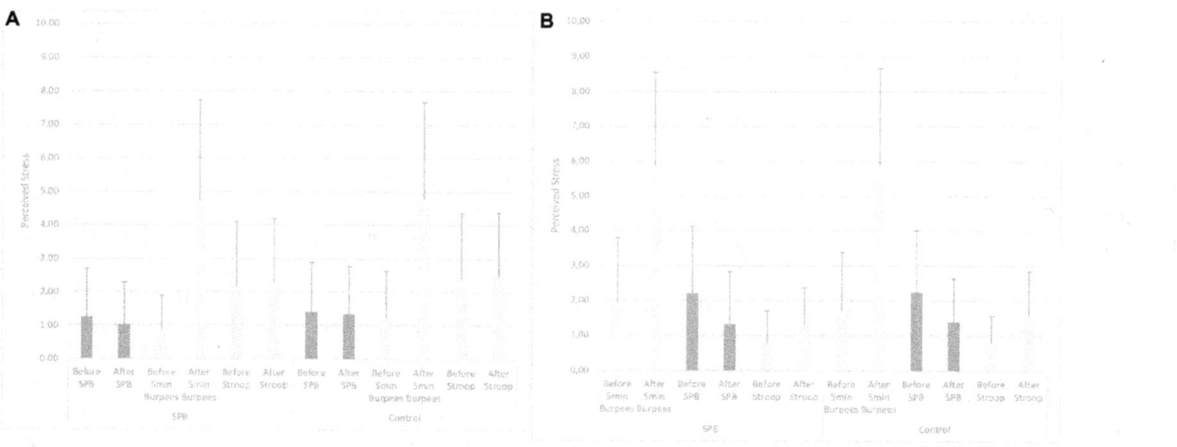

FIGURE 2 | (A,B) Perceived stress in "Relax before PE." SPB: slow-paced breathing; 5 min Burpees: 5 min Burpees exercise; Stroop: Color Word Stroop Test; "Relax before PE": Experiment in which the relaxation moment (either slow-paced breathing or watching the TV documentary) took place before the 5 min Burpees exercise; "Relax after PE": Experiment in which the relaxation moment (either slow-paced breathing or watching the TV documentary) took place after the 5 min Burpees exercise.

inferences regarding indirect effects using percentile bootstrap confidence intervals.

RESULTS

The full dataset is available in **Supplementary Material.**

Perceived Stress Manipulation Check

See **Figures 2A,B** for full descriptive statistics about PS.

Relaxation (SPB vs. Watching TV)

Greenhouse-Geisser correction was applied for the tests. Regarding PS before and after the relaxation moment, no main effect of condition was found, $F(1,105) = 1.708$, $p = 0.187$, partial $\eta^2 = 0.02$. No interaction condition × relaxation moment was found, $F(1,105) = 0.743$, $p = 0.391$, partial $\eta^2 = 0$. A main effect of time was found, $F(1,105) = 17.808$, $p < 0.001$, partial $\eta^2 = 0.15$. PS before the relaxation was higher ($M = 1.72$; $SD = 1.57$) than after the relaxation ($M = 1.45$; $SD = 1.26$), $t(106) = 3.111$, $p = 0.002$; Cohen's $d = 0.19$. An interaction effect time × relaxation moment was found, $F(1,105) = 9.108$, $p = 0.003$, partial $\eta^2 = 0.08$. Further *post hoc t*-tests were run: they showed no significant difference for PS in "Relax before PE" being higher before ($M = 1.32$; $SD = 1.31$) than after ($M = 1.18$; $SD = 1.19$) the relaxation, $t(59) = 1.359$, $p = 0.179$; Cohen's $d = 0.12$. A significant difference was found for PS being lower before relaxation in "relax before PE" ($M = 0.90$, $SD = 0.95$) in comparison to before relaxation in "relax after PE" ($M = 2.22$, $SD = 1.73$), $t(46) = 5.426$, $p < 0.001$; Cohen's $d = 0.96$. PS was significantly lower after relaxation in "relax before PE" ($M = 0.79$, $SD = 0.77$) in comparison to in "relax after PE" ($M = 1.79$, $SD = 1.29$), $t(46) = 6.795$, $p < 0.001$; Cohen's $d = 0.95$. In "relax after PE," PS was significantly lower after ($M = 1.79$, $SD = 1.29$) than before ($M = 2.22$, $SD = 1.73$) relaxation, $t(46) = 3.042$, $p = 0.004$; Cohen's $d = 0.28$. No interaction effect condition × time was found, $F(1,105) = 0.302$, $p = 0.584$, partial $\eta^2 = 0.0$. No interaction effect condition × time × relaxation moment was found, $F(1,105) = 0.178$, $p = 0.674$, partial $\eta^2 = 0.0$.

Five Minutes Burpees Exercise

Greenhouse-Geisser correction was applied for the tests. Regarding PS before and after the 5 min Burpees exercise, no main effect of condition was found, $F(1,105) = 0.197$, $p = 0.658$, partial $\eta^2 = 0$. No interaction condition × relaxation moment was found, $F(1,105) = 1.595$, $p = 0.209$, partial $\eta^2 = 0.02$. A main effect of time was found, $F(1,105) = 181.695$, $p < 0.001$, partial $\eta^2 = 0.63$. PS after the 5 min Burpees exercise was higher ($M = 5.24$; $SD = 2.73$) than before the 5 min Burpees exercise ($M = 1.37$; $SD = 1.41$), $t(106) = 13.556$, $p < 0.001$; Cohen's $d = 1.79$. No interaction effect time × relaxation moment was found, $F(1,105) = 0.310$, $p = 0.579$, partial $\eta^2 = 0$. No interaction effect condition × time was found, $F(1,105) = 0.159$, $p = 0.690$, partial $\eta^2 = 0$. No interaction effect condition × time × relaxation moment was found, $F(1,105) = 1.995$, $p = 0.161$, partial $\eta^2 = 0.02$.

Stroop Task

Greenhouse-Geisser correction was applied for the tests. Regarding PS before and after the relaxation moment, no main effect of condition was found, $F(1,105) = 2.102$, $p = 0.150$, partial $\eta^2 = 0.02$. No interaction condition × relaxation moment was found, $F(1,105) = 0.020$, $p = 0.887$, partial $\eta^2 = 0$. A main effect of time was found, $F(1,105) = 8.976$, $p = 0.003$, partial $\eta^2 = 0.08$. PS was higher after Stroop ($M = 1.94$; $SD = 1.52$) than before Stroop ($M = 1.61$; $SD = 1.54$), $t(106) = 2.696$, $p < 0.001$; Cohen's $d = 0.21$. An interaction effect time × relaxation moment was found, $F(1,105) = 4.963$, $p = 0.028$, partial $\eta^2 = 0.05$. In "relax before PE," no difference in PS before ($M = 2.27$, $SD = 1.70$) and after Stroop ($M = 2.36$, $SD = 1.69$), $t(59) = 0.500$, $p = 0.619$; Cohen's $d = 0.05$. Considering the time before the Stroop task, PS was higher in "relax before PE" ($M = 2.02$, $SD = 1.69$) in comparison to in "relax after PE" ($M = 0.77$, $SD = 0.72$);

$t(46) = 4.727$, $p < 0.001$; Cohen's $d = 0.97$. Considering the time after the Stroop task, PS was higher in "relax before PE" ($M = 2.18$, $SD = 1.66$) in comparison to "relax after PE" ($M = 2.02$, $SD = 1.69$), $t(46) = 3.034$, $p = 0.004$; Cohen's $d = 0.57$. In "relax after PE," PS was higher after the Stroop task ($M = 1.40$, $SD = 1.06$) than before the Stroop task ($M = 0.77$, $SD = 0.72$), $t(46) = 4.664$, $p < 0.001$; Cohen's $d = 0.69$. No interaction effect condition × time was found, $F(1,105) = 0.665$, $p = 0.417$, partial $\eta^2 = 0.0$. No interaction effect condition × time × relaxation moment was found, $F(1,105) = 1.099$, $p = 0.297$, partial $\eta^2 = 0.01$.

Five Minutes Burpees Exercise – Physiological Manipulation Check

Descriptive statistics for all physiological variables and all measurement points can be seen in **Tables 1A,B**, while descriptive statistics specifically related to the manipulation check of the 5 min Burpees exercise can be seen in **Figures 3A–C**.

Heart Rate

Regarding HR, a main effect of time was found, $F(1,105) = 344.906$, $p < 0.001$, partial $\eta^2 = 0.69$; with HR being higher after PE ($M = 103.93$; $SD = 13.46$) in comparison to before PE ($M = 80.85$, $SD = 12.95$).

RMSSD

Regarding RMSSD, a repeated-measures ANOVA was first ran. A main effect of time was found, $F(1,105) = 85.517$, $p < 0.001$, partial $\eta^2 = 0.40$, with RMSSD being lower after PE ($M = 13.43$; $SD = 12.53$) than before PE ($M = 24.87$; $SD = 24.23$). A linear mixed model analysis was then ran to investigate whether covariates (RF, age, gender, smoking status, BMI) were affecting the results. Relaxation moment, condition, time, and all covariates were entered as fixed effects, including intercepts, with an unstructured repeated covariance type resulting in the best model fit, with − 2 Restricted Log Likelihood = 214.341. No random effects (slopes nor intercepts) were found to improve significantly the model fit, consequently none were added to the model. Regarding the main effect of time, results remained significant within a linear mixed model analysis, $F(1,106.956) = 158.644$, $p < 0.001$, estimate of fixed effect = −0.45 ($SE = 0.04$), 95% CI = −0.52 to −0.38. From the covariates two were found to have a significant effect, RF, $F(1,263.319) = 34.114$, $p < 0.001$, estimate of fixed effect = −0.70 ($SE = 0.12$), 95% CI = −0.93 to −0.46; and BMI, $F(1,101.267) = 4.074$, $p = 0.046$; estimate of fixed effect = −0.02 ($SE = 0.01$), 95% CI = −0.04 to 0.

Respiratory Frequency

Regarding RF, a main effect of time was found, $F(1,105) = 45.262$, $p < 0.001$, partial $\eta^2 = 0.26$, with RF higher after PE ($M = 18.30$, $SD = 3.54$) than before PE ($M = 16.28$, $SD = 2.71$).

Number of Burpees

Regarding the number of Burpees performed during PE (descriptive statistics in **Table 2**), no main effect of condition was found $F(1,105) = 0.161$, $p = 0.689$, partial $\eta^2 = 0$; and no interaction effect was found with the moment of relaxation $F(1,105) = 0.524$, $p = 0.471$, partial $\eta^2 = 0.01$.

TABLE 1A | Descriptive statistics physiological variables Exp. 1 "Relax before PE."

	SPB								Control							
	Resting 1 (before relax)		Resting 2 (after relax/ PRE-PE)		Resting 3 (POST-PE/ before Stroop)		Resting 4 (after Stroop)		Resting 1 (before relax)		Resting 2 (after relax/ PRE-PE)		Resting 3 (POST-PE/ before Stroop)		Resting 4 (after Stroop)	
	M	*SD*	*M*	*SD*	*M*	*SD*	*M*	*SD*	*M*	*SD*	*M*	*SD*	*M*	*SD*	*M*	*SD*
Heart rate (bpm)	77.16	11.92	73.74	11.28	107.31	12.26	99.36	11.90	76.50	10.70	75.56	10.11	103.23	20.08	106.29	43.71
RMSSD (ms)	43.57	26.04	45.79	26.83	23.90	9.36	12.76	8.30	45.90	27.92	42.61	25.77	11.69	11.93	13.33	10.52
Respiratory frequency (cpm)	14.15	2.76	14.33	2.21	19.20	4.15	16.55	3.61	16.52	2.36	16.45	2.68	18.04	5.21	16.17	4.09

TABLE 1B | Descriptive statistics physiological variables Exp. 2 "Relax after PE."

	SPB								Control							
	Resting 1 (PRE-PE)		Resting 2 (POST-PE/ before relax)		Resting 3 (after relax/ before Stroop)		Resting 4 (after Stroop)		Resting 1 (PRE-PE)		Resting 2 (POST-PE/ before relax)		Resting 3 (after relax/ before Stroop)		Resting 4 (after Stroop)	
	M	*SD*	*M*	*SD*	*M*	*SD*	*M*	*SD*	*M*	*SD*	*M*	*SD*	*M*	*SD*	*M*	*SD*
Heart rate (bpm)	89.67	13.50	107.12	14.10	92.72	11.18	95.61	12.20	87.85	14.91	100.70	13.25	103.23	20.08	89.39	10.14
RMSSD (ms)	25.38	18.82	17.72	23.90	24.22	16.19	17.44	11.39	27.12	27.84	21.54	26.91	17.38	10.90	19.76	11.23
Respiratory frequency (cpm)	17.23	3.59	17.31	4.39	11.20	3.20	12.50	3.02	17.58	3.35	18.47	3.59	15.06	3.18	13.97	3.05

bpm: beats per minute; ms: milliseconds; cpm: cycles per minute; relax: slow-paced breathing exercise or watching TV neutral documentary; PE: physical exertion (5 min Burpees exercise); SPB: slow-paced breathing; RMSSD: root mean square of successive differences. For the manipulation check of the Burpee exercise, "PRE" refers to the 5 min resting measure realized before PE (so resting measure 1 for Exp. 1 "relax before PE" and resting measure 2 for Exp. 2 "relax after PE"). While "POST" refers to the 5 min resting measure realized after PE (so resting measure 2 for Exp. 1 "relax before PE" and resting measure 3 for Exp. 2 "relax after PE").

Main Research Question – Stroop Task

Descriptive statistics related to the variables linked to our main research question with the Stroop task are displayed in **Table 3**. Regarding Stroop interference (RT), a repeated-measures ANOVA revealed no main effect of condition $F(1,105) = 0.873$, $p = 0.352$, partial $\eta^2 = 0$. No interaction effect condition × relaxation moment was found, $F(1,105) = 0.039$, $p = 0.843$, partial $\eta^2 = 0$. Relaxation moment had an overall effect on the Stroop interference, $F(1,105) = 35.031$, $p < 0.001$, partial $\eta^2 = 0.25$, with a shorter Stroop interference found for "relax before PE" (M = 20,33; SD = 69.61) in comparison to "relax after PE" (M = 103.14; SD = 64.87).

Regarding Stroop interference (errors), we found a main effect for condition, $F(1,105) = 22.584$, $p < 0.001$, partial $\eta^2 = 0.17$, with SPB (M = 0.36, SD = 0.60) being lower than CON (M = 0.69, SD = 0.82). No main relaxation moment effect was found, $F(1,105) = 1.735$, $p = 0.191$, partial $\eta^2 = 0.02$. An interaction effect between condition and relaxation moment was found, $F(1,105) = 5.364$, $p = 0.022$, partial $\eta^2 = 0.04$. Further *post hoc* t-tests were run: they showed a significant difference between SPB-"relax before PE" (M = 0.50; SD = 0.70) and SPB-"relax after PE" (M = 0.17; SD = 0.38), with $t = 4.105$, df = 46, $p < 0.001$, Cohen's d = 0.60; a significant difference between SPB-"relax before PE" (M = 0.50, SD = 0.70) and CON-"relax before PE" (M = 0.68, SD = 0.81), with $t = 2.647$, df = 59, $p = 0.010$, Cohen's d = 0.34; a significant difference between SPB-"relax after PE" (M = 0.17, SD = 0.38) and CON-"relax after PE" (M = 0.70, SD = 0.86), $t = 3.658$, df = 46, $p < 0.001$, Cohen's d = 0.53. No significant differences were found between CON-"relax before PE" and CON-"relax after PE," $t = 0.643$, df = 46, $p = 0.523$, Cohen's d = 0.09.

Regarding RMSSD during the resting measure before starting the Stroop test: a main condition effect was found, $F(1,105) = 5.841$, $p = 0.017$, partial $\eta^2 = 0.05$, with SPB (M = 16.97, SD = 14.28) being higher than CON (M = 14.19, SD = 11.79). No interaction effect between condition and relaxation moment was found, $F(1,105) = 3.335$, $p = 0.071$, partial $\eta^2 = 0.03$. A main relaxation moment effect was found, $F(1,105) = 28.870$, $p < 0.001$, partial $\eta^2 = 0.22$, with RMSSD being higher in "relax after PE" (M = 20.80, SD = 14.15) than in "relax before PE" (M = 11.49, SD = 10.69).

A linear mixed model analysis was then ran to investigate whether covariates (RF, age, sex, smoking status, BMI) were affecting the results. Relaxation moment, condition, and all covariates were entered as fixed effects, including intercepts, with an unstructured repeated covariance type resulting in the best model fit, with − 2 Restricted Log Likelihood = 129.122. No random effects (slopes nor intercepts) were found to improve significantly the model fit, consequently none were added to the model. No main effect of condition was found, $F(1,108.835) = 0.039$, $p = 0.844$. A main effect of relaxation moment was found, $F(1,126.990) = 4.890$, $p = 0.029$, estimate of fixed effect = 0.27 (SE = 0.12), 95% CI = 0.03 to 0.51. No interaction effect condition × relaxation moment was found, $F(1,110.459) = 0.169$, $p = 0.682$. From the covariates only RF was found to have a significant effect, $F(1,143.946) = 16.814$,

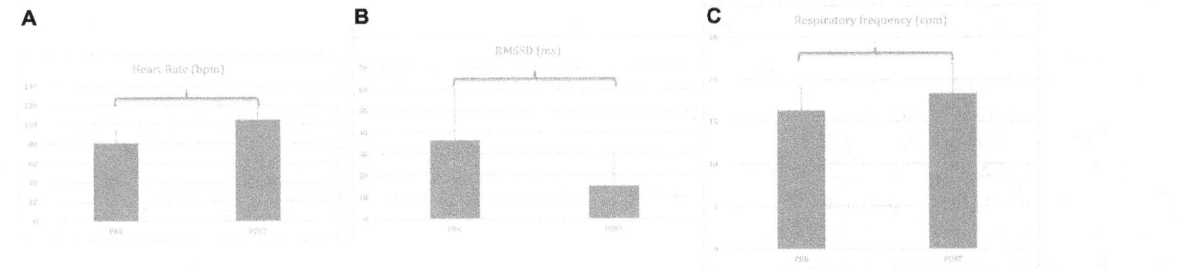

FIGURE 3 | (A) Manipulation check for time effect with heart rate before and after the 5 min Burpees exercise. **(B)** Manipulation check for time effect with RMSSD before and after the 5 min Burpees exercise. **(C)** Manipulation check for time effect with respiratory frequency before and after the 5 min Burpees exercise. For the manipulation check of the 5 min Burpee exercise (PE – physical exertion), "PRE" refers to the 5 min resting measure realized before PE (so resting measure 1 for Exp. 1 "relax before PE" and resting measure 2 for Exp. 2 "relax after PE"), while "POST" refers to the 5 min resting measure realized after PE (so resting measure 2 for Exp. 1 "relax before PE" and resting measure 3 for Exp. 2. "relax after PE"). RMSSD: root mean square of successive differences.

TABLE 2 | Descriptive statistics for the number of Burpees realized during the 5 min Burpees exercise.

	Exp. 1 – RELAX BEFORE PE				**Exp. 2 – RELAX AFTER PE**			
	Slow paced breathing		**Control**		**Slow paced breathing**		**Control**	
	M	***SD***	***M***	***SD***	***M***	***SD***	***M***	***SD***
Number of Burpees	64.27	11.54	63.00	11.64	63.60	11.69	63.19	12.20

PE: physical exertion (5 min Burpees exercise).

TABLE 3 | Descriptive statistics for the main working hypothesis.

	Exp. 1 – RELAX BEFORE PE				**Exp. 2 – RELAX AFTER PE**			
	SPB		**Control**		**SPB**		**Control**	
	M	***SD***	***M***	***SD***	***M***	***SD***	***M***	***SD***
Stroop interference (number of errors)	0.50	0.70	0.68	0.81	0.17	0.38	0.70	0.86
Stroop interference (reaction times, ms)	18.26	95.70	25.61	79.45	104.71	72.01	109.49	68.92
RMSSD (ms)	11.29	9.36	11.69	11.93	24.22	16.20	11.69	11.93
Respiratory frequency (cpm)	19.20	4.15	18.04	5.212	11.20	3.201	15.06	3.18

ms: milliseconds; cpm: cycles per minute; PE: physical exertion (5 min Burpees exercise); Stroop interference (accuracy) represents the number of errors in response to incongruent stimuli; Stroop interference (reaction time): reaction time to incongruent stimuli – reaction time to congruent stimuli; RMSSD, root mean square of successive differences; and respiratory frequency correspond to the resting measure 3 taken before the Stroop test.

$p < 0.001$, estimate of fixed effect = −0.47 (SE = 0.11), 95% CI = −0.70 to −0.24.

Finally, to test whether the effect of SPB on Stroop interference (errors) was mediated by RMSSD, the experimental group (coded SPB = 1; CON = 2) was entered as independent variable, Stroop interference (errors) was entered as dependent variable, and RMSSD was entered as mediator variable. Based on a 10,000 sampling rate, the results from bootstrapping revealed no significant indirect effect, 95% CI = −0.15 to 0.18. Rerunning the mediation analysis taking into account the covariates (RF, age, sex, smoking status, BMI) revealed no significant indirect effect, 95% CI = −0.03 to 0.10.

DISCUSSION

This research aimed to investigate the effects of SPB on the adaptation to psychological stress, and more specifically inhibition performance, after PE. At the subjective level, in line with our hypothesis, PS was increased during the 5 min Burpees exercise and the Stroop test, and decreased during the relaxation technique, however, no effect of condition was found. At the physiological level, in line with our hypothesis, our PE manipulation was successful in increasing HR, RF, and decreasing RMSSD. Our main hypothesis was partially validated, given SPB led to better Stroop interference accuracy (lower number of errors in response to incongruent stimuli), however, no differences were found regarding Stroop interference RT.

Concerning the subjective manipulation check, confirming our hypothesis, PE and CWST increased PS, while PS was decreased with relaxation. This means that PE and the Stroop task were perceived as taxing or exceeding the adaptive resources of the individual, while relaxation contributed to decreased PS (Lazarus and Folkman, 1984). However, contrary to our hypothesis based on the relaxing effects of SPB (Lehrer and Gevirtz, 2014), the effects of SPB on PS did not differ from watching the TV documentary. This could be linked to the fact that many people already use TV as means of relaxation (Conway and Rubin, 2016), and therefore associate it with an activity decreasing PS. Interestingly, the increase in PS was much higher during the 5 min Burpees exercise (partial $\eta^2 = 0.63$) in comparison to the Stroop task (partial $\eta^2 = 0.08$). This might be due to the fact the 5 min Burpees exercise was perceived as particularly exhausting by the participants.

Concerning the physiological manipulation check of the 5 min Burpees exercise, we focused specifically on the effects involving time, given we are looking for physiological changes between the resting measures before and after the Burpees. HR and RF increased overall during the 5 min Burpees exercise, while RMSSD decreased (even after controlling for RF and other covariates). Our results cannot be directly compared to previous research, given very few studies have investigated Burpees so far, and when they did it was always as part as a more global training program involving a large range of physical exercises (McRae et al., 2012; Emberts et al., 2013; Abbes et al., 2018; Sperlich et al., 2018). However, these findings would be in line with typical cardiorespiratory adaptations to PE (Stanley et al., 2013; Menz et al., 2016; Mlynczak and Krysztofiak, 2019). The number of Burpees achieved did not differ across conditions or across relaxation moment. We should note that in the 5 min Burpees exercise, the realization of the Burpees was paced for the participants, meaning they could not go faster, even if they felt that they were able to do so. Further research may investigate whether giving the instruction to perform as many Burpees as possible during 5 min (i.e., maximal performance) may have provided different results, helping to understand whether SPB influences physical performance.

Regarding our main hypothesis linked to Stroop interference errors and RTs, Stroop interference errors decreased with SPB, while no change were observed for Stroop RTs, therefore our hypothesis was only partially validated. According to the literature, with the CWST inhibition is primarily reflected by the number of errors (accuracy) made with incongruent stimuli (McDowd et al., 1995), given it shows a typical illustration of inhibition failure. This is in line with the interpretation that Stroop interference accuracy represents as well an index of the ability to maintain the task's goal temporarily in a highly retrievable state (Kane and Engle, 2003), given making a mistake linked to incongruent stimuli means that we were temporarily not successful in the aim of the task. A follow-up analysis of the condition × relaxation moment interaction shows that if Stroop interference errors were overall lower in the SPB condition in comparison to the CON condition, Stroop interference errors were lower when SPB was realized after PE than before PE. This may be explained by the time proximity of SPB to the realization of the Stroop test, and also by the fact that the physiological changes induced by PE may have influenced the effects of SPB realized beforehand.

Given no differences were observed with Stroop interference RTs, we have to conclude that SPB did not help to reduce the processing time of incongruent stimuli. Even if Stroop interference RTs are not the main marker of inhibition obtained with the Stroop test, RTs may still help us to understand mechanisms related to inhibition processing (Scarpina and Tagini, 2017). This may be linked to the fact SPB induces a general decrease of general physiological arousal (Lehrer and Gevirtz, 2014), which we also observed in this research in experiment 1 ("relax before PE"), where participants had a significantly lower HR and higher RMSSD after performing SPB in comparison to CON. The fact that physiological arousal plays a role in the Stroop interference RTs is also confirmed by our data, given Stroop interference RTs are much lower right after PE (in "relax before PE"), than 17 min later after performing SPB or CON (in "relax after PE"), with a large effect size (partial $\eta^2 = 25$), which is in line with previous research (Cooper et al., 2016). Cooper et al. (2016) found that RTs on the complex level (incongruent condition) of the Stroop were quicker (in comparison to RTs obtained before exercise) immediately following the sprint-based exercise, but did not differ after 45 min; while RTs on the simple level (congruent condition) of the Stroop were quicker 45 min following sprint-based exercise (Cooper et al., 2016), but did not differ from the rest condition right after exercise. It could be speculated that this difference may be due to changes in brain-derived neurotrophic factor (Griffin et al., 2011) and brain activation in the left dorsolateral prefrontal cortex (Yanagisawa et al., 2010), given these mechanisms were previously identified as playing a role in improving Stroop interference RTs after exercise, however, this should be investigated in further research. To sum up, we found that SPB was effective in improving Stroop interference accuracy (decreasing the number of errors to incongruent stimuli) but not RTs.

Root mean square of successive differences in the resting measure before the Stroop task was found to be higher in the SPB condition than in the CON condition, which would mean that the increase in vagal afferent activity assumed by the resonance model (Lehrer and Gevirtz, 2014) can also be observed in vagal efferent activity (CVA). However, this main effect of condition disappears when integrating covariates to the analyses, and in particular RF, given a main effect of RF on RMSSD was found. Given respiratory parameters (Hirsch and Bishop, 1981; Brown et al., 1993; Houtveen et al., 2002), and in particular RF (Hirsch and Bishop, 1981) were found to influence HRV, some authors recommend to correct HRV variables reflecting CVA for respiration in order to accurately capture CVA (e.g., Grossman et al., 1991; Grossman, 1992). However, another stream of research assumes a common neural basis for HRV and respiration, and regards a routine control of HRV for respiration problematic, given it would remove variability associated with neural control over the heartbeat, and therefore some of the variance playing a crucial role in HRV would be artificially removed, which would then not reflect normal physiology (Larsen et al., 2010; Thayer et al., 2011; Lewis et al., 2012; Dick et al., 2014). For further clarification whether SPB does increase CVA, future research should consider manipulating parasympathetic nervous activity via pharmacological blockade, for example with atropine (Lahiri et al., 2008), a parasympatholytic agent that inhibits the action of acetylcholine, the main neurotransmitter of the parasympathetic nervous system, by competitively blocking muscarine receptors (Clementi and Weber-Schöndorfer, 2015). Previous research (Du Plooy and Venter, 1995) investigating deep breathing (three deep inspirations and expirations) and HRV with atropine injection showed that RMSSD was increased during deep breathing, however, this increase was canceled by atropine, which would suggest that this increase in RMSSD was vagally driven. These findings should however be replicated with the SPB exercise used in our study in order to clarify the effects of 15 min SPB on CVA.

Finally, a mediation analysis indicates that RMSSD did not mediate the effects of SPB on Stroop interference accuracy performance. This finding is not in line with the neurovisceral integration model (Thayer et al., 2009; Smith et al., 2017), which assumes that a higher CVA is linked to higher executive performance. These results are also contrary to what was found in Albinet et al. (2016), where improvements in Stroop interference (accuracy) following a 5-month aquaerobics program were correlated to increases in RMSSD, although no mediation analysis was performed. This may suggest that other mechanisms than CVA may underlie SPB effects. For example, the high amplitude oscillations in HR provoked by SPB were recently suggested to enhance the functional connectivity in brain networks associated with emotion regulation (Mather and Thayer, 2018). Future research has to clarify whether those high amplitude oscillations in HR due to SPB also provoke changes in the functional connectivity of brain networks associated with executive (inhibitory) functioning.

The strengths of this research were conducting two experiments to thoroughly investigate the effects of SPB on the adaptation to psychological stress, specifically inhibition, following PE; as well as the use of physiological measurements (HRV) to enable the investigation of potential underlying mechanisms. However, our research is not without limitation. Firstly, the participants' sporting background (e.g., fitness level, sport experience) was not assessed. Secondly, our sample was comprised of sport students, consequently future research has to investigate whether our findings would replicate to other non-athletic samples. Thirdly, no color perception test was conducted, participants only stated if they were color-blind, however, they were only allowed to continue the experiment if they were successful during the CWST familiarization phase. Fourth, the determination of the 70% of the 5 min Burpees exercise during the pilot study was based on subjective evaluation with the Borg Scale of Perceived Exertion (Borg, 1982), and further research should also measure physiological parameters during the 5 min Burpees exercise. Fifth, due to technical problems our final sample comprised 107 participants instead of the 120 originally planned, and future studies should ensure to achieve the necessary sample size to detect whether CVA mediates executive performance following SPB, to rule out the possibility that our study was underpowered to find a mediation effect. Sixth, in order to shed more light on the underlying physiological mechanisms, other parameters should be investigated, such as gaseous exchange and brain activity for example. Future research may also consider the use of biofeedback to help the participants visualize the effects of SPB on their HRV and CVA.

CONCLUSION

The aim of this research was to investigate the role of a relaxation technique, SPB, on the adaptation to psychological stress, investigated with a measure of inhibition, following PE. Two experiments were conducted within this research. In Experiment 1, SPB (or the TV watching control condition) was realized after PE, and in Experiment 2, SPB (or the TV watching control condition) was realized before PE. Our findings showed that SPB was able to improve inhibition after PE via improving Stroop interference accuracy, meaning that participants made less errors overall after having performed SPB (either before or after PE), and the effects were stronger when SPB was performed after PE. However, SPB was not found to impact Stroop interference RTs, meaning that participants were not faster in their ability to inhibit incongruent stimuli. The applied implications of these findings are quite interesting, given athletes can consider using SPB as a quick fix to address inhibition failures. SPB may therefore help to address choking under pressure, which can be triggered by inhibition failures according to the distraction account (Roberts et al., 2017). Finally, the use of SPB could be investigated in many domains where inhibition failures would lead to unwanted behavior with serious consequences, for example police officers shooting or medical doctors operating.

ETHICS STATEMENT

This study was approved by the Ethics Committee of the German Sport University Cologne (N° 175/2016).

AUTHOR CONTRIBUTIONS

SL, TL, and FD contributed to conceiving the design of the study. TL lead the data collection, with the help of SL. SL realized the statistical analysis with the help of TH and UB, and wrote the first draft of the manuscript. EM provided the critical comments to improve the manuscript. TH, UB, and FD suggested the final adjustments on the manuscript. All authors agreed on the final version of the manuscript.

ACKNOWLEDGMENTS

We would like to acknowledge the help of Oskar Günther, Nicolas Lachner, and Adrijana Mrsic for data collection.

REFERENCES

Abbes, Z., Chamari, K., Mujika, I., Tabben, M., Bibi, K. W., Hussein, A. M., et al. (2018). Do Thirty-second post-activation potentiation exercises improve the 50-m freestyle sprint performance in adolescent swimmers? *Front. Physiol.* 9:1464. doi: 10.3389/fphys.2018.01464

Albinet, C. T., Abou-Dest, A., Andre, N., and Audiffren, M. (2016). Executive functions improvement following a 5-month aquaerobics program in older adults: role of cardiac vagal control in inhibition performance. *Biol. Psychol.* 115, 69–77. doi: 10.1016/j.biopsycho.2016.01.010

Allen, B., and Friedman, B. H. (2012). Positive emotion reduces dyspnea during slow paced breathing. *Psychophysiology* 49, 690–696. doi: 10.1111/j.1469-8986.2011.01344.x

Alves, C. R. R., Gualano, B., Takao, P. P., Avakian, P., Fernandes, R. M., Morine, D., et al. (2012). Effects of acute physical exercise on executive functions: a comparison between aerobic and strength exercise. *J. Sport Exerc. Psychol.* 34, 539–549. doi: 10.1123/jsep.34.4.539

Archer, J. A., Lee, A., Qiu, A., and Annabel Chen, S. H. (2018). Functional connectivity of resting-state, working memory and inhibition networks in perceived stress. *Neurobiol. Stress* 8, 186–201. doi: 10.1016/j.ynstr.2017.01.002

Arnsten, A. F. (2009). Stress signalling pathways that impair prefrontal cortex structure and function. *Nat. Rev. Neurosci.* 10, 410–422. doi: 10.1038/nrn2648

Aubert, A. E., Seps, B., and Beckers, F. (2003). Heart rate variability in athletes. *Sports Med.* 33, 889–919. doi: 10.2165/00007256-200333120-3

Benarroch, E. E. (1993). The central autonomic network: functional organization, dysfunction, and perspective. *Mayo Clin. Proc.* 68, 988–1001. doi: 10.1016/s0025-6196(12)62272-1

Berntson, G. G., Bigger, J. T., Eckberg, D. L., Grossman, P., Kaufmann, P. G., Malik, M., et al. (1997). Heart rate variability: origins, methods, and interpretive caveats. *Psychophysiology* 34, 623–648. doi: 10.1111/j.1469-8986.1997.tb02140.x

Borg, G. A. (1982). Psychophysical bases of perceived exertion. *Med. Sci. Sports Exerc.* 14, 377–381.

Brown, T. E., Beightol, L. A., Koh, J., and Eckberg, D. L. (1993). Important influence of respiration on human R-R interval power spectra is largely ignored. *J. Appl. Physiol.* 75, 2310–2317. doi: 10.1152/jappl.1993.75.5.2310

Brugnera, A., Zarbo, C., Tarvainen, M. P., Marchettini, P., Adorni, R., and Compare, A. (2018). Heart rate variability during acute psychosocial stress: a randomized cross-over trial of verbal and non-verbal laboratory stressors. *Int. J. Psychophysiol.* 127, 17–25. doi: 10.1016/j.ijpsycho.2018.02.016

Burpee, R. H. (1940). *Seven Quickly Administered Tests of Physical Capacity and Their Use in Detecting Physical Incapacity for Motor Activity in Men and Boys.* New York, NY: Columbia University.

Chang, Y.-K., Chi, L., Etnier, J. L., Wang, C.-C., Chu, C.-H., and Zhou, C. (2014). Effect of acute aerobic exercise on cognitive performance: role of cardiovascular fitness. *Psychol. Sport Exerc.* 15, 464–470. doi: 10.1016/j.psychsport.2014.04.007

Clementi, M., and Weber-Schöndorfer, C. (2015). "Gastro-intestinal medications, hypolipidemic agents and spasmolytics," in *Drugs During Pregnancy and Lactation*, eds C. Schaefer, P. Peters, and R. K. Miller (New York, NY: Academic Press), 93–113. doi: 10.1016/b978-0-12-408078-2.00006-8

Conway, J. C., and Rubin, A. M. (2016). Psychological predictors of television viewing motivation. *Commun. Res.* 18, 443–463. doi: 10.1177/009365091018004001

Cooper, S. B., Bandelow, S., Nute, M. L., Dring, K. J., Stannard, R. L., Morris, J. G., et al. (2016). Sprint-based exercise and cognitive function in adolescents. *Prevent. Med. Rep.* 4, 155–161. doi: 10.1016/j.pmedr.2016.06.004

Diamond, A. (2013). Executive functions. *Annu. Rev. Psychol.* 64, 135–168. doi: 10.1146/annurev-psych-113011-143750

Dick, T. E., Hsieh, Y. H., Dhingra, R. R., Baekey, D. M., Galan, R. F., Wehrwein, E., et al. (2014). Cardiorespiratory coupling: common rhythms in cardiac, sympathetic, and respiratory activities. *Prog. Brain Res.* 209, 191–205. doi: 10.1016/B978-0-444-63274-6.00010-2

Dresler, T., Meriau, K., Heekeren, H. R., and Van Der Meer, E. (2009). Emotional Stroop task: effect of word arousal and subject anxiety on emotional interference. *Psychol. Res.* 73, 364–371. doi: 10.1007/s00426-008-0154-6

Du Plooy, W. J., and Venter, C. P. (1995). The effect of atropine on parasympathetic control of respiratory sinus arrhythmia in two ethnic groups. *J. Clin. Pharmacol.* 35, 244–249. doi: 10.1002/j.1552-4604.1995.tb04054.x

Emberts, T., Porcari, J., Dobers-Tein, S., Steffen, J., and Foster, C. (2013). Exercise intensity and energy expenditure of a tabata workout. *J. Sports Sci. Med.* 12, 612–613.

Faul, F., Erdfelder, E., Lang, A. G., and Buchner, A. (2007). G*Power 3: a flexible statistical power analysis program for the social, behavioral, and biomedical sciences. *Behav. Res. Methods* 39, 175–191. doi: 10.3758/bf03193146

Folkard, S. (1990). Circadian performance rhythms: some practical and theoretical implications. *Philos. Trans. R. Soc. B Biol. Sci.* 327, 543–553. doi: 10.1098/rstb.1990.0097

Goldsmith, R. L., Bloomfield, D. M., and Rosenwinkel, E. T. (2000). Exercise and autonomic function. *Coron. Artery Dis.* 11, 129–135. doi: 10.1097/00019501-200003000-7

Griffin, E. W., Mullally, S., Foley, C., Warmington, S. A., O'Mara, S. M., and Kelly, A. M. (2011). Aerobic exercise improves hippocampal function and increases BDNF in the serum of young adult males. *Physiol. Behav.* 104, 934–941. doi: 10.1016/j.physbeh.2011.06.005

Grossman, P. (1992). Respiratory and cardiac rhythms as windows to central and autonomic biobehavioral regulation: selection of window frames, keeping the panes clean and viewing the neural topography. *Biol. Psychol.* 34, 131–161. doi: 10.1016/0301-0511(92)90013-k

Grossman, P., Karemaker, J., and Wieling, W. (1991). Prediction of tonic parasympathetic cardiac control using respiratory sinus arrhythmia: the need for respiratory control. *Psychophysiology* 28, 201–216. doi: 10.1111/j.1469-8986.1991.tb00412.x

Guo, Z., Chen, R., Liu, X., Zhao, G., Zheng, Y., Gong, M., et al. (2018). The impairing effects of mental fatigue on response inhibition: an ERP study. *PLoS One* 13:e0198206. doi: 10.1371/journal.pone.0198206

Hayes, A. F. (2013). *Introduction to Mediation, Moderation, and Conditional Process Analysis.* New York, NY: The Guilford Press.

Hill, L. K., Siebenbrock, A., Sollers, J. J., and Thayer, J. F. (2009). Are all measures created equal? Heart rate variability and respiration. *Biomed. Sci. Instrum.* 45, 71–76.

Hirsch, J. A., and Bishop, B. (1981). Respiratory sinus arrhythmia in humans: how breathing pattern modulates heart rate. *Am. J. Physiol.* 241, H620–H629.

Hoshikawa, Y., and Yamamoto, Y. (1997). Effects of Stroop color-word conflict test on the autonomic nervous system responses. *Am. J. Physiol.* 272, H1113–H1121. doi: 10.1152/ajpheart.1997.272.3.H1113

Houtveen, J. H., Rietveld, S., and de Geus, E. J. (2002). Contribution of tonic vagal modulation of heart rate, central respiratory drive, respiratory depth, and respiratory frequency to respiratory sinus arrhythmia during mental stress and physical exercise. *Psychophysiology* 39, 427–436. doi: 10.1111/1469-8986.3940427

Iellamo, F. (2001). Neural mechanisms of cardiovascular regulation during exercise. *Auton. Neurosci.* 90, 66–75. doi: 10.1016/s1566-0702(01)00269-7

Inquisit 5 [Computer Software] (2016). Available at: https://www.millisecond.com

Inzlicht, M., Schmeichel, B. J., and Macrae, C. N. (2014). Why self-control seems (but may not be) limited. *Trends Cogn. Sci.* 18, 127–133. doi: 10.1016/j.tics.2013.12.009

Johnsen, B. H., Thayer, J. F., Laberg, J. C., Wormnes, B., Raadal, M., Skaret, E., et al. (2003). Attentional and physiological characteristics of patients with dental anxiety. *J. Anxiety Disord.* 17, 75–87. doi: 10.1016/s0887-6185(02)00178-0

Johnson, L., Addamo, P. K., Selva Raj, I., Borkoles, E., Wyckelsma, V., Cyarto, E., et al. (2016). An Acute bout of exercise improves the cognitive performance of older adults. *J. Aging Phys. Act.* 24, 591–598. doi: 10.1123/japa.2015-2097

Kane, M. J., and Engle, R. W. (2003). Working-memory capacity and the control of attention: the contributions of goal neglect, response competition, and task set to Stroop interference. *J. Exp. Psychol. Gen.* 132, 47–70. doi: 10.1037/0096-3445.132.1.47

Kashihara, K., Maruyama, T., Murota, M., and Nakahara, Y. (2009). Positive effects of acute and moderate physical exercise on cognitive function. *J. Physiol. Anthropol.* 28, 155–164. doi: 10.2114/jpa2.28.155

Kotabe, H. P., and Hofmann, W. (2015). On integrating the components of self-control. *Perspect. Psychol. Sci.* 10, 618–638. doi: 10.1177/1745691615593382

Kurzban, R., Duckworth, A., Kable, J. W., and Myers, J. (2013). An opportunity cost model of subjective effort and task performance. *Behav. Brain Sci.* 36, 661–679. doi: 10.1017/S0140525X12003196

Laborde, S., Allen, M. S., Gohring, N., and Dosseville, F. (2017a). The effect of slow-paced breathing on stress management in adolescents with intellectual disability. *J. Intellect. Disabil. Res.* 61, 560–567. doi: 10.1111/jir.12350

Laborde, S., Mosley, E., and Thayer, J. F. (2017b). Heart rate variability and cardiac vagal tone in psychophysiological research - recommendations for experiment planning, data analysis, and data reporting. *Front. Physiol.* 8:213. doi: 10.3389/fpsyg.2017.00213

Laborde, S., Dosseville, F., Aloui, A., Ben Saad, H., Bertollo, M., Bortoli, L., et al. (2018a). Convergent and construct validity and test-retest reliability of the Caen Chronotype Questionnaire in six languages. *Chronobiol. Int.* 35, 1294–1304. doi: 10.1080/07420528.2018.1475396

Laborde, S., Mosley, E., and Mertgen, A. (2018b). A unifying conceptual framework of factors associated to cardiac vagal control. *Heliyon* 4:e01002. doi: 10.1016/j.heliyon.2018.e01002

Laborde, S., Mosley, E., and Ueberholz, L. (2018c). Enhancing cardiac vagal activity: factors of interest for sport psychology. *Prog. Brain Res.* 240, 71–92. doi: 10.1016/bs.pbr.2018.09.002

Laborde, S., Hosang, T., Mosley, E., and Dosseville, F. (2019). Influence of a 30-day slow paced breathing intervention compared to social media use on subjective sleep quality and cardiac vagal activity. *J. Clin. Med.* 8:193. doi: 10.3390/jcm8020193

Laborde, S., Raab, M., and Kinrade, N. P. (2014). Is the ability to keep your mind sharp under pressure reflected in your heart? Evidence for the neurophysiological bases of decision reinvestment. *Biol. Psychol.* 100C, 34–42. doi: 10.1016/j.biopsycho.2014.05.003

Lahiri, M. K., Kannankeril, P. J., and Goldberger, J. J. (2008). Assessment of autonomic function in cardiovascular disease: physiological basis and prognostic implications. *J. Am. Coll. Cardiol.* 51, 1725–1733. doi: 10.1016/j.jacc.2008.01.038

Lambourne, K., and Tomporowski, P. (2010). The effect of exercise-induced arousal on cognitive task performance: a meta-regression analysis. *Brain Res.* 1341, 12–24. doi: 10.1016/j.brainres.2010.03.091

Larsen, P. D., Tzeng, Y. C., Sin, P. Y., and Galletly, D. C. (2010). Respiratory sinus arrhythmia in conscious humans during spontaneous respiration. *Respir. Physiol. Neurobiol.* 174, 111–118. doi: 10.1016/j.resp.2010.04.021

Lautenbach, F., Laborde, S., Putman, P., Angelidis, A., and Raab, M. (2016). Attentional distraction by negative sports words in athletes under low- and high-pressure conditions: evidence from the sport emotional Stroop task. *Sport Exerc. Perform. Psychol.* 5, 296–307. doi: 10.1037/spy0000073

Lazarus, R. S., and Folkman, S. (1984). *Stress, Appraisal and Coping*. New York, NY: Springer.

Lehrer, P. M., and Gevirtz, R. (2014). Heart rate variability biofeedback: how and why does it work? *Front. Psychol.* 5:756. doi: 10.3389/fpsyg.2014.00756

Lehrer, P. M., Vaschillo, E., Lu, S. E., Eckberg, D., Vaschillo, B., Scardella, A., et al. (2006). Heart rate variability biofeedback: effects of age on heart rate variability, baroreflex gain, and asthma. *Chest* 129, 278–284. doi: 10.1378/chest.129.2.278

Lesage, F.-X., and Berjot, S. (2011). Validity of occupational stress assessment using a visual analogue scale. *Occup. Med.* 61, 434–436. doi: 10.1093/occmed/kqr037

Lewis, G. F., Furman, S. A., McCool, M. F., and Porges, S. W. (2012). Statistical strategies to quantify respiratory sinus arrhythmia: are commonly used metrics equivalent? *Biol. Psychol.* 89, 349–364. doi: 10.1016/j.biopsycho.2011.11.009

Malik, M. (1996). Heart rate variability. Standards of measurement, physiological interpretation, and clinical use. Task force of the European society of cardiology and the North American society of pacing and electrophysiology. *Eur. Heart J.* 17, 354–381.

Mather, M., and Thayer, J. F. (2018). How heart rate variability affects emotion regulation brain networks. *Curr. Opin. Behav. Sci.* 19, 98–104. doi: 10.1016/j.cobeha.2017.12.017

McDowd, J. M., Oseas-Kreger, D. M., and Filion, D. L. (1995). "Inhibitory processes in cognition and aging," in *Interference and Inhibition in Cognition*, eds F. N. Dempster and C. J. Brainerd (San Diego, CA: Academic Press), 363–400. doi: 10.1016/b978-012208930-5/50012-x

McRae, G., Payne, A., Zelt, J. G., Scribbans, T. D., Jung, M. E., Little, J. P., et al. (2012). Extremely low volume, whole-body aerobic-resistance training improves aerobic fitness and muscular endurance in females. *Appl. Physiol. Nutr. Metab.* 37, 1124–1131. doi: 10.1139/h2012-093

Menz, V., Semsch, M., Mosbach, F., and Burtscher, M. (2016). Cardiorespiratory effects of one-legged high-intensity interval training in normoxia and hypoxia: a pilot study. *J. Sports Sci. Med.* 15, 208–213.

Michael, S., Graham, K. S., and Davis, G. M. O. (2017). Cardiac autonomic responses during exercise and post-exercise recovery using heart rate variability and systolic time intervals-a review. *Front. Physiol.* 8:301. doi: 10.3389/fphys.2017.00301

Miyake, A., Friedman, N. P., Emerson, M. J., Witzki, A. H., Howerter, A., and Wager, T. D. (2000). The unity and diversity of executive functions and their contributions to complex "Frontal Lobe" tasks: a latent variable analysis. *Cogn. Psychol.* 41, 49–100. doi: 10.1006/cogp.1999.0734

Mlynczak, M., and Krysztofiak, H. (2019). Cardiorespiratory temporal causal links and the differences by sport or lack thereof. *Front. Physiol.* 10:45. doi: 10.3389/fphys.2019.00045

Ogoh, S., Tsukamoto, H., Hirasawa, A., Hasegawa, H., Hirose, N., and Hashimoto, T. (2014). The effect of changes in cerebral blood flow on cognitive function during exercise. *Physiol. Rep.* 2:e12163. doi: 10.14814/phy2.12163

Peruyero, F., Zapata, J., Pastor, D., and Cervello, E. (2017). The Acute effects of exercise intensity on inhibitory cognitive control in adolescents. *Front. Psychol.* 8:921. doi: 10.3389/fpsyg.2017.00921

Ploughman, M. (2008). Exercise is brain food: the effects of physical activity on cognitive function. *Dev. Neurorehabil.* 11, 236–240. doi: 10.1080/17518420801997007

Podstawski, R., Kasietczuk, B., Boraczyński, T., Boraczyński, M., and Choszcz, D. (2013). Relationship between BMI and endurance-strength abilities assessed by the 3 minute burpee test. *Int. J. Sports Sci. Coach.* 3, 28–35. doi: 10.5923/j.sports.20130301.06

Prinsloo, G. E., Rauch, H. G., Lambert, M. I., Muench, F., Noakes, T. D., and Derman, W. E. (2011). The effect of short duration heart rate variability (HRV) biofeedback on cognitive performance during laboratory induced cognitive stress. *Appl. Cogn. Psychol.* 25, 792–801. doi: 10.1002/acp.1750

Putman, P., and Berling, S. (2011). Cortisol acutely reduces selective attention for erotic words in healthy young men. *Psychoneuroendocrinology* 36, 1407–1417. doi: 10.1016/j.psyneuen.2011.03.015

Quintana, D. S., and Heathers, J. A. (2014). Considerations in the assessment of heart rate variability in biobehavioral research. *Front. Physiol.* 5:805. doi: 10.3389/fpsyg.2014.00805

Roberts, L. J., Jackson, M. S., and Grundy, I. H. (2017). Choking under pressure: illuminating the role of distraction and self-focus. *Int. Rev. Sport Exerc. Psychol.* 12, 325–355. doi: 10.1080/1750984x.2017.1374432

Romero, S. A., Minson, C. T., and Halliwill, J. R. (2017). The cardiovascular system after exercise. *J. Appl. Psychol.* 122, 925–932. doi: 10.1152/japplphysiol.00802.2016

Satish, P., Muralikrishnan, K., Balasubramanian, K., and Shanmugapriya. (2015). Heart rate variability changes during stroop color and word test among genders. *Indian J. Physiol. Pharmacol.* 59, 9–15.

Scarpina, F., and Tagini, S. (2017). The Stroop color and word test. *Front. Psychol.* 8:557. doi: 10.3389/fpsyg.2017.00557

Schmit, C., and Brisswalter, J. (2018). Executive functioning during prolonged exercise: a fatigue-based neurocognitive perspective. *Int. Rev. Sport Exerc. Psychol.* doi: 10.1080/1750984X.2018.1483527

Schmit, C., Davranche, K., Easthope, C. S., Colson, S. S., Brisswalter, J., and Radel, R. (2015). Pushing to the limits: the dynamics of cognitive control during exhausting exercise. *Neuropsychologia* 68, 71–81. doi: 10.1016/j.neuropsychologia.2015.01.006

Sherwood, L. (2006). *Fundamentals of Physiology: A Human Perspective*. Belmont, CA: Brooks/Cole.

Smith, R., Thayer, J. F., Khalsa, S. S., and Lane, R. D. (2017). The hierarchical basis of neurovisceral integration. *Neurosci. Biobehav. Rev.* 75, 274–296. doi: 10.1016/j.neubiorev.2017.02.003

Spangler, D. P., and Friedman, B. H. (2017). A Little goes a long way: low working memory load is associated with optimal distractor inhibition and increased vagal control under anxiety. *Front. Hum. Neurosci.* 11:43. doi: 10.3389/fnhum.2017.00043

Spangler, D. P., Gamble, K. R., McGinley, J. J., Thayer, J. F., and Brooks, J. R. (2018). Intra-individual variability in vagal control is associated with response inhibition under stress. *Front. Hum. Neurosci.* 12:475. doi: 10.3389/fnhum.2018.00475

Sperlich, B., Hahn, L. S., Edel, A., Behr, T., Helmprobst, J., Leppich, R., et al. (2018). A 4-Week intervention involving mobile-based daily 6-minute micro-sessions of functional high-intensity circuit training improves strength and quality of life, but not cardio-respiratory fitness of young untrained adults. *Front. Physiol.* 9:423. doi: 10.3389/fphys.2018.00423

Stanley, J., Peake, J. M., and Buchheit, M. (2013). Cardiac parasympathetic reactivation following exercise: implications for training prescription. *Sports Med.* 43, 1259–1277. doi: 10.1007/s40279-013-0083-4

Strauss-Blasche, G., Moser, M., Voica, M., McLeod, D. R., Klammer, N., and Marktl, W. (2000). Relative timing of inspiration and expiration affects respiratory sinus arrhythmia. *Clin. Exp. Pharmacol. Physiol.* 27, 601–606. doi: 10.1046/j.1440-1681.2000.03306.x

Stroop, J. R. (1935). Studies of interference in serial verbal reactions. *J. Exp. Psychol.* 18, 643–662. doi: 10.1037/h0054651

Subramanya, P., and Telles, S. (2015). Performance in the stroop task and simultaneously recorded heart rate variability before and after meditation, supine rest and no-intervention. *Int. J. Brain Cogn. Sci.* 4, 8–14.

Tanaka, M., Ishii, A., and Watanabe, Y. (2013). Neural correlates of central inhibition during physical fatigue. *PLoS One* 8:e70949. doi: 10.1371/journal.pone.0070949

Tarvainen, M. P., Niskanen, J. P., Lipponen, J. A., Ranta-Aho, P. O., and Karjalainen, P. A. (2014). Kubios HRV–heart rate variability analysis software. *Comput. Methods Progr. Biomed.* 113, 210–220. doi: 10.1016/j.cmpb.2013.07.024

Thayer, J. F., Hansen, A. L., Saus-Rose, E., and Johnsen, B. H. (2009). Heart rate variability, prefrontal neural function, and cognitive performance: the neurovisceral integration perspective on self-regulation, adaptation, and health. *Ann. Behav. Med.* 37, 141–153. doi: 10.1007/s12160-009-9101-z

Thayer, J. F., Loerbroks, A., and Sternberg, E. M. (2011). Inflammation and cardiorespiratory control: the role of the vagus nerve. *Respir. Physiol. Neurobiol.* 178, 387–394. doi: 10.1016/j.resp.2011.05.016

Tortora, G. J., and Derrickson, B. H. (2014). *Principles of Anatomy and Physiology*. Hoboken, NJ: John Wiley & Sons, Inc.

van Eekelen, A. P., Houtveen, J. H., and Kerkhof, G. A. (2004). Circadian variation in cardiac autonomic activity: reactivity measurements to different types of stressors. *Chronobiol. Int.* 21, 107–129. doi: 10.1081/cbi-120027983

Vaschillo, E. G., Lehrer, P., Rishe, N., and Konstantinov, M. (2002). Heart rate variability biofeedback as a method for assessing baroreflex function: a preliminary study of resonance in the cardiovascular system. *Appl. Psychophysiol. Biofeedback* 27, 1–27.

Vaschillo, E. G., Vaschillo, B., and Lehrer, P. M. (2006). Characteristics of resonance in heart rate variability stimulated by biofeedback. *Appl. Psychophysiol. Biofeedback* 31, 129–142. doi: 10.1007/s10484-006-9009-3

Vazan, R., Filcikova, D., and Mravec, B. (2017). Effect of the stroop test performed in supine position on the heart rate variability in both genders. *Auton. Neurosci. Basic Clin.* 208, 156–160. doi: 10.1016/j.autneu.2017.10.009

Vincent, C. M., and Hall, P. A. (2017). Cognitive effects of a 30-min aerobic exercise bout on adults with overweight/obesity and type 2 diabetes. *Obes. Sci. Pract.* 3, 289–297. doi: 10.1002/osp4.112

Wendt, J., Neubert, J., Koenig, J., Thayer, J. F., and Hamm, A. O. (2015). Resting heart rate variability is associated with inhibition of conditioned fear. *Psychophysiology* 52, 1161–1166. doi: 10.1111/psyp.12456

Winsley, R. (2002). Acute and chronic effects of exercise on heart rate variability in adults and children: a review. *Pediatr. Exerc. Sci.* 14, 328–344. doi: 10.1123/pes.14.4.328

Yanagisawa, H., Dan, I., Tsuzuki, D., Kato, M., Okamoto, M., Kyutoku, Y., et al. (2010). Acute moderate exercise elicits increased dorsolateral prefrontal activation and improves cognitive performance with stroop test. *Neuroimage* 50, 1702–1710. doi: 10.1016/j.neuroimage.2009.12.023

Zeki Al Hazzouri, A., Elfassy, T., Carnethon, M. R., Lloyd-Jones, D. M., and Yaffe, K. (2017). Heart rate variability and cognitive function in middle-age adults: the coronary artery risk development in young adults. *Am. J. Hypert.* 31, 27–34. doi: 10.1093/ajh/hpx125

19

Investigating Irrational Beliefs, Cognitive Appraisals, Challenge and Threat, and Affective States in Golfers Approaching Competitive Situations

Nanaki J. Chadha, Martin J. Turner and Matthew J. Slater*

Life Sciences and Education, Staffordshire University, Stoke-on-Trent, United Kingdom

***Correspondence:**
Nanaki J. Chadha
nanaki.chadha@research.staffs.ac.uk

On approach to competitive situations, affective states (emotions and anxiety) occur through the complex interaction of cognitive antecedents. Researchers have intimated that irrational beliefs might play an important role in the relationship between cognitive appraisals and affective states, but has ignored challenge and threat. In the current research, we examine the interaction between cognitive appraisals, irrational beliefs, and challenge and threat to predict golfers' pre-competitive affective states. We adopted a cross-sectional atemporal design to examine how golfers approached two different competitive situations: imagined imminent golf competition (phase 1), and actual future golf competition (phase 2). Path analysis revealed how cognitive appraisals, irrational beliefs, and challenge and threat interact to predict affective states among golfers. Serial atemporal multiple mediation analysis indicated that the relationships between cognitive appraisals and affective states were mediated by irrational beliefs and challenge and threat. Further, some differences were revealed between phase 1 and phase 2 in the serial multiple atemporal mediation results with regard to challenge. That is, at phase 1 no significant serial mediation was found for any affective outcomes, but at phase 2 significant serial mediation was found for all affective states, showing that irrational beliefs and challenge serial mediated the associations between cognitive appraisals and affective states. The finding that mediation and bivariate associations differed across phase 1 and phase 2 is echoed in the phase 1-phase 2 tests of differences. The current research makes a theoretical advancement by elucidating in more detail the complex interaction between cognitive antecedents and mediators of affective states. Specifically, the inclusion of challenge and threat alongside irrational beliefs and cognitive appraisals is an important theoretical advancement that builds on work inside of sport literature (e.g., Dixon et al., 2016) and outside of sport literature (e.g., David et al., 2002, 2005), as this constellation of theoretically related antecedents of affective states has not been examined together in the extant research.

Keywords: stress, REBT, performance, pressure, imagined, CBT

INTRODUCTION

For individuals taking part in sport, the anticipation time prior to stressful situations such as a sporting competition (Neil et al., 2011) is often daunting due to an over emphasis on winning and uncertainty of the outcome (Folkman and Lazarus, 1985). Athletes' pre-competitive anticipatory psychological states have been the focus of much research, and competition anxiety is one of the most studied areas in the discipline of sport psychology (Mellalieu et al., 2006). There are a number of frameworks that attempt to explain the occurrence of pre-competitive emotions (Jones and Uphill, 2012), but one underexplored framework that is growing in the sport literature (Turner, 2016) is Rational Emotive Behavioral Therapy (REBT; Ellis, 1957).

REBT is considered to be the original cognitive behavioral therapy (CBT), and was developed by Albert Ellis in 1955, inspired by ancient philosophers, particularly the Stoic philosopher Epictetus (1948) who proclaimed in *The Enchiridion*: "men are not disturbed by things, but by the view which they take of them." Ellis (1994) developed a framework for understanding and treating psychological disturbance known as the GABC framework. In this framework, individual goals, values, and desires (G), that are thwarted or obstructed by events and situations (A), can trigger healthy or unhealthy emotional and behavioral consequences (C), depending on one's beliefs (B) about the self, others, and the world in relation to the situation (A). If an individual's beliefs are rational (flexible, logical, and non-extreme) then healthy emotions and adaptive behaviors will occur. In contrast, if an individual's beliefs are irrational (rigid, illogical, and extreme) then unhealthy emotions and maladaptive behaviors will occur (Szentagotai and Jones, 2010). As such, irrational beliefs have attracted much research attention (e.g., Visla et al., 2016).

Within REBT, irrational and rational beliefs are the core constructs that mediate between what we experience, and our emotional responses. Since its inception in 1955 (Ellis, 1957), REBT has included irrational beliefs as the fundamental cognitions that determine psychological ill-being. In sport and exercise literature, irrational beliefs as posited in REBT have been the subject of enquiry more recently (Turner et al., 2019a), and data indicates that irrational beliefs are a risk factor for mental illness in athletes (Turner, 2016). In the current paper, we seek to gain a deeper and more complex understanding of how irrational beliefs determine athlete affective states (emotions and anxiety).

In REBT, it is suggested that individuals often adopt irrational beliefs in situations that are of utmost importance to them. Irrational beliefs have been consistently associated with various types of emotional distress (Visla et al., 2016), with the positive relationship between irrational beliefs and anxiety being particularly strong (r = 0.41). Importantly, the association between irrational beliefs and anxiety is stronger when a stressful event is real, actually present, and is personally relevant, as opposed to being experimentally induced, absent, and not personally relevant. In sport, higher irrational beliefs have been found to be related to greater emotional and physical exhaustion (Turner and Moore, 2015), and anxiety, anger, and depression (Turner et al., 2019b). Also, irrational beliefs have been targeted for intervention in athletes experiencing heightened anxiety (Turner and Barker, 2013; Turner et al., 2018a).

Although in the extant literature irrational beliefs have been found to be associated with dysfunctional emotions and maladaptive behaviors (see Turner, 2016 for a review), the precise mechanisms that explain how irrational beliefs lead to emotional and behavioral dysfunction has not yet been fully elucidated. Over the years REBT has grown into a well-established CBT, but it remains less visible in the mainstream study of emotion due to lack of experimental rigor (Still, 2001; David et al., 2002; Padesky and Beck, 2003). There is a growing body of research that places irrational beliefs within the conceptual framework of cognitive appraisal theory (CAT; Lazarus, 1991; David et al., 2002, 2005) in order to advance Ellis's cognitive theory of emotion. Therefore, the main purpose of the current study is to examine irrational beliefs as part of cognitive appraisals in the prediction of pre-competitive affective states.

Past literature has intimated that irrational beliefs might play an important role in cognitive appraisals (David et al., 2002, 2005). According to Lazarus' CAT (Lazarus and Folkman, 1984; Lazarus, 1991; Smith and Lazarus, 1993), information processing includes a transaction between the goals of the individual and the representation of environmental encounters. This transaction can be appraised as harmful, beneficial, threatening or challenging. The CAT comprises primary appraisals, which are concerned with the extent to which the encounter is relevant to one's well-being, and secondary appraisals which concerns one's resources and options for coping with the encounter (Smith and Lazarus, 1993). Specifically, primary appraisal includes motivational relevance (MR; evaluation of the extent to which the encounter is relevant to one's goals) and motivational congruence (MC; evaluation of the extent to which the encounter is consistent with one's goals). In anticipation of stressors, the components of secondary appraisal are problem-focused coping potential (PFC; evaluations of one's ability to act directly on the situation to bring it in accord with one's goals), and emotion focused coping potential (EFC; evaluations of one's ability to psychologically adjust to the situation by altering one's interpretations, desires, or beliefs; Smith and Lazarus, 1993). The primary and secondary appraisals combine to form different core-relational themes that result in emotions. For anxiety, the core relational theme is uncertain, existential threat (Lazarus, 1991) where primary appraisals of high MR and low MC combine with secondary appraisals of low EFC (Smith and Lazarus, 1993).

Researchers have explored the links between irrational beliefs and cognitive appraisals, finding that anxiety is most effectively predicted by a combination of high MR, low MC, low EFC, and irrational beliefs (David et al., 2002, 2005). Clearly, there are some demonstrable relationships between the concepts of irrational beliefs proposed by Ellis, and CAT proposed by Lazarus. Ellis and Lazarus recognized this potential relationship in their works, with Ellis recognizing the influence of Lazarus on his thinking (Ellis, 1994), and with Lazarus explicitly addressing the overlap between REBT and the Lazarusian CAT (Lazarus, 1989). To explain the potential links between REBT and the CAT, Ziegler (2001) suggests that cognitive appraisals (both primary and secondary) are thoroughly couched in, and interconnected with, beliefs in the GABC model. For example, a golfer is anticipating the tee-off for an important competition with a lucrative reward (reflecting G in the REBT model, and MR in the CAT). The golfer has not competed in such a prestigious event before and is unsure whether he will perform well (reflecting A in the REBT model, and low MC in the CAT) and believes that he absolutely must perform well and he could not tolerate underperforming (reflecting irrational beliefs in the REBT model). Because the prospect of underperforming (A) is rendered highly dangerous to his goals (G) by the irrational beliefs, the golfer is likely to appraise the situation as a threat (Lazarus, 1999). If the golfer believes that he cannot psychologically adjust to the encounter (low EFC), and is not flexible in his coping abilities (Ziegler, 2001), then he is more likely to experience dysfunctional anxiety (David et al., 2002) in anticipation of the tee-off. Importantly, cognitive appraisals and irrational beliefs are seen as co-occurring simultaneously rather than occurring in a sequential and fixed order.

Within a sporting context, researchers have investigated the association between irrational beliefs and challenge and threat, finding irrational beliefs to be positively associated with threat and no association to be found with challenge (Dixon et al., 2016). Similarly, another study (Evans et al., 2018) found that soccer athletes who received a rational team talk (promoting rational beliefs) at half-time reported significantly lower threat compared to athletes who received an irrational team talk (promoting irrational beliefs). Research has also examined the effect of irrational and rational beliefs on performance within golf (Turner et al., 2018a,b). One study (Turner et al., 2018b) found that when golfers used rational self-talk they performed more accurately in a putting task than when they used irrational self-talk. Similarly, Turner et al. (2018a) used an REBT intervention with amateur golfers and found that as irrational beliefs decreased so to did golf-specific anxiety and in addition, golf performance improved. However, this fledgling research fails to examine how irrational beliefs and challenge and threat interact to predict competitive affective states. In the present study, cognitive appraisals, irrational beliefs, and challenge and threat are assessed in relation to upcoming competitive situations. Based on past research, it is the combination of these psychological constructs that gives rise to emotions in competitive situations (Neil et al., 2011).

The constructs of challenge and threat have been the subject of growing research in sport literature (e.g., Blascovich et al., 2004), spawning theories of challenge and threat that attempt to predict athletic performance (Jones et al., 2009; Vine et al., 2016). Challenge and threat are important constructs in Lazarus's appraisal process and are labeled as relational meanings in his appraisal theory (Lazarus, 2000). Threat appraisal refers to evaluation of future harm or loss; whereas challenge appraisal occurs when an individual perceives a future gain (Lazarus, 1991). In extant theory, challenge and threat result in emotional responses, where challenge is said to be associated with more positive emotions, whereas threat is associated with more negative emotions (Skinner and Brewer, 2004; Jones et al., 2009). Furthermore, positive emotions are proposed to be interpreted as facilitative for performance in challenge whereas negative emotions as debilitative in threat (Skinner and Brewer, 2004; Jones et al., 2009). With regards to anxiety, research evidence demonstrates that threat is positively associated with greater cognitive and somatic anxiety and a more debilitative interpretation of anxiety compared to challenge (Williams et al., 2010; Quested et al., 2011; Moore et al., 2012). Therefore, challenge and threat are important antecedents to affective states that should be studied alongside cognitive appraisals, and irrational beliefs.

The current research is the first to investigate and understand how affective states occur through the complex interaction of antecedent cognitive appraisals, irrational beliefs and challenge and threat within a specific sporting population. This integrative examination might facilitate a more complete understanding of how affective states occur through the complex interaction of cognitive antecedents.

The Current Research

The main aim of the current study is to examine the interaction between, cognitive appraisals, irrational beliefs, and challenge and threat, to predict pre-competitive affective states. To achieve this main aim, two study phases are reported; phase 1 meets the main aim in an imagined imminent golf competition, and phase 2 meets the main aim in an actual future golf competition. For the two phases, we illustrate our hypotheses in **Figure 1**, which are informed and supported by past research. Based on past research, it is hypothesized that (H1) golfers' cognitive appraisals will be negatively associated with irrational beliefs (David et al., 2002, 2005), (H2) high irrational beliefs will be positively associated with threat and negatively with challenge (Dixon et al., 2016), (H3) cognitive appraisals will be negatively associated with threat and positively with challenge (Lazarus, 1999), (H4) challenge will be positively associated with positive emotions, and threat will be positively associated with negative emotions (Jones et al., 2009), (H5) threat will be positively associated with cognitive and somatic anxiety, and challenge will be negatively associated with cognitive and somatic anxiety (Moore et al., 2012), and (H6) threat will be negatively associated with facilitative perceptions of anxiety, and challenge will be positively associated with facilitative perceptions of anxiety (Quested et al., 2011). It is also hypothesized that (H7) the relationship between cognitive appraisals and affective states will be mediated by irrational beliefs (David et al., 2002, 2005) and challenge and threat (Jones et al., 2009). Further, on the basis of meta-analytical data (Visla et al., 2016) where stronger associations were found between irrational beliefs and affective states during a real-stressor, we hypothesize that (H8) the associations between target variables will be stronger in phase 2 than in phase 1. Lastly, we examine differences in variables between study phases 1 and 2, and hypothesize that (H9) in phase 2 golfers will report greater cognitive appraisals, irrational beliefs, threat and affective states and lower challenge, positive emotions and facilitative perceptions of anxiety in comparison to phase 1.

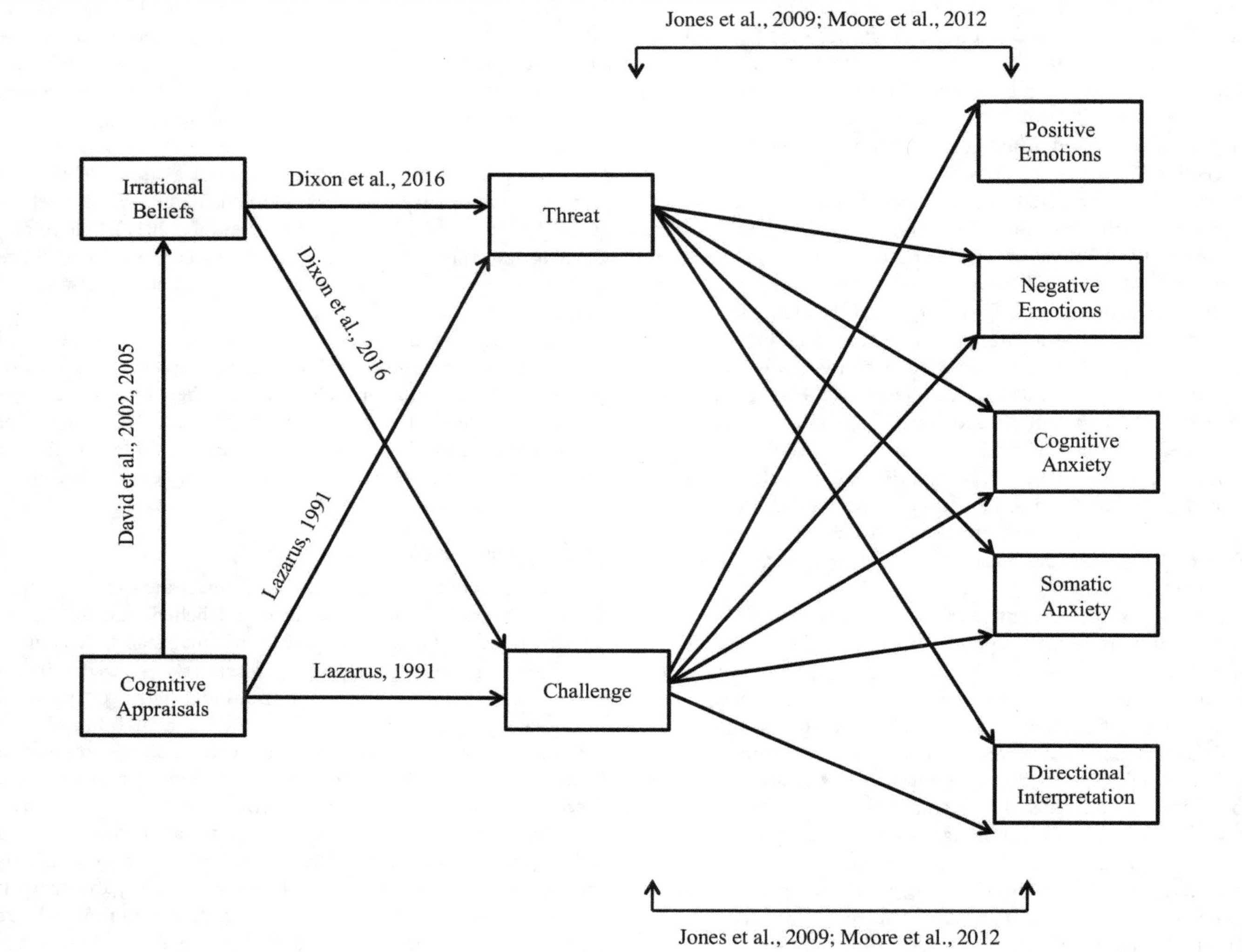

FIGURE 1 | Proposed theoretical model.

MATERIALS AND METHODS

Participants

In phase 1, 287 participants (*Male* = 232, *Female* = 55; *M*age = 38.7 ± 15.20) with a golf handicap between 0 and 31 (*M*handicap = 8.85 ± 7.13) took part in the study. The participants encompassed Indians (*n* = 220), British (*n* = 41) and other ethnic origins (*n* = 26). They had an average of 11.85 years (± 8.31) golfing experience and were competing at a club (*n* = 115), amateur (*n* = 120) and professional (*n* = 52) level. In phase 2, 212 golfers (*Male* = 169, *Female* = 43; *M*age = 38.55 ± 15.08) with a handicap between 0 and 31 (*M*handicap = 8.68 ± 7.16) completed the study. The participants encompassed Indians (*n* = 161), British (*n* = 30) and other ethnic origins (*n* = 21). They had an average of 12.28 years (± 8.38) of golfing experience and were competing at the club (*n* = 83), amateur (*n* = 86) and professional (*n* = 43) level. No incentive was offered to the participants for taking part in the research. Ethical approval was granted from the ethics committee of Staffordshire University and individual informed consent was obtained prior to data collection. The participants were recruited by contacting local golf clubs on their willingness to participate in the research project. The lead author approached golf clubs and golf organizations in India to recruit golfers. Further, the distribution of an online survey resulted in snowball sampling that helped in the recruitment of golfers.

Measures

Irrational Performance Beliefs

The irrational Performance Beliefs Inventory (iPBI; Turner et al., 2018) was used as a performance specific measure of irrational beliefs. It comprises 28-items representing four core irrational beliefs; primary belief and three secondary beliefs (Ellis and Dryden, 1997). The primary irrational belief is stated to be demandingness (DEM), which refers to rigid, absolutistic requirements expressed in the form of "musts," "shoulds," and "oughts" (e.g., "I must attain my goals"). The three secondary irrational beliefs comprise of awfulizing (AWF), low frustration tolerance (LFT) and depreciation (DEP). AWF refers to the beliefs that an individual holds where unpleasant situations are assessed in the greatest negative manner (e.g., "If I don't attain my goals it is awful"). LFT reflects an individuals evaluation that they are absolutely incapable of enduring a given situation, accompanied with the view that they will not experience any happiness if what they want does not exist (e.g., "If I don't attain my goals I can't stand it"), and DEP appears when individuals tend to be excessively critical about themselves, others or the world when they fail to live up to their self-imposed demands (e.g., "If I don't attain my goals, I am a complete failure"; Ellis, 1994). The responses are made on a 5-point Likert-scale ranging from 1 (*strongly disagree*) to 5 (*strongly agree*) to a series of performance belief statements. The iPBI has previously been used with athletes (Turner et al., 2019b) including golfers (Turner et al., 2018a) and has demonstrated good internal validity and reliability among sporting populations (Turner and Allen, 2018). However, due to a novel and relatively homogenous sample population in the current study, confirmatory factor analysis (CFA) was conducted to test the four-factor structure of the iPBI. One item from DEM showing factor loading less than 0.40 was eliminated from further analyses (Comrey and Lee, 1992; Tabachnick and Fidell, 2007). Cronbach's alphas from the current sample were 0.76 for DEM, 0.84 for AWF, 0.87 for LFT, and 0.87 for DEP.

Cognitive Appraisals

The primary and secondary cognitive appraisals were assessed with five single-item questions used in previous research (David et al., 2002), modified from Smith and Lazarus (1993). The single-item questions were answered on a 11-points Likert-scale ranging from 1 (*not at all*) to 11 (*extremely*). The measure assesses motivational relevance (MR), motivational congruence (MC; 2-items), problem-focused coping potential (PFC), and emotion-focused coping (EFC). A total cognitive appraisal score was obtained by calculating the mean score of all the items. Higher cognitive appraisals indicated more positive appraisals.

Challenge and Threat

The Challenge and Threat in Sport scale (CAT-Sport; Rossato et al., 2016), comprises 12-items representing two subscales; challenge and threat. The responses are made on a 6-point Likert-scale ranging from 1 (*totally disagree*) to 6 (*totally agree*) in anticipation of a competition. The CAT-Sport has only recently been developed, so confirmatory factor analysis (CFA) was conducted to test the two-factor structure. One item from challenge displaying factor loading less than 0.40 was eliminated from further analyses (Comrey and Lee, 1992; Tabachnick and Fidell, 2007). The CAT-Sport has previously demonstrated good internal validity and reliability in athlete populations (Rossato et al., 2016) and the Cronbach's alphas from the current sample were 0.90 for threat, and 0.77 for challenge in phase 1, and 0.91 for threat and 0.82 for challenge in phase 2.

Emotion

The Positive and Negative Affect Schedule (PANAS; Watson et al., 1988) incorporates two 10-item subscales based on a bi-dimensional theory of emotion. Individuals can experience a mixture of positive affect (PA; e.g., "enthusiastic") and negative affect (NA; e.g., "afraid") during a specific period of time (Watson and Tellegen, 1985; Watson and Clark, 1997). The items are scored on a 5-point Likert scale ranging from 1 (*very slightly or not at all*) to 5 (*extremely*). The PANAS has previously demonstrated good internal validity and reliability in athlete populations (Watson et al., 1988) and the Cronbach's alphas from the current sample were 0.87 for PA and 0.84 for NA in phase 1, and 0.90 for PA and 0.91 for NA in phase 2.

Anxiety

The Competitive State Anxiety Inventory-2 (CSAI-2; Martens et al., 1990; Jones and Swain, 1992) was used to assess the intensity and directional interpretation of cognitive and somatic anxiety symptoms. Cognitive anxiety (CA) assesses the mental component of anxiety caused by negative expectations about success or negative self-evaluation (e.g., "I am concerned about losing") and somatic anxiety (SA) is associated with the physiological or affective component of anxiety (e.g., "My hands are clammy"). The items are scored on a 4-point Likert-scale ranging between 1 (*not at all*) to 4 (*very much so*) for intensity. Further, the directional interpretation of the anxiety symptoms was assessed using a single-item question on a 7-point Likert-scale ranging from −3 (*very negative/debilitative*) to + 3 (*very positive/facilitative*). The CSAI-2 has previously demonstrated good internal validity and reliability in athlete populations (Burton, 1998) and the Cronbach's alphas from the current sample were 0.88 for CA and 0.89 for SA in phase 1, and 0.88 for CA and 0.89 for SA in phase 2.

Design

The current study is a cross-sectional, single time-point atemporal design that examines golfers' approach to competitive situations; an imagined imminent golf competition (phase 1), and an actual future golf competition (phase 2). Specifically, we examine how irrational beliefs interact with cognitive appraisals and challenge and threat to predict affective states (emotions and anxiety) across the two phases. The study was introduced in the form of an online survey to explore the ways in which golfers approach motivated performance situations (golf competition). In phase 1, we adopted an experimental vignette methodology (EVM, Aguinis and Bradley, 2014), where participants were presented with a vignette that represented a real-life scenario in which golfers imagined themselves approaching an imminent golf competition, followed by questionnaires exploring their thoughts and affective states about this event. The vignette was adapted from Skinner and Brewer (2002) to represent a stressful golfing situation, and was presented to players in written form. The personal meaning of the scenario was enhanced by emphasizing the prestige of the tournament, and the composition of the audience. In addition, expectations of other personnel, the final reward, and the presence of other competitors from all across the country emphasized the importance of the event and ensured high levels of pressure. Further, ego-threatening instructions were included, as in line with past golf research (Wilson et al., 2009; Turner et al., 2018) where poor performance represented lack of skill to play at a competitive level. Participants took on average 26 min to complete the survey. The scenario presented to the golfers was as follows:

> *You are at an important competition waiting for your name to be announced by the starter at which point you will collect your score card. As you approach the first tee box to start your round, you notice there is a large and dense crowd, more than you have seen before, waiting for you to tee off. This competition is crucial because it is the most prestigious event you have played in and the prize money is the most you've competed for. There are high expectations for your performance from friends, family, and the crowd. If you don't play well then people will think you are not capable of playing at this level and therefore you probably won't be invited next year. In addition, there is a really strong field of competitors from all over the country. As you step up to the tee, you notice the drastic change in weather conditions.... the wind has picked up and it is now raining. You take your position and ready yourself to tee off...*

In phase 2, participants were asked to provide details about their next actual important golf competition and complete questionnaires about their thoughts and affective states in relation to that important event. The aim of phase 2 is to extend phase 1 by examining how golfers' irrational beliefs interact with cognitive appraisals and challenge and threat to predict affective states in relation to an actual future golf competition. Therefore, the real-life event of an actual upcoming competition allows us to explore the phenomenon in relation to a real-life stressor. This is important, because irrational beliefs are implicated in affectivity different for real vs. imagined stressors (Visla et al., 2016).

Analytic Strategy

Data for both the phases were examined for missing values. In phase 1, little's MCAR test revealed that across each variables data between 2.4 and 10.5% were missing at random, $\chi^2 = 462.55$, df = 425, $p > 0.05$. In phase 2, little's MCAR test revealed that across each variables the data between 2.8 and 4.7% were missing at random, $\chi^2 = 192.37$, df = 169, $p > 0.05$. In the current research, since the missing values were scattered throughout the data, the employment of the deletion technique where missing values are discarded would have resulted in substantial loss of participants, thus reducing the total sample size and further resulting in loss of power (Tabachnick and Fidell, 2007; Baraldi and Enders, 2010). Therefore, we used expectation maximisation (EM) method, a simple and reasonable approach to estimate the missing values (Graham, 2009), and providing a complete data set for the main analyses (Quinton et al., 2018). Further, in line with previous research (e.g., Dixon and Yuen, 1974; Orr et al., 1991; Smith, 2011) the data were checked for outliers and data points with z scores greater than 2 were winsorized which involved replacing extreme values to reduce the influence of outliers on the data. For phase 1, items for DEM (n = 15), AWF (n = 14), LFT (n = 8), DEP (n = 13), MR (n = 13), MC (n = 14), PFC (n = 12), EFC (n = 14), challenge (n = 14), threat (n = 7), positive emotions (n = 11), negative emotions (n = 11), cognitive anxiety (n = 9), somatic anxiety (n = 10), and directional interpretation (n = 11) were windsorized. For phase 2, items for MR (n = 10), MC (n = 8), PFC (n = 8), EFC (n = 13), challenge (n = 6), threat (n = 10), positive emotions (n = 8), negative emotions (n = 15), cognitive anxiety (n = 10), somatic anxiety (n = 10), and directional interpretation (n = 15) were windsorized.

Prior to the main analyses, since the data was collected from the same participants in regards to the imagined imminent golf competition (phase 1), and an actual future golf competition (phase 2), it was important to examine differences in cognitive appraisals, challenge and threat, affective states (emotions and anxiety) and directional interpretations of anxiety, between the two phases. To compare the means for each dependent variable between the imagined imminent golf competition and the actual future golf competition, three repeated measures multivariate analysis of covariance (MANCOVA) were conducted, one for cognitive appraisals, one for challenge and threat, and one for affective states. In addition, one repeated measure analysis of covariance (ANCOVA) was conducted for directional interpretations of anxiety. Age and handicap were included as covariates in all analyses in both phases, and in phase 2, the number of weeks until the next important competition was also included as a covariate. The result of Shapiro-Wilk for number of weeks, $W_{(212)} = 0.67$, $p = 0.000$, indicated that this variable was not normally distributed. Therefore, the variable was transformed using log transformation to overcome the heteroscedastic errors (i.e., large error variance) associated with the variable and to make it more homogenous (Nevill, 1997).

Main analyses for both phases were conducted in three main stages. First, descriptive statistics and Pearson's correlations were calculated for all self-report variables to examine associations between cognitive appraisals, irrational beliefs, challenge and threat, and affective states. Second, path analysis was employed in conjunction with bootstrapping procedures to test the hypothesized model using AMOS. Since most of the variables were moderately to strongly correlated, it was possible to introduce a structure to the correlation matrix in accordance with the path diagram (see **Figure 1**). The model fit was evaluated using the chi-square statistic (χ^2), comparative fit index (CFI), the root-mean-square error of approximation (RMSEA). CFI provides an indication of how the theoretical model better fits the data in comparison to a base model constraining all constructs to be uncorrelated with one another. A non-significant χ^2 and CFI value of 0.90 or above is considered a good fit (Bentler, 1990; Hu and Bentler, 1998; Vandenbergh and Lance, 2000). Further, a RMSEA value of <0.06 indicates a close fit whereas a value < 0.08 is also considered an acceptable fit (Browne and Cudek, 1993). Vandenbergh and Lance (2000) suggest that a cut-off value of 0.10 for RMSEA is acceptable.

Lastly, serial atemporal multiple mediation analysis (SAMM) were conducted using PROCESS version 2.10 for IBM SPSS (Hayes, 2013), to understand the direct and indirect effects of cognitive appraisal, irrational beliefs, and challenge and threat, on affective states. Considering practical implications, PROCESS was employed for multiple mediation as it calculates relevant statistics automatically and efficiently in comparison to structural equation modeling (SEM) programmes such as AMOS that require greater effort and programming skills to gain relevant output. In addition, literature suggests (Hayes et al., 2017) that where the models are entirely based on observed variables, the results yielded from PROCESS and AMOS programmes are substantively identical. Thus, the current methodology is in line with Monteiro et al. (2018), where SEM was used to analyze the relationship between different variables and serial multiple mediation was used to access direct and indirect mediation effects of independent variables on dependent variables. **Figure 2** represents a generic model of SAMM with two mediators for illustrative purposes. In the current study in both phases, the independent variable (X) was cognitive appraisals and dependent variables (Y) were affective states (positive or negative emotions, cognitive and somatic anxiety, and directional interpretation of anxiety). Since, there is an established causation from cognitive appraisals to affective states (Lazarus, 1991), in the current research, we treated affective states as the Y variable and cognitive antecedents of affective states as the X and M variables. The data is available on request from the first author of the current study.

RESULTS

Repeated Measures Comparison of Phase 1 and Phase 2

Cognitive Appraisals

The results of the MANCOVA indicated a significant main effect for cognitive appraisals, Wilks' $\Lambda = 0.92$, $F(1, 199) = 4.28$, $p < 0.01$ $\eta^2 = 0.08$. A significant within-subjects effect was revealed for MC, $F(1, 199) = 6.02$, $p < 0.01$, $\eta^2 = 0.03$, with pairwise comparisons indicating that golfers perceive goals to be less motivationally congruent in anticipation of the imagined imminent golf competition ($M = 6.94 \pm 1.71$) compared to an actual future golf competition ($M = 7.32 \pm 1.89$). Similarly, a significant within-subjects effect was revealed for PFC, $F(1, 199) = 9.31$, $p < 0.01$, $\eta^2 = 0.04$, with pairwise comparisons indicating that golfers perceived more problem focused coping potential in anticipation of the imagined imminent golf competition ($M = 7.81 \pm 1.85$) compared to an actual future golf competition ($M = 7.59 \pm 2.17$).

Challenge and Threat

The results of the MANCOVA indicated a significant main effect for challenge and threat, Wilks' $\Lambda = 0.92$, $F(1, 203) = 8.16$, $p < 0.001$, $\eta^2 = 0.07$. A significant within-subjects effect was revealed for threat, $F(1, 203) = 15.68$, $p < 0.01$, $\eta^2 = 0.07$, with pairwise comparisons indicating golfers reported greater threat in anticipation of the imagined imminent golf competition ($M = 2.79 \pm 1.10$) compared to an actual future golf competition ($M = 2.22 \pm 1.02$).

Affect

The results of the MANCOVA indicated a significant main effect for emotions, Wilks' $\Lambda = 0.84$, $F(1, 199) = 8.98$, $p < 0.001$, $\eta^2 = 0.15$. A significant within-subjects effect was revealed for negative emotion, $F(1, 199) = 12.09$, $p < 0.01$, $\eta^2 = 0.06$, with pairwise comparisons indicating golfers experienced more negative emotions in anticipation of the imagined imminent golf competition ($M = 1.87 \pm 0.55$) compared to an actual future golf competition ($M = 1.53 \pm 0.56$). A significant within-subjects effect was revealed for cognitive anxiety, $F(1, 199) = 8.53$, $p < 0.01$, $\eta^2 = 0.04$, with pairwise comparisons indicating golfers reported greater cognitive anxiety in anticipation of the imagined imminent golf competition ($M = 2.05 \pm 0.64$) compared to an actual future golf competition ($M = 1.79 \pm 0.58$). Also, a significant within-subjects effect was revealed for somatic anxiety, $F(1, 199) = 34.63$, $p < 0.001$, $\eta^2 = 0.15$, with pairwise comparisons indicating golfers experienced more somatic anxiety in anticipation of the imagined imminent golf competition

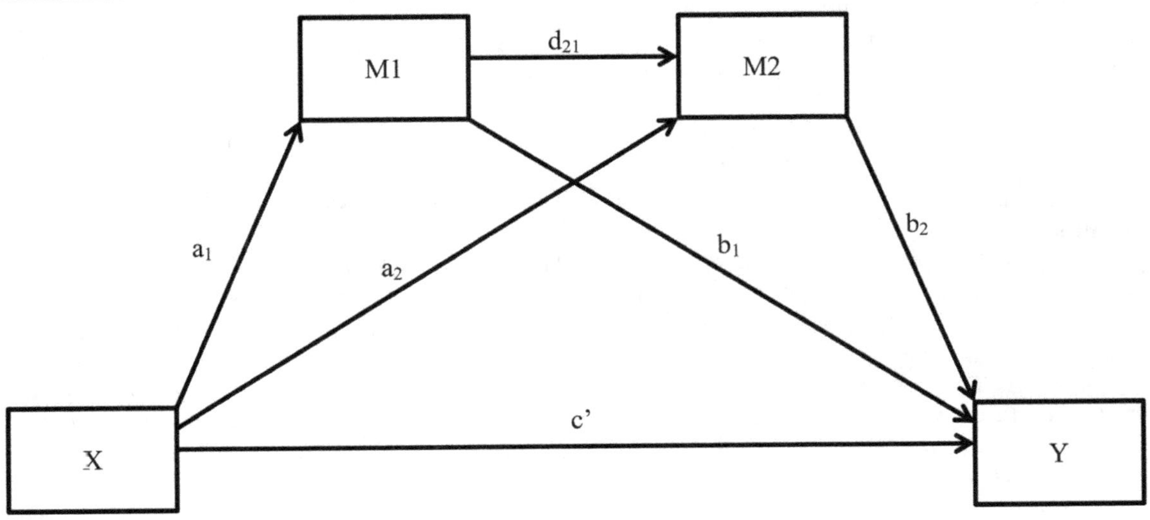

FIGURE 2 | Serial atemporal multiple mediation model with two mediators. X = independent variable; Y = dependent variable; M1, M2 = mediators. a1, a2, b1, b2, d21, c' = regression coefficients.

(M = 2.04 ± 0.57) in comparison to an actual future golf competition (M = 1.60 ± 0.50).

Directional Interpretation of Anxiety

The results of the ANCOVA indicated a significant main effect for directional interpretation of anxiety, Wilks' $\Lambda = 0.91$, $F(1, 199) = 18.51$, $p < 0.01$, $\eta^2 = 0.08$, with pairwise comparisons indicating that golfers perceived their anxiety as less facilitative in anticipation of the imagined imminent golf competition (M = 1.72 ± 1.26) compared to an actual future golf competition (M = 2.01 ± 1.01).

PHASE 1 RESULTS

Table 1 displays descriptive statistics and Pearson's correlations for all variables.

Test of the Model

Path analysis revealed that the hypothesized model demonstrated an acceptable fit to the data $\chi^2(21) = 60.39$, $p < 0.05$, CFI = 0.97, RMSEA = 0.08. The standardized path coefficients for each individual path are displayed in **Figure 3**, demonstrating patterns consistent with study hypotheses. Overall, cognitive appraisals and irrational beliefs accounted for 33% of total variance in threat and 23% of total variance in challenge. With regards to affective states (emotions and anxiety), cognitive appraisals, irrational beliefs, and challenge and threat accounted for 35% of variance in positive emotion, 47% of variance in negative emotion, 52% of variance in cognitive anxiety, 37% of variance in somatic anxiety, and 35% of variance in directional interpretation of anxiety.

Serial Atemporal Multiple Mediation Analyses (SAMM)

A total of ten SAMM were conducted to assess the direct and indirect effects of cognitive appraisals on affective states (positive and negative emotions, and cognitive and somatic anxiety, and directional interpretation of anxiety), through irrational beliefs, and challenge and threat. Age and handicap were included as covariates. The results of SAMM are presented in **Tables 2–4**. Total effects for cognitive appraisals on affective states and directional interpretation of anxiety were significant in all the ten mediation models tested. Furthermore, SAMM generated the following results:

Positive Emotion

There were significant indirect effects for cognitive appraisals on positive emotion through challenge (β = 0.24, 95% CI = 0.16–0.31) and through threat (β = 0.06, 95% CI = 0.02–0.11). The indirect effect for cognitive appraisals on positive emotion through irrational beliefs (β = −0.03, 95% CI = −0.06 to −0.01) was significant when threat was included in the model (i.e., model 6). Furthermore, there was a significant indirect effect for cognitive appraisals on positive emotion through both irrational beliefs and threat (β = 0.01, 95% CI = 0.003–0.03). In sum, there was a significant positive direct effect for cognitive appraisals on positive emotion when both mediators (i.e., irrational beliefs and challenge or threat) were included.

Negative Emotion

There were significant indirect effects for cognitive appraisals on negative emotion through challenge (β = −0.12, 95% CI = −0.19 to −0.06) and through threat (β = −0.18, 95% CI = −0.23 to −0.12). The indirect effect for cognitive appraisals on negative emotion through irrational beliefs (β = −0.04, 95% CI = −0.08 to −0.02) was significant when challenge was included in the model (i.e., model 2). Furthermore, there was a significant indirect effect for cognitive appraisals on negative emotion through both irrational beliefs and threat (β = −0.04, 95% CI = −0.07 to −0.01). In sum, there was a significant negative direct effect for cognitive appraisals on negative emotion when both mediators (i.e., irrational beliefs and challenge or threat) were included.

Cognitive Anxiety

There were significant indirect effects for cognitive appraisals on cognitive anxiety through irrational beliefs when challenge (β = −0.07, 95% CI = −0.11 to −0.02) or threat (β = −0.02, 95% CI = −0.05 to −0.01) were included in the model (i.e., model 3 and 8). The indirect effects for cognitive appraisals on cognitive anxiety were significant through challenge (β = −0.09, 95% CI = −0.16 to −0.04) and also through threat (β = −0.18, 95% CI = −0.25 to −0.13). Furthermore, there was a significant indirect effect for cognitive appraisals on cognitive anxiety through both irrational beliefs and threat (β = −0.04, 95% CI = −0.07 to −0.01). In sum, there was a significant negative direct effect for cognitive appraisals on cognitive anxiety when both mediators (i.e., irrational beliefs and challenge or threat) were included.

Somatic Anxiety

There were significant indirect effects for cognitive appraisals on somatic anxiety through challenge (β = −0.11, 95% CI = −0.18 to −0.05) and through threat (β = −0.15, 95% CI = −0.21 to −0.10). The indirect effect for cognitive appraisals on somatic anxiety through irrational beliefs (β = −0.04, 95% CI = −0.08 to −0.01) was significant when challenge was included in the model (i.e., model 4). Furthermore, there was a significant indirect effect for cognitive appraisals on somatic anxiety through both irrational beliefs and threat (β = −0.03, 95% CI = −0.06 to −0.01). In sum, there was a significant negative direct effect for cognitive appraisals on somatic anxiety when both mediators (i.e., irrational beliefs and challenge or threat) were included.

Directional Interpretation

There were significant indirect effects for cognitive appraisals on directional interpretation of anxiety through challenge (β = 0.17, 95% CI = 0.11–0.24) and through threat (β = 0.10, 95% CI = 0.06–0.15). The indirect effect for cognitive appraisals on directional interpretation of anxiety through irrational beliefs (β = 0.02, 95% CI = 0.002–0.04) was significant when challenge was included in the model (i.e., model 5). Furthermore, there was a significant indirect effect for cognitive appraisals on directional interpretation of anxiety through both irrational beliefs and threat (β = 0.02, 95% CI = 0.01–04). In sum, there was a significant positive direct effect for cognitive appraisals on

TABLE 1 | Mean Scales, Standard Deviations and Correlations among all variables regarding imagined imminent golf competition.

N = 287	*M*	*SD*	Age	Handi	Exp	DEM	AWF	LFT	DEP	iBs	MR	MC	PFC	EFC	Cog App	Chall	Threat	Post Emo	Neg Emo	CA	SA	DI
Age	38.71	15.20	–	0.65**	0.53**	–0.04	–0.06	–0.18**	–0.06	–0.11	–0.11	0.07	–0.01	0.02	0.01	–0.01	–0.14*	–0.06	–0.28**	–0.12*	–0.22**	0.16**
Handi	8.85	7.13		–	0.10	0.04	0.04	–0.11	0.08	0.01	–0.00	–0.07	–0.08	–0.09	–0.10	–0.07	0.05	–0.09	–0.14*	0.06	–0.13*	0.10
Exp	11.86	8.31			–	–0.02	–0.03	–0.08	–0.03	–0.05	–0.09	0.18**	0.07	–0.01	0.08	0.04	–0.06	01	–0.12*	–0.08	–0.05	0.05
DEM	20.59	3.82				–	0.76**	0.53**	0.45**	0.81**	0.12	–0.19**	–0.04	–0.08	–0.10	0.01	0.35**	0.08	0.21**	0.35**	0.19**	–0.09
AWF	21.77	4.66					–	0.64**	0.54**	0.89**	0.15*	–0.21**	–0.13*	–0.17**	–0.17**	–0.06	0.46**	0.00	0.31**	0.42**	0.30**	–0.16**
LFT	23.35	5.48						–	0.46**	0.83**	0.17**	–0.17**	–0.11	–0.10	–0.10	0.00	0.30**	0.13*	0.22**	0.35**	0.28**	–0.16**
DEP	14.85	4.85							–	0.75**	0.04	–0.22**	–0.11	–0.30**	–0.25**	–0.22**	0.47**	–0.21**	0.37**	0.40**	0.25**	–0.24**
iBs	20.14	3.85								–	0.15*	–0.24**	–0.12*	–0.20**	–0.19**	–0.08	0.48**	0.00	0.34**	0.46**	0.32**	–0.20**
MR	8.59	1.91									–	0.09	0.15*	0.07	0.44**	0.17**	0.03	0.32**	0.05	0.11	0.10	0.15*
MC	13.78	3.18										–	0.34**	0.31**	0.77**	0.32**	–0.33**	0.22**	–0.28**	–0.35**	–0.29**	0.32**
PFC	7.86	1.86											–	0.41**	0.69**	0.40**	–0.33**	0.38**	–0.28**	–0.36**	–0.30**	0.40**
EFC	8.53	2.10												–	0.67**	0.38**	–0.38**	0.28**	–0.41**	–0.34**	–0.37**	0.33**
Cog App	9.69	1.49													–	0.48**	–0.40**	0.44**	–0.37**	–0.38**	–0.35**	0.46**
Chall	4.93	0.70														–	–0.38**	0.59**	–0.36**	–0.33**	–0.34**	0.49**
Threat	2.78	1.09															–	–0.27**	0.65**	0.72**	0.57**	–0.45**
PostEmo	3.97	0.55																–	–0.24**	–0.22**	–0.22**	0.48**
NegEmo	1.86	0.54																	–	0.65**	0.71**	–0.48**
CA	2.05	0.62																		–	0.71**	–0.51**
SA	2.02	0.55																			–	–0.48**
DI	1.66	1.24																				–

*$p < 0.05$, **$p < 0.01$.

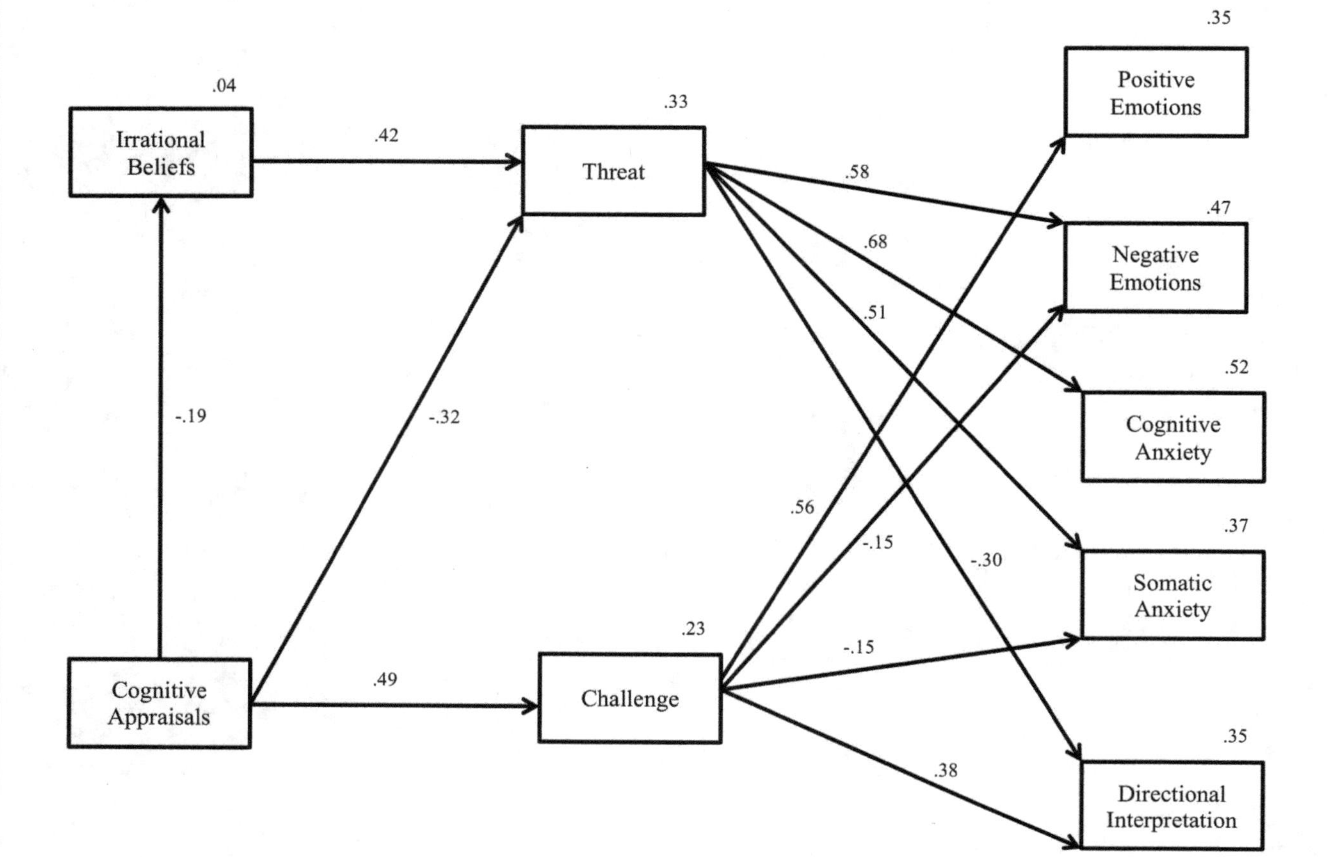

FIGURE 3 | Path analysis testing the theoretical model for imagined imminent golf competition. The model The model indicates all significant paths.

directional interpretation of anxiety when both mediators (i.e., irrational beliefs and challenge or threat) were included.

In summary, the data shows that the relationship between cognitive appraisals and affective states is mediated by irrational beliefs and threat in all models, and by irrational beliefs and challenge in some models. In other words, the cognitive appraisals, irrational beliefs and threat are seen as essential antecedents in predicting affective states among golfers.

PHASE 2 RESULTS

Table 5 displays descriptive statistics and Pearson's correlations for all variables.

Test of the Model

Path analysis revealed that the hypothesized model demonstrated an acceptable fit to the data $\chi^2(31) = 107.31, p < 0.05$, CFI = 0.94, RMSEA = 0.11. The standardized path coefficients for each individual path are displayed in **Figure 4**, demonstrating patterns consistent with study hypotheses. Overall, cognitive appraisals and irrational beliefs accounted for 37% of total variance in threat and 57% of total variance in challenge. With regards to affective states (emotions and anxiety), cognitive appraisals, irrational beliefs, and challenge and threat accounted for 46% of variance in positive emotion, 41% of variance in negative emotion, 53% in cognitive anxiety, 40% in somatic anxiety, and 34% in directional interpretation of anxiety.

Serial Atemporal Multiple Mediation Analysis (SAMM)

A total of ten SAMM analyses were conducted to assess the indirect effects of cognitive appraisals on affective states (positive and negative emotions, cognitive and somatic anxiety, and directional interpretation or anxiety), through irrational beliefs and challenge and threat. Age, handicap and number of weeks to the next important competition were included as covariates. The results of SAMM are presented in **Tables 6–8**. Total effects of cognitive appraisals on affective states and directional interpretation of anxiety were significant in all the ten mediation models tested. Furthermore, SAMM generated the following results:

Positive Emotion

There were significant indirect effects for cognitive appraisals on positive emotion through challenge (β = 0.36, 95% CI = 0.27–0.45) and through threat (β = 0.08, 95% CI = 0.03–0.15). The indirect effect for cognitive appraisals on positive emotion

TABLE 2 | Serial atemporal multiple mediation analysis for imagined imminent golf competition.

Model No.	(M1) iBs	(M2) appraisals	(Y) outcome	$YR^2 = F(,) = , P$	Total $c = t(df) = , P$	Direct $c' = t(df) = , P$	Indirect# = effect, [to]	
1		Challenge	PostEmo	$R^2 = 0.38$ $F(5, 281) = 35.24$, $P < 0.001$	0.16 $t(283) = 8.12$, $P = 0.00$	0.08 $t(283) = 3.94$, $P = 0.00$	Tot = 0.22 [0.15 to 0.30]	Ind1 = −0.01 [−0.03 to 0.002]; Ind2 = 0.24 [0.16 to 0.32]; Ind 3 = −0.001 [−0.01 to 0.008]
2			NegEmo	$R^2 = 0.32$ $F(5, 281) = 26.46$, $P < 0.001$	−0.13 $t(283) = -6.85$, $P = 0.00$	−0.07 $t(283) = -3.48$, $P = 0.00$	Tot = −0.17 [−0.24 to −0.10]	Ind1 = −0.04 [−0.08 to −0.02]; Ind2 = −0.12 [−0.19 to −0.06]; Ind3 = 0.0003 [−0.005 to 0.01]
3			CogAnxiety	$R^2 = 0.35$ $F(5, 281) = 29.77$, $P < 0.001$	−0.15 $t(283) = -6.67$, $P = 0.00$	−0.08 $t(283) = -3.60$, $P = 0.00$	Tot = −0.16 [−0.24 to −0.08]	Ind1 = −0.07 [−0.11 to −0.02]; Ind2 = −0.09 [−0.16 to −0.03]; Ind3 = 0.0003 [−0.003 to 0.005]
4			SomAnxiety	$R^2 = 0.26$ $F(5, 281) = 20.17$, $P < 0.001$	−0.13 $t(283) = -6.38$, $P = 0.00$	−0.07 $t(283) = -3.29$, $P = 0.00$	Tot = −0.15 [−0.24 to −0.08]	Ind1 = −0.04 [−0.08 to −0.01]; Ind2 = −0.11 [−0.18 to −0.05]; Ind3 = 0.0003 [−0.004 to 0.01]
5			DI	$R^2 = 0.35$ $F(5, 281) = 30.11$, $P < 0.001$	0.38 $t(283) = 8.87$, $P = 0.00$	0.22 $t(283) = 4.83$, $P = 0.00$	Tot = 0.19 [0.12 to 0.27]	Ind1 = 0.02 [0.002 to 0.04]; Ind2 = 0.17 [0.11 to 0.24]; Ind3 = −0.0005 [−0.01 to 0.01]
6		Threat	PostEmo	$R^2 = 0.23$ $F(5, 281) = 16.81$, $P < 0.001$	0.16 $t(283) = 8.12$, $P = 0.00$	0.14 $t(283) = 6.72$, $P = 0.00$	Tot = 0.05 [0.004 to 0.10]	Ind1 = −0.03 [−0.06 to −0.01]; Ind2 = 0.06 [0.02 to 0.11]; Ind3 = 0.01 [0.003 to 0.03]
7			NegEmo	$R^2 = 0.48$ $F(5, 281) = 52.02$, $P < 0.001$	−0.13 $t(283) = -6.85$, $P = 0.00$	−0.05 $t(283) = -3.03$, $P = 0.00$	Tot = −0.22 [−0.29 to −0.16]	Ind1 = −0.004 [−0.02 to 0.01]; Ind2 = −0.18 [−0.24 to −0.12]; Ind3 = −0.04 [−0.07 to −0.01]
8			CogAnxiety	$R^2 = 0.55$ $F(5, 281) = 67.86$, $P < 0.001$	−0.15 $t(283) = -6.67$, $P = 0.00$	−0.046 $t(283) = -2.48$, $P = 0.01$	Tot = −0.25 [−0.33 to −0.18]	Ind1 = −0.02 [−0.05 to −0.01]; Ind2 = −0.18 [−0.25 to −0.13]; Ind3 = −0.04 [−0.07 to −0.02]
9			Som Anxiety	$R^2 = 0.38$ $F(5, 281) = 34.01$, $P < 0.001$	−0.13 $t(283) = -6.38$, $P = 0.00$	−0.06 $t(283) = -2.99$, $P = 0.00$	Tot = −0.19 [−0.26 to −0.13]	Ind1 = −0.01 [−0.03 to 0.01]; Ind2 = −0.15 [−0.21 to −0.10]; Ind3 = −0.03 [−0.06 to −0.01]
10			DI	$R^2 = 0.32$ $F(5, 281) = 26.47$, $P < 0.001$	0.38 $t(283) = 8.87$, $P = 0.00$	0.28 $t(283) = 6.34$, $P = 0.00$	Tot = 0.12 [0.08 to 0.17]	Ind1 = −0.003 [−0.03 to 0.02]; Ind2 = 0.10 [0.06 to 0.15]; Ind3 = 0.02 [0.01 to 0.04]

TABLE 3 | Regression weights for serial atemporal multiple mediation models for imagined imminent golf competition.

	Mediators			Regression weights				
Model No.	**(M1) iBs**	**(M2)**	**(Y) outcome**	a_1	b_1	d_{21}	b_2	a_2
1		Challenge	PostEmo	−0.46**	0.01	0.00	0.39**	0.22**
2			NegEmo	−0.46**	0.03**	0.00	−0.19**	0.22**
3			CogAnxiety	−0.46**	0.06**	0.00	−0.17**	0.22**
4			SomAnxiety	−0.46**	0.03**	0.00	−0.18**	0.22**
5			DI	−0.46**	−0.04*	0.00	0.64**	0.22**
6		Threat	PostEmo	−0.46	0.02**	0.11**	−0.11**	−0.23**
7			NegEmo	−0.46**	0.00	0.11**	0.28**	−0.23**
8			CogAnxiety	−0.46**	0.02**	0.11**	0.34**	−0.23**
9			Som Anxiety	−0.46**	0.01	0.11**	0.24**	−0.23**
10			DI	−0.46**	0.01	0.11**	−0.37**	−0.23**

*$p < 0.05$, **$p < 0.01$.

TABLE 4 | Causal chain according to models (X-M-M-Y) for imagined imminent golf competition.

SAMM				
Ind1	Cog appraisals	iBs	Post Emo	
Ind2	**Cog appraisals**	**Challenge**	**Post Emo**	
Ind3	Cog appraisals	iBs	Challenge	Post Emo
SAMM				
Ind1	**Cog appraisals**	**iBs**	**Neg Emo**	
Ind2	**Cog appraisals**	**Challenge**	**Neg Emo**	
Ind3	Cog appraisals	iBs	Challenge	Neg Emo
SAMM				
Ind1	**Cog appraisals**	**iBs**	**Cog anxiety**	
Ind2	**Cog appraisals**	**Challenge**	**Cog anxiety**	
Ind3	Cog appraisals	iBs	Challenge	Cog anxiety
SAMM				
Ind1	**Cog appraisals**	**iBs**	**Som anxiety**	
Ind2	**Cog appraisals**	**Challenge**	**Som anxiety**	
Ind3	Cog appraisals	iBs	Challenge	Som anxiety
SAMM				
Ind1	**Cog appraisals**	**iBs**	**DI**	
Ind2	**Cog appraisals**	**Challenge**	**DI**	
Ind3	Cog appraisals	iBs	Challenge	DI
SAMM				
Ind1	**Cog appraisals**	**iBs**	**Post Emo**	
Ind2	**Cog appraisals**	**Threat**	**Post Emo**	
Ind3	**Cog appraisals**	**iBs**	**Threat**	**Post Emo**
SAMM				
Ind1	Cog appraisals	iBs	Neg Emo	
Ind2	**Cog appraisals**	**Threat**	**Neg Emo**	
Ind3	**Cog appraisals**	**iBs**	**Threat**	**Neg Emo**
SAMM				
Ind1	**Cog appraisals**	**iBs**	**Cog anxiety**	
Ind2	**Cog appraisals**	**Threat**	**Cog anxiety**	
Ind3	**Cog appraisals**	**iBs**	**Threat**	**Cog anxiety**
SAMM				
Ind1	Cog appraisals	iBs	Som anxiety	
Ind2	**Cog appraisals**	**Threat**	**Som anxiety**	
Ind3	**Cog appraisals**	**iBs**	**Threat**	**Som anxiety**
SAMM				
Ind1	Cog appraisals	iBs	DI	
Ind2	**Cog appraisals**	**Threat**	**DI**	
Ind3	**Cog appraisals**	**iBs**	**Threat**	**DI**

Values in bold indicate significant SAMM paths.

through irrational beliefs (β = −0.05, 95% CI = −0.10 to −0.01) was significant when threat was included in the model (i.e., model 6). Furthermore, there was a significant indirect effect for cognitive appraisals on positive emotion through both irrational beliefs and challenge (β = −0.02, 95% CI = −0.04 to −0.002) or threat (β = 0.02, 95% CI = 0.003–0.04). In sum, there was a significant positive direct effect for cognitive appraisals on positive emotion when both mediators (i.e., irrational beliefs and challenge or threat) were included.

Negative Emotion

There were significant indirect effects for cognitive appraisals on negative emotion through challenge (β = −0.21, 95% CI = −0.31 to −0.11) and through threat (β = −0.19, 95% CI = −0.27 to −0.11). The indirect effect for cognitive appraisals on negative emotion through irrational beliefs (β = −0.05, 95% CI = −0.09 to −0.01) was significant when challenge was included in the model (i.e., model 2). Furthermore, there was a significant indirect effect for cognitive appraisals on negative emotion through both irrational beliefs and challenge (β = 0.01, 95% CI = 0.001–0.03) or threat (β = −0.04, 95% CI = −0.07 to −0.01). In sum, there was a non-significant negative direct effect for cognitive appraisals on negative emotion when both mediators (i.e., irrational beliefs and challenge) were included.

Cognitive Anxiety

There were significant indirect effects for cognitive appraisals on cognitive anxiety through irrational beliefs when challenge (β = −0.08, 95% CI = −0.15 to −0.03) or threat (β = −0.03, 95% CI = −0.07 to −0.01) were included in the model (i.e., model 3 and 8). The indirect effects for cognitive appraisals on cognitive anxiety were significant through challenge (β = −0.12, 95% CI = −0.21 to −0.03) and also through threat (β = −0.22, 95% CI = −0.30 to −0.13). Furthermore, there was a significant indirect effect for cognitive appraisals on cognitive anxiety through both irrational beliefs and challenge (β = 0.01, 95% CI = 0.0003–0.02) or threat (β = −0.05, 95% CI = −0.08 to −0.02). In sum, there was a non-significant negative direct effect for cognitive appraisals on cognitive anxiety when both mediators (i.e., irrational beliefs and challenge or threat) were included.

Somatic Anxiety

There were significant indirect effects for cognitive appraisals on somatic anxiety through challenge (β = −0.20, 95% CI = −0.30 to −0.10) and through threat (β = 0.18, 95% CI = −0.26 to −0.11). The indirect effect for cognitive appraisals on somatic anxiety through irrational beliefs (β = −0.05, 95% CI = −0.10 to −0.01) was significant when challenge was included in the model (i.e., model 4). Furthermore, there was a significant indirect path for cognitive appraisals on somatic anxiety through both

TABLE 5 | Mean Scales, Standard Deviations and Correlations among all variables for actual future golf competition.

N = 212	M	SD	Age	Handi	Exp	No. of weeks	DEM	AWF	LFT	DEP	Total iBs	MR	MC	PFC	EFC	Cog App	Chall	Threat	Post Emo	Neg Emo	CA	SA	DI
Age	38.55	15.08	–	0.62**	0.53**	−0.07	−0.04	−0.07	−0.18**	−0.07	−0.12	−0.18**	−0.04	−0.25**	−0.04	−0.16*	−0.10	−0.20**	−0.01	−0.27**	−0.18**	−0.19**	0.04
Handi	8.68	7.15		–	0.09	−0.10	0.07	0.10	−0.08	0.14*	0.06	−0.23**	−0.18**	−0.29**	−0.17*	−0.29**	−0.12	0.04	−0.08	−0.09	−0.02	−0.12	0.02
Exp	12.81	8.38			–	−0.15*	−0.05	−0.10	−0.13	−0.06	−0.10	−0.16*	0.01	−0.06	−0.04	−0.07	−0.07	−0.08	−0.08	−0.13	−0.10	−0.05	−0.03
No. of weeks	1.16	1.07				–	−0.06	0.00	−0.07	−0.01	−0.04	0.07	−0.02	0.02	0.03	0.02	−0.05	0.14*	0.07	0.12	0.15*	0.15*	−0.04
DEM	20.53	3.83					–	0.77**	0.57**	0.47**	0.82**	0.06	−0.14*	−0.07	−0.15*	−0.11	0.13	0.31**	0.11	0.10	0.31**	0.13	0.00
AWF	21.79	4.75						–	0.67**	0.57**	0.90**	0.04	−0.25**	−0.12	−0.16*	−0.18**	−0.00	0.43**	0.02	0.26**	0.40**	0.26**	−0.15*
LFT	23.59	5.52							–	0.47**	0.83**	0.14*	−0.22**	0.01	−0.11	−0.09	0.14*	0.27**	0.12	0.15*	0.29**	0.16*	−0.09
DEP	14.90	5.11								–	0.77**	0.01	−0.36**	−0.13	−0.34**	−0.30**	−0.15*	0.51**	−0.15*	0.39**	0.47**	0.37**	−0.27**
Total iBs	20.20	3.98									–	0.08	−0.30**	−0.09	−0.23**	−0.21**	0.03	0.46**	0.03	0.28**	0.45**	0.28**	−0.16*
MR	7.82	2.48										–	0.30**	0.30**	0.21**	0.62**	0.40**	−0.13	0.43**	0.03	0.05	0.01	0.20**
MC	14.78	3.63											–	0.32**	0.47**	0.80**	0.42**	−0.41**	0.30**	−0.38**	−0.38**	−0.40**	0.44**
PFC	7.60	2.19												–	0.53**	0.69**	0.44**	−0.20**	0.34**	−0.11	−0.14*	−0.17*	0.33**
EFC	8.44	2.21													–	0.74**	0.41**	−0.35**	0.33**	−0.36**	−0.33**	−0.40**	0.50**
Cog App	9.66	1.90														–	0.58**	−0.40**	0.48**	−0.31**	−0.30**	−0.35**	0.51**
Chall	4.96	0.73															–	−0.39**	0.66**	−0.37**	−0.25**	−0.39**	0.54**
Threat	2.24	1.00																–	−0.30**	0.63**	0.73**	0.61**	−0.40**
PostEm	3.98	0.65																	–	−0.27**	−0.18**	−0.25**	0.43**
NegEm	1.53	0.53																		–	0.72**	0.82**	−0.40**
CA	1.80	0.57																			–	0.73**	−0.40**
SA	1.61	0.49																				–	−0.46**
DI	1.99	1.00																					–

$^{*}p < 0.05$, $^{**}p < 0.01$.

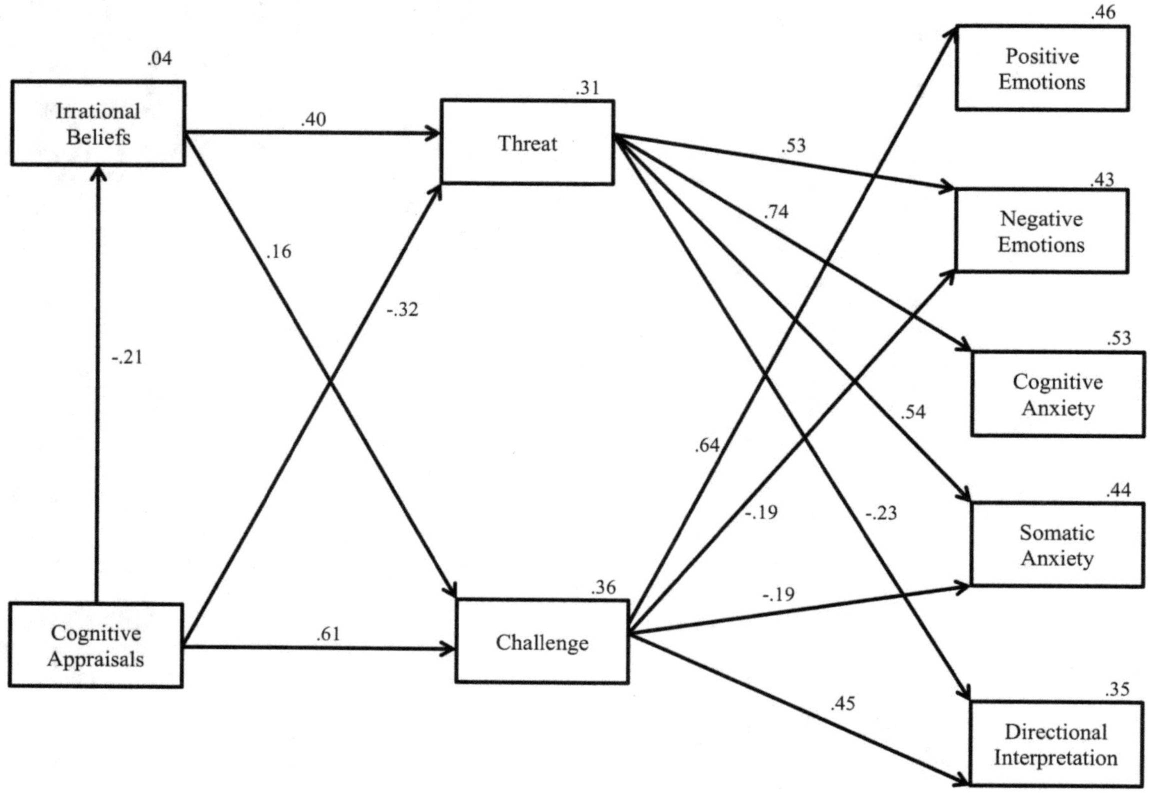

FIGURE 4 | Path analysis testing the theoretical model for an actual future golf competition. The model indicates all significant paths.

irrational beliefs and challenge (β = 0.01, 95% CI = 0.001–0.02) or threat (β = −0.04, 95% CI = −0.07 to −0.01). In sum, there was a significant negative direct effect for cognitive appraisals on somatic anxiety when both mediators (i.e., irrational beliefs and challenge or threat) were included.

Directional Interpretation

There were significant indirect effects for cognitive appraisals on directional interpretation of anxiety through challenge (β = 0.24, 95% CI = 0.14–0.34) and also through threat (β = 0.08, 95% CI = 0.03–0.14). The indirect effect for cognitive appraisals on directional interpretation of anxiety through irrational beliefs (β = 0.02, 95% CI = 0.0005–0.06) was significant when challenge was included in the model (i.e., model 5). Furthermore, there was a significant indirect path for cognitive appraisals on directional interpretation of anxiety through both irrational beliefs and challenge (β = −0.01, 95% CI = −0.03 to −0.001) or threat (β = 0.02, 95% CI = 0.003–0.04). In sum, there was a significant positive direct effect for cognitive appraisals on directional interpretation of anxiety when both mediators (i.e., irrational beliefs and challenge or threat) were included.

In summary, data analyses demonstrate that the relationships between cognitive appraisals and affective states and directional interpretation of anxiety is mediated by irrational beliefs and challenge and threat in all models. In other words, the interaction of cognitive appraisals, irrational beliefs, and challenge and threat, emerged as antecedent to the golfers' affective states on approach to both imagined imminent, and actual future golf competitions.

DISCUSSION

The main aim of the current study was to examine the interaction between cognitive appraisals, irrational beliefs, and challenge and threat, in anteceding pre-competitive affective states (emotions and anxiety) and directional interpretation of anxiety in golfers. To achieve this main aim, two study phases were undertaken where golfers considered an imagined imminent golf competition (phase 1), and an actual future golf competition (phase 2). The current study is the first to investigate how affective states occur through the complex interaction of antecedent cognitive appraisals, irrational beliefs, and challenge and threat, within a specific sporting population.

In accordance with study hypotheses, the results of path analyses across both the study phases revealed that threat was positively associated with negative emotions (H4) and both cognitive and somatic anxiety (H5). Threat was also negatively associated with directional interpretation of anxiety, such that greater threat was associated with less facilitative perceptions of anxiety (H6). In addition, threat was positively associated with irrational beliefs (H2) and negatively associated with

TABLE 6 | Serial atemporal multiple mediation analysis for actual future golf competition.

Model No.	(M1) iBs	(M2) appraisals	(Y) outcome	$YR^2 = F(,) =, P$	Total $c = t(df) =, P$	Direct $c' = t$ (df) $=, P$	Indirect# = effect, [to]	
1		Challenge	PostEmo	$R^2 = 0.47$ $F(6, 205) = 30.44$, $P < 0.001$	0.17 $t(207) = 7.89$, $P = 0.00$	0.06 $t(207) = 2.52$, $P = 0.01$	Tot = 0.33 [0.24 to 0.43]	Ind1 = −0.01 [−0.04 to 0.01] Ind2 = 0.36 [0.27 to 0.45] Ind3 = −0.02 [−0.04 to −0.002]
2			NegEmo	$R^2 = 0.32$ $F(6, 205) = 15.81$, $P < 0.001$	−0.10 $t(207) = -5.55$, $P = 0.00$	−0.03 $t(207) = -1.45$, $P = 0.15$	Tot = −0.25 [−0.35 to −0.14]	Ind1 = −0.05 [−0.09 to −0.01] Ind2 = −0.21 [−0.31 to −0.11] Ind3 = 0.01 [0.001 to 0.03]
3			Cog anxiety	$R^2 = 0.32$ $F(6, 205) = 16.42$, $P < 0.001$	−0.10 $t(207) = -4.98$, $P = 0.00$	−0.040 $t(207) = -1.76$, $P = 0.08$	Tot = −0.20 [−0.31 to −0.09]	Ind1 = −0.08 [−0.15 to −0.03] Ind2 = −0.12 [−0.21 to −0.03] Ind3 = 0.01 [0.0003 to 0.02]
4			Som anxiety	$R^2 = 0.31$ $F(6, 205) = 15.63$, $P < 0.001$	−0.11 $t(207) = -6.47$, $P = 0.00$	−0.04 $t(207) = -2.33$, $P = 0.02$	Tot = −0.24 [−0.35 to −0.14]	Ind1 = −0.05 [−0.10 to −0.01] Ind2 = −0.20 [−0.30 to −0.10] Ind3 = 0.01 [0.001 to 0.02]
5			DI	$R^2 = 0.39$ $F(6, 205) = 22.11$, $P < 0.001$	0.30 $t(207) = 9.34$, $P = 0.00$	0.17 $t(207) = 4.44$, $P = 0.00$	Tot = 0.25 [0.15 to 0.35]	Ind1 = 0.02 [0.0005 to 0.06] Ind2 = 0.24 [0.14 to 0.34] Ind3 = −0.01 [−0.03 to −0.001]
6		Threat	PostEmo	$R^2 = 0.30$ $F(6, 205) = 14.58$, $P < 0.001$	0.17 $t(207) = 7.89$, $P = 0.00$	0.15 $t(207) = 6.59$, $P = 0.00$	Tot = 0.05 [−0.01 to 0.13]	Ind1 = −0.05 [−0.10 to −0.01] Ind2 = 0.08 [0.03 to 0.15] Ind3 = 0.02 [0.003 to 0.04]
7			NegEmo	$R^2 = 0.43$ $F(6, 205) = 26.21$, $P < 0.001$	−0.10 $t(207) = -5.55$, $P = 0.00$	−0.04 t(207) = −2.18, $P = 0.03$	Tot = −0.22 [−0.31 to −0.14]	Ind1 = 0.003 [−0.02 to 0.03] Ind2 = −0.19 [−0.27 to −0.11] Ind3 = −0.04 [−0.07 to −0.01]
8			Cog anxiety	$R^2 = 0.55$ $F(6, 205) = 42.40$, $P < 0.001$	−0.10 $t(207) = -4.98$, $P = 0.00$	−0.01 $t(207) = -0.66$, $P = 0.51$	Tot = −0.29 [−0.39 to −0.20]	Ind1 = −0.031 [−0.07 to −0.01] Ind2 = −0.22 [−0.30 to −0.13] Ind3 = −0.05 [−0.08 to −0.02]
9			Som anxiety	$R^2 = 0.43$ $F(6, 205) = 25.64$, $P < 0.001$	−0.107 $t(207) = -6.47$, $P = 0.00$	−0.049 $t(207) = -3.18$, $P = 0.00$	Tot = −0.22 [−0.31 to −0.15]	Ind1 = −0.002 [−0.03 to 0.02] Ind2 = −0.18 [−0.26 to −0.11] Ind3 = −0.04 [−0.07 to −0.01]
10			DI	$R^2 = 0.34$ $F(6, 205) = 17.48$, $P < 0.001$	0.30 $t(207) = 9.34$, $P = 0.00$	0.25 $t(207) = 7.24$, $P = 0.00$	Total = 0.09 [0.04 to 0.16]	Ind1 = −0.01 [−0.04 to 0.02] Ind2 = 0.08 [0.03 to 0.14] Ind3 = 0.02 [0.003 to 0.04]

TABLE 7 | Regression weights for serial atemporal multiple mediation models for actual future golf competition.

Model No.	(M1) iBs	(M2) Mediators	(Y) outcome	a_1	b_1	d_{21}	b_2	a_2
1		Challenge	PostEmo	−0.43**	0.01	0.03*	0.51**	0.24**
2			NegEmo	−0.43**	0.03**	0.03*	−0.24**	0.24**
3			Cog anxiety	−0.43**	0.06**	0.03*	−0.15*	0.24**
4			Som anxiety	−0.43**	0.03**	0.03*	−0.22**	0.24**
5			DI	−0.43**	−.03*	0.03*	0.52**	0.24**
6		Threat	PostEmo	−0.43**	0.04**	0.09**	−0.16**	−0.18**
7			NegEmo	−0.43**	−0.00	0.09**	0.29**	−0.18**
8			Cog anxiety	−0.43**	0.02**	0.09**	0.36**	−0.18**
9			Som anxiety	−0.43**	0.00	0.09**	0.26**	−0.18**
10			DI	−0.43**	0.01	0.09**	−0.24**	−0.18**

*$p < 0.05$, **$p < 0.01$.

TABLE 8 | Causal chain according to models (X-M-M-Y) for actual future golf competition.

SAMM				
Ind1	Cog appraisals	iBs	Post Emo	
Ind2	**Cog appraisals**	**Challenge**	**Post Emo**	
Ind3	**Cog appraisals**	**iBs**	**Challenge**	**Post Emo**
SAMM				
Ind1	**Cog appraisals**	**iBs**	**Neg Emo**	
Ind2	**Cog appraisals**	**Challenge**	**Neg Emo**	
Ind3	**Cog appraisals**	**iBs**	**Challenge**	**Neg Emo**
SAMM				
Ind1	**Cog appraisals**	**iBs**	**Cog anxiety**	
Ind2	**Cog appraisals**	**Challenge**	**Cog anxiety**	
Ind3	**Cog appraisals**	**iBs**	**Challenge**	**Cog anxiety**
SAMM				
Ind1	**Cog appraisals**	**iBs**	**Som anxiety**	
Ind2	**Cog appraisals**	**Challenge**	**Som anxiety**	
Ind3	**Cog appraisals**	**iBs**	**Challenge**	**Som anxiety**
SAMM				
Ind1	**Cog appraisals**	**iBs**	**DI**	
Ind2	**Cog appraisals**	**Challenge**	**DI**	
Ind3	**Cog appraisals**	**iBs**	**Challenge**	**DI**
SAMM				
Ind1	**Cog appraisals**	**iBs**	**Post Emo**	
Ind2	**Cog appraisals**	**Threat**	**Post Emo**	
Ind3	**Cog appraisals**	**iBs**	**Threat**	**Post Emo**
SAMM				
Ind1	Cog appraisals	iBs	Neg Emo	
Ind2	**Cog appraisals**	**Threat**	**Neg Emo**	
Ind3	**Cog appraisals**	**iBs**	**Threat**	**Neg Emo**
SAMM				
Ind1	**Cog appraisals**	**iBs**	**Cog anxiety**	
Ind2	**Cog appraisals**	**Threat**	**Cog anxiety**	
Ind3	**Cog appraisals**	**iBs**	**Threat**	**Cog anxiety**
SAMM				
Ind1	Cog appraisals	iBs	Som anxiety	
Ind2	**Cog appraisals**	**Threat**	**Som anxiety**	
Ind3	**Cog appraisals**	**iBs**	**Threat**	**Som anxiety**
SAMM				
Ind1	Cog appraisals	iBs	DI	
Ind2	**Cog appraisals**	**Threat**	**DI**	
Ind3	**Cog appraisals**	**iBs**	**Threat**	**DI**

Values in bold indicate significant SAMM paths.

cognitive appraisals (H3). Challenge was negatively associated with negative emotions (H4) and somatic anxiety (H5), and positively associated with positive emotions (H4) and more facilitative perceptions of anxiety (H6). Also, cognitive appraisals were negatively associated with irrational beliefs (H1). Further, challenge was positively related to cognitive appraisals (H3), and in phase 2 was positively associated with irrational beliefs (H2), but unrelated to irrational beliefs in phase 1.

In other words, a golfer approaching competition with low cognitive appraisals, that report high irrational beliefs, is more likely to be threatened, and less likely to be challenged. As a result, the golfer will likely experience greater negative emotions and anxiety and is more likely to perceive their anxiety symptoms as less facilitative for their performance in that competition.

The findings of current research support some extant research (e.g., David et al., 2002, 2005) in revealing the interaction between irrational beliefs and cognitive appraisals in the prediction of affective states. The current research extends previous research by investigating and understanding the complex interaction of antecedents to affective states within a golf specific sport setting. David et al. (2002, 2005) did not consider challenge and threat in their studies. Our findings that challenge and threat mediate the relationship between cognitive appraisals and affective states alongside irrational beliefs is an important extension of our knowledge of how affective states occur. Also, our research takes into account the interpretation of anxiety, previously unexplored in research. The current research also makes methodological advancements by using more sophisticated analytical procedures (SEM and SAMM).

The inclusion of challenge and threat in the current study, alongside irrational beliefs and cognitive appraisals, is a particularly important extension of past research because it more comprehensively reflects the antecedents of affective states in anticipation of personally relevant situations. Researchers have found irrational beliefs to be positively associated with threat (Dixon et al., 2016; Evans et al., 2018), but the current study develops this research by offering an integration of cognitive appraisals, irrational beliefs, and challenge and threat. The finding that challenge and threat are associated differentially with affective states is in line with the postulations of prominent theories (e.g., Skinner and Brewer, 2004; Jones et al., 2009). That is, challenge was associated with positive affective states, and more facilitative perceptions of anxiety, whilst threat was related to negative affective states, and less facilitative perceptions of anxiety. The findings concerning anxiety in the current study are in line with previous research that demonstrates threat to be associated with greater cognitive and somatic anxiety and a more debilitative interpretation of anxiety responses compared to a challenge (e.g., Williams et al., 2010; Quested et al., 2011;

Moore et al., 2012). Specifically, Moore et al. (2012) found that the golfers who received challenge instructions reported lower levels of cognitive anxiety compared to golfers who received threat instructions. In addition, golfers who received challenge instructions interpreted anxiety to be more facilitative for their performance in comparison to golfers who received threat instructions.

Beyond the bivariate associations emerging from path analyses, SAMM provided some important evidence concerning the mechanisms that could explain the relationships between cognitive appraisals and affective states. There were significant indirect effects across both study phases, implying that the association between cognitive appraisals and affective states was mediated by irrational beliefs and threat (H7). This is in support of previous research in which irrational beliefs are associated with cognitive appraisals (David et al., 2002, 2005), and where higher irrational beliefs are associated with greater threat, and lesser challenge (Dixon et al., 2016). That irrational beliefs and threat mediated the relationship between cognitive appraisal and affective states in serial suggests that it is the interaction between cognitive appraisals, irrational beliefs, and threat, that is particularly important for understanding anticipatory affective states on approach to competitive golf situations.

With regards to challenge, there were some differences between phase 1 and phase 2 in the serial multiple atemporal mediation results. With challenge in the mediation model, at phase 1 no significant serial mediation was found for any affective outcomes, although simple mediation was revealed. However, in phase 2, significant serial mediation was found for all affective states, showing that irrational beliefs and challenge (H7) in serial mediated the association between cognitive appraisals and affective states. This lack of serial mediation in phase 1 could be due to a variety of factors. First, there is no significant relationship between irrational beliefs and challenge in phase 1, revealed in bivariate correlations (**Table 1**), and in the path analysis. Second, in phase 1 participants approached an imagined competition scenario, whereas in phase 2 they approached a real future competition. It might be that the imagined event induced greater psychological pressure than what the participants might face in their next actual competition. In phase 1, we induced pressure using ego-threat, but in phase 2, we did not induce pressure at all. Therefore, challenge might have been more salient in phase 2 where a participant's next competition might be one in which they are facing less pressure to perform because some participants are unlikely to be performing under the pressured conditions reflected in phase 1. Therefore, challenge is more likely to emerge on approach to a less pressured competition (Blascovich and Mendes, 2000).

The finding that mediation and bivariate associations differed across phase 1 and phase 2 is also echoed in the phase 1-phase 2 tests of differences, and differences in the strength of relationships between the two phases, reported in the results. Specifically, the results revealed that golfers appraised the imagined imminent competition as less motivationally congruent and perceived greater problem focused coping potential during phase 1 than in phase 2. Also, the golfers reported greater threat greater negative emotions and anxiety in phase 1. PFC reflects the potential to act directly on the situation with the purpose of changing the situation or bringing it in accordance with one's desires (Lazarus, 1999). However, in the current study, PFC is unrealistic for the golfers because the imagined competition is imminent and unchangeable. For instance, if a golfer perceives the situation to be incongruent with his or her goals, focuses on problem focused coping and evaluates the competition as a threat, then he or she is more likely to experience greater negative emotions and anxiety before an imminent golf competition.

The phase 1-phase 2 differences were unexpected and contrary to our hypotheses (H8, 9). We expected golfers to experience stronger negative emotions during phase 2 (H9), and we expected stronger associations between variables in phase 2 (H8), because research indicates that real events are more stressful and should elicit bivariate associations (Visla et al., 2016). It is important however to consider past literature, which suggests that temporal proximity is an important factor when measuring responses to stressful events. For instance, research has extensively investigated the temporal patterning of competitive anxiety (Cerin et al., 2000) and the findings of the studies revealed that the intensity of the somatic component of competitive anxiety increases as competition nears (Slaughter et al., 1994), whereas the cognitive anxiety component can increase (Swain and Jones, 1992; Slaughter et al., 1994) or remain stable (Caruso et al., 1990) on approach to competition. Our findings that affective states were lower in the real event (phase 2) in comparison to the imminent imagined situation (phase 1) could be because the next event for each participant varied in proximity ranging from a few days to months.

The results of the present study indicate the importance of using various procedural and data analytical methods to investigate the associations between cognitive appraisals, irrational beliefs, challenge and threat, and affective states. Although, there were some differences between phases 1 and phase 2, overall path analytical and atemporal mediational models were broadly consistent across both the phases. The findings of the current paper may have some important theoretical implications, in part because we offer a more complex model than has previously need proposed and tested (e.g., David et al., 2002). It is essential and advantageous to consider cognitive appraisals, irrational beliefs, and challenge and threat, in the occurrence of affective states. The model proposed and tested in the current study provides a more accurate and comprehensive explanation concerning the antecedents of affective states on approach to competitive situations. Importantly, cognitive appraisals and irrational beliefs are seen as co-occurring simultaneously rather than occurring in a sequential and fixed order (Ziegler, 2001).

The consistency in SEM and SAMM results between phases 1 and 2 demonstrate the utility of experimental vignettes that represent real-life golf scenarios. The current research has not investigated REBT interventions *per se*, however, it has provided useful information for the readers with regards to potential practical implications. That is, by having golfers imagine approaching an upcoming competition, we were able to identify their beliefs and trigger affective states similar to what was reported for a real golf competition. Thus, practitioners in the field can encourage athletes to imagine upcoming situations in order to trigger cognitive appraisals and irrational beliefs for the purposes of more accurate assessment and intervention. Indeed, in REBT Rational Emotive Imagery (REI) is an oft-used technique (Maultsby, 1971) with athletes (Turner and Bennett, 2018). REI involves athletes visualizing the situation that elicits unhealthy negative emotions and then emotional change is brought about by encouraging them to change their irrational beliefs into rational beliefs.

Researchers have not yet investigated the effects of REI within sporting performance, but motivational general arousal (MG-A) imagery has been suggested as an effective intervention for the enhancement of athletes overall affect experiences and interpretation of pre-competitive symptoms (Mellalieu et al., 2009). Clearly, there is some overlap between MG-A imagery and REI, where imagery focuses upon the emotional experiences associated with stress, anxiety and arousal (Vadocz et al., 1997). However, in MG-A imagery the athletes are asked to imagine arousal reducing images (e.g., imagine oneself in a relaxed place) whereas, in REI the athletes are asked to alter their irrational beliefs in order to change their unhealthy emotional responses to the imagined situation. Further, imagery has been used in research to manipulate challenge and threat (Hale and Whitehouse, 1998; Williams et al., 2010; Williams and Cumming, 2012) and deemed as a useful strategy to help athletes evaluate the competitive situation as a challenge prior to their performance. Additionally, the findings of the current research have established associations between cognitive appraisals, irrational beliefs, and challenge and threat (David et al., 2002; Dixon et al., 2016; Evans et al., 2018). Therefore, practitioners can promote the use of REI combined with MG-A imagery with athletes during consultation. For instance, athletes can be asked to imagine themselves in events or situations (A) that obstruct their goals (G), and trigger unhealthy emotional and behavioral consequences (C), depending on their beliefs about the self, others, and the world in relation to the situation (A). If the athletes beliefs (B) are irrational (rigid, illogical, and extreme) then the practitioner can help them change their irrational beliefs into rational beliefs (flexible, logical, and non-extreme), which in turn can influence athletes to appraise the competition as a challenge, thus, leading to healthy emotional and behavioral responses (C) prior competition. Thus, similar to the imaged situations, REI can be a useful practical tool for practitioners to use with athletes to encourage healthy affective states among athletes in competitions (Ellis and Dryden, 1997).

The current research is not without its limitations. The primary limitation is that we adopted a cross-sectional single time point atemporal design. Cognitions and affective states change in the lead up to important events (e.g., Skinner and Brewer, 2002), and cognitive appraisals are most accurately considered to be iterative, rather than static and singular occurrences (Blascovich and Mendes, 2000; Lerner and Keltner, 2000; Schneider, 2008). Therefore, future research should explore the role that irrational beliefs play in the temporal changes in cognitive appraisals and affective states in the lead up to a sport competition.

Furthermore, the current research uses self-report measures, which can result in biases when investigating cognitive appraisals (e.g., Paunonen and LeBel, 2012). It is possible that the hypothetical scenario in the current paper influenced appraisals unconsciously, outside of the conscious awareness of the participants. Indeed, it may be that only some aspects of cognitive appraisal are consciously accessible with an even smaller section of those perceptions considered acceptable to report by individuals (e.g., Greenwald and Banaji, 1995; LeDoux, 1998; Blascovich and Mendes, 2000; Quigley et al., 2002). To overcome such a limitation, future research using longitudinal designs could investigate emotional experience using more objective psychophysiological markers (see Jones et al., 2009). Also, future researchers would benefit from the development of a sport specific measure for primary and secondary cognitive appraisals. Further, the current research lacks objective measure of sport performance, and researchers should aim to explore how irrational beliefs and cognitive appraisals interact to predict affective states, and in turn, athletic performance. The current sample also involves higher proportion of male golfers in comparison to females. The sex-imbalance with the sport of golf, with 15% of golf club members being female (England Golf, 2018) makes it difficult to make comparisons, therefore future research should look at recruiting equal numbers of males and females for a detailed comparisons (Turner et al., 2018b). In addition, the substantial time delay from completion of the questionnaires to the next competition for some golfers meant that there is great variability in the time to event data. Indeed, due to the variability, we transformed the variable number of weeks to allow us to include it in the analyses (make it more homogenous). Nevertheless, future research might consider recruiting participants within the same time proximity to the next competition to understand the phenomenon in a more homogenous data set. Lastly, within current research, the participants were not recruited based upon a specific range of handicap. The current research aimed to recruit golfers competing at all different levels being club, amateur golfers and professional golfers. Hence, the participants differed across a wide range of handicaps. However, the main aim of the current research was to make an initial investigation concerning how cognitive appraisals, irrational beliefs, and challenge and threat, relate to affective states among competitive golfers. Future researcher could restrict the handicap to more elite athletes and examine the differences between low and high handicap golfers.

CONCLUSION

In conclusion, the findings of the current study indicate that irrational beliefs interact with cognitive appraisals and challenge and threat to determine affective states within golfers. The data shows that the relationship between cognitive appraisals and affective states is mediated by irrational beliefs and challenge or threat. In other words, cognitive appraisals, irrational beliefs, and challenge and threat, are seen as interacting antecedents to pre-competitive affective states among golfers. It is hoped that this study stimulates further research and discussion concerning cognitive appraisal in anticipation of competitive situations.

ETHICS STATEMENT

This study was carried out in accordance with the recommendations of "Staffordshire University Ethics Committee" with written informed consent from all subjects. All subjects gave written informed consent in accordance with the Declaration of Helsinki. The protocol was approved by the "Staffordshire University Ethics Committee."

AUTHOR CONTRIBUTIONS

NC, MT, and MS conceived the research idea, and structured and drafted the manuscript. NC collected and analyzed the data. MT and MS edited the manuscript and made comments on the final version.

REFERENCES

Aguinis, H., and Bradley, K. J. (2014). Best-practice recommendations for designing and implementing experimental vignette methodology studies. *Organ. Res. Methods* 17, 351–371. doi: 10.1177/1094428114547952

Baraldi, A. N., and Enders, C. K. (2010). An introduction to modern missing data analyses. *J. Sch. Psychol.* 48, 5–37. doi: 10.1016/j.jsp.2009.10.001

Bentler, P. M. (1990). Comparative fit indexes in structural models. *Psychol. Bull.* 107, 238–246. doi: 10.1037//0033-2909.107.2.238

Blascovich, J., and Mendes, W. B. (2000). "Challenge and threat appraisals: the role of affective cues," in *Feeling and Thinking: The Role of Affect in Social Cognition*, ed. J. P. Forgas, (Cambridge: Cambridge University Press), 59–82.

Blascovich, J., Seery, M. D., Mugridge, C. A., Norris, K., and Weisbuch, M. (2004). Predicting athletic performance from cardiovascular indexes of challenge and threat. *J. Exp. Soc. Psychol.* 40, 683–688. doi: 10.1016/j.jesp.2003.10.007

Browne, M. W., and Cudek, R. (1993). "Alternative ways of assessing model fit," in *Testing Structural Equation Models*, eds K. A. Bollen, and J. S. Long, (Newbury Park, CA: Sage), 136–162.

Burton, D. (1998). "Measuring competitive state anxiety," in *Advances in Sport and Exercise Psychology Measurement*, ed. J. L. Duda, (Morgantown, WV: Fitness Information Technology, Inc.), 129–148.

Caruso, C. M., Dzewaltowski, D. A., Gill, D. L., and McElroy, M. A. (1990). Psychological and physiological changes in competitive state anxiety during noncompetition and competitive success and failure. *J. Sport Exerc. Psychol.* 12, 6–20. doi: 10.1123/jsep.12.1.6

Cerin, E., Szabo, A., Hunt, N., and Williams, C. (2000). Temporal patterning of competitive emotions: a critical review. *J. Sport Sci.* 18, 605–626. doi: 10.1080/02640410050082314

Comrey, A. L., and Lee, H. B. (1992). *A First Course in Factor Analysis*, 2nd Edn. Hillsdale, NJ: Lawrence Erlbaum Associates, Inc.

David, A., Ghinea, C., Macavei, B., and Eva, K. (2005). A search for "hot" cognitions in a clinical and non-clinical context: appraisal, attributions, core relational themes, irrational beliefs, and their relations to emotion. *J. Cogn. Behav. Psychother.* 5, 1–42.

David, D., Schnur, J., and Belloiu, A. (2002). Another search for the "hot" cognitions: appraisal, irrational beliefs, attributions, and their relation to emotion. *J. Ration. Emot. Cogn. Behav. Ther.* 20, 93–131. doi: 10.1023/A:1019876601693

Dixon, M., Turner, M. J., and Gillman, J. (2016). Examining the relationships between challenge and threat cognitive appraisal and coaching behaviors in football in football coaches. *J. Sports Sci.* 35, 2446–2452. doi: 10.1080/02640414.2016.1273538

Dixon, W. J., and Yuen, K. K. (1974). Trimming and winsorization: a review. *Statist. Hefte* 15, 150–170. doi: 10.1007/BF02922904

Ellis, A. (1957). Rational psychotherapy and individual psychology. *J. Individ. Psychol.* 13, 38–44.

Ellis, A. (1994). *Reason and Emotion in Psychotherapy*. Secaucus, NJ: Carol publishing group.

Ellis, A., and Dryden, W. (1997). *The Practice of Rational-Emotive Behavior Therapy*. New York, NY: Springer Publishing Company.

England Golf, (2018). *Women & girls*. Available at: https://statistics.laerd.com/spss-tutorials/ancova-using-spss-statistics.php (accessed April 24, 2018).

Epictetus. (1948). *The Enchiridion*. Indianapolis, IN: Bobbs-Merrill.

Evans, A. L., Turner, M. J., Pickering, R., and Powditch, R. (2018). The effects of rational and irrational coach team talks on the cognitive appraisal and achievement goal orientation of varsity football athletes. *Int. J. Sports Sci. Coach.* 13, 431–438. doi: 10.1177/1747954118771183

Folkman, S., and Lazarus, R. S. (1985). If it changes it must be a process: study of emotion and copying during three stages of a college examination. *J. Pers. Soc. Psychol.* 48, 150–170. doi: 10.1037/0022-3514.48.1.150

Graham, J. W. (2009). Missing data analysis: making it work in the real world. *Annu. Rev. Psychol.* 60, 549–576. doi: 10.1146/annurev.psych.58.110405.085530

Greenwald, A. G., and Banaji, M. R. (1995). Implicit social cognition: attitudes, self-esteem, and stereotypes. *Psychol. Rev.* 102, 4–27. doi: 10.1037/0033-295X.102.1.4

Hale, B. D., and Whitehouse, A. (1998). The effects of imagery manipulated appraisal on intensity and direction of competitive anxiety. *Sport Psychol.* 12, 40–51. doi: 10.1123/tsp.12.1.40

Hayes, A. F. (2013). *Methodology in the Social Sciences. Introduction to mediation, moderation and conditional process analysis: A regression based approach.* New York, NY: The Guilford Press.

Hayes, A. F., Montoya, A. K., and Rockwood, N. J. (2017). The analysis of mechanisms and their contingencies: PROCESS versus structural equation modeling. *Austr. Mark. J.* 25, 76–81. doi: 10.1016/j.ausmj.2017.02.001

Hu, L., and Bentler, P. M. (1998). Fit indices in covariance structure modelling: sensitivity to underparameterized model misspecifications. *Psychol. Method* 4, 424–453. doi: 10.1037//1082-989X.3.4.424

Jones, G., and Swain, A. B. J. (1992). Intensity and direction dimensions of competitive state anxiety and relationships with competitiveness. *Percept. Motor Skills* 74, 467–472. doi: 10.2466/pms.1992.74.2.467

Jones, M., Meijen, C., McCarthy, P. J., and Sheffield, D. (2009). A theory of challenge and threat states in athletes. *Int. Rev. Sport Exerc. Psychol.* 2, 161–180. doi: 10.1080/17509840902829331

Jones, M. V., and Uphill, M. (2012). "Emotion in sport: antecedents and performance consequences," in *Coping and Emotion in Sport*, eds J. Thatcher, M. V. Jones, and D. Lavallee, (London: Routledge), 33–61. doi: 10.4324/9780203852293_chapter_2

Lazarus, R. S. (1989). "Cognition and emotion from the RET viewpoint," in *Inside Rational-Emotive Therapy*, eds M. E. Bernard, and R. DiGiuseppe, (San Diego, CA: Academic Press), 47–68.

Lazarus, R. S. (1991). *Emotion and Adaptation*. New York, NY: Oxford University Press.

Lazarus, R. S. (1999). *Stress and Emotion. A New Synthesis*. New York, NY: Springer.

Lazarus, R. S. (2000). How emotions influence performance in competitive sports. *Sport Psychol.* 14, 229–252. doi: 10.1123/tsp.14.3.229

Lazarus, R. S., and Folkman, S. (1984). *Stress, Appraisal, and Coping*. New York, NY: Springer.

LeDoux, J. (1998). *The Emotional Brain*. New York, NY: Simon & Schuster.

Lerner, J. S., and Keltner, D. (2000). Beyond valence: toward a model of emotion-specific influences on judgment and choice. *Cogn. Emot.* 14, 473–493. doi: 10.1080/026999300402763

Martens, R., Burton, D., Vealey, R. S., Bump, L. A., and Smith, D. E. (1990). "Development and validation of the competitive state anxiety inventory-2," in *Competitive Anxiety in Sport*, eds R. Martens, R. D. Vealey, and D. Burton, (Champaign, IL: Human Kinetics), 117–118.

Maultsby, M. (1971). Rational emotive imagery. *Ration. Liv.* 6, 24–27.

Mellalieu, S. D., Hanton, S., and Fletcher, D. (2006). "A competitive anxiety review: recent directions in sport psychology research," in *Literature Reviews in Sport Psychology*, eds S. Hanton, and S. D. Mellalieu, (Hauppage, NY: Nova Science), 1–45.

Mellalieu, S. D., Hanton, S., and Thomas, O. (2009). The effects of a motivational general-arousal imagery intervention upon preperformance symptoms in male rugby union players. *Psychol. Sport Exerc.* 10, 175–185. doi: 10.1016/j.psychsport.2008.07.003

Monteiro, D., Teixeira, D. S., Travassos, B., Duarte-Mendes, P., Moutão, J., Machado, S., et al. (2018). Perceived effort in football athletes: the role of achievement goal theory and self-determination theory. *Front. Psychol.* 9:15–75. doi: 10.3389/fpsyg.2018.01575

Moore, L. J., Vine, S. J., Wilson, M. R., and Freeman, P. (2012). The effect of challenge and threat states on performance: an examination of potential mechanisms. *Psychophysiology* 49, 1417–1425. doi: 10.1111/j.1469-8986.2012.01449.x

Neil, R., Hanton, S., Mellalieu, S. D., and Fletcher, D. (2011). Competition stress and emotions in sport performers: the role of further appraisals. *Psychol. Sport Exerc.* 12, 460–470. doi: 10.1016/j.psychsport.2011.02.001

Nevill, A. (1997). Why will the analysis of performance variables recorded on a ratio scale will invariably benefit from log transformation. *J. Sport Sci.* 15, 457–458.

Orr, J. M., Sackett, P. R., and DuBois, C. L. Z. (1991). Outlier detection and treatment in I/O psychology: a survey of researcher beliefs and an empirical illustration. *Pers. Psychol.* 44, 473–486. doi: 10.1111/j.1744-6570.1991.tb02401.x

Padesky, C. A., and Beck, A. T. (2003). Science and philosophy: comparison of cognitive therapy and rational emotive behaviour therapy. *J. Cogn. Psychother.* 17, 211–224. doi: 10.1891/jcop.17.3.211.52536

Paunonen, S. V., and LeBel, E. P. (2012). Socially desirable responding and its elusive effects on the validity of personality assessments. *J. Pers. Soc. Psychol.* 103, 158–175. doi: 10.1037/a0028165

Quested, E., Bosch, J. A., Burns, V. E., Cumming, J., Ntoumanis, N., and Duda, J. L. (2011). Basic psychological need satisfaction, stress-related appraisals, and dancer's cortisol and anxiety responses. *J. Sport Exerc. Psychol.* 33, 828–846. doi: 10.1123/jsep.33.6.828

Quigley, K. S., Barrett, L. F., and Weinstein, S. (2002). Cardiovascular patterns associated with threat and challenge appraisals: individual responses across time. *Psychophysiology* 39, 1–11. doi: 10.1017/S0048577201393046

Quinton, M. L., Cumming, J., and Williams, S. E. (2018). Investigating the mediating role of positive and negative mastery imagery ability. *Pychol. Sport Exerc.* 35, 1–9. doi: 10.1016/j.psychsport.2017.10.011

Rossato, C. J. L., Uphill, M. A., Swain, J., and Coleman, D. A. (2016). The development and preliminary validation of the challenge and threat in sport (CAT-Sport) scale. *Int. J. Sport Exerc. Psychol.* 14, 1–14. doi: 10.1080/1612197X.2016.1182571

Schneider, T. R. (2008). Evaluations of stressful transactions: what's in an appraisal? *Stress Health* 24, 151–158. doi: 10.1002/smi.1176

Skinner, N., and Brewer, N. (2002). The dynamics of threat and challenge appraisals prior to stressful achievement events. *J. Pers. Soc. Psychol.* 83, 678–692. doi: 10.1037/0022-3514.83.3.678

Skinner, N., and Brewer, N. (2004). Adaptive approaches to competition: challenge appraisals and positive emotion. *J. Sport Exerc. Psychol.* 26, 283–305. doi: 10.1123/jsep.26.2.283

Slaughter, S., Selder, D., and Patterson, P. (1994). "Gender differences in competitive state anxiety prior to and during competition," in *Proceedings of the 10th Commonwealth and International Scientific Congress: Access to Active Living*, eds F. I. Bell, and G. H. Van Gyn, (Melbourne: Victoria University), 393–398.

Smith, A. C., and Lazarus, R. (1993). Appraisal components, core relational theme, and the emotions. *Cogn. Emot.* 7, 233–269. doi: 10.1080/02699939308409189

Smith, M. (2011). *Research Methods in Accounting*, 2nd Edn. London: Sage.

Still, A. (2001). Marginalisation is not unbearable. Is it even undesirable? *J. Ration. Emot. Cogn. Behav. Ther.* 19, 55–66. doi: 10.1023/A:1007847300779

Swain, A., and Jones, G. (1992). Relationships between sport achievement orientation and competitive state anxiety. *Sport Psychol.* 6, 42–54. doi: 10.1123/tsp.6.1.42

Szentagotai, A., and Jones, J. (2010). "The behavioral consequences of irrational beliefs," in *Rational and Irrational Beliefs: Research, Theory, and Clinical Practice*, eds D. David, S. J. Lynn, and A. Ellis, (New York, NY: Oxford University Press), 75–97.

Tabachnick, B. G., and Fidell, L. S. (2007). *Using Multivariate Statistics*, 5th Edn. New York, NY: Allyn and Bacon.

Turner, M. J. (2016). Rational emotive behavior therapy (REBT), irrational and rational beliefs, and the mental health of athletes. *Front. Psychol.* 7:14–23. doi: 10.3389/fpsyg.2016.01423

Turner, M. J., and Allen, M. (2018). Confirmatory factor analysis of the irrational performance beliefs inventory (iPBI) in a sample of amateur and semi-professional athletes. *Psychol. Sport Exerc.* 35, 126–130. doi: 10.1016/j.psychsport.2017.11.017

Turner, M. J., Allen, M. S., Slater, M. J., Barker, J. B., Woodcock, C., Harwood, C. G., et al. (2018). The development and initial validation of the irrational performance beliefs inventory (iPBI). *Eur. J. Psychol. Assess.* 34, 174–180. doi: 10.1027/1015-5759/a000314

Turner, M. J., Aspin, G., and Gillman, J. (2019a). Maladaptive schemas as a potential mechanism through which irrational beliefs relate to psychological distress in athletes. *Psychol. Sport Exerc.* 44, 9–16. doi: 10.1016/j.psychsport.2019.04.015

Turner, M. J., Carrington, S., and Miller, A. (2019b). Psychological distress across sport participation groups: the mediating effects of secondary irrational beliefs on the relationship between primary irrational beliefs and symptoms of anxiety, anger, and depression. *J. Clin. Sport Psychol.* 12, 1–38. doi: 10.1123/jcsp.2017-0014

Turner, M. J., and Barker, J. B. (2013). Examining the efficacy of rational-emotive behavior therapy (REBT) on irrational beliefs and anxiety in elite youth cricketers. *J. Appl. Sport Psychol.* 25, 131–147. doi: 10.1080/10413200.2011.574311

Turner, M. J., and Bennett, R. (2018). *Rational Emotive Behavior Therapy in Sport and Exercise*. New York, NY: Routledge.

Turner, M. J., Ewen, D., and Barker, J. B. (2018a). An idiographic single-case study examining the use of rational emotive behavior therapy (REBT) with three amateur golfers to alleviate social anxiety. *J. Appl. Sport Psychol.* 0, 1–19. doi: 10.1080/10413200.2018.1496186

Turner, M. J., Kirkman, L., and Wood, A. G. (2018b). Teeing up for success: the effects of rational and irrational self-talk on the putting performance of amateur golfers. *Psychol. Sport Exerc.* 38, 148–153. doi: 10.1016/j.psychsport.2018.06.012

Turner, M. J., and Moore, M. (2015). Irrational beliefs predict increased emotional and physical exhaustion in Gaelic football athletes. *Int. J. Sport Psychol.* 47, 187–199. doi: 10.7352/IJSP2016.47.187

Vadocz, E. A., Hall, C. R., and Moritz, S. E. (1997). The relationship between competitive anxiety and imagery use. *J. Appl. Sport Psychol.* 9, 241–253. doi: 10.1080/10413209708406485

Vandenbergh, R. J., and Lance, C. E. (2000). A review and synthesis of the measurement invariance literature: suggestions, practices and recommendations for organisational research. *Organ. Res. Methods* 3, 4–70. doi: 10.1177/109442810031002

Vine, S. J., Moore, L. J., and Wilson, M. R. (2016). An integrative framework of stress, attention, and visuomotor performance. *Front. Psychol.* 7:1–10. doi: 10.3389/fpsyg.2016.01671

Visla, A., Fluckiger, C., Grosse Holtforth, M., and David, D. (2016). Irrational beliefs and psychological distress: a meta-analysis. *Psychother. Psychosomat.* 85, 8–15. doi: 10.1159/000441231

Watson, D., and Clark, L. A. (1997). Measurement and mismeasurement of mood: recurrent and emergent issues. *J. Pers. Assess.* 68, 267–296. doi: 10.1207/s15327752jpa6802_4

Watson, D., Clark, L. A., and Tellegen, A. (1988). Development and validation of brief measures of positive and negative affect: the PANAS scales. *J. Pers. Soc. Psychol.* 54, 1063–1070. doi: 10.1037/0022-3514.54.6.1063

Watson, D., and Tellegen, A. (1985). Toward a consensual structure of mood. *Psychol. Bull.* 98, 219–235. doi: 10.1037/0033-2909.98.2.219

Williams, S. E., and Cumming, J. (2012). Challenge vs. threat imagery: investigating the effect of using imagery to manipulate cognitive appraisal of a dart throwing task. *Sport Exerc. Psychol. Rev.* 8, 4–21.

Williams, S. E., Cumming, J., and Balanos, G. M. (2010). The use of imagery to manipulate challenge and threat appraisals in athletes. *J. Sport Exerc. Psychol.* 32, 339–358. doi: 10.1123/jsep.32.3.339

Wilson, M. R., Wood, G., and Vine, S. J. (2009). Anxiety, attentional control, and performance impairment in penalty kicks. *J. Sport Exerc. Psychol.* 31, 761–775. doi: 10.1123/jsep.31.6.761

Ziegler, D. J. (2001). The possible place of cognitive appraisal in the ABC model underlying rational emotive behavior therapy. *J. Ration. Emot. Cogn. Behav. Ther.* 19, 137–152. doi: 10.1023/A:1011172915691

20

A Path Analysis of Adolescent Athletes' Perceived Stress Reactivity, Competition Appraisals, Emotions, Coping, and Performance Satisfaction

Darren M. Britton[1]*, Emma J. Kavanagh[2] and Remco C. J. Polman[3]*

[1] School of Sport, Health, and Social Sciences, Solent University, Southampton, United Kingdom, [2] Department of Sport & Physical Activity, Bournemouth University, Bournemouth, United Kingdom, [3] School of Exercise and Nutrition Sciences, Queensland University of Technology, Brisbane, QLD, Australia

***Correspondence:**
Darren M. Britton
darren.britton@solent.ac.uk
Remco C. J. Polman
remco.polman@qut.edu.au

This study examined a path analysis of adolescent athletes' individual differences in perceived stress reactivity, competition appraisals, emotions, coping, and performance satisfaction. The study aimed to extend an analysis by Nicholls et al. (2012) and further validate the use of the Perceived Stress Reactivity Scale for Adolescent Athletes (PSRS-AA). Adolescent athletes (N = 229, M age = 18.55, SD = 2.40) completed the PSRS-AA followed by a measure of competition appraisals less than 1 h before a competitive event. Within an hour after the competitive event, participants completed a retrospective assessment of emotions, coping strategies, and subjective performance. A path analysis revealed that perceived stress reactivity had direct and indirect effects on the appraisal of higher stressor intensity, lower perceived control, higher perceived threat, negative emotions, and maladaptive coping. Increased threat, positive and negative emotions, and maladaptive coping were associated with performance satisfaction. However, task-orientated coping was not associated with performance satisfaction. The present study enhances and refines the validity of the PSRS-AA for assessing adolescent athletes' perceived stress reactivity. Further strengths and weaknesses of the present study are discussed, along with recommendations for practitioners aiming to support adolescent athletes with high levels of stress reactivity.

Keywords: stress reactivity, stress appraisal, emotion, coping, adolescence, performance

INTRODUCTION

Stress is an ongoing transaction between an individual and their environment (Lazarus and Folkman, 1987). Environmental demands encountered by individuals are commonly referred to as "stressors" (Lazarus and Folkman, 1987; Fletcher et al., 2012). Stressors, depending upon how they are appraised, can produce numerous negative physical, psychological, and behavioral responses from an individual that can significantly affect athletic performance and satisfaction, particularly if individuals do not cope with them adaptively (Lazarus and Folkman, 1987; Lazarus, 2000; Fletcher et al., 2006; Nicholls et al., 2012; Laborde et al., 2016; Arnold et al., 2017). Specifically, based upon a path analysis performed by Nicholls et al. (2012), appraisals of challenge prior to sporting competition are associated with positive emotions, task orientated coping strategies, and increased performance satisfaction, while threat appraisals are associated with negative emotions, distraction and disengagement orientated coping strategies and decreased performance satisfaction.

Competitive sport can produce multiple stressors which young athletes must contend with (Nicholls et al., 2005; Reeves et al., 2009). These include stressors related directly and indirectly to their sports performance (Neil et al., 2011), and those associated with the physical, emotional, and social developments of adolescence (Compas et al., 2001; van Rens et al., 2016). An inability to cope with stressors has been cited as one of the main causes of both burnout and dropout in youth sport (Goodger et al., 2007; Crane and Temple, 2015), and one of the reasons why some talented youth athletes fail to achieve success (Holt and Dunn, 2004). Therefore, assisting young athletes in coping more adaptively with the stressors they experience during this challenging period is important not just for enhancing performance in active individuals, but also maintaining levels of participation and protecting health.

Adolescence is an important period where an individual's stress reactivity (SR), plus their repertoire of coping strategies, develops (Blakemore and Choudhury, 2006; Nicholls et al., 2009; Romeo, 2010). SR has been defined as an individual difference reflecting the broad variability in responses to stressors (Boyce and Ellis, 2005; Ellis et al., 2005; Schlotz et al., 2011a,b; Schlotz, 2013). Hyper-reactivity in adolescents has been associated with internalizing symptoms (negative emotionality, anxiety, and depression; Granger et al., 1994; Allwood et al., 2011; Marceau et al., 2012; Lopez-Duran et al., 2015).

Given the large number of stressors adolescent athletes face (Nicholls et al., 2005; Reeves et al., 2009), one's level of SR would be a significant risk factor to youth athletes, increasing or decreasing the likelihood of experiencing more adverse reactions to environmental demands. More intense stress reactions in response to these demands would likely be harder to cope with, thus increasing the potential for burnout and dropout from sport. Furthermore, exposure to a large number of stressors during adolescence (sport-related or otherwise) is also likely to affect and influence one's level of SR (Romeo, 2010).

The development of SR is highly dependent on environmental influences during childhood and adolescence, particularly exposure to both adversity and support (Boyce and Ellis, 2005; Romeo, 2010). A recent meta-analysis has revealed how an increased exposure to adverse childhood experiences influences the development of maladaptive reactivity to stress (Hughes et al., 2017). However, exposure to a moderate level of adverse experiences among athletic populations have been associated with adaptive physiological responses under pressure (Moore et al., 2018).

Numerous individual differences and personal factors have been associated with the way in which athletes appraise and cope with stressors (see **Figure 1**; Kerdijk et al., 2016), including gender (Kaiseler et al., 2012b) the Big Five personality traits (Kaiseler et al., 2012a), mental toughness, (Kaiseler et al., 2009), and maturity (Nicholls et al., 2009, 2013, 2015). However, less research has focussed upon individual differences in adolescent athletes' SR.

Adolescent athletes' perceived SR has been associated with a number of outcomes, including greater perceived strain (negative symptoms associated with stress) and lesser hedonic well-being (i.e., life satisfaction; Britton et al., 2017). Self-report measures of perceived SR (such as the PSRS-AA; Britton et al., 2017) provide a less costly, less invasive, and more ecologically valid alternative to lab-based measures of SR, such as cortisol sampling. Moreover, assessing SR physiologically during athletic performance runs the risk of being unable to distinguish between responses to physical demands of competition and psychological demands (Polman et al., 2010).

The perceived influence of SR on the performance of adolescent athletes, via the process of appraisal and coping, is currently not known (Britton et al., 2017). Further research is also required to examine the relationship between appraisals, emotions, coping, and performance satisfaction among adolescents, by replicating the path analysis performed by Nicholls et al. (2012). This is significant given that adolescents are known to appraise and cope with stressors differently to adults (Compas et al., 2001).

THE PRESENT STUDY

The purpose of this study was to extend Nicholls et al.'s (2012) path analysis in two key ways: (1) To examine the direct and indirect effects of Perceived Stress Reactivity (PSR) as a dispositional variable on the stress, emotion, and coping process. (2) To examine the relationships between competition appraisals, emotions, coping and performance satisfaction within a sample of exclusively adolescent athletes, rather than adults. The hypothesized model is illustrated in **Figure 2**, with PSR the main predictor of the model. Arrows indicate a direct effect, plus signs infer a positive relationship, and minus signs a negative relationship.

A number of hypotheses were made regarding the different variables within the model: (1) PSR would have a direct effect on competition appraisal. In addition, it was predicted that PSR would positively predict stressor intensity (primary appraisal), and negatively predict perceived control (secondary appraisal). This was due to previous research associating adolescent athletes' PSR with personality traits associated with greater stressor intensity and perceived lower control (Kaiseler et al., 2012a; Britton et al., 2017).

(2) Perceived Stress Reactivity would have both direct and indirect effects (via competition appraisals) on relational meaning. Specifically, PSR would positively predict perceived threat, and negatively predict perceived challenge. This is because PSR has been associated with increased threat appraisals in previous research (Schlotz et al., 2011a). It was also predicted that participants would make threat appraisals when they appraised themselves as having little perceived control, and challenge appraisals when appraising high perceived control, replicating Nicholls et al.'s (2012) findings.

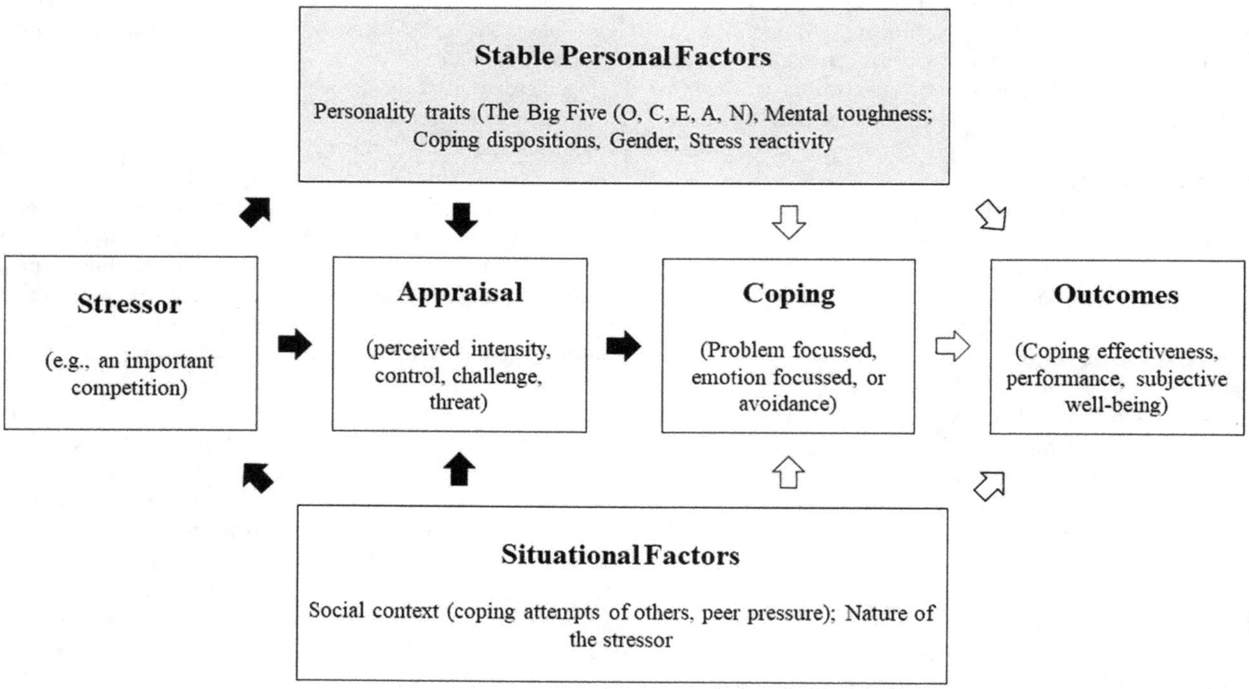

FIGURE 1 | Conceptual framework illustrating how stable and situational factors directly and indirectly influence the stress and coping response (Kerdijk et al., 2016). Black arrows represent direct effects, while white arrows indicate indirect effects. (Adapted with permission granted from corresponding author R. Polman).

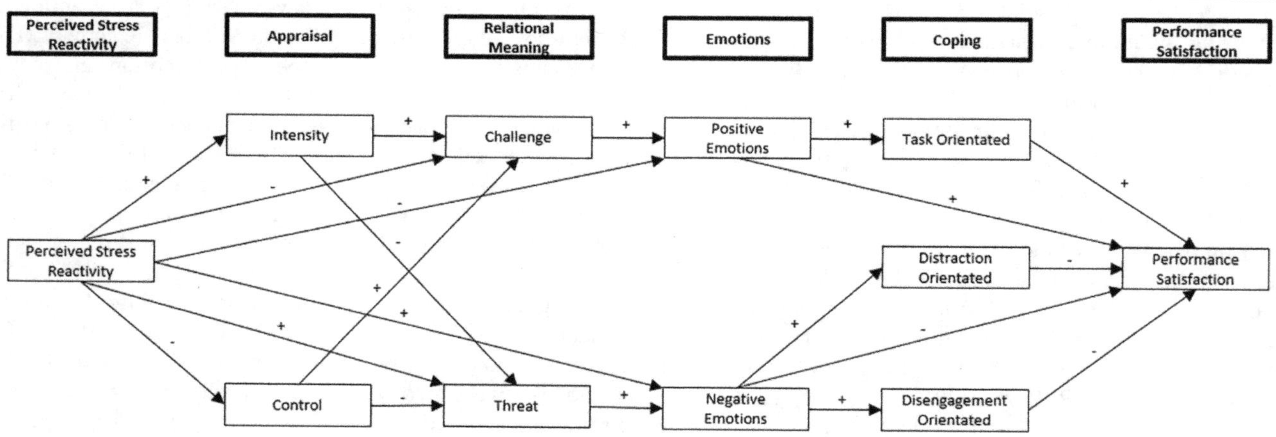

FIGURE 2 | Initial hypothesized model for the relationships between PSR, competition appraisals, relational meanings, emotions, coping, and performance satisfaction.

(3) Perceived Stress Reactivity would have both direct and indirect effects (via competition appraisal and relational meaning) on emotion. It was predicted that PSR would positively predict negative emotion, and negatively predict positive emotion. This is because SR has been associated with negative emotionality in adolescents, and PSR has been associated with greater perceived strain overtime in adolescent athletes (Marceau et al., 2012; Britton et al., 2017). It was also predicted that threat appraisals would be associated with greater negative emotions, and challenge appraisals with positive emotions (Nicholls et al., 2012).

(4) Perceived Stress Reactivity would have an indirect effect on coping via competition appraisals, relational meaning, and emotion. PSR would positively affect disengagement and distraction orientated coping, and negatively affect task orientated coping. This was predicted because adolescent athletes' PSR has been related to personality traits associated with coping, namely high levels of PSR with neuroticism, and

low levels with emotional stability (Kaiseler et al., 2012a; Britton et al., 2017). It was also predicted that positive emotions would predict task-orientated coping, and negative emotions would predict both distraction and disengagement-orientated coping (Nicholls et al., 2012).

(5) Perceived Stress Reactivity would have a negative indirect effect on subjective performance via competition appraisals, relational meaning, emotion, and coping. Furthermore, it was predicted that emotion would have a direct and indirect effect (via coping) on subjective performance, with positive emotion predicting increased performance satisfaction and negative emotion decreased performance satisfaction. A direct effect of coping on subjective performance satisfaction was predicted, as both are affective variables, and likely to correlate irrespective of coping (Nicholls et al., 2012). Finally, coping would have a direct effect on subjective performance, with task-orientated coping predicting increased performance satisfaction, and both distraction and disengagement-orientated coping predicting decreased performance satisfaction.

No predictions were made regarding potential negative relationships between, for example, positive emotions and disengagement coping, or negative emotions and task-orientated coping, in order to avoid reducing the power of the model (Byrne, 2016).

MATERIALS AND METHODS

Participants

Participants were 229 adolescent athletes (male n = 150; female n = 79; M age = 18.55, SD = 2.40) who competed at international/national (n = 8), regional (n = 11), county/academy (n = 85), club (n = 93), or school/university (n = 32) levels in the United Kingdom. Participants were recruited opportunistically from numerous sports clubs, academies, schools, and universities. They needed to be participating in competitive sport and between the ages of 12 and 22. The sample consisted of 167 adolescents from team sports (including rugby, football, and cricket) and 62 from individual sports (including golf, karate, and badminton). All participants received an information sheet and were asked to sign a consent form prior to the study. For all participants under the age of 16, parents or guardians were also sent an information sheet and asked to provide written consent.

Materials and Methods

PSR

The PSRS-AA (Britton et al., 2017) was used to assess individual differences in PSR. The PSRS-AA consists 23 items over five subscales assessing reactivity to different domains: reactivity to social evaluation ("When I have to perform in front of other people. . ."), reactivity to social conflict ("When I have arguments with team-mates and coaches. . ."), reactivity to failure ("When I fail at something. . ."), reactivity to work overload ("When all my different training sessions and matches build up and become hard to manage. . ."), and prolonged reactivity ("When I want to relax after a hard training session or match. . ."). The aggregate score from these five subscales create an overall score of total reactivity. Each item is assessed using three descriptive multiple-choice options of differing levels of reactivity in response to a proposed stressful situation (e.g., When I have little time to prepare for a match: (a). I usually stay calm, (b). I usually feel uneasy, (c). I usually get quite unsettled). The answers reflecting lowest reactivity are scored zero, while the answers reflecting highest reactivity are scored with two. Intermediate answers are scored one. Subscales scores are calculated via the mean, with each mean subscale score being summed to calculate the aggregate measure of total reactivity. Britton et al. (2017) confirmed the hierarchal structure of the adapted scale using a second order model. The PSRS-AA's subscales demonstrate only marginal reliability (α = 0.62 –0.73). However, the overall aggregate score of total reactivity had good reliability (α = 0.87).

Competition Appraisals and Relational Meanings

A version of the "stress thermometer" was used to assess primary appraisal in the form of perceived stressor intensity prior to competition (Kowalski and Crocker, 2001), with a 10 cm visual analog scale (VAS) measuring from 0 (not at all stressful) to (extremely stressful) 100. The stress thermometer has previously demonstrated normal distribution within a sample of adolescent athletes and has been utilized in many studies measuring athletes' stressor appraisals (Kowalski and Crocker, 2001; Kaiseler et al., 2012a). In order to maintain similarity with the measure of primary appraisal, a 10-cm VAS was also used to measure secondary appraisal in the form of perceived overall control prior to competition (Kaiseler et al., 2012a), measuring from 0 (no control) to 100 (total control). To maintain further similarity and consistency with the measure of primary and secondary appraisal, levels of both challenge and threat experienced prior to competition were also measured with separate VASs, measuring from 0 (not at all a threat; not at all a challenge) to 100 (very much a threat; very much a challenge). Nicholls et al.'s (2012) original path analysis utilized the 28 item Stress Appraisal Measure (Peacock and Wong, 1990). However, it was decided that a briefer method of assessing appraisals was more suitable for the current study, in order not to burden adolescents with copious items prior to competing, especially given the addition of the 23 item PSRS-AA within this battery of tests, and thus to allow for the completion of the assessments as close to the beginning of competition as possible. The use of VAS are increasingly adopted in order to assess athletes' appraisals of stressors and relational meaning (Turner et al., 2012; Kaiseler et al., 2012a,b; Turner et al., 2014).

Emotions

The Sport Emotion Questionnaire (SEQ; Jones et al., 2005) was used to retrospectively assess the emotions experienced during competition. The SEQ assesses five emotions grouped into two higher order dimensions: positive emotions (excitement and happiness) and negative emotions (anxiety, dejection, and anger). The scale contains 22 items scored on a 5-point Likert scale from 0 = "not at all" to 4 = "extremely." The SEQ has been reported to have excellent reliability for its scales, with Cronbach's alpha ranging from 0.81 to 0.90 (Jones et al., 2005).

Coping

The Coping Inventory for Competitive Sport (CICS; Gaudreau and Blondin, 2002) was used to retrospectively assess how participants coped during competition. The CICS measures ten coping subscales grouped into three coping dimensions: task-orientated coping (thought control, mental imagery, relaxation, effort expenditure, logical analysis, and support seeking), distraction-orientated coping (distancing and mental distraction), and disengagement-coping (disengagement and venting). Nine of the subscales feature four items, while one features three items. The scale uses a 5-point Likert scale to assess the extent to which the coping strategy described corresponds with what the athlete did during competition, ranging from 1 = "does not correspond at all" to 5 = "corresponds very strongly." The CICS's measure of three coping dimensions feature adequate to good levels of reliability (α = 0.73 to 0.87) and has been utilized with adolescent athlete populations (Nicholls et al., 2009).

The transactional model of stress and coping typically refers to three different dimensions of coping: Problem-focussed (coping designed to eliminate a source of stress), emotion-focussed (coping which addresses the emotional distress caused by a stressor), and avoidance (physically or mentally withdrawing from a stressor, Lazarus and Folkman, 1987). However, this study chose to use Gaudreau and Blondin's (2002) task, distraction, and disengagement-orientated dimensions instead for two reasons. Firstly, this was the measure used by Nicholls et al. (2012) which this study aimed to extend. Secondly, the CICS assesses coping within the specific context of sports performance, rather than measures of Lazarus and Folkman's dimensions, which refer to coping in much broader contexts. Therefore, it was concluded that the CICS was the most appropriate measure for assessing coping within this context.

Performance Satisfaction

Participants subjectively rated how satisfied they were with their performance on a VAS ranging from 0 ("not at all satisfied") to 100 ("totally satisfied"; Pensgaard and Duda, 2003). This subjective measure of performance was used instead of an objective measure in order to compare performance across a range of different sports and positions within sports (Terry, 1995; Males and Kerr, 1996). Furthermore, subjective satisfaction provides a more sensitive measure of performance, as it can be compared between participants despite differences in environmental factors such as playing conditions, weather, or opponents' skill levels (Nicholls et al., 2012).

Procedure

University ethics board approval was obtained prior to data collection. Participants firstly completed the PSRS-AA prior to competition. The VAS measures of competition appraisals and relational meaning were then completed less than 1 h before competing at a time and place agreed with by the researcher, participant, and coach if one was present. The SEQ, CICS and VAS measure of performance satisfaction was completed less than 1 h after competing also at an agreed time.

Data Analysis

The proposed path analysis containing PSR, competition appraisals, relational meanings, emotions, coping, and performance satisfaction was tested in SPSS Amos (v.24) using maximum likelihood estimation. This allows for the simultaneous examination of direct and indirect effect paths throughout the model, while also testing the overall fit of the data to the hypothesized model (Byrne, 2016). For structural equation models, 200 cases are considered a minimum requirement as a rule of thumb (Kline, 1998). The following variables were originally entered: PSR, stressor intensity, perceived control, threat, challenge, negative emotions, positive emotions, task-orientated coping, distraction-orientated coping, disengagement-orientated coping, and performance satisfaction (see **Figure 2**). The error terms of distraction and disengagement-orientated coping were allowed to co-vary with one another, as they were anticipated to correlate. No other co-variances between shared antecedents were drawn, as no more correlations were predicted based on existing theory. Bivariate correlations were calculated in order to initially analyze the relationships between the variables entered into the model.

A number of indices were used to assess overall model fit. The chi-square statistic assesses the magnitude of discrepancy between the data sample and the co-variance matrix predicted by the model (Hu and Bentler, 1999). However, chi-square is notably sensitive to sample size. Therefore, the chi-square/degrees of freedom ratio (CMIN/DF) was used in order to minimize the effect of sample size on determining model fit (Hooper et al., 2008). A threshold of 3 was used to indicate an acceptable model fit (Kline, 1998). The comparative fit index (CFI) was assessed in order to indicate the extent to which the theoretical model better fitted the data in comparison to a base model where all constructs are constrained to be correlated with one another, with greater than or equal to 0.95 indicating good model fit, and 0.90 indicating adequate fit (Hu and Bentler, 1999; Hooper et al., 2008). Root mean square error of approximation (RMSEA) was calculated in order to provide an estimate of the average absolute difference between estimated model covariances and the observed covariances, with less than 0.06 indicating good model fit (Hu and Bentler, 1999; Hooper et al., 2008). A p-value testing the null hypothesis (PCLOSE) of the RMSEA was also assessed, with a non-significant result greater than 0.05 required to reject the null.

Standardized regression (beta) weights were used to examine the size and significance of the direct effects of PSR specified within the model (Byrne, 2016). To examine the indirect effects of PSR through the model, the probability associated with the standardized indirect effects and their respective confidence intervals (90%) were estimated using a bias-corrected confidence interval bootstrap test (using 500 samples; Byrne, 2016).

Data Preparation

Prior to conducting the path analysis, data were screened for outliers and normality. Univariate normality was assessed using skewness and kurtosis values, while multivariate normality was examined using Malhalanobis distances. Seven cases were removed from the analyses due to the presence of multivariate outliers. To test the validity of the questionnaire measures used, confirmatory factor analyses (CFA) using SPSS Amos (v.24) were performed on the SEQ and the CICS. This was to test the fit of the scales and subscales to their proposed higher order structures, so modifications (such as item co-variances or removals) could be made to the scales if required. This would confirm validity of the scale for use with the sample population. The same goodness of fit indices were used.

The positive emotion dimension of the SEQ provided good model fit once two co-variances were drawn between the error terms of items 5 and 10, and items 10 and 20 on the happiness subscale (CMIN/DF = 1.73; CFI = 0.99; RMSEA = 0.06; PCLOSE = 0.34). The negative emotion dimension provided good model fit once two co-variances were drawn between the error terms of items 2 and 7 on the dejection subscale and 9 and 19 on the anger subscale, and item 1 was removed from the anxiety subscale due to multiple high modification indices with items on other subscales (CMIN/DF = 1.95; CFI = 0.98; RMSEA = 0.06; PCLOSE = 0.11). The combined model for the whole questionnaire, however, produced questionable model fit (CMIN/DF = 1.98; CFI = 0.95; RMSEA = 0.07; PCLOSE = 0.01). This may have been due to large covariances between the anxiety subscale and happiness subscale from the positive dimension. Mean scores for the subscales and dimensions of the SEQ were then calculated based upon these modifications.

The task-orientated dimension of the CICS provided adequate model fit after co-variances were drawn between the error terms of items 18 and 28 on the relaxation subscale, and items 9 and 29 on the logical analysis subscale (CMIN/DF = 1.73; CFI = 0.91; RMSEA = 0.06; PCLOSE = 0.12). The distraction subscale provided good model fit once item 3 was removed from the social withdrawal subscale due to large co-variances with items on the mental distraction subscale (CMIN/DF = 1.79; CFI = 0.96; RMSEA = 0.06; PCLOSE = 0.31). The disengagement subscale provided adequate model fit once items 22 and 32 were removed from the venting subscale due to large co-variances with the disengagement subscale (CMIN/DF = 2.99; CFI = 0.97; RMSEA = 0.09; PCLOSE = 0.04). However, no further modifications were made, as CFI indicated good model fit. The three dimensions combined into one model also provided questionable model fit, with no indications that further modifications would improve the model (CMIN/DF = 1.85; CFI = 0.84; RMSEA = 0.06; PCLOSE = 0.00). However, given that the individual dimensions provided good to adequate model fits, analysis proceeded. Mean scores for the subscales and dimensions of the CICS were then calculated based upon these modifications.

TABLE 1 | Mean and standard deviations for variables used in model and Cronbach's alpha coefficients.

Scales	Mean	SD	α
Prolonged Reactivity	0.42	0.36	0.48
Reactivity to Work Overload	0.45	0.38	0.57
Reactivity to Social Conflict	0.62	0.40	0.68
Reactivity to Failure	0.93	0.40	0.68
Reactivity to Social Evaluation	0.57	0.42	0.66
Total Reactivity	3.01	1.45	0.85
Intensity	42.25	23.63	
Control	61.57	23.52	
Challenge	61.46	20.96	
Threat	35.27	22.70	
Excitement	2.61	0.91	0.81
Happiness	2.63	1.09	0.89
Positive emotions	2.62	0.92	0.90
Anxiety	1.53	0.97	0.89
Dejection	1.15	0.88	0.88
Anger	1.58	0.94	0.87
Negative emotions	1.42	0.77	0.90
Thought control	2.95	0.87	0.68
Mental imagery	2.75	0.84	0.68
Relaxation	2.33	0.98	0.84
Effort	3.96	0.72	0.75
Logical analysis	2.76	0.84	0.68
Seeking support	2.21	0.91	0.76
Task-orientated coping	2.83	0.61	0.89
Social withdrawal	1.79	0.70	0.55
Mental distraction	1.60	0.62	0.67
Distraction orientated coping	1.70	0.57	0.73
Venting	2.47	1.21	0.72
Disengagement	1.44	0.60	0.76
Disengagement orientated coping	1.96	0.73	0.68
Performance satisfaction	63.90	22.56	

RESULTS

Table 1 provides means, standard deviations, and Cronbach's alpha coefficients for all the variables entered in the model, including discrete emotions and coping strategies. **Table 2** provides Pearson's r correlations between all variables entered into the model. **Table 3** provides correlations between the discrete coping strategies measured by the CICS and performance satisfaction.

To examine the overall fit of all the data collected, the model shown in **Figure 2** was tested. The fit of the model produced inadequate model fit (CMIN/DF = 4.29; CFI = 0.79; RMSEA = 0.12; PCLOSE < 0.01). Based upon modification indices and correlations within the data set, modifications were made to the model in the form of additional paths. These modifications were only made if they were theoretically sound and did not fundamentally change the nature of the path (Nicholls et al., 2012). An additional path was drawn from control to both negative emotions, and from control to task-orientated coping, as both demonstrated high modification indices, and existing theory would suggest that secondary appraisal of control and coping resources has the potential to directly influence the experience of negative emotions and the use of adaptive coping strategies (Lazarus and Folkman, 1987; Lazarus, 1999; Fletcher et al., 2006).

The overall revised model, however, still produced inadequate fit (CMIN/DF = 3.96; CFI = 0.82; RMSEA = 0.12;

TABLE 2 | Pearson's *r* correlations between all variables entered into the model.

Scales	1	2	3	4	5	6	7	8	9	10
1. Total reactivity										
2. Intensity	0.34**									
3. Control	−0.23**	−0.15*								
4. Challenge	0.15*	0.52**	−0.04							
5. Threat	0.29**	0.54**	−0.07	0.47**						
6. Positive emotions	0.10	−0.02	0.10	0.02	−0.05					
7. Negative emotions	0.21**	0.24**	−0.21**	0.27**	0.21**	−0.04				
8. Task orientated coping	−0.04	−0.12	0.25**	0.05	0.01	0.42**	0.06			
9. Distraction orientated coping	0.08	0.00	0.07	0.07	0.04	0.08	0.18**	0.48**		
10. Disengagement orientated coping	0.26**	0.14*	0.00	0.09	0.15*	−0.02	0.40**	0.15*	0.29**	
11. Performance satisfaction	−0.06	0.12	0.22**	−0.07	−0.10	0.52**	−0.36**	0.15*	−0.16*	−0.29**

Note. *$p < 0.05$., ** $p < 0.01$.

TABLE 3 | Pearson's *r* correlations between discrete coping strategies and performance satisfaction.

Scales	1	2	3	4	5	6	7	8	9	10
1. Thought control										
2. Relaxation	0.49**									
3. Effort	0.33**	0.19**								
4. Logical analysis	0.52**	0.59**	0.33**							
5. Mental imagery	0.51**	0.50**	0.39**	0.66**						
6. Seeking support	0.25**	0.36**	0.20**	0.39**	0.38**					
7. Mental distraction	0.26**	0.23**	0.03	0.20**	0.30**	0.27**				
8. Social withdrawal	0.41**	0.48**	0.07	0.43**	0.36**	0.31**	0.49**			
9. Venting	0.24**	0.01	0.01	0.19**	0.15*	0.06	0.11	0.18**		
10. Disengagement	0.07	0.10	−0.24**	0.05	0.00	0.16*	0.31**	0.30**	0.23**	
11. Performance satisfaction	0.07	0.02	0.32**	0.10	0.20**	0.01	−0.10	−0.17*	−0.17*	−0.38**

Note. *$p < 0.05$, **$p < 0.01$.

PCLOSE < 0.01). **Figures 3.1, 3.2** both illustrate the final model, with separate figures for the "positive" and "negative" paths used for ease of illustration. The significance levels of each path coefficient are included. **Table 4** details the direct and indirect effects (plus bias corrected confidence intervals) for PSR and all other variables included in the final model.

DISCUSSION

In this study, a path analysis was used to examine adolescent athletes' PSR, competition appraisals and relational meanings prior to competition, emotions and coping strategies during competition, and subjective performance satisfaction. This was to explore the direct and indirect effects of PSR on the stress and coping process of adolescent athletes, plus to further extend the path analysis conducted by Nicholls et al. (2012). The revised models (**Figures 3.1, 3.2**) did not provide adequate model fit, which limits the overall conclusions which can be drawn from the model. However, there were several significant direct and indirect effects observed within the model relating to the a-priory predictions (see **Table 4**). These will be discussed in turn. The study extends the understanding of how perceived SR influences the stress, emotion, and coping process among adolescent athletes. The study also provides a further examination of stress appraisal and coping measures, and their validity among adolescent athlete populations.

Perceived Stress Reactivity demonstrated direct effects on competition appraisals of intensity and control, relational meanings of threat, and negative emotions. PSR also demonstrated indirect effects on threat, challenge, negative emotions, and maladaptive coping (distraction and disengagement-orientated coping). However, PSR failed to demonstrate effects (direct or indirect) on positive emotions, task-orientated coping, or performance satisfaction. Although the analyses shared some similarities with Nicholls et al. (2012), there were also a number of divergences. Overall, these findings provide new information on how PSR influences the stress and coping process, as well as how competition appraisals, emotions, and coping impact upon the performance satisfaction of adolescent athletes (see **Table 4**). In addition, findings suggest there are some differences in the stress and coping process in adolescents compared to adult athletes.

In relation to the first set of hypotheses, participants with higher levels of PSR were more likely to appraise the impending competition as more stressful, and to appraise themselves as having less control, and thus not have the resources to cope. This is consistent with previous research which has found individual

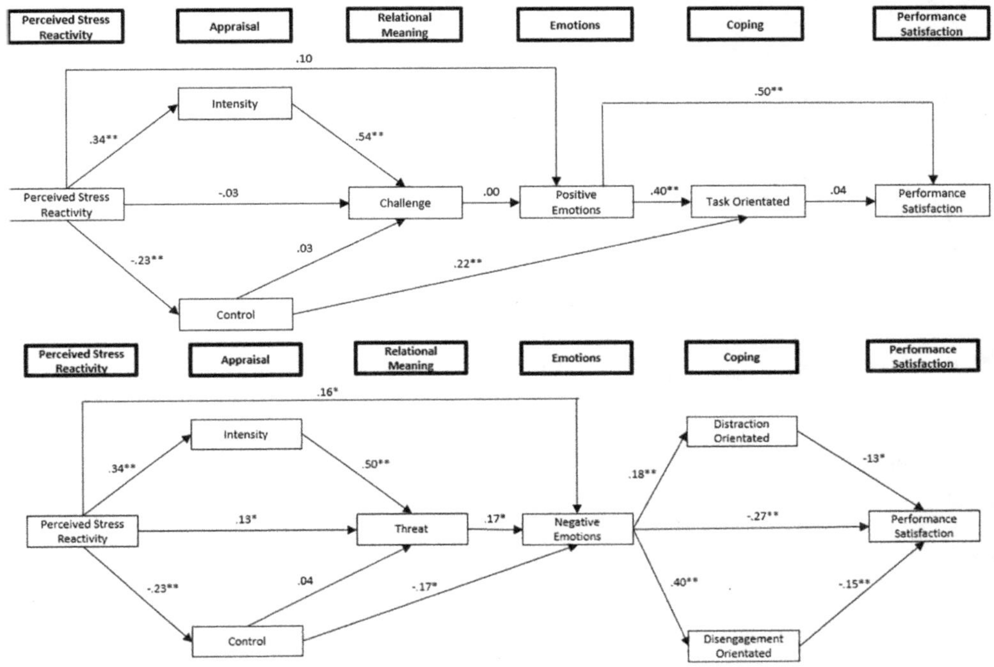

FIGURE 3 | Revised model of relationships between PSR, competition appraisals, challenge, positive emotions, task-orientated coping, and performance satisfaction. Revised model of relationships between PSR, competition appraisals, threat, negative emotions, distraction and disengagement orientated coping, and performance satisfaction.

differences (most notably neuroticism) to predict athletes' appraisals of stressor intensity and perceived control (Kaiseler et al., 2012a). These are among the strongest effects within the model, confirming that an adolescent athletes' perception of how reactive they are to stressors in general has a direct effect on how they cognitively appraise sporting competitions.

With regards to the second set of hypotheses, adolescent athletes with a higher level of PSR were more likely to form a relational meaning of threat in relation to the impending competition. This was partially due to their increased likelihood of scoring the stress relating to the impending competition as more intense. This is consistent with previous research which has associated measures of PSR with increased threat appraisals (Schlotz et al., 2011a). However, participants with higher levels of PSR were also more likely to appraise the impending competition as a challenge, via the increased appraisal of intensity. This suggests that appraisal is not dichotomous, and that athletic competition can be appraised with a level of challenge and threat at the same time. This supports previous research that has suggested that challenge and threat appraisals can co-occur (Lazarus, 1999). In this sample, it is possible that adolescent athletes with high levels of PSR were more likely to appraise competitions with greater personal relevance (primary appraisal), hence greater appraisals of both challenge and threat.

Control appraisals, however, did not influence the relational meaning of either threat or challenge. Such a finding does not support theory and previous empirical findings with adult populations that has associated secondary stressor appraisals with relational meanings of challenge and threat (Lazarus and Folkman, 1987; Fletcher et al., 2006; Nicholls et al., 2012). This might suggest that, for adolescent athletes, factors outside of their own perceived personal control of the situation, may account for the secondary appraisals that determine relational meanings of challenge or threat (e.g., perceived social support from others). In Nicholls et al.'s (2012) original model, the full 28 item SAM was used, which assesses not only controllability by the self, but also the perceived controllability of stressors by others. By using only a single item in this study, this may not have sufficiently captured the full nature of secondary appraisal, and how an adolescent athlete perceives the resources available to them, thus determining whether situations of high personal relevance and stressfulness are perceived as either challenges or threats.

Adolescent athletes who viewed themselves as having greater control prior to competition did experience fewer negative emotions and used more task-focussed coping strategies. This is consistent with previous empirical findings and theory, suggesting that if adolescent athletes were to perceive themselves as having a high level of control the impending competition, they would have significant resources available to cope and thus would likely experience less negative emotions and have a larger repertoire of task-focussed coping strategies (Lazarus and Folkman, 1987; Amiot et al., 2004; Fletcher et al., 2006; Neil et al., 2011; Nicholls et al., 2012).

In relation to the third set of hypotheses, adolescent athletes with higher levels of PSR were more likely to experience negative emotions during competition. This is explained directly by an

TABLE 4 | Direct and indirect effects of variables entered into the model.

Independent Variable	Dependent Variables	Direct	Indirect	
			Sum	90% CI
PSR	Intensity	0.34**		
	Control	−0.23**		
	Challenge	−0.03	0.18**	0.11.25
	Threat	0.13*	0.16**	0.10,0.23
	Positive Emotions	0.10	0.00	−0.02,0.02
	Negative Emotions	0.16*	0.09**	0.04,0.15
	Task-orientated		−0.01	−0.07,0.05
	Distraction-orientated		0.04**	0.01,0.08
	Disengagement-orientated		0.08**	0.03,0.12
	Performance satisfaction		−0.02	−0.09,0.05
Intensity	Challenge	0.54**		
	Threat	0.50**		
	Positive Emotions		0.00	−0.06,0.06
	Negative Emotions		0.08*	0.02,0.16
	Task-orientated		0.00	−0.03,0.02
	Distraction-orientated		0.01*	0.00,0.03
	Disengagement-orientated		0.03*	0.01,0.07
	Performance satisfaction		−0.03	−0.07,0.01
Control	Challenge	0.03		
	Threat	0.04		
	Positive Emotions		0.00	−0.00,0.00
	Negative Emotions	−0.17*	0.01	−0.01,0.02
	Task-orientated	0.22**	−0.00	−0.00,0.00
	Distraction-orientated		0.04*	0.01,0.08
	Disengagement-orientated		0.08*	0.03,0.12
	Performance satisfaction		−0.02*	−0.09,0.05
Challenge	Positive Emotions	0.00		
	Task-orientated		0.00	−0.04,0.05
	Performance satisfaction		0.00	−0.06,0.06
Threat	Negative Emotions	0.17*		
	Distraction-orientated		0.03*	0.01,0.06
	Disengagement-orientated		0.07*	0.02,0.12
	Performance satisfaction		−0.06*	−0.11, −0.01
Positive Emotions	Task-orientated	0.40**		
	Performance satisfaction	0.50**	0.02	−0.02,0.06
Negative Emotions	Distraction-orientated	0.18**		
	Disengagement-orientated	0.40**		
	Performance satisfaction	−0.27**	−0.08**	−0.14, −0.03
Task-orientated	Performance satisfaction	0.04		
Distraction-orientated	Performance satisfaction	−0.13*		
Disengagement-orientated	Performance satisfaction	−0.15**		

Note. *$p < 0.05$, **$p < 0.01$.

adolescent athletes PSR, and indirectly via cognitive appraisal. This supports previous research that has associated increased reactivity in adolescents with negative emotionality (Marceau et al., 2012). PSR, however, did not feature any direct or indirect effects on positive emotions. Like appraisal, negative and positive emotions can co-exist (Folkman, 1997; Polman and Borkoles, 2011). Adolescent athletes' experience of positive emotions is likely to be determined by other factors which we did not measure in the current study. With regards to appraisals predicting emotions, supporting previous findings, threat was positively associated with negative emotions (Lazarus, 2000; Nicholls et al., 2012). Similarly, decreased control also predicted negative emotions. However, challenge did not predict positive emotions as expected. As indicated previously, the sample characteristics (adolescent athletes) and the way appraisal was measured in the present study might explain this finding. The notion that positive emotions experienced by adolescent athletes are not predicted by any antecedents within the present study supports findings that the stress-coping process in adolescents is different compared to that of adults (Davis and Compas, 1986; Compas et al., 2001).

With regards to the fourth set of hypotheses, adolescent athletes with high levels of PSR were more likely to use coping strategies during competition that are considered maladaptive, via increased threat appraisals and negative emotions. This supports previous research which has observed an association between athletes' individual differences and maladaptive coping (e.g., Kaiseler et al., 2012a). However, no effects were observed between PSR and task-orientated coping. These findings point toward the notion that the PSR is more likely to predict the maladaptive aspects of high SR (more negative emotions, maladaptive coping) but that less SR is not automatically associated with adaptive outcomes (positive emotions, adaptive coping). However, although no relationship was found between PSR and adaptive coping, it is possible that low levels of PSR may be facilitative via other processes not observed within the model (e.g., via lower levels of negative emotion). Supporting previous findings (Nicholls et al., 2012; Laborde et al., 2016), positive emotions predicted the use of task-orientated coping, and negative emotions predicted both distraction and disengagement-orientated coping.

In relation to the fifth and final set of hypotheses, PSR was found to have no indirect effect on subjective performance satisfaction via the stress and coping process experienced prior to and during competition. This suggests that, in the short-term, high levels of PSR do not have an impact upon the subjective performance of adolescent athletes on the day of competition. However, this is not to say that PSR does not impact upon adolescent athletes' actual and subjective performance and well-being in the long-term. Youth athletes' PSR is associated with increased strain over a 30 day period and decreased life-satisfaction (Britton et al., 2017). Furthermore, athletes experience multiple organizational stressors, other than those in competition, which can impact upon performance (Mellalieu et al., 2009; Arnold et al., 2017). Therefore, PSR may influence the appraisal of other organizational stressors experienced by adolescent athletes (such as conflicts with team-mates or training) which may in turn impact upon emotions, coping, and performance in the long-term.

Similar to Nicholls et al. (2012), positive emotions in the adolescent athletes were directly associated with higher and negative emotions with lower levels of subjective performance satisfaction. This association is not unexpected because both are affective variables. At the dimensional level the use of distraction and disengagement coping significantly predicted lower levels of subjective performance satisfaction as expected. However, task-oriented coping was not directly associated with higher levels of performance satisfaction. The correlation matrix showed that the only task-oriented coping strategies associated with subjective performance were mental imagery and effort (see **Table 3**). This suggests that the majority of the task-orientated coping strategies proposed by Gaudreau and Blondin (2002) are not associated with increased performance. This is not consistent with adult samples which have found a much wider range of coping strategies from the CICS to predict performance satisfaction (see Nicholls et al., 2012). This suggests that adolescent athletes have a much smaller range of effective coping strategies compared to adults. The effectiveness of these strategies, and thus the effect on performance satisfaction, may be explained by maturational processes, as adolescent athletes' coping effectiveness has been shown to increase with emotional and social maturity (Nicholls et al., 2013, 2015).

Similar to Nicholls et al. (2012), negative emotions indirectly predicted subjective performance satisfaction via distraction and disengagement-oriented coping. However, there was no indirect effect for positive emotions. Overall, the direct and indirect effects on subjective performance satisfaction suggest that adolescent athletes' emotions experienced during competition are greater predictors of performance satisfaction than the coping strategies they use. Specifically, although maladaptive coping strategies predict decreased performance satisfaction, the task-orientated strategies considered effective by adults (Gaudreau and Blondin, 2002; Nicholls et al., 2012) are not associated with increased performance satisfaction among adolescents.

Practical Implications

For applied practitioners, these findings have a number of implications. Firstly, practitioners can use the PSRS-AA to identify adolescent athletes most likely to appraise competitions with greater intensity, less perceived control, greater perceived threat, more likely to experience negative emotions, and more likely to use maladaptive coping strategies. Having identified adolescents at greatest risk, practitioners could employ a range of interventions to help athletes manage the effects of reactivity on stress and its outcomes. Given that stress is a recursive process (Lazarus, 1999) and that reactivity is a variable disposition (Schlotz et al., 2011b), successful interventions could bring about long-term adaptations in reactivity over time.

Specifically, given the findings within this sample, adolescent athletes with high levels of PSR could be prioritized for interventions that address control appraisals prior to competitive performances. Although control appraisals were not related to relational meanings of challenge or threat within this sample, they were associated with fewer negative emotions during competition and the greater use of task-orientated coping strategies. Manipulating athletes' appraisals of their resources available to them has been found to positively impact upon physiological responses to pressure situations (Turner et al., 2014).

Given the recursive nature of stress (Lazarus, 1999), coping interventions could also prove effective in assisting adolescent athletes with high level of PSR. Enhancing and refining an adolescent's coping repertoire is likely to affect future control appraisals, by increasing coping self-efficacy (Reeves et al., 2011). Although previous research has recommended that athletes use a wide range of task-orientated strategies to enhance performance (Gaudreau and Blondin, 2002; Nicholls et al., 2012), correlations within the present data set would suggest that effort expenditure and mental imagery could be taught as coping strategies to adolescent athletes to enhance their performance (see **Table 3**).

Finally, given the direct and indirect effects of PSR on the negative emotions, interventions based upon the processes of emotion regulation could also be recommended for young athletes measuring highly on the PSRS-AA (Lane et al., 2012; Wagstaff, 2014).

Study Strengths

This study has several strengths and provides a number of novel findings. Few studies have examined the associations between competition appraisals, emotions, coping, and performance satisfaction using longitudinal data, let alone with adolescents. The focus on adolescents in this study extends the work Nicholls et al. (2012) with adult athletes. Furthermore, this study also extends existing research by examining the direct and indirect effects of a dispositional factor (PSR) on the stress and coping process. Specifically, the strong associations between PSR and competition appraisals (perceived intensity and control) enhance the validity of the PSRS-AA as a measure of adolescent athletes' individual differences in reactivity, capable of predicting psychological responses to competition stressors.

Study Limitations

A general weakness of the study can be found within the reliance on self-report measures, which are associated with numerous biases (Furnham, 1986). Furthermore, there appear to be specific limitations with the single item VAS measures of appraisal and relational meaning utilized within the study. The measures of relational meaning (challenge and threat) were significantly positively correlated and were not associated with secondary appraisals of control. This brings into question the validity and reliability of the use of single item VAS scales to measure stress appraisal, despite their use in previous research (Kaiseler et al., 2012a,b; Turner et al., 2012, 2014). In other words, single item VAS scales may not be sufficient for capturing the complex nature of stress appraisal adolescent athletes undergo prior to competition.

The SAM (Peacock and Wong, 1990) used by Nicholls et al. (2012) may have been a more comprehensive measure of appraisal and relational meaning, despite the burden its length may have placed upon participants required to complete it close to the start of competition. Alternatively, given that athletes experience multiple stressors prior to competition other than just the competition itself (Mellalieu et al., 2009), assessing just the appraisals and relational meanings of the competition may have been too broad for capturing the dynamic nature of stressors experienced.

The measures of task-orientated coping and distraction-orientated coping were also correlated within the sample. This is a relationship not previously observed between these two variables in both adult or adolescent samples, given that task-orientated strategies are considered adaptive, while distraction-orientated strategies are considered maladaptive (Gaudreau and Blondin, 2002; Nicholls et al., 2009; Nicholls et al., 2012). Given the dynamic nature of sporting competition, athletes, have been known to use coping strategies from across dimensions (Nicholls et al., 2007; Nicholls and Polman, 2007). Only effort and mental imagery from the task-orientated dimension correlated with performance satisfaction. However, coping strategies perceived as effective are not always associated with performance satisfaction (Didymus and Fletcher, 2017). Therefore, future research may wish to further explore the validity of the CICS for use with adolescent athletes or use alternative measures of coping validated for use with adolescent athletes (Kowalski and Crocker, 2001).

The positive and negative dimensions of the SEQ when combined also produced poor model fit. Co-variances were observed between items on the anxiety and happiness subscales, suggesting that both positive and negative emotions co-occurred within the sample, rather than being experienced distinctly. This would imply that, within adolescent athletes, SEQ may not be able to successfully distinguish between discrete positive and negative emotions as expected.

Finally, a number of potentially significant negative relationships were not specified within the model, in order to avoid reducing the overall power of the model. Low levels of negative emotion may have facilitated task orientated coping, for example, or threat appraisals associated with low levels of positive emotion. These negative associations would be expected theoretically (Lazarus and Folkman, 1987; Lazarus, 1999). However, adding too many co-variances within such a path analysis is likely to risk reducing the overall power of the model (Byrne, 2016).

Future Research

Future research may wish to examine the factors that contribute to the development of SR in adolescent athletes. With a growing understanding of the outcomes associated with PSR in adolescent athletes (Britton et al., 2017), and how its influences the stress and coping process, youth sport organizations may benefit from an understanding of the developmental factors which contribute to some adolescent athletes having higher levels of reactivity than others. Exposure to stressors and support during childhood have already been associated with the development of reactivity in the wider population (Boyce and Ellis, 2005; Hughes et al., 2017). Future research could examine the relationship between adolescent athletes' history of stressors and support experienced within youth support environments and their PSR using the PSRS-AA.

Given that PSR appears to be related almost exclusively to negative constructs within the analysis (threat, negative emotion, maladaptive coping), future research may also wish to examine further salutogenic constructs that may explain more positive outcomes (challenge appraisals, positive emotion, task-orientated coping). For example, mental toughness has already been associated with increased appraisals of control, and greater use of effective coping strategies (Kaiseler et al., 2009). Future studies may also wish to examine the relationship between SR and salutogenic constructs such as mental toughness or resilience.

CONCLUSION

In conclusion, this study demonstrates the direct and indirect effects of individual differences in adolescent athletes' PSR on competition appraisals, emotions, and coping. Furthermore, the study extends previous research by examining the relationship between competition appraisals, emotions, coping, and performance satisfaction within adolescent athletes. Overall model fit was not achieved, limiting the overall conclusions that can be made regarding the stress-coping process. However, several significant direct and indirect effects were observed within the path analysis, partially replicating previous research (Nicholls et al., 2012) and supporting the extant theory to some extent (Lazarus and Folkman, 1987; Lazarus, 1999; Fletcher et al., 2006). This has implications for applied practitioners, as the PSRS-AA could be used to identify young athletes who are at greater risk of experiencing negative emotions and employing maladaptive coping strategies. Practitioners' resources could therefore be more efficiently allocated to adolescents at greatest risk. However, to inform future research further, researchers may wish to explore the validity of measures used to assess adolescent athletes' appraisals (particularly challenge and threat) and use of coping strategies, due to divergent and null findings within the present data. Furthermore, future research may also wish to investigate which factors influence the development of SR in adolescent athletes.

ETHICS STATEMENT

This study was carried out in accordance with the recommendations of Bournemouth University's Research Ethics Code of Practice, with written informed consent from all subjects. For all subjects under the age of 16, written and informed consent was also provided by a parent or guardian. All subjects gave written informed consent in accordance with the Declaration of Helsinki. The protocol was approved by Bournemouth University's Research Ethics Committee (ref: 12462).

AUTHOR CONTRIBUTIONS

DB, EK, and RP conceived and designed the study and experiments and edited, critically revised manuscript and approved the final version of manuscript. DB analyzed the data and drafted manuscript and prepared table/figures. DB and RP interpreted results of research.

REFERENCES

Allwood, M. A., Handwerger, K., Kivlighan, K. T., Granger, D. A., and Stroud, L. R. (2011). Direct and moderating links of salivary alpha-amylase and cortisol stress-reactivity to youth behavioral and emotional adjustment. *Biol. Psychol.* 88, 57–64. doi: 10.1016/j.biopsycho.2011.06.008

Amiot, C. E., Gaudreau, P., and Blanchard, C. M. (2004). Self-Determination, coping, and goal attainment in sport. *J. Sport Exerc. Psychol.* 26, 396–411. doi: 10.1123/jsep.26.3.396

Arnold, R., Fletcher, D., and Daniels, K. (2017). Organisational stressors, coping, and outcomes in competitive sport. *J. Sports Sci.* 35, 694–703. doi: 10.1080/02640414.2016.1184299

Blakemore, S.-J., and Choudhury, S. (2006). Development of the adolescent brain: implications for executive function and social cognition. *J. Child Psychol. Psychiatry* 47, 296–312. doi: 10.1111/j.1469-7610.2006.01611.x

Boyce, W. T., and Ellis, B. J. (2005). Biological sensitivity to context: I. An evolutionary-developmental theory of the origins and functions of stress reactivity. *Dev. Psychopathol.* 17, 271–301. doi: 10.1017/S0954579405050145

Britton, D., Kavanagh, E., and Polman, R. (2017). The perceived stress reactivity scale for adolescent athletes. *Pers. Individ. Dif.* 116, 301–308. doi: 10.1016/j.paid.2017.05.008

Byrne, B. M. (2016). *Structural Equation Modelling with Amos: Basic Concepts, Applications, and Programming*, 3rd Edn. New York, NY: Routledge.

Compas, B. E., Connor-Smith, J. K., Saltzman, H., Thomsen, A. H., and Wadsworth, M. E. (2001). Coping with stress during childhood and adolescence: problems, progress, and potential in theory and research. *Psychol. Bull.* 127, 87–127. doi: 10.1037/0033-2909.127.1.87

Crane, J., and Temple, V. (2015). A systematic review of dropout from organized sport among children and youth. *Eur. Phy. Educ. Rev.* 21, 114–131. doi: 10.1177/1356336x14555294

Davis, G. E., and Compas, B. E. (1986). Cognitive appraisal of major and daily stressful events during adolescence: a multidimensional scaling analysis. *J. Youth Adolesc.* 15, 377–388. doi: 10.1007/BF02143520

Didymus, F. F., and Fletcher, D. (2017). Organizational stress in high-level field hockey: examining transactional pathways between stressors, appraisals, coping and performance satisfaction. *Int. J. Sports Sci. Coach.* 12, 252–263. doi: 10.1177/1747954117694737

Ellis, B. J., Essex, M. J., and Boyce, W. T. (2005). Biological sensitivity to context: II. Empirical explorations of an evolutionary-developmental theory. *Dev. Psychopathol.* 17, 303–328. doi: 10.1017/S0954579405050157

Fletcher, D., Hanton, S., and Mellalieu, S. D. (2006). "An organizational stress review: conceptual and theoretical issues in competitive sport," in *Literature Reviews in Sport Psychology*, eds S. Hanton and S. D. Mellalieu (Hauppauge, NY: Nova), 321–373.

Fletcher, D., Hanton, S., Mellalieu, S. D., and Neil, R. (2012). A conceptual framework of organizational stressors in sport performers. *Scand. J. Med. Sci. Sports* 22, 545–557. doi: 10.1111/j.1600-0838.2010.01242.x

Folkman, S. (1997). Positive psychological states and coping with severe stress. *Soc. Sci. Med.* 45, 1207–1221. doi: 10.1016/s0277-9536(97)00040-3

Furnham, A. (1986). Response bias, social desirability and dissimulation. *Pers. Individ. Dif.* 7, 385–400. doi: 10.1016/0191-8869(86)90014-0

Gaudreau, P., and Blondin, J. P. (2002). Development of a questionnaire for the assessment of coping strategies employed by athletes in competitive sport settings. *Psychol. Sport Exerc.* 3, 1–34. doi: 10.1016/S1469-0292(01)00017-6

Goodger, K., Gorely, T., Lavallee, D., and Harwood, C. (2007). Burnout in sport: a systematic review. *Sport Psychol.* 21, 125–151.

Granger, D. A., Weisz, J. R., and Kauneckis, D. (1994). Neuroendocrine reactivity, internalizing behavior problems, and control-related cognitions in clinic-referred children and adolescents. *J. Abnorm. Psychol.* 103, 267–276. doi: 10.1037/0021-843X.103.2.267

Holt, N. L., and Dunn, J. G. H. (2004). Toward a grounded theory of the psychosocial competencies and environmental conditions associated with soccer success. *J. Appl. Sport Psychol.* 16, 199–219. doi: 10.1080/10413200490437949

Hooper, D., Coughlan, J., and Mullen, M. R. (2008). Structural equation modelling: guidelines for determining model fit. *Electron. J. Bus. Res. Methods* 6, 53–59. doi: 10.1016/j.acap.2015.07.001

Hu, L. T., and Bentler, P. M. (1999). Cutoff criteria for fit indexes in covariance structure analysis: conventional criteria versus new alternatives. *Struct. Equ. Modeling* 6, 1–55. doi: 10.1080/10705519909540118

Hughes, K., Bellis, M. A., Hardcastle, K. A., Sethi, D., Butchart, A., Mikton, C., et al. (2017). The effect of multiple adverse childhood experiences on health: a systematic review and meta-analysis. *Lancet Public Health* 2, e356–e366. doi: 10.1016/S2468-2667(17)30118-4

Jones, M. V., Lane, A. M., and Bray, S. R. (2005). Development and validation of the sport emotion questionnaire. *J. Sport Exerc. Psychol.* 27, 407–431. doi: 10.1080/02640414.2014.955520

Kaiseler, M., Polman, R., and Nicholls, A. R. (2009). Mental toughness, stress, stress appraisal, coping and coping effectiveness in sport. *Pers. Individ. Dif.* 47, 728–733. doi: 10.1016/j.paid.2009.06.012

Kaiseler, M., Polman, R. C. J., and Nicholls, A. R. (2012a). Effects of the big five personality dimensions on appraisal coping, and coping effectiveness in sport. *Eur. J. Sport Sci.* 12, 62–72. doi: 10.1080/17461391.2010.551410

Kaiseler, M., Polman, R. C. J., and Nicholls, A. R. (2012b). Gender differences in appraisal and coping: an examination of the situational and dispositional hypothesis. *Int. J. Sport Psychol.* 43, 1–14.

Kerdijk, C., van der Kamp, J., and Polman, R. (2016). The Influence of the social environment context in stress and coping in sport. *Front. Psychol.* 7:875. doi: 10.3389/fpsyg.2016.00875

Kline, R. B. (1998). *Principles and Practice of Structural Equation Modeling*, 1st Edn. Marquette, NE: Guilford.

Kowalski, K. C., and Crocker, P. R. E. (2001). Development and validation of the coping function questionnaire for adolescents in sport. *J. Sport Exerc. Psychol.* 23, 136–155. doi: 10.1080/02640414.2012.747692

Laborde, S., Dosseville, F., Wolf, S., Martin, T., and You, M. (2016). Consequences and antecedents of debilitative precompetitive emotions. *Psychol. Française* 61, 303–317. doi: 10.1016/j.psfr.2016.05.002

Lane, A. M., Beedie, C. J., Jones, M. V., Uphill, M., and Devonport, T. J. (2012). The BASES expert statement on emotion regulation in sport. *J. Sports Sci.* 30, 1189–1195. doi: 10.1080/02640414.2012.693621

Lazarus, R. S. (1999). *Stress and Emotion: A New Synthesis*. New York, NY: Springer Publishing Co.

Lazarus, R. S. (2000). How emotions influence performance in competitive sports. *Sport Psychol.* 14, 229–252. doi: 10.1123/tsp.14.3.229

Lazarus, R. S., and Folkman, S. (1987). Transactional theory and research on emotions and coping. *Eur. J. Pers.* 1, 141–169. doi: 10.1002/per.2410010304

Lopez-Duran, N. L., McGinnis, E., Kuhlman, K., Geiss, E., Vargas, I., and Mayer, S. (2015). HPA-axis stress reactivity in youth depression: evidence of impaired regulatory processes in depressed boys. *Stress* 18, 545–553. doi: 10.3109/10253890.2015.1053455

Males, J. R., and Kerr, J. H. (1996). Stress, emotion, and performance in elite slalom canoeists. *Sport Psychol.* 10, 17–36. doi: 10.1123/tsp.10.1.17

Marceau, K., Dorn, L. D., and Susman, E. J. (2012). Stress and puberty-related hormone reactivity, negative emotionality, and parent–adolescent relationships. *Psychoneuroendocrinology* 37, 1286–1298. doi: 10.1016/j.psyneuen.2012.01.001

Mellalieu, S. D., Neil, R., Hanton, S., and Fletcher, D. (2009). Competition stress in sport performers: stressors experienced in the competition environment. *J. Sports Sci.* 27, 729–744. doi: 10.1080/02640410902889834

Moore, L. J., Young, T., Freeman, P., and Sarkar, M. (2018). Adverse life events, cardiovascular responses, and sports performance under pressure. *Scand. J. Med. Sci. Sports* 28, 340–347. doi: 10.1111/sms.12928

Neil, R., Hanton, S., Mellalieu, S. D., and Fletcher, D. (2011). Competition stress and emotions in sport performers: the role of further appraisals. *Psychol. Sport Exerc.* 12, 460–470. doi: 10.1016/j.psychsport.2011.02.001

Nicholls, A. R., Holt, N. L., Polman, R. C. J., and James, D. W. G. (2005). Stress and coping among international adolescent golfers. *J. Appl. Sport Psychol.* 17, 333–340. doi: 10.1080/10413200500313644

Nicholls, A. R., Levy, A. R., and Perry, J. L. (2015). Emotional maturity, dispositional coping, and coping effectiveness among adolescent athletes. *Psychol. Sport Exerc.* 17, 32–39. doi: 10.1016/j.psychsport.2014.11.004

Nicholls, A. R., Perry, J. L., Jones, L., Morley, D., and Carson, F. (2013). Dispositional coping, coping effectiveness, and cognitive social maturity among adolescent athletes. *J. Sport Exerc. Psychol.* 35, 229–238. doi: 10.1123/jsep.35.3.229

Nicholls, A. R., Polman, R., Levy, A. R., Taylor, J., and Cobley, S. (2007). Stressors, coping, and coping effectiveness: gender, type of sport, and skill differences. *J. Sports Sci.* 25, 1521–1530. doi: 10.1080/02640410701230479

Nicholls, A. R., Polman, R., Morley, D., and Taylor, N. J. (2009). Coping and coping effectiveness in relation to a competitive sport event: pubertal status, chronological age, and gender among adolescent athletes. *J. Sport Exerc. Psychol.* 31, 299–317. doi: 10.1123/jsep.31.3.299

Nicholls, A. R., and Polman, R. C. J. (2007). Coping in sport: a systematic review. *J. Sports Sci.* 25, 11–31. doi: 10.1080/02640410600630654

Nicholls, A. R., Polman, R. C. J., and Levy, A. R. (2012). A path analysis of stress appraisals, emotions, coping, and performance satisfaction among athletes. *Psychol. Sport Exerc.* 13, 263–270. doi: 10.1016/j.psychsport.2011.12.003

Peacock, E. J., and Wong, P. T. P. (1990). The stress appraisal measure (SAM): a multidimensional approach to cognitive appraisal. *Stress Health* 6, 227–236. doi: 10.1002/smi.2460060308

Pensgaard, A. M., and Duda, J. L. (2003). Sydney 2000: the interplay between emotions, coping, and the performance of olympic-level athletes. *Sport Psychol.* 17, 253–267. doi: 10.1123/tsp.17.3.253

Polman, R., and Borkoles, E. (2011). The fallacy of directional anxiety. *Int. J. Sport Psychol.* 42, 303–306.

Polman, R., Clough, P., and Levy, A. (2010). "Personality and coping in sport: the big five and mental toughness," in *Coping in Sport: Theory, Methods, and Related Constructs*, ed. A. R. Nicholls (New York, NY: Nova Science), 141–157.

Reeves, C. W., Nicholls, A. R., and McKenna, J. (2009). Stressors and coping strategies among early and middle adolescent premier league academy soccer players: differences according to age. *J. Appl. Sport Psychol.* 21, 31–48. doi: 10.1080/10413200802443768

Reeves, C. W., Nicholls, A. R., and McKenna, J. (2011). The effects of a coping intervention on coping self-efficacy, coping effectiveness, and subjective performance among adolescent soccer players. *Int. J. Sport Exerc. Psychol.* 9, 126–142. doi: 10.1080/1612197x.2011.567104

Romeo, R. D. (2010). Adolescence: a central event in shaping stress reactivity. *Dev. Psychobiol.* 52, 244–253. doi: 10.1002/dev.20437

Schlotz, W. (2013). "Stress reactivity," in *Encyclopedia of Behavioral Medicine*, eds M. Gellman and J. Turner (New York, NY: Springer), 1891–1894.

Schlotz, W., Hammerfald, K., Ehlert, U., and Gaab, J. (2011a). Individual differences in the cortisol response to stress in young healthy men: testing the roles of perceived stress reactivity and threat appraisal using multiphase latent growth curve modeling. *Biol. Psychol.* 87, 257–264. doi: 10.1016/j.biopsycho.2011.03.005

Schlotz, W., Yim, I. S., Zoccola, P. M., Jansen, L., and Schulz, P. (2011b). The perceived stress reactivity scale: measurement invariance, stability, and validity in three countries. *Psychol. Assess.* 23, 80–94. doi: 10.1037/a0021148

Terry, P. (1995). The efficacy of mood state profiling with elite performers: a review and synthesis. *Sport Psychol.* 9, 309–324. doi: 10.1123/tsp.9.3.309

Turner, M. J., Jones, M. V., Sheffield, D., Barker, J. B., and Coffee, P. (2014). Manipulating cardiovascular indices of challenge and threat using resource appraisals. *Int. J. Psychophysiol.* 94, 9–18. doi: 10.1016/j.ijpsycho.2014.07.004

Turner, M. J., Jones, M. V., Sheffield, D., and Cross, S. L. (2012). Cardiovascular indices of challenge and threat states predict competitive performance. *Int. J. Psychophysiol.* 86, 48–57. doi: 10.1016/j.ijpsycho.2012.08.004

van Rens, F. E. C. A., Borkoles, E., Farrow, D., Curran, T., and Polman, R. C. J. (2016). Development and initial validation of the role strain questionnaire for junior athletes (RSQ-JA). *Psychol. Sport Exerc.* 24, 168–178. doi: 10.1016/j.psychsport.2016.02.004

Wagstaff, C. R. (2014). Emotion regulation and sport performance. *J. Sport Exerc. Psychol.* 36, 401–412. doi: 10.1123/jsep.2013-0257

PERMISSIONS

All chapters in this book were first published by Frontiers; hereby published with permission under the Creative Commons Attribution License or equivalent. Every chapter published in this book has been scrutinized by our experts. Their significance has been extensively debated. The topics covered herein carry significant findings which will fuel the growth of the discipline. They may even be implemented as practical applications or may be referred to as a beginning point for another development.

The contributors of this book come from diverse backgrounds, making this book a truly international effort. This book will bring forth new frontiers with its revolutionizing research information and detailed analysis of the nascent developments around the world.

We would like to thank all the contributing authors for lending their expertise to make the book truly unique. They have played a crucial role in the development of this book. Without their invaluable contributions this book wouldn't have been possible. They have made vital efforts to compile up to date information on the varied aspects of this subject to make this book a valuable addition to the collection of many professionals and students.

This book was conceptualized with the vision of imparting up-to-date information and advanced data in this field. To ensure the same, a matchless editorial board was set up. Every individual on the board went through rigorous rounds of assessment to prove their worth. After which they invested a large part of their time researching and compiling the most relevant data for our readers.

The editorial board has been involved in producing this book since its inception. They have spent rigorous hours researching and exploring the diverse topics which have resulted in the successful publishing of this book. They have passed on their knowledge of decades through this book. To expedite this challenging task, the publisher supported the team at every step. A small team of assistant editors was also appointed to further simplify the editing procedure and attain best results for the readers.

Apart from the editorial board, the designing team has also invested a significant amount of their time in understanding the subject and creating the most relevant covers. They scrutinized every image to scout for the most suitable representation of the subject and create an appropriate cover for the book.

The publishing team has been an ardent support to the editorial, designing and production team. Their endless efforts to recruit the best for this project, has resulted in the accomplishment of this book. They are a veteran in the field of academics and their pool of knowledge is as vast as their experience in printing. Their expertise and guidance has proved useful at every step. Their uncompromising quality standards have made this book an exceptional effort. Their encouragement from time to time has been an inspiration for everyone.

The publisher and the editorial board hope that this book will prove to be a valuable piece of knowledge for researchers, students, practitioners and scholars across the globe.

LIST OF CONTRIBUTORS

Mark A. Uphill, Jon Swain and Jamie O'Driscoll
Section of Sport Exercise Sciences, Canterbury Christ Church University, Canterbury, United Kingdom

Claire J. L. Rossato
Department of Psychology, Social Work and Counselling, Old Royal Naval College, University of Greenwich, London, United Kingdom

Tengfei Guo, Yakun Ni and Qiaoling Li
School of Educational Science, Henan University, Kaifeng, China

Hao Hong
School of Physical Education, Henan University, Kaifeng, China

Chris G. Harwood and Lucy Frearson
School of Sport, Exercise and Health Sciences, Loughborough University, Loughborough, United Kingdom

Sam N. Thrower
School of Sport, Exercise and Health Sciences, Loughborough University, Loughborough, United Kingdom
Department of Life Sciences, University of Roehampton, London, United Kingdom

Faye F. Didymus
Institute for Sport, Physical Activity and Leisure, Leeds Beckett University, Leeds, United Kingdom

Mary Louise Quinton, Jet Veldhuijzen van Zanten, Gavin P. Trotman, Jennifer Cumming and Sarah Elizabeth Williams
University of Birmingham, Birmingham, United Kingdom

Francesca Vitali, Cantor Tarperi, Jacopo Cristini, Andrea Rinaldi and Federico Schena
Department of Neurosciences, Biomedicine and Movement Sciences, University of Verona, Verona, Italy

Arnaldo Zelli
Department of Movement, Human and Health Sciences, Foro Italico University of Rome, Rome, Italy

Fabio Lucidi
Department of Developmental and Social Psychology, La Sapienza University of Rome, Rome, Italy

Laura Bortoli and Claudio Robazza
BIND–Behavioral Imaging and Neural Dynamics Center, Department of Medicine and Aging Sciences, Università degli Studi G. d'Annunzio Chieti e Pescara, Chieti, Italy

Lee J. Moore and Emma Solomon-Moore
Department for Health, University of Bath, Bath, United Kingdom

Paul Freeman and Adrian Hase
School of Sport, Rehabilitation, and Exercise Sciences, University of Essex, Colchester, United Kingdom

Marie Ottilie Frenkel, Robin-Bastian Heck and Henning Plessner
Institute of Sports and Sports Sciences, Heidelberg University, Heidelberg, Germany

Joana Brokelmann
Psychological Institute, Goethe University Frankfurt, Frankfurt, Germany

Arne Nieuwenhuys
Department of Exercise Sciences, The University of Auckland, Auckland, New Zealand
Behavioural Science Institute, Radboud University, Nijmegen, Netherlands

Christian Kasperk
Department of Internal Medicine I and Clinical Chemistry, Steroid Laboratory, University Hospital Heidelberg, Heidelberg, Germany

Martin Stoffel
Institute of Medical Psychology, University Hospital Heidelberg, Heidelberg, Germany

Gareth A. Roberts, Rachel Arnold, James E. Turner and James Bilzon
Department for Health, University of Bath, Bath, United Kingdom

Martin Colclough
Help for Heroes Sports Recovery, Tidworth, United Kingdom

Michel Nicolas
Laboratory of Psychology, Psy-DREPI (EA7458), Faculty of Sport Sciences, Université Bourgogne Franche-Comté (UBFC), Dijon, France

Mickaël Campo
Laboratory of Psychology, Psy-DREPI (EA7458), Faculty of Sport Sciences, Université Bourgogne Franche-Comté (UBFC), Dijon, France
Department d'Accompagnement Mental à la Performance, Fédération Française de Rugby (FFR), Marcoussis, France

Guillaume Martinent
L-VIS (EA 7428), Faculty of Sports Sciences, Université Claude Bernard Lyon 1, Lyon, France

Benoît Louvet
CETAPS (EA 3832), Faculty of Sports Sciences, Normandie Université, Rouen, France

Montse C. Ruiz and Saara Haapanen
Faculty of Sport and Health Sciences, University of Jyväskylä, Jyväskylä, Finland

Asko Tolvanen
Faculty of Education and Psychology, University of Jyväskylä, Jyväskylä, Finland

Joan L. Duda
School of Sport, Exercise and Rehabilitation Sciences, University of Birmingham, Birmingham, United Kingdom

Ross Wadey
Faculty of Sport, Health, and Applied Sciences, St Mary's University, Twickenham, United Kingdom

Lynne Evans, Sheldon Hanton and Helen Oliver
School of Sport and Health Sciences, Cardiff Metropolitan University, Cardiff, United Kingdom

Mustafa Sarkar
School of Science and Technology, Nottingham Trent University, Nottingham, United Kingdom

Laura A. Ceccarelli and Ryan J. Giuliano
Department of Psychology, University of Manitoba, Winnipeg, MB, Canada

Cheryl M. Glazebrook and Shaelyn M. Strachan
Faculty of Kinesiology and Recreation Management, University of Manitoba, Winnipeg, MB, Canada

Mark A. Wetherell
Psychobiology Research Group, Department of Psychology, Northumbria University, Newcastle upon Tyne, United Kingdom

Douglas MacDonald
Psychobiology Research Group, Department of Psychology, Northumbria University, Newcastle upon Tyne, United Kingdom
Scottish Canoe Association, Edinburgh, United Kingdom

Paul Davis, Anton Halvarsson and Wictor Lundström
Department of Psychology, Umeå University, Umeå, Sweden

Carolina Lundqvist
Department of Behavioural Sciences and Learning, Linköping University, Linköping, Sweden

Alena Kröhler and Stefan Berti
Department of Clinical Psychology and Neuropsychology, Institute for Psychology, Johannes Gutenberg-University Mainz, Mainz, Germany

Chris Hartley and Pete Coffee
Faculty of Health Sciences and Sport, University of Stirling, Stirling, United Kingdom

Tandy Haughey and Conor McGeown
Sport and Exercise Sciences Research Institute, Ulster University, Newtownabbey, United Kingdom

Stephen Shannon and Gavin Breslin
Sport and Exercise Sciences Research Institute, Ulster University, Newtownabbey, United Kingdom Institute of Mental Health Sciences, Ulster University, Derry, United Kingdom

Donncha Hanna
School of Psychology, Queen's University Belfast, Belfast, United Kingdom
Centre for Evidence and Social Innovation, Queen's University Belfast, Belfast, United Kingdom

Gerard Leavey
Bamford Centre for Mental Health and Wellbeing, School of Psychology, Ulster University, Coleraine, United Kingdom

Theresa Lentes and Uirassu Borges
Department of Performance Psychology, German Sport University Cologne, Cologne, Germany

Sylvain Laborde
Department of Performance Psychology, German Sport University Cologne, Cologne, Germany Normandie Université, UFR STAPS, EA 4260, Cesams, Caen, France

Thomas J. Hosang
Experimental Psychology Unit, Department of Psychology, Helmut Schmidt University, Hamburg, Germany

Emma Mosley
Southampton Solent University, Southampton, United Kingdom

Fabrice Dosseville
Normandie Université, UMR-S 1075 COMETE, Caen, France
INSERM, UMR-S 1075 COMETE, Caen, France

Nanaki J. Chadha, Martin J. Turner and Matthew J. Slater
Life Sciences and Education, Staffordshire University, Stoke-on-Trent, United Kingdom

Darren M. Britton
School of Sport, Health, and Social Sciences, Solent University, Southampton, United Kingdom

Emma J. Kavanagh
Department of Sport & Physical Activity, Bournemouth University, Bournemouth, United Kingdom

Remco C. J. Polman
School of Exercise and Nutrition Sciences, Queensland University of Technology, Brisbane, QLD, Australia

Index

www.ingramcontent.com/pod-product-compliance
Lightning Source LLC
LaVergne TN
LVHW080931210926
848485LV00004B/772